AF814212

Recommended by **Teachers**
Trusted by **Toppers**

All in One®

ECONOMICS

Class 12

EVERYTHING YOU NEED TO SCORE

- Simplified NCERT Theory
- All Types of Exam Pattern Questions
- CBQs; MCQs, A-R, Case Based
- Board Questions Upto 2025
- Sample Question Papers

CBSE Exams 2026

Author
Dr. Ginni Juneja Nanda

arihant
SUCCESS AND NOTHING LESS

arihant
SUCCESS AND NOTHING LESS

ARIHANT PRAKASHAN
(School Division Series)

卐 ADMINISTRATIVE & PRODUCTION OFFICES

Regd. Office

'Ramchhaya' 4577/15, Agarwal Road, Darya Ganj, New Delhi -110002
Tele: 011- 47630600, 43518550; Fax: 011- 23280316

卐 *Head Office*

Kalindi, TP Nagar, Meerut (UP) - 250002, Tel: 0121-7156203, 7156204

卐 SALES & SUPPORT OFFICES

Agra, Ahmedabad, Bengaluru, Bareilly, Chennai, Delhi, Guwahati, Hyderabad, Jaipur, Jhansi, Kolkata, Lucknow, Nagpur & Pune.

PO No : TXT-XX-XXXXXXX-X-XX

Published By Arihant Publications (India) Ltd.

For further information about the books published by Arihant, log on to www.arihantbooks.com or e-mail at info@arihantbooks.com

Follow us on

卐 PRICE ₹ 525.00

PRODUCTION TEAM

Publishing Managers
Mahendra Singh Rawat & Keshav Mohan

Cover Designer
Salman Shaikh

Inner Designer
Ankit Tyagi

Project Head
Saurabh Gupta

Page Layouting
Amit Bansal

Proof Reader
Apoorvi

Index *cum* Study Planner

One Book- Endless Features

to Help you Succeed

In this Chapter

At the start of each chapter, all the chapter topics have been listed, so that students may know what they are going to study.

01

CHAPTER

Macroeconomics and Circular Flow of Income

"Macroeconomic theory is that part of economics which studies the overall averages and aggregates of the system."
— *Kenneth E. Boulding*

YOUR STUDY GOALS

1.1 Macroeconomics
1.2 Some Basic Macroeconomic Concepts
1.3 Circular Flow of Income

YOUR PRACTICE GOAL

- Objective Type Questions (64 Qs ; MCQs, A-R, Statements, Matching, Concept Identification)
- Subjective Questions (26 SAs, 7 LAs)
- Self Assessment Test (8 MCQs, 6 SAs, 3 LAs)

1.1 Macroeconomics

Macroeconomics is that branch of economics which deals with economic issues or aggregates related to the economy as a whole. It examines economic challenges like inflation and unemployment, which impact all economic agents.

Economic agents are individuals and institutions that make decisions related to production, consumption and expenditure.

Flowchart

To quickly recall the concepts, flow charts are given at many places.

Complete Theory in Each Chapter

Each chapter has Complete, Easy to Understand and Simplified theory covering latest syllabus and latest NCERT Textbook. Theory is developed in such a way that it is suitable for all types of learners.

Functions of Money

Functions of money are placed in two categories

Functions of Money

- Primary
  - Medium of Exchange
  - Measure of Value
- Secondary
  - Standard of Deferred Payments
  - Store of Value
  - Transfer of Value

Primary Functions

These are basic functions of money, which it must perform in every country. They include

1. **Medium of Exchange**
   - Money is used to make payments for transactions involving goods and services. It allows buyers and sellers to trade independently, facilitating economic transactions.
   - This function eliminates the need for a double coincidence of wants, which was a major drawback of the barter system.

2.1 National Income

It is defined as the sum total of factor incomes earned by normal residents of a country, within the domestic territory of a country and from rest of the world, during a period of an accounting year.

Important Concepts Related to National Income

Concept	Explanation
Normal Resident of a Country	A person or institution, who ordinarily resides in a country for a period of one year or more and whose centre of economic interest, i.e. earnings, spendings and accumulation lies in that country.
Citizenship and Residential Status	**Citizenship** is a legal concept which is based on the birth place of person or when some legal provisions allow a person to be a citizen of a country. **Residential Status** is an economic concept which is based on economic activities performed by a person. A person can be a citizen of one country and at the same time, he can be the resident of another country.
Domestic Territory of a Country	According to the United Nations, domestic territory or economic territory of a country is the geographical territory, administrated by the government of that country within which persons, goods and capital circulate freely.

Point to Remember

While relating to the concept of domestic territory in economics, students should not keep in mind the political map of India. Rather, it is basically an area of operation, where people or goods or capital of a country can move and circulate freely to add to economic interest of country. In economics, domestic territory basically means the 'economic territory' of country.

One Book- Endless Features

to Help you Succeed

Boxed Matter

Information in the boxes is given to focus on important points related to the concepts.

Problem of Double Counting

Double counting refers to counting of an output more than once while passing through various stages of production. While measuring national income, only the value of final goods and services should be included. However, when the value of intermediate goods is also included along with the value of final goods, then the problem of double counting arises.

Exam Pattern Questions

To make students completely prepared for examination, Exam Pattern Questions are provided after theory. These questions cover all types of questions, like; MCQs, Case Based Questions, Assertion-Reason, SA & LA Type Questions. All the questions are fully explained helping students to understand, how to write the answers to get full marks in the exam.

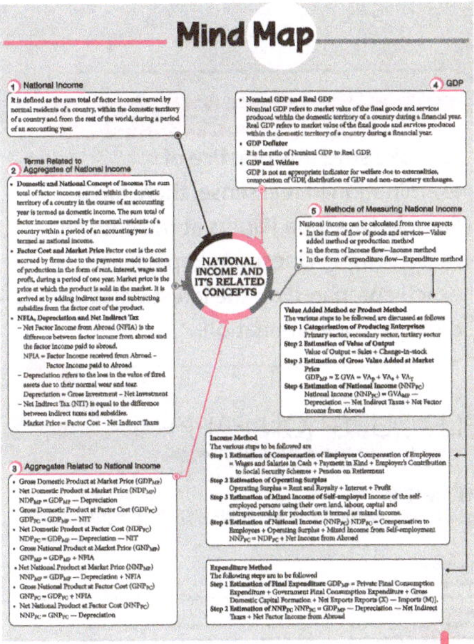

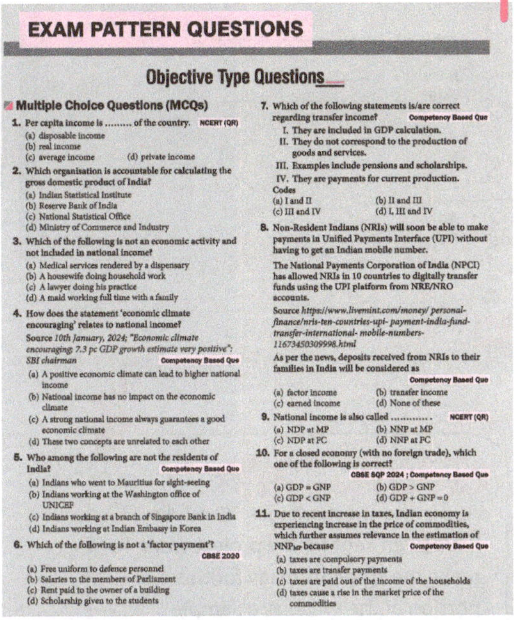

EXAM PATTERN QUESTIONS

Objective Type Questions

Multiple Choice Questions (MCQs)

1. Per capita income is .... of the country. NCERT (QR)
(a) disposable income
(b) real income
(c) average income (d) private income

2. Which organisation is accountable for calculating the gross domestic product of India?
(a) Indian Statistical Institute
(b) Reserve Bank of India
(c) National Statistical Office
(d) Ministry of Commerce and Industry

3. Which of the following is not an economic activity and not included in national income?
(a) Medical services rendered by a dispensary
(b) A housewife doing household work
(c) A lawyer doing his practice
(d) A maid working full time with a family

4. How does the statement 'economic climate encouraging' relates to national income?
Source *10th January, 2024; "Economic climate encouraging: 7.3 pc GDP growth estimate very positive": SBI chairman* Competency Based Que
(a) A positive economic climate can lead to higher national income
(b) National income has no impact on the economic climate
(c) A strong national income always guarantees a good economic climate
(d) These two concepts are unrelated to each other

5. Who among the following are not the residents of India? Competency Based Que
(a) Indians who went to Mauritius for sight-seeing
(b) Indians working at the Washington office of UNICEF
(c) Indians working at a branch of Singapore Bank in India
(d) Indians working at Indian Embassy in Korea

6. Which of the following is not a 'factor payment'? CBSE 2020
(a) Free uniform to defence personnel
(b) Salaries to the members of Parliament
(c) Rent paid to the owner of a building
(d) Scholarship given to the students

7. Which of the following statements is/are correct regarding transfer income? Competency Based Que
I. They are included in GDP calculation.
II. They do not correspond to the production of goods and services.
III. Examples include pensions and scholarships.
IV. They are payments for current production.
Codes
(a) I and II (b) II and III
(c) III and IV (d) I, III and IV

8. Non-Resident Indians (NRIs) will soon be able to make payments in Unified Payments Interface (UPI) without having to get an Indian mobile number.
The National Payments Corporation of India (NPCI) has allowed NRIs in 10 countries to digitally transfer funds using the UPI platform from NRE/NRO accounts.
Source *https://www.livemint.com/money/ personal-finance/nris-ten-countries-upi- payment-india-fund-transfer-international- mobile-numbers-11673450309998.html*
As per the news, deposits received from NRIs to their families in India will be considered as Competency Based Que
(a) factor income (b) transfer income
(c) earned income (d) None of these

9. National income is also called .... NCERT (QR)
(a) NDP at MP (b) NNP at MP
(c) NDP at FC (d) NNP at FC

10. For a closed economy (with no foreign trade), which one of the following is correct? CBSE SQP 2024 ; Competency Based Que
(a) GDP = GNP (b) GDP > GNP
(c) GDP < GNP (d) GDP + GNP = 0

11. Due to recent increase in taxes, Indian economy is experiencing increase in the price of commodities, which further assumes relevance in the estimation of NNP_{MP} because Competency Based Que
(a) taxes are compulsory payments
(b) taxes are transfer payments
(c) taxes are paid out of the income of the households
(d) taxes cause a rise in the market price of the commodities

Mind Map

A quick revision visual tool for the complete chapter.

One Book- Endless Features

to Help you Succeed

Self Assessment Test

A Complete Test of Chapter in Exam Format

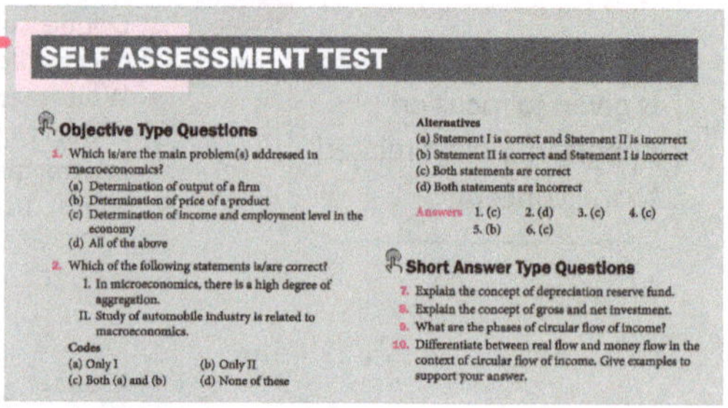

SELF ASSESSMENT TEST

Objective Type Questions

1. Which is/are the main problem(s) addressed in macroeconomics?
   (a) Determination of output of a firm
   (b) Determination of price of a product
   (c) Determination of income and employment level in the economy
   (d) All of the above
2. Which of the following statements is/are correct?
   I. In microeconomics, there is a high degree of aggregation.
   II. Study of automobile industry is related to macroeconomics.
   Codes
   (a) Only I (b) Only II
   (c) Both (a) and (b) (d) None of these

Alternatives
(a) Statement I is correct and Statement II is incorrect
(b) Statement II is correct and Statement I is incorrect
(c) Both statements are correct
(d) Both statements are incorrect

Answers 1. (c) 2. (d) 3. (c) 4. (c) 5. (b) 6. (c)

Short Answer Type Questions

7. Explain the concept of depreciation reserve fund.
8. Explain the concept of gross and net investment.
9. What are the phases of circular flow of income?
10. Differentiate between real flow and money flow in the context of circular flow of income. Give examples to support your answer.

Sample Project

EVOLUTION OF MONEY

Name : ....
Class : ....
Roll No. : ....
School : ....

Submitted by .... Submitted to ....

Project Work

455

Sample Question Papers

To make students practice of examination in real sense, there are 3 Sample Question Papers at the end. All these Sample Questions Papers are exactly prepared on the latest syllabus & pattern of examination.

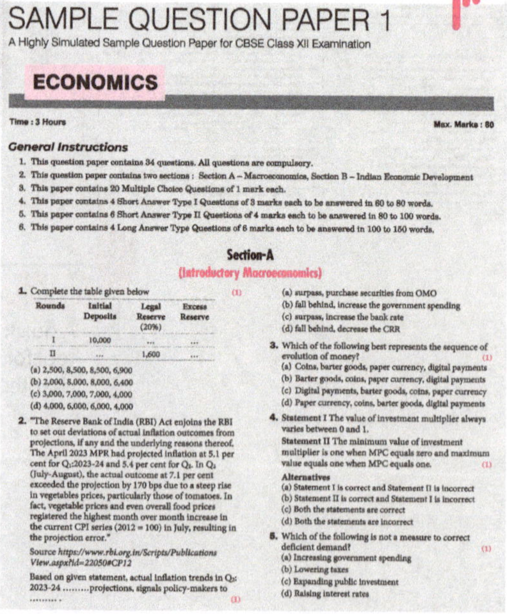

SAMPLE QUESTION PAPER 1

A Highly Simulated Sample Question Paper for CBSE Class XII Examination

ECONOMICS

Time : 3 Hours Max. Marks : 80

General Instructions

1. This question paper contains 34 questions. All questions are compulsory.
2. This question paper contains two sections : Section A – Macroeconomics, Section B – Indian Economic Development
3. This paper contains 20 Multiple Choice Questions of 1 mark each.
4. This paper contains 4 Short Answer Type I Questions of 3 marks each to be answered in 60 to 80 words.
5. This paper contains 6 Short Answer Type II Questions of 4 marks each to be answered in 80 to 100 words.
6. This paper contains 4 Long Answer Type Questions of 6 marks each to be answered in 100 to 150 words.

Section-A
(Introductory Macroeconomics)

1. Complete the table given below (1)

Rounds	Initial Deposits	Legal Reserve (20%)	Excess Reserve
I	10,000	...	...
II	...	1,600	...

(a) 2,500, 8,500, 8,500, 6,900
(b) 2,000, 8.000, 8,000, 6,400
(c) 3,000, 7,000, 7,000, 4,000
(d) 4,000, 6,000, 6,000, 4,000

2. "The Reserve Bank of India (RBI) Act enjoins the RBI to set out deviations of actual inflation outcomes from projections, if any and the underlying reasons thereof. The April 2023 MPR had projected inflation at 5.1 per cent for Q_1:2023-24 and 5.4 per cent for Q_2. In Q_2 (July-August), the actual outcome at 7.1 per cent exceeded the projection by 170 bps due to a steep rise in vegetables prices, particularly those of tomatoes. In fact, vegetable prices and even overall food prices registered the highest month over month increase in the current CPI series (2012 = 100) in July, resulting in the projection error."
   Source *https://www.rbi.org.in/Scripts/Publications View.aspx?id=22050#CP12*
   Based on given statement, actual inflation trends in Q_2: 2023-24 ....projections, signals policy-makers to .... (1)
   (a) surpass, purchase securities from OMO
   (b) fall behind, increase the government spending
   (c) surpass, increase the bank rate
   (d) fall behind, decrease the CRR
3. Which of the following best represents the sequence of evolution of money? (1)
   (a) Coins, barter goods, paper currency, digital payments
   (b) Barter goods, coins, paper currency, digital payments
   (c) Digital payments, barter goods, coins, paper currency
   (d) Paper currency, coins, barter goods, digital payments
4. Statement I The value of investment multiplier always varies between 0 and 1.
   Statement II The minimum value of investment multiplier is one when MPC equals zero and maximum value equals one when MPC equals one. (1)
   Alternatives
   (a) Statement I is correct and Statement II is incorrect
   (b) Statement II is correct and Statement I is incorrect
   (c) Both the statements are correct
   (d) Both the statements are incorrect
5. Which of the following is not a measure to correct deficient demand? (1)
   (a) Increasing government spending
   (b) Lowering taxes
   (c) Expanding public investment
   (d) Raising interest rates

Project Work

As per the latest syllabus, 20 marks have been kept for the project work. To make the students ready for this portion of the syllabus, a Sample Project Report has been given.

Latest Course Structure

Theory : 80 Marks

Project : 20 Marks

Units		Marks
Part A	Introductory Macroeconomics	
1	National Income and Related Aggregates	10
2	Money and Banking	6
3	Determination of Income and Employment	12
4	Government Budget and the Economy	6
5	Balance of Payments	6
		40
Part B	Indian Economic Development	
6	Development Experience (1947-90) and Economic Refroms Since 1991	12
7	Current Challenges facing Indian Economy	20
8	Development Experience of Inida - A Comparison with Neighbours	08
		40
Part C	Project Work	20

Part A Introductory Macroeconomics

Unit 1 National Income and Related Aggregates

What is Macroeconomics ?

Basic Concepts: Consumption Goods, Capital Goods, Final Goods, Intermediate Goods; Stocks and Flows; Gross Investment and Depreciation.

Circular Flow of Income (two sector model), Methods of Calculating National Income - Value Added or Product Method, Expenditure Method, Income Method.

Aggregates Related to National Income: Gross National Product (GNP), Net National Product (NNP), Gross and Net Domestic Product (GDP and NDP) - at Market Price, at Factor Cost; Real and Nominal GDP. GDP Deflator, GDP and Welfare

UNIT 2 Money and Banking

Money - Meaning and Functions, Supply of Money - Currency Held by the Public and Net Demand Deposits Held by Commercial Banks.

Money Creation by the Commercial Banking System.

Central Bank and Its Functions (example of the Reserve Bank of India): Bank of issue, Govt. Bank, Banker's Bank, Control of Credit through Bank Rate, CRR, SLR, Repo Rate and Reverse Repo Rate, Open Market Operations, Margin Requirement.

UNIT 3 Determination of Income and Employment

Aggregate Demand and its Components.
Propensity to Consume and Propensity to Save (average and marginal).

Short-run Equilibrium Output; Investment Multiplier and its Mechanism.

Meaning of Full Employment and Involuntary Unemployment.

Problems of Excess Demand and Deficient Demand; Measures to Correct Them - Changes in Government Spending, Taxes and Money Supply.

UNIT 4 Government Budget and the Economy

Government Budget - Meaning, Objectives and Components.

Classification of Receipts - Revenue Receipts and Capital Receipts; Classification of Expenditure – Revenue Expenditure and Capital Expenditure.

Balanced, Surplus and Deficit Budget - Measures of Government Deficit

UNIT 5 Balance of Payments

Balance of Payments Account - Meaning and Components; Balance of Payments-Surplus and Deficit.

Foreign Exchange Rate - Meaning of Fixed and Flexible Rates and Managed Floating.

Determination of Exchange Rate in a Free Market, Merits and Demerits of Flexible and Fixed Exchange Rate. Managed Floating Exchange Rate System.

Part B Indian Economic Development

UNIT 6 Development Experience (1947-90) and Economic Reforms Since 1991

A brief introduction of the State of Indian Economy on the Eve of Independence.

Indian Economic System and Common Goals of Five Year Plans.

Main Features, Problems and Policies of Agriculture (Institutional Aspects and New Agricultural Strategy), Industry (IPR 1956 ; SSI-role & importance) and Foreign Trade.

Economic Reforms since 1991

Features and appraisals of Liberalisation, Globalisation and Privatisation (LPG Policy);

Concepts of Demonetisation and GST

Unit 7 Current Challenges facing Indian Economy

Human Capital Formation: How people become resource; Role of Human Capital in Economic Development; Growth of Education Sector in India.

Rural Development: Key Issues-Credit and Marketing - Role of Cooperatives; Agricultural Diversification; Alternative Farming - Organic Farming.

Employment: Growth and Changes in workforce participation rate in formal and informal sectors; Problems and Policies.

Sustainable Economic Development: Meaning, Effects of Economic Development on Resources and Environment, Including Global Warming.

Unit 8 Development Experience of India

A Comparison with Neighbours.

India and Pakistan.

India and China.

Issues: Economic Growth, Population, Sectoral Development and other Human Developmental Indicators.

Part C Projects in Economics

Prescribed Books:

1. Statistics for Economics, NCERT
2. Indian Economic Development, NCERT
3. Introductory Microeconomics, NCERT
4. Macroeconomics, NCERT
5. Supplementary Reading Material in Economics, CBSE

Note : The above publications are also available in Hindi Medium.

PART A
Introductory Macroeconomics

01 CHAPTER

Macroeconomics and Circular Flow of Income

"Macroeconomic theory is that part of economics which studies the overall averages and aggregates of the system." — *Kenneth E. Boulding*

YOUR STUDY GOALS

1.1 Macroeconomics
1.2 Some Basic Macroeconomic Concepts
1.3 Circular Flow of Income

YOUR PRACTICE GOAL

- Objective Type Questions (64 Qs ; MCQs, A-R, Statements, Matching, Concept Identification)
- Subjective Questions (26 SAs, 7 LAs)
- Self Assessment Test (6 MCQs, 6 SAs, 3 LAs)

1.1 Macroeconomics

Macroeconomics is that branch of economics which deals with economic issues or aggregates related to the economy as a whole.

It examines economic challenges like inflation and unemployment, which impact all economic agents.

Economic agents are individuals and institutions that make decisions related to production, consumption and expenditure.

Subject Matter of Macroeconomics

Name	Explanation
Theory of Employment	• Studies determination of employment in the economy. • Includes study of full employment, underemployment, voluntary and involuntary unemployment.
Theory of National Income Determination	• Studies determination of domestic and national income by different methods.
Theory of General Pricing	• Studies the determination of general price level. • Includes issues like inflation, excess/deficient demand.
Theory of Money	• Explains the importance of money and banking in functioning of the economy.
Theory of International Trade	• Studies all international transactions between home country and rest of the world. • Determination of foreign exchange rate and balance of payment are also covered under subject matter of macroeconomics.

Importance of Macroeconomics

- It assesses the economy's performance through National Income (NI) estimates, unemployment rates and government budgets.
- It aids in developing strategies for growth and development.
- It supports government in policy formulation.
- It helps to understand income distribution among various demographic groups.
- It is crucial for addressing monetary issues that adversely affect the economy.
- It enables international comparisons.

Interdependence between Macroeconomics and Microeconomics

Microeconomics and macroeconomics are interdependent, as explained through following points

- Macroeconomics deals with aggregates at economy level where as microeconomics deals with aggregates of goods, but with lesser degree of aggregation.

  Example Demand for cars in India is a macroeconomics subject, while city demand is a microeconomics subject. Demand computation at city level is less aggregation intensive.
- Policy changes at the macro level impact the micro level.

  Example Changes in government policy on personal taxes or subsidies affect individual income and consumption demand.

1.2 Some Basic Macroeconomic Concepts

Some of the important concept of macroeconomics, such as types of goods produced in the economy, investment, depreciation, stock, flow, etc. are discussed ahead.

1. Types of Goods Produced in the Economy

S.No.	Type	Meaning	Example
1.	**Final Goods**	These are the goods which have crossed the boundary line of production and are ready for use by their final users, such as consumers and producers.	Smartphone, packaged meal, etc.
	Types of Final Goods		
	• **Final Consumer Goods**	The goods which are ready to be used by the consumers for satisfaction of their wants. Expenditure on these goods is termed as **consumption expenditure**.	Eatables like milk, bread, etc.
	• **Final Producer Goods**	The goods which are ready to be used by the producers in the production process. Expenditure on these goods is termed as **investment expenditure**.	Machinery, etc.
2.	**Intermediate Goods**	These are the goods which are within the boundary line of production and are not ready for use by their final users. Expenditure on intermediate goods by producers during an accounting year is termed as **intermediate consumption**.	Wheat purchased by a baker, readymade shirts purchased by a trader, etc.
3.	**Consumer/ Consumption Goods**	These are the goods which are directly used for the satisfaction of human wants.	Ice-cream and milk used by the households.
	Types of Consumer/Consumption Goods		
	• **Durable Goods**	These are consumer goods which can be used for several years and are generally expensive.	TV, AC, etc.
	• **Semi-durable Goods**	These are consumer goods which have a life span of one year or more, but they are not of very high value.	Crockery, clothes, etc.
	• **Non-durable Goods**	These are consumer goods which are used in single act of consumption, i.e. they cannot be re-used.	Fruits, vegetables, milk, etc.
	• **Services**	These are intangible goods, that directly satisfy human wants.	Services of doctor, lawyer, etc.

S.No.	Type	Meaning	Example
4.	**Capital Goods**	These are those goods which are used in the process of production for several years and which are of high value. "All capital goods are producer goods but not *vice-versa*, as producer goods include both intermediate as well as capital goods."	Fixed assets of the producers like building, plant and machinery, etc.

Production Boundary

In sugar production, growing sugarcane, processing it in a mill to make raw sugar and refining it to produce white and brown sugar, all fall within the production boundary because each step adds value, creating a product for the market.

2. Investment

Investment is the process of capital formation by a firm or addition to the stock of capital of a country.
It can be represented as,

$$I = \Delta K$$

Here, I = Investment ; ΔK = Change in capital stock during the year

Components of Investment

Fixed Investment

- Refers to increase or addition in the stock of fixed assets of the production units during an accounting year.
- e.g. Plant and machinery

Inventory Investment

- Refers to the change in the inventory stock over the period of a year.
- Includes stock of finished goods, semi-finished goods and raw materials. It can be planned or unplanned.
- Inventory Investment = Closing Stock – Opening Stock

Types of Investment

Type	Meaning	Formula
Gross Investment	The total addition to existing stock of capital during a given time period including depreciation. **Components** Gross fixed investment and inventory investment.	Gross Investment = Expenditure on Purchase of Fixed Asset in an Accounting Year + Expenditure on Inventory Stock in an Accounting Year *or* Gross Investment = Net Investment + Depreciation
Net Investment	The actual increase in stock of capital during an accounting year. It is also termed as new capital formation.	Net Investment = Gross Investment – Depreciation

3. Depreciation

Depreciation is the loss in the value of fixed assets in use on account of normal wear and tear, accidental damages and expected or foreseen obsolescence. It does not take into account unexpected obsolescence or sudden destruction of capital asset due to accidents, natural calamities, etc. It is also called **consumption of fixed capital**.

It can be calculated as

$$\text{Depreciation} = \text{Gross Investment} - \text{Net Investment}$$

Depreciation Reserve Fund (DRF)

- It is a fund created by the producers to meet the upcoming depreciation losses in the process of production.
- Every year, from the profits, an amount is appropriated to DRF to purchase new asset when required.

4. Stock and Flow

Basis	Stock	Flow
Meaning	A stock variable is defined as any quantity, which is measured at a particular point of time.	A flow variable is defined as any quantity, which is measured over a period of time.
Time	It is not time dimensional.	It is time dimensional.
Concept	It is a static concept.	It is a dynamic concept.
Example	Quantity of money, wealth, etc.	Consumption, investment, etc.
Diagrammatic View	**State Bank of India** ₹ 25,000 balance in savings account as at 1st April, 2020	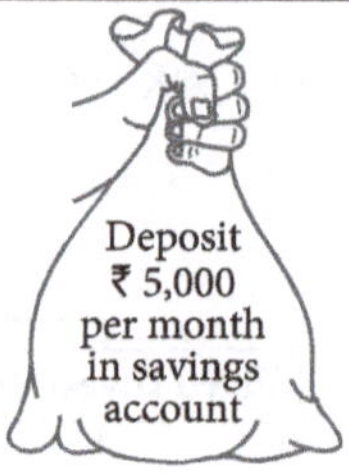

Sectors of an Economy

Different sectors, which are present within an economy are

1. **Household Sector** It is engaged in the consumption of goods and services and is also the provider of factor services.
2. **Producing Sector** It is engaged in the production of goods and services. It is also referred to as 'firms'.
3. **Government Sector** It is engaged in such activities which are related to taxation and subsidies as well as consumption and production.
4. **Rest of the World/External Sector** It is engaged in exports and imports.

Market

In macroeconomics, there are two types of markets

1. **Product Market** Market for goods and services.
2. **Factor Market** Market for factors of production.

1.3 Circular Flow of Income

Circular flow means the unending flow of production of goods and services and income and expenditure in an economy from one sector of an economy to another.

It shows the redistribution of income in a circular manner between production units and household.

Phases of Circular Flow of Income

There are three different phases of circular flow of income, which includes

1. **Production Phase** Firms produces goods and services with help of factors services.
2. **Distribution Phase** Involves the flow of factor income from firms to households.
3. **Expenditure Phase** Income received by factor of production, is spent on purchase of goods and services produced by firms.

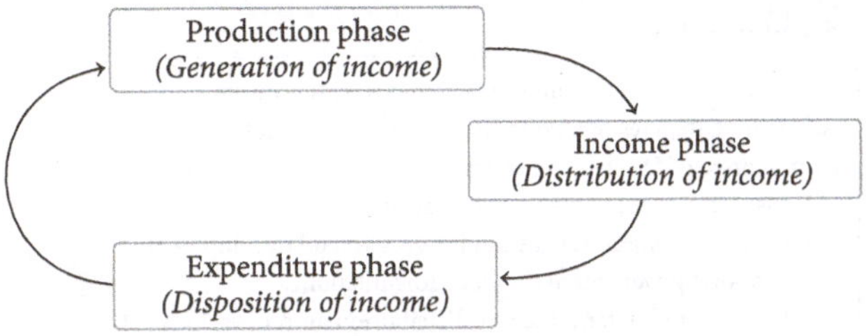

Types of Circular Flow

Real Flow	Money Flow
It explains the flow of factor services by the households to firms as well as the flow of the goods and services produced by the firms to households.	It explains the flow of factor payments by firms to households for their factor services as well as the flow of money from households to firms in the form of purchase of goods and services.
It is also termed as **physical flow.**	It is also termed as **nominal flow.**

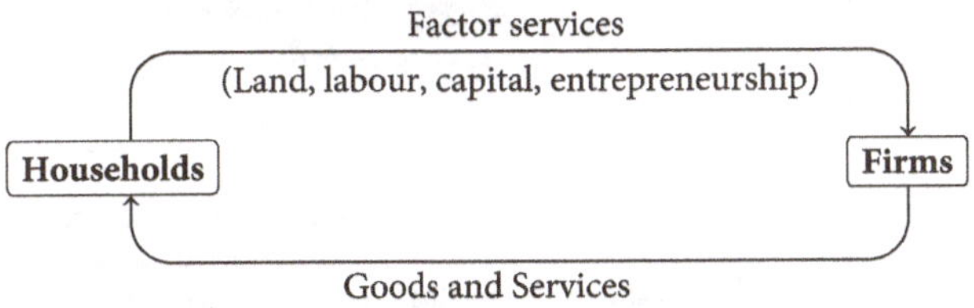

Real flow in a two-sector economy

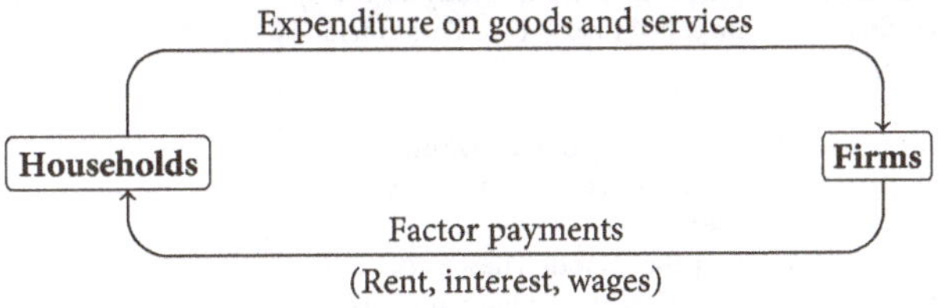

Money flow in a two-sector economy

Circular Flow in Two-Sector Economy

In a two-sector economy, there are only two sectors of economic activity, namely households and firms. Households supply factor services to firms and firms hire factor services from households.

Households spend their entire income on consumption of goods and services. Firms sell what is produced by the households. This leads to intersectoral flows.

The diagram is prepared on following assumptions

- The economy consists of just two sectors i.e. producers and households.
- Factor payments by firms equals factor incomes of households.
- There are no savings because the households spend all of their income.
- There are no imports or exports since the domestic economy is closed.
- Total production equals total consumption.

In this type of economy, intersectoral circular flow can be explained with the help of the following

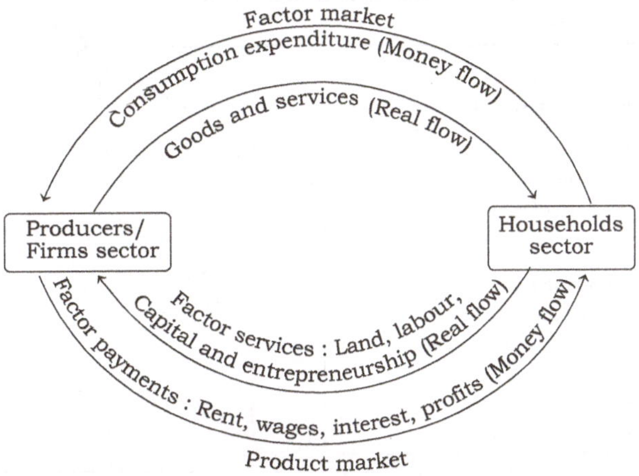

Leakages and Injections in Circular Flow

Leakages	Injections
It means withdrawal from the circular flow.	It means introduction of income into the circular flow.
When households and firms save part of their incomes, it constitutes leakages.	When households and firms borrow, they constitute injections.
e.g. Saving, tax payments, imports.	e.g. Investment, exports, government spending.

Mind Map

MACROECONOMICS AND CIRCULAR FLOW OF INCOME

1 Macroeconomics

It is that branch of economics which deals with economic issues or aggregates related to the economy as a whole.

Importance of Macroeconomics

- It assesses the economy's performance
- It aids in developing strategies for growth and development
- It supports government in policy formulation
- It helps to understand income distribution among various demographic groups
- It is crucial for addressing monetary issues
- It enables international comparisons

2 Types of Goods Produced in the Economy

1. **Final Goods** Goods which have crossed the boundary line of production and are ready for use by their final users, are called final goods. These include
   - Final consumer goods
   - Final producer goods
2. **Intermediate Goods** These goods are within the boundary line of production and are not ready for use by their final users.
3. **Consumer/Consumption Goods** These goods are directly used for the satisfaction of human wants. These include
   - Durable goods
   - Non-durable goods
   - Semi-durable goods
   - Services
4. **Capital Goods** These goods are used in the process of production for several years and which are of high value.

3 Investment

It is the process of capital formation by a firm or addition to the stock of capital of a country.

$I = \Delta K$

Components

- Fixed investment
- Inventory investment

Types

- Gross investment
- Net investment

4 Depreciation

It is the loss in the value of fixed assets in use on account of normal wear and tear, accidental damages and expected or foreseen obsolescence. It is also called consumption of fixed capital.

Depreciation = Gross Investment – Net Investment

5 Stock and Flow

- A stock variable is defined as any quantity, which is measured at a particular point of time whereas a flow variable is defined as any quantity, which is measured over a period of time.
- Stock is not time dimensional whereas flow is time dimensional.
- Stock is a static concept whereas flow is a dynamic concept.

6 Sectors of an Economy

- **Household Sector** Engaged in the consumption of goods and services and is also the provider of factor services.
- **Producing Sector** Engaged in the production of goods and services. It is also referred to as 'firms'.
- **Government Sector** Engaged in such activities which are related to taxation and subsidies as well as consumption and production.
- **Rest of the World/External Sector** Engaged in exports and imports.

Market In macroeconomics, there are two types of markets

- **Product Market** Market for goods and services.
- **Factor Market** Market for factors of production.

7 Circular Flow of Income

Circular flow means the unending flow of production of goods and services and income and expenditure in an economy from one sector of an economy to another.

Phases

- Production phase
- Distribution phase
- Expenditure phase

8 Types of Circular Flow

- **Real Flow** It explains the flow of factor services by the households to firms as well as the flow of goods and services produced by the firms to households.
- **Money Flow** It explains the flow of factor payments by firms to households for their factor services as well as the flow of money form households to firms in the form of purchase of goods and services.

9 Circular Flow in Two-Sector Economy

In a two-sector economy, there are only two sectors of economic activity, namely households and firms. Households supply factor services to firms and firms hire factor services from households. Households spend their entire income on consumption of goods and services. Firms sell what is produced by the households. This leads to intersectoral flows.

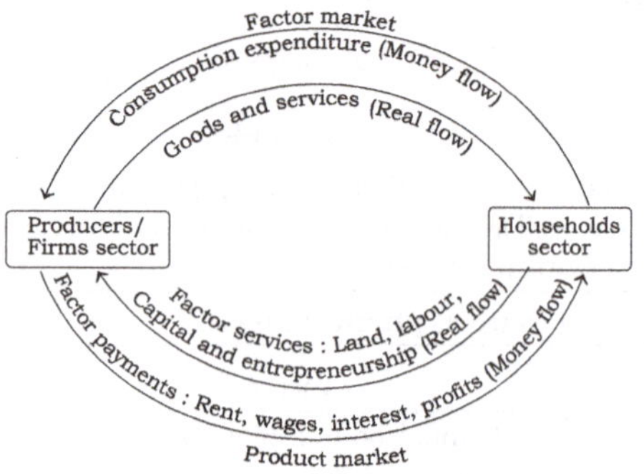

EXAM PATTERN QUESTIONS

Objective Type Questions

Multiple Choice Questions (MCQs)

1. Macroeconomics is also called ...... economics.

(a) experimental (b) applied
(c) aggregated (d) individual

2. **In 1936, macroeconomics become a separate branch of economics, after a book published by**

(a) Adam Smith (b) JB Say
(c) John Maynard Keynes (d) Alfred Marshall

3. **Which of the following is/are under the scope of macroeconomics?** Competency Based Que

I. To estimate the national income.
II. To analyse the consumer's behaviour.
III. To determine the employment level.
IV. To facilitate international trade.

Codes

(a) I, II, III and IV (b) I and II
(c) Only I (d) I, III and IV

4. **Macroeconomics provides tools to analyse the effects of ...., which are crucial for managing inflation and economic growth.**

(a) marketing strategies
(b) government policies
(c) product promotions
(d) consumer surveys

5. **What does the picture emphasise about the scope of modern macroeconomics?**

(a) It focuses solely on domestic economic policies and performance
(b) It considers only individual national economies in isolation
(c) It recognises the increasing role of international trade and globalisation
(d) It emphasises the limited impact of external factors on national economies

6. **Which of the following statements are true about relation between microeconomics and macroeconomics?** Competency Based Que

I. Macroeconomic trends are often influenced by microeconomic decisions.
II. Individual markets and sectors can sometimes significantly affect the broader economy.
III. Microeconomics has no impact on macroeconomic outcomes.

Codes

(a) I and II (b) I and III (c) II and III (d) I, II and III

7. **.......... of the goods is the principle basis of classifying the goods into intermediate and final goods.**

(a) Production (b) Consumption
(c) End-use (d) Expenditure

8. **Crockery, clothes, etc. are examples of**

(a) durable goods (b) semi-durable goods
(c) non-durable goods (d) None of these

9. **Purchase of machinery by a producer is a/an .... good.**

(a) intermediate (b) capital
(c) consumer (d) None of these

10. **"Building, plant and machinery are capital goods." In the light of this statement, following are the characteristics of capital goods excluding** Competency Based Que

(a) they are of high value
(b) they are the assets of the company
(c) they are used for less than one year
(d) they are used in production process

11. **...... is addition to the stock of fixed assets of producers during an accounting year.**

(a) Current investment (b) Fixed investment
(c) Inventory investment (d) Gross investment

12. **When the firms have unsold goods, which it had not anticipated during the year then these are referred to as ...... of the business.**

(a) fixed investment (b) inventory investment
(c) planned inventory stock (d) unplanned inventory stock

13. Which of the following is not considered investment in economics?

I. A person putting funds into a term deposit.
II. A farmer who replaces an old fence with a new fence.
III. A business updates its computer.
IV. A new factory that is built. **Competency Based Que**

Codes

(a) Only I (b) I and IV
(c) II and III (d) Only II

14. Depreciation of fixed capital assets refers to

(a) normal wear and tear (b) foreseen obsolescence
(c) Both (a) and (b) (d) unforeseen obsolescence

15. Depreciation is equal to **NCERT (QR)**

(a) Personal Income – Personal Taxes
(b) Gross National Product – Personal Income
(c) Gross National Product – Net National Product
(d) None of the above

16. Which of the following statements is/are correct?

I. Unexpected obsolescence is a component of depreciation.
II. Inventory is a stock variable.

CBSE 2020 (M); Competency Based Que

Codes

(a) Only I (b) Only II
(c) Both I and II (d) None of these

17. Which variables are defined as any quantity measured at a particular point of time?

(a) Stock (b) Flow
(c) Investment (d) Inventory

18. Identify the concept depicted in the picture given below.

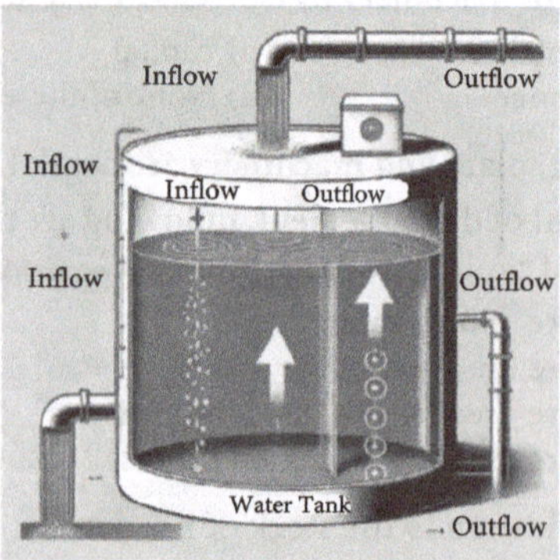

(a) Stock (b) Flow
(c) Investment (d) Depreciation reserve

19. The .... model depicts the relationship between households, firms and the government in terms of production, consumption and income generation.

(a) circular flow of income (b) capital formation
(c) supply and demand
(d) national income accounting

20. Circular flow of income refers to cycle of .... in the production process, its distribution among the factors of production and finally, its circulation from households to firms in the form of consumption expenditure on goods and services produced by them.

Competency Based Que

(a) generation of income (b) generation of goods
(c) generation of services (d) generation of gain

21. There are two sides to every transaction. When you purchase a piece of computer software, you give money to the seller and the seller gives the software to you.

You might literally hand over rupee bills and receive a CD, or you might enter a credit card number into a website entitling you to a download. The idea is the same either way. There is a flow of money from you to the seller and a flow of goods or services from the seller to you, this is true for all transactions. This movement of money from the buyers to the sellers refers to which phase of circular flow of income? **Competency Based Que**

(a) Phase of production
(b) Phase of income generation
(c) Phase of disposal
(d) Both (b) and (c)

22. Read the following figure carefully and choose the correct pair from the alternatives given below.

CBSE SQP 2024

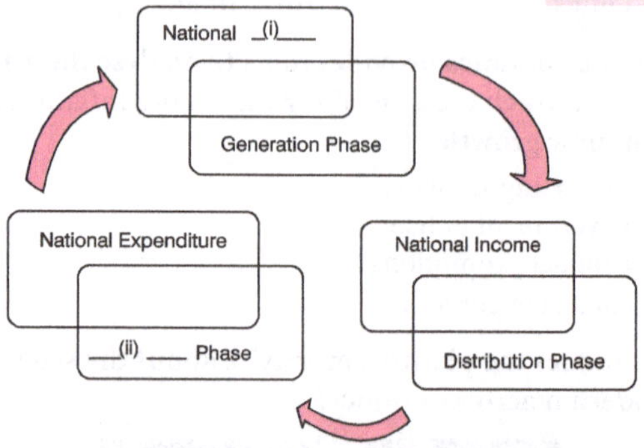

(a) Output, Production (b) Value added, Production
(c) Output, Disposition (d) Wealth, Development

23. In the context of the circular flow of income in a two-sector economy, identify the flow shown in the image below.

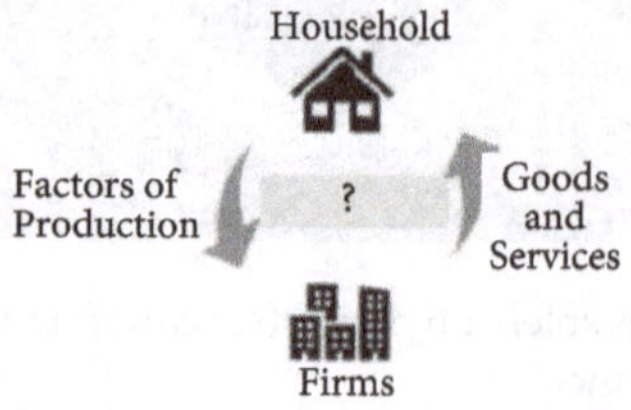

(a) Real Flow (b) Money Flow
(c) Government Flow (d) Financial sector Flow

24. **Which of the following is the money flow that corresponds to the real flow of resources?**

(a) Incomes (b) Consumption
(c) Factors of production (d) Goods and services

25. **Identify the circular flow of income from the image given below.**

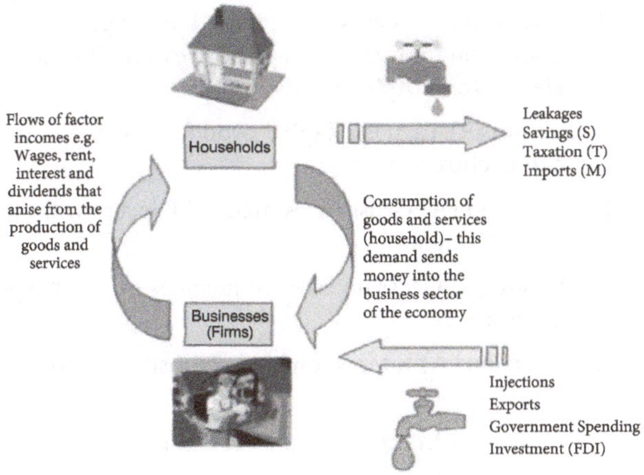

(a) Real flow (b) Money flow
(c) Both (a) and (b) (d) Neither (a) nor (b)

26. **In the circular flow model, if there were only a real flow but no money flow, which of the following would be the most likely outcome?** Competency Based Que

(a) Goods and services would be produced, but households and workers would receive no income in return
(b) Households would continue to receive income, but firms would struggle to produce goods and services
(c) Firms would incur higher production costs due to the lack of monetary transactions
(d) Both firms and households would experience increased savings due to reduced expenditures

27. **"Unemployment rate falls to a 10-year low, boosting consumer confidence and spending."**

What component of the circular flow of income is directly affected by this news? Competency Based Que

(a) Savings (b) Investment
(c) Consumption expenditure (d) Factor income

28. **"Local businesses experience higher revenues after increasing worker wages."**

In the two-sector circular flow model, what is the most likely explanation for this outcome? Competency Based Que

(a) Increased wages reduce profits, causing a decline in production and revenue
(b) Wages have no effect on business revenues in a two-sector model
(c) Higher wages increase household spending, leading to higher business revenues
(d) Higher wages only influence household savings, not business revenues

29. **The circular flow of income model assumes that**

(a) there is no international trade
(b) all markets are perfectly competitive
(c) the price level remains constant
(d) All of the above

30. **In a two-sector economy, aggregate demand can be determined by adding ....** CBSE SQP 2025

(a) autonomous consumption, induced consumption and induced investment
(b) autonomous consumption, autonomous investment and induced investment
(c) autonomous consumption and autonomous investment
(d) autonomous consumption, induced consumption and autonomous investment

Direction *Read the case study and answer the questions 31 to 34 on the basis of the same*

Kamakshi is an entrepreneur. She manufactures decorative items. She is at the helm of affairs. She hires wage labour from the market, she employs the services of capital and land as well. After hiring these inputs, she undertakes the task of production. Her motive for producing goods and services (referred to as output) is to sell them in the market and earn profits. She also sells her products online on international e-commerce sites and then ships the products to America, Belgium, Germany, etc.

In the process, she undertakes risks and uncertainties. e.g. She may not get a high enough price for the goods she is producing and this may lead to fall in the profits that she earns or the goods shipped may be damaged. However, she tries her best to mitigate such risks and uncertainties.

31. **For procuring capital from the market, Kamakshi will be required to pay ....**

32. **Divij works as a dispatch officer with Kamakshi. He will get .... for his services.**

(a) rent (b) interest (c) wages (d) salary

33. **Kamakshi earns .... for her efforts.**

34. **Kamakshi undertakes .... and ....**

(a) risks (b) benefits
(c) uncertainties (d) Both (a) and (c)

Direction *Read the case study and answer the questions 35 to 38 on the basis of the same*

Arjun runs a successful electronics retail store that sells a wide range of goods, including smartphones, laptops and home appliances.

He sources these final goods from manufacturers who produce them using various intermediate goods, such as electronic components and packaging materials. Arjun understands that his business relies not only on the stock of these goods in his store but also on the continuous flow of new inventory to meet customer demand.

To optimise his sales strategy, he closely monitors market trends and adjusts his orders accordingly. Arjun also makes strategic investments in advertising and store upgrades, which represent a form of capital investment. These investments aim to enhance customer experience and attract more foot traffic to his store. The balance between maintaining adequate stock levels of final goods and ensuring a steady flow of new products is crucial for maximising sales and profitability. By understanding these dynamics, Arjun positions his retail business to thrive in a competitive market place.

35. Arjun's electronics store primarily sells ...., which are designed for direct consumption by individuals.
(a) intermediate goods (b) capital goods
(c) consumer goods (d) final goods

36. The funds Arjun allocates for upgrading his store and improving marketing efforts are examples of .... that aim to enhance his business's operational capacity.
(a) capital goods (b) intermediate goods
(c) investments (d) consumer goods

37. The components used in the manufacturing of smart-phones, which do not directly reach consumers as finished products and are essential for the production process are known as ....

38. The synchronisation between Arjun's available stock and incoming customer orders reflects a careful management of the .... of his retail operations, ensuring smooth transactions and satisfied customers.

Assertion-Reason

Direction (Q.No. 39 to 46) *Read the following Assertion (A) and Reason (R) and choose the correct alternative from the following*

Alternatives

(a) Both Assertion (A) and Reason (R) are true and Reason (R) is the correct explanation of Assertion (A)
(b) Both Assertion (A) and Reason (R) are true, but Reason (R) is not the correct explanation of Assertion (A)
(c) Assertion (A) is true, but Reason (R) is false
(d) Assertion (A) is false, but Reason (R) is true

39. Assertion (A) Macroeconomics is the study of a single commodity unit.

Reason (R) The fundamental instruments of microeconomics are supply and demand.

40. Assertion (A) Macroeconomics plays a crucial role in assessing the standard of living across different countries.

Reason (R) By analysing indicators such as GDP per capita and income distribution, macroeconomics provides valuable insights into overall economic well-being.

41. Assertion (A) Goods that are used in the process of production for several years and are of high value, are referred to as capital goods.

Reason (R) Yarn is a capital good for a textile manufacturer.

42. Assertion (A) Gross investment still occurs without any net investment.

Reason (R) Gross investment includes value of expected obsolescence.

43. Assertion (A) Interest on bank deposits is a stock concept.

Reason (R) Interest is earned over a period of time.

44. Assertion (A) In income phase, factor incomes flow from firms to households.

Reason (R) Firms distribute the revenue received from the sale of goods and services as rent, interest, profit and wages.

45. Assertion (A) Real flow is also known as physical flow.

Reason (R) Real flow involves flow of factor payments between firms and households.

46. Assertion (A) Real flow and money flow are one or the same thing, presented in a different form.

Reason (R) In money flow, there is no involvement of goods in its physical form.

Two Statements Based MCQs

Direction (Q.No. 47 to 54) *Read the following statements carefully and choose the correct alternative*

Alternatives

(a) Statement I is correct and Statement II is incorrect
(b) Statement II is correct and Statement I is incorrect
(c) Both the statements are correct
(d) Both the statements are incorrect

47. Statement I The study of microeconomics focuses on how a nation's economy can be strengthened by its government.

Statement II The field of macroeconomics studies depression.

48. Statement I Producers and consumers are examples of institutional agents.

Statement II The goal of individual economic agents is to minimise their own utility and maximise social benefit.

49. **Statement I** Durable goods are items that have a long lifespan and are used over time.

Statement II Services such as haircuts are categorised as durable goods.

50. **Statement I** All capital goods are producer goods but not all producer goods are capital goods.

Statement II Capital goods are used for longer periods, whereas producer goods can be either intermediate or capital goods.

51. **Statement I** Depreciation reserve fulfils the need for replacement investment.

Statement II Loss in the value of fixed assets owing to sudden accident or natural calamity is also accounted in depreciation reserve fund.

52. **Statement I** Net investment is a stock concept.
Statement II Capital is a flow concept.

53. **Statement I** Savings by household sector leads to decrease in the circular flow of income.

Statement II Borrowings by the firms leads to increase in the circular flow of income.

54. **Statement I** Total production is equal to total consumption in the case of circular flow in a two-sector economy.

Statement II The household sector supplies factor services only to firms and the firm hire factor services only from households.

Matching

55. From the set of the statement in Column I and Column II, choose the correct pair of statement

Column I	Column II
A. Aggregate variables	(i) Deals with individual economic units like consumers, firms and markets.
B. Economic growth and development	(ii) Deals with the government's spending and taxation policies.
C. Economic fluctuations	(iii) Analyses the ups and downs of economic activity over time.
D. Short-run and long-run analysis	(iv) Studies the relationship between aggregate demand and aggregate supply.

Codes
(a) A-(i) (b) B-(ii) (c) C-(iii) (d) D-(iv)

56. Identify the correct sequence of alternatives given in Column II by matching them with respective item in Column I **Competency Based Que**

Column I	Column II
A. Fixed investment	(i) Demand for all good and services in the economy.
B. Aggregate demand	(ii) Raises productive capacity of the producers.
C. General equilibrium	(iii) Considered for the estimation of depreciation.
D. Expected obsolescence	(iv) Simultaneous equilibrium across all the market in economy.

Codes

	A	B	C	D		A	B	C	D
(a)	(iii)	(ii)	(iv)	(i)	(b)	(ii)	(i)	(iv)	(iii)
(c)	(iv)	(iii)	(i)	(ii)	(d)	(i)	(ii)	(iii)	(iv)

57 Match the options of Column I with their correct options in Column II

Column I (Feature)	Column II (Type of Good)
A. Goods that are ready to use by their final users.	(i) Final or capital goods.
B. Goods that are usedup in a single act of consumption.	(ii) Intermediate goods.
C. Goods which have not crossed the boundary line of production.	(iii) Final goods.
D. Goods of high value which are used by producers for several years.	(iv) Non-durable consumer goods.

Codes

	A	B	C	D		A	B	C	D
(a)	(i)	(ii)	(iii)	(iv)	(b)	(ii)	(iii)	(iv)	(i)
(c)	(iii)	(iv)	(ii)	(i)	(d)	(iv)	(iii)	(ii)	(i)

58. Match the options of Column I with their correct options in Column II.

Column I (Flow Chart)	Column II (Type of Circular Flow)
A. 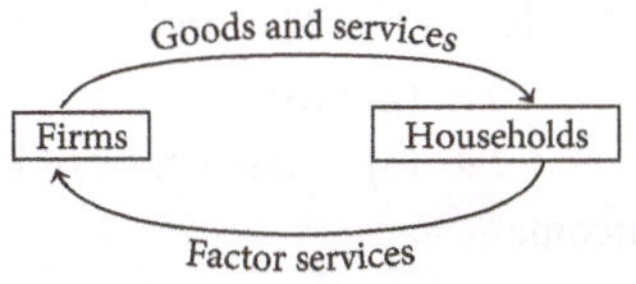	(i) Nominal flow
B. 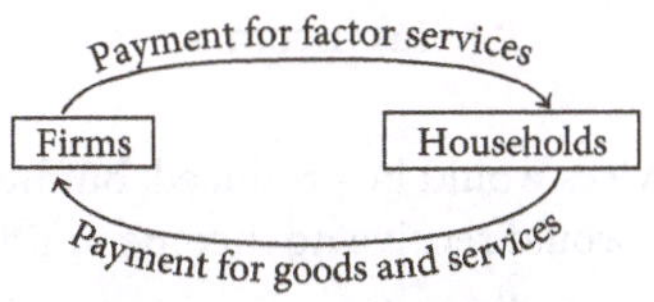	(ii) Real flow
	(iii) No flow

Codes

	A	B		A	B
(a)	(i)	(ii)	(b)	(ii)	(iii)
(c)	(iii)	(i)	(d)	(ii)	(i)

59. Identify the correct sequence of alternatives given in Column II by matching them with respective item in Column I

Column I	Column II
A. Injection	(i) Provides labour and receives wages
B. Leakage	(ii) Exports and investments
C. Household sector	(iii) Savings and taxes
D. Firm sector	(iv) Receives factors of production and provides goods and services

Codes

	A	B	C	D
(a)	(ii)	(iii)	(iv)	(i)
(b)	(ii)	(i)	(iv)	(iii)
(c)	(iv)	(iii)	(i)	(ii)
(d)	(ii)	(iii)	(i)	(iv)

Concept Identification

60. Items with a short lifespan, typically consumed or used up quickly usually in single act of consumption.

61. The loss of value of fixed asset while not in use.

62. Goods that can be used for a period of one year or slightly more and are not of very high value.

63. The process of increase in the stock of capital.

64. The movement of goods and services, along with the flow of money, between various sectors of the economy.

Answers

1. (c) Macroeconomics is basically concerned with the following three aggregates
   (i) Measurement national aggregates (i.e. GDP).
   (ii) Fluctuations in national aggregates (i.e. inflation).
   (iii) Growth in national aggregates (i.e. real GDP).
2. (c) John Maynard Keynes
3. (d) I, III and IV
4. (b) government policies
5. (c) It recognises the increasing role of international trade and globalisation
6. (a) I and II
7. (c) End-use
8. (b) semi-durable goods
9. (b) capital
10. (c) they are used for less than one year
11. (b) Fixed investment
12. (d) unplanned inventory stock
13. (a) Only I
14. (c) Both (a) and (b)
15. (c) Gross National Product – Net National Product
16. (b) Only II
17. (a) Stock
18. (b) Flow
19. (a) circular flow of income
20. (a) generation of income
21. (c) Phase of disposal
22. (c) Output, Disposition
23. (a) Real Flow
24. (a) Incomes
25. (c) Money flow
26. (a) Goods and services would be produced, but households and workers would receive no income in return
27. (c) Consumption expenditure (as consumer confidence and spending rise).
28. (c) Higher wages increase household spending, leading to higher business revenues
29. (d) All of the above
30. (a) autonomous consumption, induced consumption and induced investment
31. interest
32. (d) salary
33. profits
34. (d) Both (a) and (c)
35. (c) consumer goods
36. (c) investments
37. intermediate goods
38. flow
39. (d) Macroeconomics is concerned with the economy as a whole, focusing on aggregates such as total output, total employment, national income and overall price levels.
40. (a) Both Assertion (A) and Reason (R) are true and Reason (R) is the correct explanation of Assertion (A)
41. (b) Both Assertion (A) and Reason (R) are true, but Reason (R) is not the correct explanation of Assertion (A)
42. (a) Both Assertion (A) and Reason (R) are true and Reason (R) is the correct explanation of Assertion (A)
43. (d) Interest is a flow concept because it is earned over time.
44. (b) Both Assertion (A) and Reason (R) are true, but Reason (R) is not the correct explanation of Assertion (A)
45. (c) Real flow involves flow of goods and services between firms and households.
46. (d) Real flow and money flow are not the same thing; they represent different aspects of economic transactions.

Real flow refers to the physical movement of goods and services, while money flow refers to the transfer of money between economic agents. In money flow, money is transferred without involving the physical movement of goods or services.

47. (b) Policy formulation to strengthen the economy is a subject matter of macroeconomics.

48. (d) Producers and consumers are examples of economic agents, not institutional agents. The primary goal of individual economic agents (like producers and consumers) is typically to maximise their own utility or profit, rather than maximising social benefit.

49. (a) Services like haircuts are categorised as non-durable goods because they are consumed immediately and do not have a long lifespan.

50. (c) Both the statements are correct

51. (a) Unexpected obsolescence or sudden destruction is not accounted.

52. (d) Net investment is a flow concept because it represents the addition to the capital stock over a specific period. Capital is a stock concept because it represents the total assets or wealth available at a particular point in time, not over a period.

53. (c) Both the statements are correct

54. (c) Both the statements are correct

55. (c) C-(iii)

56. (b) (ii) (i) (iv) (iii)

57. (c) (iii) (iv) (ii) (i)

58. (d) (ii) (i)

59. (d) (ii) (iii) (i) (iv)

60. Non-durable goods

61. Capital loss

62. Semi-durable consumer goods

63. Investment

64. Intersectoral flows

Subjective Questions

Short Answer Type Questions

1. Describe 'The Great Depression' of 1929. NCERT

Ans. The Great Depression took place in 1929 which adversely affected the developed economies of Europe and North America. There was extreme fall in aggregate demand due to fall in income, which led to a vicious circle of poverty.

Demand for goods in the market was low. Many factors of production were lying idle and workers were thrown out of their jobs. The consequences of Great Depression gave birth to the study of macroeconomics.

2. What are the key areas of study within macroeconomics?

Ans. The key areas of study within macroeconomics are as follows

(i) **Theory of Employment**
It studies determination of employment in the economy, which further includes study of full employment, underemployment, voluntary and involuntary unemployment, etc.

(ii) **Theory of National Income**
It studies determination of domestic income and national income by different methods.

(iii) **Theory of General Pricing**
Issues related to inflation, deflation, excess demand, deficient demand, etc. are studied under this theory.

(iv) **Theory of Money**
It explains the important role of money and banking in the functioning of the economy.

(v) **Theory of International Trade**
It studies all international transactions between home country and rest of the world.

3. What is the difference between microeconomics and macroeconomics? NCERT

Ans. Differences between microeconomics and macroeconomics are

Basis	Microeconomics	Macroeconomics
Meaning	It studies economic problems at the level of an individual.	It studies economic problems at the level of an economy as a whole.
Constant Varibles	It assumes all the macrovariables to be constant as national income, consumption, saving, etc.	It assumes all the microvariables to be constant as demand of households, supply of firms, prices of individual products, etc.
Objective	It determines the output and price for an individual firm.	It determines an aggregate output and general price level in the whole economy.
Examples	Demand and supply.	Aggregate demand and aggregate supply.

4. "Final goods include only those goods which are consumed by the households." Defend or refute the given statement with valid reasons. CBSE 2020; Competency Based Que

Ans. I refute the given statement that "final goods include only those goods which are consumed by the households."

Final goods are products that have completed the production process and are ready for end-use. They are not subject to further transformation or resale within the current economic period. Final goods include both consumer goods (used by households, like food and clothing) and capital goods (used by businesses for production, like machinery and equipment).

Capital goods, though not consumed by households, are still final goods because they are the end products for businesses and are not meant for resale or further production within the period.

Thus, the statement is incorrect because it limits final goods to only consumer goods, ignoring capital goods. Final goods, therefore, include goods consumed by households as well as those used by firms for production.

5. The given below two images depict the 'micro' and 'macro' picture. Explain both the concepts with illustrations. Competency Based Que

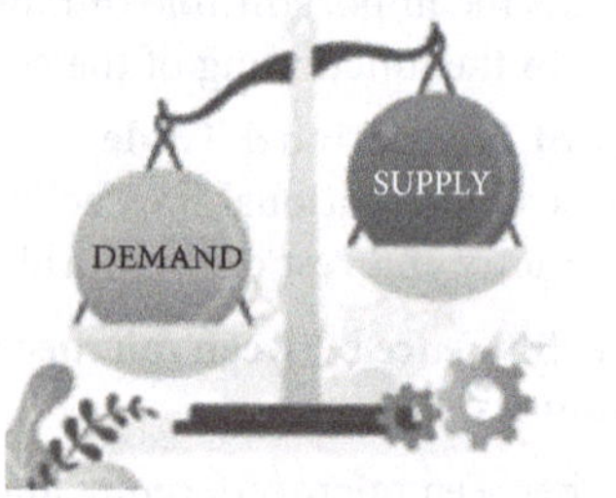

Picture A

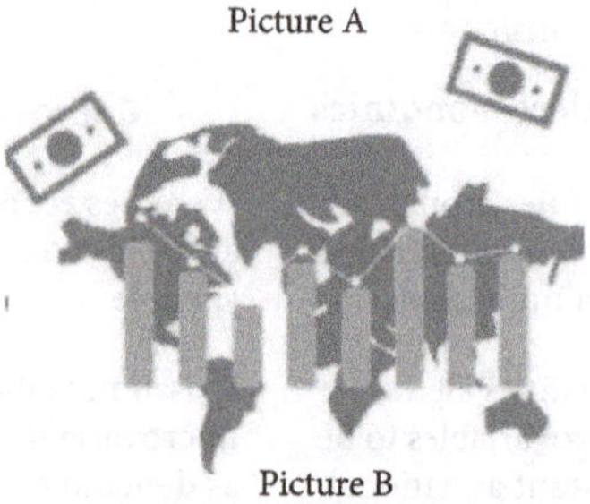
Picture B

Ans. Picture A represents 'microeconomic' concept while Picture B represents 'macroeconomic' concept.

The two concepts are discussed as follows

(i) Microeconomics examines choices and shortages at the individual, home, business and industry levels. For instance, microeconomics examines how a customer makes decisions about what products and services to purchase, in order to maximise his satisfaction with a given amount of income.

In contrast, macroeconomics examines choices and shortages at the level of the entire economy. For instance, macroeconomics examines how the nation's resources are allocated to promote the well-being of all citizens, whether through the production of consumer or defence goods.

(ii) The determination of output and price for a specific firm or industry is the focus of microeconomics. On the other hand, macroeconomics studies how the whole economy's general price level and total output are determined.

6. Differentiate between final goods and intermediate goods. CBSE 2024 C

Or

How do final goods and intermediate goods differ with each other?

Ans. Differences between final and intermediate goods are

Basis	Final Goods	Intermediate Goods
Meaning	They are those goods which are out of the production boundary and available for direct consumption by their buyers.	They are those goods which are still within the production boundary, i.e. either value need to be added or are meant for resale.
Purpose or Use	These goods are not resold by the firms to make profits during the accounting year.	These goods may be resold by the firms to make profits during the accounting year.
Consumption	These goods are ready to be consumed by their final users.	These goods are not ready to be consumed by their final users.
Value Addition	Value is not to be added to these goods.	Value is yet to be added to these goods.
Example	Machinery purchased by producer.	Wheat purchased by a baker.

7. Provide an example to illustrate the rationale behind the division of goods into final and intermediate categories.

Ans. The basis of classification is the end-use of the product. Goods which are used by the producers in the process of production such as raw material or goods purchased for resale, are known as intermediate goods.

e.g. Shirt purchased by a firm for resale. These goods are still within the production boundary.

Goods which are outside the boundary line of production and are ready for use by their final users are called final goods. e.g. Shirt purchased by a consumer.

8. Giving reason, classify the following into intermediate products and final products. Competency Based Que

(i) Computers installed in an office.

(ii) Mobile sets purchased by a mobile dealer.

Ans. (i) Computers installed in an office are final products.

Reason Offices buy computers as long-term durable products and invests in them. That's why, they are considered as a final products.

(ii) Mobile sets purchased by a mobile dealer are intermediate products.

Reason A mobile dealer purchases mobile sets for reselling. That's why, they are intermediate products.

9. Which among the following are final goods and which are intermediate goods? Give reasons.

(i) Milk purchased by a tea stall.

(ii) Bus purchased by a school.

(iii) Juice purchased by a student from the school canteen. Competency Based Que

Ans. (i) 'Milk purchased by a tea stall' is intermediate good.

Reason It will be used as a raw material for making tea and involves value addition.

(ii) 'Bus purchased by a school' is final good.

Reason School purchases bus as long-term durable product and it is an investment for school. It is not for resale.

(iii) 'Juice purchased by a student from school canteen' is final good.

Reason Here juice is purchased for direct satisfaction of student's need, i.e. juice is being consumed by its end user.

10. Schools across the country are playing a major role in bridging the educational gap. These institutions are using variety of goods like chalks, dusters, furniture, school bus, etc.

Categorise the goods used by schools based upon durability. Also which of the goods depreciates with time? Competency Based Que

Ans. Chalks and dusters used by the school are considered as intermediate goods as these goods get used up within one year while furniture and buses are final goods as these have a longer life shelf of more than one year. Capital goods like buses and furniture depreciates with time while chalks and dusters gets used up thus doesn't depreciate.

11. What are the distinctions between capital goods and consumer goods?

Ans. Differences between capital goods and consumer goods are

Basis	Consumer Goods	Capital Goods
Meaning	These goods are purchased by consumers for the satisfaction of their wants and not for resale.	These goods are purchased by manufacturers and producers for the production of other goods. These goods are not meant for resale.
Use	These are for own use.	These are used for production of goods and services.
Demand	High	Comparatively less
Examples	Bread, butter, jam, etc.	Machinery, equipment, etc.

12. Giving reason, classify the following into capital goods and consumer goods. Competency Based Que

(i) Ice-cream purchased by a consumer.

(ii) Plant and machinery of XYZ company.

Ans. (i) Ice-cream purchased by a consumer is a consumer good.

Reason Here, ice-cream is purchased for the direct satisfaction of human wants

(ii) Plant and machinery of XYZ company is a capital good.

Reason XYZ company uses plant and machinery in the process of production to produce final products.

13. "All producer goods are not capital goods." Do you agree? Competency Based Que

Ans. Yes, I agree that all producer goods are not capital goods, because producer goods includes

(i) Goods which are used as raw material, like wood used to make furniture.

(ii) Goods which are used as fixed assets like plant and machinery.

Capital goods include only fixed assets of the producers. These are durable goods. On the other hand, goods used as raw material are not capital goods as these are not repeatedly used in the process of production.

Thus, all producer goods are not capital goods.

14. What is the difference between depreciation and depreciation reserve fund?

Ans. Differences between depreciation and depreciation reserve fund are

Basis	Depreciation	Depreciation Reserve Fund
Concept	It is the loss in the value of fixed assets in use, on account of normal wear and tear and foreseen obsolescence.	It is a provision of funds created by producers to cope up with depreciation losses.

Basis	Depreciation	Depreciation Reserve Fund
Effect	It leads to correct computation of profit.	These funds are used for the replacement of fixed assets when they are worn out.
Reason	Expected or foreseen obsolescence, normal wear and tear.	Obsolete/Outdated assets need to be replaced.

15. "Machine purchased by a firm is always a capital good." Do you agree with the given statement? Give valid reasons for your answer. CBSE SQP 2023; Competency Based Que

Ans. No. I do not agree with the statement.

Capital goods are those final goods which help in the production of other goods and services. A machine purchased by a firm will be a capital good when it is used for the production of other goods and services.

However, if it is purchased by a firm for resale purposes in the same year, it will be considered as an intermediate good and not a capital good.

16. Give reasons and categorise the following into stock and flow. Competency Based Que

(i) Capital (ii) Saving
(iii) Gross domestic product
(iv) Wealth (v) Net investment

Ans. (i) **Capital**
It is a man-made means of production. It is a stock because it is measured at a given point of time.

(ii) **Saving**
It is the surplus of production over consumption. It is a flow as it is measured during a period of time.

(iii) **Gross Domestic Product**
It is a flow as it is the market value of final goods and services produced within the domestic territory, measured during a period of time.

(iv) **Wealth**
It is a stock as it is measured at a particular point of time.

(v) **Net Investment**
It is the addition to the stock of capital and it is measured during a period of time, hence it is a flow concept.

17. Differentiate between stock variables and flow variables with suitable example. CBSE 2024 C

Ans. Differences between stock and flow are

Basis	Stock	Flow
Meaning	It is that quantity of an economic variable which is measured at a particular point of time.	It is that quantity of an economic variable which is measured during a period of time.
Time	It has no time dimension.	It has time dimension as per hour, per day, per month.
Concept	It is a static concept.	It is a dynamic concept.
Examples	Quantity of money, wealth, etc.	Consumption, investment, etc.

18. Describe the four major sectors in an economy according to the macroeconomic point of view. NCERT

Ans. An economy is generally classified into the following four sectors

(i) **Household Sector**
It is engaged in the consumption of goods and services.

(ii) **Producing Sector**
It is engaged in the production of goods and services.

(iii) **Government Sector**
It is engaged in such activities which are related to taxation and subsidies as well as consumption and production.

(iv) **Rest of the World/External Sector**
It is engaged in exports and imports.

19. Describe the concept of the circular flow of income in an economy.

Ans. Circular flow means the unending flow of production of goods and services and income and expenditure in an economy from one sector of an economy to another. It shows the redistribution of income in a circular manner between production units and households.

This circulation happens in terms of income in the production process and distribution between the factors of production. Households provide factors of production (such as labour and capital) to firms, which in turn produce goods and services.

Firms pay wages, rent, interest and profits to households as income for their contributions. Households then spend this income on goods and services produced by firms, creating demand. This spending generates revenue for firms, completing the cycle.

20. What is the principle of circular flow of income and product?

Ans. It involves two basic principles

(i) Real flow of income implies the flow of factor services from the households sector to the producing sector.

(ii) Flow of income across different sectors always implies the identity between payments and receipts.

21. Explain the three phases of the circular flow of income.

Ans. The three different phases in the circular flow of income are as follows

(i) **Production Phase**

In this phase, the firm manufactures the goods and services with the assistance of factor services.

(ii) **Distribution Phase**

This phase involves the flow of factor income, which comprises rent, interests, wages and profit from the firm to the household.

(iii) **Expenditure Phase**

Here, the income collected by the factors of production is used on the goods and services manufactured by a firm.

22. "Disposition phase of circular flow of income involves flow of factor income, which comprises of rent, wages, interest and profits from firms to households."

Defend or refute the statement, giving valid reasons in support of your answer.

CBSE 2024; Competency Based Que

Ans. I defend the statement, as it accurately describes the disposition/expenditure phase of the circular flow of income. It highlights the movement of factor income from firms to households, which is a important aspect of economic activity within the circular flow model.

The reasons are as follows

(i) **Disposition Phase**

This phase involves the flow of factor income from firms to households.

(ii) **Factors of Production**

The statement mentions the flow of factor income, which comprises rent, wages, interest and profits. These are indeed the primary forms of factor income.

(iii) **Flow from Firms to Households**

This reflects the movement of factor payments from firms, which utilise the factors of production, to households, which provide these factors.

23. Discuss the difference between real flow and money flow.

Ans. Differences between real flow and money flow are

Basis	Real Flow	Money Flow
Meaning	Real flow explains the flow of goods and services between the two sectors of an economy, i.e. households and firms.	Money flow explains the flow of money between the two sectors of an economy; i.e. households and firms.
Exchange	The households provide factor services to firms and on the other hand, the firms provide goods and services to the households for consumption purpose.	The households receive factor payments from the firms in the form of income and this income is then spent by the households on the purchase of goods and services.
Known as	It is also termed as physical flow.	It is also termed as nominal flow.

24. "Circular flow of income in a two-sector economy is based on the axiom that one's expenditure is other's income."

Do you agree with the given statement? Support your answer with valid reasons. **Competency Based Que**

Or

"Circular flow principle is based on the assumption that one's expenditure will become other's income." Explain the given statement. **CBSE 2020**

Ans. Yes, I agree with the given statement. In a two-sector economy, the firms produce goods and services and make factors payments to the households. The factor income earned by the households will be used to buy the goods and services which would be equal to income of firms.

Thus, the aggregate consumption expenditure by the households in the economy is equal to the aggregate expenditure on goods and services produced by the firms in the economy (income of the producers).

25. Viaan and Rohan are two partners in a business. Over the year, both of them have expanded their production and sales around the globe. In order to meet domestic demands for goods, they sometimes import raw material from abroad. Also, they meet the demand for domestic goods by producing both domestically and abroad.

Identify the leakages and injections in the circular flow of income. Also explain the impact on the overall circular flow of income of the above transactions.

Competency Based Que

Ans. Exports of goods by Viaan and Rohan is an injection to the circular flow of income as it leads to inflow of currency while import of raw materials are leakages from the circular flow as it leads to outflow of currency.

The overall impact on the circular flow of income depends upon the magnitude of exports and imports by the two partners. If the value of exports exceeds the value of imports, then there will be growth in the circular flow of income and if imports exceeds exports, it will lead to weakening of the circular flow.

26. **Based upon the image given below, answer the following questions**

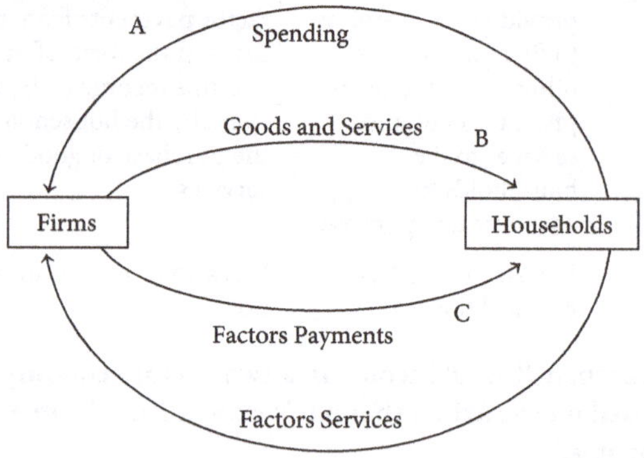

(i) What do the arrows labelled 'goods and services' and 'factors services' represent in the diagram?

(ii) Explain how an injection or leakage, could affect the flow of income in this model.

Competency Based Que

Ans. (i) • 'Goods and services' arrows represent the flow of goods and services from firms to households.

• 'Factors services' arrows represent the flow of labour, land, capital and entrepreneurship from households to firms.

(ii) Injections (like investment) and leakages (like savings) disrupt the circular flow of income. Injections add money to the economy, stimulating production and increasing firms' income, which can lead to economic growth.

Leakages, such as savings, reduce spending on goods and services, potentially decreasing firms' income and slowing economic activity.

If leakages exceed injections, overall economic activity declines; if injections exceed leakages, the economy expands.

Long Answer Type Questions

27. **How can the importance of macroeconomics be emphasised?**

Ans. Macroeconomics is important for several reasons

(i) It provides a comprehensive overview of the economy.

(ii) It offers guidance on growth and development.

(iii) It aids in achieving economic stability through suitable monetary and fiscal policies.

(iv) It helps to determine a country's Balance of Payments (BoP) status, which reveals performance of the economy in relation to rest of the world.

(v) It provides insights into issues like poverty, unemployment, inflation, foreign exchange rate as well as environmental pollution.

(vi) Data on macroeconomic variables is crucial for crafting policies aimed at national growth and development.

28. **What are consumer goods? Categorise them and explain each category with the help of an example.**

Ans. These are the goods which are directly used for the satisfaction of human wants. e.g. Ice-cream and milk used by the households. Consumer goods are broadly classified into four categories, as under

(i) **Durable Goods**

These are those consumer goods which can be used for several years and are generally expensive. e.g. TV, AC, etc.

(ii) **Semi-durable Goods**

These are those consumer goods which have a life span of one year or more but they are not of very high value, like crockery, clothes, etc.

(iii) **Non-durable Goods**

These are those consumer goods which are used in single act of consumption, i.e. they cannot be re-used, like fruits, vegetables, milk, etc.

(iv) **Services**

These are intangible goods, that cannot be seen or touched, but their benefit can be enjoyed, i.e. they directly satisfy human wants. e.g. Watching a movie in a cinema hall, getting treatment from a doctor.

29. (i) **"Basis of classification of final goods into consumption and capital goods depend on the economic nature of its use."**

Defend or refute the statement, with the help of a suitable example.

(ii) **"Natural calamities in the hill states of India have led to massive destruction of capital assets."**

Identify the type of loss (depreciation or capital loss) indicated in the aforesaid statement. Give valid reasons in support of your answer.

CBSE 2024 C; Competency Based Que

Ans. (i) The statement is defended. The classification of final goods into consumption goods and capital goods is determined by their purpose or use in the economy.

• **Consumption Goods**

These goods are used directly by consumers to satisfy their needs and provide immediate utility. e.g. Milk, bread and clothes are classified as consumption goods because they fulfill household needs.

• **Capital Goods**

These goods are used in the production process to produce other goods and services. e.g. Machinery and tools used by producers are capital goods, as they aid in generating income and economic value.

Thus, the classification of goods into these two categories is dependent on whether the good satisfies consumer needs directly (consumption) or contributes to production (capital).

(ii) The loss described in the statement is capital loss, not depreciation. Depreciation accounts for the wear and tear, obsolescence or gradual reduction in the value of fixed assets over time. In contrast, capital loss refers to the sudden destruction of assets due to unforeseen events such as natural calamities, accidents or disasters, which cannot be predicted or accounted for systematically as depreciation. Hence, the loss due to natural calamities is categorised as a capital loss because it involves an unexpected and immediate reduction in the value of capital assets.

30. Explain circular flow of income in a two-sector economy.

Ans. Circular flow means the unending flow of production of goods and services and income and expenditure in an economy from one sector of an economy to another.

In a two-sector economy, there are only two sectors of economic activity, namely households and firms. In this type of economy, intersectoral circular flow can be explained with the help of the following diagram

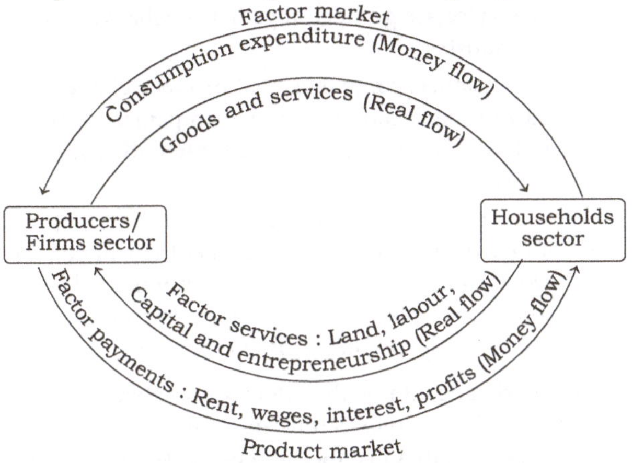

(i) The upper half of the diagram represents the factor market, while the lower half represents the commodity market.

(ii) The factors of production flow from households to firms. The firms use these factors to produce goods and services required by households. Thus, goods flow from the households to the firms and from the firms back to the households. It is called product flow.

(iii) Similarly, money flows from firms to households in the form of factor payments such as rent, wages, interest, and profit. Households use this income to purchase goods and services.

Thus, money flows from the firms to the households and from the households back to the firms. It is called money flow.

In the circular flow of income, production generates factor income, which is converted into expenditure. This flow of income continues as production is a continuous activity due to never-ending human wants. It makes the flow of income circular.

31. Explain with the help of diagrams, real flow and money flow of income.

Ans. Real Flow

Real flow explains the flow of factor services by the households to firms as well as the flow of the goods and services produced by the firms to households. It is also termed as physical flow.

The households provide factor services in the form of wage labour, capital, land and entrepreneurship to firms. On the other hand, the firms provide goods and services to the households for consumption purpose.

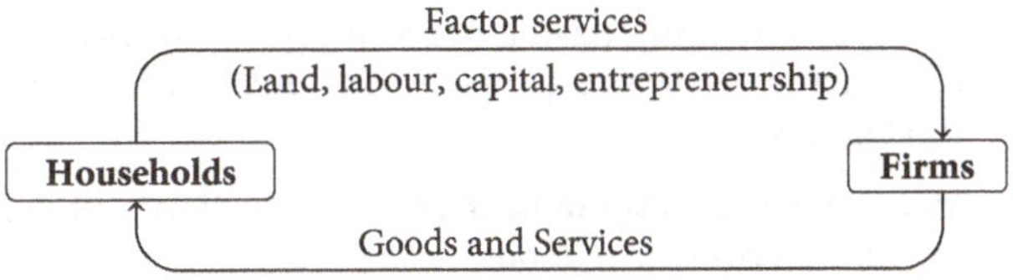

Real flow in a two-sector economy

Money Flow

Money flow explains the flow of factor payments by firms to households for their factor services as well as the flow of money from households to firms in the form of purchase of goods and services. It is also termed as nominal flow.

The households receive wages, rent, interest and profits from the firms in the form of income.

This income is then spent by the households on the purchase of goods and services produced by the firms. So, money first flows from firms to households and then from households to firms.

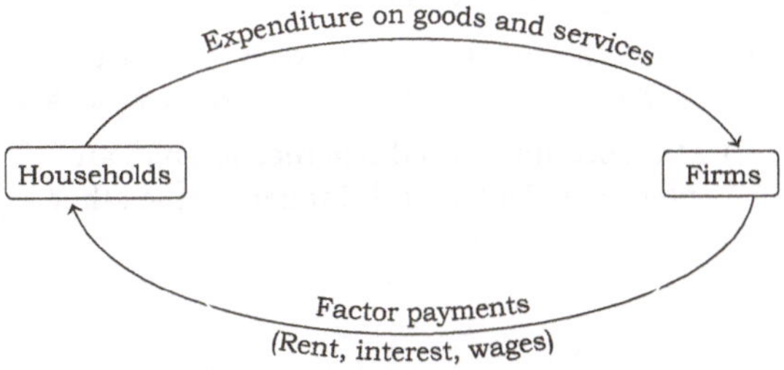

Money flow in a two-sector economy

32. **There are majorly two branches of economics, namely microeconomics and macroeconomics. In actual sense, micro and macroeconomics are interdependent.**

The theories regarding the behaviour of some macroeconomic aggregates (but not all) are derived from theories of individual behaviour.

For instance, the theory of investment, which is a part and parcel of the microeconomic theory, is derived from the behaviour of individual entrepreneur.

According to this theory, an individual entrepreneur in his investment activity is governed by the expected rate of profit on the one hand and rate of interest on the other.

Also, the production decision in the market is dependent upon consumer choices or consumption goods demand and so is the aggregate investment function. Similarly, the theory of aggregate consumption function is based upon the behaviour patterns of individual consumers.

In the production decision of an entrepreneur, they come across variety of goods, broadly intermediate and final goods.

Intermediate goods can be used in production, but they can also be consumer goods.

How it is classified depends on who buys it. If a consumer buys a bag of sugar to use at home, it is a consumer good. But if a manufacturer purchases sugar to use during the production of another product, it becomes an intermediate good.

Capital goods, on the other hand, are assets that are used in the production of consumer goods. That means they are purchased to help in the production process.

So, the baker who bakes the bread will buy an oven to use in the production process which will be considered as capital good, that doesn't transform or change shape, unlike the wheat.

(i) Explain the interdependence between the two branches of economics.

(ii) Explain the interlink between the consumer goods and producer goods. **Competency Based Que**

Ans. (i) Microeconomics and macroeconomics are interdependent as each influences the other.

Microeconomics, which studies individual decisions by consumers and firms, shapes macroeconomic outcomes like national income and inflation through aggregated consumer spending and business investment.

Conversely, macroeconomic policies, like interest rate changes or tax policies, impact individual choices and business strategies by affecting costs, income and demand. This interaction forms a continuous cycle: changes in macroeconomic conditions (like recessions) affect micro-level decisions, while these individual choices impact the broader economy.

Understanding both is essential for effective policy-making and economic analysis.

(ii) A society's economy is based on creating wealth through selling and buying. The people who do the selling and buying are producers and consumers.

Producers create or produce goods and provide services and consumers buy those goods and services with money. Most people are both producers and consumers.

Producers can be individuals or companies. Companies that produce a particular kind of good or service are grouped together in what is known as an industry.

For instance, companies that produce clothes are part of the fashion industry. Companies within the fashion industry compete with each other for consumers.

Consumers are the people who buy the goods and services. Most consumers get their money by working for companies. This economic cycle creates jobs for people. People with jobs, or workers, have money to spend on goods and services.

33. **In a market economy, the interaction between firms and households is fundamental. Firms are organisations that produce goods and services. They utilise various inputs, such as labour, capital and natural resources, to create products that are sold in output markets.**

To acquire these inputs, firms purchase resources in factor markets. On the other hand, households provide labour and other resources to firms and receive income in the form of wages, rent and dividends.

Households then spend this income on goods and services in the product markets. This interdependence creates a continuous flow of money and resources between firms and households.

Source *Adapted from "Economic Fundamentals: A Comprehensive Guide," Economic Insights, 2023.*

(i) **Define the term 'factor market' and explain its role in the economy.**

(ii) **What does the term 'circular flow of income' signify? Discuss its importance in understanding economic dynamics.** **Competency Based Que**

Ans. (i) A 'factor market' refers to the marketplace where services of the factors of production, such as labour, capital, land and entrepreneurship, are bought and sold. In this market

- firms demand factors of production to use in the production of goods and services.
- households supply these factors, such as labour, in exchange for income.

The **role** of the factor market is crucial as it facilitates the allocation of resources for production and determines the distribution of income among households. The efficiency of this market influences overall economic productivity and growth.

(ii) The circular flow of income represents the continuous movement of money between producers (firms) and consumers (households) in an economy.

It shows how different sectors of an economy interact and depend on each other.

This model illustrates how production, income generation and expenditure are interconnected

- Households provide labour and resources to firms.
- Firms produce goods and services and pay households for these resources.
- Households use the income earned to purchase goods and services from firms.

The significance of the circular flow of income includes

- **Interdependence of Sectors**
  The circular flow model highlights the interdependence between different sectors of the economy.
  It shows how households and firms rely on each other for resources and goods/services, creating a network of economic activities.
- **Measurement of Economic Activity**
  By examining the circular flow of income, economists can measure key economic indicators like Gross Domestic Product (GDP), national income and national output. It helps in understanding the overall economic performance.
- **Understanding Economic Equilibrium**
  The circular flow model helps in analysing the equilibrium state of an economy where total production equals total consumption. It assists in identifying imbalances that may lead to inflation or recession.

SELF ASSESSMENT TEST

Objective Type Questions

1. Which is/are the main problem(s) addressed in macroeconomics?
   (a) Determination of output of a firm
   (b) Determination of price of a product
   (c) Determination of income and employment level in the economy
   (d) All of the above

2. Which of the following statements is/are correct?
   I. In microeconomics, there is a high degree of aggregation.
   II. Study of automobile industry is related to macroeconomics.

   Codes
   (a) Only I (b) Only II
   (c) Both (a) and (b) (d) None of these

3. Which of the following is not an example of depreciation?
   (a) A plant producing rubber shoes becomes obsolete when demand shift from rubber shoes to leather shoes
   (b) A plant producing black and white televisions becomes obsolete when technology is discovered to produce colour televisions
   (c) Fall in the market value of the assets during the period of economic recession
   (d) Fall in the value of your school building

4. In the two-sector model of circular flow, the two main participants in the economy are
   (a) households and government
   (b) firms and foreign sector
   (c) households and firms
   (d) government and foreign sector

5. In the two-sector model, circular flow equilibrium is achieved when
   (a) total income is greater than total expenditure
   (b) total income equals total expenditure
   (c) total savings equal total investments
   (d) total production equals total exports

6. **Statement I** Macroeconomics and microeconomics are interdependent as policies aimed at one level often impact the other.

   Statement II A change in national income, a macroeconomic factor, can influence demand for individual goods and services, a microeconomic consideration.

   Alternatives
   (a) Statement I is correct and Statement II is incorrect
   (b) Statement II is correct and Statement I is incorrect
   (c) Both statements are correct
   (d) Both statements are incorrect

Answers 1. (c) 2. (d) 3. (c) 4. (c) 5. (b) 6. (c)

Short Answer Type Questions

7. Explain the concept of depreciation reserve fund.
8. Explain the concept of gross and net investment.
9. What are the phases of circular flow of income?
10. Differentiate between real flow and money flow in the context of circular flow of income. Give examples to support your answer.
11. "In response to rising inflation and increasing unemployment rates, the government has introduced a fiscal stimulus package aimed at boosting aggregate demand and creating jobs." — The Economic Times

    Based on the statement above, explain the importance of macroeconomics in addressing national economic issues such as inflation and unemployment. How does macroeconomics help policy-makers design strategies to stabilise the economy?
12. Describe the four major sectors in an economy according to the macroeconomics point of view.

Long Answer Type Questions

13. Discuss in brief the scope of macroeconomics.
14. Discuss briefly the types of goods produced in an economy.
15. Read the following statement and answer the question that follows

    "In the wake of the economic downturn, households are tightening their budgets while firms are experiencing a decrease in demand for goods and services, leading to a significant impact on the circular flow of income."
    — Financial Express

    Based on the statement above, explain the two-sector circular flow of income, including the roles of households and firms in this model.

02

"National income is the total amount of services received by consumers from their material and human environments."

— *Irving Fisher*

YOUR STUDY GOALS

2.1 National Income

2.2 Methods of Measuring National Income
- Value Added Method
- Income Method
- Expenditure Method

YOUR PRACTICE GOAL

- Objective Questions (80 Qs ; MCQs, A-R, Statements, Matching, Concept Identification)
- Subjective Questions (41 SAs, 9 LAs)
- 63 Numerical Questions
- Self Assessment Test (7 MCQs, 7 SAs, 2 LAs, 4 Numerical)

National Income and its Related Concepts

2.1 National Income

It is defined as the sum total of factor incomes earned by normal residents of a country, within the domestic territory of a country and from rest of the world, during a period of an accounting year.

Important Concepts Related to National Income

Concept	Explanation
Normal Resident of a Country	A person or institution, who ordinarily resides in a country for a period of one year or more and whose centre of economic interest, i.e. earnings, spendings and accumulation lies in that country.
Citizenship and Residential Status	**Citizenship** is a legal concept which is based on the birth place of person or when some legal provisions allow a person to be a citizen of a country. **Residential Status** is an economic concept which is based on economic activities performed by a person. A person can be a citizen of one country and at the same time, he can be the resident of another country.
Domestic Territory of a Country	According to the United Nations, domestic territory or economic territory of a country is the geographical territory, administrated by the government of that country within which persons, goods and capital circulate freely.

Point to Remember

While relating to the concept of domestic territory in economics, students should not keep in mind the political map of India. Rather, it is basically an area of operation, where people or goods or capital of a country can move and circulate freely to add to economic interest of country. In economics, domestic territory basically means the 'economic territory' of country.

Factor Income and Transfer Income

Basis	Factor Income	Transfer Income
Meaning	It refers to income received by the owners of factors of production for rendering factor services in the production process.	It refers to income received without rendering any productive service in return.
Nature	It is included in both national income and domestic income.	It is neither included in national income nor in domestic income.
Concept	It is a earning concept.	It is a receipt concept.
Example	Land-rent, labour-wages, capital-interest, entrepreneur-profit.	Subsidies, old age pensions, scholarships, unemployment allowance, etc.

Terms Related to Aggregates of National Income

1. Domestic and National Concept of Income

- The sum total of factor incomes earned within the domestic territory of a country in the course of an accounting year is termed as **domestic income**. This income can be earned by normal residents or non-residents.

Domestic Income = Domestic Product

- The sum total of factor incomes earned by the normal residents of a country within a period of an accounting year is termed as **national income**. This income can be earned within or outside the domestic territory of the country.

National Income = National Product

2. Factor Cost and Market Price

- Factor cost is the cost accrued by firms due to the payments made to the factors of production in the form of rent, interest, wages and profit, during a period of one year.
- Market price is the price at which the product is sold in the market. It is arrived at by adding indirect taxes and subtracting subsidies from the factor cost of the product.

3. NFIA, Depreciation and Net Indirect Tax

Concept	Meaning	Formula	Conversion
Net Factor Income from Abroad (NFIA)	It is the difference between factor income from abroad and the factor income paid to abroad.	NFIA = Factor Income received from Abroad − Factor Income paid to Abroad	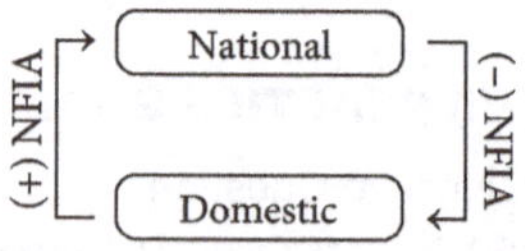
Depreciation	It refers to the loss in the value of fixed assets due to their normal wear and tear.	Depreciation = Gross Investment − Net Investment	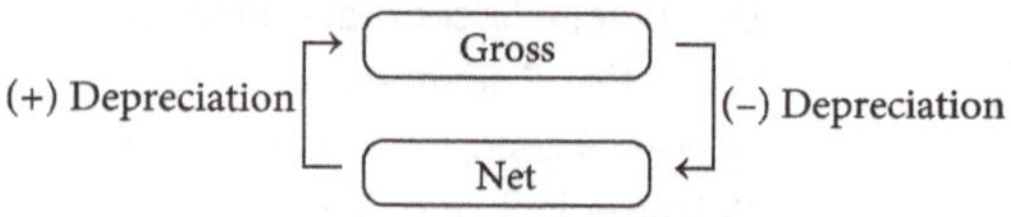
Net Indirect Tax (NIT)	It is equal to the difference between indirect taxes and subsidies.	Market Price = Factor Cost − Net Indirect Taxes	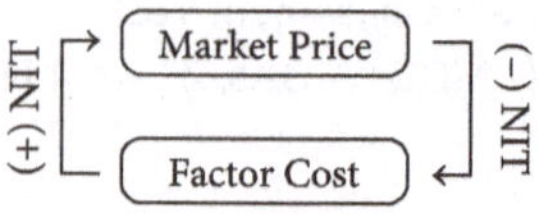

Points to Consider

- **Factor Income from Abroad** The income earned by the normal residents of a country from the Rest of the World (RoW) in the form of wages and salaries, rent, interest, dividend and retained earnings.
- **Factor Income to Abroad** The factor income paid to the normal residents of other countries (i.e. non-residents) for their factor services within the economic territory.
- **Indirect Taxes** These taxes are imposed by the government on production of goods and services. e.g. Goods and Services Tax (GST), custom duty, etc.
- **Subsidies** It is a form of financial aid given by the government to the firms and households, with the aim of promoting economic and social policy. e.g. Subsidy on cooking gas.

Aggregates Related to National Income

There are eight aggregates of national income, which are as follows

Aggregate	Meaning	Formula
Gross Domestic Product at Market Price (GDP_{MP})	It is the market value of the final goods and services produced during a year within the domestic territory of a country by residents or non-residents. It includes the value of depreciation or consumption of fixed capital.	—
Net Domestic Product at Market Price (NDP_{MP})	It is the market value of the final goods and services produced within the domestic territory of a country during a year, exclusive of depreciation.	$NDP_{MP} = GDP_{MP}$ – Depreciation
Gross Domestic Product at Factor Cost (GDP_{FC})	It is the sum total of factor cost incurred on the production of final goods and services within the domestic territory of a country along with consumption of fixed capital during the year. It is exclusive of Net Indirect Taxes (NIT).	$GDP_{FC} = GDP_{MP}$ – NIT
Net Domestic Product at Factor Cost (NDP_{FC})	It is the sum total of factor cost incurred on the production of final goods and services within the domestic territory of a country during a year, exclusive of depreciation.	$NDP_{FC} = GDP_{MP}$ – Depreciation – NIT *or* $NDP_{FC} = GDP_{FC}$ – Depreciation
Gross National Product at Market Price (GNP_{MP})	It is the market value of the final goods and services produced in the economy, during a year, inclusive of Net Factor Income from Abroad (NFIA).	$GNP_{MP} = GDP_{MP}$ + NFIA
Net National Product at Market Price (NNP_{MP})	It is the market value of the final goods and services produced in the economy during an accounting year, exclusive of depreciation and inclusive of Net Factor Income from Abroad (NFIA).	$NNP_{MP} = GDP_{MP}$ – Depreciation + NFIA *or* $NNP_{MP} = GNP_{MP}$ – Depreciation
Gross National Product at Factor Cost (GNP_{FC})	It is the sum total of factor incomes earned by normal residents of a country, inclusive of depreciation during an accounting year and Net Factor Income from Abroad (NFIA).	$GNP_{FC} = GDP_{FC}$ + NFIA
Net National Product at Factor Cost (NNP_{FC})	It is the sum total of all the factor incomes earned by normal residents of a country during the period of an accounting year. It is net of depreciation and inclusive of Net Factor Income from Abroad (NFIA). In economic sense, it is the national income of the country.	$NNP_{FC} = GNP_{FC}$ – Depreciation *or* $NNP_{FC} = NDP_{FC}$ + NFIA

Relationship between Domestic Product Concepts

Domestic product concepts include GDP_{MP}, NDP_{MP}, GDP_{FC} and NDP_{FC}.

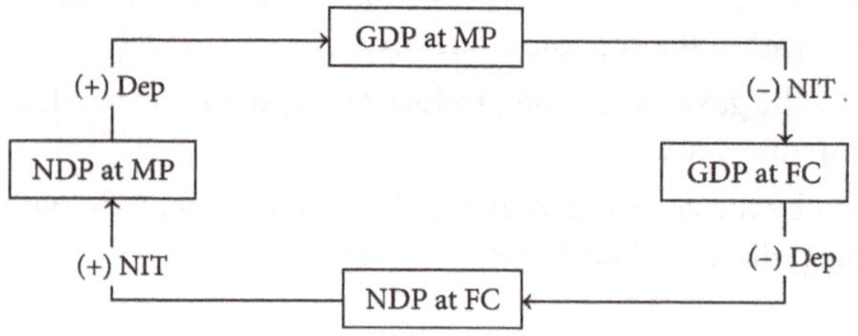

Relationship between National Product Concepts

National product concepts include GNP_{MP}, NNP_{MP}, GNP_{FC} and NNP_{FC}.

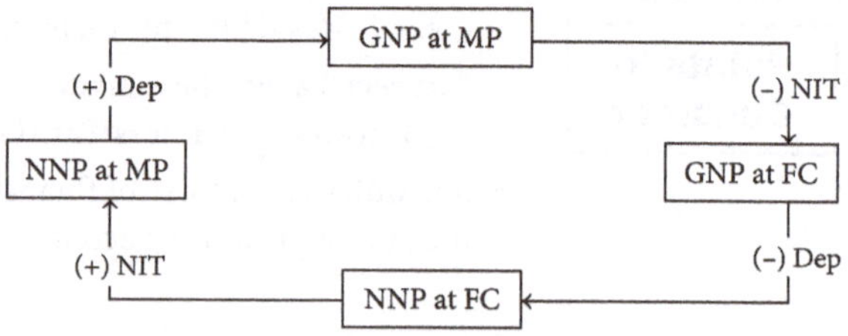

Nominal GDP and Real GDP

GDP may be estimated at current prices or constant prices. These are explained as follows

Basis	Nominal GDP/GDP at Current Prices	Real GDP/ GDP at Constant Prices
Meaning	It refers to market value of the final goods and services produced within the domestic territory of a country during a financial year, as estimated using the current year prices. It is also called monetary GDP.	It refers to market value of the final goods and services produced within the domestic territory of a country during a financial year, as estimated using the base year prices. It increases only when there is increase in the quantum of output in an economy.
Formula	It is calculated in the following manner $Y = Q \times P$ Where, Y = GDP at Current Prices Q = Quantity of goods and services produced during an accounting year P = Price of goods and services prevailing during an accounting year	It is calculated in the following manner $Y' = Q \times P'$ Where, Y' = GDP at constant prices Q = Quantity of goods and services produced during an accounting year P' = Price of goods and services prevailing during the base year

GDP Deflator

It is the ratio of Nominal GDP to Real GDP. It measures average price changes in all goods and services that add upto GDP. It is calculated as

$$\text{GDP Deflator/Price Index} = \frac{\text{Nominal GDP}}{\text{Real GDP}} \times 100$$

GDP and Welfare

GDP may be a good indicator of economic growth but it is not considered as a good measure of welfare of people or economic welfare. Welfare of people refers to the greater and equitable availability of goods and services per person. GDP is not an appropriate indicator for welfare due to following reasons

1. **Externalities** They refer to benefits or harms of an activity caused by a firm or an individual, for which they are not charged or penalised. e.g. Environmental pollution caused by industrial plants is a **negative externality** and building a flyover is a **positive externality.**
2. **Distribution of GDP** When GDP is unevenly distributed, increase in GDP does not result in increase in welfare.
3. **Non-monetary Exchanges** Many activities in an economy are not evaluated in monetary terms, they are not included in GDP, due to non-availability of data.

Better Measure of Welfare: Nominal or Real GDP

As Nominal GDP gives us an indication of increase in the level of output only, Real GDP is definitely a better measure.

The following points can be put forward to prove it

- It helps to compare the increase or decrease in physical output across different years.
- It measures the actual increase or decrease in the level of physical output in terms of quantity and not due to prices.
- It helps to make international comparisons.

Real GDP

2.2 Methods of Measuring National Income

National income can be calculated from three aspects

- In the form of flow of goods and services – Value Added Method or Production Method
- In the form of income flow – Income Method
- In the form of expenditure flow – Expenditure Method

Value Added Method or Product Method

This method is based on the aspect that national income is the sum total of value added by all producing units in the economy during a financial year.

Under this method, from the value of output, the value of intermediate consumption is deducted to find the value added to the product by a firm during an accounting year. The value added by all the firms, i.e. the sum total of value added by all the firms give us Gross Domestic Product at Market Price (GDP_{MP}).

The various steps to be followed are discussed as follows

***Step* 1** **Categorisation of Producing Enterprises**

Primary sector, secondary sector, tertiary sector

***Step* 2** **Estimation of Value of Output**

Value of Output = Sales + Change-in-stock

where, Change-in-stock = Closing Stock – Opening Stock

***Step* 3** **Estimation of Gross Value Added at Market Price** (GVA_{MP})

$GVA_{MP} = GDP_{MP} = \Sigma GVA = VA_P + VA_S + VA_T$

Where, ΣGVA = Summation of gross value added; VA_P = Value added in primary sector; VA_S = Value added in secondary sector; VA_T = Value added in tertiary sector

***Step* 4** **Estimation of National Income** (NNP_{FC})

National Income (NNP_{FC}) = GVA_{MP} – Depreciation – Net Indirect Taxes + Net Factor Income from Abroad

Precautions while using Value Added Method

- The value of intermediate goods should not be included.
- Purchase and sale of second-hand goods should not be included.
- Imputed or estimated value of self-consumed goods should be included but self-consumed services should not be included.
- Own account production should be included.
- Commission earned on account of sale and purchase of second-hand goods is included.
- Double counting should be avoided. For this, final output method or value added method can be adopted.

Problem of Double Counting

Double counting refers to counting of an output more than once while passing through various stages of production. While measuring national income, only the value of final goods and services should be included. However, when the value of intermediate goods is also included along with the value of final goods, then the problem of double counting arises.

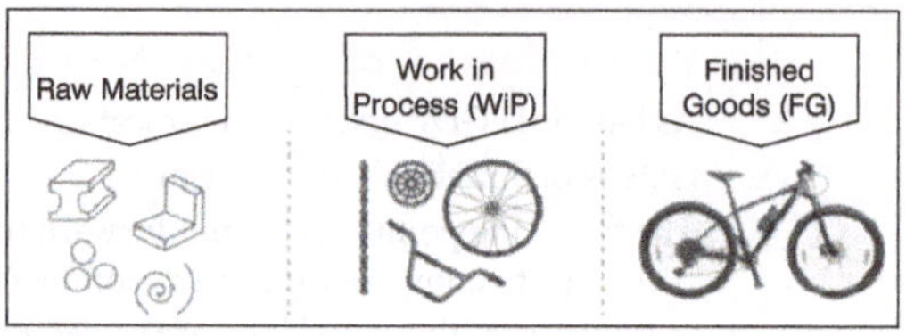

Income Method

In this method, national income is measured in terms of factor payments (wages, rent, interest and profit) to the owners of factors of production (labour, land, capital and enterprise), during an accounting year. This method is also called **Share Method** or **Factor Payment Method**.

The sum of factor payments give us NDP_{FC}.

The various steps to be followed are discussed ahead

***Step* 1** **Estimation of Compensation of Employees**

Compensation of Employees = Wages and Salaries in Cash + Payment in Kind + Employer's Contribution to Social Security Schemes + Pension on Retirement

***Step* 2** **Estimation of Operating Surplus**

Operating Surplus = Rent and Royalty + Interest + Profit

where, Profit = Dividend/Distributed Profits + Corporate Dividend Tax + Undistributed Profits

***Step* 3** **Estimation of Mixed Income of Self-employed**

Income of the self-employed persons using their own land, labour, capital and entrepreneurship for production is termed as mixed income.

***Step* 4** **Estimation of National Income** (NNP_{FC})

NDP_{FC} = Compensation to Employees + Operating Surplus + Mixed Income from self-employment

$NNP_{FC} = NDP_{FC}$ + Net Income from Abroad

Precautions while using Income Method

- Income from illegal activities like smuggling, theft, gambling, etc. should not be included.
- Commission paid on the sale and purchase of second hand goods are to be included.
- Income in terms of windfall gains should not be included.
- Imputed rent of the owner occupied houses is to be treated along with rent as a component of factor incomes.
- Income tax is paid out of compensation of employees. It should not be separately added in the estimation of national income.
- Brokerage on the sale/purchase of shares and bonds is to be included.
- Transfer earnings like old age pensions, unemployment allowances, scholarships, pocket expenses, etc. should not be included.

Expenditure Method

According to this method, national income is measured in terms of expenditure on the purchase of final goods and services produced in an economy, during an accounting year. This method is also called **income disposal method**.

Estimation of expenditure on the final goods and services produced during the year is equal to GDP_{MP}. Then, it is adjusted to find national income (NNP_{FC}).

The following steps are to be followed

Step 1 Estimation of Final Expenditure

GDP_{MP} = Private Final Consumption Expenditure + Government Final Consumption Expenditure + Gross Domestic Capital Formation + Net Exports (Exports (X) – Imports (M)).

Where, Gross Domestic Capital Formation = Gross Domestic Fixed Capital Formation + Change in Stock

Step 2 Estimation of NNP_{FC}

$NNP_{FC} = GDP_{MP}$ – Depreciation – Net Indirect Taxes + Net Factor Income from Abroad

Precautions while using Expenditure Method

- Only final expenditure is to be taken into account to avoid error of double counting.
- Expenditure on second hand goods is not to be included.
- Expenditure on transfer payments by government is not to be included.
- Imputed value of expenditure on goods produced for self-consumption should be taken into account.
- Expenditure on shares and bonds is not to be included in total expenditure.

Triple Identity

National income estimated on the basis of all the three methods, amount to be the same. Now, it can safely be said that national income, national product and national expenditure are always the same i.e.

National Product = National Income = National Expenditure

This is known as **triple identity**.

A Summarised View of Methods of Measuring National Income

Value Added Method	Income Method	Expenditure Method
GVA_{MP} of Primary Sector + GVA_{MP} of Secondary Sector + GVA_{MP} of Tertiary Sector ↓ Gross Domestic Product at Market Price (GDP_{MP}) – Depreciation ↓ NVA_{MP} *or* NDP_{MP} – NIT ↓ NDP_{FC} + NFIA ↓ NNP_{FC}	Compensation of Employees + Operating Surplus + Mixed Income of Self-employed ↓ NDP_{FC} + NFIA ↓ NNP_{FC}	Private Final Consumption Expenditure + Government Final Consumption Expenditure + Gross Domestic Capital Formation + Net Exports ↓ GDP_{MP} – Depreciation ↓ NDP_{MP} – NIT ↓ NDP_{FC} + NFIA ↓ NNP_{FC}

Mind Map

NATIONAL INCOME AND IT'S RELATED CONCEPTS

1 National Income

It is defined as the sum total of factor incomes earned by normal residents of a country, within the domestic territory of a country and from the rest of the world, during a period of an accounting year.

2 Terms Related to Aggregates of National Income

- **Domestic and National Concept of Income** The sum total of factor incomes earned within the domestic territory of a country in the course of an accounting year is termed as domestic income. The sum total of factor incomes earned by the normal residents of a country within a period of an accounting year is termed as national income.
- **Factor Cost and Market Price** Factor cost is the cost accrued by firms due to the payments made to factors of production in the form of rent, interest, wages and profit, during a period of one year. Market price is the price at which the product is sold in the market. It is arrived at by adding indirect taxes and subtracting subsidies from the factor cost of the product.
- **NFIA, Depreciation and Net Indirect Tax**
  - Net Factor Income from Abroad (NFIA) is the difference between factor income from abroad and the factor income paid to abroad.
    NFIA = Factor Income received from Abroad – Factor Income paid to Abroad
  - Depreciation refers to the loss in the value of fixed assets due to their normal wear and tear.
    Depreciation = Gross Investment – Net Investment
  - Net Indirect Tax (NIT) is equal to the difference between indirect taxes and subsidies.
    Market Price = Factor Cost – Net Indirect Taxes

3 Aggregates Related to National Income

- Gross Domestic Product at Market Price (GDP_{MP})
- Net Domestic Product at Market Price (NDP_{MP})
  $NDP_{MP} = GDP_{MP}$ — Depreciation
- Gross Domestic Product at Factor Cost (GDP_{FC})
  $GDP_{FC} = GDP_{MP}$ — NIT
- Net Domestic Product at Factor Cost (NDP_{FC})
  $NDP_{FC} = GDP_{MP}$ — Depreciation — NIT
- Gross National Product at Market Price (GNP_{MP})
  $GNP_{MP} = GDP_{MP}$ + NFIA
- Net National Product at Market Price (NNP_{MP})
  $NNP_{MP} = GDP_{MP}$ — Depreciation + NFIA
- Gross National Product at Factor Cost (GNP_{FC})
  $GNP_{FC} = GDP_{FC}$ + NFIA
- Net National Product at Factor Cost (NNP_{FC})
  $NNP_{FC} = GNP_{FC}$ — Depreciation

4 GDP

- **Nominal GDP and Real GDP**
  Nominal GDP refers to market value of the final goods and services produced within the domestic territory of a country during a financial year. Real GDP refers to market value of the final goods and services produced within the domestic territory of a country during a financial year.
- **GDP Deflator**
  It is the ratio of Nominal GDP to Real GDP.
- **GDP and Welfare**
  GDP is not an appropriate indicator for welfare due to externalities, composition of GDP, distribution of GDP and non-monetary exchanges.

5 Methods of Measuring National Income

National income can be calculated from three aspects
- In the form of flow of goods and services—Value added method or production method
- In the form of income flow—Income method
- In the form of expenditure flow—Expenditure method

Value Added Method or Product Method
The various steps to be followed are discussed as follows
Step 1 Categorisation of Producing Enterprises
Primary sector, secondary sector, tertiary sector
Step 2 Estimation of Value of Output
Value of Output = Sales + Change-in-stock
Step 3 Estimation of Gross Value Added at Market Price
$GDP_{MP} = \Sigma GVA = VA_p + VA_s + VA_T$
Step 4 Estimation of National Income (NNP_{FC})
National Income (NNP_{FC}) = GVA_{MP} — Depreciation — Net Indirect Taxes + Net Factor Income from Abroad

Income Method
The various steps to be followed are
Step 1 Estimation of Compensation of Employees Compensation of Employees = Wages and Salaries in Cash + Payment in Kind + Employer's Contribution to Social Security Schemes + Pension on Retirement
Step 2 Estimation of Operating Surplus
Operating Surplus = Rent and Royalty + Interest + Profit
Step 3 Estimation of Mixed Income of Self-employed Income of the self-employed persons using their own land, labour, capital and entrepreneurship for production is termed as mixed income.
Step 4 Estimation of National Income (NNP_{FC}) NDP_{FC} = Compensation to Employees + Operating Surplus + Mixed Income from Self-employment
$NNP_{FC} = NDP_{FC}$ + Net Income from Abroad

Expenditure Method
The following steps are to be followed
Step 1 Estimation of Final Expenditure GDP_{MP} = Private Final Consumption Expenditure + Government Final Consumption Expenditure + Gross Domestic Capital Formation + Net Exports Exports (X) — Imports (M)].
Step 2 Estimation of NNP_{FC} $NNP_{FC} = GDP_{MP}$ — Depreciation — Net Indirect Taxes + Net Factor Income from Abroad

EXAM PATTERN QUESTIONS

Objective Type Questions

Multiple Choice Questions (MCQs)

1. **Per capita income is .... of the country.** **NCERT (QR)**

(a) disposable income
(b) real income
(c) average income
(d) private income

2. **Which organisation is accountable for calculating the gross domestic product of India?**

(a) Indian Statistical Institute
(b) Reserve Bank of India
(c) National Statistical Office
(d) Ministry of Commerce and Industry

3. **Which of the following is not an economic activity and not included in national income?**

(a) Medical services rendered by a dispensary
(b) A housewife doing household work
(c) A lawyer doing his practice
(d) A maid working full time with a family

4. **How does the statement 'economic climate encouraging' relates to national income?**

Source *10th January, 2024; "Economic climate encouraging; 7.3 pc GDP growth estimate very positive": SBI chairman* **Competency Based Que**

(a) A positive economic climate can lead to higher national income
(b) National income has no impact on the economic climate
(c) A strong national income always guarantees a good economic climate
(d) These two concepts are unrelated to each other

5. **Who among the following are not the residents of India?** **Competency Based Que**

(a) Indians who went to Mauritius for sight-seeing
(b) Indians working at the Washington office of UNICEF
(c) Indians working at a branch of Singapore Bank in India
(d) Indians working at Indian Embassy in Korea

6. **Which of the following is not a 'factor payment'?** **CBSE 2020**

(a) Free uniform to defence personnel
(b) Salaries to the members of Parliament
(c) Rent paid to the owner of a building
(d) Scholarship given to the students

7. **Which of the following statements is/are correct regarding transfer income?** **Competency Based Que**

I. They are included in GDP calculation.
II. They do not correspond to the production of goods and services.
III. Examples include pensions and scholarships.
IV. They are payments for current production.

Codes

(a) I and II
(b) II and III
(c) III and IV
(d) I, III and IV

8. **Non-Resident Indians (NRIs) will soon be able to make payments in Unified Payments Interface (UPI) without having to get an Indian mobile number.**

The National Payments Corporation of India (NPCI) has allowed NRIs in 10 countries to digitally transfer funds using the UPI platform from NRE/NRO accounts.

Source *https://www.livemint.com/money/ personal-finance/nris-ten-countries-upi-payment-india-fund-transfer-international- mobile-numbers-11673450309998.html*

As per the news, deposits received from NRIs to their families in India will be considered as **Competency Based Que**

(a) factor income
(b) transfer income
(c) earned income
(d) None of these

9. **National income is also called ....** **NCERT (QR)**

(a) NDP at MP
(b) NNP at MP
(c) NDP at FC
(d) NNP at FC

10. **For a closed economy (with no foreign trade), which one of the following is correct?** **CBSE SQP 2024 ; Competency Based Que**

(a) GDP = GNP
(b) GDP > GNP
(c) GDP < GNP
(d) GDP + GNP = 0

11. **Due to recent increase in taxes, Indian economy is experiencing increase in the price of commodities, which further assumes relevance in the estimation of NNP_{MP} because** **Competency Based Que**

(a) taxes are compulsory payments
(b) taxes are transfer payments
(c) taxes are paid out of the income of the households
(d) taxes cause a rise in the market price of the commodities

12. **Which of the following statements is incorrect?** CBSE 2020

(a) Gross Domestic Product (GDP) at Market Price = GDP at Factor Cost plus Net Indirect Taxes
(b) Net National Product (NNP) at Market Price = NNP at Factor Cost
(c) Gross National Product (GNP) at Market Price = GDP at Market Price plus Net Factor Income from Aborad
(d) Net National Product (NNP) at Factor Cost = National Income

13. **Which of the following correctly represents the components of Gross National Product (GNP) at factor cost?**

(i) GDP at market price
(ii) Net indirect taxes
(iii) Net factor income from abroad
(iv) Depreciation Competency Based Que

Codes
(a) (i) + (iv) – (ii) (b) (i) + (ii) – (iii)
(c) (i) – (iii) – (iv) (d) (i) + (iii) – (ii)

14. **On the basis of the given chart, complete the equation by choosing the correct alternative.**

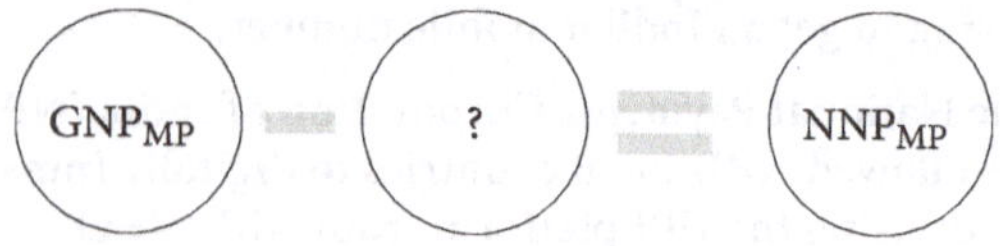

(a) Depreciation (b) Net exports
(c) Net factor income from abroad
(d) Net indirect taxes

15. **If NFIA is positive,**

(a) $NDP_{FC} = NNP_{FC}$ (b) $NDP_{FC} > NNP_{FC}$
(c) $NDP_{FC} < NNP_{FC}$ (d) None of these

16. **Find domestic income when GNP_{MP} = ₹ 2,40,000, indirect taxes = ₹ 40,000, consumption of fixed capital = ₹ 10,000 and factor income from rest of the world = ₹ 6,000.** Competency Based Que

(a) ₹ 1,90,000 (b) ₹ 2,00,000
(c) ₹ 1,94,000 (d) ₹ 1,84,000

17. **If the country is facing rise in prices of goods and services, then nominal national income will**

(a) rise (b) fall
(c) either rise or fall (d) None of these

18. **National income computed at constant prices is also referred to as**

(a) nominal national income
(b) real national income
(c) gross national income (d) None of the above

19. **RBI 7th December, 2023 "The country's Gross Domestic Product (GDP), a measure of economic output, surprised everyone by growing 7.6 per cent in the second quarter of financial year 2023-24 (Q2FY24). Real GDP grew at 7.8 per cent in the first quarter."**

In reference to above statement, the difference between nominal GDP and real GDP is Competency Based Que

(a) nominal GDP includes transfer payments, while real GDP does not
(b) real GDP is always higher than nominal GDP
(c) nominal GDP is measured in current prices, while real GDP is adjusted for inflation
(d) there is no difference between nominal and real GDP

20. **When Nominal Gross Domestic Product (GDP) is ₹ 840 crore and price index is 120, then the Real Gross Domestic Product (GDP) will be ....** CBSE 2020; Competency Based Que

(a) ₹ 700 crore (b) ₹ 900 crore
(c) ₹ 800 crore (d) ₹ 500 crore

21. **Due to the setting-up of a factory near a residential area, the locality is experiencing an increase in .... but decreases in ....** Competency Based Que

(a) welfare, GDP
(b) GDP, welfare
(c) equality, welfare
(d) GDP, employment opportunities

22. **Observe the image given below and choose the correct statement about GDP based upon the same.**

(a) Unequal distribution of GDP
(b) Equitable distribution of GDP
(c) GDP is comprised of everyone's contribution
(d) All of the above

23. **With a rise in real national income, welfare of the people**

(a) rises (b) falls
(c) remains unchanged (d) None of these

24. **The graph below shows a rising trend in India's GDP. What does this indicate about the Indian economy?**

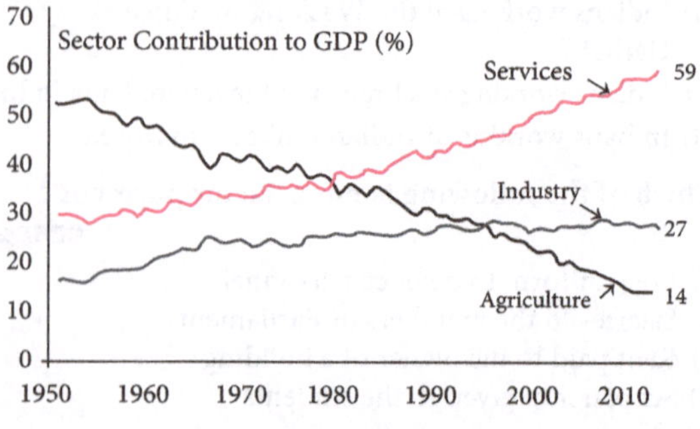

(a) Stagnant economic growth
(b) Declining living standards
(c) Increasing overall production of goods and services
(d) Decreasing unemployment

25. **Which aggregate of national income is constituted from the value added method?**

(a) NDP_{FC}
(b) GDP_{MP}
(c) GDP_{FC}
(d) NDP_{MP}

26. **Complete the table** **CBSE 2023; Competency Based Que**

Producer	Value of Output	Intermediate Consumption	Value Added
Farmer	2,000	—	2,000
Baker	...(i)...	2,000	2,000
Retail Seller	4,400	...(iii)...	400
Total	...(ii)...	6,000	...(iv)...

(a) 4,000, 10,400, 4,000, 4,000
(b) 4,000, 10,400, 4,000, 4,400
(c) 2,000, 6,000, 6,000, 4,400
(d) 4,000, 10,400, 6,000, 4,000

27. **Complete the table**

S.No.	Particulars	₹ (in crores)
(i)	Sales	90
(ii)	Closing Stock	25
(iii)	Opening Stock	?
(iv)	Change-in-stock	10
(v)	GVO_{MP}	?
(vi)	Intermediate Consumption	40

(a) 10, 100 (b) 15, 115
(c) 10, 60 (d) 15, 100

28. **Compensation of Employees + Operating Surplus + Mixed Income of Self-employed = ...**

(a) NNP_{FC} (b) NNP_{MP}
(c) NDP_{FC} (d) NDP_{MP}

29. **To arrive at the value of Gross Value Added at Market Price (GVA_{MP}) .... must be added to Gross Value Added (GVA) at basic prices.** **CBSE SQP 2025**

(a) product taxes
(b) net product taxes
(c) production taxes
(d) net production taxes

30. **This image depicts a bustling stock market. Which component of India's national income is directly related to this activity?**

(a) Wages and salaries (b) Rent
(c) Interest (d) Profits

31. **Which of the following affects national income?** **CBSE 2018**

(a) Goods and services tax (b) Corporation tax
(c) Subsidies (d) None of these

32. **Identify, which of the following items will not be included in estimating national income of India.** **CBSE 2025**

(a) Salary to Indian residents working at the Russian Embassy in India
(b) Income generated from smuggling
(c) Payments to farm workers in the form of foodgrains
(d) Interest paid by a firm to a bank

33. **Kindly consider the following data for an economy**

S.No.	Particulars	₹ (in crores)
(i)	Interest	700
(ii)	Employees' Salaries	?
(iii)	NIT	500
(iv)	Rent and Profit	700
(v)	Mixed Income	28,000
(vi)	Net Domestic Income	53,400

Calculate employees' salaries. **Competency Based Que**

(a) ₹ 24,000 (b) ₹ 23,300 (c) ₹ 22,800 (d) ₹ 23,500

34. **The Consumption Expenditure (C) component in the expenditure method includes which of the following?**

I. **Spending on food and beverages by households.**
II. **Business spending on office furniture.**
III. **Purchase of clothing by households.**
IV. **Purchase of a new factory by a company.**

Codes **Competency Based Que**

(a) I and III (b) II and IV
(c) I, II and III (d) All of these

35. **Which of the following is not a component of gross fixed capital formation?**

(a) Gross business fixed investment
(b) Inventory investment
(c) Gross residential construction investment
(d) Gross public investment

36. **Kindly consider the following data for an economy**

S.No.	Particulars	₹ (in crores)
(i)	Gross Investment	90
(ii)	Net Exports	10
(iii)	Net Indirect Taxes	5
(iv)	Depreciation	15
(v)	Net Factor Income from Abroad	(–) 5
(vi)	Private Consumption Expenditure	?
(vii)	Government Purchase of Goods and Services	100
(viii)	GDP_{MP}	550

Calculate private consumption.

(a) ₹ 350 (b) ₹ 340 (c) ₹ 450 (d) ₹ 365

37. **India's former chief statistician and now Chair, Standing Committee on Statistics Pronab Sen says "There are three ways of calculating GDP – from production, from incomes and from expenditures. If you had perfect measurement, the three would give you exactly the same result. The problem is that different countries have data sources which enable them to use one or maybe two at most of these three approaches.**

In our case, we rely on the production approach because that's where the data is the best."

In India, the preferred method for calculating GDP is the production approach. Why? Competency Based Que

(a) It provides the most accurate data
(b) The income and expenditure data are unreliable
(c) It best reflects the size of the informal economy
(d) It aligns with international standards

Direction *Read the case study and answer the questions 38 to 41 on the basis of the same*

It is not that countries which are endowed with a bounty of natural weath-minerals or forests or the most fertile lands are naturally the countries with high national income. In fact, the resource rich Africa and Latin America have some of the countries with lowest national income in the world, whereas many countries with high national income have scarcely any natural wealth. There was a time when possession of natural resources was the most important consideration but even then the resources have to be transformed through a production process.

The economic well-being of a country thus does not necessarily depend on the mere possession of resources; the point is how these resources are used in generating a flow of production and how, as a consequence, income and wealth are generated from that process.

38. **Countries with more natural resources necessarily have a higher level of national income. State true or false.**

39. **Countries of .... are rich in natural resources.**

(a) Africa (b) Latin America
(c) Both (a) and (b) (d) Asia

40. **The economic well being of a country depends on how ...... are used in generating a flow of production.**

41. **Income and wealth are generated from the process of ....**

Direction *Read the case study and answer the questions 42 to 45 on the basis of the same*

The budget estimate of total spending for 2021-22 is ₹ 34.83 lakh crore. The Revised Estimate (RE) for total central spending in 2020-21 is ₹ 34.5 lakh crore. The Gross Domestic Product (GDP) deflator — if one takes 14.4% nominal GDP growth projection for 2021-22 given in the budget and 11% real GDP forecast given in the latest economic survey comes to 3.4%. This means that central spending should have increased to at least ₹ 35.7 lakh crore to keep it unchanged in real terms.

The fact that it has not happened implies that the 2021-22 budget entails a negative fiscal stimulus to the economy. To be sure, one could argue that 2020-21 was an abnormal year — and therefore, the government is justified in rolling back its welfare spending push, as the economy gets unlocked and vaccination gains momentum. CBSE QB

42. **With the rise in real national income, the economic welfare of the people ....**

43. **If GDP Deflator = 125, Nominal GDP = ₹ 15,000 crore then Real GDP is equal to ....**

44. **Assertion** (A) Real GDP is always equal to Nominal GDP.

Reason (R) Real GDP is a better measure to make periodic comparison in the physical output of goods and services over different years.

Alternatives

(a) Assertion (A) is true and Reason (R) is false
(b) Assertion (A) is false and Reason (R) is true

45. **State the significance of GDP deflator.**

Direction *From the following data answer the questions 46 to 49 on the basis of the same*

S.No.	Particulars	₹ (in crores)
(i)	Compensation of Employees	800
(ii)	Private Final Consumption Expenditure	1,200
(iii)	Profit	500
(iv)	Rent	200
(v)	Government Final Consumption Expenditure	800
(vi)	Interest	150
(vii)	Net Factor Income from Abroad	20
(viii)	Net Indirect Taxes	190

S.No.	Particulars	₹ (in crores)
(ix)	Mixed Income of Self-employed	630
(x)	Net Exports	– 30
(xi)	Net Domestic Capital Formation	500
(xii)	Consumption of Fixed Capital	150

46. The value of operating surplus for the given data is .... lakh.

47. The value of NNP_{FC} for the given data is ₹ ...... lakh.

48. Identify the correct formula for NDP_{MP}.

(a) Compensation of Employees + Operating Surplus + Net Indirect Tax

(b) Compensation of Employees + Mixed Income of Self-employed + Depreciation + Net Indirect Tax

(c) Compensation of Employees + Operating Surplus + Mixed Income of Self-employed + Net Indirect Tax

(d) Compensation of Employees + Operating Surplus + Mixed Income of Self-employed + Depreciation – Net Indirect Tax

49. Assertion (A) Operating surplus does not arise in the general government sector.

Reason (R) General government produces goods and services with the aim of earning profit without any intention of social welfare.

Alternatives

(a) Both Assertion (A) and Reason (R) are true and Reason (R) is the correct explanation of Assertion (A)

(b) Both Assertion (A) and Reason (R) are true, but Reason (R) is not the correct explanation of Assertion (A)

(c) Assertion (A) is true, but Reason (R) is false

(d) Assertion (A) is false, but Reason (R) is true

Assertion-Reason

Direction (Q.No. 50 to 59) *Read the following Assertion (A) and Reason (R) and choose the correct alternative from the following*

Alternatives

(a) Both Assertion (A) and Reason (R) are true and Reason (R) is the correct explanation of Assertion (A)

(b) Both Assertion (A) and Reason (R) are true, but Reason (R) is not the correct explanation of Assertion (A)

(c) Assertion (A) is true, but Reason (R) is false

(d) Both Assertion (A) and Reason (R) are false

50. Assertion (A) Income earned by foreigners working in a foreign bank in India is a part of gross domestic income.

Reason (R) It is included in gross domestic income because foreign bank is located within the domestic territory of the country.

51. Assertion (A) Profits earned by a company situated in India but owned by a non-resident is a part of gross national income of India.

Reason (R) It is included in gross national income because it is earned by a person who is not a resident of India.

52. Assertion (A) In the calculation of GDP of India, profits earned by a branch of foreign bank in India will be included.

Reason (R) Profit are earned within the domestic territory of India.

53. Assertion (A) The concept of Net National Product (NNP) is essential for understanding the sustainability of economic growth.

Reason (R) NNP adjusts the Gross National Product (GNP) for depreciation, providing a more accurate measure of the net addition to the nation's wealth.

54. Assertion (A) Real Gross Domestic Product (GDP) is a better indicator of economic growth of a nation as compared to Nominal Gross Domestic Product.

Reason (R) Real Gross Domestic Product (GDP) measures the value of goods and services at current year prices. **CBSE 2024**

55. Assertion (A) Government scholarships provided to students are considered as factor payments.

Reason (R) Factor payments entail compensating individuals regardless of their contribution to the production of goods and services.

56. Assertion (A) Double counting occurs when the value of a product is tallied multiple times in calculations.

Reason (R) Intermediate goods' values are included because each producer regards the commodity they sell as the final product.

57. Assertion (A) The value added method includes the imputed rental value of owner occupied houses in national income calculations.

Reason (R) Imputing rental value for owner occupied houses is necessary because owner occupiers do not pay rent but derive housing services that contribute to overall economic output.

58. Assertion (A) National income calculated using the income method includes only the factor income generated from the production of goods and services within the country.

Reason (R) Factor incomes received from abroad are not included in the domestic national income but are added to the Gross National Product (GNP).

59. Assertion (A) The expenditure method includes household consumption expenditure as a component of national income.

Reason (R) Household consumption expenditure reflects the demand for final goods and services in the economy.

Two Statement Based MCQs

Direction (Q.No. 60 to 69) *Read the following statements carefully and choose the correct alternative*

Alternatives

(a) Statement I is correct and Statement II is incorrect
(b) Statement II is correct and Statement I is incorrect
(c) Both the statements are correct
(d) Both the statements are incorrect

60. **Statement I** Commission charged on sale of goods will be excluded from national product.

Statement II Depreciation is charged on the fixed assets.

61. **Statement I** Old age pensions are excluded from national product.

Statement II Interest paid by a firm to the government is included in the domestic product.

62. **Statement I** GDP at market prices and GDP at factor cost are the same.

Statement II Personal income is the income received by individuals and households after deduction of direct taxes and other deductions.

63. **Statement I** Net National Product (NNP) is obtained by deducting depreciation from Gross National Product (GNP).

Statement II Depreciation represents the value of worn-out capital during the production process.

64. **Statement I** Gross National Product (GNP) can be greater than Gross Domestic Product (GDP) in a two-sector economy.

Statement II Net factor income from abroad is zero in a two-sector economy. **CBSE 2024 C**

65. **Statement I** The GDP deflator measures the change in prices of all goods and services included in the Gross Domestic Product (GDP).

Statement II The GDP deflator is considered a more comprehensive measure of inflation than the Consumer Price Index (CPI) because it includes all goods and services produced domestically, not just those purchased by consumers.

66. **Statement I** Externalities are a limitation in assessing welfare on the basis of GDP.

Statement II Production of services for self-consumption are not included in national income.

67. **Statement I** Value added method and expenditure method give slightly different national income.

Statement II Value added method is not as reliable as expenditure method in calculation of national income.

68. **Statement I** The expenditure method of calculating national income sums up all spending by households, businesses, government and net exports.

Statement II Government spending on subsidies should be included in the expenditure method as it directly contributes to economic output.

69. **Statement I** Intermediate goods should be included in national income to accurately reflect all production activities in an economy.

Statement II To avoid double counting in the product method of national income calculation, only the value added at each stage of production should be included.

Matching

70. Match the following **NCERT (QR)**

Column I		Column II
A. PCI (Per Capita Income)	(i)	The increase of wealthy class per capita above the majority population
B. Purchasing power parity	(ii)	Compares the income level of different countries
C. If the income distribution is skewed	(iii)	Income per person

Codes

	A	B	C
(a)	(i)	(ii)	(iii)
(b)	(iii)	(ii)	(i)
(c)	(iii)	(i)	(ii)
(d)	(ii)	(iii)	(i)

71. Match the following

Column I		Column II
A. Factor income	(i)	Consumption of fixed capital
B. Depreciation	(ii)	Scholarship
C. Transfer income	(iii)	Difference between national income and domestic income
D. Net factor income from abroad	(iv)	Rent

Codes

	A	B	C	D
(a)	(i)	(ii)	(iii)	(iv)
(b)	(iii)	(ii)	(iv)	(i)
(c)	(iv)	(i)	(ii)	(iii)
(d)	(ii)	(iii)	(i)	(iv)

72. Match the following

Column I	Column II
A. GNP_{FC}	(i) NNP_{FC} – NFIA + NIT
B. NDP_{FC}	(ii) GDP_{FC} + NFIA
C. NNP_{FC}	(iii) GDP_{MP} – Depreciation – NIT
D. NDP_{MP}	(iv) GNP_{FC} – Depreciation

Codes

	A	B	C	D		A	B	C	D
(a)	(i)	(ii)	(iii)	(iv)	(b)	(iii)	(ii)	(iv)	(i)
(c)	(iv)	(i)	(ii)	(iii)	(d)	(ii)	(iii)	(i)	(iv)

73. From the set of statement given in Column I and Column II, choose the correct pair of statement

Column I	Column II
A. Mixed income	(i) Income of the casual worker
B. Change-in-stock	(ii) Opening stock – closing stock
C. Unemployment allowance	(iii) Not included in the estimation of national income
D. Free services by the government	(iv) A part of net factor income to abroad

Codes

(a) A-(i) (b) B-(ii) (c) C-(iii) (d) D-(iv)

74. Identify the correctly matched items in Column I to that of Column II **Competency Based Que**

Column I	Column II
A. Social welfare	(i) Total of economic and non-economic welfare
B. Comparison of GDP of different countries	(ii) GDPs evaluated at current market prices
C. Economic welfare	(iii) Situation of unemployment
D. GDP deflator	(iv) Includes prices of imported goods

Codes

(a) A-(i) (b) B-(ii)
(c) C-(iii) (d) D-(iv)

75. Identify the correctly matched items in Column I to that of Column II

Column I	Column II
A. Vegetables grown in the personal garden	(i) Non-marketing activity
B. A car used as a taxi	(ii) Consumer good
C. An air-conditioner used by household	(iii) Capital good
D. Scholarship given to students by government	(iv) Factor income

Codes

(a) A-(i)
(b) B-(ii)
(c) C-(iii)
(d) D-(iv)

Concept Identification

76. Market value of final goods and services produced within the domestic territory of the country within one year, inclusive of depreciation. **CBSE 2019**

77. Market value of the final goods and services produced within the domestic territory of a country during an accounting year, as estimated using the base year prices. **CBSE 2020**

78. Positive or negative impact of an economic activity on the others without involving any price or penalty.

79. Income received in form of rent and from investments made in an entrepreneurial venture. **CBSE 2020**

80. Combined factor income, which can't be separated into various factor income components. **CBSE 2020**

Answers

1. (c) average income
2. (c) National Statistical Office
3. (b) A housewife doing household work
4. (a) A positive economic climate can lead to higher national income
5. (b) Indians working at the Washington office of UNICEF
6. (d) Scholarship given to the students
7. (b) II and III
8. (b) transfer income
9. (d) NNP at FC
10. (a) GDP = GNP
11. (d) taxes cause a rise in the market price of the commodities
12. (b) Net National Product (NNP) at Market Price = NNP at Factor Cost
13. (d) (i) + (iii) – (ii)
14. (a) Depreciation
15. (c) $NDP_{FC} < NNP_{FC}$

16. (d) Domestic Income or NDP at FC = GNP at MP – Depreciation (Consumption of Fixed Capital) – Net Factor Income from Abroad – Net Indirect Taxes = Indirect Taxes – Subsidies

NDP at FC = 2,40,000 – 10,000 – 6,000 – 40,000
(40,000 – 0) = ₹ 1,84,000

17. (a) rise

18. (b) real national income

19. (c) nominal GDP is measured in current prices, while real GDP is adjusted for inflation

20. (a) $\text{Price Index} = \frac{\text{Nominal GDP}}{\text{Real GDP}} \times 100$

21. (b) GDP, welfare

22. (a) Unequal distribution of GDP

23. (a) rises

24. (c) Increasing overall production of goods and services

25. (b) GDP_{MP}

26. (b) Gross Value Added = Value of Output – Intermediate Consumption

(i) Baker

2,000 = Value of Output – 2,000

∴ Value of Output = 4,000

(ii) Total of Value of Output = 2,000 + 4,000 + 4,400
= 10,400

(iii) Total of Intermediate Consumption = Farmer + Baker + Retail Seller

6,000 = 0 + 2,000 + Retail Seller

∴ Retail Seller = 4,000

(iv) Total of Value Added = 2,000 + 2,000 + 400 = 4,400

27. (d) Change in Stock = Closing Stock – Opening Stock
GVO_{MP} = Sales + Change in Stock

28. (c) NDP_{FC}

29. (a) product taxes

30. (d) Profits (profits earned by companies listed on the stock market).

31. (b) It affects national income because it is a part of corporate profits.

32. (b) Income generated from smuggling

33. (a) Net Domestic Income (NDP_{FC}) = Mixed Income + Employees' Salaries + Operating Surplus

53,400 = 28,000+ Employees's Salaries + (700 + 700)

53,400 = 29,400 + Employees's Salaries

24,000 = Employees's Salaries

34. (a) I and III

35. (b) Inventory investment

36. (a) GDP_{MP} = Gross Investment + Net Exports + Private Consumption Expenditure + Government Purchases of Goods and Services

550 = 90 + 10 + Private Consumption Expenditure + 100

Private Consumption Expenditure = 550 – (90 + 10 + 100)
= ₹ 350 crore

37. (b) The income and expenditure data are unreliable

38. False. Usage and not possession of natural resources is an important determinant of national income.

39. (c) Both (a) and (b)

40. natural resources

41. production

42. rises

43. ₹ 12,000 crore $\left(\text{Real GDP} = \frac{\text{Nominal GDP}}{\text{GDP Deflator}} \times 100 \right)$

44. (b) Assertion (A) is false and Reason (R) is true

45. GDP deflator is a tool that shows changes in the price level of the economy over a given period of time.

46. ₹ 850 [500 (Profit) + 200 (Rent) + 150 (Interest)]

47. NDP_{FC} = Compensation of Employees + Operating Surplus + Mixed Income of Self-employed
= 800 + 850 + 630 = ₹ 2,280 crore

So, NNP_{FC} = NDP_{FC} + Net Factor Income from Abroad
2280 + 20 = ₹ 2,300 crore

48. (c) Compensation of Employees + Operating Surplus + Mixed Income of Self-employed + Net Indirect Tax

49. (c) Operating surplus does not arise in the general government sector as the government produces goods and services for the welfare of the society, not for profit.

50. (a) Both Assertion (A) and Reason (R) are true and Reason (R) is the correct explanation of Assertion (A)

51. (d) Since the profits are earned by a foreign owned company operating in India, they contribute to India's GDP but not its GNI. Since GNI represents the income earned by a nation's residents and their overseas investments.

52. (a) Both Assertion (A) and Reason (R) are true and Reason (R) is the correct explanation of Assertion (A)

53. (a) Both Assertion (A) and Reason (R) are true and Reason (R) is the correct explanation of Assertion (A)

54. (c) Real Gross Domestic Product (GDP) serves as a superior indicator of economic growth compared to nominal GDP because it accounts for changes in prices by measuring the value of goods and services using base year prices.

55. (d) Scholarships given to students is not a factor payment, it is a transfer payment and it will not be included in national income. Reason is also false because factor payments are given in return for contributions to production. They specifically reward the use of resources (labour, capital, etc.) in the production process.

56. (b) Both Assertion (A) and Reason (R) are true, but Reason (R) is not the correct explanation of Assertion (A)

57. (a) Both Assertion (A) and Reason (R) are true and Reason (R) is the correct explanation of Assertion (A)
58. (b) Both Assertion (A) and Reason (R) are true, but Reason (R) is not the correct explanation of Assertion (A)
59. (a) Both Assertion (A) and Reason (R) are true and Reason (R) is the correct explanation of Assertion (A)
60. (b) Commission and brokerage paid to facilitate the sale of goods is included in the national income because it is an income earned for rendering productive services.
61. (c) Both the statements are correct
62. (b) GDP at market prices and GDP at factor cost are not the same. GDP at market prices is the total value of goods and services produced within a country's borders, including indirect taxes (taxes on production and imports) but excluding subsidies. On the other hand, GDP at factor cost is calculated by subtracting indirect taxes and adding subsidies from GDP at market prices.
63. (c) Both the statements are correct
64. (b) Since there is no foreign income, GNP and GDP will be equal in two sector economy.
65. (c) Both the statements are correct
66. (c) Both the statements are correct
67. (d) Both methods are accurate and yield same results.
68. (a) Government spending on subsidies is not directly included in the expenditure method of national income calculation. Subsidies are considered transfer payments because they do not correspond to the production of goods or services.
69. (b) Intermediate goods are not included in national income calculations because their value is already included in the value of final goods. Including intermediate goods would result in double counting and an overestimation of national income.
70. (b) (iii) (ii) (i)
71. (c) (iv) (i) (ii) (iii)
72. (b) (iii) (ii) (iv) (i)
73. (c) C-(iii)
74. (a) A-(i)
75. (a) A-(i)
76. Gross domestic product at market price
77. Real Gross Domestic Product (GDP)
78. Externalities
79. Income from property and entrepreneurship
80. Mixed income of self-employed

Subjective Questions

Short Answer Type Questions

1. Why should the aggregate final expenditure of an economy be equal to the aggregate factor payments? Explain. NCERT

Ans. In a simplified economy, income is spent on the purchase of final goods and services. Expenditure of income on final goods represents final consumption expenditure. In such an economy, there are no savings, taxes or trasactions with the rest of the world. Also, this expendi- ture is distributed among the factors of production in the form of wages and salaries, rent, interest and profit. These constitute transfer payments of the firm. So, we can say that the final expenditure in an economy is equal to transfer payments made by the firm.

2. "Factors of production within the domestic territory determine domestic factor income." Do you agree? Give reason. Competency Based Que

Ans. Yes, this is correct. Factors of production like land, labour, capital, organisation, etc. falling in the domestic territory of the country, generate income like rent, wages, interest and profit. Since, these incomes are generated within the domestic territory, therefore, they determine domestic factor income.

3. Government of India has recently launched 'Jan-Dhan Yojana' aimed at every household in the country to have atleast one bank account.

Explain how deposits made under the plan are going to affect national income of the country. CBSE 2018; Competency Based Que

Ans. 'Jan-Dhan Yojana' was launched with the aim to bring every individual into the financial market, and a large number of bank accounts have also been opened, which has led to increase in the deposits with the commercial banks and hence it has enhanced their capacity to create credit in the economy.

Increase in money supply would lead to increase in the rate of transactions and aggregate demand, leading to increase in national income of the economy.

4. Differentiate between factor income and transfer income. CBSE 2024 C ; Term II 2022

Ans. Differences between factor income and transfer income are

Basis	Factor Income	Transfer Income
Meaning	Income received by factors of production for rendering factor services in the production process.	Income received without rendering any productive services in return.

Basis	Factor Income	Transfer Income
Nature	It is included in both national income and domestic income.	It is neither included in national income nor in domestic income.
Mechanism	It is earned through the market mechanism.	It is provided through non-market mechanism.

5. Identity the concept and explain the difference between them. Competency Based Que

A  vs B 

Ans. In picture A, domestic income is highlighted while picture B relates to national income. Differences between these two are

Basis	Domestic Income	National Income
Definition	Refers to the total income earned by residents of a country within the country's borders.	Refers to the total income earned by all country residents, including those living abroad.
Components	Salaries, rents, interests and profits earned within a country.	Salaries, rents, interests and profits earned within a country's limits and beyond by the country's citizens.
Scope	Includes economic activities within a country's limits.	Includes both domestic and foreign economic activities.
Importance	Helps to understand the economic well-being of its residents.	Helps to estimate the global economic position of a country.

6. Define Net Factor Income from Abroad (NFIA) and discuss its components. CBSE 2025

Ans. Net factor income from abroad is the difference between the factor income earned from abroad by normal residents of a country (i.e. India) and the factor income earned by non-residents (foreigners) in the domestic territory of that country (i.e. India).

Following are its three main components

(i) Net compensation of employees.

(ii) Net income from property and entrepreneurship (rent, interest, profit).

(iii) Net retained earnings of resident companies abroad.

7. "Subsidies to the producers should be treated as transfer payments." Defend or refute the given statement with valid reason. CBSE 2020; Competency Based Que

Ans. No, subsidies given to the producers should not be treated as transfer payments. Subsidies are given to reduce the market price of socially desirable goods such as fertilisers, LPG gas, etc. so, that they can be afforded by the poorer sections of society. Transfer payments, on the other hand, are given to fulfill social objectives. Examples of transfer payments are old age pension, unemployment allowance, etc.

Transfer payments are not taken into account while computing the GDP of the country, but subsidies are considered in the computation of GDP.

8. Differentiate between gross domestic product at market price and net national product at factor cost.

Ans. Differences between gross domestic product at market price and net national product at factor cost are

Basis	Gross Domestic Product at Market Price	Net National Product at Factor Cost
Depreciation	It includes depreciation.	It excludes depreciation.
Area of Production	It is produced within the domestic territory by normal residents as well as non-residents.	It is produced within and outside the domestic territory by the normal residents only.
NFIA	It does not include net factor income from abroad.	It includes net factor income from abroad.
NIT	It includes net indirect taxes.	It excludes net indirect taxes.

9. Are the following a part of country's net domestic product at market price? Explain.

(i) Net indirect taxes (ii) Net exports

(iii) Net factor income from abroad

(iv) Consumption of fixed capital

Ans. (i) Net indirect taxes are a part of NDP_{MP}, as we add Net indirect taxes to NDP_{FC}, to obtain NDP_{MP}.

(ii) Net exports are a part of NDP_{MP}, while calculating NDP_{MP} by expenditure method.

(iii) Net factor income from abroad is not a part of NDP_{MP}, as the income is not generated in domestic territory of the country.

(iv) Consumption of fixed capital is not a part of NDP_{MP}, as we subtract it from GDP_{MP} to obtain NDP_{MP}.

10. GNP is the estimated value of the total worth of production and services earned by the normal residents of a country. But to find out NNP, why should we deduct depreciation from GNP? Competency Based Que

Ans. The productive power of physical capital stock of a country diminishes gradually because of the wear and tear in the process of production. When the machine becomes totally unproductive, it has to be replaced by new machine. So, a sum of money is set aside every year into depreciation account and new machine can be purchased by utilising this accumulated sum.

So, depreciation is deducted from GNP in order to get more accurate measure of the sustainable production of goods and services in a country in a given year to find NNP.

11. Giving reasons, explain the treatment assigned to the following while estimating national income
(i) Social security contributions by employees.
(ii) Pension paid after retirement.
(iii) Interest paid by banks on deposits by individuals.
(iv) National debt interest.** Competency Based Que

Ans. (i) Social security contributions by employees are not separately included in the estimation of national income as these are paid out of compensation of employees.

(ii) Pension paid after retirement is included in the estimation of national income because this is a kind of deferred wage payment and is therefore, treated as a component of compensation of employees.

(iii) Interest paid by banks on deposits by individuals should be included in the estimation of national income as it is treated as factor income.

(iv) National debt interest should not be included in estimation of national income as it is assumed that government borrows for consumption and hence, it is treated as transfer payment.

12. How will you treat the following while estimating national income of India?
(i) Dividend received by an Indian from his investment in shares of a foreign company.
(ii) Money received by a family in India from relatives working abroad.
(iii) Interest received on loans given to a friend for purchasing a car.** Competency Based Que

Ans. (i) Dividend received by an Indian from his investment in shares of a foreign company is included in national income of India because it is a part of net factor income from abroad.

(ii) Money received by a family in India from relatives working abroad is not included in national income of India because it is a kind of transfer income.

(iii) Interest received on loans given to a friend for purchasing a car is not included in national income because loans are not used for production purpose.

13. How will you treat the following while estimating national income? Give reasons for your answer.
(i) Capital gain on sale of a house.
(ii) Prize won in a lottery.
(iii) Interest on public debt.** Competency Based Que

Ans. (i) Capital gain on sale of a house is not included in the national income estimation because it does not add to the flow of goods and services in the economy.

(ii) Prize won in a lottery is not included in national income estimation because it is a part of transfer payments.

(iii) Interest on public debt is deemed as transfer payment. Hence, it is not included in the estimation of national income.

14. How will you treat the following in estimating national income of India? Give reasons for your answer.
(i) Value of bonus shares received by shareholders of a company.
(ii) Fees received from students.
(iii) Interest received on loan given to a foreign company in India.** Competency Based Que

Ans. (i) Values of bonus shares received by shareholders of a company is not included in the estimation of national income of India because these are just financial transactions, not contributing to the flow of goods and services in the economy.

(ii) From the students' point of view, expenditure on fees is to be treated as a part of private final consumption expenditure. Accordingly, it is to be included in national income when expenditure method is used to estimate it.

(iii) Interest received on loan given to a foreign company in India is included in estimating national income of India as a part of net factor income from abroad.

15. Will the following factor incomes be included in domestic income of India? Give reasons for your answer.
(i) Compensation of employees to the residents of Japan working in Indian Embassy in Japan.
(ii) Profits earned by a branch of foreign bank in India.
(iii) Rent received by an Indian resident from Russian Embassy in India.
(iv) Profits earned by a branch of State Bank of India in England.** Competency Based Que

Ans. (i) It is a part of domestic factor income in India, because Indian Embassy in Japan is a part of domestic territory of India.

(ii) It is a part of domestic factor income of India, because the branch of foreign bank is within the domestic territory of India.

(iii) It is not a part of domestic factor income of India, because Russian Embassy in India is not a part of domestic territory of India.

(iv) It is not a part of domestic factor income of India, because the branch of State Bank of India in England, is not a part of domestic territory of India.

16. Giving valid reasons, explain how the following would be treated while estimating domestic income?

(i) Payment made by a Japanese tourist for goods purchased in India.

(ii) Broker's commission on the sale of second hand goods.

(iii) Expenditure on free services provided by government.

(iv) Payment of interest by a government firm.

Competency Based Que

Ans. (i) Goods purchased by Japanese tourist is an export for India as goods are produced in the domestic territory of India. Therefore, included in domestic income.

(ii) Sale of second hand car is a productive service. Hence, broker commission should be included in domestic income.

(iii) Expenditure on free services provided by government should be included in the estimation of national income, as it is a final· expenditure of the government.

(iv) Payment of interest by a government firm should not be included in the estimation of national income, as it is a transfer payment.

17. How will you treat the following while estimating domestic product of a country? Give reasons for your answer.

(i) Profits earned by branches of country's bank in other countries.

(ii) Gifts given by an employer to his employees on Independence Day.

(iii) Salaries of Indians working in the Russian embassy in India.

Competency Based Que

Ans. (i) It is not included while estimating the domestic product of a country as these profits are not earned within the domestic territory of the country.

(ii) It is not included while estimating the domestic product of a country as it is a transfer payment.

(iii) This will not be included in the domestic product of India as Russian embassy in India is not a part of India's domestic territory.

18. Giving reason, explain how the following are treated in estimating national income

(i) Wheat grown by farmer, but used entirely for family's consumption.

(ii) Earning of shareholders from the sale of shares.

(iii) Expenditure by government on providing free education.

Competency Based Que

Ans. (i) Wheat grown by farmer, but used entirely for family's consumption will be included while estimating national income, as the production is done for self-consumption purpose.

(ii) Earning of shareholders from the sale of shares will not be included while estimating national income, as it will be considered as transfer payment.

(iii) Expenditure by government on providing free education will be included while estimating national income, as it is a part of government final consumption expenditure.

19. Giving reasons, explain whether the following are included in national income

(i) Profits earned by a branch of foreign bank.

(ii) Interest paid by an individual on a loan taken to buy a car.

(iii) Expenditure on machines for installation in a factory.

Competency Based Que

Ans. (i) Profits earned by a branch of foreign bank will not be included while estimating national income, as it is a factor income to abroad.

(ii) Interest paid by an individual on a loan taken to buy a car will not be included while estimating National Income, as loan is taken for consumption purpose.

(iii) Expenditure on machines for installation in a factory will be included while estimating national income, as it is a final consumption expenditure by factory management.

20. Giving reason, explain how the following should be treated in the estimation of national income

Competency Based Que

(i) Payment of interest by a firm to a bank.

(ii) Payment of interest by a bank to an individual.

(iii) Payment of interest by an individual to a bank.

Ans. (i) It will be included in the estimation of national income, as it is a factor income. Also firms take loans for investment purposes.

(ii) It will be included in the estimation of national income as it is a factor income.

(iii) It will not be included in the estimation of national income as consumer takes loan for consumption purposes.

21. **Giving valid reasons, explain how the following would be treated while estimating domestic income?** CBSE SQP 2024; Competency Based Que

(i) **Payment made by American tourist for goods purchased in India.**

(ii) **Tomatoes grown by Ms. Puja in her kitchen garden.**

Ans. (i) Yes, it will be included in domestic income as goods purchased by American tourist is the expenditure made by him in India and will be included as exports.

(ii) No, it will not be included in domestic income because it is difficult to ascertain their market value. Moreover, such transactions are not undertaken for any monetary consideration.

22. **Will the following be included in the national income of India? Give reasons for your answer.** Competency Based Que

(i) **Financial assistance to flood victims.**

(ii) **Expenditure by a firm on payment of fees to a chartered accountant.**

(iii) **Payment of corporate tax by a firm.**

(iv) **Purchase of refrigerator by a firm for own use.**

Ans. (i) It will not be included in the national income of India as it is a form of transfer payment. It does not add to the stock of goods and services in the economy.

(ii) Expenditure by a firm on payment of fees to a chartered accountant is an intermediate expenditure, so it is not included in national income.

(iii) Payment of corporate tax by a firm is a transfer payment, so it is not included in national income.

(iv) Purchase of refrigerator by a firm for its own use will be treated as investment expenditure and thereby will be included in estimating national income.

23. **Why are export receipts excluded from net factor income from abroad?**

Ans. Export refers to the purchase of domestically produced goods by the rest of the world. Export receipts refer to revenue of the firms from the sale of its output.

These are not the receipts of factor incomes from abroad which are to be in the form of rent, interest, profit and wages. Hence, they are not a part of net factor income from abroad.

24. **Distinguish between Real Gross Domestic Product (GDP) and Nominal Gross Domestic Product (GDP).** CBSE 2025

Ans. Differences between Real GDP and Nominal GDP are

Basis	Real GDP	Nominal GDP
Definition	GDP at constant prices, representing the market value of final goods and services produced within a country during an accounting year, using base year prices.	GDP at current prices, representing the market value of final goods and services produced within a country during an accounting year, using current year prices.
Price Changes	Adjusted for inflation, reflecting actual production changes.	Affected by inflation or deflation.
Usefulness	Useful for long-term comparisons and assessing real economic growth.	Useful for current economic analysis and comparisons within the same year.

25. **Use following information of an imaginary country**

Year	2014-15	2015-16	2016-17
Nominal GDP	6.5	8.4	9
GDP Deflator	100	140	125

(i) **For which year is Real GDP and Nominal GDP same and why?**

(ii) **Calculate Real GDP for the given years. Is there any year for which Real GDP falls?** Competency Based Que

Ans. (i) Real GDP and Nominal GDP is same for year 2014-2015. It is so because 2014-2015 is the base year.

(ii)

Year	2014-15	2015-16	2016-17
Nominal GDP	6.5	8.4	9
GDP Deflator	100	140	125
Real GDP	6.5	6	7.2

$$\text{Real GDP} = \frac{\text{Normal GDP}}{\text{GDP Deflator}} \times 100$$

The Real GDP declined in the year 2015-2016. It could be due to high rate of inflation or price levels.

26. **"Externalities can be classified into negative or positive, however it is not necessary that they will be directly correlated with the gross domestic product."**

Do you agree with the given statement? Give valid reasons in support of your answer. CBSE 2024 C

Ans. Yes, I agree with the statement.

Externalities, whether positive (e.g. Education) or negative (e.g. Pollution), impact societal welfare but are not necessarily reflected in GDP.

GDP measures market driven economic activities, while externalities often occur outside market transactions. For instance, industrial production may increase GDP but cause environmental harm, a negative externality that reduces welfare.

Similarly, the benefits of education, a positive externality, improve societal well-being but are not fully captured in GDP.

27. Explain with the help of given picture, how depicted issue affect GDP and welfare. Competency Based Que

Ans. GDP is often used as an index to measure the welfare of people.

Welfare here refers to the sense of material well-being amongst people. The welfare of people depends upon the per head availability of goods and services.

However, higher GDP does not necessarily implies higher level of welfare of people because of the following limitations

(i) **Distribution of GDP**
Sometimes a higher GDP results in the rise in inequalities in the income distribution amongst people. Therefore, in some cases, a rise in GDP does not mean an increase in the welfare of people.

(ii) **Change in Prices**
Sometimes the GDP of an economy increases because of the increase in the price of the goods and services, but not because of the rise in physical output of goods and services.
In these cases, taking GDP as an index to measure welfare is not reliable.

(iii) **Externalities**
Externalities mean any benefit or harm of an activity that is caused by an individual or an organisation for which they are not paid or penalised.
There are two types of externalities i.e. positive externalities and negative externalities. Positive externalities are those activities that benefit other people and negative externalities result in a decrease in welfare.

28. "In the past few decades, Indian economy has been fairly benefitted by positive externalities created by rapid rise in infrastructure." Justify the given statement with valid arguments. CBSE 2024; Competency Based Que

Ans. The term 'positive externality' describes the advantages that one party experiences as a result of another party's actions. The nation's gross domestic product does not account for positive externalities.

It is accurate to state that the positive externalities brought about by the infrastructure have helped the Indian economy in the following ways

(i) Increased productivity. (ii) Better connectivity.
(iii) Increased investment and employment.
(iv) Social development.
(v) Increase inflow of foreign direct investment.

29. Describe how the 'distribution of gross domestic product' limits the use of GDP as a welfare indicator.

Ans. Even if the Gross Domestic Product (GDP) of a country is rising significantly, it may not necessarily indicate welfare. This is because the rise in GDP may be concentrated in the hands of very few individuals or firms.

It means the gap between the rich and poor is widening due to these inequalities in the distribution of income. So, it can be concluded that welfare of the common people does not rise with the rise in GDP.

30. Explain the likely impact of construction of 2,000 new schools providing high quality education in a nation or Gross Domestic Product (GDP) and welfare in an economy. CBSE 2025; Competency Based Que

Ans. The construction of 2,000 new schools providing high quality education will have a positive impact on both Gross Domestic Product (GDP) and welfare in the economy

(i) **Increase in GDP**
The construction process will create jobs, boosting income and demand. In the long-run, a better educated workforce enhances productivity, innovation and economic growth, leading to a higher GDP.

(ii) **Improved Human Capital**
High quality education develops skilled workers, increasing employability and wages. This leads to higher earnings and better economic opportunities.

(iii) **Enhanced Welfare**
Education improves living standards by reducing poverty and inequality. An educated population makes better health and social choices, leading to overall well-being and sustainable economic development.

31. **"The public investment on the construction of a multi-lane flyover may reduce traffic congestion."**

On the basis of the above statement, discuss its likely impact on Gross Domestic Product (GDP) and welfare in an economy. **CBSE SQP 2025; Competency Based Que**

Ans. **Impact on GDP**

Public investment in constructing a multi-lane flyover will directly increase GDP as it involves large-scale infrastructure development, which adds to economic output. It contributes to the growth of sectors like construction, steel, cement and labour-intensive industries, boosting overall production and employment.

Impact on Welfare

The flyover reduces traffic congestion, saving time and fuel costs for commuters, thereby improving productivity and quality of life.

Reduced congestion also lowers air pollution, contributing to better environmental and health outcomes, enhancing societal welfare.

While public investment increases GDP through infrastructure development, its broader benefits like reduced congestion and environmental improvements enhance welfare beyond what GDP alone can measure.

32. **What is the difference between planned and unplanned inventory accumulation? Write down the relation between change in inventories and value added of a firm.** **NCERT**

Ans. Difference between planned and unplanned inventory accumulation are

Planned Inventory Accumulation

In case of an expected fall in sales, the firm will have unsold stock of goods which has been anticipated. Hence, there will be planned accumulation of inventories.

Unplanned Inventory Accumulation

In case of an unexpected fall in sales, the firm have unsold goods which it had not anticipated. Hence, there will be unplanned accumulation of inventories.

Relation between Change in Inventories and Value Added

Value Added = Value of Output − Intermediate Consumption

Also,

Value of Output = Sales + Change in Inventory

So, it can be summarised as follows

Value Added = Sales + Change in Inventory − Intermediate Consumption

Change in inventory is the difference between closing stock and opening stock. If it is positive, then value added will increase and if it is negative then value added will decrease.

33. **Distinguish between 'value of output' and 'value addition.'** **CBSE SQP 2023**

Ans. Differences between value of output and value addition are

Basis	Value of Output	Value Addition
Definition	The total market value of all goods and services produced by an enterprise during an accounting year.	The value added to raw materials (intermediate goods) by a firm through its productive activities.
Calculation	Calculated as the market value of goods and services produced.	Calculated as the difference between the value of output and the value of intermediate inputs.
Focus	Focuses on the total production value of the enterprise.	Focuses on the additional value created by the enterprise beyond the cost of intermediate goods.

34. **Define the problem of double counting in the computation of national income. State any two approaches to correct the problem of double counting.** **CBSE 2019**

Or **Suppose that there are only two kinds of producers in the economy. They are the wheat producers (or the farmers) and the bread makers (the bakers). The wheat producers grow wheat and they do not need any input other than human labour.**

They sell a part of the wheat to the bakers. The bakers do not need any other raw material besides wheat to produce bread.

Let us suppose that in a year, the total value of wheat that the farmers have produced is ₹ 400. He sold this to the flour mill. The flour mill sells this to the baker for ₹ 600.

Baker sells this to the retailer for ₹ 800 and retailer sells this to the consumer for ₹ 900. Which problem has been shown in the above case and how this problem can be avoided? **Competency Based Que**

Ans. The above case is indicating the problem of double counting. Problem of double couning means including the value of some goods and services more than once in the estimation of national income. In other words, the counting of the value of commodity more than once is called double counting. This leads to over estimation of the value of goods and services produced.

To avoid the problem of double counting, following two methods are used

(i) **Final Output Method**
According to this method, the value of intermediate goods is not considered. Only the value of final goods and services is considered.

(ii) **Value Added Method**
Another method to avoid the problem of double counting is to estimate the total value added at each stage of production. This is done by using the following formula
Value Added = Value of Output – Intermediate Cost

35. What precautions are necessary while using value added method of measuring national income?

Ans. The following are the various precautions to be taken in value added method

(i) Intermediate goods are not to be included in the national income since such goods are included in the value of final goods if they are included again it will lead to double counting.

(ii) Sale and purchase of second hand goods is not included as they do not add to current flow of goods and services. However, any commission or brokerage on sale or purchase of such goods will be included in the national income as it is a productive service.

(iii) Production of services for self-consumption are not included since it is difficult to measure their market value such as services of housewife.

(iv) Change in stock of goods will be included as it is a part of capital formation.

36. Identify the concept highlighted in the given image and explain the returns earned by different components. **Competency Based Que**

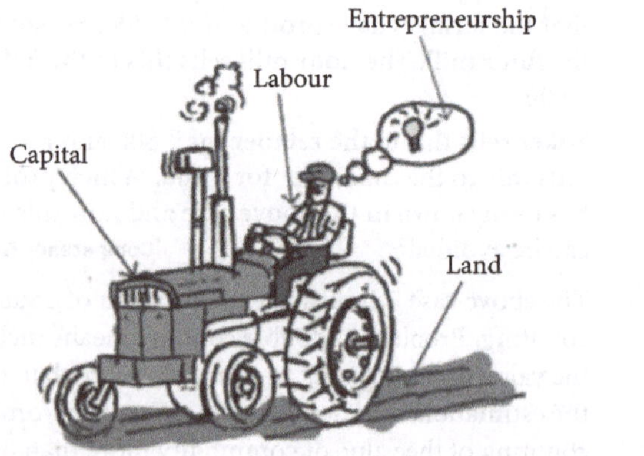

Ans. The concept illustrated in the image is the 'factors of production'. These are the essential inputs used in the production process to generate goods and services.

The main factors of production are as follows

(i) **Land**
It is a free gift of nature and it is called as a natural, original or primary factor of production.

(ii) **Labour**
Person or people engaged in some physical work form the labour force which is a factor of production.

(iii) **Capital**
It means wealth, money or income which is invested in a business to boost production.

(iv) **Entrepreneur**
It is the work of an entrepreneur to bring the required factors together and make them work harmoniously.

The remuneration to them are as follows

(i) **Land** Rent is a reward for the use of land.
(ii) **Labour** Wages are the reward for labour.
(iii) **Capital** Interest is the reward for capital.
(iv) **Entrepreneur** Profit is the reward for an entrepreneur.

37. Distinguish between rent and royalty. **CBSE SQP 2023**

Ans. Differences between rent and royalty are

Basis	Rent	Royalty
Definition	Income earned by the owners for lending physical assets like land, buildings, etc.	Income earned for granting rights to use intellectual property or subsoil assets (e.g. Minerals, oil).
Type of Asset	Physical assets (tangible) like land and buildings.	Intangible assets like intellectual property or natural resources.
Examples	Payment received for leasing land or renting out a building.	Payment for using copy-rights, patents or natural resources like minerals.

38. As per a news dated 11th April, 2023: "Electric vehicle sales crossed one million mark in FY 2023." Analyse its impact on Gross Domestic Product (GDP) and economic welfare. **CBSE 205; Competency Based Que**

Ans. The rise in Electric Vehicle (EV) sales crossing one million in FY 2023 has a significant impact on Gross Domestic Product (GDP) and economic welfare

(i) **Increase in GDP**
Higher EV sales boost production, creating demand for raw materials, labour and services.

This leads to increased industrial output, job creation and overall economic growth.

(ii) **Technological Advancement and Investment**
Growth in the EV sector encourages innovation, research and investment in infrastructure like charging stations, further strengthening the economy.

(iii) **Improved Economic Welfare**
EV adoption reduces air pollution, leading to better public health and a cleaner environment. Lower fuel dependency also enhances energy security, contributing to long-term sustainable development.

39. State the three components of income from property and entrepreneurship. CBSE 2020

Ans. The three components of income from property and entrepreneurship are as follows

(i) **Rent**
It is the income earned by providing fixed natural resource (land).

(ii) **Interest**
It is the income earned by providing capital.

(iii) **Profit**
It is the income earned by an entrepreneur.

40. What precautions are necessary while using income method of measuring national income?

Ans. While using income method, following precautions should be followed

(i) Income from illegal activities like smuggling, theft, gambling, etc. should not be included.

(ii) Commission paid on the sale and purchase of second hand goods are to be included.

(iii) Imputed rent of the owner occupied houses is to be treated along with rent as a component of factor incomes.

(iv) Income tax is paid out of compensation of employees. It should not be separately added in the estimation of national income.

(v) Transfer earnings like old age pensions, unemployment allowances, scholarships, pocket expenses etc. should not be included.

41. Explain the precautions that should be taken while estimating national income by expenditure method.

Ans. Precautions regarding calculation of national income by expenditure method are

(i) Expenditure on only final goods and services should be included in the national income estimation while intermediate consumption expenditure should not be included.

(ii) Similarly, expenditure on the purchase of second hand goods should not be included in the national income estimation of the current accounting year. This is because they have already been included in the national income of the accounting year in which they were originally purchased.

(iii) Expenditure on shares and bonds is not included. This is because these are mere financial assets and do not reflect any production activity of the goods or services.

(iv) Expenditure on transfer payments by the government should not be included. This is because such payments are not related to any production activity in an economy.

Long Answer Type Questions

42. Write down some of the limitations of using GDP as an index of welfare of a country. NCERT

Or **"Gross Domestic Product (GDP) as an indicator of welfare loses its significance if the distribution of income turns unequal." Justify the given statement with valid reason.** CBSE Term II 2022; Competency Based Que

Or **"Higher Gross Domestic Product (GDP) means greater per capita availability of goods in the economy." Do you agree with the given statement? Give valid reasons in support of your answer.** CBSE 2019

Or **"Gross Domestic Product (GDP) does not give us a clear indication of economic welfare of a country." Defend or refute the given statement with valid reason.** CBSE 2019

Ans. Following are the limitations of using GDP as an index of welfare of a country

(i) With every increase in the level of GDP, distribution of GDP is getting more unequal, welfare level of the society may not rise.

(ii) Composition of GDP may not be welfare oriented even when the level of GDP tends to rise, i.e. rise in GDP may be concentrated in few hands.

(iii) Because of non-monetary transactions, GDP remains under estimated and therefore, there is no proper index of welfare.

(iv) Impact of externalities (positive or negative impact of an activity) is not accounted in the index of social welfare in terms of GDP.

So, higher GDP does not means greater per capita availability of goods in the economy and neither does it gives a clear indication of economic welfare of a country.

43. Define the following

(i) Value addition **(ii) Gross domestic product**
(iii) Flow variables
(iv) Income from property and entrepreneurship

CBSE 2019

Ans. (i) **Value Addition**

It refers to difference in the value of output and intermediate expenses incurred in the production process.

Value Added = Value of Output − Intermediate Expenses

Where

Value of Output = Sales + Change in Stock

Change in Stock = Closing Stock − Opening Stock

(ii) **Gross Domestic Product** (GDP)

It refers to total value of final goods and services produced within the domestic teritory of an economy in a fiscal year. It only includes the value of final goods and services.

(iii) **Flow Variables**

It refers to a variable which is measured over a period of time. It is dynamic in nature. e.g. Savings.

(iv) **Income from Property and Entrepreneurship**

If refers to income received in the form of rent and from investment made in an entrepreneurial venture, i.e. profit. e.g. Rent received by an Indian from his property abroad.

44. Explain the concepts of net national product at factor cost and net national product at market price. Highlight the difference between these concepts.

Ans. **National Income at Factor Cost**

(i) Net national product at factor cost is also called national income.

(ii) Net national product at factor cost is equal to sum total of value added at factor cost or net domestic product at factor cost and net factor income from abroad.

(iii) NNP at Factor Cost = NNP at Market Price − Net Indirect Tax

(iv) Factor cost is the total cost of all the factors of production consumed or used in producing a good or service.

National Income at Market Price

(i) It refers to the total market value of all the final goods and services produced by the normal residents of a country both within the domestic territory as well as outside the country.

(ii) National Income at Market Price = National Income at Factor Cost + Net Indirect Taxes

Differences between these two concepts are

Basis	Net National Product at Factor Cost	Net National Product at Market Price
Definition	The value of all final goods and services produced by residents, measured at the cost of factors of production.	The total market value of all final goods and services produced by residents, including taxes.
Inclusion of Taxes and Subsidies	Excludes indirect taxes and includes subsidies, representing production costs alone.	Includes indirect taxes and excludes subsidies, reflecting the final prices paid by consumers.
Formula	NNP at Factor Cost = NNP at Market Price − Net Indirect Taxes	NNP at Market Price = NNP at Factor Cost + Net Indirect Taxes

45. Write down the three identities of calculating the GDP of a country by the three methods. Also briefly explain why each of these should give us the same value of GDP.

Ans. Three identities of calculating GDP are as follows

(i) **Product Method or Value Added Method**

It is that method which measures national income in terms of value addition by each producing enterprise in the economy.

It is calculated as

Gross Value Added in the Primary Sector at Market Price + Gross Value Added in the Secondary Sector at Market Price + Gross Value Added in the Tertiary Sector at Market Price = GDP_{MP}.

GDP_{MP} − Depreciation = Net Domestic Product at Market Price (NDP_{MP})

NDP_{MP} − Net Indirect Tax = Net Domestic Product at Factor Cost (NDP_{FC})

NDP_{FC} + NFIA = National Income

(ii) **Income Method**

Under this method, national income is measured in terms of factor payments to the owners of factors of production. It is calculated as

Compensation of Employees + Operating Surplus + Mixed Income of the Self-employed = Net Domestic Income at Factor Cost

Net Domestic Income at Factor Cost + NFIA = National Income

(iii) **Expenditure Method**

Under this method, national income is measured in terms of expenditure on the purchase of final goods and services produced in the economy.

It is calculated as

Private Final Consumption Expenditure + Government Final Consumption Expenditure + Gross Domestic Fixed Capital Formation + Change in Stock + Net Exports = GDP_{MP}

GDP_{MP} − Depreciation = Net Domestic Product at Market Price (NDP_{MP})

NDP_{MP} − Net Indirect Tax = NDP_{FC}

NDP_{FC} + NFIA = National Income

These three methods give us the same value of GDP because

National Product (Value Added Method) = National Income (Income Method) = National Expenditure (Expenditure Method)

This is known as triple identity.

46. Explain the value added method of national income estimation.

Ans. Value Added Method or Product Method

This method is based on the aspect that national income is the sum total of value added by all producing units in the economy during a financial year.

Under this method, from the value of output, the value of intermediate consumption is deducted to find the value added to the product by a firm during an accounting year. The value added by all the firms, i.e. the sum total of value added by all the firms give us Gross Domestic Product at Market Price (GDP_{MP}).

Main steps involved in the measurement of National Income (NI) through the production/value added method are

Step I Classification of the producing enterprises into industrial sectors like-primary secondary and tertiary sector.

Step II Estimation of the NVA at factor cost (NVA_{FC}) by each producing enterprise by taking the following sub-steps

(i) Estimate the value of output by adding sales and change in stock.

(ii) Estimate the value of Intermediate Consumption (IC) and deduct the same from value of output to arrive at Gross Value Added at Market Price. (GVA_{MP}).

(iii) Deduct depreciation and Net Indirect Taxes (NIT) from GVA_{MP} to arrive at Net Value Added at Factor Cost NVA_{FC}.

$$NVA_{FC} = \text{Value of Output} - IC - \text{Dep.} - NIT$$

Step III Take the sum of NVA_{FC} by all the producing enterprises to arrive at NDP_{FC}), i.e. NDP_{FC}, i.e. $NDP_{FC} = \Sigma NVA_{FC}$.

Step IV Finally add Net Factor Income from Abroad to the NDP_{FC} to arrive at NNP_{FC}.

Symbolically NNF_{FC} *or* $NI = NDP_{FC} + NFIA$

Precautions of Value Added Method

While using value added method, items to be included or excluded in the calculation of national income are

(i) The value of intermediate goods should not be included.

(ii) Purchase and sale of second hand goods should be excluded.

(iii) Commission earned on account of sale and purchase of second hand goods should be included.

(iv) Imputed value of self-consumed goods should be included.

(v) Own account production should be included.

(vi) Value of self-consumed services should not be included in the estimation of national income.

(vii) Imputed rent of the owner occupied house is to be taken into the account.

47. Discuss in detail the income method of estimating national income.

Or **State the steps pertaining to the estimation of national income under the income method.** **CBSE SQP 2025**

Ans. In this method, national income is measured in terms of factor payments (wages, rent, interest and profit) to the owners of factors of production (labour, land, capital and enterprise), during an accounting year.

This method is also called share method or factor payment method.

The sum of factor payments give us NDP_{FC}. To this, we add Net Factor Income from Abroad (NFIA) to get the National Income (NNP_{FC}).

The various steps to be followed are discussed ahead

Step I Classify the production units into industrial sectors namely into primary, secondary and tertiary sector.

Step II Estimate the factor incomes paid out by each industrial sector.

The sum of (i) Compensation of Employees (ii) Rent and Royalty (iii) Interest (iv) Profit and (v) Mixed Income of the Self-employed, represents the contribution of the sector to the domestic factor income and equals NVA_{FC}.

Step III Take the sum of the factor incomes paid out by all the industrial sectors to arrive at $NDP_{FC} = \Sigma NVA_{FC}$

Step IV Finally, add net factor income from abroad to NDP_{FC} to arrive at NNP_{FC} *or* Domestic Income + NFIA $= NNP_{FC}$

Precautions of Income Method

While using income method, items included and excluded in the calculation of national income are

(i) Income from illegal activities like smuggling, theft, gambling, etc. should not be included.

(ii) Commission paid on the sale and purchase of second hand goods are to be included.

(iii) Income in terms of windfall gains should not be included.

(iv) Imputed rent of the owner occupied houses is to be treated alongwith rent as a component of factor incomes.

48. Discuss in detail the expenditure method of estimating national income.

Ans. According to this method, national income is measured in terms of expenditure on the purchase of final goods and services produced in an economy, during an accounting year. This method is also called income disposal method.

Estimation of expenditure on the final goods and services produced during the year is equal to GDP_{MP}. Then, it is adjusted to find national income (NNP_{FC}).

Main steps involved in the measurement of national income by the 'expenditure method' are

Step I Classify the domestic economic factors—households, corporations, the government and international trade—are responsible for production costs in the nation.

Step II Estimate final expenditure on goods and services produced by these industrial sectors, by way of Private Final Consumption Expenditure (PFCE), Government Final Consumption Expenditure (GFCE), Gross Domestic Capital Formation (GDCF) and Net Exports (X–M) and add them up to obtain GDP_{MP}

Symbolically,

$GDP_{MP} = PFCE + GFCE + GDCF + (X - M)$

Step III Deduct consumption of fixed capital and net indirect taxes to arrive at NDP_{FC} i.e.

GDP_{MP} – Consumption of Fixed Capital – Net Indirect Taxes = NDP_{FC} *or* Domestic Income.

Step IV Add Net Factor Income from abroad to NDP_{FC} to arrive at National Income/NNP_{FC}

$NDP_{FC} + NFIA = NNP_{FC}$ *or* National Income

While using expenditure method, items included and excluded in the calculation of national income are

(i) Only final expenditure is to be taken into account to avoid error of double counting.

(ii) Expenditure on second hand goods is not to be included, because value of second hand goods has already been accounted for during the year of their production.

(iii) Expenditure on shares and bonds is not to be included in total expenditure, as these are mere paper claims and are not related to the production of final goods and services.

(iv) Expenditure on transfer payments by the government is to be excluded.

(v) Imputed value/Estimated value of expenditure on goods produced for self-consumption should be taken into account, as these goods are reflected in the estimation of GDP.

49. (i) **"Domestic/Household services performed by a woman may not be considered as an economic activity." Defend or refute the given statement with valid reason.**

(ii) **Compensation to the victims of a cyclone is an example of a welfare measure taken by the government. State with valid reason, should it be included/not included in the estimation of national income of India.**

CBSE SQP 2022; Competency Based Que

Ans. (i) The given statement is defended, as it is difficult to measure the monetary value of the services performed by a woman (homemaker). Also, the motive behind these services is not 'generation of income.' Therefore, these services are not considered as a productive activity.

(ii) Compensation given to the victims of a cyclone is an example of a social welfare measure taken by the government. However, it is not included in estimation of national income as it is a transfer payment which does not lead to corresponding flow of goods and services.

50. The overall objective of political activities in democratic societies is to ensure the highest possible level of welfare for the country's citizens now and in the future. When politicians, macroeconomists and others discuss welfare and economic development in Denmark they often focus on the Gross Domestic Product, GDP. e.g. The overall goal of the government's 2020 plan is for Denmark to be among the 10 richest countries in the world in 2020 in terms of GDP per capita.

GDP is a measure of the economic prosperity of a country compiled as output or income. There is a strong correlation between the development in GDP and changes in several important social factors, including tax payments and unemployment and to a lesser extent, health and education.

It is therefore no mere coincidence that GDP plays a key role in the public debate. However, GDP is regularly criticised for not presenting a fair view of welfare. If GDP is a poor measure of welfare, focusing one-sidedly on increasing GDP may lead to misguided political decisions. e.g. Nobel laureate Joseph Stiglitz has argued that the objective of the highest possible GDP growth will result in reduced welfare.

The criticism of GDP is not new and over the last 30-40 years efforts have been made to put together alternative objectives. The debate has revived recently, partly as a result of the publication of a recent report concerning the limitations of GDP as a measure of economic performance and social progress.

The report was written by the two Nobel laureates for economy, Joseph Stiglitz and Amartya Sen, among others.

The criticism of GDP as a measure of welfare is two-fold. Firstly, there are a number of compilation problems, including the breakdown by price and quantity changes and the calculation of public output. These problems can cause both the level of GDP and GDP growth to deviate from actual output.

Furthermore, changes in the terms of trade may cause income to develop differently from output. As a result, applying the level of GDP and GDP growth as measures of economic prosperity is not fully possible.

Secondly, a number of factors of major significance to welfare are not included in GDP. Accordingly, a number of alternative measures of welfare, so-called welfare indicators, have been proposed. Some welfare indicators are based on the national accounts.

A number of other factors affecting welfare, e.g. Leisure time, health condition and level of education, are subsequently included. These welfare indicators do not seem to provide a significantly better picture of welfare due to the strong correlation between e.g. Health and education and GDP.

Instead, other welfare indicators attempt to measure welfare directly, including by means of questionnaires on the subjective feeling of happiness. The patterns of these indicators are different from that of GDP.

There is a strong cross-country correlation between GDP and happiness, but measured over time, happiness seems to be independent of the development in GDP. One explanation of this apparent paradox is that happiness is related to the relative position in the income hierarchy rather than to the absolute level of income.

Consequently, the feeling of happiness is not increased by higher income if everyone else has also become more affluent. **Competency Based Que**

(i) Briefly explain why GDP is not considered as a measure of economic well-being?

(ii) Is it reasonable to treat a person's income level as his or her level of well-being? Give reason.

Ans. (i) GDP is not considered as a measure of economic well-being due to the following limitations

- **Non-monetary Exchanges**
  GDP measures the goods and services produced in an economy during a particular period of time. However, it does not take into account those transactions that do not come under monetary terms. In less developed countries there are non-monetary exchanges, particularly in rural areas. Hence, these transactions remain outside the domain of GDP. The household sector and volunteer sectors get ignored in GDP.
- **Inflation**
  GDP does not take into account the level of prices in a country. Because of inflation, the cost of living increases leading to a decrease in the standard of living. The loss of welfare due to this decrease is not taken into consideration by GDP as an index of welfare.
- **Externalities**
  Increase in the national income is associated with increased levels of pollution, accidents, disasters, shortage and depletion of natural resources, etc. These factors affect human health and lead to ecological degradation. GDP fails to consider the costs or valuations of such factors.

(ii) Yes, in the study, happiness and well-being were compared in wealthier countries and poorer countries across the globe. The data showed a direct link between well-being, specifically that sense that people were living the best possible life they could, and GDP. More than half of the variations in well-being could be explained by a countries overall prosperity or poverty level.

Numerical Questions

Numerical 1

Assuming real income to be ₹ 200 crore and price index to be 145, calculate nominal income.

Sol. Given Real Income = ₹ 200 crore

Price Index = 145

We know that Price Index $= \frac{\text{Nominal Income}}{\text{Real Income}} \times 100$

$$145 = \frac{\text{Nominal Income}}{200} \times 100$$

⇒ Nominal Income = ₹ 290 crore

Numerical 2

The value of the nominal GNP of an economy was ₹ 3,500 crore in a particular year. The value of GNP of that count evaluated at the same base year prices for the year was ₹ 5,000 crore. Calculate the value of the GNP deflator of the year in percentage terms.

Also calculate the price fall in percentage terms.

Sol. GNP Deflator $= \frac{\text{Nominal GDP}}{\text{Real GDP}} \times 100 = \frac{3{,}500}{5{,}000} \times 100 = 70\%$

Price Fall = 100% − GNP Deflator = 100 − 70 = 30%

Numerical 3

If the Real GDP is ₹ 600 crore and Nominal GDP is ₹ 900 crore, calculate the price index (base = 100).

Sol. Given, Real GDP = ₹ 600 crore

Nominal GDP = ₹ 900 crore

Price Index $= \frac{\text{Nominal GDP}}{\text{Real GDP}} \times 100 = \frac{900}{600} \times 100 = 150$

Numerical 4

If the Nominal GDP is ₹ 480 crore and price index in ₹ 120 (base = 100), calculate the Real GDP.

Sol. Nominal GDP = ₹ 480 crore

Price Index = 120

Price Index $= \frac{\text{Nominal GDP}}{\text{Real GDP}} \times 100$

⇒ $120 = \frac{480}{\text{Real GDP}} \times 100$

⇒ Real GDP = ₹ 400 crore

Numerical 5

Suppose only one Good 'X' is produced in the country. Output of Good X during year 2018 and 2019 were 100 units and 110 units respectively. The market price of the product during the two years was ₹ 50 and ₹ 55 per unit respectively. Calculate the percentage change in Real Gross Domestic Product (GDP) in year 2019 using 2018 as the base year. CBSE 2023

Sol. Assuming the Base Year Price Index = 100

We know, Q of 2018 is 100 units and that of 2019 is 110 units.

So, Real GDP of 2018 = Base Year Price Index × Quantity of 2018

= 100 × 100 = 10,000

Real GDP of 2019

= Base Year Price Index × Quantity of 2019

= 100 × 110 = 11,000

Percentage change in Real GDP = 1,000/10,000 × 100 = 10%

Numerical 6

Suppose the Gross Domestic Product (GDP) of Nation X was ₹ 2,000 crore in 2018-19, whereas the gross domestic product of Nation Y in the same year was ₹ 71,20,000 crore. If the gross domestic product of Nation X rises to ₹ 4,000 crore in 2019-20 and the gross domestic product of Nation Y rises to ₹ 72,00,000 crore in 2019-20, compare the rate of change of GDP of Nations X and Y, taking 2018-19 as base year. CBSE SQP 2022

Sol.

Nations/ Years	2018-19 (₹)	2019-20 (₹)	Growth Rate of GDP $= \frac{\text{Change in GDP}}{\text{Base Year GDP}} \times 100$ (Base Year = 2018-19)
X	2,000 crore	4,000 crore	$= \frac{2{,}000}{2{,}000} \times 100 = 100\%$
Y	1,20,000 crore	2,00,000 crore	$= \frac{80{,}000}{1{,}20{,}000} \times 100 = 66.67\%$

Nation X has a GDP growth rate of 100% and has performed better on the front of GDP rise as compared to Nation Y which has a GDP growth rate of 66.67%.

Numerical 7

S.No.	Items	₹ (in crores)
(i)	GNP_{MP}	15,000
(ii)	Depreciation or Consumption of Fixed Capital	1,000
(iii)	Indirect Taxes	500
(iv)	Subsidies	150
(v)	Net Factor Income from Abroad	650

On the basis of the above information, calculate

(i) NNP_{MP} (ii) NNP_{FC} (iii) NDP_{FC} (iv) GDP_{MP}

Sol. (i) $NNP_{MP} = GNP_{MP}$ – Depreciation

$= 15{,}000 - 1{,}000 =$ ₹ 14,000 crore

(ii) $NNP_{FC} = GNP_{MP}$ – Depreciation – Net Indirect Taxes

$= 15{,}000 - 1{,}000 - (500 - 150)$

$= 14{,}000 - 350 =$ ₹ 13,650 crore

[∵ NIT = Indirect Taxes – Subsidies]

(iii) $NDP_{FC} = GNP_{MP}$ – Depreciation – Net Factor Income from Abroad – Net Indirect Taxes

$= 15{,}000 - 1{,}000 - 650 - (500 - 150)$

= ₹ 13,000 crore

(iv) $GDP_{MP} = GNP_{MP}$ – Net Factor Income from Abroad

$= 15{,}000 - 650 =$ ₹ 14,350 crore

Numerical 8

Calculate Domestic Income (NDP_{FC}) from the data given below **CBSE 2025**

S.No.	Particulars	₹ (in lakhs)
(i)	Gross National Product at Market Price	2,500
(ii)	Consumption of Fixed Capital	200
(iii)	Goods and Services Tax	20
(iv)	Subsidies	50
(v)	Net Factor Income from Abroad	50
(vi)	Changes in Stocks	30
(vii)	Unexpected Loss of a Fixed Asset	500

Sol. Net National Product at Market Price (NNP_{MP})

= Gross Domestic Product at Market Price (GDP_{MP}) – Depreciation = 2,500 – 200 = ₹ 2,300 lakh

Net National Product at Market Price (NNP_{MP})

= Net Domestic Product at Market Price (NDP_{MP}) + Net Factor Income from Abroad (NFIA)

⇒ Net Domestic Product at Market Price (NDP_{MP})

= 2,300 – 50 = ₹ 2,250 lakh

Now, Net Domestic Product at Factor Cost (NDPFC)

= Net Domestic Product at Market Price (NDP_{MP}) – Goods and Services Tax + Subsidies

= 2,250 – 20 + 50 = ₹ 2,280 lakh

Numerical 9

Find out the amount of subsidies from the information given.

S.No.	Items	₹ (in crores)
(i)	GNP_{FC}	13,855
(ii)	Depreciation	2,000
(iii)	Indirect Taxes	60
(iv)	Net Factor Income to Abroad	100
(v)	NDP_{MP}	12,000

Sol. We know that,

Net Indirect Taxes = Indirect Taxes – Subsidies $= 60 - x$

Now, $GNP_{FC} = NDP_{MP}$ + Depreciation – Net Factor Income to Abroad – Net Indirect Taxes

So, $13{,}855 = 12{,}000 + 2{,}000 - 100 - (60 - x)$

$13{,}855 = 13{,}900 - 60 + x$

$13{,}855 = 13{,}840 + x$

⇒ $x = 13{,}855 - 13{,}840 =$ ₹ 15 crore

So, Subsidies = ₹ 15 crore

Numerical 10

Calculate factor income to abroad.

S.No.	Items	₹ (in crores)
(i)	GNP_{MP}	9,000
(ii)	Replacement of Fixed Capital	200
(iii)	Indirect Taxes	600
(iv)	Subsidies	400
(v)	Factor Income from Abroad	1,400
(vi)	NDP_{FC}	7,800

Sol. We know that,

Net Indirect Taxes = Indirect Taxes – Subsidies

= 600 – 400 = ₹ 200 crore

Net Factor Income from Abroad

= Factor Income from Abroad – Factor Income to Abroad

$= 1{,}400 - x$

Now,

$GNP_{MP} = NDP_{FC}$ + Replacement of Fixed Capital + Net Factor Income from Abroad + Net Indirect Taxes

$9{,}000 = 7{,}800 + 200 + (1{,}400 - x) + 200$

$9{,}000 = 9{,}600 - x = 9{,}600 - 9{,}000 =$ ₹ 600 crore

So, Factor Income to Abroad = ₹ 600 crore

Numerical 11

Find Gross Value Added at Market Price.

S.No.	Items	₹ (in lakhs)
(i)	Depreciation	20
(ii)	Domestic Sales	200
(iii)	Net Change in Stocks	(–) 10
(iv)	Exports	10
(v)	Single use Producer Goods	120

Sol. Gross Value Added at Market Price (GVA_{MP})

$= \text{Domestic Sales} + \text{Exports} + \text{Net Change in Stocks} - \text{Single use Producer Goods}$

$= 200 + 10 + (-10) - 120$

$GVA_{MP} = ₹\ 80 \text{ lakh}$

Numerical 12

Find net value added at market price.

S.No.	Items	₹ (in lakhs)
(i)	Fixed Capital Good with Life Span of 5 Years	30
(ii)	Raw Materials	12
(iii)	Sales	50
(iv)	Net Change-in-stock	(–) 4
(v)	Taxes on Production	2

Sol. Net Value Added at Market Price (NVA_{MP})

$= \text{Sales} + \text{Net Change-in-stock} - \text{Raw Material} - \text{Depreciation on Fixed Capital Good}$

$= 50 + (-4) - 12 - \frac{30}{5} = ₹\ 28 \text{ lakh}$

Numerical 13

On the basis of the given data, estimate the value of Net Value Added at Factor Cost (NVA_{FC}) **CBSE 2024 C**

S.No.	Items	₹ (in crores)
(i)	Sales	1,000
(ii)	Change in Stock	150
(iii)	Purchase of Raw Material	300
(iv)	Gross Investment	100
(v)	Net Investment	80
(vi)	Net Indirect Taxes	20

Sol. NVA_{FC}

$= \text{Sales} + \text{Change in Stock} - \text{Raw Material Purchase} - \text{Depreciation} - \text{Net Indirect Taxes}$

$NVA_{FC} = 1{,}000 + 150 - 300 - (100 - 80) - 20$

$NVA_{FC} = 1{,}000 + 150 - 300 - 40$

$NVA_{FC} = ₹\ 810 \text{ crore}$

Numerical 14

Calculate Net Value Added at Factor Cost (NVA_{FC}) from the following data **CBSE 2020**

S.No.	Items	₹ (in crores)
(i)	Value of Output	800
(ii)	Intermediate Consumption	200
(iii)	Indirect Taxes	30
(iv)	Depreciation	20
(v)	Subsidies	50
(vi)	Purchase of Machinery	50

Sol. Net Value Added at Factor Cost (NVA_{FC})

$= \text{Value of Output} - \text{Intermediate Consumption} - \text{Depreciation} - \text{Net Indirect Taxes}$

$= 800 - 200 - (-20) = 800 - 200 - 20 + 20$

$= ₹\ 600 \text{ crores}$

Here, Net Indirect Taxes = Indirect Taxes – Subsidy

Numerical 15

From the data given below, calculate net value added at factor cost

S.No.	Items	₹ (in crores)
(i)	Total Sales	500
(ii)	Decrease in Stock	35
(iii)	Production for Self-consumption	60
(iv)	Purchase of Raw Materials	150
(v)	Exports	75
(vi)	Electricity Charges	25
(vii)	Wealth Tax	10
(viii)	Goods and Services Tax (GST)	35
(ix)	Subsidy	20

Sol. $NVA_{FC} = \text{Value of Output} + \text{Change in Stock} - \text{Intermediate Consumption} - \text{Net Indirect Taxes}$

$= (\text{Total Sales} + \text{Production for Self-consumption}) - \text{Decrease in Stock} - (\text{Purchase of Raw Material} + \text{Electricity Charges}) - (\text{GST} - \text{Subsidy})$

$= (500 + 60) - 35 - (150 + 25) - (35 - 20)$

$= 560 - 35 - 175 - 15 = 560 - 225 = ₹\ 335 \text{ crore}$

Notes
- Production for self-consumption is included in the value of output.
- Total sales are given, hence exports will not be considered.
- Electricity charges are a part of intermediate consumption.
- Wealth tax is a direct tax.

Numerical 16

Calculate national income from the following data

S.No.	Items	₹ (in lakhs)
(i)	Sales	800
(ii)	Purchase of Raw Materials from Domestic Market	400
(iii)	Import of Raw Material	100
(iv)	Subsidies	30

S.No.	Items	₹ (in lakhs)
(v)	Consumption of Fixed Capital	40
(vi)	Change-in-stock	50
(vii)	Rent	70
(viii)	Net Factor Income from Abroad	10

Sol. National Income = Sales + Change-in-Stock – (Purchase of Raw Material from Domestic Market + Import of Raw Material) – Consumption of Fixed Capital + Subsidies + NFIA

= 800 + 50 – (400 + 100) – 40 + 30 + 10

= (880 – 540 + 10) = ₹ 350 lakh

Numerical 17

From the information given below, calculate

(a) Value added by Firm A and Firm B.

(b) Gross Domestic Product at Market Price.

S.No.	Items	₹ (in crores)
(i)	Sales by Firm B to General Government	500
(ii)	Sales by Firm A	2,500
(iii)	Sales by Firm B to Households	1,750
(iv)	Change in Stock of Firm A	100
(v)	Closing Stock of Firm B	200
(vi)	Opening Stock of Firm B	150
(vii)	Purchases by Firm A	1,600
(viii)	Indirect Taxes Paid by Both the Firms	375
(ix)	Sales by Firm A to B	1,000

Sol. (a) **Value Added by Firm A**

= Sales by Firm A + Change in Stock of Firm A – Purchases by Firm A

= 2,500 + 100 – 1,600

= ₹ 1,000 crore

Value Added by Firm B

= Sales by Firm B to General Government + Sales by Firm B to Households + Change in Stock of Firm B – Purchases by Firm B from Firm A (Intermediate Consumption)

= 500 + 1,750 + (200 – 150) – 1,000

= ₹ 1,300 crore

(b) GDP_{MP}

= Value Added by Firm A + Value Added by Firm B

= 1,000 + 1,300 = ₹ 2,300 crore

Numerical 18

In an economy, following transactions took place. Calculate value of output and value added by Firm B.

(i) Firm A sold to Firm B goods of ₹ 80 crore, to Firm C ₹ 50 crore; to household ₹ 30 crore and goods of value ₹ 10 crore remains unsold.

(ii) Firm B sold to Firm C goods of ₹ 70 crore; to Firm D ₹ 40 crore; goods of value ₹ 30 crore were exported and goods of value ₹ 5 crore was sold to government.

CBSE SQP 2019

Sol. (i) Value of Output of Firm B = Sales of Firm B to Firm C + Sales of Firm B to Firm D + Exports + Sales of Firm B to Government

= 70 + 40 + 30 + 5 = ₹ 145 crore

(ii) Value Added by Firm B = Value of Output by Firm B – Purchases by Firm B from Firm A

= 145 – 80 = ₹ 65 crore

Numerical 19

There are only two producing sectors A and B in an economy. Calculate

(a) Gross Value Added at Market Price by A and B.

(b) National Income.

S.No.	Items	₹ (in crores)
(i)	Net Factor Income from Abroad	20
(ii)	Sales by A	500
(iii)	Sales by B	600
(iv)	Indirect Tax by A and B	80
(v)	Depreciation by A and B	30
(vi)	Exports by A	45
(vii)	Net Change-in-stock of A	10
(viii)	Intermediate Consumption of A	200
(ix)	Net Change-in-stock of B	(–) 10
(x)	Intermediate Consumption of B	300

Sol. (a) GVA_{MP} by A

= Sales by A + Net Change-in-stock of A – Intermediate Consumption of A

= 500 + 10 – 200 = ₹ 310 crore

GVA_{MP} by B = Sales by B + Net Change-in-stock of B – Intermediate Consumption of B

= 600 + (–10) – 300 = ₹ 290 crore

GVA_{MP} by A and B = 310 + 290 = ₹ 600 crore

(b) National Income (NNP_{FC})

= GVA_{MP} by A and B – Indirect Taxes by A and B – Depreciation by A and B + Net Factor Income from Abroad

= 600 – 80 – 30 + 20 = 620 – 110 = ₹ 510 crore

Numerical 20

Suppose, there are only three firms in a hypothetical economy, *viz.* A, B and C. During a given period of time, the following transactions were undertaken by them

(i) Firm A sold goods worth ₹ 2,000 to Firm B and ₹ 1,200 to Firm C.

(ii) Firm B sold goods worth ₹ 1,100 to Firm A and ₹ 3,500 to Firm C.

(iii) Firm C sold to households for final consumption, goods worth ₹ 5,700.

Estimate the value of Net Domestic Product at Market Price (NDP_{MP}) assuming depreciation to be ₹ 120.

CBSE 2025

Sol. Value Added by Firm A = Sales (to B and C) – Purchases + Change in Stock

= (2,000 + 1,200) – 1,100 = ₹ 2,100

Value Added by Firm B = Sales (to A and C) – Purchases

= (3,500 + 1,100) – 2,000 = ₹ 2,600

Value Added by Firm C = Sales (to Market) – Purchases (from A and B)

= 5,700 – (1,200 + 3,500) = ₹ 1,000

Now, GDP_{MP} = Value Added by Firm A + B + C

= 2,100 + 2,600 + 1,000 = ₹ 5,700

So, NDP_{MP} = GDP_{MP} – Depreciation = 5,700 – 120

= ₹ 5,580

Numerical 21

Calculate Gross Value Added at Factor Cost (GVA_{FC}).

S.No.	Items	₹ (in crores)
(i)	Units of Output Sold	2,000
(ii)	Price Per Unit	30
(iii)	Depreciation	2,000
(iv)	Intermediate Cost	24,000
(v)	Closing Stock	6,000
(vi)	Opening Stock	4,000
(vii)	Excise	5,000

Sol. Sales = Units of Output Sold × Price Per Unit

= 2,000 × 30 = ₹ 60,000 crore

Value of Output = Sales + Change-in-stock

= 60,000 + (6,000 – 4,000)

= ₹ 62,000 crore

GVA_{FC} = Value of Otput – Intermediate Cost – Net Indirect Taxes (Excise + Sales Tax)

= 62,000 – 24,000 – (5,000) = ₹ 33,000 crore

Numerical 22

Calculate net value added at factor cost.

S.No.	Items	₹ (in crores)
(i)	Consumption of Fixed Capital	900
(ii)	Import Duty	600
(iii)	Output Sold (units)	3,000
(iv)	Price Per Unit of Output	10
(v)	Net Change-in-stock	(–) 75
(vi)	Intermediate Cost	15,000
(vii)	Subsidy	750

Sol. Sales = Output sold × Price Per Unit

= 3,000 × 10 = ₹ 30,000 crore

Value of Output = Sales + Net Change-in-stock

= 30,000 + (– 75) = 29,925

GVA_{MP} = Value of Output – Intermediate Cost

= 29,925 – 15,000 = 14,925

NVA_{FC} = GVA_{MP} – Consumption of Fixed Capital – Net Indirect Tax

= 14,925 – 900 – (600 – 750) = ₹ 14,175 crore

Numerical 23

Given the following data, find net value added at factor cost by Sambhav (a farmer) producing wheat

CBSE Term II 2022

S.No.	Items	₹ (in crores)
(i)	Sale of Wheat by the Farmer in the Local Market	6,800
(ii)	Purchase of Tractor	5,000
(iii)	Procurement of Wheat by the Government from the Farmer	200
(iv)	Consumption of Wheat by the Farming Family during the Year	50
(v)	Expenditure on the Maintenance of Existing Capital Stock	100
(vi)	Subsidy	20

Sol. Net Value Added at Factor Cost (NVA_{FC})

= Sale of Wheat by the Farmer in the Local Market + Procurement of Wheat by the Government from the Farmer + Consumption of Wheat by the Farming Family during the Year + Subsidy – Expenditure on the Maintenance of Existing Capital Stock

= 6,800 + 200 + 50 + 20 – 100

= ₹ 6,970 crore

Numerical 24

Calculate the value of output from the following data

S.No.	Items	₹ (in crores)
(i)	Net Value Added at Factor Cost	800
(ii)	Intermediate Consumption	600
(iii)	Goods and Services Tax (GST)	160
(iv)	Subsidy	40
(v)	Depreciation	80

Sol. We know that,

NVA_{FC} = Value of Output − Intermediate Consumption − Depreciation − Net Indirect Taxes

$800 = x - 600 - 80 - (160 - 40)$

$800 = x - 680 - 120 \Rightarrow 800 = x - 800$

$\Rightarrow x = 800 + 800 =$ ₹ 1,600 crore

So, Value of Output = ₹ 1,600 crore

Numerical 25

Calculate sales from the following data.

S.No.	Items	₹ (in lakhs)
(i)	Subsidies	200
(ii)	Opening Stock	100
(iii)	Closing Stock	600
(iv)	Intermediate Consumption	2000
(v)	Consumption of Fixed Capital	500
(vi)	Profit	900
(vii)	Net Value Added at Factor Cost	1500

Sol. Gross Value Added at Market Price, (GVP_{MP})

= Value of Output − Intermediate Consumption

Further GVA_{MP} = Sales + Change in stock − Intermediate Consumption

$\Rightarrow$ 1800 = Sales + (600 − 100) − 2,000

Sales = 1,800 − 500 + 2,000

Sales = ₹ 3,300 lakh

Numerical 26

Calculate the value of 'change-in-stock' from the following data **CBSE 2020**

S.No.	Items	₹ (in crores)
(i)	Sales	400
(ii)	Net Value Added at Factor Cost (NVA_{FC})	200
(iii)	Subsidies	10
(iv)	Change in Stock	?
(v)	Depreciation	40
(vi)	Intermediate Consumption	100

Sol. $GVA_{MP} = NVA_{FC}$ + Depreciation + Net Indirect Tax

$GVA_{MP} = 200 + 40 + (0 - 10)$

$GVA_{MP} = 230$

Value Added = Value of Output − Intermediate Consumption

Value of Output = 230 + 100 = 330

Value of Output = Sales + Change in Stock

Change in Stock = 330 − 400

Change in Stock = (−) ₹ 70 crore

Numerical 27

Calculate 'intermediate consumption' from the following data

Items	₹ (in crores)
Value of Output	480
Net Value Added at Factor Cost	120
Sales Tax	40
Subsidy	10
Depreciation	25

Sol. Intermediate Consumption

= Value of Output − Net Value Added at Factor Cost − Net Indirect Taxes (Sales Tax − Subsidy) − Depreciation

= 480 − 120 − (40 − 10) − 25

= 480 − 120 − 30 − 25 = ₹ 305 crore

Numerical 28

Suppose in a hypothetical economy there are only two Firms A and B, Firm A sold goods for ₹ 2,000 to Firm B and purchased goods for ₹ 1,000. Firm B exported goods for ₹ 2,500 and had domestic sales of ₹ 1,500. Calculate net domestic product at market price, if consumption of fixed capital is ₹ 200. **CBSE SQP 2023**

Sol.

	Value of Output (₹)	Intermediate Consumption (₹)	Value Addition (₹)
A.	2,000 (to B)	1,000 (purchases)	2,000 − 1,000 = 1,000
B.	2,500 (exports) + 1,500 (domestic sales) = 4,000	2,000 (purchased from A)	4,000 − 2,000 = 2,000
Total	6,000	3,000	3,000

Net Domestic Product at MP

= Gross Domestic Product at MP − Consumption of Fixed Capital

= 3,000 − 200 = ₹ 2,800

Numerical 29

Suppose in a financial year, the Gross Domestic Product (GDP) at Market Price of a country was ₹ 1,100 crore. Net factor income from Abroad was ₹ 100 crore, the net indirect taxes was ₹ 150 crore and national income was ₹ 850 crore. Calculate the value of depreciation, on the basis of above information. **CBSE 2023**

Sol. GDP_{MP} = ₹ 1,100 crore

Net Factor Income from Abroad = ₹ 100 crore

Net Indirect Taxes = ₹ 150 crore

National Income (NNP_{FC}) = ₹ 850 crore

National Income (NNP_{FC}) = Gross Value Added at Market Prices (GDP_{MP}) − Depreciation − Net Indirect Taxes + NFIA

So, Depreciation = Gross Value Added at Market Prices (GDP_{MP}) − National Income (NNP_{FC}) − Net Indirect Taxes + NFIA

= 1,100 − 850 − 150 + 100 = ₹ 200 crore

Numerical 30

From the following data, calculate the value of operating surplus

S.No.	Items	₹ (in crores)
(i)	Royalty	5
(ii)	Rent	75
(iii)	Interest	30
(iv)	Net Domestic Product at Factor Cost	400
(v)	Profit	45
(vi)	Dividends	20

Sol. Operating Surplus = Rent + Royalty + Interest + Profit

= 75 + 5 + 30 + 45 = ₹ 155 crore

Numerical 31

(a) Define net factor income from abroad. How is it different from net exports?

(b) Calculate the value of Rent from the following data **CBSE 2019**

S.No.	Items	₹ (in crores)
(i)	Gross Domestic Product at Market Price	18,000
(ii)	Mixed Income of Self-employed	7,000
(iii)	Subsidies	250
(iv)	Interest	800
(v)	Rent	?
(vi)	Profit	975
(vii)	Compensation of Employees	6,000
(viii)	Consumption of Fixed Capital	1,000
(ix)	Indirect Tax	2,000

Sol. (a) Net factor income from abroad is the difference between the factor incomes earned by domestic residents from abroad i.e. factor incomes received and factor incomes paid to non-residents for their services in the domestic country.

Symbolically,

NFIA = Factor Incomes Received − Factor Incomes Paid

On the other hand, net exports refers to the difference between the value of exports and value of imports of goods i.e. visible trade.

Symbolically,

Net Exports = Exports (X) − Imports (M)

(b) By Income Method,

NDP_{FC} = Compensation of Employees + Operating Surplus + Mixed Income of Self-employed ...(i)

Where,

Operating Surplus = Rent + Interest + Profits and

NDP_{FC} = GDP_{MP} − Depreciation − NIT

= 18,000 − 1,000 − (2,000 − 250) = ₹ 15,250

Now, putting values in eq. (i)

15,250 = 6,000 + (Rent + 800 + 975) + 7,000

15,250 = 14,775 + Rent

∴ Rent = ₹ 475 crore

Numerical 32

Study the table given below which has information about two firms of an economy. **CBSE SQP 2023**

	Wages (₹)	Profits (₹)	Interest (₹)	Rent (₹)
Firm A	50	150	100	100
Firm B	90	210	100	100

Further, it should be noted that

(i) Net factor income from abroad is (−) ₹ 20.

(ii) Employee's contribution to the social security fund by Firm A and Firm B is ₹ 5 and ₹ 10 respectively.

Calculate the national income.

Sol. NDP_{FC} = 50 + 150 + 90 + 210 + 100 + 100 + 100 + 100

= ₹ 900

National Income = Net National Product at Factor Cost

= Net Domestic Product at Factor Cost + Net Factor Income from Abroad

NI = NNP at Factor Cost

= 900 + (−) 20 = ₹ 880

Numerical 33

From the following data, calculate the value of Compensation of Employees (CoE).

S.No.	Items	₹ (in crores)
(i)	Old Age Pension	2,000
(ii)	Wages and Salaries in Cash	60,000
(iii)	Rent Free Accommodation to Employees	30,000
(iv)	Employer's Contribution to Provident Fund	7,500
(v)	Payment of Life Insurance Premium by the Employees	2,500
(vi)	Contribution to Provident Fund by Employees	35,000

Sol. Compensation of Employees (CoE)

= Wages and Salaries in Cash + Rent Free Accommodation to Employees + Employer's Contribution to Provident Fund

= 60,000 + 30,000 + 7,500 = ₹ 97,500 crore

Numerical 34

Calculate the value of Mixed Income of Self-employed from the following data

S.No.	Items	₹ (in crores)
(i)	Compensation of Employees	17,300
(ii)	Interest	1,200
(iii)	Consumption of Fixed Capital	1,100
(iv)	Mixed Income of Self-employed	?
(v)	Subsidies	750
(vi)	Gross Domestic Product at Market Price	27,500
(vii)	Indirect Taxes	2,100
(viii)	Profit	1,800
(ix)	Rent	2,000

Sol. Let Mixed Income of Self-employed $= x$

We know,

NDP_{FC} = Compensation of Employees + Operating Surplus + Mixed Income of Self-employed

Where, Operating Surplus = Rent + Interest + Profits

Also, $NDP_{FC} = GDP_{MP}$ − Depreciation − NIT

= 27,500 − 1,100 − (2,100 − 750) = ₹ 25,050 crore

Now, putting values in eq. (i)

25,050 = 17,300 + (200 + 1,200 + 1,800) + x

∴ x = Mixed Income of Self-employed = ₹ 4,550 crore

Numerical 35

On the basis of the given data, estimate the value of Net Value Added at Factor Cost (NVA_{FC}) **CBSE 2024 C**

S.No.	Items	₹ (in crores)
(i)	Sales	2,500
(ii)	Purchase of Raw Material	700
(iii)	Change in Stock	100
(iv)	Gross Investment	500
(v)	Net Indirect Taxes	300
(vi)	Net Investment	400

Sol. NVA_{FC} = Sales + Change in Stock − Raw Material Purchase − Depreciation − Net Indirect Taxes

NVA_{FC} = 2,500 + 100 − 700 − (500 − 400) − 300

NVA_{FC} = 2,500 + 100 − 1,100

NVA_{FC} = ₹ 1,500 crore

Numerical 36

Calculate Net Domestic Product at Factor Cost.

S.No.	Items	₹ (in lakhs)
(i)	Interest	700
(ii)	Compensation of Employees	3,000
(iii)	Net Indirect Taxes	500
(iv)	Rent and Profit	700
(v)	Transfer Payments by Government	10

Sol. Net Domestic Product at Factor Cost (NDP_{FC})

= Compensation of Employees + Interest + Rent and Profit

= 3,000 + 700 + 700 = ₹ 4,400 crore

Numerical 37

Calculate net domestic product at factor cost by income method.

S.No.	Items	₹ (in crores)
(i)	Dividend	60
(ii)	Wages and Salaries	2,000
(iii)	Social Security Contribution by Employers	100
(iv)	Rent	300
(v)	Corporation Tax	30
(vi)	Retained Earnings of Private Corporations	10
(vii)	Interest	300

Sol. By Income Method,

Net Domestic Product at Factor Cost (NDP_{FC})

= Wages and Salaries + Social Security Contribution by Employers + Corporation Tax + Retained Earnings of Private Corporations + Dividend + Rent + Interest

= 2,000 + 100 + 30 + 10 + 60 + 300 + 300 = ₹ 2,800 crore

Notes
- The sum of wages and salaries and social security contribution gives us the compensation of employees.
- The sum of corporation tax, retained earnings of private corporations and dividend gives us profit.
- Retained earnings of private corporations is the same as undistributed profits.

Numerical 38

Calculate value of Domestic Income from below data

CBSE 2023

S.No.	Items	₹ (in crores)
(i)	Rent and Royalties	1,300
(ii)	Net Indirect Taxes	200
(iii)	Wages and Salaries (in cash and in kind)	1,700
(iv)	Corporate Tax	400
(v)	Depreciation	400
(vi)	Retained Earnings	300
(vii)	Dividends	400
(viii)	Net Factor Income from Abroad	(–) 120
(ix)	Mixed Income of Self Employed	1,400
(x)	Change in Stock	(–) 200

Sol. Domestic Income (NDP_{FC})

= Wages and Salaries + Rent and Royalties + Corporate Tax + Dividends + Retained Earnings + Mixed Incomes of Self-employed

= 1,700 + 1300 + 400 + 400 + 300 + 1,400

= ₹ 5,500 crore

Numerical 39

Calculate (a) Gross Domestic Product at Market Price and (b) Factor Income from Abroad from the following data

S.No.	Items	₹ (in crores)
(i)	Gross National Product at Factor Cost	6,150
(ii)	Net Exports	(–)50
(iii)	Compensation of Employees	3,000
(iv)	Rent	800
(v)	Interest	900
(vi)	Profit	1,300
(vii)	Net Indirect Taxes	300
(viii)	Net Domestic Capital Formation	800
(ix)	Gross Fixed Capital Formation	850
(x)	Change in Stock	50
(xi)	Dividend	300
(xii)	Factor Income to Abroad	80

Sol. (a) GDP_{MP} = Compensation of Employees + Rent + Interest + Profit + Net Indirect Taxes + Consumption of Fixed Capital

= 3,000 + (800 + 900 + 1,300) + 300 + (850 + 50 – 800) = ₹ 6,400 crore

Note Depreciation = Gross Domestic Fixed Capital Formation + Change in Stock – Net Domestic Capital Formation

(b) GNP_{FC} = GDP_{MP} – Net Indirect Taxes + Factor Income from Abroad – Factor Income to Abroad

⇒ 6,150 = 6,400 – 300 + Factor Income from Abroad – 80

⇒ 6,150 = 6,020 + Factor Income from Abroad

⇒ Factor Income from Abroad = 6,150 – 6,020 = ₹ 130 crore

Numerical 40

Calculate from following data

(a) Gross domestic product at market price.

(b) Factor income from abroad.

S.No.	Items	₹ (in crores)
(i)	Profits	1,000
(ii)	Exports	80
(iii)	Compensation of Employees	3,000
(iv)	Gross National Product at Factor Cost	5,600
(v)	Net Current Transfers from Rent of World	180
(vi)	Rent	600
(vii)	Interest	800
(viii)	Factor Income to Abroad	240
(ix)	Net Indirect Taxes	500
(x)	Net Domestic Capital Formation	1,300
(xi)	Gross Fixed Capital Formation	1,400
(xii)	Change-in-stock	100

Sol. (a) Net Domestic Product at Factor Cost (NDP_{FC})
= Compensation of Employees + Rent + Profits + Interest

$\Rightarrow NDP_{FC} = 3{,}000 + 600 + 1{,}000 + 800 =$ ₹ 5,400 crore

$GDP_{MP} = NDP_{FC}$ + Net Indirect Taxes + Depreciation

$= 5{,}400 + 500 + (1{,}400 - 1{,}300 + 100) =$ ₹ 6,100 crore

(b) $GNP_{FC} = GDP_{MP}$ − Net Indirect Taxes + Factor Income from Abroad − Factor Income to Abroad

$5{,}600 = 6{,}100 - 500$ + Factor Income from Abroad − 240

Factor Income from Abroad = ₹ 240 crore

Numerical 41

Find out (a) Net National Product at Market Price and (b) Gross Domestic Product at Factor Cost from the following data

S.No.	Items	₹ (in crores)
(i)	Net Current Transfers from Abroad	(−) 10
(ii)	Wages and Salaries	1,000
(iii)	Net Factor Income from Abroad	(−) 20
(iv)	Social Security Contributions by Employers	100
(v)	Net Indirect Tax	80
(vi)	Rent	300
(vii)	Consumption of Fixed Capital	120
(viii)	Corporation Tax	50
(ix)	Undistributed Profits	60
(x)	Dividend	200
(xi)	Interest	400

Sol. (a) NDP_{FC} = Wages and Salaries + Social Security Contribution by Employers + Rent + Corporation Tax + Dividend + Undistributed Profit + Interest

$= 1{,}000 + 100 + 300 + 50 + 200 + 60 + 400$

= ₹ 2,110 crore

$NNP_{MP} = NDP_{FC}$ + Net Indirect Tax + Net Factor Income from Abroad

$= 2{,}110 + 80 + (-20)$

= ₹ 2,170 crore

(b) $GDP_{FC} = NDP_{FC}$ + Consumption of Fixed Capital

$= 2{,}110 + 120 =$ ₹ 2,230 crore

Numerical 42

On the basis of the given data, estimate the value of Domestic Income (NDP_{FC}). **CBSE SQP 2025**

S.No.	Items	₹ (in crores)
(i)	Household Consumption Expenditure	800
(ii)	Gross Business Fixed Capital Formation	150
(iii)	Gross Residential Construction Investment	120
(iv)	Government Final Consumption Expenditure	170
(v)	Excess of Imports over Exports	20
(vi)	Inventory Investment	140
(vii)	Gross Public Investment	500
(viii)	Net Indirect Taxes	75
(ix)	Net Factor Income from Abroad	(−) 50
(x)	Consumption of Fixed Capital	40

Sol. NDP_{FC} = Private Final Consumption Expenditure + Government Final Consumption Expenditure + Gross Investment + Net Exports − Net Indirect Taxes − Consumption of Fixed Capital

$NDP_{FC} = 800 + 170 + (150 + 120 + 140 + 500) - 20 - 70 - 40$

$= 1{,}860 - 70 - 40 =$ ₹ 1,750 crore

Numerical 43

Calculate gross national product at market price from following data.

S.No.	Items	₹ (in crores)
(i)	Compensation of Employees	1,000
(ii)	Interest	250
(iii)	Rent	350
(iv)	Profits	400
(v)	Employer's Contribution to PF	100
(vi)	Dividends	150
(vii)	Mixed Income of Self-employed	750
(viii)	Net Indirect Taxes	125
(ix)	Net Factor Income to Abroad	75
(x)	Consumption of Fixed Capital	50

Sol. NDP_{FC} = Compensation of Employees + Interest + Rent + Profits + Mixed Income of Self-employed

$= 1{,}000 + 250 + 350 + 400 + 750 =$ ₹ 2,750 crore

$GNP_{MP} = NDP_{FC}$ + Net Indirect Taxes − Net Factor Income to Abroad + Consumption of Fixed Capital

$= 2{,}750 + 125 - 75 + 50$

$\Rightarrow GNP_{MP} =$ ₹ 2,850 crore

Numerical 44

Calculate 'national income' from the following information.

S.No.	Items	₹ (in crores)
(i)	Rent	200
(ii)	Net Factor Income to Abroad	10
(iii)	National Debt Interest	15
(iv)	Wages and Salaries	700
(v)	Current Transfers from Government	10
(vi)	Undistributed Profits	20
(vii)	Corporation Tax	30
(viii)	Interest	150
(ix)	Social Security Contributions by Employers	100
(x)	Net Domestic Product Accruing to Government	250
(xi)	Net Current Transfers to Rest of the World	5
(xii)	Dividends	50

Sol. NDP_{FC} = Rent + Wages and Salaries + Corporation Tax + Interest + Social Security Contribution by Employers + Dividends + Undistributed Profits

$NDP_{FC} = 200 + 700 + 30 + 150 + 100 + 50 + 20$

$=$ ₹ 1,250 crore

$NNP_{FC} = NDP_{FC} + NFIA$

$= 1{,}250 + (-10) =$ ₹ 1,240 crore

Numerical 45

Calculate (a) Net National Product at Market Price and (b) Gross Domestic Product at Factor Cost. **CBSE 2018**

S.No.	Items	₹ (in crores)
(i)	Rent and Interest	6,000
(ii)	Wages and Salaries	1,800
(iii)	Undistributed Profit	400
(iv)	Net Indirect Taxes	100
(v)	Subsidies	20
(vi)	Corporation Tax	120
(vii)	Net Factor Income to Abroad	70
(viii)	Dividends	80
(ix)	Consumption of Fixed Capital	50
(x)	Social Security Contribution by Employers	200
(xi)	Mixed Income	1,000

Sol. (a) NNP_{MP} = Compensation of Employee + Operating Surplus + Mixed Income + NFIA + Net Indirect Taxes

$= (1{,}800 + 200) + (6{,}000 + 400 + 120 + 80) + 1{,}000 + (-70) + 100$

$=$ ₹ 9,630 crore

(b) GDP_{FC} = Compensation of Employee + Operating Surplus + Mixed Income + Consumption of Fixed Capital

$= 1{,}800 + 200 + 6{,}000 + 400 + 120 + 80 + 1{,}000 + 50$

$=$ ₹ 9,650 crore

Numerical 46

Calculate gross national product at market price by production method and income method.

S.No.	Items	₹ (in crores)
(i)	Value of Output by Primary Sector	1,000
(ii)	Indirect Tax	200
(iii)	Compensation of Employees	780
(iv)	Net Factor Income to Abroad	100
(v)	Intermediate Purchases by all Sectors	2,900
(vi)	Value of Output by Secondary Sector	2,000
(vii)	Rent	300
(viii)	Subsidy	50
(ix)	Interest	600
(x)	Consumption of Fixed Capital	120
(xi)	Value of Output by Tertiary Sector	3,000
(xii)	Profits	320
(xiii)	Mixed Income of Self-employed	830

Sol. By Production Method,

GNP_{MP} = (Value of Output by Primary Sector + Value of Output by Secondary Sector + Value of Output by Tertiary Sector) − Intermediate Purchase by all Sectors − Net Factor Income to Abroad

$= (1{,}000 + 2{,}000 + 3{,}000) - 2{,}900 - 100$

$= 6{,}000 - 3{,}000 =$ ₹ 3,000 crore

By Income Method,

GNP_{MP} = Compensation of Employees + Rent + Interest + Profits + Mixed Income of the Self-employed + Net Indirect Taxes (Indirect Taxes – Subsidy) – Net Factor Income to Abroad + Consumption of Fixed Capital

$= 780 + 300 + 600 + 320 + 830 + (200 - 50) - 100 + 120$

$= 3{,}100 - 100 =$ ₹ 3,000 crore

Numerical 47

Calculate national income by the expenditure method.

S.No.	Items	₹ (in crores)
(i)	Government Final Consumption Expenditure	150
(ii)	Private Final Consumption Expenditure	750
(iii)	Consumption of Fixed Capital	150
(iv)	Net Indirect Taxes	120
(v)	Net Factor Income from Abroad	20
(vi)	Net Domestic Fixed Capital Formation	220
(vii)	Change-in-stock	(–) 20
(viii)	Net Imports	50

Sol. By Expenditure Method, National Income (NNP_{FC})

= Private Final Consumption Expenditure + Government Final Consumption Expenditure + Net Domestic Fixed Capital Formation + Change in Stock – Net Imports – Net Indirect Taxes + Net Factor Income from Abroad

$= 750 + 150 + 220 + (-20) - 50 - 120 + 20$

$= 1{,}140 - 190 =$ ₹ 950 crore

Numerical 48

Find out the national income.

S.No.	Items	₹ (in crores)
(i)	Net Imports	(–) 10
(ii)	Net Domestic Fixed Capital Formation	100
(iii)	Private Final Consumption Expenditure	600
(iv)	Consumption of Fixed Capital	60
(v)	Change-in-stock	(–) 50
(vi)	Government Final Consumption Expenditure	200
(vii)	Net Factor Income to Abroad	20
(viii)	Net Indirect Tax	70
(ix)	Factor Income from Abroad	10

Sol. GDP_{MP} = Private Final Consumption Expenditure + Government Final Consumption Expenditure + Net Domestic Fixed Capital Formation + Change-in-stock + Consumption of Fixed Capital – Net Imports

$= 600 + 200 + 100 + (-50) + 60 - (-10)$

$= 970 - 50 =$ ₹ 920 crore

National Income (NNP_{FC})

= GDP_{MP} – Net Factor Income to Abroad – Net Indirect Tax – Consumption of Fixed Capital

$= 920 - 20 - 70 - 60 =$ ₹ 770 crore

Numerical 49

Find out National Income.

S.No.	Items	₹ (in crores)
(i)	Factor Income from Abroad	15
(ii)	Private Final Consumption Expenditure	600
(iii)	Consumption of Fixed Capital	50
(iv)	Government Final Consumption Expenditure	200
(v)	Net Current Transfer to Abroad	(–)5
(vi)	Net Domestic Fixed Capital Formation	110
(vii)	Net Factor Income to Abroad	10
(viii)	Change-in-stock	(–) 10
(ix)	Net Imports	(–) 20
(x)	Net Indirect Taxes	70

Sol. NDP_{MP} = Private Final Consumption Expenditure + Government Final Consumption Expenditure + Net Domestic Fixed Capital Formation + Change-in-stock – Net Imports

$NDP_{MP} = 600 + 200 + 110 + (-10) - (-20) =$ ₹ 920 crore

National Income (NNP_{FC})

= NDP_{MP} – Net Factor Income to Abroad – Net Indirect Taxes

$= 920 - 10 - 70 =$ ₹ 840 crore

Numerical 50

On the basis of the following hypothetical data (all figures in ₹ crores)

Year	Nominal GDP	Nominal GDP Adjusted to Base Year Prices
2020	3,000	4,000
2023	4,000	4,500

Calculate the percentage change in real gross domestic product in the year 2023 using 2020 as the base year.

CBSE SQP 2025

Sol. To calculate the percentage change in Real GDP, use the formula

Percentage Change in Real GDP

$$= \frac{\text{Real GDP in 2023} - \text{Real GDP in 2020}}{\text{Real GDP in 2020}} \times 100$$

Real GDP in 2020 (adjusted to base year prices)

= ₹ 4,000 crore

Real GDP in 2023 (adjusted to base year prices)

= ₹ 4,500 crore

$$\text{Percentage Change in Real GDP} = \frac{4{,}500 - 4{,}000}{4{,}000} \times 100$$

$$= \frac{500}{4{,}000} \times 100 = 12.5\%$$

Numerical 51

Calculate (a) National Income and (b) GNP_{MP} from the following

S.No.	Items	₹ (in arabs)
(i)	Net Current Transfers to Abroad	(–) 15
(ii)	Private Final Consumption Expenditure	600
(iii)	Subsidies	20
(iv)	Government Final Consumption Expenditure	100
(v)	Indirect Tax	120
(vi)	Net Imports	20
(vii)	Consumption of Fixed Capital	35
(viii)	Net Change in Stocks	10
(ix)	Net Factor Income to Abroad	5
(x)	Net Domestic Capital Formation	110

Sol. (a) National Income (NNP_{FC})

= Private Final Consumption Expenditure
+ Government Final Consumption Expenditure
+ Net Domestic Capital Formation – Net Imports
– Net Indirect Tax – Net Factor Income to Abroad
= 600 + 100 + 110 – 20 – (120 – 20) – 5
= 810 – 125 = ₹ 685 arab

(b) GNP_{MP} = NNP_{FC} + (Depreciation)+Net Indirect Tax
685 + 35 + 20 = ₹ 740 arab

Numerical 52

Calculate

(a) Gross National Product at Market Price

(b) NNP_{FC}

S.No.	Items	₹ (in crores)
(i)	Private Final Consumption Expenditure	3,000
(ii)	Net Factor Income to Abroad	100
(iii)	Government Final Consumption Expenditure	800
(iv)	Net Export	(–) 200
(v)	Net Current Transfers from Rest of the World	300
(vi)	Gross Domestic Fixed Capital Formation	600
(vii)	Change-in-stock	(–) 20
(viii)	Net Indirect Taxes	400
(ix)	Factor Income from Abroad	50
(x)	Net Domestic Capital Formation	500
(xi)	Depreciation	30
(xii)	Indirect Tax	50
(xiii)	Subsidies	20

Sol. (a) Gross National Product at Market Price (GNP_{MP})

= Private Final Consumption Expenditure
+ Government Final Consumption Expenditure
+ Gross Domestic Fixed Capital Formation
+ Change-in-stock Net Export – Net Factor Income to Abroad
= 3,000 + 800 + 600 + (–20) + (– 200) – 100
= 4,400 – 320 = ₹ 4,080 crore

(b) NNP_{FC} = GNP_{MP} – Depreciation – Net Indirect Taxes
4,080 – 30 – (50 – 20)= ₹4,020 crore

Numerical 53

Calculate Net National Product at Market Price and GNP_{FC}.

S.No.	Items	₹ (in crores)
(i)	Transfer Payments by Government	7
(ii)	Government Final Consumption Expenditure	50
(iii)	Net Imports	(–) 10
(iv)	Net Domestic Fixed Capital Formation	60
(v)	Private Final Consumption Expenditure	300
(vi)	Private Income	280
(vii)	Net Factor Income to Aboad	(–) 5
(viii)	Closing Stock	8
(ix)	Opening Stock	8
(x)	Depreciation	12
(xi)	Corporate Tax	60
(xii)	Retained Earnings of Corporations	20
(xiii)	Net Indirect Tax	7

Sol. NNP_{MP} = Private Final Consumption Expenditure + Government Final Consumption Expenditure + (Net Domestic Fixed Capital Formation + Depreciation) + Change-in-stock − Net Imports − Depreciation − Net Factor Income to Abroad

$= 300 + 50 + 60 + 12 + (8 - 8) - (-10) - 12 - (-5)$

NNP_{MP} = ₹ 425 crore

$GNP_{FC} = NNP_{MP} - NIT + Depreciation$

$= 425 - 7 + 12$ = ₹ 430 crore

Numerical 54

Estimate the value of Net National Product at Factor Cost (NNP_{FC}), using the following information. **CBSE 2024**

S.No.	Items	₹ (in crores)
(i)	Household Consumption Expenditure	1,200
(ii)	Business Fixed Investment Expenditure	800
(iii)	Government Final Consumption Expenditure	500
(iv)	Excess of Imports over Exports	100
(v)	Net Indirect Taxes	150
(vi)	Change in Inventory	(−) 50
(vii)	Consumption of Fixed Capital	200
(viii)	Net Factor Income from Abroad	80
(ix)	Public Fixed Investment	70

Sol. According to Expenditure Method

NNP_{FC} = Household Consumption Expenditure + Business Fixed Investment Expenditure + Government Final Consumption Expenditure − Excess of Imports over Exports + Change in Inventory + Public Fixed Investment − Net Indirect Taxes − Public Fixed Investment − Net Indirect Taxes − Consumption of Fixed Capital + Net Factor Income From Abroad

$= 1{,}200 + 800 + 500 - 100 + (-)\,50 + 70 - 150 - 200 + 80$

= ₹ 2,150 crore

Numerical 55

Calculate Gross National Product at Factor Cost from the following data by

(a) Income method (b) Expenditure method

S.No.	Items	₹ (in crores)
(i)	Private Final Consumption Expenditure	1,000
(ii)	Net Domestic Capital Formation	200
(iii)	Profits	400
(iv)	Compensation of Employees	800
(v)	Rent	250
(vi)	Government Final Consumption Expenditure	500
(vii)	Consumption of Fixed Capital	60
(viii)	Interest	150
(ix)	NFIA	(−) 10
(x)	Net Exports	(−) 20
(xi)	Net Indirect Tax	80

Sol. (a) By Income Method,

GNP_{FC} = Compensation of Employees + (Profits + Rent + Interest) + Consumption of Fixed Capital + Net Factor Income from Abroad

$= 800 + (400 + 250 + 150) + 60 + (-10)$

= ₹ 1,650 crore

(b) By Expenditure Method, GNP_{FC}

= Private Final Consumption Expenditure + Government Final Consumption Expenditure + Net Domestic Capital Formation + Consumption of Fixed Capital + Net Export − Net Indirect Taxes + Net Factor Income from Abroad

$= 1{,}000 + 500 + 200 + 60 + (-20) - 80 + (-10)$

$= 1{,}760 - 110$ = ₹ 1,650 crore

Numerical 56

From the following data, show that the National Income will be same from both income method and expenditure method. **CBSE 2022**

S.No.	Items	₹ (in crores)
(i)	Net Exports	(−) 60
(ii)	Net Indirect Taxes	150
(iii)	Operating Surplus	740
(iv)	Compensation of employees	1,400
(v)	Net Factor Income from Abroad	40
(vi)	Mixed Income of Self-employed	1,000
(vii)	Net Domestic Fixed Capital Formation	500
(viii)	Change-in-stock	(−) 100
(ix)	Depreciation	100

S.No.	Items	₹ (in crores)
(x)	Private Final Consumption Expenditure	1,950
(xi)	Government Final Consumption Expenditure	1,000

Sol. Income Method

National Income

= Compensation of Employees + Operating Surplus + Mixed Income of Self-employed + Net Factor Income from Abroad

= 1,400 + 740 + 1,000 + 40 = ₹ 3,180 crore

Expenditure Method

National Income

= Private Final Consumption Expenditure + Government Final Consumption Expenditure + Net Domestic Fixed Capital Formation + Change-in-stock + Net Exports – Net Indirect Taxes + Net Factor Income from Abroad

= 1,950 + 1,000 + 500 + (–) 100 + (–) 60 – 150 + 40

= ₹ 3,180 crore

Numerical 57

Calculate Net Domestic Product at Factor Cost by Expenditure Method and Production Method.

S.No.	Items	₹ (in crores)
(i)	Value of Output in Economic Territory	4,100
(ii)	Net Imports	(–) 50
(iii)	Intermediate Purchase by Primary Sector	600
(iv)	Private Final Consumption Expenditure	1,450
(v)	Intermediate Purchases by Secondary Sector	700
(vi)	Government Final Consumption Expenditure	400
(vii)	Net Domestic Fixed Capital Formation	200
(viii)	Intermediate Purchases by Tertiary Sector	700
(ix)	Net Change in Stock	(–) 50
(x)	Net Indirect Taxes	100
(xi)	Consumption of Fixed Capital	50

Sol. By Expenditure Method, NDP_{FC}

= Private Final Consumption Expenditure + Government Final Consumption Expenditure + Net Domestic Fixed Capital Formation + Net Change in Stock – Net Imports – Net Indirect Taxes

$= 1,450 + 400 + 200 + (-50) - (-50) - 100$

= ₹ 1,950 crore

By Production Method, NDP_{FC}

= Value of Output in Economic Territory – (Intermediate Purchase by Primary Sector + Intermediate Purchase by Secondary Sector + Intermediate Purchase by Tertiary Sector) – Consumption of Fixed Capital – Net Indirect Taxes

$= 4,100 - (600 + 700 + 700) - 50 - 100$

$= 4,100 - 2,150$

= ₹ 1,950 crore

Numerical 58

Given the following data, find the values of 'Gross Domestic Capital Formation' and 'Operating Surplus'.

All India 2019

S.No.	Items	₹ (in crores)
(i)	National Income (NI)	22,100
(ii)	Wages and Salaries	12,000
(iii)	Private Final Consumption Expenditure (PFCE)	7,200
(iv)	Net Indirect Taxes (NIT)	700
(v)	Gross Domestic Capital Formation (GDCF)	?
(iv)	Depreciation	500
(vii)	Government Final Consumption Expenditure (GFCE)	6,100
(viii)	Mixed Income of Self-employed	4,800
(ix)	Operating Surplus	?
(x)	Net Exports (NX)	3,400
(xi)	Rent	1,200
(xii)	Net Factor Income from Abroad	(–) 150
(xiii)	Net Indirect Tax	700

Sol. Let Gross Domestic Capital Formation = x and Operating Surplus = y

We know,

(a) $GDP_{MP} = PFCE + GFCE + NX$ ...(i)

Also, $GDP_{MP} = NNP_{FC}$ + Depreciation – NFIA + NIT

$= 22,100 + 500 - (-150) + 700$

= ₹ 23,450 crore

Now, putting values in eq. (i).

$23,450 = 7,200 + 6,100 + x + 3,400$

$\therefore \quad x = 6,750$

Thus, Gross Domestic Capital Formation

$= ₹\ 6{,}750$ crore

(b) NDP_{FC} = CoE + Operation Surplus + Mixed Income ...(i)

Also, $NDP_{FC} = NNP_{FC} - NFIA$

$= 22{,}100 - (-150)$

$= ₹\ 22{,}250$

Now, putting value in eq. (i)

$22{,}250 = 12{,}000 + y + 4{,}800$

$\therefore \quad y = 5{,}450$

Thus, operating surplus = ₹ 5,450 crore

Numerical 59

Given the following data, find the missing values of Gross Domestic Capital Formation and Wages and Salaries.

Delhi 2019

S.No.	Items	₹ (in crores)
(i)	Mixed Income of Self-employed	3,500
(ii)	Net Indirect Taxes	300
(iii)	Wages and Salaries	?
(iv)	Government Final Consumption Expenditure (GFCE)	14,000
(v)	Net Exports	3,000
(vi)	Consumption of Fixed Capital	300
(vii)	Net Factor Income from Abroad	700
(viii)	Operating Surplus	12,000
(ix)	National Income	30,000
(x)	Profits	500
(xi)	Gross Domestic Capital Formation (GDCF)	?
(xii)	Private Final Consumption Expenditure (PFCE)	11,000

Sol. Let Gross Domestic Capital Formation = x

Wages and Salaries = y

We know,

NDP_{FC} = COE + Operating Surplus + Mixed Income of Self-employed

$NDP_{FC} = NNP_{FC} - NFIA = 30{,}000 - 700 = ₹\ 29{,}300$ crore

$\therefore 29{,}300 = y + 12{,}000 + 3{,}500$

y = Wages and Salaries (Compensation of Employees)

$= ₹\ 13{,}800$ crore

Also,

GDP_{MP} = PFCE + GFCE + Gross Domestic Capital Formation + Net Exports

$GDP_{MP} = NDP_{FC}$ + Depreciation + NIT

$= 29{,}300 + 300 + 300 = ₹\ 29{,}900$ crore

$\therefore 29{,}900 = 11{,}000 + 14{,}000 + x + 3{,}000$

x = GDCF = ₹ 1,900 crore

Numerical 60

Given the following data, find the missing value of 'Government Final Consumption Expenditure' and 'Mixed Income of Self-employed'.

S.No.	Items	₹ (in crores)
(i)	National Income	71,000
(ii)	Gross Domestic Capital Formation	10,000
(iii)	Government Final Consumption Expenditure	?
(iv)	Mixed Income of Self-employed	?
(v)	Net Factor Income from Abroad	1,000
(vi)	Net Indirect Taxes	2,000
(vii)	Profits	1,200
(viii)	Wages and Salaries	15,000
(ix)	Net Exports	5,000
(x)	Private Final Consumption Expenditure	40,000
(xi)	Consumption of Fixed Capital	3,000
(xii)	Operating Surplus	30,000

Sol. $NNP_{FC} = 71{,}000$ (given)

$GDP_{MP} = NNP_{FC}$ − Net Factor Income from Abroad + Depreciation + Net Indirect Taxes

$= 71{,}000 - 1{,}000 + 3{,}000 + 2{,}000 = ₹\ 75{,}000$

Now, Let Government Final Consumption Expenditure = x

GDP_{MP} = Private Final Consumption Expenditure + Government Final Consumption Expenditure + Gross Domestic Capital Formation + Net Exports

$75{,}000 = 40{,}000 + x + 10{,}000 + 5{,}000$

$\therefore \quad x$ = Government Final Consumption Expenditure

$= ₹\ 20{,}000$ crore

Also, Let Mixed Income of Self-employed = y

NDP_{FC} = Wages and Salaries + Operating surplus + Mixed Income of Self-employed

$$70{,}000 = 15{,}000 + 30{,}000 + y$$

So, y = Mixed Income of Self-employed
= ₹ 25,000 crore

Note $NDP_{FC} = NNP_{MP} - NFIA = 71{,}000 - 1{,}000 =$ ₹ 70,000

Numerical 61

Given the following data, find the missing values of 'Private Final Consumption Expenditure' and 'Operating Surplus'. **Delhi 2019**

S.No.	Items	₹ (in crores)
(i)	National Income	50,000
(ii)	Net Indirect Taxes (NIT)	1,000
(iii)	Private Final Consumption Expenditure (PFCE)	?
(iv)	Gross Domestic Capital Formation (GDCF)	17,000
(v)	Profits	1,000
(vi)	Government Final Consumption Expenditure (GFCE)	12,500
(vii)	Wages and Salaries	20,000
(viii)	Consumption of Fixed Capital	700
(ix)	Mixed Income of Self-employed	13,000
(x)	Operating Surplus	?
(xi)	Net Factor Income from Abroad	500
(xii)	Net Exports (NX)	2,000

Sol. Private Final Consumption Expenditure = y and Operating Surplus = x

We know,

NDP_{FC} = Compensation of Employees + Operating Surplus + Mixed Income of Self-employed

Where,

Operating Surplus = Rent + Interest + Profits

Also,

$$NDP_{FC} = NNP_{FC} - NFIA$$
$$= 50{,}000 - 500 = ₹\ 49{,}500 \text{ crore}$$

$$\therefore \quad 49{,}500 = 20{,}000 + x + 13{,}000$$
$$49{,}500 = 33{,}000 + x$$

x = Operating Surplus
$= 49{,}500 - 33{,}000 =$ ₹ 16,500 crore

Also, $GDP_{MP} = PFCE + GFCE + GDCF + NX$

$GDP_{MP} = NDP_{FC} + \text{Depreciation} + NIT$
$= 49{,}500 + 700 + 100 =$ ₹ 51,200 crore

$$\therefore \quad 51{,}200 = y + 12{,}500 + 17{,}00 + 2{,}000$$

$\therefore y$ = Private Final Consumption Expenditure
= ₹ 19,700 crore

Numerical 62

Calculate Gross Value Added at Market Price. **CBSE 2020**

S.No.	Items	₹ (in lakhs)
(i)	Depreciation	20
(ii)	Domestic Sales	200
(iii)	Change-in-stock	(–) 10
(iv)	Exports	10
(v)	Single Use Producer Goods	120

Sol. Gross Value Added at Market Price (GVA_{MP})
= Domestic Sales + Exports + Change-in-stock – Single Use Producer Goods
$= 200 + 10 + (-10) - 120$

GVA_{MP} = ₹ 80 lakh

Numerical 63

Prove the 'triple identify' using following data

	Particulars	(₹ in crores)
(i)	Value of Output of Primary Sector	1,000
(ii)	Value of Output of Other Sectors	400
(iii)	Raw Material Purchased by Primary Sector	500
(iv)	Raw Material Purchased by Other Sectors	300
(v)	Factor Income received from Rest of the World	10
(vi)	Factor Income paid to Rest of the World	15
(vii)	Depreciation	55
(viii)	Indirect Taxes (GST)	100
(ix)	Subsidies	20
(x)	Mixed Income of Self-employed	200
(xi)	Compensation of Employees	170
(xii)	Rent	40
(xiii)	Interest	30
(xiv)	Profit	25
(xv)	Private final consumption expenditure	200
(xvi)	Government final consumption expenditure	300
(xvii)	Exports	80
(xviii)	Imports	30

Particulars		(₹ in crores)
(xix)	Gross Domestic Fixed Capital Formation	40
(xx)	Change-in-stock	10

Sol. We will find national income by three methods and conclude that national income by all three methods is same.

(i) **Income Method**

NDP_{FC} = COE + OS + MI

= Compensation of Employees + (Rent + Interest + Profit) + Mixed Income of Self-employed

= 170 + (40 + 30 + 25) + 200

= 170 + 95 + 200

= ₹465 crore

$NNP_{FC} = NDP_{FC}$ + NFIA

= 465 +(10 – 15) = 465 – 5 = ₹ 460 crore

(ii) **Expenditure Method**

GDP_{MP} = PFCE + GFCE + GDCF + Net Exports

= 200 + 300 +(40 +10) +(80 – 30)

= 200 + 300 + 50 + 50 = ₹ 600 crore

$NNP_{FC} = GDP_{MP}$ – Depreciation + NFIA – NIT

= 600 – 55 + (10 – 15) – (100 – 20)

= 600 – 55 – 5 – 80

= ₹ 460 crore

(iii) **Output/Product Method**

$GDP_{MP} = GVA_{MP}$ – Intermediate Consumption

= (Value of Output of Primary Sector + Value of Output of Other Sectors) – (Raw Material Purchased by Primary Sector + Raw Material Purchased by Other Sector)

= (1,000 + 400) – (500 +300)

= 1,400 – 800 = ₹ 600 crore

$NNP_{FC} = GDP_{MP}$ – Depreciation + NFIA – NIT

= 600 – 55 + (10 – 15) – (100 – 20)

= 600 – 55 – 5 – 80

= 600 – 140

= ₹ 460 crore

Hence, national income by all three methods gives the same answer, therefore

Production = Income = Expenditure.

SELF ASSESSMENT TEST

Objective Type Questions

1. Which of the following does not directly contribute to GDP?
   (a) Government spending
   (b) Private consumption
   (c) Transfer payments
   (d) Business investments
2. If Gross National Product at Market Price (GNP_{MP}) = ₹ 15,000 and depreciation = ₹ 1,000 then find Net National Product at Market Price (NNP_{MP})?
   (a) ₹ 10,000 (b) ₹ 16,000
   (c) ₹ 15,000 (d) ₹ 14,000
3. Which of the following GDP (Gross Domestic Product) helps to achieve a sustainable use of natural resources and equitable distribution of national income?
   (a) Real GDP (b) Current GDP
   (c) Green GDP (d) Nominal GDP
4. If Nominal GDP is ₹ 21,000 crore and Real GDP is ₹ 20,000 crore, find GDP deflator?
   (a) 100% (b) 104% (c) 105% (d) 95.24%
5. Which approach involves adding up all the incomes earned by factors of production within a nation?
   (a) Expenditure method (b) Income method
   (c) Production method (d) Value added method
6. Which of the following statements is/are correct?
   I. GDP may be a good indicator of economic growth but not economic welfare.
   II. GDP can never be equal to NDP.

   Codes
   (a) Only I (b) Only II
   (c) Both I and II (d) None of these
7. **Statement I** National income is always equal to the sum of consumption, investment and government expenditure.

   Statement II The expenditure approach considers only the value of goods produced in the current year.

   Alternatives
   (a) Both the statements are correct
   (b) Both the statements are incorrect
   (c) Statement I is correct and Statement II is incorrect
   (d) Statement I is incorrect and Statement II is correct

Answers 1. (c) 2. (d) 3. (c) 4. (c) 5. (b) 6. (c) 7. (c)

Short Answer Type Questions

8. Who is regarded as the normal resident of a country?
9. Explain the concept of 'GDP deflator.' How is it used to measure inflation?
10. Why is the concept of 'depreciation' important in national income accounting?
11. What is meant by double counting? Explain with the help of example.
12. Distinguish between secondary sector and tertiary sector.
13. "Gross Domestic Product (GDP) has several limitations when used as an index of welfare. It fails to account for societal factors, environmental degradation and non-market activities."

    Do you agree with the statement? Support your answer with valid argument.
14. What precautions are to be taken while measuring national income by income method?

Long Answer Type Questions

15. An economy is just maintaining its capital intact all over time. What can you say about its level of production, consumption, net investment over the same period?
16. Explain the expenditure method of calculating national income.

Numerical Questions

17. Calculate intermediate consumption from the following data

S.No.	Items	₹ (in lakhs)
(i)	Value of Output	200
(ii)	Net Value Added to Factor Cost	80
(iii)	Sales Tax	15
(iv)	Subsidy	5
(v)	Depreciation	20

18. Find out
    (i) Gross national product at market price and
    (ii) Net current transfers from abroad

S.No.	Items	₹ (in crores)
(i)	Private Final Consumption Expenditure	1,000
(ii)	Depreciation	100
(iii)	Net National Disposable Income	1,500
(iv)	Closing Stock	20
(v)	Government Final Consumption Expenditure	300
(vi)	Net Indirect Tax	50
(vii)	Opening Stock	20
(viii)	Net Domestic Fixed Capital Formation	110
(ix)	Net Exports	15
(x)	Net Factor Income to Abroad	(–) 10

19. Calculate gross national product at market price.

S.No.	Items	₹ (in crores)
(i)	Net Current Transfer from Abroad	(-) 10
(ii)	Compensation of Employees	800
(iii)	Net Indirect Tax	50
(iv)	Social Security Contributions by Employers	80
(v)	Consumption of Fixed Capital	30
(vi)	Rent	300
(vii)	Net Factor Income to Abroad	10
(viii)	Interest Paid by Production Units	400
(ix)	Royalty	40
(x)	National Debt Interest	40
(xi)	Profit after Tax	250
(xii)	Retained Earnings	20
(xiii)	Corporation Tax	50

20. From the following data, calculate
(i) Gross domestic product at factor cost and
(ii) Factor income to abroad

S.No.	Items	₹ (in crores)
(i)	Compensation of Employees	800
(ii)	Profits	200
(iii)	Dividends	50
(iv)	Gross National Product at Market Price	1,400
(v)	Rent	150
(vi)	Interest	100
(vii)	Gross Domestic Capital Formation	300
(viii)	Net Fixed Capital Formation	200
(ix)	Change-in-stock	50
(x)	Factor Income from Abroad	60
(xi)	Net Indirect Taxes	120

03
CHAPTER

Money and Banking

Money is a means of payment and thus lubricant that facilitates exchange. It also acts as a store of value and a unit of account. *–Koontz and O' Donnell*

▼ **YOUR STUDY GOALS**

3.1 Money
3.2 Money Supply
3.3 Commercial Banks
3.4 Central Bank

▼ **YOUR PRACTICE GOAL**

- Objective Questions (75 Qs ; MCQs, A-R, Statements, Matching, Concept Identification)
- Subjective Questions (32 SAs, 8 LAs)
- Self Assessment Test (7 MCQs, 6 SAs, 3 LAs)

3.1 Money

In its most basic form, money can be defined as anything which is commonly accepted as a medium of exchange. However, money is much more than just a medium of exchange.

In other words, money can be defined as "anything that is generally acceptable as a means of exchange and at the same time, acts as a measure of value, store of value and as a standard of deferred payments."

e.g. In India, the Rupee is the accepted medium of exchange and thus considered money. But this was not always the case, before the invention of money, barter system of exchange was prevalent.

Barter System of Exchange

- Before the invention of money, goods were exchanged for goods. This system was known as the barter system of exchange.
- Barter economy is also termed to as C-C economy, where commodities were exchanged for commodities.

Drawbacks of the Barter System

1. **Lack of Double Coincidence of Wants** Double coincidence of wants implies that two individuals must have such goods which the other wants to exchange to satisfy their wants. e.g. If a person with rice wants wheat, there must be another person who has wheat and wants rice, which was rare.

2. **Lack of Store of Value** Due to absence of money in barter system, wealth was stored in terms of goods, leading to problems such as
   (i) **Cost of Storage** Maintaining and storing goods incurs costs.
   (ii) **Loss of Value** Perishable goods like milk and vegetables spoil over time.
   (iii) **Transfer Difficulty** Moving goods from one place to another is cumbersome.
3. **Lack of Common Measure of Value** In the barter system, there was no common unit of measurement to measure the value of goods and services. e.g. Cloth is measured in meters (length) while milk is measured in liters (capacity), thus both cannot be measured in a single unit, complicating valuation and exchange process.
4. **Lack of Standard of Deferred Payments** Deferred payments or future payments, were difficult in barter system due to following reasons
   (i) **Quantity and Quality** Goods to be returned might not match the original quantity and quality.
   (ii) **Value Changes** The value of goods could change over time, affecting repayment.

Transition to Money

Necessity
To overcome the drawbacks of the barter system and smoothen exchanges, an intermediary was needed.

Solution
Money was introduced as this intermediary, accepted by both buyers and sellers.

Evolution of Money

Money, as we see it in its present form, has evolved after a long process of evolution. Initially, **commodity money** was used as a medium of exchange, followed by **metallic money**, which was made from metals like gold, silver and copper.

With further advancement, **paper money** was introduced as currency notes along with the introduction of **credit money.**

The most modern form of money is **plastic money** in the form of debit and credit cards or **e-money**, which is stored electronically in devices like mobile phones and computer systems.

Types of Money

Type	Definition	Example
Fiat Money	It is issued by the order or authority of the government, such as notes and coins. Unlike gold or silver coins, fiat money does not have intrinsic value. It is also known as **legal tender** as it cannot be refused by any citizen for settling transactions.	Indian Rupee notes and coins. 
Fiduciary Money	This type of money relies on mutual trust between the payer and the payee for its acceptance. It is also known as **optional** or **voluntary money**.	A bank cheque, drafts, bills of exchange.
Full-bodied Money	It refers to coins whose commodity value equals their money value. This type of money is also known as **standard money**.	A 1 rupee silver coin from the British era contained an amount of silver equal to the value of 1 rupee.
Credit Money	It has a face value significantly greater than its intrinsic value (the value of commodity from which it is made).	A hundred rupee note's paper and printing cost is much less than its face value of ₹ 100.

Functions of Money

Functions of money are placed in two categories

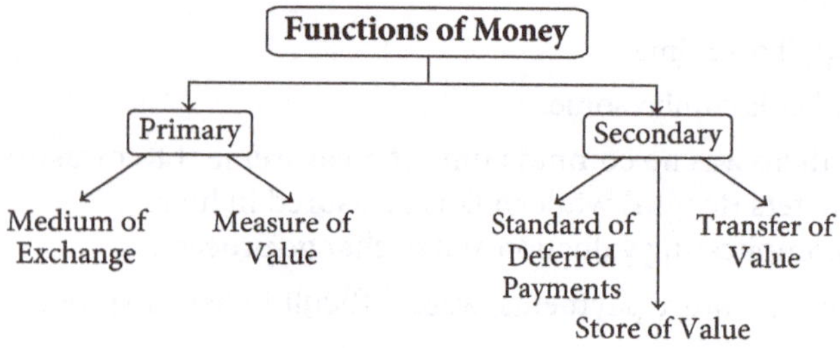

Primary Functions

These are basic functions of money, which it must perform in every country. They include

1. **Medium of Exchange**
   - Money is used to make payments for transactions involving goods and services. It allows buyers and sellers to trade independently, facilitating economic transactions.
   - This function eliminates the need for a double coincidence of wants, which was a major drawback of the barter system.
2. **Measure of Value**
   - Money serves as a common unit to measure the value of all goods and services, simplifying the calculation of relative prices.
   - It acts as a 'unit of account,' facilitating the maintenance of business accounts.

Medium of Exchange
When you go to a supermarket and purchase groceries, you use money to pay for your items. This transaction demonstrates how money facilitates the exchange of goods.

Secondary Functions

These functions are also known as derived functions as they are derived from primary functions. They include

1. **Standard of Deferred Payments**
   - Money acts as a 'standard' for making future payments, simplifying borrowing and lending operations.
   - This function aids in capital formation and economic development by creating financial institutions.
2. **Store of Value**
   - Money can be stored conveniently and economically for future use, providing a secure way to save wealth and earnings.
   - It offers protection against contingencies and emergencies, and allows individuals to pay future debts.
3. **Transfer of Value** Money facilitates the transfer of value, enabling the buying and selling of goods domestically and internationally.

Store of Value
People deposit money in savings accounts to store their wealth for future use. The money can be accessed when needed for emergencies, investments or planned future expenses.

3.2 Money Supply

The total stock of money held by the public in an economy at a particular point in time is called money supply.

It is a **stock** variable as it is measured at a particular point of time. It excludes the money held by the government and banking system as they are suppliers of money.

Measures of Money Supply

1. **M_1 Measure of Money Supply**
   - It is also known as **transaction money**, as it can be directly used for making transactions.
   - **Components**
     - **CU** (Currency) Notes and coins held by the public.
     - **DD** (Demand Deposits) Net demand deposits held by commercial banks. Only the public's deposits are included, not interbank deposits.
     - **OD** (Other Deposits) *Includes*
       (a) Demand deposits with RBI of public financial institutions.
       (b) Demand deposits with RBI of foreign central banks and governments.
       (c) Demand deposits of international financial institutions.

   Excludes government deposits with RBI and commercial banks' deposits with RBI.

- **Formula** $M_1 = CU + DD + OD$

High Powered Money

High powered money consists of currency held by the public and reserves of commercial banks which include vault cash and bank's deposits with RBI.

Therefore, High Powered Money = Currency Held by Public + Reserves of Commercial Banks (including vault cash)

2. **M_2 Measure of Money Supply**
   - It includes all components of M_1 plus savings deposits of the public with post offices.
   - **Formula** $M_2 = M_1$ + Savings Deposits with Post Office Savings Banks
3. **M_3 Measure of Money Supply**
   - It includes all components of M_1 plus net time deposits (fixed/term deposits) of public with commercial banks.
   - **Formula** $M_3 = M_1$ + Net Time Deposits of Commercial Banks
4. **M_4 Measure of Money Supply**
   - It includes all components of M_3 plus total deposits of public with post office savings banks, excluding National Savings Certificates (NSCs).
   - **Formula** $M_4 = M_3$ + Total Deposits with Post Office Savings Organisations (excluding NSCs)

These measures help in understanding the liquidity in the economy and the potential for spending and investment by the public.

Points to Remember

- M_1 is the most liquid and M_4 is the least liquid.
- M_1 and M_2 are called as narrow money supply or traditional money supply concepts, while M_3 and M_4 are called as broader money supply or modern money supply concepts.
- M_3 is mostly used measure of money supply and also known as aggregate monetary resource.

Indian Monetary System

- India uses an inconvertible paper currency standard with the rupee (₹) as the standard money.
- The Reserve Bank of India (RBI) manages currency issuance, including notes from two to five hundred rupees.
- The RBI maintains a minimum reserve of ₹ 200 crore in gold and foreign exchange to issue currency notes.

3.3 Commercial Banks

Commercial banks are financial institutions that accept public deposits from the public and lend out this money (loan) to consumers, aiming to earn profits.

They offer a **borrowing rate** for deposits and charge a **lending rate** for loans. The difference between these rates, known as the **spread**, represents the bank's profit.

Functions of Commercial Banks

Commercial banks perform following functions

Primary Functions

(i) **Accepting Deposits** Deposits may be accepted from public in following forms

Basis \ Types	Current Account Deposits	Fixed Deposits	Saving Deposits
Meaning	These deposits are repayable by bank on demand. Banks do not pay any interest on these deposits.	It is deposited with banks for fixed period of time, which is not repayable on demand. These carry high rate of interest.	These carry combined features of fixed deposits and current accounts. They carry a nominal interest rate with limited number of withdrawal transactions.
Example	A business deposits daily earnings and uses cheques for transactions.	A retiree invests ₹ 1,00,000 in a fixed deposit for higher interest.	A student saves pocket money and earns interest.

2. **Advancing Loans** Money collected in various forms by banks is advanced as loans to eligible applicants in following forms

Basis \ Types	Cash Credit	Loans and Advances
Meaning	It refers to loans given by banks to the borrowers up to a specified limit against current assets/securities. Interest is charged upon the amount actually withdrawn and not on sanctioned amount.	Entire loan amount is credited to borrower's account on interest which is payable in fixed time either in lumpsum or in installments.
Example	A small business uses a cash credit line for day-to-day expenses.	A homebuyer takes a loan for buying a house and repays it monthly.

Other Functions

1. **Secondary functions** like providing overdraft facility and discounting of bills of exchange. e.g. A company uses an overdraft to cover short-term expenses.
2. **Agency functions** such as funds transfer, sale/ purchase of securities, Forex etc. and collections of cheques, interest or dividends. e.g. A bank transfers funds for a car purchase and collects dividends on stocks.
3. **General utility functions** like providing locker facilities, issue letter of credit, underwriting securities, etc. e.g. A customer rents a safe deposit box and gets a letter of credit for international trade.

Money Creation or Credit Creation by Commercial Banks

It means the creation of secondary deposits through initial deposits.

Through the process of money creation, commercial banks are able to create credit, which is in far excess of the initial deposits.

The process of money creation is based on the following **assumptions**

- The whole of the commercial banking system is treated as 'one unit'.
- All monetary exchanges in an economy are routed through banks.
- Banks also assume that all the depositors will not withdraw their deposits at the same time.

The capacity of banks to create money or credit depends on two factors

- Amount of initial fresh deposits or primary deposits.
- **Legal Reserve Ratio** (LRR), which is fixed by the Central Bank of the country, is the minimum ratio of deposit legally required to be kept as cash by banks. It has two components
  - Cash Reserve Ratio (CRR)
  - Statutory Liquidity Ratio (SLR)

An Illustration to Understand Process of Credit Creation

- Let the LRR be 20% and there is a fresh deposit of ₹ 10,000. As required, banks keep 20%, i.e. ₹ 2,000 as cash.
- Suppose the banks lend the remaining ₹ 8,000. The money lended is transferred to the bank account of the borrower. Also, those who borrow, use this money for making payments.
- As assumed, those who receive payments, put the money back into the banks. In this way, bank receives fresh deposits of ₹ 8,000.
- The banks again keep 20% of fresh deposits of ₹ 8,000, i.e. ₹ 1,600 as cash and lend ₹ 6,400, which is also 80% of the last deposits. The money again comes back to the bank leading to a rise in bank deposits by ₹ 6,400.
- In this way, the money goes on multiplying and ultimately total money creation is ₹ 50,000.

The table below will help you to understand process easily

Credit Creation by Commercial Banks

Round	Deposit (₹)	Reserves (₹) (CRR = 20%)	Loans (₹)
Ist Round	10,000	2,000	8,000
IInd Round	8,000	1,600	6,400
IIIrd Round	6,400	1,280	5,120
IVth Round	5,120	1,024	4,096
–	–	–	–
Total	50,000	10,000	40,000

The table shows the process that how the bank is able to create total deposits of ₹ 50,000 with the help of initial deposits of ₹ 10,000. Thus, given the amount of initial deposit and the LRR, the total money creation is

$$\text{Money Creation} = \text{Initial Deposit} \times \frac{1}{\text{Legal Reserve Ratio}}$$

So on substituting the variables, we get,

$$\text{Money Creation} = 10{,}000 \times \frac{1}{20\%} = ₹\ 50{,}000$$

Money or Credit Multiplier

It shows the number of times the commercial banks can create credit per unit of their cash reserves with RBI.

It is calculated as

$$\text{Money Multiplier} = \frac{1}{\text{LRR}}$$

Where, LRR comprises CRR and SLR. It should be remembered that higher the value of LRR, lower is the value of money multiplier and less money is created by the banking system and *vice-versa.*

Example If the Legal Reserve Ratio (LRR) is 20%, calculate the money multiplier and also determine how much money can the banking system create from an initial deposit of ₹ 5,000?

Sol. Money Multiplier = 1/Liquidity Reserve Ratio

$\Rightarrow$ Money Multiplier = 1/20% = 5

Total Money Created = Initial Deposit × Money Multiplier

$\Rightarrow$ Total Money Created = 5,000 × 5 = ₹ 25,000

3.4 Central Bank

A central bank is an apex institution of a country which operates, controls, directs and regulates the monetary and financial system of the country.

It does not engage itself in ordinary banking activities, such as accepting deposits and advancing loans to the public. Reserve Bank of India (RBI) is the Central Bank of India.

Functions of Central Bank

Functions of central bank are as follows

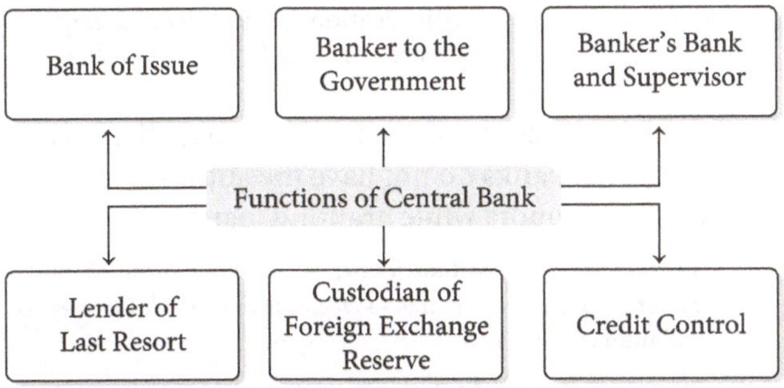

1. **Bank of Issue** The central bank is responsible for issuing paper currency notes (excluding one-rupee notes and coins) and ensuring that these notes are legal tender, which are backed by assets like gold or foreign securities of equal value. It helps to maintain public confidence in paper currency.

   This function is also referred to as 'Currency Authority Function of Central Bank'.

2. **Banker to the Government** Central bank plays following roles as banker to central or state government.

   Banker Keeps cash balances and carries out banking business of government;

   Agent Buys and sells government securities;

   Advisor Advises government on various economic, monetary and financial matters.

3. **Banker's Bank and Supervisor** The central bank acts as a bank for commercial banks by providing loans, accepting their deposits and offering clearing house services.

   As a supervisor, it regulates and controls the working of commercial banks to ensure their stability and compliance with regulations.

4. **Lender of Last Resort** When commercial banks fail to obtain funds from other sources, the central bank provides loans to them against approved securities. By offering loans to commercial banks in situation of emergencies, it ensures that money market remains stable and banking system does not suffer a setback.

5. **Custodian of Foreign Exchange Reserves** It manages the nation's foreign exchange reserves to promote international trade and stabilise the exchange rate to an agreed limit.

6. **Credit Control** The central bank regulates the credit creation capacity of commercial banks to control the money supply and influence economic stability through its monetary policy.

Bank of Issue

The Reserve Bank of India (RBI) issues currency notes, including denominations from ₹ 2 to ₹ 500. RBI has ceased printing ₹ 2,000 notes since 2018-19, having fulfilled the currency needs that arose after the 2016 demonetisation.

Credit Control Policy of Central Bank

Credit control policy of central bank includes following instruments

I. Quantitative Instruments

Instrument	Effects of Rise/Sale	Effect of Fall/Purchase
1. **Bank Rate** It is the rate of interest at which the RBI lends money to the commercial bank.	***Rise in the Bank Rate*** → Rise in the market rate of interest → Rise in the cost of capital → Fall in demand for credit → Fall in the supply of money → Inflation is controlled	***Fall in the Bank Rate*** → Fall in the market rate of interest → Fall in the cost of capital → Rise in demand for credit → Rise in the supply of money → Deflation is controlled
2. **Open Market Operations** It means the sale/purchase of securities in the open market by RBI on the behalf of government.	***Sale of Securities by RBI*** → Contracts the liquidity and leads to fall in cash reserves of commercial banks → Fall in credit creation of commercial banks → Fall in money supply → Inflation is controlled	***Purchase of Securities by RBI*** → Expands the liquidity and leads to a rise in cash reserves of commercial banks → Rise in credit creation of commercial banks → Rise in money supply → Deflation is controlled
3. **Cash Reserve Ratio** (CRR) It refers to the minimum percentage of commercial bank's total deposits required to be kept with the RBI.	***Rise in CRR*** → Rise in cash reserves for a given amount of demand deposits → Fall in money supply of commercial banks → Inflation is controlled	***Fall in CRR*** → Fall in cash reserves for a given amount of demand deposits → Rise in money supply of commercial banks → Deflation is controlled
4. **Statutory Liquidity Ratio** Every bank is required to maintain a fixed percentage of its assets in form of liquid assets with itself, called SLR.	***Rise in SLR*** → Rise in liquid assets to be held by commercial banks with themselves → Fall in availability of funds for CRR deposits with RBI → Fall in money supply of commercial banks → Inflation is controlled	***Fall in SLR*** → Fall in liquid assets to be held by commercial banks with themselves → Rise in availability of funds for CRR deposits with RBI → Rise in money supply of commercial banks → Deflation is controlled
5. **Repo Rate** It is the rate at which RBI offers the short period loans to the commercial banks by buying the government securities in the open market.	***Rise in Repo Rate*** → Rise in cost of capital → Fall in demand for credit → Fall in supply of money by commercial banks → Inflation is controlled	***Fall in Repo Rate*** → Fall in cost of capital → Rise in demand for credit → Rise in supply of money by commercial banks → Deflation is controlled
6. **Reverse Repo Rate** It is the rate at which RBI accepts deposits from the commercial banks (through government securities).	***Rise in Reverse Repo Rate*** → More funds parked by commercial banks with RBI to generate interest → Less funds used as CRR funds with RBI for credit creation → Supply of money decreases → Inflation is controlled	***Fall in Reverse Repo Rate*** → Less funds parked by commercial banks with RBI to generate interest → More funds used as CRR funds with RBI for credit creation → Supply of money increases → Deflation is controlled

II. Qualitative Instruments

These instruments focus on select sectors of the economy.

1. **Margin Requirements** Margin is the difference between the value of security offered for and the amount of loan sanctioned.

   Rise in Margin Requirement → Fall in demand for credit → Fall in supply of credit by commercial banks → Fall in money supply → Inflation is controlled

   Fall in Margin Requirement → Rise in demand for credit → Rise in supply of credit by commercial banks → Rise in money supply → Deflation is controlled

2. **Rationing of Credit** It refers to fixation of credit quotas for different business activities. The RBI fixes credit quota for different activities and commercial banks do not have the authority to exceed such quota while granting loans.

   Introduction of Credit Rationing → Reduction of supply of credit by commercial banks → Decrease in supply of money → Inflation is controlled

   Withdrawal of Credit Rationing → Expansion of supply of credit by commercial banks → Increase in supply of money → Deflation is controlled

3. **Moral Suasion** Central bank can issue directives to member banks in the form of directional control, prohibiting loans of particular type or giving advice to grant loan to priority sectors.

Mind Map

MONEY AND BANKING

1 Money

Money can be defined as anything that is generally acceptable as a means of exchange and at the same time, acts as a measure of value, store of value and as a deferred payments.

2 Barter System of Exchange

Before the invention of money, goods were exchanged for goods. This system was known as the barter system of exchange.

Drawbacks
- Lack of double coincidence of wants
- Lack of store of value
- Lack of common measure of value
- Lack of standard of deferred payments

3 Types of Money

- **Fiat Money** Issued by the order or authority of the government, such as notes and coins.
- **Fiduciary Money** Relies on mutual trust between the payer and the payee for its acceptance.
- **Full-bodied Money** Refers to coins whose commodity value equals their money value.
- **Credit Money** It has a face value significantly greater than its intrinsic value.

4 Functions of Money

Primary Functions
These are basic functions of money, which it must perform in every country. They include
- Medium of exchange
- Measure of value

Secondary Functions
These are known as derived functions and include
- Standard of deferred payments
- Store of value
- Transfer of value

5 Money Supply

The total stock of money held by the public in an economy at a particular point in time is called money supply.

Measures
- **M_1 Measure of Money Supply** It is also known as transaction money, as it can be directly used for making transactions. $M_1 = CU + DD + OD$
- **M_2 Measure of Money Supply** It includes all components of M_1 plus savings deposits of the public with post offices.
- **M_3 Measure of Money Supply** It includes all components of M_1 plus net time deposits (fixed/term deposits) of public with commercial banks.
- **M_4 Measure of Money Supply** It includes all components of M_3 plus total deposits of public with post office savings banks, excluding National Savings Certificates (NSCs).

6 Commercial Banks

Commercial banks are financial institutions that accept public deposits from the public and lend out this money to consumers, aiming to earn profits.

7 Functions of Commercial Banks

Primary Functions
- **Accepting Deposits** Deposits may be accepted from public in the form of current account, fixed and saving deposits.
- **Advancing Loans** Money collected in various forms by banks is advanced as cash credit & loans and advances to eligible applicants.

Other Functions
- **Secondary functions** like overdraft facility, discounting of bills of exchange.
- **Agency functions** such as funds transfer, interest or dividends, etc.
- **General utility functions** like providing locker facilities, issue letter of credit, etc.

Money Creation or Credit Creation
It means the creation of secondary deposits through initial deposits. The capacity to create money depends upon amount of initial fresh deposits and legal reserve ratio.
Money or credit multiplier shows the number of times the commercial banks can create credit per unit of their cash reserves with RBI. It is calculated as

$$\text{Money Multiplier} = 1/LRR$$

8 Central Bank

It is an apex institution of a country which operates, controls, directs and regulates the monetary and financial system of the country.

9 Functions of Central Bank

- **Bank of Issue** Central Bank issues paper currency notes and ensures that these are legal tender.
- **Banker to the Government** Central bank plays the role of banker, agent and advisor for the government.
- **Banker's Bank and Supervisor** Central bank acts as a bank for commercial banks and regulates their working.
- **Lender of Last Resort** It provides loans to commercial banks in case of emergencies.
- **Custodian of Foreign Exchange Reserves** It manages the nation's foreign exchange reserves.
- **Credit Control** It regulates the credit creation capacity of commercial banks to control the money supply.

10 Credit Control Policy of Central Bank

Quantitative Instruments
- **Bank Rate** Rate of interest at which RBI lends money to the commercial bank.
- **Open Market Operations** Sale/Purchase of securities in the open market on the behalf of the government.
- **Cash Reserve Ratio** Minimum percentage of commercial bank's total deposits required to be kept with RBI.
- **Statutory Liquidity Ratio** Every bank is required to maintain a fixed percentage of its assets in form of liquid assets with itself, called SLR.
- **Repo Rate** It is the rate at which RBI offers the short period loans to the commercial banks by buying the government securities in the open market.
- **Reverse Repo Rate** It is the rate at which RBI accepts deposits from the commercial banks (through government securities).

Qualitative Instruments
- **Margin Requirements** Margin is the difference between the value of security offered for and the amount of loan sanctioned.
- **Rationing of Credit** Refers to fixation of credit quotas for different business activities.
- **Moral Suasion** Central Bank can issue directives to member banks.

EXAM PATTERN QUESTIONS

Objective Type Questions

Multiple Choice Questions (MCQs)

1. **In the barter system, the value of a good or service is determined by**

(a) market price
(b) intrinsic worth
(c) relative availability
(d) perceived usefulness to traders

2. **What is the main challenge faced by the barter system depicted in the image?**

Barter

Exchange of Goods take place without money

Source *https://www.wallstreetmojo.com/barter/*

(a) Lack of government regulation and oversight
(b) Difficulty in calculating exchange value
(c) Limited variety of goods and services available
(d) Inefficiency in facilitating large-scale transactions

3. **Money is most liquid of all assets because …… .**

(a) it includes shares and equities
(b) money itself is a medium of exchange
(c) it does not have general acceptability
(d) it has many functions

4. **Money was evolved to remove the problems of barter system of exchange. Find the correct sequence of evolution of money concepts.** Competency Based Que

(i) Paper money **(ii) Plastic money**
(iii) Metallic money **(iv) e-money**

Codes

(a) (iii), (i), (iv), (ii)
(b) (i), (ii), (iii), (iv)
(c) (iii), (iv), (i), (ii)
(d) (iii), (i), (ii), (iv)

5. **……… backs fiduciary money in the economy.**

(a) Physical commodities
(b) Government guarantee
(c) The gold standard
(d) International reserves

6. **The money whose value as money is significantly greater than its intrinsic value is referred to as …….. .**

(a) fiat money
(b) fiduciary money
(c) full-bodied money
(d) credit money

7. **Identify the correct reason(s) that explains the primary functions of money.**

I. Transfer of value **II. Measure of value**
III. Medium of exchange
IV. Standard of deferred payment

Codes

(a) I and II
(b) II and III
(c) III and IV
(d) I and IV

8. **"The value of all goods and services can be expressed in monetary units."**
On the basis of the given statement, identify the function performed by money. CBSE SQP 2024; Competency Based Que

(a) Medium of exchange
(b) Store of value
(c) Unit of account
(d) Means of standard of deferred payments

9. **"Money facilitates comparison of the value of different goods and services."**
On the basis of the given statement, identify the function performed by money. Competency Based Que

(a) Medium of exchange
(b) Store of value
(c) Measure of value
(d) Standard of deferred payment

10. **"Money is an asset which can be stored for use in future." In the light of given statement, identify the function performed by money.** CBSE 2023; Competency Based Que

(a) A measure of value
(b) A standard of deferred payment
(c) A store of value
(d) A medium of exchange

11. **……… is the total volume of money held by the public, for the purpose of disposing off, at a particular point of time.** CBSE 2024 C

(a) Term deposits
(b) Demand for money
(c) Money supply
(d) Credit creation

12. Narrow money includes NCERT (QR)

(a) $M_2 + M_3$ (b) $M_1 + M_2$
(c) $M_1 + M_3$ (d) M_4

13. What is the order of money supply from narrowest to broadest?

(a) M_4, M_3, M_2, M_1 (b) M_1, M_2, M_3, M_4
(c) M_2, M_1, M_3, M_4 (d) M_3, M_2, M_1, M_4

14. Identify the incorrect feature(s) of the money supply in an economy, from the following

(i) It is measured during a period of time.
(ii) It includes stock of money held by the government of a nation.
(iii) It always represents the currency held with Central Bank of the nation. CBSE 2024; Competency Based Que

Codes

(a) Only (i) (b) (ii) and (iii)
(c) (i) and (ii) (d) (i), (ii) and (iii)

15. Identify the correct differences between time deposits and demand deposits. Competency Based Que

I. Time deposits generally offer higher interest rates than demand deposits.
II. Demand deposits are less liquid than time deposits due to withdrawal restrictions.
III. Time deposits have a fixed maturity period, whereas demand deposits can be withdrawn at any time.
IV. Demand deposits typically incur penalties for early withdrawal, unlike time deposits.

Codes

(a) I and II (b) I and III
(c) III and IV (d) I, II and III

16. What economic role of banks is depicted in this image?

(a) Monitoring government policy
(b) Providing savings and credit facilities
(c) Regulating exchange rates
(d) Implementing fiscal policy

17. The credit multiplier is

(a) the ratio of loans to deposits
(b) the ratio of deposits to loans
(c) the ratio of reserves to deposits
(d) the ratio of deposits to reserves

18. Suppose in a hypothetical economy, the Central Bank increases the reserve ratio from 10% to 25%. Keeping the amount of initial deposits constant at ₹ 1,000 crore, the amount of total money creation would be ₹ ...... crore. CBSE 2024 C

(a) 10,000 (b) 4,000
(c) 6,000 (d) 5,000

19. Process of credit creation by commercial banks comes to an end when .... CBSE Term I 2021

(a) fresh deposits with banks become zero
(b) reserve ratio become zero
(c) money multiplier becomes zero
(d) total money reserves become equals to initial deposit

20. If the total credit created by the banks is ₹ 500 and reserve ratio is 20%, the value of primary deposits would be .... CBSE 2025; Competency Based Que

(a) ₹ 200 (b) ₹ 300
(c) ₹ 100 (d) ₹ 500

21. Calculate the legal reserve requirement if the initial deposit of ₹ 400 crore led to the creation of ₹ 3,200 crore of credit in the economy. Competency Based Que

(a) 10% (b) 12.5%
(c) 14% (d) 12%

22.

Round	Primary Deposits	Loans	Demand Deposits
Round I	1,000	900	100
Round II	(i)	(ii)	(iii)
(and so on till all excess reserves are exhausted)			
Total	10,000	9,000	1,000

The value of primary deposits, loans and demand deposits in Round II are (i) .... , (ii) .... and (iii) .... respectively. Competency Based Que

(a) 800, 720, 80
(b) 900, 810, 90
(c) 900, 800, 100
(d) 1,000, 900, 90

23. Statutory liquidity ratio implies to that percentage of .... CBSE Term I 2021

(a) total deposits of the commercial banks which must be kept in the current account, with the Reserve Bank of India

(b) total deposits of the commercial banks which must be kept in the form of liquid assets, with the Reserve Bank of India
(c) net time and demand deposit liabilities of the commercial banks which must be kept in the form of cash, with the Reserve Bank of India
(d) net time and demand deposit liabilities of the commercial bank which must be kept with themselves in the form of liquid assets

24. **The higher the reserve ratio, the ....**
(a) higher the level of credit creation
(b) lower the level of credit creation
(c) more profitable the bank becomes
(d) higher the interest rate

25. **In the context of commercial bank, which of the following statements are not correct?** **Competency Based Que**

I. Note issuing authority of the country.
II. Creates credit on the basis of cash reserve.
III. Accepts deposits of the general public.
IV. Acts as a banker to the government.

Codes
(a) I and III
(b) II and III
(c) III and IV
(d) I and IV

26. **What is the primary difference between the two banks depicted in the image below?**

Source *https://currentaffairs.adda247.com/rbi-approves-sbis-establishment-of-operations-support-subsidiary/*
(a) Commercial banks (like SBI) are owned by the government, while central banks (like RBI) are privately owned
(b) Commercial banks focus on providing services to individuals and businesses, while central banks focus on managing the nation's monetary system
(c) Commercial banks are responsible for printing currency notes, while central banks are responsible for setting interest rates
(d) Commercial banks are regulated by the government, while central banks are independent

27. **How does the central bank help move the economy from an unstable to a stable state according to the diagram?**

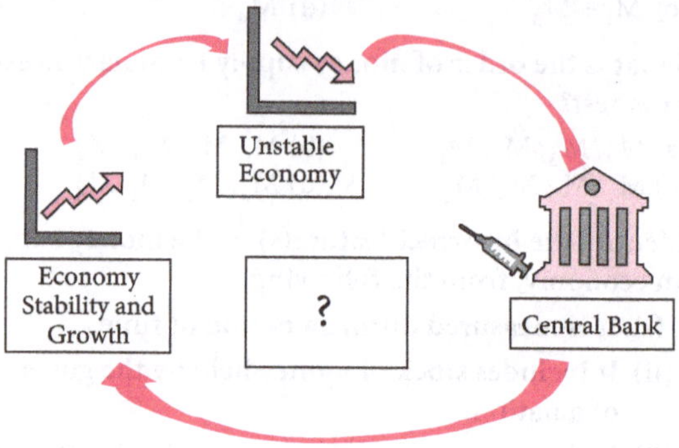

(a) By increasing government spending
(b) By setting trade policies
(c) By injecting monetary policy and controlling the money supply
(d) By raising taxes on businesses

28. **Central bank as ...., manages public debt of the government.** **CBSE Term I 2021**
(a) custodian of foreign exchange
(b) agent
(c) financial advisor
(d) supervisor

29. **Which of the following statements do not support with the function of RBI as supervisor to the commercial banks?** **CBSE Term I 2021**
(a) Regulates the expansion, merger, acquisition, etc. of the bank
(b) Formulates all rules and regulations for commercial bank
(c) Extend loans to the commercial bank
(d) Inspection of operations of banks

30. **What is the main objective of the central bank's foreign exchange policy?**
(a) To maintain a fixed exchange rate
(b) To prevent excessive fluctuations in the exchange rate
(c) To maximise the country's foreign exchange reserves
(d) To control the flow of foreign capital

31. **As per the Reserve Bank of India (RBI) Press Release: 2019-2020/2082, dated 18/03/2020**

RBI announces OMO purchase of government of India dated securities: On a review of the current liquidity and financial conditions, the Reserve Bank has decided to conduct open market operations on 20th March, 2020 (Friday) in the form of purchase of an aggregate amount of ₹ 10,000 crore of the government securities.

Analyse the impact of OMO planned by RBI on the state of Indian economy. **Competency Based Que**

(a) No change in money supply
(b) Increase in money supply
(c) Decrease in money supply
(d) Have mixed effect on money supply

32. **What is the purpose of the policy instrument represented by the following image?**

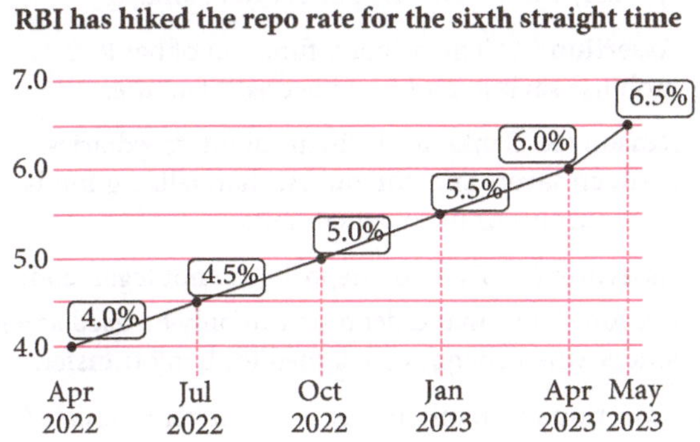

Source *https://www.bankbazaar.com/home-loan/repo-rate.html*

(a) Influencing inflation
(b) Controlling credit growth
(c) Managing foreign exchange reserves
(d) Providing financial assistance to banks

33. **When there is surplus liquidity in the banking system, the central bank may increase the .... rate to encourage banks to park excess funds with the central bank.**

(a) reverse repo (b) repo
(c) discount (d) base

34. **Central bank can decrease the money supply in the economy by........... .** **CBSE 2025, 24; Competency Based Que**

(a) lowering the cash reserve
(b) increasing the bank rate
(c) lowering the bank rate
(d) purchase of G-Secs (Government Securities)

35. **The Reserve Bank of India (RBI) recently hiked the repo rate by 35 bps, the fifth such increase in 2022. The repo rate currently stands at 6.25 per cent. The first time RBI hiked the repo rate was in May when the central bank's rate setting panel unanimously hiked the benchmark lending rate by 40 bps.**

This was followed by an increase of 50 bps each in June, August and September. In total, the RBI has hiked the rate by 190 bps.

Source *https://www.zeebiz.com/economy-infra/news-year-ender-2022-rbis-repo-rate-hike-impact-on-your-money-banks-economy-214605*

The above news is an action that has been taken to deal with which of the following situations in the economy? **Competency Based Que**

(a) Inflationary gap (b) Deflationary gap
(c) Economic recession (d) All of these

36. **To fight recession, RBI needs to** **Competency Based Que**

I. Lower bank rate **II. Lower CRR**
III. Increase SLR **IV. Increase repo rate**

Codes

(a) I and III (b) II and III
(c) III and IV (d) I and II

37. **Moral persuasion is**

(a) a legal requirement for banks to follow central bank guidelines
(b) a direct order from the central bank to restrict credit
(c) a method of influencing bank behaviour through speeches, seminars and meetings
(d) an incentive programme for promoting investment

Direction *Read the case study and answer the questions 38 to 41 on the basis of the same*

The Central Bank of India (Reserve Bank of India) is the apex institution that controls the entire financial market. It's one of the major functions is to maintain the reserve of foreign exchange. Also, it intervenes in the foreign exchange market to stabilise the excessive fluctuations in the foreign exchange rate.

In other words, it is the central bank's job to control a country's economy through monetary policy. If the economy is moving slowly or going backward, there are steps that central bank can take to boost the economy. These steps, whether they are asset purchases or printing more money, all involve injecting more cash into the economy.

The simple supply and demand economic projection occur and currency will devalue. When the opposite occurs, and the economy is growing, the central bank will use various methods to keep that growth steady and in-line with other economic factors such as wages and prices.

Whatever the central bank does or in fact don't do, will affect the currency of that country. Sometimes, it is within the central bank's interest to purposefully affect the value of a currency. e.g. If the economy is heavily reliant on exports and their currency value becomes too high, importers of that country's commodities will seek cheaper supply; hence directly affecting the economy.

38. **......... and .... tools are employed by central bank to regulate the money supply in the domestic economy.**

39. **Money supply is a .... concept.**

40. **In the event that the foreign currency rate rises excessively, which of the following actions should the central bank take?**

(a) Provide foreign currency from its stock
(b) Increase demand for other foreign currency
(c) Permit commercial banks to operate in a less restrictive setting
(d) Both (b) and (c)

41. **Dear money policy of central bank, which is used to keep the growth steady and in-line with other economic factors, refers to**

(a) tighten the money supply in the economy
(b) ease the money supply in the economy
(c) allow commercial banks to work under less strict environment
(d) Both (b) and (c)

Direction *Read the hypothetical information and answer the questions 42 to 45 on the basis of same*

Round	Primary Deposits	Loans	LRR = 20%
Round I	1,000	800	200
Round II	? A	640	160
Round III	640	? B	? C
(and so on till all excess reserves are exhausted)			
Total	5,000	4,000	? D

42. **The process of credit creation in an economy is affected by .... and ....**

43. **The value of primary deposits in Round II is ₹ ....**

44. **The value of loans created and value of reserve ratio in round III is .... and .... respectively.**

(a) 512, 128
(b) 1,440, 360
(c) 512, 360
(d) 1,440, 128

45. **When initial deposits .... legal reserves of ...., the process of credit creation comes to the end.**

(a) exceeds, ₹ 1,000
(b) is lower, ₹ 5,000
(c) equal, ₹ 1,000
(d) exceeds, ₹ 4,000

Assertion-Reason

Direction (Q.No. 46 to 55) *Read the following Assertion (A) and Reason (R) and choose the correct alternative from the following*

Alternatives

(a) Both Assertion (A) and Reason (R) are true and Reason (R) is the correct explanation of Assertion (A)
(b) Both Assertion (A) and Reason (R) are true, but Reason (R) is not the correct explanation of Assertion (A)
(c) Assertion (A) is true, but Reason (R) is false
(d) Assertion (A) is false, but Reason (R) is true

46. **Assertion** (A) We can still encounter barter system in modern economic system.

Reason (R) People exchange old clothes for utensils.

47. **Assertion** (A) Paper currency is accepted as a medium of exchange because it has intrinsic value.

Reason (R) The value of paper currency is determined by the trust and guarantee of the issuing authority, typically the government or central bank.

48. **Assertion** (A) The primary function of banks is to mobilise savings and provide credit facilities.

Reason (R) Banks act as financial intermediaries between savers and borrowers, channelising funds from surplus units to deficit units.

49. **Assertion** (A) Demand deposits are not legal tender.

Reason (R) Demand deposits can only be used as a legal tender when cheques are issued for bank transfer.

50. **Assertion** (A) Bank money is the currency created by central bank.

Reason (R) It is the sole responsibility of central bank of a country to print and circulate currency.

51. **Assertion** (A) Credit creation power of commercial banks is indirectly proportional to Legal Reserve Ratio (LRR).

Reason (R) When LRR is increased, the overall liquidity of commercial banks is decreased.

52. **Assertion** (A) Reverse repo rate is the rate at which central bank of a country lends funds to commercial bank.

Reason (R) When reverse repo rate is raised, it encourages banks to park their funds with the central bank.

53. **Assertion** (A) Reserve ratio and credit creation power of commercial bank are directly related.

Reason (R) Credit creation is the product of the reciprocal of Reserve Ratio (RR) and primary deposit.

CBSE Term I 2021

54. **Assertion** (A) Inflation tends to decrease the purchasing power of money.

Reason (R) When the general price level rises, each unit of currency buys fewer goods and services.

55. **Assertion** (A) The government can reduce the deflationary gap by purchasing government securities in the open market.

Reason (R) The Central Bank purchases government securities in the open market to increase the lending capacity of commercial banks. **CBSE SQP 2025**

Two Statement Based MCQs

Direction (Q.No. 56 to 65) *Read the following statements carefully and choose the correct alternative*

Alternatives

(a) Statement I is correct and Statement II is incorrect
(b) Statement II is correct and Statement I is incorrect
(c) Both the statements are correct
(d) Both the statements are incorrect

56. **Statement I** In the barter system, there is a lack of divisibility of goods, which can complicate trade for smaller transactions.

Statement II The barter system facilitates the efficient allocation of resources as goods are directly exchanged without any intermediary.

57. **Statement I** All the coins are issued by Finance Ministry in India.

Statement II All the currency notes are issued by Reserve Bank of India.

58. **Statement I** Full-bodied money is that money whose money value and commodity value are equal in the market.

Statement II When money value of money is less than commodity value of money, it is called credit money.

59. **Statement I** M_1 measure of money supply includes currency held by the public and other deposits with the reserve bank.

Statement II In M_1, other deposits does not include deposits of the government of the country with RBI as well as deposits of the country's banking system with RBI.

60. **Statement I** Bank money is the money which is generated in the form of credit creation.

Statement II High powered money is the money held by the people, vault cash of the commercial banks as well as cash reserves of the commercial banks with RBI.

61. **Statement I** Fixed deposits allow customers to withdraw their funds at any time without penalty.

Statement II Savings accounts typically offer lower liquidity compared to fixed deposits.

62. **Statement I** The central bank acts as a 'lender of last resort' to the government to maintain financial stability in the banking system.

Statement II By serving as a lender of last resort, the central bank provides unlimited liquidity to any financial institution in distress, regardless of its financial health.

63. **Statement I** Increase in repo rate enhances the credit creating power of commercial banks.

Statement II The ability of commercial bank to create credit is controlled by central bank.

64. **Statement I** The reverse repo rate is a tool used by the RBI to control liquidity in the banking system.

Statement II When the reverse repo rate is increased, banks prefer to deposit their excess funds with the RBI, reducing the availability of money for lending in the economy.

65. **Statement I** Selective credit control is the qualitative tool of monetary policy.

Statement II Bank rate offers short-term loans to the commercial banks.

Matching

66. **Match the columns with correct explanation**

Column I	Column II
A. Reserve Bank of India	(i) Borrowers and lenders
B. Commercial bank	(ii) Regulating authority
C. Credit creation	(iii) Tool to influence money supply
D. Open market operations	(iv) Multiple expansion of deposits

Codes

	A	B	C	D		A	B	C	D
(a)	(iii)	(ii)	(iv)	(i)	(b)	(ii)	(i)	(iii)	(iv)
(c)	(ii)	(i)	(iv)	(iii)	(d)	(i)	(ii)	(iii)	(iv)

67. **Write the correct sequence of options in Column II by matching them with options of Column I**

Column I	Column II
A. Full-bodied money	(i) Optional voluntary money
B. Credit money	(ii) Commodity value = Value in money
C. Fiat money	(iii) Legal tender
D. Fiduciary money	(iv) Commodity value < Value in money

Codes

	A	B	C	D
(a)	(i)	(ii)	(iii)	(iv)
(b)	(ii)	(iv)	(iii)	(i)
(c)	(iii)	(ii)	(i)	(iv)
(d)	(iv)	(iii)	(ii)	(i)

68. **Match the functions of commercial banks in Column I with their descriptions in Column II**

Column I	Column II
A. Accepting deposits	(i) Providing a safe place to keep valuables
B. Acting as an agent for various services	(ii) Enabling secure and convenient transfer of funds.
C. Issuing bank drafts and clearing cheques	(iii) Meeting the financial needs of individuals and businesses.
D. Providing locker facilities	(iv) Offering a range of financial services beyond banking

Codes

	A	B	C	D
(a)	(iii)	(ii)	(iv)	(i)
(b)	(iii)	(iv)	(ii)	(i)
(c)	(iv)	(iii)	(i)	(ii)
(d)	(i)	(ii)	(iii)	(iv)

69. **Write the correct sequence of options in Column II by matching them with options of Column I**

Column I	Column II
A. Bank rate	(i) Minimum percentage of bank's total deposits required to be kept with Central Bank
B. Repo rate	(ii) Commercial banks park their surplus funds with Central Bank
C. Cash reserve ratio	(iii) Minimum rate at which the Central Bank gives credit to commercial banks
D. Reverse repo rate	(iv) Rate at which Central Bank offers short-term loans to commercial banks

Codes

	A	B	C	D
(a)	(i)	(ii)	(iii)	(iv)
(b)	(ii)	(iii)	(iv)	(i)
(c)	(iii)	(iv)	(i)	(ii)
(d)	(iv)	(iii)	(ii)	(i)

70. Choose the correct pair **Competency Based Que**

Column I	Column II
A. Increase in bank rate	(i) Credit expands
B. Decrease in SLR	(ii) Credit contracts
C. Decrease in margin requirement	(iii) Credit contracts
D. Withdrawal of credit rationing	(iv) Credit expands

Codes
(a) A-(i)
(b) B-(ii)
(c) C-(iii)
(d) D-(iv)

Concept Identification

71. A financial institution that accepts deposits from individuals and businesses and lends money to borrowers.

72. The difference between the borrowing rate and lending rate. It is the profit of the banks.

73. Deposits created by commercial banks when they lend out a portion of the primary deposits after keeping a reserve.

74. The central bank's tool to control the money supply in the economy by influencing the availability and cost of credit.

75. The ratio of a bank's reserves to its deposits, which determines the bank's ability to lend money.

Answers

1. (d) perceived usefulness to traders
2. (b) Difficulty in calculating exchange value
3. (b) money itself is a medium of exchange
4. (d) (iii), (i), (ii), (iv)
5. (b) Government guarantee
6. (d) credit money
7. (b) II and III
8. (c) Unit of account
9. (c) Measure of value
10. (c) A store of value
11. (c) Money supply
12. (b) $M_1 + M_2$
13. (b) M_1, M_2, M_3, M_4
14. (d) (i), (ii) and (iii)
15. (b) I and III
16. (b) Providing savings and credit facilities
17. (d) the ratio of Deposits to reserves
18. (b) Total Money Creation = Initial Deposit/Reserve Ratio
$= 1{,}000/0.25 = 4{,}000$
19. (d) total money reserves become equals to initial deposit
20. (c) $\text{Credit Multiplier} = \dfrac{1}{\text{Reserve Ratio}}$

Total Credit = ₹ 500

Reserve Ratio = 20% *or* 0.20

So, Multiplier $= \frac{1}{0.20} = 5$

Now, Total Credit = Primary Deposits × Money Multiplier

500 = Primary Deposits × 5

∴ Primary Deposits = ₹ 100

21. (b) Money Multiplier = Credit Created/Initial Deposit

$$= \frac{3,200}{400} = 8$$

$$\text{Legal Reserve ratio} = \frac{1}{\text{Money Multiplier}} \times 100$$

$$= \frac{1}{8} \times 100 = 12.5\%$$

22. (b) **Primary Deposit for Round II** This is the amount lent out in Round I, which is ₹ 900.

Loan in Round II The bank keeps 10% of ₹ 900 as a reserve and lends out the remaining amount.

- Reserve = 10% of ₹ 900 = ₹ 90
- Loan = 900 − 90 = ₹ 810

Demand Deposit in Round II The reserve for Round II is ₹ 90, which becomes the new demand deposit.

Therefore, the values for Round II are

- Primary Deposit (i) = ₹ 900 • Loan (ii) = ₹ 810
- Demand Deposit (iii) = ₹ 90

23. (d) net time and demand deposit liabilities of the commercial bank which must be kept with themselves in the form of liquid assets
24. (b) lower the level of credit creation
25. (d) I and IV
26. (b) Commercial banks focus on providing services to individuals and businesses, while central banks focus on managing the nation's monetary system.
27. (c) By injecting monetary policy and controlling the money supply
28. (b) agent
29. (a) Regulates the expansion, merger, acquisition, etc. of the bank
30. (b) To prevent excessive fluctuations in the exchange rate
31. (b) Increase in money supply
32. (a) Influencing inflation
33. (a) reverse repo
34. (b) increasing the bank rate
35. (a) Inflationary gap
36. (d) I and II
37. (c) a method of influencing bank behaviour through speeches, seminars and meetings.
38. Quantitative, qualitative
39. stock
40. (a) Provide foreign currency from its stock
41. (a) tighten the money supply in the economy
42. amount of initial deposits, LRR
43. The primary deposit for Round II is the amount loaned in Round I, which is ₹ 800.
44. (a) **Primary Deposit for Round III**
    - The primary deposit for Round III is the amount loaned in Round II, which is ₹ 640.

    Reserve in Round III
    - Reserve Ratio (LRR) = 20%
    - Reserve = 20% of ₹ 640 = ₹ 128

    Loan in Round III
    - Loan = Primary Deposit − Reserve
    - Loan = 640 − 128 = ₹ 512

    So, the values for Round III are
    - Loan created = ₹ 512
    - Reserve = ₹ 128
45. (c) Credit creation ends when initial deposits equal legal reserves of ₹ 1,000.
46. (a) Both Assertion (A) and Reason (R) are true and Reason (R) is the correct explanation of Assertion (A)
47. (d) Paper currency does not have intrinsic value; its acceptance as a medium of exchange is based on the trust and authority of the issuing government or central bank, which guarantees its value as legal tender. The value of paper currency depends on this trust rather than any intrinsic worth.
48. (a) Both Assertion (A) and Reason (R) are true and Reason (R) is the correct explanation of Assertion (A)
49. (c) Demand deposits themselves are never legal tender, regardless of how they are transferred. They can facilitate transactions, but they do not transform into legal tender merely by the act of issuing a cheque.
50. (d) Bank money refers to the money created through the banking system, mainly in the form of deposits (such as savings accounts and checking accounts) that banks create through lending. The Central Bank does create the physical currency (cash) that circulates in the economy, but bank money is primarily created by commercial banks through the lending process.
51. (a) Both Assertion (A) and Reason (R) are true and Reason (R) is the correct explanation of Assertion (A)
52. (d) The reverse repo rate is actually the rate at which the central bank borrows funds from commercial banks. In this context, when commercial banks deposit their excess funds with the central bank, they receive interest at the reverse repo rate.
53. (d) Credit creation is linked to the reserve ratio, as the credit multiplier (which indicates the potential maximum amount of credit that can be created) is inversely related to the reserve ratio.

Since a higher reserve ratio restricts lending, while a lower reserve ratio enhances the capacity for credit creation.

54. (a) Both Assertion (A) and Reason (R) are true and Reason (R) is the correct explanation of Assertion (A)

55. (a) Both Assertion (A) and Reason (R) are true and Reason (R) is the correct explanation of Assertion (A)

56. (a) While the barter system allows for direct exchange of goods without intermediaries, it does not necessarily facilitate efficient allocation of resources.

The barter system can lead to issues such as the double coincidence of wants, where each party must want what the other has, which can hinder efficient trade and resource allocation.

57. (a) All currency notes except ₹ 1 note, are issued by Reserve Bank of India. ₹ 1 note is issued by Government of India.

58. (a) When the money value of money is less than its commodity value, it is not referred to as credit money. Instead, it may indicate that the money is overvalued or that there is a scarcity of the commodity. Credit money refers to money that is backed by a promise to pay (like bank notes or deposits) and does not have intrinsic value tied to a commodity.

59. (b) M_1 does not include deposits with the Reserve Bank (central bank); rather, it focuses on the currency in the hands of the public and demand deposits at commercial banks.

60. (c) Both the statements are correct

61. (d) Fixed deposits have a maturity period and withdrawing early usually incurs penalties. Savings accounts generally offer higher liquidity than fixed deposits, which have restrictions on withdrawals.

62. (d) The central bank acts as a 'lender of last resort' primarily to commercial banks and other financial institutions, not to the government.

It typically does not provide unlimited liquidity without conditions; the support is selective and aims to stabilise the financial system rather than bail out unsound institutions.

63. (b) An increase in the repo rate actually makes borrowing from the central bank more expensive for commercial banks, which typically reduces their ability to create credit. Higher borrowing costs lead banks to tighten lending, decreasing their credit creation power.

64. (c) Both the statements are correct

65. (a) The bank rate is the rate at which a country's central bank lends money to commercial banks, typically for long-term loans, not short-term loans. Short-term loans to commercial banks are generally offered through the repo rate or other short-term lending facilities.

66. (c) (ii) (i) (iv) (iii)

67. (b) (ii) (iv) (iii) (i)

68. (b) (iii) (iv) (ii) (i)

69. (c) (iii) (iv) (i) (ii)

70. (d) D-(iv)

71. Commercial bank

72. Spread

73. Secondary deposits

74. Monetary policy

75. Reserve ratio

Subjective Questions

Short Answer Type Questions

1. How come the issue of 'lacking a reliable store of value' was a significant challenge during the barter system era, despite the availability of easily storable commodities like diamonds and gold? Competency Based Que

Ans. It is true that value can be stored in the form of gold or diamond for future use, however it again has certain drawbacks such as

(i) Being limited in supply, these were not available in abundance.

(ii) These involved certain transaction cost in exchange of goods.

(iii) These were not liquid form of exchange, because not everyone was able to accept them.

(iv) Divisibility was also a problem while dealing in these goods.

Therefore, while gold and diamonds held intrinsic value, their limitations made them ineffective as a universal store of value in the barter system.

2. Sarah, a budding entrepreneur, is facing challenges in sustaining her small business. In an effort to expand her operations, she contemplates exchanging goods in kind as a means to facilitate growth. However, Sarah lacks clarity on the potential drawbacks associated with this approach.

So, help Sarah by explaining her the problems that she may face in exchanging goods in kind. Competency Based Que

Ans. The potential drawbacks associated with barter system or exchange of goods in kinds include

(i) **Lack of Double Coincidence of Wants**

It was a major drawback of the barter system as it was very rare when the owner of some goods or services could find someone who wanted his goods or services and possessed those goods or services that the first person wanted. No exchange was possible, if the double coincidence of wants was not there.

(ii) **Lack of Common Measure of Value**

In barter system, there was absence of a common unit of measurement in which the value of goods and services can be measured.

In the absence of common unit, proper valuation was not possible.

(iii) **Lack of Standard for Deferred Payments**

Deferred payments means future payments. In barter system, it was difficult to return value in future in terms of goods of same quantity and quality.

Therefore, future payments regarding interest and loans became difficult.

(iv) **Lack of Store of Value**

Due to absence of money in barter system, wealth was stored in terms of goods. Storing of goods carried some problems like cost of storage, loss of value, difficult to transfer from one place to other, etc.

So, in case of commodities, it was difficult for people to store their purchasing power.

3. Identify the system depicted in the image and explain two major drawbacks of this system in an economy.

Ans. The image depicts a barter system, where goods and services are directly exchanged for other goods and services without the use of money.

Two major drawbacks of a barter system are

(i) **Double Coincidence of Wants**

It is difficult for two individuals to have exactly what the other wants at the same time, making exchange inconvenient and inefficient.

(ii) **Lack of a Unit of Account**

Measuring the value of different goods and services becomes complex and subjective without a standard unit of measurement.

4. "Money is dynamic in nature." How?

Competency Based Que

Ans. Money is a dynamic factor because

(i) It has facilitated exchange beyond limits.

(ii) It has facilitated accumulation of wealth for the purpose of investment.

(iii) It has facilitated flow of capital from one place to other and from developed countries to less developed countries of the world.

So, we can say that, money is a dynamic factor because it helps economic stability and promotes the process of growth and development.

5. Identify the type of money used in the image and explain how it is created in the modern banking system.

Competency Based Que

Ans. The image shows the use of plastic money, specifically credit and debit cards, which facilitate cashless transactions. Debit cards are linked to bank accounts, allowing purchases to be made directly from available funds, while credit cards enable users to borrow money for purchases up to a specified limit, which must be repaid monthly. The modern banking system creates credit through following steps

(i) **Deposits and Loans**

Customers deposit money, which banks use to give loans.

(ii) **Multiplier Effect**

This lending and redepositing cycle increases the money supply.

Through this system, banks enable us to use plastic money, making transactions easier and cashless.

6. Elaborate the different classification of money.

Ans. Money can be classified as

(i) **Full-bodied Money**

It is the money whose value as commodity is equal to its value as money. e.g. Gold, silver.

(ii) **Credit Money**

It is that money whose value as money is more than the commodity value of the material which is used to make the money.

(iii) **Fiat Money**

It refers to money issued by the order or authority of the government, e.g. Notes and coins. They do not have intrinsic value like gold or silver coin.

(iv) **Fiduciary Money**
It refers to the money where acceptance is based on mutual trust between the payer and the payee. Drafts, cheques, bills of exchange, etc. are examples of fiduciary money.

7. Why can money be considered both a medium of exchange and a commodity? Competency Based Que

Ans. Money can be considered both a medium of exchange and a commodity because it has evolved from forms that held intrinsic value (like gold or silver) to forms that represent value based on government backing or societal trust.

(i) **As a Medium of Exchange**
Money facilitates transactions by providing a widely accepted method for trading goods and services. It eliminates the complexities of a barter system by creating a standard unit of account, which makes exchanging goods much simpler and more efficient.

(ii) **As a Commodity**
Historically, certain forms of money were commodities themselves, like gold, silver or other valuable items, which had intrinsic value. These materials were valued for their own properties (like durability, rarity and appeal) and people accepted them not only for transactions but also for their intrinsic worth.

In conclusion, money serves the dual roles of simplifying transactions and holding value.

8. "In the context of modern economies, money serves as a fundamental tool in facilitating various economic activities."
Discuss the primary functions of money and explain how they contribute to the smooth functioning of an economy. Competency Based Que

Ans. Money has overcome the problems under the barter system and thus, performs many functions.
All the functions that money performs, can be broadly classified as

(i) Primary functions
(ii) Secondary functions

Primary functions include basic functions of money, which it must perform in every country.
These are as follows

(i) **Medium of Exchange**
It means that money can be used to make payments for all the transactions of goods and services. It is an essential function of money which facilitates trade and helps in conducting transactions in an economy.
This function of money has removed the difficulty of lack of double coincidence of wants and inconveniences associated with the barter system.

(ii) **Measure of Value**
Money serves as a common denomination, expressing the value of goods and services. Money is also regarded as unit of account' as it helps in calculating relative prices of goods and services.
This function of money facilitates maintenance of business accounts, which would be otherwise impossible.

9. What is high powered money? NCERT

Ans. High powered money consist of currency held by the public and reserves of the commercial banks, which include vault cash (cash that a bank keeps in its vault for daily transactions) and bank's deposits with RBI.

10. How has money solved the problem of 'standard of deferred payment' found under barter?

Ans. Deferred payments means future payments. Money serves as the measure by which the value of future payments is regulated. In modern economic system, loans are generally given and taken and the repayment is generally postponed for a future date.
As with money, exact amount to be repaid can easily be calculated, money is therefore, used as a standard of deferred payments.
In barter system, it was difficult to return value in future in terms of goods of same quantity and quality.
Therefore, future payments regarding interest and loans became difficult. But money has solved this problem. Loans can be re-paid back in money and interest payments can also be made in money.

11. What is the function of money represented in the image? Briefly explain its importance in economic transactions. Competency Based Que

Ans. The image represents the store of value function of money. Gold coins, along with other precious metals, were historically used as money because they could retain their value over time.
This function is important because it allows individuals to save their wealth for future use without worrying about its value depreciating. This encourages investment and economic growth.

12. "In the present era of growth of monetary economy, near money assets have came into existence."

What do you understand by near money assets? Give examples. Competency Based Que

Ans. Near money assets refer to those financial assets which perform some of the functions of money like general acceptability, store of value, etc. however it is not as liquid as cash. e.g. Cheques, credit cards. Due to growing credit transactions, importance of these near money assets have increased.

13. What are the alternative definitions of money supply in India? NCERT

Ans. RBI publishes figures for four alternative measures of money supply, *viz*, M_1, M_2, M_3 and M_4.

They are defined as

(i) M_1 measure of money supply is also referred to as transaction money. It includes $M_1 = CU + DD + OD$

Where, CU is Currency (notes plus coins) held by the public, DD is net Demand Deposits held by commercial banks and OD is for Other Deposits.

(ii) M_2 Measure of Money Supply $= M_1$ + Savings Deposits with Post Office Savings Banks

(iii) M_3 Measure of Money Supply $= M_1$ + Net time Deposits of Commercial Banks

(iv) M_4 Measure of Money Supply $= M_3$ + Total Deposits with Post Office Savings Organisations (excluding National Savings Certificates)

14. Explain the difference between money and high powered money.

Ans. Differences between money and high powered money are

Basis	Money	High Powered Money
Meaning	Money consists of currency with public and demand deposits.	The high powered money consists of currency with public and cash reserves with commercial banks. It is also known as 'monetary base'.
Control	Controlled by both banks and central banks through lending and borrowing.	Directly controlled by the central bank, as they can increase or decrease this through monetary policy.
Formula	Money = CU + DD, where CU is the currency with the public and DD is the demand deposits.	High Powered Money = CU + R, where CU is the currency with the public and R is the cash reserves of banks. (reserves of commercial banks which include vault cash and bank's deposits with RBI).

15. India's money supply surge signals pandemic-related uncertainty, not growth. Heightened uncertainty in India caused by the coronavirus pandemic has led to a surge in currency in circulation as people hoard cash or park money in accessible deposits to safeguard themselves against salary cuts or job losses.

According to RBI data, India's M_3 money supply rose 6.7% in the first five months of this year compared with the same period last year, the highest growth in seven years. Currency in circulation, which measures money with the public and in banks has also surged.

A rise in money supply usually is seen as a leading indicator of growth in consumption and business investments, but the rise this time is unlikely to bolster either, analysts said.

"We suspect that the recent increase reflects higher cash withdrawals by depositors to meet needs during the lockdown period, until normalcy returns," said Radhika Rao, an economist at DBS Bank.

Source *Economic Times*

Mention the components of M_1. Will there be any increase in India's M_1 money supply? Is this rise in money supply good for economy? Give reason. Competency Based Que

Ans. M_1 is comprised of currency with public, demand deposits with bank and other deposits with RBI.

Yes, there is an increase in India's M_1 money supply as people are parking money in banks and with themselves to safeguard themselves. No, because this rise in money supply is for cash withdrawals to meet basic needs and not for business investments.

16. Study the following image.

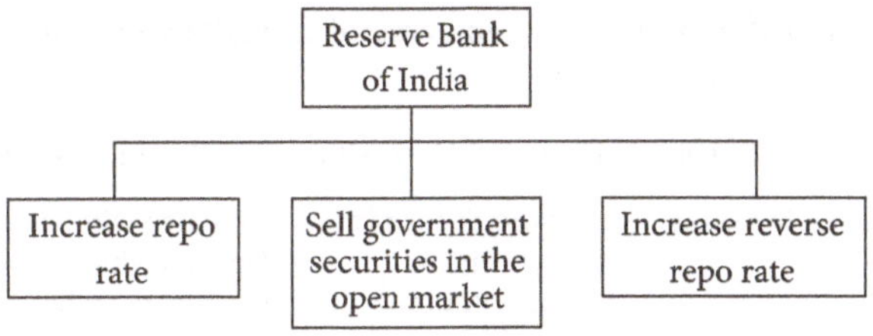

(i) Identify the indicated situation.

(ii) Explain any two steps which may be taken by RBI to correct the situation. CBSE 2024 C

Ans. (i) The situation represents inflation where the RBI uses contractionary monetary policy to reduce excess money supply in the economy.

(ii) Steps by RBI to correct the situation are

- **Increase Repo Rate**
  Makes borrowing costlier for banks, reducing money supply.
- **Sell Government Securities**
  Absorbs excess liquidity from the market.

17. Amit, a young professional, is considering opening a savings account in a bank. Describe to him the functions of a commercial bank and the benefits of having a savings account. Competency Based Que

Or **Explain the functions of a commercial bank.** NCERT

Ans. A commercial bank serves as a financial institution that offers various services to individuals, businesses and governments. Its primary functions include

(i) **Accepting Deposits**

Commercial banks accept deposits from individuals, businesses and other entities in various forms such as savings accounts, current accounts, fixed deposits, and recurring deposits.

(ii) **Providing Loans**

Commercial banks primarily lend money to individuals and businesses for various purposes, with interest charged on these loans accounting for a significant portion of a bank's revenue.

(iii) **Facilitating Payment Services**

Commercial banks provide efficient payment services like issuing checks, debit cards, credit cards and electronic funds transfers for individuals and businesses.

(iv) **Offering Investment Products**

Banks offer various investment products like mutual funds, stocks, bonds and retirement accounts to help customers achieve their financial goals over time.

The benefits of opening a savings account with a commercial bank are as follows

- Safety of funds
- Interest earnings

18. Differentiate between demand deposits and time deposits.

Ans.

Basis	Demand Deposits	Time Deposits
Meaning	Demand deposits are the deposits which can be withdrawn on demand at any point of time.	Time deposits are the deposits which cannot be withdrawn before a specified period of time.
Facility	These are chequable deposits, i.e. cheques can be drawn against such deposits.	These deposits are non-chequable, i.e. one cannot draw cheques against such deposits.
Time Period	A demand deposit has no fixed time period for its kind.	There is a fixed time period under term deposits.
Includes	(i) Current account deposits (ii) Savings account deposits	(i) Fixed deposits (ii) Recurring deposits

19. What is credit creation?

Ans. It refers to the creation of demand deposits with the commercial banks on the basis of their cash reserves or it means the creation of secondary deposits through initial deposits.

Through the process of credit creation commercial banks are able to create secondary deposits which exceeds the amount of initial deposits.

Credit creation can be ascertained by using the given formula

$$\text{Credit Creation} = \text{Initial Deposits} \times \frac{1}{\text{LRR}}$$

Where, LRR = Legal Reserve Ratio.

20. What is money multiplier? What determines the value of this multiplier? NCERT

Ans. Money multiplier measures the amount of money that the banks are able to create in the form of deposits with every unit of money, they keep in reserves.

It is calculated as

$$\text{Money Multiplier} = \frac{1}{\text{Legal Reserve Ratio}}$$

Legal Reserve Ratio (LRR) comprises of Cash Reserve Ratio (CRR) and Statutory Liquidity Ratio (SLR).

It can be said that LRR determines the value of multiplier.

21. Describe how the banking system's ability to create credit is impacted by an increase in the reserve deposit ratio using a numerical example.

Ans. The amount of credit created is given as

$$\text{Credit Creation} = \text{Initial Deposits} \times \frac{1}{\text{LRR}}$$

where LRR is the sum of CRR and SLR and is also referred to as reserve deposit ratio. It inversely affects the credit creation power of the banking system.

If reserve deposit ratio increases, the amount of credit created decreases and *vice-versa.*

The following numerical example will make it easy to understand

Let the amount of initial deposits be ₹ 10,000 and reserve deposit ratio be 20%. So, credit created will be

$$\text{Credit Creation} = 10{,}000 \times \frac{1}{20\%} = ₹\ 50{,}000$$

Now, the reserve deposit ratio falls to 10%.

So, now the credit created will be

$$\text{Credit Creation} = 10{,}000 \times \frac{1}{10\%} = ₹\ 1{,}00{,}000$$

So, we see that when reserve deposit ratio is reduced, the credit created increases.

22. Describe the role of the central bank in the 'bank of note issue'.

Ans. Central bank is the apex institution of a country which regulates the entire banking system. e.g. RBI in India. Central bank is considered as the bank of issue as, only central bank of the country has the authority to issue currency which gives it the monopoly power to change the supply of money in the economy according to the need. Also, it ensures uniformity in the currency issue and hence becomes easy to check fake frequency.

23. "In the 1990s, on the advice of Reserve Bank of India (RBI), the Government of India took a decision of hypothecation of gold reserves to different nations."

In the light of above statement, discuss briefly the role of Central Bank as banker, agent and advisor to the government. CBSE 2025; Competency Based Que

Or **Discuss the function of Central Bank as 'banker, agent and advisor' to the government.** All India 2020

Or **Explain the role of Central Bank as government's agent and advisor.** CBSE 2023

Ans. The Central Bank plays a crucial role as the banker, agent and advisor to the government. It helps in managing the financial transactions of the Central and State Governments, implements monetary policies and provides expert guidance on economic matters.

(i) **As a Banker**
The Central Bank maintains the government's accounts, provides short-term loans and advances, and manages public debt by issuing and redeeming government securities.

(ii) **As an Agent**
It carries out financial transactions on behalf of the government, such as buying and selling government securities in the open market. It also manages the issuance of new currency and foreign exchange reserves.

(iii) **As an Advisor**
It advises the government on monetary policy, inflation control, credit regulation and overall economic stability. The Central Bank provides recommendations to frame policies that ensure growth and financial stability in the economy.

24. Explain the function of Central Bank as 'banker's bank and supervisor'. CBSE 2024, 20

Or **Explain 'banker's bank' function of the Central Bank.**

Ans. Central Bank keeps the cash balances of commercial banks and issues loans to them on requirements, in the same manner as the commercial banks do for its customers.
A Central Bank has almost the same relation with the other commercial banks of the country that the commercial banks have with the common public.
That is why, the Central Bank is also called as bankers' bank. The Central Bank also supervises the working of the commercial banks. It grants licences and controls branch expansion, liquidity of assets, mergers and winding-ups of the banks.

25. State the role played by the Central Bank as the 'lender of last resort'. NCERT

Ans. It means that if a commercial bank fails to get financial accommodation from anywhere, it approaches the Central Bank as a last resort.

Central Bank advances loan to such banks against approved securities.

By offering loans to the commercial banks in situations of emergency, the Central Bank ensures that

(i) The banking system of the country does not suffer from any set back.
(ii) Money market remains stable.

26. Elaborate how does a Central Bank stabilise money supply through 'bank rate'. CBSE 2020

Or **Explain how 'bank rate' is helpful in controlling credit creation.**

Ans. The bank rate is the minimum rate at which the Central Bank of a country is prepared to give credit to the commercial banks.

The increase in bank rate increases the rate of interest and credit becomes dear. Accordingly, the demand for credit is reduced.

On the other hand, decrease in bank rate lowers the market rate of interest and credit becomes cheap.

Accordingly, demand for credit expands. The Central Bank adopts dear money policy when supply of credit needs to be reduced during periods of inflation. It adopts cheap money policy when credit needs to be expanded during deflation.

27. Illustrate how open market operations aid in limiting the creation of credit.

Ans. Under open market operations, RBI purchases or sells government securities to general public for the purpose of increasing or decreasing the stock of money in an economy. The purchase or sale of securities controls the money in the hands of public as they deposit or withdraw the money from commercial banks. Thus, money creation by commercial banks get affected.

Suppose, the Central Bank purchases securities of ₹ 1,000 from a bond holder by issuing a cheque. The seller of the bond deposits this cheque of ₹ 1,000 in his bank. The commercial bank credits the account of the seller by ₹ 1,000 and the deposits of the bank goes up by ₹ 1,000, which increases the credit creation capacity of the banks.

Thus, purchase of security increases the money creation of commercial banks and similarly, sale of securities decreases the credit creation of commercial banks.

Thus, the Central Bank controls the process of money creation by commercial banks by open market operations.

28. Explain the role of Cash Reserve Ratio in controlling credit creation.

Ans. Cash Reserve Ratio (CRR) is the fraction of total deposits that each commercial bank must keep with the Central Bank of the country, as a part of fractional reserve system. CRR is an important tool in controlling the credit creation in the country.

When the Central Bank wants to decrease the level of credit creation in the economy, it increases the CRR. As the CRR increases, the loanable deposits left with the commercial bank decreases.

This reduces the lending powers of the bank and as a result the process of credit creation falls.

If on the other hand, the Central Bank wants to increase the level of credit creation in the country, it lowers the CRR.

As the CRR decreases, the loanable deposits left with the commercial banks increases. This increases the lending powers of the banks and as a result the level of credit creation in the country rises.

29. Define reverse repo rate. Discuss briefly, how this instrument helps in controlling credit creation by commercial banks. **CBSE 2023**

Or

Explain the role of reverse repo rate in controlling money supply.

Ans. Reverse repo rate is the rate of interest at which commercial banks can deposit their surplus funds with the Central Bank, for a short period of time.

It is an important quantitative tool for controlling money supply in the economy. If the Central Bank wants to increase money supply in the economy, then, it reduces the reverse repo rate.

With fall in reverse repo rate the commercial banks reduce the deposits of surplus funds with the Central Bank, thereby increasing the money supply.

On the other hand, if the Central Bank wants to decrease money supply, then it increases the reverse repo rate. With rise in reverse repo rate, the commercial banks increase the deposits of surplus funds with the Central Bank, thereby decreasing the money supply. Thus, reverse repo rate plays an important role in controlling money supply.

30. "The Reserve Bank of India lowered the repo rate from 6% to 5.5%."

This policy change is likely to stimulate economic activity. Explain how the repo rate cut can achieve this? **Competency Based Que**

Ans. The Reserve Bank of India's decision to lower the repo rate from 6% to 5.5% aims to boost economic activity by reducing borrowing costs for banks.

The repo rate is the rate at which the central bank lends money to commercial banks. When this rate is lowered, it becomes cheaper for banks to borrow funds, allowing them to offer loans to businesses and consumers at lower interest rates.

With cheaper loans, businesses are more likely to borrow for investments, like expanding their operations, while consumers may find it more affordable to finance major purchases such as homes or cars.

This increase in lending can lead to higher levels of investment and consumption in the economy, which drives demand for goods and services and, ultimately, promotes economic growth.

31. What is the relationship between the variables shown in the graph?

Explain how the central bank can influence economic activity using this relationship. **Competency Based Que**

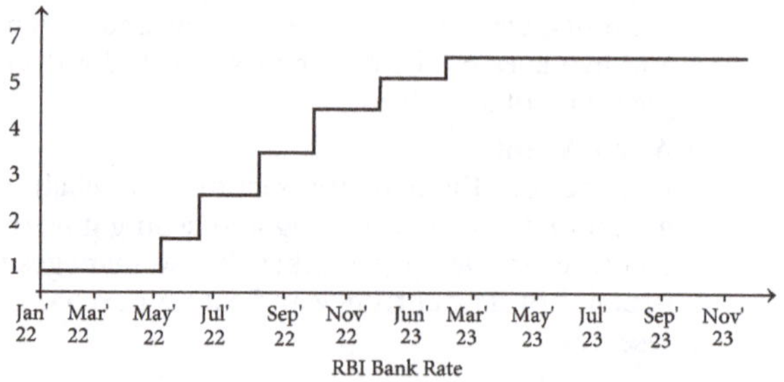

Source *https://www.ceicdata.com/en/india/bank-interest-rate/bank-rate*

Ans. The graph shows the relationship between interest rates and money supply. Generally, when interest rates increase, the money supply decreases and *vice-versa*.

The central bank can influence economic activity by adjusting interest rates. Lowering interest rates encourages borrowing and spending, stimulating economic growth, while raising interest rates can curb inflation and cool down an overheating economy.

32. Distinguish between 'qualitative and quantitative tools' of credit control as may be used by a central bank. **All India 2019**

Ans. Central bank uses different instrument to control money supply.

These tools can be broadly classified as

Basis	Quantitative Tools	Qualitative Tools
Meaning	These are those which directly impacts the quantity of money supply in the economy.	These are those which impacts the quality of money supply not volume.
Effectiveness	These tools are very effective to either increase or decrease money supply.	These are not much effective tool to control money supply.
Includes	(i) Bank rate (ii) Legal reserve ratio (iii) Open market operations (iv) Repo and reverse repo rate	(i) Margin requirement (ii) Moral suasion (iii) Selective credit control

Long Answer Type Questions

33. Define credit multiplier. What role does it play in determining the credit creation power of the banking system? Use a numerical illustration to explain. **Delhi 2019**

Ans. Money multiplier measures the amount of money that the banks are able to create in the form of deposits with every unit of money, they keep in reserves.

It is calculated as

$$\text{Money Multiplier} = \frac{1}{\text{Legal Reserve Ratio}}$$

Legal Reserve Ratio (LRR) comprises of Cash Reserve Ratio (CRR) and Statutory Liquidity Ratio (SLR). It can be said that LRR determines the value of multiplier.

Role of Credit Multiplier in determining the Credit Creation Power of the Banking System

The greater the credit multiplier, the more will be the credit creation power of the banking system and *vice-versa*.

The following numerical example will make this more clear

Let initial deposits be ₹ 10,000 and LRR be 10%. So, now,

$$\text{Money/Credit Multiplier} = \frac{1}{\text{LRR}} = \frac{1}{10\%} = 10$$

$$\text{Credit Creation} = \text{Initial Deposits} \times \text{Credit Multiplier} = 10{,}000 \times 10 = ₹\ 1{,}00{,}000$$

Now, let us assume that LRR falls to 5%.

So, now, Money/Credit Multiplier

$$= \frac{1}{\text{LRR}} = \frac{1}{5\%} = 20$$

$$\text{Credit Creation} = \text{Initial Deposits} \times \text{Credit Multiplier} = 10{,}000 \times 20 = ₹\ 2{,}00{,}000$$

So, we see that when credit multiplier increases, the level of credit creation also increases.

34. "The central bank is the cornerstone of a nation's financial stability." Critically analyse this statement, explaining the key functions of a central bank that contribute to economic stability. **Competency Based Que**

Or

"The Reserve Bank of India (RBI) performs the same function for the government as the commercial banks perform for the general public."

Discuss briefly any two such functions performed by the Central Bank for the Government of India. **CBSE 2024 C**

Ans. Central bank is an apex bank that controls and regulates the entire banking system of a country.

The various functions performed by the central bank are

(i) **Bank of Issuing Notes**
Central bank has monopoly rights of issuing notes. This is called the currency authority function of central banks. All notes issued by the central bank are unlimited legal tender in the country.

(ii) **Banker to the Government**
Central bank is a banker, agent, and financial adviser to the government. It manages the account of the government, it buys and sells the securities of the government and it frames policies to regulate the money market.

(iii) **Custodian of Foreign Currency**
The central bank maintains a minimum reserve of international currency all the time in order to meet emergency requirements of foreign exchange and overcome adverse requirements of deficit in the balance of payments.

(iv) **Lender of Last Resort**
The central bank also lends money to commercial banks. When the commercial banks are facing a liquidity crunch or any type of insolvency, the central bank is the last resort to provide loans against treasury bills, government securities and bills of exchange.

(v) **Maintains Cash Reserves of Commercial Banks**
The central bank takes care of the cash reserves of commercial banks. Commercial banks are required to keep a certain amount of public deposits as cash reserve, with the central bank.

(vi) **Control of Credit**
The central bank has power to regulate credit creation by commercial banks.

The credit creation depends upon the amount of deposits, cash reserves and rate of interest given by commercial banks. All these are directly or indirectly controlled by the central bank. Therefore, they have the power to control the amount of credit creation of commercial banks.

35. What are the instruments of monetary policy of RBI? NCERT

Ans. The following are the instruments of monetary policy of Reserve Bank of India (RBI)

(i) **Quantitative Instruments**

These instruments affect the overall supply of credit in the economy.

These are as follows

- **Bank Rate** The bank rate is the minimum rate at which the Central Bank of a country lends money to the commercial banks.
- **Open Market Operations** It refers to the sale and purchase of securities in open market by the Central Bank (RBI) on behalf of the government.
  By selling the securities, the Central Bank withdraws cash balances from the economy and by buying the securities, the Central Bank add to the cash balances in economy.
- **Cash Reserve Ratio** It refers to the minimum percentage of a commercial bank's total deposits required to be kept with the Central Bank.
- **Statutory Liquidity Ratio** Every bank is required to maintain a fixed percentage of its assets in the form of cash or other liquid assets, called SLR with itself. The major components of liquid assets are cash in hand, reserves with the Central Bank and government and unencumbered approved securities.
- **Repo Rate** It is the rate at which the Central Bank offers short-term loans to commercial banks by buying government securities in the open market.
- **Reverse Repo Rate** It is the rate of interest at which commercial banks can park their surplus funds with the Central Bank, for short period of time through purchase of government securities.

(ii) **Qualitative Instruments**

These instruments seek to influence the quality of credit in the economy.

These are as follows

- **Margin Requirements** Margin is the difference between the value of security offered for and the amount of loan sanctioned.
- **Rationing of Credit** It refers to fixation of credit quotas for different business activities.
- **Moral Suasion** The Central Bank is often empowered to issue directives to member banks. Such direct orders are in the form of directional control, prohibiting loans of particular type or giving advice to grant loan to priority sectors.

36. **(i) State any two components of M_1 measure of money supply.**

(ii) Elaborate any two instruments of credit control as exercised by Reserve Bank of India. Delhi 2019

(iii) Among all alternatives which is widely used measure of money supply?

Ans. (i) Component of M_1 measure of money supply are C = Currency held by the public. It includes both paper currency and coins.

DD = Demand deposits in the banks. Here we will not include the demand deposits of bank made in another bank i.e. interbank deposits are to be excluded.

(ii) Refer to Q.No. 35 of long answer type questions.

(iii) M_3 is widely used measure of money supply and also known as aggregate monetary resources.

37. Distinguish between central bank and commercial bank.

Ans. Differences between central bank and commercial bank are

Basis	Central Bank	Commercial Bank
Status	Central Bank is the banker of all the banks. It is an apex body.	Commercial banks operate under the control of Central Bank.
Credit Flow	It controls the flow of credit within the economy.	It creates credit within the economy.
Objective	The objective of Central Bank is social welfare.	The objective of commercial banks is profit maximisation.
Banker	It is the banker to the government and banks.	It is the banker of the common public.
Custody of Foreign Exchange	It is the custodian of nation's foreign reserve.	It is not the custodian of foreign reserve.
Currency Issue	It has the authority to issue currency.	It has no authority to issue currency.
Function	It acts as an advisor to the government and enforces monetary policy regulations.	It does not have the right to give advise to the government. It has to follow the monetary policy guidelines laid down by Central Bank.

38. **"Reserve ratio and credit creation are inversely related." Do you agree with given statement? Justify your answer.** CBSE SQP 2023; Competency Based Que

Ans. Yes, I agree with the given statement that reserve ratio and credit creation are inversely related. The reserve ratio is the portion of deposits that commercial banks are required to hold in reserve, while credit creation is the process by which commercial banks create credit by making loans to customers.

The relationship between reserve ratio and credit creation can be explained by the following example

Let's say that the Reserve Bank of India (RBI) sets the reserve ratio at 10%.

This means that commercial banks are required to hold 10% of their deposits in reserve and can use the remaining 90% for lending to customers.

Assuming that the total deposits in the banking system are ₹ 1,000 crores, the commercial banks would be required to hold reserves of ₹ 100 crores (10% of total deposits) and can lend the remaining ₹ 900 crores.

If the RBI decides to increase the reserve ratio to 20%, the commercial banks would be required to hold reserves of ₹ 200 crores (20% of total deposits) and can lend only ₹ 800 crores. This means that the credit creation capacity of the commercial banks has been reduced.

On the other hand, if the RBI decides to decrease the reserve ratio to 5%, the commercial banks would be required to hold reserves of ₹ 50 crores (5% of total deposits) and can lend ₹ 950 crores. This means that the credit creation capacity of the commercial banks has been increased.

Thus, we can see that an increase in the reserve ratio reduces the credit creation capacity of the commercial banks, while a decrease in the reserve ratio increases the credit creation capacity.

This is because a higher reserve ratio means that commercial banks have less money available for lending, while a lower reserve ratio means that they have more money available for lending. Therefore, we can conclude that the reserve ratio and credit creation are inversely related.

39. ***Economic Slowdown*** **The Indian economy is experiencing a slowdown, with GDP growth falling below 5%. Inflation is also declining, but remains above the central bank's target of 4%. Unemployment is rising, particularly among young people.**

(i) Analyse the role of the Reserve Bank of India (RBI) in addressing this situation. Discuss any three monetary policy tools it can use (e.g. Repo rate, CRR) and their potential impact on economic performance.

(ii) What are the challenges that RBI faces in managing the trade-off between inflation and growth? Competency Based Que

Ans. (i) The Reserve Bank of India (RBI) plays a crucial role in addressing economic slowdowns by formulating and implementing monetary policies aimed at stabilising the economy. In the current scenario, where GDP growth is below 5% and inflation remains above the central bank's target of 4%, the RBI faces the challenge of balancing growth and price stability.

The RBI can use a variety of tools to address the economic slowdown.

- Lowering the repo rate can make borrowing cheaper for businesses and individuals, stimulating investment and consumption.
- Lowering the reverse repo rate encourages banks to lend more, thus boosting economic activity.
- Reducing the CRR can also increase the amount of money available for lending by commercial banks.

(ii) The RBI faces a trade-off between controlling inflation and promoting economic growth. Lowering interest rates can boost growth but may also lead to higher inflation. Conversely, raising interest rates can fight inflation but may slow down the economy.

In conclusion, the RBI faces a complex task in managing the trade-off between inflation and growth during an economic slowdown.

That is why central bank carefully calibrate its monetary policy tools while navigating various challenges to achieve price stability and sustainable economic growth.

40. **As societies developed from hunters and gatherers, the material needs of human beings increased – to build a house, wear clothes, make weapons and implements, etc. Since these needs could not be produced individually, people had to purchase them from others. These purchases, for example, were paid initially by barter – a leather skin cloak for a spear. As barter had its limits – how many cloaks for a spear – barter got standardised in terms of metals or cowrie shells. Now people knew the value of both the cloak and the spear in terms of bronze or cowrie shells.**

This was still barter, as both bronze and shells had intrinsic value (shells were desired for their beauty). This system evolved over time into metal currencies. Gold and silver coinage were the offshoot of this system where they had features of barter (both gold and silver had intrinsic value) as well as money (they were standardised representation of value).

In respect of money two facts emerge historically

- **Money has taken the form of either commodities (which have intrinsic value) or in terms of debt instruments.**
- **Money is usually issued by a sovereign (or a Central Bank as its representative).**

In modern economies, currency is a form of money that is issued exclusively by some competent authority (Central Bank). It is a liability of the issuing Central Bank and an asset of the holding public. Currency is usually issued in paper (or polymer) form, but the form of currency is not its defining characteristic.

In the recent past, the Reserve Bank of India, issued Central Bank Digital Currency (CBDC). A CBDC is the currency issued by a Central Bank in a digital form. It serves all the purposes of a paper currency in a different form.

The introduction of CBDC has the potential to provide significant benefits, such as reduced dependency on cash, lower transaction costs, reduced settlement risk. Introduction of CBDC would possibly lead to a more robust, efficient, trusted, regulated payments option. There are associated risks such as cyber-attacks and technology preparedness, but they need to be carefully evaluated against the potential benefits.

Source *https://website.rbi.org.in/web/rbi/-/speeches-interview/central-bank-digital-currency-is-this-the-future-of-money-1111 (adapted and modified)*

On the basis of the given text and common understanding, answer the following questions

(i) "Over the centuries, money has evolved in various forms."
In the light of the given statement, state and discuss briefly any two forms of money.

(ii) "Various economists have formed a strong opinion that, in the modern times digital currency (like CBDC) is quite essential. However, it comes with its own benefits and potential risks."
Do you agree with the given statement, giving valid arguments in support of your answer.

CBSE SQP 2025; Competency Based Que

Ans. (i) Money has undergone significant evolution over centuries. Two prominent forms of money include

- **Commodity Money** Commodity money refers to items that have intrinsic value and are used as a medium of exchange. Examples include metals like gold and silver or cowrie shells, which were widely accepted due to their inherent value. In ancient times, these items served both as a measure of value and a medium of exchange, but they posed challenges like divisibility and portability.
- **Fiat Money** Fiat money has no intrinsic value but is declared as legal tender by a government or central authority. Its value is derived from public trust in the issuing authority, such as the central bank.

(ii) I agree with the statement that digital currency, such as the Central Bank Digital Currency (CBDC), is essential in modern economies, but it comes with both benefits and risks.

Benefits

- **Reduced Dependency on Cash** CBDCs offer an efficient alternative to physical cash, reducing production and handling costs. It also lowers the risks associated with cash storage and transport.
- **Improved Transaction Efficiency** Digital currencies enable faster and cheer transactions with lower settlement risks. They are particularly advantageous for cross-border payments, which often involve high costs and delays.

Risks

- **Cyber Security Concerns** CBDCs are vulnerable to cyber attacks, hacking and fraud. The Central Bank must ensure robust technological systems to mitigate these risks.
- **Technology Preparedness** Developing countries may face challenges in implementing CBDCs due to inadequate technological infrastructure and digital literacy among the population.

In conclusion, while CBDCs have significant potential to revolutionise the monetary system, the associated risks must be carefully addressed to maximise their benefits. Governments and central banks need to ensure a secure and efficient implementation.

SELF ASSESSMENT TEST

Objective Type Questions

1. Which of the following is showing problem of perishability involved in barter exchange system?
   (a) Lack of double coincidence of wants
   (b) Lack of common measure of value
   (c) Lack of store of value
   (d) All of the above

2. The money backed by order or authority of the government and do not have instrinsic value like gold and silver coins are called
   (a) legal tender money
   (b) credit money
   (c) high powered money
   (d) fiduciary money

3. Which of the following functions is not a primary function of money?
   (a) Medium of exchange (b) Store of value
   (c) Unit of account (d) Transfer of wealth

4. The term 'broad money' refers to
   (a) M_1 (b) M_2 (c) M_3 (d) M_0

5. Which of the following is an example of near money?
   (a) Demand deposits (b) Fixed deposits
   (c) Coins and currency (d) Credit cards

6. When the Reserve Bank of India wants to reduce the money supply in the economy, it may
   (a) reduce the cash reserve ratio
   (b) increase the repo rate
   (c) lower the statutory liquidity ratio
   (d) purchase government securities

7. Which of the following statements is/are correct?
   I. The capacity of banks to create credit depends only on LRR.
   II. SLR is component of LRR which is to be kept with the bank themselves.

   Codes
   (a) Only I (b) Only II
   (c) Both I and II (d) None of these

Answers 1. (c) 2. (a) 3. (d) 4. (c) 5. (b) 6. (b) 7. (b)

Short Answer Type Questions

8. "Indian paper currency is inconvertible." Discuss.
9. Define fiduciary money and explain its significance in the context of the modern economy.
10. "While commercial banks primarily accept deposits and provide loans, they also engage in services like investment services, payment processing and financial consulting."
    In light of statement, explain the other functions of commercial banks that extend beyond their primary roles.
11. Differentiate between 'demand deposits' and 'time deposits' and provide examples of each.
12. What is the role of repo rate in controlling the money supply?
13. "In its recent quarterly report, the central bank urged banks to exercise caution in lending to sectors with high default rates. The governor highlighted the importance of prioritising lending to sectors that contribute to long-term economic stability and sustainable growth."
    Identify and explain the measure the central bank is using to control credit in this context.

Long Answer Type Questions

14. "In a recent article discussing the banking sector, it was reported that commercial banks significantly contribute to the economy by creating credit through the lending process, effectively multiplying the initial deposits they receive."
    Do you agree with the given statement? Give valid arguments and example in support of your answer.
15. Explain the functions of central bank.
16. What are the instruments of monetary policy of RBI? Explain them briefly.

04
CHAPTER

We study Aggregate Demand (AD) and Aggregate Supply (AS) to understand the overall functioning of an economy and how factors like inflation, unemployment and economic growth are interrelated.

Aggregate Demand and Supply & Other Related Concepts

YOUR STUDY GOALS

4.1 Concept of Aggregate Demand (AD)
4.2 Concept of Aggregate Supply (AS)
4.3 Consumption Function (Propensity to Consume)
4.4 Saving Function (Propensity to Save)
4.5 Concept of Investment Multiplier

YOUR PRACTICE GOAL

- Objective Questions (77 Qs ; MCQs, A-R, Statements, Matching, Concept Identification)
- Subjective Questions (21 SAs, 11 LAs)
- 36 Numerical Questions
- Self Assessment Test (6 MCQs, 5 SAs, 2 LAs, 4 Numerical)

4.1 Concept of Aggregate Demand (AD)

Aggregate demand is the value of total expenditure that people plan to spend on all goods and services in an economy at a given level of income during a fiscal year.

The following points related to the concept of 'aggregate demand' should be kept in mind

- It is different from market demand.
- It is the amount that people wish or plan to spend on purchase of goods and services during a fiscal year.
- It is measured in terms of money spent.
- It is a flow concept.
- There is positive and direct relationship with the level of income and aggregate demand corresponding to it.
- There exists a positive and direct relationship with the level of employment and aggregate demand corresponding to it.

Components of Aggregate Demand

1. **Household Consumption Demand or Expenditure** (C)
   - It refers to the total planned expenditure to be incurred by all households on purchase of goods and services. e.g. Households demand for food, clothing, housing, etc.

- It is also known as private consumption expenditure.
- It is determined by the level of disposable income in the economy, i.e.
  ↑ Level of disposable income → ↑ Private consumption expenditure.

2. **Investment Expenditure by Firms** (I)
   - It refers to the planned expenditure by private entrepreneurs on creation of new capital assets like machines, buildings and inventory.
   - It is also known as private investment expenditure.
   - Investment expenditure can be induced or autonomous.

Basis \ Type	Induced Investment	Autonomous Investment
Definition	It is positively related to the level of income and profitability in an economy.	It is an investment which is not influenced by expected profitability or level of income.
Motive	The motive behind induced investment is profit. It means that it depends on profit expectations.	The motive behind autonomous investment is social welfare.
Graph	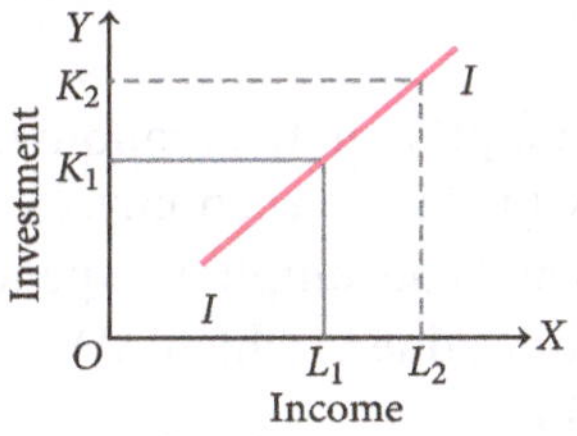 **Induced Investment**	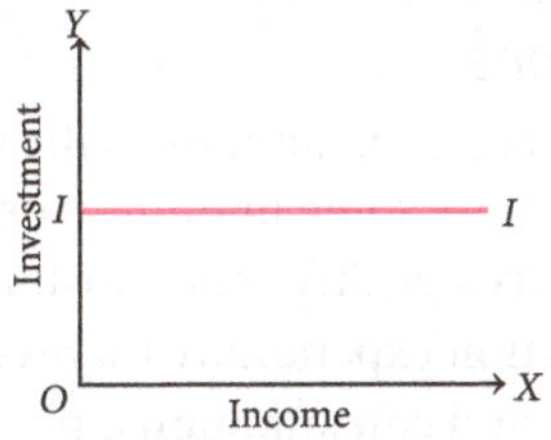 **Autonomous Investment**

Note Investment is an addition to capital stock. The relationship between investment demand and rate of interest is called **investment demand function**. Higher the market rate of interest, lower is the investment expenditure as rate of interest is considered as cost of borrowings.

3. **Government Expenditure** (G)
   - It refers to government's total planned expenditure on purchase of consumer and capital goods to fulfill the common needs of the society.
   - This includes provision for schools, transport, hospitals, roads, parks, etc.

4. **Net Export** (X – M)
   - It is defined as the difference between the demand for goods produced within the domestic country by foreign countries and domestic country's demand for goods produced in foreign countries.
   - It depends upon foreign exchange rate, terms of trade, trade policy, etc.

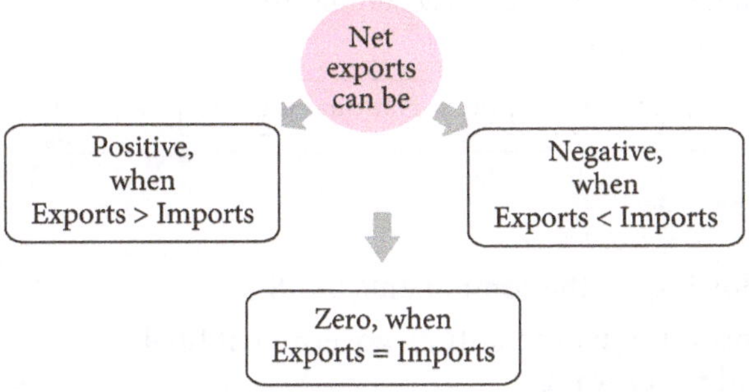

Sectors of an Economy and Aggregate Demand

- In a two sector economy, comprising of households and firms, AD $= C + I$
- In a three sector economy, comprising of households, firms and governments, AD $= C + I + G$
- In a four sector economy, comprising of households, firms, government and external sector, AD $= C + I + G + X - M$

Aggregate Demand in Two Sector Economy

Two sector economic model is a simple closed economic set-up where it is assumed that there are only two sectors in an economy, i.e. households and firms.

$$AD = C + I$$

The concept, using an imaginary aggregate demand schedule of a two sector economy and graph are given below

Income (Y)	Consumption (C)	Investment (I)	Aggregate Demand (C + I)
0	100	100	200
200	200	100	300
400	300	100	400
600	400	100	500
800	500	100	600
1,000	600	100	700

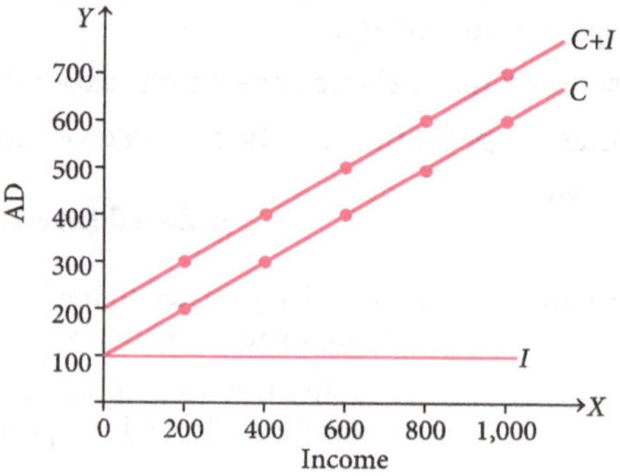

Observations

- Autonomous consumption is the minimum level of consumption in the economy, even when income is zero. It is so because some minimum expenditure is always essential in an economy.
- There exists a positive relationship between income level and consumption expenditure in the economy.
- Consumption expenditure increases with increase in income, due to which AD curve slopes upwards.
- AD curve and consumption curve run parallel to each other.
- At higher level of income (Y), percentage increase in expenditure is often less than the percentage increase in income, as people are now able to save a part of their income.

4.2 Concept of Aggregate Supply (AS)

Aggregate supply is the money value of the final goods and services that the firms are willing to supply in an economy during one year.

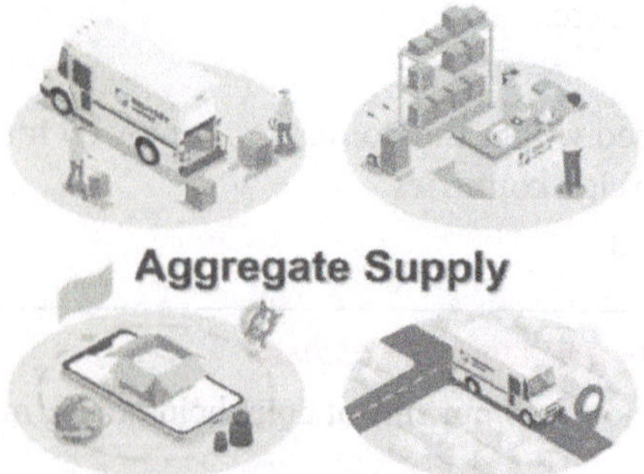

Understanding 'Aggregate Supply'

- It is the planned or desired production and not the actual production.
- It implies flow of goods and services or flow of income in an economy during a fiscal or accounting year.
- It is also a flow concept.

Aggregate Supply = National Income

Components of Aggregate Supply (AS)

Income generated is either consumed or saved. So, accordingly, following are the components of AS

1. **Consumption Expenditure** (C) It is the total of private final consumption expenditure, government final consumption expenditure, gross domestic capital formation and net exports.
2. **Savings** (S) It constitutes the part of income that is not consumed.

$$AS = Y = C + S$$

Did You Know

Consumption expenditure is same as the expenditure method of national income

The table reflects consumption expenditure's significant role in GDP calculation using the expenditure method, showing how it contributes to national income. Year-wise trends (2021-24) illustrate changes in GDP driven by consumption spending, emphasising its critical impact.

Share in GDP (%)	**2021-22** (2nd RE)	**2022-23** (2nd RE)	**2023-24** (2nd RE)
Private Final Consumption Expenditure (PFCE)	58.1	58.0	55.6
Government Final Consumption Expenditure (GFCE)	9.9	10.0	9.6
Gross Fixed Capital Formation (GFCF)	33.4	33.3	34.1
Changes in Stock (CIS)	1.1	1.1	1.1
Valuables	1.9	1.4	1.5
Exports	22.6	23.9	22.6
Imports	23.6	24.4	25.1
Discrepancies	(–) 3.3	(–) 3.4	0.7
GDP	100.0	100.0	100.0

Source *Second Advance Estimates of National Income and Expenditure Components of GDP, 2023-24 (at 2011-12 Prices)*

Aggregate Supply in a Two Sector Economy

The concept of aggregate supply using a schedule of a two sector economy and graph are given below

Income (*Y*)	**Consumption** (*C*)	**Saving** (*S*)	**Aggregate Supply** (*C* + *S*)
0	80	– 80	0
200	240	– 40	200
400	400	0	400
600	560	40	600
800	720	80	800
1,000	880	120	1,000

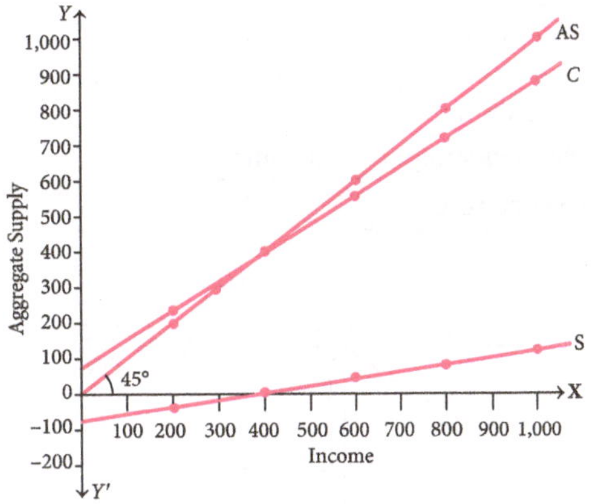

AS is presented by 45° line from the origin
⇒ AS = Y

Observations

- When income is zero, aggregate supply is also zero.
- When income is zero, consumption is not zero and savings are negative, also referred to as 'dissavings'.
- Consumption curve originates from positive coordinate of Y-axis and slopes upward.
- Saving curve originates from negative coordinate of Y-axis signifying dissavings at zero level of income.
- AS starts at the origin and slopes upward forming a 45° angle, based on the assumption of excess capacity in the economy.
- Due to the excess capacity in the economy, AS increases in proportion to AD.

4.3 Consumption Function (Propensity to Consume)

The relationship between the consumption expenditure and income is known as consumption function (propensity to consume). It is expressed as

$$C = f(Y)$$

Where, C = Consumption expenditure, Y = Income and
$C = f(Y)$ denotes that consumption expenditure is a function of income.

The algebraic expression of consumption function (propensity to consume) is

$$C = \bar{c} + bY$$

Where,

C = Consumption expenditure; $\bar{c}$ = Autonomous consumption, i.e. consumption at zero level of income

b = Marginal propensity to consume; Y = Disposable income, i.e. income after tax

Types of Propensity to Consume

Basis\Type	Average Propensity to Consume (APC)	Marginal Propensity to Consume (MPC)
Meaning	The ratio between the total consumption expenditure and total income at a given level of income, is called average propensity to consume.	The ratio between the change in consumption expenditure (ΔC) and the change in income (ΔY) is called marginal propensity to consume.
Formula	It represents the fraction of total income which is consumed i.e. $APC = C/Y$.	It refers to the fraction of changed income which is consumed. i.e. $MPC = \Delta C / \Delta Y$
Observation	APC > 1, when consumption > income. APC =1, when consumption = income. This is referred to as 'break-even point'. APC < 1, when consumption < income.	MPC =1, signify entire additional income is spent. MPC = 0, signify entire additional income is saved.
Value	APC can never be zero.	MPC lies between 0 to 1.
Graph		

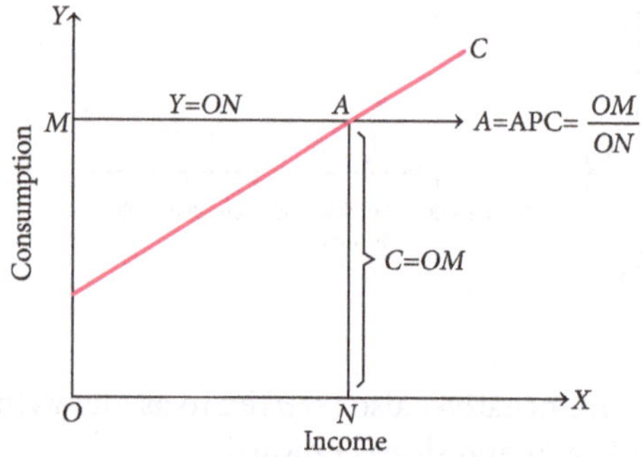

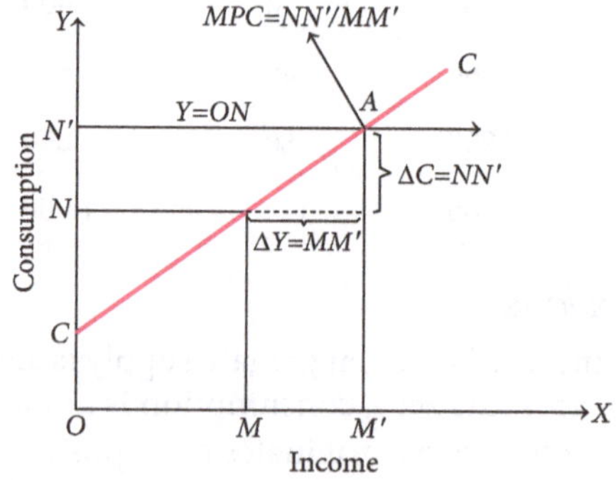

Explanation of consumption function with the help of an imaginary schedule and graph. It also summarises the effect of ΔY and ΔC on APC and MPC

Income (Y)	Consumption (C)	APC (C/Y)	ΔC	ΔY	MPC ($\Delta C/\Delta Y$)
0	300	—	—	—	—
200	350	1.75	50	200	0.25
400	400	1	50	200	0.25
600	450	0.75	50	200	0.25
800	500	0.625	50	200	0.25
1,000	550	0.55	50	200	0.25

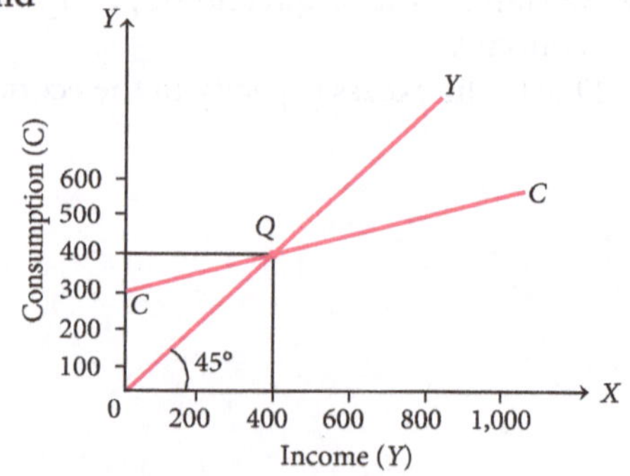

Observations from Consumption Curve

- *CC* is the consumption function, showing the behaviour of *C* with respect to *Y*.
- *CC* is a linear function.
- Consumption curve always starts above origin. There is minimum level of consumption called autonomous consumption ($\bar{c}$).
- There is positive relation between *Y* and *C*, i.e. as $Y \uparrow \rightarrow C \uparrow$.
- *CC* has a positive slope indicating rise in consumption with rise in income.
- The rate of increase in *C* often trails behind the rate of increase in *Y*.
- When income is less than consumption, the gap is covered by dissaving.
- Break-even point: when $C = Y$.

> **Point to Remember**
>
> Slope of consumption function is calculated by MPC, not by using APC

4.4 Saving Function (Propensity to Save)

Saving is the excess income which is left with the consumer after doing all the consumption expenditure.

$$S = Y - C$$

The relationship between savings and income is known as saving function. It is expressed as

$$S = f(Y)$$

Where, S = Saving, Y = Income and $S = f(Y)$ denotes that savings are a function of income.
The algebraic expression of saving function (propensity to save) is

$$S = (-)\bar{s} + sY$$

Where S = Saving ; $\bar{s}$ = Autonomous saving, i.e. level of saving when income is zero
s = Marginal Propensity to Save (MPS) ; Y = Disposable income

Types of Propensity to Save

Basis \ Type	**Average Propensity to Save** (APS)	**Marginal Propensity to Save** (MPS)
Meaning	The ratio between Aggregate Saving (*S*) and Aggregate Income (*Y*) is called Average Propensity to Save (APS).	The ratio between change in saving (Δ*S*) and change in income (Δ*Y*) is called Marginal Propensity to Save (MPS).
Formula	It refers to the fraction of total income which is saved, i.e. APS = *S*/*Y*.	It refers to the fraction of changed income which is saved i.e. MPS= Δ*S*/Δ*Y*.
Observation	APS increase with increase in income. APS can be negative when there are dissavings. APS can be zero when whole income is consumed.	MPS = 1, If entire additional income is saved. MPS = 0, If entire additional income is consumed.
Value	APS can be less than one.	MPS lies between 0 to 1.

Graph

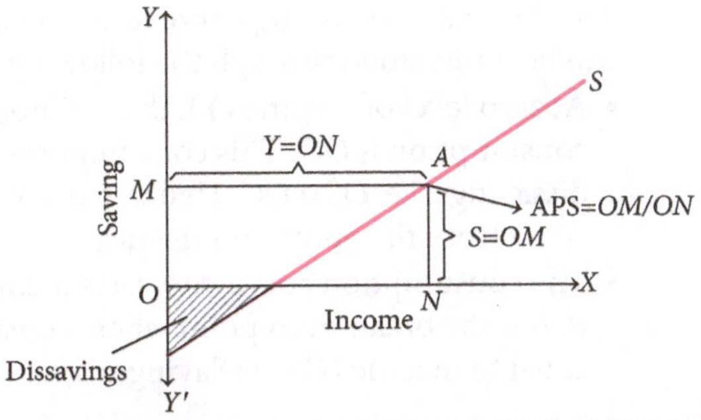

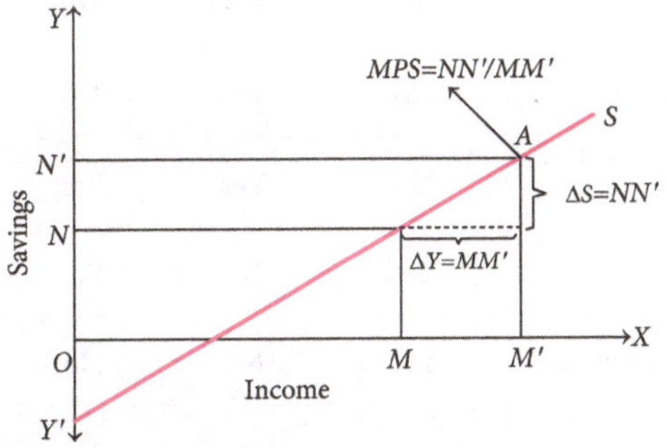

Explanation of saving function with the help of an imaginary schedule and graph. It also summarises the effect of ΔY and ΔS on APS and MPS

Income (Y)	Consumption (C)	Saving (S)	APS (S/Y)	ΔS	ΔY	MPS ($\Delta S/\Delta Y$)
0	300	–300	—	—	—	—
200	350	–150	–0.75	150	200	0.75
400	400	0	0	150	200	0.75
600	450	150	0.25	150	200	0.75
800	500	300	0.375	150	200	0.75
1,000	550	450	0.45	150	200	0.75
1,200	600	600	0.50	150	200	0.75

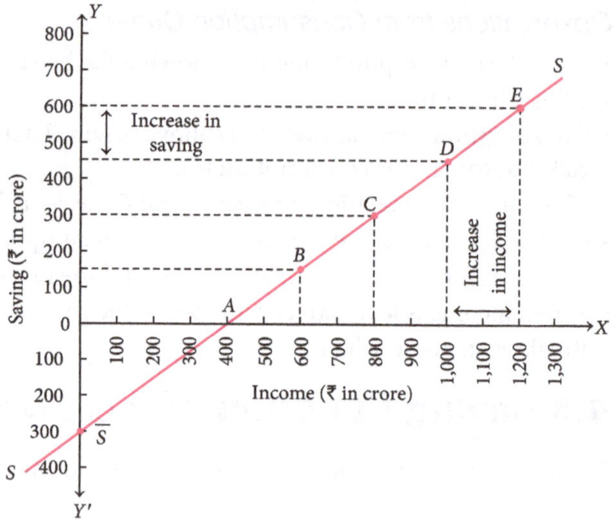

Observations from Saving Curve

- SS is the saving function, showing the behaviour of S with respect to Y.
- Saving curve start from point $\bar{S}$ on Y-axis. S is negative, when $C > Y$.
- The saving function is linear.
- Autonomous savings ($\bar{s}$) is equal to the intercept made by the savings function on the negative coordinate of Y-axis and value of MPS (s) is the slope of saving function.
- SS has a positive slope, indicating positive relationship between saving and income.
- Break-even point: when $C = Y$, $S = 0$.
- After break-even point, saving is positive.

Point to Remember

Slope of saving function is calculated by MPS, not by using APS.

Relation between APC and APS

$\text{APC} = \frac{C}{Y}$; $\text{APS} = \frac{S}{Y}$; The sum of APC and APS = 1

As we know that, $Y = C + S$

So, $\text{APC} + \text{APS} = \left[\frac{C}{Y} + \frac{S}{Y}\right] = \frac{C+S}{Y} = \frac{Y}{Y} = 1$

or $\text{APC} + \text{APS} = 1$; $\text{APC} = 1 - \text{APS}$

$\text{APS} = 1 - \text{APC}$

Relation between MPC and MPS

$\text{MPC} = \frac{\Delta C}{\Delta Y}$; $\text{MPS} = \frac{\Delta S}{\Delta Y}$; The sum of MPC and MPS = 1

As we know that, $\Delta Y = \Delta C + \Delta S$

So, $\text{MPC} + \text{MPS} = \left[\frac{\Delta C}{\Delta Y} + \frac{\Delta S}{\Delta Y}\right] = \frac{\Delta C + \Delta S}{\Delta Y} = \frac{\Delta Y}{\Delta Y} = 1$

or $\text{MPC} + \text{MPS} = 1$; $\text{MPC} = 1 - \text{MPS}$

$\text{MPS} = 1 - \text{MPC}$

Values of APC, APS, MPC and MPS at a Glance

Value	APC	APS	MPC	MPS
Negative	No	Yes	No	No
Zero	No	Yes	Yes	Yes
One	Yes	No	Yes	Yes
More than one	Yes	No	No	No

Derivation of Saving Curve from Consumption Curve

The derivation of saving curve from consumption curve can be understood through the following points

- At zero level of income (Y), the autonomous consumption is $O\bar{C}$. This consumption is equal to dissavings, i.e. $O\bar{S} = O\bar{C}$. Hence, the saving curve starts from the point $\bar{s}$ on the negative Y-axis.
- The consumption curve intersects income line at point B. B is the break-even point where consumption is equal to income ($C = Y$; Saving = 0).

- The consumption is less than income beyond point E. It means the excess income after consumption is saved and hence, the saving curve moves toward positive direction above X-axis with the increase in the level of income.

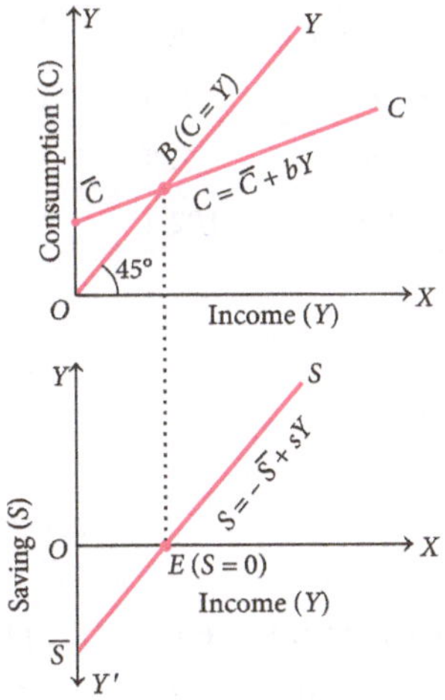

Derivation of Consumption Curve from Saving Curve

The derivation of consumption curve from saving curve can be understood through the following points

- Autonomous savings is equal to $-O\bar{S}$. If we take the vertical distance between O and $-\bar{S}$, then $-O\bar{S} = O\bar{C}$. Thus, $\bar{C}$ becomes the starting point of consumption curve.
- The savings curve intersects income line at point E. E is the break-even point, where $C = Y$.
- Draw a straight line from point O which cuts the 45° income curve at point B. The consumption curve intersects income curve at point B.
  Also, at this point, saving is equal to zero, thus it is known as **break-even point**. From here, consumption curve slopes upward with increase in income.

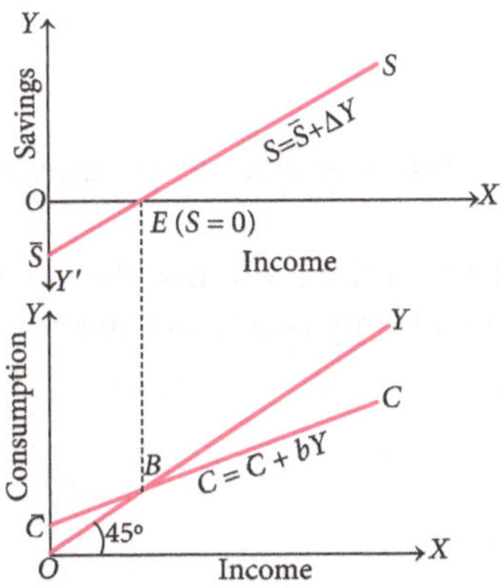

4.5 Concept of Investment Multiplier

Investment multiplier or output multiplier refers to the increase in the aggregate income of the economy as a result of an increase in the investments in an economy.

Keynes believed that an initial increment in investment increases the final income by many times. Thus, multiplier expresses the relationship between these two components.

It is measured as the ratio between change in output/income and change in investment, i.e.

$$K = \frac{\Delta Y}{\Delta I}$$

Where, K = Multiplier

ΔY = Change in output/income

ΔI = Change in investment

The multiplier can be shown graphically using AD and AS approach.

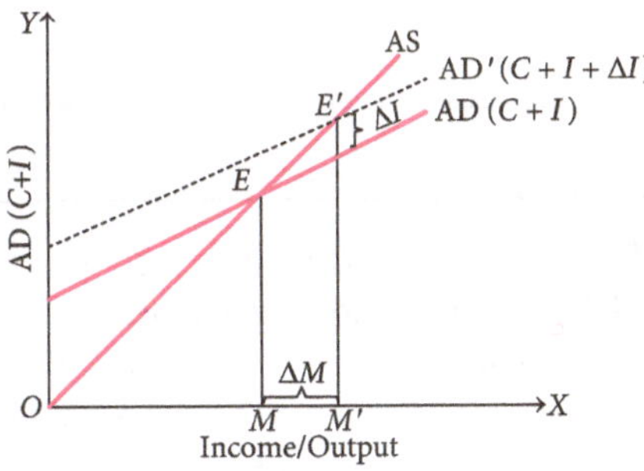

In the above graph, investment changes by ΔI, income change by ΔM.

Mechanism of Multiplier

The multiplier works on the assumption that one person's expenditure is another person's income.

Given example will help us to understand this

- Government invests ₹ 1,000 crore in an expressway, generating an initial income of ₹ 1,000 crore in 1st round.
- With MPC = 0.80, 80% (₹ 800 crore) is spent on consumption, saving the remaining amount. This increases income in the second round by ₹ 800 crore.
- In the next round, 80% of ₹ 800 crore (₹ 640 crore) is spent, further increasing income by ₹ 640 crore.

This multiplier process will go on. It is shown in the table below

Mechanism of Multiplier

Round	Increase in Investment (ΔI)	Increase in Income (ΔY)	Increase in Expenditure (ΔC)	Increase in Savings (ΔS)
1st	1,000	1,000	800 (1,000 × 0.8)	200
2nd	–	800	640 (800 × 0.8)	160
3rd	–	640	512 (640 × 0.8)	128
4th	–	512	409.6 (512 × 0.8)	102.4
5th	–	409.6	–	–
6th	–	–	–	–
Total	1,000	5,000	4,000	1,000

Note The maximum value of multiplier can be infinity while its minimum value is 1.

Relationship of Investment Multiplier with MPC and MPS

Relationship between Investment Multiplier and MPC	Relationship between Investment Multiplier and MPS
There is a direct relationship between investment multiplier and MPC.	There is an inverse relationship between investment multiplier and MPS.
Higher the value of MPC, higher the multiplier and *vice-versa.*	Higher the value of MPS, lower the multiplier and *vice-versa.*
Multiplier is estimated using the equation $K = \frac{1}{1 - \text{MPC}}$	Multiplier is estimated using the equation $K = \frac{1}{1 - \text{MPC}}$ *or* $\frac{1}{\text{MPS}}$ as $1 - \text{MPC} = \text{MPS}$
This equation establishes a direct relationship between MPC and *K*.	This equation establishes an inverse relationship between MPS and *K*.

Derivation of Relationship between MPC and K

It is derived in the following manner

We know that, $Y = C + I$

So, $\Delta Y = \Delta C + \Delta I$

Dividing both sides by ΔY, we will get

$$\frac{\Delta Y}{\Delta Y} = \frac{\Delta C}{\Delta Y} + \frac{\Delta I}{\Delta Y} \Rightarrow 1 = \text{MPC} + \frac{1}{K} \left[\frac{\Delta Y}{\Delta Y} = 1; \frac{\Delta C}{\Delta Y} = \text{MPC}; \frac{\Delta I}{\Delta Y} = \frac{1}{K}\right]$$

$$\Rightarrow K = \frac{1}{1 - \text{MPC}}$$

Point to Remember

Change in GDP = Multiplier × Initial Change in Spending

Ex-ante and Ex-post Saving and Investment

Ex-ante and ex-post are two important concepts that help in comparing the planned or estimated values and the actual value of the variables like savings and investment.

Ex-ante refers to the anticipated or planned or estimated value of the variables that the economy plans to spend. On the other hand, ex-post is the actual or realised value of the variables that the economy is actually able to spend.

Aspects of Savings and Investments

Ex-ante Savings	Ex-post Savings	Ex-ante Investment	Ex-post Investment
It refers to the desired savings or planned savings by households during the period of one year.	It refers to the actual savings in the economy from the given level of income during the period of one year.	It refers to the desired investment or planned investment by firms during the period of one year.	It refers to the actual investment in the economy during the period of one year.
It is given by saving function.	It is the sum total of planned as well as unplanned savings.	It is determined by the relation between investment demand and rate of interest.	It is the sum of total of planned as well as unplanned investment.

Paradox of Thrift

If all the people of the economy increase the proportion of income they save, the total value of savings in the economy will not increase but it will either decline or remain unchanged. This result is known as the paradox of thrift, which states that as people become more thrifty they end up saving less or same as before.

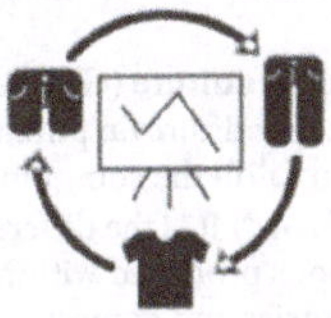

Important Formulae

1. Consumption Function

$\therefore \quad C = \bar{C} + bY$

Where, C = Consumption

$\bar{C}$ = Autonomous consumption

b = MPC

Y = Income

2. $\text{APC} = \dfrac{C}{Y}$

C = Consumption and Y = Income

3. $\text{MPC} = \dfrac{\Delta C}{\Delta Y}$

ΔC = Change in Consumption and

ΔY = Change in Income

4. Saving Function

$\therefore \quad S = -\bar{S} + sY$

Where, S = Saving

$\bar{S}$ = Autonomous saving

s = MPS

Y = Income

5. $\text{APS} = \dfrac{S}{Y}$; S = Saving and Y = Income

$\text{APC} + \text{APS} = 1$

$\Rightarrow \quad \text{APC} = 1 - \text{APS}$

or $\quad \text{APS} = 1 - \text{APC}$

$\text{MPC} + \text{MPS} = 1$

$\Rightarrow \quad \text{MPC} = 1 - \text{MPS}$

or $\quad \text{MPS} = 1 - \text{MPC}$

6. $\text{MPS} = \dfrac{\Delta S}{\Delta Y}$; ΔS = Change in saving and

ΔY = Change in income

7. Investment Multiplier

$\therefore \quad K = \dfrac{1}{1 - \text{MPC}} \text{ or } \dfrac{1}{\text{MPS}} \text{ or } \dfrac{\Delta Y}{\Delta I}$

Where, K = Investment Multiplier

MPC = Marginal Propensity to Consume

MPS = Marginal Propensity to Save

ΔY = Change in Income

ΔI = Change in Investment

Mind Map

AGGREGATE DEMAND AND SUPPLY & OTHER RELATED CONCEPTS

1 Aggregate Demand and its Components

Aggregate demand is the value of total expenditure that people plan to spend on all goods and services in an economy at a given level of income during a fiscal year.

Components

- **Household Consumption Demand or Expenditure** (C) It refers to the total planned expenditure to be incurred by all households on purchase of goods and services.
- **Investment Expenditure by Firms** (I) It refers to the planned expenditure by private entrepreneurs on creation of new capital assets. Investment can be induced or autonomous.
- **Government Expenditure** (G) It refers to government's total planned expenditure on purchase of consumer and capital goods to fulfill the common needs of the society.
- **Net Export** (X —M) It is the difference between the demand for goods produced within the domestic country by foreign countries and domestic country's demand for goods produced in foreign countries.

$$AD = C + I + G + X - M$$

2 Aggregate Supply and its Components

Aggregate supply is the money value of the final goods and services that the firms are willing to supply in an economy during one year.

Components

- **Consumption Expenditure** (C) It is the total of private final consumption expenditure, government final consumption expenditure, gross domestic capital formation and net exports.
- **Savings** (S) It constitutes the part of income that is not consumed.

$$AS = Y = C + S$$

3 Consumption Function

The relationship between the consumption expenditure and income is known as consumption function (propensity to consume). It is expressed as

$$C = f(Y)$$

Where, C = Consumption expenditure, Y= Income and $C = f(Y)$ denotes that consumption expenditure is a function of income.

The algebraic expression of consumption function (propensity of consume) is

$$\boxed{C = I + bY}$$

Where,

C = Consumption expenditure

I = Autonomous consumption, i.e. consumption at zero level of income

b = Marginal propensity to consume

Y = Disposable income, i.e. income after tax

Types of Propensity of Consume

- **Average Propensity to Consume** (APC) It is the ratio between the total consumption expenditure and total income at a given level of income.
- **Marginal Propensity to Consume** (MPC) It is the ratio between the change in consumption expenditure and the change in income.

4 Saving Function

Saving is the excess income which is left with the consumer after doing all the consumption expenditure.

$$S = Y—C$$

The relationship between savings and income is known as saving function. It is expressed as

$S = f(Y)$ where, S = Saving, Y = Income and $S = f(Y)$ denotes that savings are a function of income.

The algebraic expression of saving function (propensity to save) is

$$\boxed{S = (-) = \bar{s} + sY}$$

Where S = Saving

$\bar{s}$ = Autonomous saving, i.e. level of saving when income is zero

s = Marginal Propensity to Save (MPS); Y = Disposable income

Types of Propensity to Save

- **Average Propensity to Save** (APC) It is the ratio between Aggregate Saving (S) and Aggregate Income (Y) is called Average Propensity to Save (APS).
- **Marginal Propensity to Save** (MPS) It is the ratio between change in saving and change in income is called Marginal Propensity to Save (MPS).

5 Concept of Investment Multiplier

Investment multiplier or output multiplier refers to the increase in aggregate income of the economy as a result of an increase in the investments in an economy.

$$\boxed{K = \frac{\Delta Y}{\Delta I}}$$

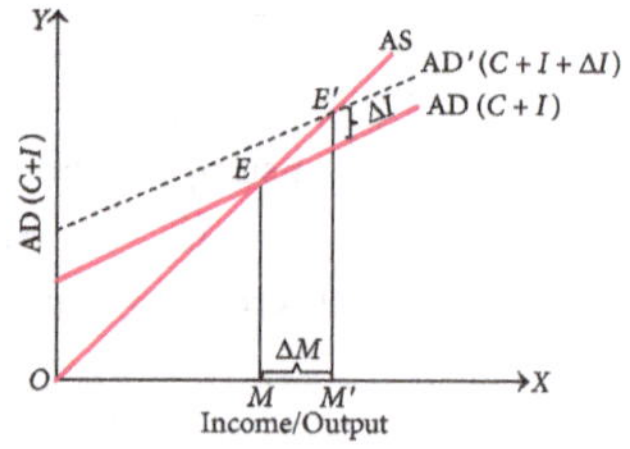

Mechanism of Multiplier

The multiplier works on the assumption that one person's expenditure is another person's income.

Relationship of Investment Multiplier with MPC and MPS

- There is a direct relationship between investment multiplier and MPC, i.e. higher the value of MPC, higher the multiplier and *vice-versa*.
- There is an inverse relationship between investment multiplier and MPS, i.e. higher the value of MPS, lower the multiplier and *vice-versa*.

6 Ex-ante and Ex-post Saving and Investment

Ex-ante and ex-post are two important concepts that help in comparing the planned or estimated values and the actual value of the variables like savings and investment. Ex-ante refers to the anticipated or planned or estimated value of the variables that the economy plans to spend. On the other hand, ex-post is the actual or realised value of the variables that the economy is actually able to spend.

Aspects

- **Ex-ante Savings** It is given by saving function.
- **Ex-post Savings** It is the sum total of planned as well as unplanned savings.
- **Ex-ante Investment** It is determined by the relation between investment demand and rate of interest.
- **Ex-post Investment** It is the sum total of planned as well as unplanned investment.

EXAM PATTERN QUESTIONS

Objective Type Questions

Multiple Choice Questions (MCQs)

1. Aggregate demand curve starts from
(a) the origin
(b) point below the origin
(c) point above the origin
(d) None of the above

2. **"Surge in stock market due to positive job report and optimistic economic forecasts."**

Which component of aggregate demand is most likely to be boosted by the events mentioned in the headline? **Competency Based Que**

(a) Consumption (b) Investment
(c) Government spending (d) Net exports

3. **On the basis of the below image, answer the following question.**

What does *OL* in the given diagram signify?

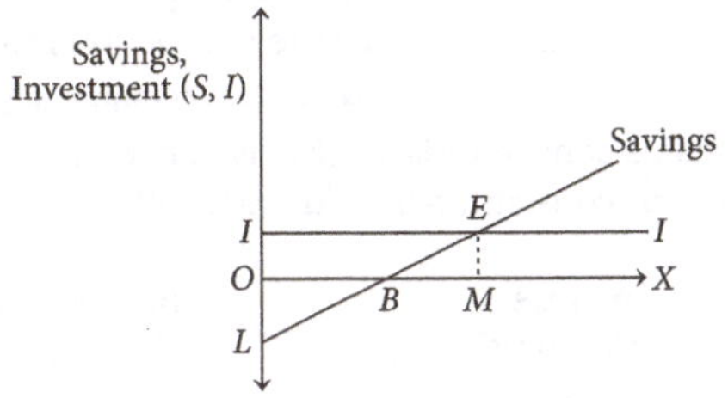

(a) Minimum consumption expenditure
(b) Minimum income level
(c) Dissaving
(d) Autonomous consumption

4. **Investment is an addition to ....**
(a) supply (b) current stock
(c) capital stock (d) None of these

5. **Autonomous investment curve**
(a) slopes upward originating from origin
(b) slopes upward originating from X-axis
(c) runs parallel to X-axis
(d) runs parallel to Y-axis

6. **"Trade war escalates, leading to higher tariffs and disrupted supply chains. Businesses delay investments and consumers tighten their belts."**

Which component of aggregate demand is most likely to be negatively affected by the news in the headline? **Competency Based Que**

(a) Autonomous consumption
(b) Induced investment
(c) Government expenditure
(d) Net exports

7. **If the net exports are positive, the aggregate demand curve will** **NCERT (QR)**
(a) shift to right (b) shift downward
(c) no effect (d) shift to left

8. **Graphically, aggregate demand function can be obtained by vertically adding the .... and .... function.** **CBSE SQP 2024**
(a) consumption, saving
(b) consumption, investment
(c) investment, saving
(d) aggregate supply, consumption

9. **Global supply chain disruptions due to the Covid-19 pandemic have increased the costs of trade between countries. Given the interconnectedness of the US economy with the rest of the world, higher trade costs can have important impacts on US labour markets.**

Source *https://www.frbsf.org/economic-research/publications/economic-letter/2023/january/supply-chain-disruptions-trade-costs-and-labour-markets/*

What will be the impact of the Covid outbreak on the aggregate demand of the US economy? **Competency Based Que**

(a) Increase (b) Decrease
(c) Constant (d) Either (a) or (b)

10. Choose the correct statement. **Competency Based Que**

I. Aggregate Demand = Consumption + Investment (for a two-sector economy)
II. Aggregate Supply = Consumption + Saving (for a two-sector economy)
III. Aggregate Demand = Consumption + Investment + Government Expenditure + Net Exports (for an open economy)
IV. Aggregate Supply = Consumption + Saving (Income) (for a two-sector economy)

Codes
(a) I and IV (b) II and IV
(c) Only III (d) I, II and III

11. 'Consumption curve is a straight line', due to

(a) zero income level
(b) constant marginal propensity to consume
(c) inverse in consumption
(d) All of the above

12. **Identify, which of the following options exhibits the proportional relation between consumption and disposable income.** CBSE 2024 C

(a) Marginal Propensity to Consume (MPC) > Average Propensity to Consume (APC)
(b) Marginal Propensity to Consume (MPC) < Average Propensity to Consume (APC)
(c) Marginal Propensity to Consume (MPC) = Average Propensity to Consume (APC)
(d) Marginal Propensity to Consume = 1

13. **At break-even point**

(a) $Y = C$ (b) $C = S$ (c) $S = 0$ (d) $Y < C$

14. **An increase in the MPC will**

(a) shift the saving function upwards
(b) lead to a steeper slope of consumption function
(c) shift the consumption function upwards
(d) shift the consumption function downwards

15. **Which of the following statements is the correct description of propensity to save?**

(a) It is the additional income that does not get saved
(b) It denotes the ratio of the savings to income
(c) It denotes the actual level of income at which it is equal to the savings
(d) It indicates the total amount of savings in the economy

16. **Which of the following statements is correct about the relationship between the Average Propensity to Save (APS) and Average Propensity to Consume (APC)?**

(a) Both APS and APC rise in case of an increase in the national income
(b) Both APS and APC fall in case of an increase in the national income
(c) APC rises, but APS falls in case of an increase in the national income
(d) APS rises, but APC falls in case of an increase in the national income

17. **In an economy, break-even level of income can be determined, when ....**

(i) Marginal Propensity to Consume (MPC) = Marginal Propensity to Save (MPS)
(ii) Income (Y) = Consumption (C)
(iii) Savings (S) = 0
(iv) Average Propensity to Consume (APC) = Average Propensity to Save (APS) CBSE 2024 C

Codes

(a) Only (i) (b) (i) and (ii)
(c) (ii) and (iii) (d) (i) and (iv)

18. **Observe the graph given below of saving function, APS will be calculated by**

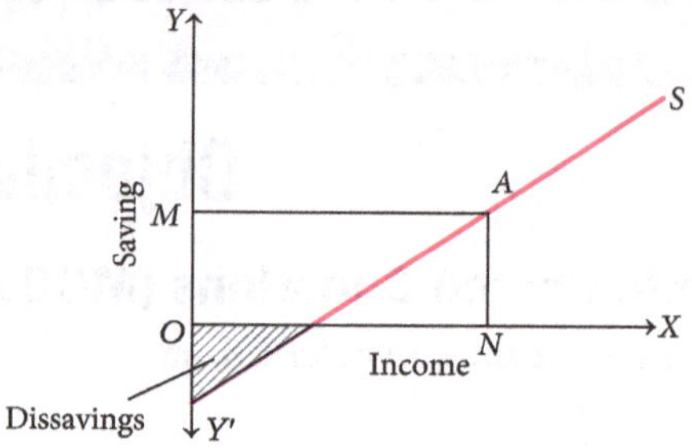

(a) ON/OM (b) AM/AN
(c) OM/ON (d) ON/MA

19. **If a straight line consumption function makes a positive intercept at the Y-axis, it implies that the marginal propensity to consume .... and average propensity to consume .... as the level of income rises.** CBSE 2024

(a) remains constant, rises (b) rises, rises
(c) falls, falls (d) remains constant, falls

20. **If an upward sloping straight line consumption function makes an intercept at the Y-axis at a positive coordinate, it implies that Marginal Propensity to Consume (MPC) .... and Average Propensity to Consume (APC) .... as the income increases.** CBSE 2025; Competency Based Que

(a) remains constant, rises (b) rises, rises
(c) remains constant, falls (d) falls, falls

21.

Income (₹ in crores)	Consumption (₹ in crores)
80	64
100	78

On the basis of the above mentioned information, identify the slope of MPS. Competency Based Que

(a) 0.20 (b) 0.30 (c) 0.70 (d) 0.78

22. **Using the given information, complete the following table** CBSE 2025; Competency Based Que

Income (Y) (in ₹ crore)	Savings (in ₹ crore)	Consumption (C) (in ₹ crore)	Average Propensity to Consume (APC)
0	...(i)...	30	—
100	0	...(ii)	1
200	30	170	0.85
300	60	240	0.8

(a) −30, 120 (b) 30, 120
(c) 0, 70 (d) −30, 100

23. From the given table, identify that level of income, where Average Propensity to Save (APS) becomes zero. **CBSE 2024**

Income (₹ crore)	0	50	100	200	300	400
Consumption (₹ crore)	50	75	100	150	200	250

(a) 50 (b) 100 (c) 200 (d) 0

24. Consider the graph given below

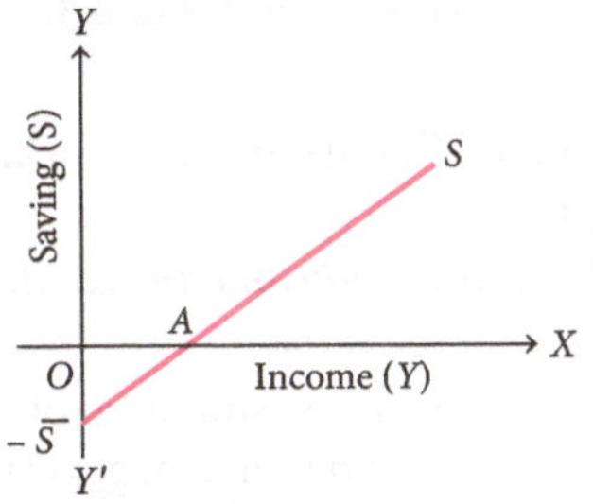

At point A, APC will be

(a) 0.2 (b) 0 (c) 1 (d) 1.2

25. Find the missing figures and choose the correct alternatives **Competency Based Que**

Income (₹)	Consumption (₹)	Average Propensity to Consume (APC)
0	20	—
20	60	...(iii)...
40	...(ii)...	2.5
60	140	...(iv)...
...(i)...	170	2.125

Codes

(a) 100, 100, 1.3, 2 (b) 70, 100, 3, 1.33
(c) 80, 100, 3, 2.33 (d) 110, 90, 2, 3.33

26. If the value of Average Propensity to Consume (APC) is 0.8 and national income is ₹ 4,000 crore, the value of savings will be .... **CBSE 2020; Competency Based Que**

(a) ₹ 100 crore (b) ₹ 200 crore
(c) ₹ 800 crore (d) ₹ 500 crore

27. If the value of Average Propensity to Save (APS) is 0.2 and and national income is ₹ 4,000 crore, then consumption will be ...... **CBSE 2020; Competency Based Que**

(a) ₹ 4,000 crore (b) ₹ 3,200 crore
(c) ₹ 3,800 crore (d) ₹ 2,600 crore

28. "A recent survey finds that, on average, Indian households spend 70% of their income on consumption and save 30%." Which of the following statements is true about the propensities in this scenario? **Competency Based Que**

(a) MPC = MPS (b) APC = APS
(c) APC > APS (d) APS > APC

29. Complete the following table **Competency Based Que**

Income (Y)	APS	Saving (S)	MPC
500	0.25	...(i)...	–
700	0.45	315	...(ii)...

(a) 125, 0.95 (b) 185, 0.55
(c) 385, 0.75 (d) 200, 0.7

30. Which of the following statements about investment multiplier is incorrect?

(a) Maximum value of investment multiplier is ∞
(b) Minimum value of investment multiplier is 0
(c) $K = \Delta Y/\Delta I$
(d) There is a direct relationship between investment multiplier and MPC

31. There is ...... relationship between MPS and investment multiplier.

(a) positive (b) inverse
(c) direct (d) None of these

32. If Marginal Propensity to Save (MPS) is 0.25 and initial change in investment is ₹ 250 crore, then the final change in income would be .... **CBSE 2020; Competency Based Que**

(a) ₹ 1,000 crore
(b) ₹ 1,200 crore
(c) ₹ 500 crore
(d) ₹ 3,500 crore

33. Observe the image given below carefully and identify the value of investment multiplier from the same, given that an initial investment has resulted in a total increase of ₹ 1,000 crore in income. **Competency Based Que**

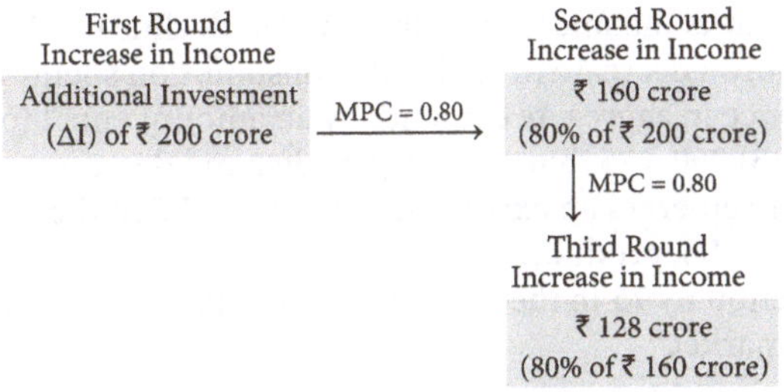

(a) 8 (b) 5
(c) 4 (d) 2

34. Complete the following table **Competency Based Que**

MPC	MPS	Multiplier (K)
0	1	1
...(i)...	0.75	...(ii)...
0.50	0.50	...(iii)...

(a) 0.25, 1.23, 2 (b) 0.25, 1.33, 2
(c) 0.50, 1.33, 1 (d) 0.25, 4, 2

35. .... **refers to the amount of savings that households plan to make in a given period whereas** .... **is the actual amount of investment that firms have made during the period.**

(a) Ex-ante investment, ex-post savings
(b) Ex-post investment, ex-ante savings
(c) Ex-ante savings, ex-post investment
(d) Ex-post savings, ex-ante investment

36. If in an economy, the value of investment multiplier is 4 and autonomous consumption is ₹ 30 crore, the relevant consumption function would be CBSE SQP 2023; Competency Based Que

(a) $C = 30 + 0.75\ Y$ (b) $C = (-)\ 30 + 0.25\ Y$
(c) $C = 30 - 0.75\ Y$ (d) $C = 30 - 0.25\ Y$

37. If the value of investment multiplier (K) is 5, the relevant saving function would be .... CBSE 2025

(a) $S = -60 + 0.25\ Y$ (b) $S = -60 + 0.75\ Y$
(c) $S = -60 + 0.20\ Y$ (d) $S = -60 + 0.60\ Y$

Direction *Read the case study and answer the questions 38 to 41 on the basis of the same*

If all the people of the economy increase the proportion of income they save (i.e. if the MPS of the economy increases) the total value of savings in the economy will not increase it will either decline or remain unchanged.

This result is known as the **Paradox of Thrift** which states that as people become more thrifty they end up saving less or same as before. Let us understand it with the help of an example. Suppose at the initial level, income $(Y) = 250$, MPC = 0.8 and MPS = 0.2. Now, people decide to cut down their expenditure as there is a threat of an imminent war. Hence the MPS of the economy increases or alternatively, the MPC decreases from 0.8 to 0.5.

At the initial income level of this sudden decline in MPC will imply a decrease in aggregate consumption spending and hence in aggregate demand, by an amount equal to $(0.8 - 0.5)\ 250 = 75$. But as aggregate demand decreases by 75, there emerges an excess supply equal to 75 in the economy. So, producers decide to cut the value of production by 75 in the next round to restore equilibrium in the market.

But that would mean a reduction in factor payments in the next round and hence a reduction in income by 75. As income decreases people reduce consumption proportionately but, this time, according to the new value of MPC which is 0.5. Consumption expenditure and hence aggregate demand, decreases by (0.5) 75, which creates again an excess supply in the market. In the next round, therefore, producers reduce output further by (0.5)75.

Income of the people decreases accordingly and consumption expenditure and aggregate demand goes down again by $(0.5)^2 75$. So, as income decreases, savings also decreases.

38. When all the people in the country save more, the total value of savings in the country will also ....

(a) increase (b) decrease
(c) constant (d) Can't be determined

39. Decrease in consumption expenditure leads to a decrease in the level of AD. The statement is

(a) true (b) false
(c) partialy true (d) Can't say

40. When MPC decreases from 0.8 to 0.5, MPS will rise from .... **to** ....

41. A decrease in MPC leads to .... **in consumption expenditure.**

Direction *Read the case study and answer the questions 42 to 45 on the basis of the same*

Aggregate demand curve is the sum total of consumption expenditure, investment expenditure, government expenditure and the net export and indicates the planned for ex-ante demand. So, all the consumption investment and saving function influence aggregate demand.

In the IS-LM model the demand curve is derived from the investment saving curve and is influenced by the investment multiplier. The slope of the curve depends on the value of the multiplier as well.

42. Aggregate demand curve indicates .... **demand in the economy.**

43. What effect does the value of the investment multiplier have on the aggregate demand curve?

(a) It changes only the position but not the slope of the curve
(b) It has no effect on either the slope or the position of the curve
(c) It affects both the slope and the position of the aggregate demand curve
(d) It affects only the slope of the aggregate supply curve

44. The ratio of a change in income to a given change in investment is called ....

45. The value of multiplier will be .... **if entire additional income is converted into additional consumption.**

(a) infinity (b) zero
(c) one (d) double the consumption

Direction *Read the hypothetical information carefully and answer the questions 46 to 49 on the basis of the same*

Income (₹)	Savings (₹)
0	− 12
20	− 6
40	0
60	6

46. **The value of autonomous consumption will be**

(a) ₹ 12 (b) ₹ 30
(c) ₹ 20 (d) ₹ 0

47. **APS at income level of ₹ 60 will be ....**

(a) 0.4 (b) 0
(c) 0.2 (d) 0.1

48. **Calculate the slope of consumption function.**

(a) 0.5 (b) 0.6
(c) 0.7 (d) 0.8

49. **Assertion** (A) There is a positive relationship between saving and income.

Reason (R) Savings are positive even at zero level of national income.

Alternatives

(a) Both Assertion (A) and Reason (R) are true and Reason (R) is the correct explanation of Assertion (A)
(b) Both Assertion (A) and Reason (R) are true, but Reason (R) is not the correct explanation of Assertion (A)
(c) Assertion (A) is true but Reason (R) is false
(d) Assertion (A) is false but reason (R) is true

Assertion-Reason

Direction (Q.No. 50 to 59) Read the following Assertion (A) and Reason (R) and choose the correct alternative from the following

Alternatives

(a) Both Assertion (A) and Reason (R) are true and Reason (R) is the correct explanation of Assertion (A)
(b) Both Assertion (A) and Reason (R) are true, but Reason (R) is not the correct explanation of Assertion (A)
(c) Assertion (A) is true, but Reason (R) is false
(d) Both Assertion (A) and Reason (R) are false

50. **Assertion** (A) Aggregate demand is a flow concept.

Reason (R) It is measured for the period of a fiscal year.

51. **Assertion** (A) Aggregate demand is zero at zero level of income.

Reason (R) When income is zero, people do not have money to spend on consumption expenditure and hence AD is also zero.

52. **Assertion** (A) Autonomous consumption leads to negative savings.

Reason (R) People have to spend on such consumption from their past savings.

53. **Assertion** (A) In the short-run, the aggregate supply curve is upward sloping.

Reason (R) This is because as output increases, firms face higher costs and prices rise.

54. **Assertion** (A) Consumption curve makes an intercept on the Y-axis, some point above the origin.

Reason (R) People need certain basic goods and services to sustain themselves, even if income is zero.

55. **Assertion** (A) Saving curve makes a negative intercept on the vertical axis at zero level of income.

Reason (R) Saving function refers to the functional relationship between saving and income. **CBSE SQP 2023**

56. **Assertion** (A) The sum of APC and APS is equal to one.

Reason (R) Income is either used for consumption or for saving.

57. **Assertion** (A) Average propensity to save is always positive.

Reason (R) APS shows percentage saving per unit of income.

58. **Assertion** (A) Higher the value of MPC, more is the value of multiplier.

Reason (R) Multiplier is indirectly related to MPC.

59. **Assertion** (A) In the determination of equilibrium output, only ex-ante saving and ex-ante investment are considered.

Reason (R) Ex-ante saving and ex-ante investment are always equal to each other.

Two Statements Based MCQs

Direction (Q.No. 60 to 67) *Read the following statements carefully and choose the correct alternative*

Alternatives

(a) Statement I is correct and Statement II is incorrect
(b) Statement II is correct and Statement I is incorrect
(c) Both the statements are correct
(d) Both the statements are incorrect

60. **Statement I** In a two sector economy, consumption expenditure and investment expenditure are the two components of aggregate demand.

Statement II Aggregate demand curve always start from point of origin with positive slope. **CBSE 2023**

61. **Statement I** The consumption curve is an upward sloping straight line curve due to the direct relationship between income and consumption and the assumption of constant marginal propensity to consume.

Statement I Aggregate demand curve and consumption curve are parallel to each other. **CBSE SQP 2023**

62. **Statement I** Average Propensity to Consume (APC) represents the change in total income with respect to a given change in total consumption.

Statement II When income changes, change in consumption (ΔC) can never exceed the change in income (ΔY). **CBSE 2024 C**

63. **Statement I** The value of marginal propensity to consume can be greater than one.

Statement II The value of marginal propensity to save can be negative as well.

64. **Statement I** At the break-even point, consumption is equal to national income.

Statement II APC falls continuously with an increase in income as the proportion of income spent on consumption keeps on decreasing.

65. **Statement I** The size of the investment multiplier depends on the Marginal Propensity to Save (MPS).

Statement II The investment multiplier is always greater than 1, as an initial increase in investment leads to a larger increase in national income due to successive rounds of consumption and saving.

66. **Statement I** In a simple economy, ex-ante savings equals ex-ante investment as part of the national income accounting.

Statement II Ex-post savings is generally equal to ex-ante savings at the end of the period, as there are no changes in savings behaviour.

67. **Statement I** The maximum value of Marginal Propensity to Consume (MPC) can be unity.

Statement II As the income of an economy increases, the proportionate increase in the level of consumption is always more than the increase in the level of income.

CBSE SQP 2025

Matching

68. Match the following

Column I	Column II
A. Originates from positive coordinate of Y-axis	(i) Autonomous investment curve
B. Originates from origin	(ii) Consumption curve
C. Originates from negative coordinates of Y-axis	(iii) Savings curve
D. Runs parallel to X-axis	(iv) Aggregate supply curve

Codes

	A	B	C	D		A	B	C	D
(a)	(i)	(ii)	(iii)	(iv)	(b)	(ii)	(iii)	(iv)	(i)
(c)	(iii)	(iv)	(i)	(ii)	(d)	(iv)	(i)	(iii)	(ii)

69. Choose the correct pair

Column I	Column II
A. Aggregate demand	(i) Stock concept
B. Investment	(ii) Addition to capital stock
C. Aggregate supply	(iii) It has three components, *viz.* consumption, investment and net exports

Codes

(a) A-(i)
(b) B-(ii)
(c) C-(iii)
(d) None of these

70. Match the following

Column I	Column II
A. Can have a negative value	(i) MPC
B. Its value can never be zero	(ii) APS
C. Its value can be 1	(iii) APC

Codes

	A	B	C		A	B	C
(a)	(i)	(ii)	(iii)	(b)	(ii)	(iii)	(i)
(c)	(iii)	(i)	(ii)	(d)	(iii)	(ii)	(i)

71. Choose the correctly matched pair from the following

Competency Based Que

Column I	Column II
A. If, MPC =1	(i) $K = \infty$
B. If, K =1	(ii) MPC = 1
C. If, APS = 0	(iii) APC = 0
D. If, $Y = C$	(iv) Savings is zero

Codes

(a) A–(i)
(b) B–(ii)
(c) C–(iii)
(d) All of these

72. Choose the correctly matched pair from the following

Column I	Column II
A. Induced investment	(i) An investment which is influenced by expected profitability.
B. Ex-ante investment	(ii) It refers to actual investments at different levels of Income.
C. Autonomous investment	(iii) It refers to planned investments at different levels of income which is influenced by expected profitability.
D. Investment multiplier	(iv) Ratio between change in income to change in savings.

Codes

(a) A-(i) (b) B-(ii) (c) C-(iii) (d) D-(iv)

Concept Identification

73. It shows the relationship between investment demand and rate of interest.

74. It is the planned production of goods and services in an economy during an accounting year.

75. It is the functional relationship between consumption (C) and income (Y) denoted as $C = C + bY$.

76. It is the ratio of change in saving to change in income.

77. It is the ratio of a change in income to a given change in investment.

Answers

1. (c) point above the origin
2. (a) An optimistic outlook and increased employment suggest higher consumer confidence and business investment, both contributing to consumption.
3. (c) Dissaving
4. (c) capital stock
5. (c) runs parallel to X-axis
6. (b) This creates uncertainty for businesses, making them less likely to invest in new projects or expand existing ones. This directly impacts induced investment, which is investment spending driven by changes in income or output.
7. (a) shift to right
8. (b) consumption, investment
9. (b) Decrease
10. (d) I, II and III
11. (b) constant marginal propensity to consume
12. (c) Marginal Propensity to Consume (MPC) = Average Propensity to Consume (APC)
13. (a) $Y = C$
14. (c) shift the consumption function upwards
15. (b) It denotes the ratio of the savings to income
16. (d) APS rises, but APC falls in case of an increase in the national income
17. (c) (ii) and (iii)
18. (c) OM/ON ($APS = S/Y$)
19. (c) falls, falls
20. (a) remains constant, rises
21. (b) $\Delta Y = 100 - 80 =$ ₹ 20 crore

    $\Delta C = 78 - 64 =$ ₹ 14 crore

    $S = Y - C$

    Initial savings = $80 - 64 =$ ₹ 16 crore

    Final savings = $100 - 78 =$ ₹ 22 crore

    So,

    ΔS = Final Savings − Initial Savings = $22 - 16 =$ ₹ 6 crore

    $MPS = \Delta S/\Delta Y$

    $MPS = 6/20 = 0.30$
22. (d) Savings = Income − Consumption

    (i) $S = 0 - 30 = -30$ (ii) $0 = 100 - C \Rightarrow C = 100$
23. (b) Savings = Income − Consumption

    For Income = 0, Savings = $0 - 50 = -50$

    For Income = 50, Savings = $50 - 75 = -25$

    For Income = 100, Savings = $100 - 100 = 0$

    Therefore, APS becomes zero at this level of income.
24. (b) 0
25. (c) $APC = C/Y$
26. (c) $APS = 1 - APC = 1 - 0.8 = 0.2$

    Also, $APS = \frac{\text{Savings}}{\text{National Income}}$

    $\Rightarrow \quad 0.2 = \frac{\text{Savings}}{4{,}000} \Rightarrow$ ₹ 800 crore
27. (b) $APC = 1 - APS = 1 - 0.2 = 0.8$

    Also, $APC = \frac{\text{Consumption } (C)}{\text{Income } (Y)}$

    $= \frac{C}{4{,}000} = 0.8$

    $\therefore C = 4{,}000 \times 0.8 =$ ₹ 3,200 crore
28. (c) APC > APS
29. (a) (i) Finding Savings (S) when $Y = 500$, $APS = 0.25$

    $APS = S/Y$

    $S = APS \times Y$

    $S = 0.25 \times 500 = 125$

    (ii) $\Delta S = 315 - 125 = 190$

    $\Delta Y = 700 - 500 = 200$

    $MPS = 190/200 = 0.95$
30. (b) The minimum value of investment multiplier is 1.
31. (b) inverse
32. (a) $K = \frac{1}{MPS} \Rightarrow \frac{1}{0.25} \Rightarrow 4$

    Also, $K = \frac{\Delta Y}{\Delta I} \Rightarrow 4 = \frac{\Delta Y}{250}$

    $\Rightarrow \Delta Y =$ ₹ 1,000 crore
33. (b) $K = \Delta Y/\Delta I = 1{,}000/200 = 5$
34. (b) $MPC + MPS = 1$

    $K = 1/MPS$

    (i) $MPS = 0.75$

    $MPC = 1 - MPS = 1 - 0.75 = 0.25$

    (ii) $MPS = 0.75$

    $K = 1/MPS = 1/0.75 = 1.33$

    (iii) $MPC = 0.50$ and $MPS = 0.50$

    $K = 1/MPS = 1/0.50 = 2$
35. (c) Ex-ante savings, ex-post investment
36. (a) Investment Multiplier (K) = 4

    Autonomous Consumption (C) = 30 crore

    $K = 1/1 - MPC$

    $4 = 1/1 - MPC$

    $MPC = 1 - 1/4 = 0.75$

Consumption Function

$$C = \overline{C} + \text{MPC}\,(Y)$$

$$C = 30 + 0.75\,Y$$

37. (c) $K = \dfrac{1}{1-\text{MPC}}$

$$5 = \frac{1}{1-\text{MPC}}$$

$$\therefore \quad 1-\text{MPC} = \frac{1}{5}$$

$$1-\text{MPC} = 0.2$$

$$\text{MPC} = 0.8$$

So, $\text{MPS} = 1 - 0.8 = 0.2$

38. (b) decrease
39. (a) true
40. 0.2, 0.5
41. decrease
42. ex-ante
43. (c) It affects both the slope and the position of the aggregate demand curve
44. investment multiplier
45. (b) zero
46. (a) $C = \text{Income} - \text{Savings}$

At an income of ₹ 0, the savings are – ₹ 12, so
$C = 0 - (-12) =$ ₹ 12

47. (d) APS at income level of ₹ 60

To calculate APS, use the formula
APS = Savings/Income
APS = 6/60 = 0.1

48. (c) Change in Consumption = 54 – 40 = ₹ 14
Change in Income = 60 – 40 = ₹ 20
Thus, the slope (MPC) is $C/Y = 14/20 = 0.7$

49. (c) At zero level of income, there is some amount of consumption which means autonomous consumption. Since $Y - C = S$, so at zero level of income savings will be negative.
50. (a) Both Assertion (A) and Reason (R) are true and Reason (R) is the correct explanation of Assertion (A)
51. (d) Even when income is zero, there is still some consumption that takes place, which is called autonomous consumption.

This consumption is necessary for survival. Even when income is zero, people still consume basic necessities, such as food. This means that consumption is never zero and therefore Aggregate Demand (AD) is also never zero.

52. (a) Both Assertion (A) and Reason (R) are true and Reason (R) is the correct explanation of Assertion (A)
53. (a) Both Assertion (A) and Reason (R) are true and Reason (R) is the correct explanation of Assertion (A)
54. (a) Both Assertion (A) and Reason (R) are true and Reason (R) is the correct explanation of Assertion (A)
55. (b) Both Assertion (A) and Reason (R) are true, but Reason (R) is not the correct explanation of Assertion (A)
56. (a) Both Assertion (A) and Reason (R) are true and Reason (R) is the correct explanation of Assertion (A)
57. (d) Both Assertion (A) and Reason (R) are false
58. (c) The multiplier is not indirectly related to MPC; it is directly related. As MPC increases, the multiplier increases. This means a higher MPC leads to a larger multiplier, not an indirect relationship.
59. (c) Ex-ante savings and ex-ante investment are not always equal because at different level of income aggregate demand is not equal to aggregate supply.
60. (a) Aggregate demand curve originates from Y-axis and then slopes upwards. It originates from Y-axis because at zero level of income, consumption expenditure is not zero. When income increases, consumption expenditure also increases, because of which AD curve slope upwards.
61. (a) The Aggregate Demand (AD) curve and the consumption curve are not necessarily parallel to each other. The AD curve includes not only consumption but also other components such as investment, government spending and net exports.
62. (b) Statement II is correct and Statement I is incorrect
63. (d) The value of MPC cannot be greater than one. MPC is the ratio of additional consumption to additional income ($\Delta C/\Delta Y$). Since additional consumption (ΔC) is only a part of the additional income and cannot be greater than the additional income itself.

Marginal propensity to save is the ratio between additional saving and additional income which is always positive because of a positive relationship between saving and income.

64. (c) Both the statement are correct
65. (c) Both the statements are correct
66. (a) Ex-post savings may not always equal ex-ante savings because savings behaviour can change during the period due to various factors such as unexpected income changes or consumption habits.
67. (a) Statement I is correct and Statement II is incorrect
68. (d) (iv) (i) (iii) (ii)
69. (b) B-(ii)
70. (b) (ii) (iii) (i)
71. (a) When $K = 1$ then MPC = 0 ; when APS = 0 then APC = 1.
72. (a) A-(i)
73. Investment demand function
74. Aggregate supply
75. Consumption function
76. Marginal propensity to save
77. Investment multiplier

Subjective Questions

Short Answer Type Questions

1. What is aggregate demand? State its components.

***Or* List the components of aggregate demand.**

Ans. Aggregate demand is the value of total expenditure on all goods and services in an economy during a fiscal year.

So, $AD = C + I$

Where, AD = Aggregate Demand

C = Consumption

I = Investment

Components of aggregate demand in a four sector economy are as follows

(i) Household consumption expenditure (C)

(ii) Private investment expenditure (Fixed Capital Formation + Change in Stock) (I)

(iii) Government expenditure (G)

(iv) Net exports ($X-M$)

So, $AD = C + I + G + (X - M)$

2. Elaborate the concept of aggregate supply.

Ans. Aggregate supply is the money value of the final goods and services or national product produced in an economy during one year. It is equal to income generated.

So, $AS = Y = C + S$

Where, AS = Aggregate Supply

C = Consumption

S = Savings

3. Differentiate between aggregate demand and market demand.

Ans. Differences between aggregate demand and market demand are

Basis	Aggregate Demand	Market Demand
Meaning	It refers to the total demand of goods and services in the economy.	It refers to the demand of goods in the market.
Concept	It is a macro concept.	It is a micro concept.
Relation	It is positively sloped which establishes positive relationship between income and demand.	It is negatively sloped which shows the inverse relationship between price and demand.
Graph	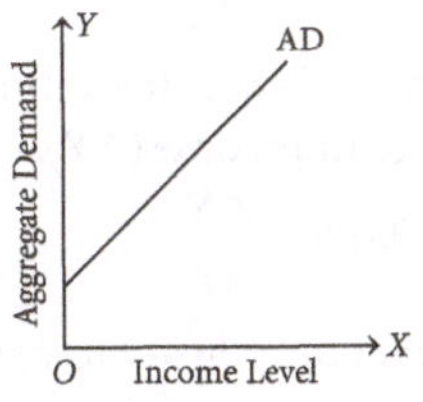	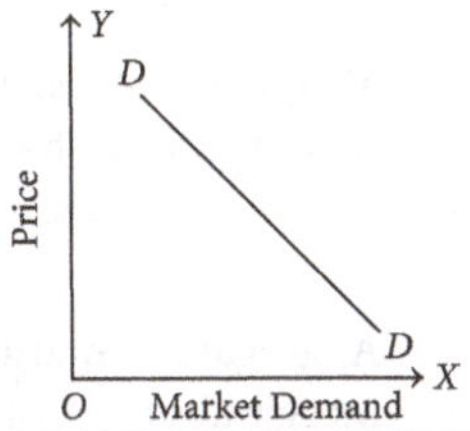

4. What is the significance of 45 degree line in the Keynesian economics?

Ans. The 45 degree line is a line of reference and shows all those points where aggregate expenditure and output are equal. It indicates that vertical axis measurement is equal to horizontal axis measurement.

A 45 degree line represents the aggregate supply curve drawn from the origin.

5. Describe the concept of saving function.

Ans. Saving function refers to the standard equation of savings which defines the relationship between savings and income where savings value can be derived at each level with the use of income value.

The algebraic expression of saving function is

$$S = -\bar{s} + Y(1 - b)$$

Where, $-\bar{s}$ = Autonomous savings,

$(1 - b)$ = Marginal Propensity to Save and Y = Income

6. Answer the following questions on the basis of given figure CBSE 2020; Competency Based Que

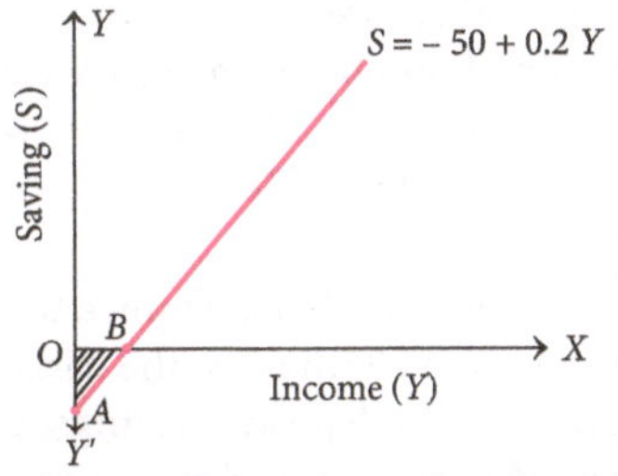

(i) What does the shaded area *AOB* indicate?

(ii) What is the significance of point *B*?

Ans. (i) The shaded area AOB indicates negative savings or dissavings.

(ii) Point B is the point of equilibrium. At point B, savings are zero and level of aggregate demand is equal to the level of aggregate supply in the economy.

7. What is marginal propensity to consume? How is it related to marginal propensity to save? NCERT

Ans. Marginal Propensity to consume is the ratio of change in consumption expenditure (ΔC) to change in income (ΔY).

So, $$\text{MPC} = \frac{\Delta C}{\Delta Y}$$

Marginal Propensity to Save is the ratio of change in saving (ΔS) to change in income (ΔY).

$$\text{MPS} = \frac{\Delta S}{\Delta Y}$$

Aggregate of marginal propensity to consume and marginal propensity to save is equal to one.

or $$\text{MPC} + \text{MPS} = 1$$

This is because $$\frac{\Delta C}{\Delta Y} + \frac{\Delta S}{\Delta Y} = \frac{\Delta Y}{\Delta Y} = 1 \quad [\because \Delta C + \Delta S = \Delta Y]$$

So, $\text{MPC} + \text{MPS} = 1$ *or* $\text{MPC} = 1 - \text{MPS}$

or $\text{MPS} = 1 - \text{MPC}$

8. "Economists are generally concerned about the rising Marginal Propensity to Save (MPS) in an economy." Explain why? Competency Based Que

Ans. Economists are generally concerned about the rising Marginal Propensity to Save (MPS) in an economy as rising MPS implies falling MPC (Marginal Propensity to Consume). A cut in MPC leads to a cut in the rate at which consumption increases when income rises.

This leads to a fall in the rate at which AD rises. A fall in the rate of rise in AD will lead to a fall in investment.

Because, demand is a significant determinant of investment by the producers. Ultimately this would mean a fall in the rate of GDP growth.

Also, lower MPC implies lower value of multiplier.

9. State Bank of India's latest edition of Ecowrap has noted that many households may have marginal propensity to consume less because several types of spending are not easily available amid social distancing constraints.

Analysing the trends in deposits since the lockdown was first imposed, on 25th May, the bank noted that the data revealed that deposits (savings, current and term) increased significantly during Lockdown-1 as people were apprehensive in the beginning about spending and turned frugal.

During Lockdown-2, there was a 25% decline in bank deposits, but term deposit accrual was very healthy.

Source *Business Standard; 2nd June, 2020*

Briefly explain the impact on aggregate demand due the above situation. Competency Based Que

Ans. In the above situation, due to the impact of lockdown, people started to spend more on consumption either due to fear of storage of goods or due to withdrawal of savings. This action leads to rise in marginal propensity to consume by the consumer. A rise in MPC leads to rise in consumption expenditure and hence aggregate demand will rise.

10. "High propensity to consume is a virtue, while high propensity to save is not." Do you agree? Why or why not? Competency Based Que

Ans. The above statement is correct that high propensity to consume is a virtue as consumption is considered as an injection to the circular flow of income by increasing demand, as increased demand leads to increased production of goods and services, leading to increase in induced investment and hence, national income.

On the other hand, savings are considered as leakages from the circular flow of income by reducing consumption demand and hence production, investment and national income also fall.

11. How are average propensity to consume and average propensity to save related? Is it possible for the APS value to be negative? If so, under what circumstances does this occur?

Ans. Average Propensity to Consume (APC) is the ratio of Consumption expenditure (C) and Income (Y), which indicates the average percentage of income that is spent on consumption.

$$\text{APC} = C/Y$$

Average Propensity to Save (APS) is the ratio of Saving (S) and Income (Y), expressing the average percentage of income that is saved.

$$\text{APS} = S/Y$$

The relation between Average Propensity to Consume (APC) and Average Propensity to Save (APS) is that their sum is always equal to unity, i.e. APC + APS = 1. It is so because the money income can either be spent on consumption or it can be saved.

Yes, APS can be negative, when saving is negative or when $C > Y$.

12. Answer the following questions based on the figure given below CBSE 2020; Competency Based Que

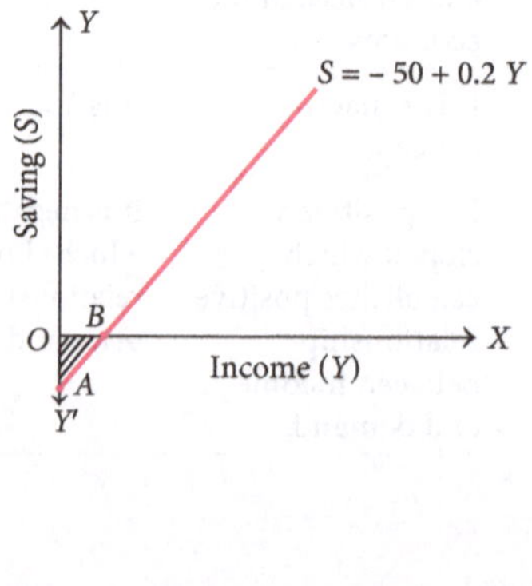

(i) **At which level of income, average propensity to consume will be equal to one and why?**

(ii) **What is the significance of saving curve above the point *B*?**

Ans. (i) Average Propensity to Consume (APC) will be equal to one at point *B*. At point *B*, savings will be zero. So, this implies that all that is earned is consumed. So, APC will be equal to one.

(ii) Saving curve above point *B* represents positive savings. It shows that consumption is less than income and people are saving a part of their income. It also shows that there is a positive relationship between income and savings. As income increases, savings also increase and *vice-versa*.

13. "When ex-ante Aggregate Demand (AD) falls short of ex-ante Aggregate Supply (AS) it resuls in fall in unintended inventories." Defend or refute the given statement, giving valid arguments.

CBSE 2024 C; Competency Based Que

Ans. I refute the statement. When ex-ante Aggregate Demand (AD) falls short of ex-ante Aggregate Supply (AS), it results in an unintended accumulation of inventories, not a fall. This happens because firms produce more than what is demanded, leading to unsold goods. These unsold goods get added to inventories, creating an imbalance between planned expenditure (AD) and planned production (AS). Thus, the given statement is incorrect, as a shortfall in AD relative to AS leads to an increase in unintended inventories rather than a decrease.

14. Answer the following questions based on the figure given below **CBSE 2020; Competency Based Que**

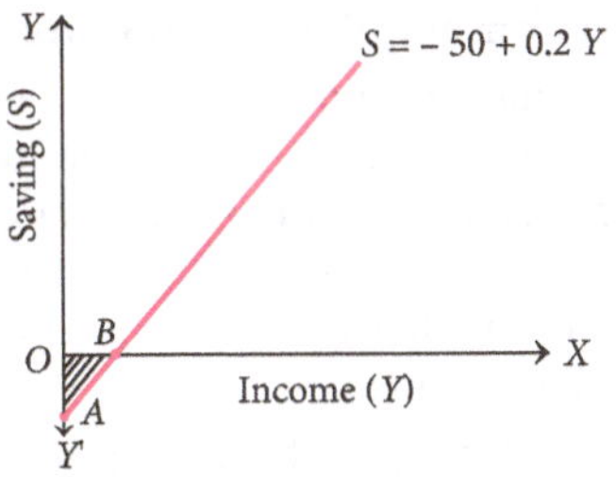

(i) **At which level of income, Average Propensity to Save (APS) will be equal to zero and why?**

(ii) **What does '*OA*' signify with respect to consumption function?**

Ans. (i) At point *B* on the graph, APS will be zero as at this level, saving is equal to zero and APS is the ratio of saving and income.

(ii) *OA* signifies Autonomous Consumption ($\overline{C}$) with respect to consumption function.

Autonomous consumption represents consumption at zero level of income.

15. Giving reasons, state whether the following statements are true or false.

(i) **Average propensity to save is always greater than zero.**

(ii) **Value of investment multiplier varies between zero and infinity.**

Ans. (i) No, the statement is false. When consumption is greater than the income level, the value of average propensity to save is less than zero or negative.

(ii) No, the statement is false.

We know that, $K = \dfrac{1}{1 - MPC}$

So, even if the MPC will have its minimum value, i.e. zero, the investment multiplier will be 1.

Similarly, when MPC = 1, the value of investment multiplier is infinity.

So, we can say that the value of investment multiplier varies between 1 and infinity.

16. Giving reasons, state whether the following statements are true or false.

(i) **When MPC is zero, the value of investment multiplier will also be zero.**

(ii) **Value of average propensity to consume can never be less than zero.**

Ans. (i) No, the statement is false. When MPC is zero, the value of investment multiplier will be 1.

$$K = \frac{1}{1 - MPC} \quad or \quad K = \frac{1}{1-0} = \frac{1}{1} = 1$$

(ii) Yes, the statement is true. As consumption can never be zero or negative, hence, APC is always positive.

17. Create a diagram illustrating both the consumption curve and saving curve together and indicate the point of 'break-even point'.

Ans. *AC* is the consumption curve and *A'S* is the saving curve.

OA is the autonomous consumption and '*Q*' is the break-even point where the income = consumption and savings = 0.

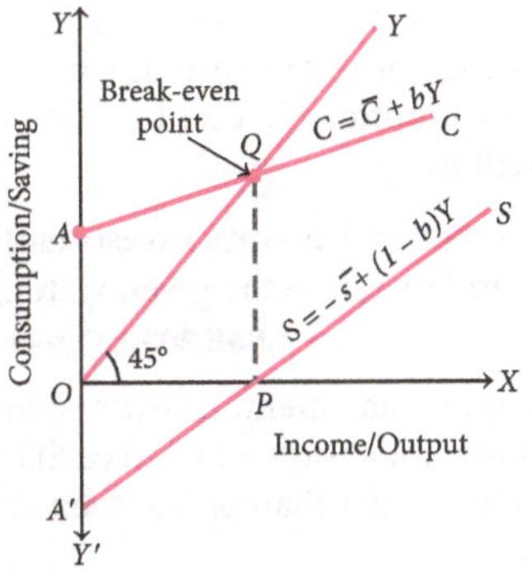

18. **What is the difference between ex-ante investment and ex-post investment?** NCERT

Ans. Differences between planned (ex-ante) and actual (ex-post) investment are

Basis	Planned Investment	Actual Investment
Meaning	It refers to the desired level of investment.	It refers to the realised level of investment.
Reaction with Savings	In an accounting year, planned investment may or may not be equal to planned savings.	In an accounting year, actual investment is always equal to actual savings. (This is according to the principle of national income accounting).
Determination of Income	Equilibrium level of income is determined where planned investment is equal to planned savings.	Actual investment does not determine the equilibrium level of income.

19. **Elaborate using a hypothetical numerical example, how a given initial increase in investment affects the level of final income of the economy.** CBSE 2025

Ans. The effect of an initial increase in investment on the final income of an economy can be explained using the investment multiplier concept.

The multiplier (K) is given by $K = 1/1 - \text{MPC}$

where, MPC (Marginal Propensity to Consume) represents the fraction of additional income that households spend on consumption.

Numerical Example

Suppose an economy experiences an initial increase in investment of ₹ 100 crore and the MPC = 0.8.

The multiplier (K) is calculated as

$$K = 1/1 - 0.8 = 1/0.2 = 5$$

The total increase in income is given by

Total Income = $K \times$ Initial Investment

Thus, an initial investment of ₹ 100 crore leads to a final income increase of ₹ 500 crore in the economy due to the multiplier effect. This happens because the additional investment generates income, which increases consumption, further boosting demand and production.

20. **"Ex-ante savings and ex-ante investments are always equal." Defend or refute the given statement with valid reasons.** CBSE 2020; Competency Based Que

Ans. I refute the given statement. Ex-ante savings and ex-ante investment are not always equal to each other. Ex-ante savings can be greater than or less than ex-ante investment.

The reason for the difference between these parameters is because they are both 'planned' or 'desired' parameters.

Additionally, the economic entities that plan investments and savings are distinct from one another i.e. producers plan investments, whereas households plan savings.

A distinct set of factors governs producers as investors and households as savers. Producers plan their investments in anticipation of future demand, while households plan their savings based on transactional and speculative motives.

21. **Explain paradox of thrift.** NCERT

Ans. **Paradox of Thrift** If all the people of the economy increase the proportion of income they save, the total value of savings in the economy will not increase but it will either decline or remain unchanged. This result is known as the paradox of thrift, which state that as people become more thrifty they end up saving less or same as before.

Long Answer Type Questions

22. **Discuss in detail the concept of aggregate demand and its components.**

Ans. Aggregate demand implies the total demand of final goods and services by all the people in an economy. In this manner, it can be defined as the actual aggregate expenditure incurred by all the people in the economy on different goods and services.

The components of aggregate demand are enlisted below

(i) **Private Consumption Expenditure** (C)

Private consumption expenditure refers to the total expenditure incurred by all the households in an economy on different types of final goods and services in order to satisfy their wants. Consumption depends on the level of the disposable income.

There are two types of consumption expenditure *viz* autonomous consumption expenditure and induced consumption expenditure.

(ii) **Private Investment Expenditure** (I)

Private investment expenditure refers to the planned (ex-ante) total expenditure incurred by all the private investors on the creation of capital goods such as expenditure incurred on new machinery, tools, buildings, raw materials, etc. Broadly, investment can be categorised in two types *viz.* autonomous investment expenditure and induced investment expenditure.

(iii) **Government Expenditure** (G)

Government expenditure refers to the total planned expenditure incurred by the government on consumption and investment purposes to enhance the welfare of the society and to achieve higher economic growth rates.

(iv) **Net Exports** $(X–M)$

Net exports refer to the difference between the demand for domestically produced goods and services by the rest of the world (exports) and the demand for goods and services produced abroad by the residents of a country.

In other words, it is the difference between the exports and imports.

$$AD = C + I + G + (X - M)$$

23. Explain the aggregate demand in two sector economy utilising an appropriate schedule and diagram.

Ans. Two sector economic model is a simple closed economic set-up where it is assumed that there are only two sectors in an economy, i.e. households and firms.

Let us discuss the concept using schedule and graph.

An imaginary aggregate demand schedule of a two sector economy is given below

Income (Y)	C	I	Aggregate Demand $(C + I)$
0	100	100	200
200	200	100	300
400	300	100	400
600	400	100	500
800	500	100	600
1,000	600	100	700

The diagrammatic presentation of AD schedule is depicted below

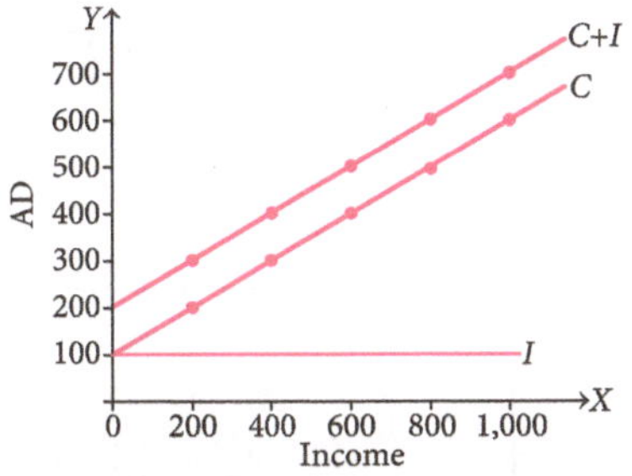

Observations drawn from the above schedule and diagram are

(i) When income is zero, consumption is not zero. This is the minimum level of consumption in an economy. This is termed as autonomous consumption because some minimum expenditure is always essential in an economy. Past savings or borrowings may be the source of such consumption expenditure.

(ii) Consumption curve starts above the origin and slopes upward, depicting a positive relationship between level of income and consumption expenditure in the economy.

(iii) Autonomous investment curve is a straight line parallel to X-axis as it is independent of the level of income in the economy.

24. Explain consumption function, with the help of a schedule and diagram.

Ans. The relationship between the consumption expenditure and the income is known as consumption function.

$$C = f(Y)$$

The algebraic expression of consumption function is

$$C = \overline{C} + bY$$

Where, C = Consumption expenditure,

$\overline{C}$ = Autonomous consumption i.e. consumption at zero level of income,

b = Marginal Propensity to Consume

Y = Income

Consumption function can be understood with the help of the following schedule and diagram

Income (Y)	Consumption (C)	APC $\left(\frac{C}{Y}\right)$	ΔC	ΔY	MPC $\left(\frac{\Delta C}{\Delta Y}\right)$
0	100	–	–	–	–
100	170	1.7	70	100	0.7
200	240	1.2	70	100	0.7
300	310	1.33	70	100	0.7
400	380	0.95	70	100	0.7
500	450	0.9	70	100	0.7

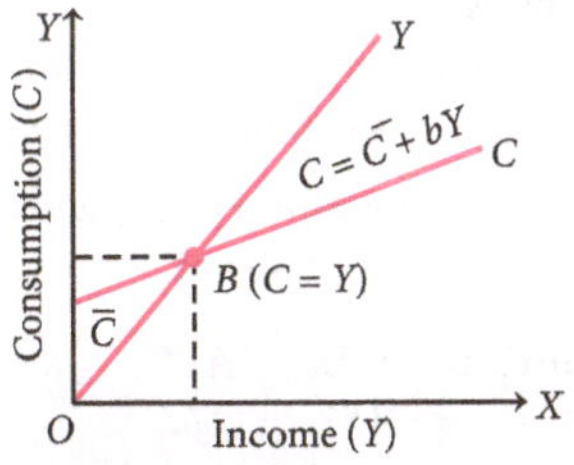

The point B in the diagram represents the break-even point where the consumption expenditure equals to the income.

25. Differentiate between marginal and average propensity to consume. Give a numerical illustration.

Ans. Differences between marginal propensity to consume and average propensity to consume are

Basis	Marginal Propensity to Consume (MPC)	Average Propensity to Consume (APC)
Meaning	The ratio between the change in consumption expenditure and the change in income is called the marginal propensity to consume.	The ratio between the total consumption expenditure and total income, at a given level of income is called the average propensity to consume.
Represents	It represents the part of increased income which is spent on consumption.	It represents the part of total income which is spent on consumption.
Symbolically	MPC = $\frac{\text{Change in Consumption } (\Delta C)}{\text{Change in Income } (\Delta Y)}$	APC $= \frac{\text{Total Consumption } (C)}{\text{Total Income } (Y)}$

The numerical example given below will help to understand the computation of MPC and APC

Income (Y)	Consumption (C)	APC (C/Y)	ΔC	ΔY	MPC (ΔC/ΔY)
0	300	—	—	—	—
200	350	1.75	50	200	0.25
400	400	1	50	200	0.25
600	450	0.75	50	200	0.25
800	500	0.625	50	200	0.25
1,000	500	0.55	50	200	0.25

26. Explain saving function with the help of a schedule and diagram.

Ans. The relationship between the savings and income is known as saving function.

$$S = f(Y)$$

The algebraic expression of saving function is

$$S = -\bar{S} + sY$$

Where, S = Saving

$-\bar{S}$ = Saving at zero level of income

s = Marginal Propensity to Save ; Y = Income

Saving function can be understood with the help of the following schedule and diagram

Income (Y)	Consumption (C)	Saving (S)	APS (S/Y)	ΔS	ΔY	MPS $\left(\frac{\Delta S}{\Delta Y}\right)$
0	100	−100	–	–	–	–
100	160	−60	−0.6	40	100	0.4
200	220	−20	−0.1	40	100	0.4
300	280	20	0.067	40	100	0.4
400	340	60	0.15	40	100	0.4
500	400	100	0.2	40	100	0.4
600	460	140	0.233	40	100	0.4

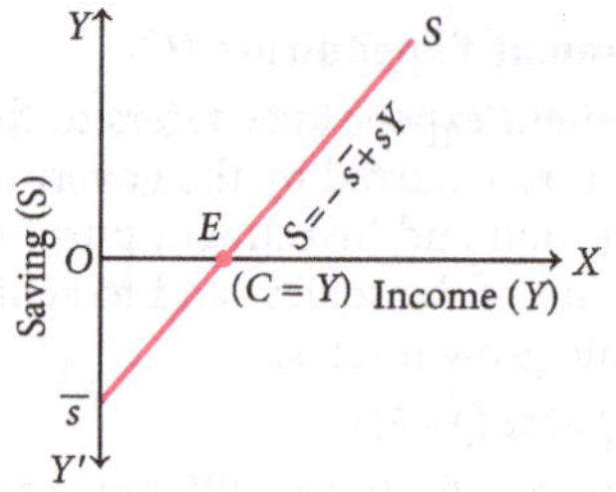

In the diagram, E is the point when savings become zero from negative. Beyond E, saving is positive.

27. Derive a saving curve from a consumption curve and explain the procedure involved.

Or **"Saving curve can be derived from the consumption curve." Justify the statement, citing valid steps with the help of a well-labelled diagram.** **CBSE SQP 2025**

Ans. The derivation of saving curve from consumption curve is discussed through following points

(i) At zero level of income (Y), the autonomous consumption is $O\bar{C}$. This consumption is equal to dissavings, i.e. $O\bar{S} = O\bar{C}$.

Hence, the saving curve starts from the point $\bar{S}$ on the negative Y-axis.

(ii) The consumption curve intersects income line at point B. B is the break-even point where consumption is equal to income $(C = Y)$. At this point, saving will be zero as all the income is consumed. Hence, the saving curve will intersect the X-axis (at point E) at this income level.

(iii) The consumption is less than income beyond point E. It means the excess income after consumption is saved and hence, the saving curve moves toward positive direction above X-axis with the increase in the level of income.

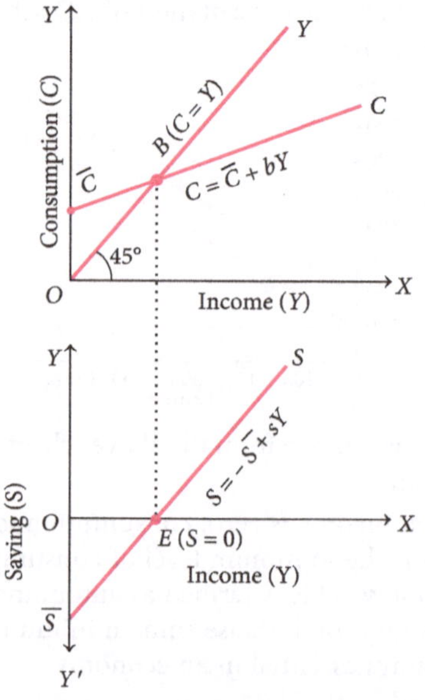

28. Construct a graph representing the economy's savings and then establish the consumption curve. Explain the process of deriving this curve and indicate a specific point on it where the average propensity to consume equals 1. **Competency Based Que**

Ans. Following figure shows how consumption curve is derived from the saving curve

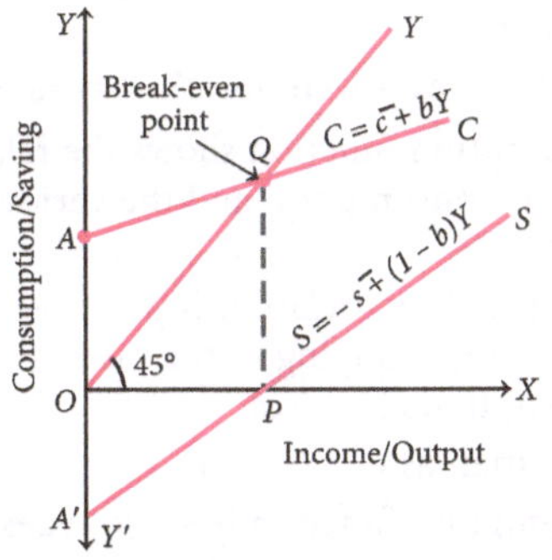

It involves the following steps

(i) We take $OA = OA'$. Because OA' = negative saving, when $Y = 0$ and this is exactly equal to minimum consumption when $Y = 0$.

(ii) Point Q on the Y-line (45° angle) is marked corresponding to point P on the saving curve. Because at P, saving = 0 and at point Q, consumption = income (implying that $S = 0$).

(iii) Joining points A and Q and stretching it to form a straight line, we get C curve. C function is linear as it is derived from a linear S function.

Since, MPC + MPS = 1, MPS = 1 − MPC. So that, while in C function, MPC is indicated by b, in S function, it is indicated by $1 - b$. Point Q on the consumption curve is the point at which APC = 1.

29. "Investment multiplier and Marginal Propensity to Consume (MPC) are directly related to each other." Explain with the help of numerical example. **CBSE Term II 2022; Competency Based Que**

Or **Define multiplier. What is the relation between marginal propensity to consume and multiplier? Calculate the marginal propensity to consume if the value of multiplier is 4.** **CBSE 2018**

Ans. Multiplier It is measured as the ratio between change in income and change in investment.

$$K = \frac{\Delta Y}{\Delta I}$$

Relation between Marginal Propensity to Consume and Multiplier There is direct and positive relationship between MPC (Marginal Propensity to Consume) and multiplier. Higher the MPC, higher will be the value of multiplier and *vice-versa*.

$$K = \frac{1}{1 - \text{MPS}}$$

If multiplier is 4

$$K = \frac{1}{\text{MPS}} \Rightarrow 4 = \frac{1}{\text{MPS}}$$

$$\text{MPS} = \frac{1}{4} = 0.25$$

$$\text{MPS} + \text{MPS} = 1$$

$$\text{MPC} + 0.25 = 1$$

$$\text{MPC} = 0.75$$

30. "Union Finance Minister stated, that investments in infrastructure and productive capacity have a large multiplier impact on growth and employment and in view of this, capital investment outlay is being proposed to increase steeply in the Budget 2023-24 by 1,000 crore."

Based on the given text and common understanding, explain the working process of the increase in investment on the national income, assuming the Marginal Propensity to Save (MPS) as 20%. **CBSE SQP 2025**

Ans. Formula for Multiplier $K = 1/\text{MPS}$

Change in National Income $(\Delta Y) = K \times \Delta I$

Calculate Multiplier (K)

Substituting MPS = 0.2

$$K = \frac{1}{0.2} = 5$$

Calculate Change in National Income (ΔY)

Substituting $K = 5$ and $\Delta I = 1{,}000$

$$\Delta Y = K \times \Delta I = 5 \times 1{,}000 = ₹\ 5{,}000 \text{ crore}$$

When the government increases capital investment by ₹ 1,000 crore, it creates a multiplier effect in the economy due to increased demand for goods and services. The multiplier effect amplifies the initial investment, leading to a five fold increase in national income (ΔY=5,000 crore). This increase boosts growth, employment and productivity across various sectors of the economy.

The increase in national income will be ₹ 5,000 crore. This highlights the significant impact of capital investment through the multiplier effect.

31. Keynes' multiplier is known as investment or income multiplier. The essence of multiplier is that total increase in income, output or employment is manifold the original increase in investment. e.g. If investment equal to ₹ 100 crore is made, then the income will not rise by ₹ 100 crore only but a multiple of it.

The total cost will amount to ₹ 100 crore. This will increase income of the people equal to ₹ 100 crore. But this is not all. The people who receive ₹ 100 crore will spend a good part of them on consumer goods.

Suppose, marginal propensity to consume of the people is 4/5 or 80%, then out of ₹ 100 crore, they will spend ₹ 80 crore on consumer goods, which would increase income of those people who supply consumer goods equal to ₹ 80 crore.

But those who receive these ₹ 80 crore will also in turn spend this income, depending upon their marginal propensity to consume. If their marginal propensity to consume is also 4/5, then they will spend ₹ 64 crore on consumer goods.

Thus, this will further increase income of some other people equal to ₹ 64 crore. It is thus clear that if the marginal propensity to consume is 4/5, the investment of ₹ 100 crore will lead to the increase in the national income by ₹ 500 crore. Therefore, multiplier here is equal to 5. **Competency Based Que**

(i) What is the meaning of investment multiplier?

(ii) Investment multiplier has both forward and backward operations. Do you agree? Explain.

Ans. (i) The term investment multiplier relates to the concept that any increase in public or private investment spending has a more than proportionate positive impact on aggregate income and the general economy.

Thus, the investment multiplier refers to the stimulative effects of public or private investments. The extent of the investment multiplier depends on two factors, i.e. the Marginal Propensity to Consume (MPC) and the Marginal Propensity to Save (MPS). A higher investment multiplier suggests that the investment will have a larger stimulative effect on the economy.

(ii) Multiplier is a double-edged weapon. It works in the backward direction as much as in the forward direction. The process of income propagation through multiplier does not work in the forward direction only. The higher the MPC, the greater the value of the multiplier and greater the cumulative decline in income.

In economics, a multiplier broadly refers to an economic factor that when increased or changed, causes increases or changes in many other related economic variables. In terms of gross domestic product, the multiplier effect causes gains in total output to be greater than the change in spending that caused it.

32. **Consumption expenditure refers to that portion of income which is spent on the purchase of goods and services at the given level of income. Consumption function refers to functional relationship between consumption and national income.**

It represents the willingness of households to purchase goods and services at a given level of income during a given time period.

It also shows the consumption level at different levels of income in an economy.

It is a psychological concept as it is influenced by subjective factors like consumer's preferences, habits, etc.

(i) Elaborate the functional relation of consumption function.

(ii) Explain the slope of consumption curve with help of diagram.

(iii) What is break-even point? **Competency Based Que**

Ans. (i) Consumption function shows the relationship between consumption and the various levels of income.

There is a direct relationship between consumption and income implying as the income rises, consumption also rises.

It is written as $C = \overline{C} + bY$

Consumption function has two types

- **Autonomous Consumption**
  It means that the level of consumption is independent of the changes in income.
  This is an amount of consumption which will take place even when the income is zero. In the above equation, $\overline{C}$ is the autonomous consumption.
- **Induced Consumption**
  It means the level of consumption which changes with the change in income. As the income rises, consumption also rises. In the equation, 'bY' represents induced consumption.

(ii) Slope of C-line (indicating consumption function) refers to the rate at which C increases in response to a given increase in Y.

It indicates the proportion of additional income that goes to consumption. This is measured as the ratio between AC (increase in C) and AY (increase in Y). This is known as Marginal Propensity to Consume (MPC).

Figure below shows the estimation of MPC as the slope of C-line.

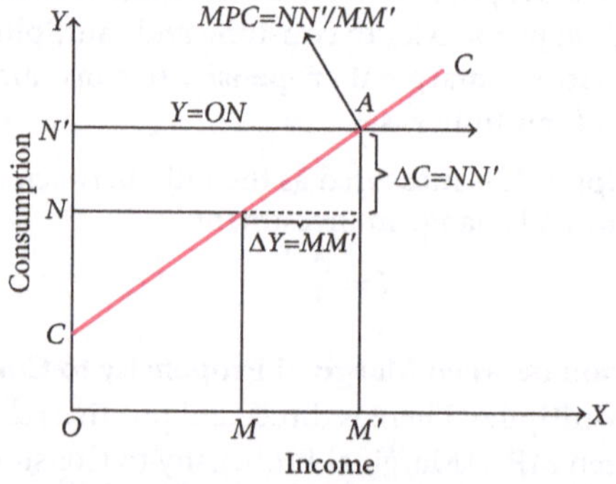

(iii) At break-even point consumption becomes equal to income and saving is 0.

Numerical Questions

Numerical 1

Complete the following table

Income (₹)	Saving (₹)	Average Propensity to Consume (APC)	Marginal Propensity to Consume (MPC)
0	–40	—	—
50	–20	...	...
100	0	...	0.6
150	30	0.8	...
200	50	...	...

Sol. $C = Y - S$; APC = C/Y; MPC $= \frac{\Delta C}{\Delta Y}$

Income (*Y*) (₹)	Saving (*S*) (₹)	Consumption (*C*) (₹)	APC (*C*/*Y*)	ΔC	ΔY	MPC $\left(\frac{\Delta C}{\Delta Y}\right)$
0	–40	40	—	—	—	—
50	–20	70	**1.4**	30	50	**0.6**
100	0	100	**1**	30	50	0.6
150	30	120	0.8	20	50	**0.4**
200	50	150	**0.75**	30	50	**0.6**

Numerical 2

Complete the following table

Consumption Expenditure (₹)	Saving (₹)	Income to Consume	Marginal Propensity to Consume (MPC)
100	50	150	—
175	75	...	...
250	100	...	...
325	125	...	...

Sol. Income to Consume = Consumption Expenditure + Savings

$$\text{MPC} = \frac{\Delta C}{\Delta Y}$$

Consumption Expenditure (*C*) (₹)	Saving (*S*) (₹)	Income to Consume (*Y*)	ΔC	ΔY	MPC $\left(\frac{\Delta C}{\Delta Y}\right)$
100	50	150	—	—	—
175	75	**250**	75	100	**0.75**
250	100	**350**	75	100	**0.75**
325	125	**450**	75	100	**0.75**

Numerical 3

Complete the following table

Income (*Y*)	Marginal Propensity to Consume (MPC)	Saving (*S*)	Average Propensity to Save (APS)
0	–	– 90	–
100	0.4	...	...
200	0.4	...	...
300	0.4	...	...

Sol.

Y	MPC	MPS	*S*	APS
0	–	–	90	–
100	0.4	0.6	60	0.6
200	0.4	0.6	120	0.6
300	0.4	0.6	180	0.6

$$S = Y - C;\quad \text{APS} = \frac{S}{Y}$$

Numerical 4

Complete the following table

Income (₹)	Consumption Expenditure (₹)	Marginal Propensity to Save (MPS)	Average Propensity to Save (APS)
0	80	—	—
100	140	0.4	...
200	...	...	0
...	240	...	0.20
...	260	0.8	0.35

Sol. $Y = C + S$; $S = Y - C$; MPS $= \frac{\Delta S}{\Delta Y}$; APS $= \frac{S}{Y}$

Income (*Y*)(₹)	Consumption Expenditure (*C*) (₹)	Saving (*S*) (₹)	ΔS	ΔY	MPS $\left(\frac{\Delta S}{\Delta Y}\right)$	APS $\left(\frac{S}{Y}\right)$
0	80	–80	—	—	—	—
100	140	–40	40	100	0.4	**–0.4**
200	**200**	0	–40	100	**– 0.4**	0
300	240	60	60	100	**0.6**	0.20
400	260	140	80	100	0.8	0.35

Numerical 5

Complete the following table

Income	Saving	MPC	APS
0	−15	—	—
50	0	...	...
100	15	...	...
150	30	...	...

Sol. $C = Y - S$; $MPC = \frac{\Delta C}{\Delta Y}$; $APS = \frac{S}{Y}$

Income (Y)	Saving (S)	C	ΔY	ΔC	MPC	APS
0	−15	15	–	–	–	–
50	0	50	50	35	**0.7**	**0**
100	15	85	50	35	**0.7**	**0.15**
150	30	120	50	35	**0.7**	**0.2**

Numerical 6

Complete the following table

Income (Y)	Consumption (C)	MPS	APC
0	6	—	—
20	23	...	...
40	40	...	...
60	57	...	...

Sol.

Y	C	S	ΔS	ΔY	MPS	APS
0	6	−6	–	–	–	–
20	23	−3	3	20	**0.15**	**1.15**
40	40	0	3	20	**0.15**	**1.00**
60	57	3	3	20	**0.15**	**0.95**

Numerical 7

The consumption function in an economy is $C = 20 + 0.75Y$. Determine the level of income where average propensity to consume will be one.

Sol. As we know $APC = \frac{C}{Y}$

For APC = 1; $C = Y$

$Y = 20 + 0.75\,Y$; $0.25\,Y = 20$

Therefore at $Y = 80$, APC = 1

Numerical 8

Find change in savings when 1/3rd of income is always spent as consumption expenditure and current income is 50% more than the initial income of ₹ 40,000.

Sol. Current income = 50% of 40,000 + 40,000

= 20,000 + 40,000 = ₹ 60,000

Initial income = ₹ 40,000

Change in income (ΔY) = 60,000 − 40,000 = ₹ 20,000

MPC = 1/3 (Given)

MPS = 1 − MPC = 1 − 1/3 = 2/3

Also,

$$MPS = \Delta S/\Delta Y$$

$$2/3 = \Delta S/20{,}000$$

$$\Delta S = 13{,}333.33$$

Thus, change in savings = ₹ 13,333.33

Numerical 9

If marginal propensity to consume is 70% and is constant at all levels of income and the autonomous consumption is ₹ 400 crore, find consumption function of the given hypothetical economy.

Sol. Given, Marginal Propensity to Consume (MPC) = 70% = 0.7

Autonomous Consumption ($\overline{C}$) = ₹ 400 crore

Consumption function would be

$$C = \overline{C} + MPC\,(Y)$$

$$= 400 + 0.7Y$$

Numerical 10

Given that the national income is ₹ 120 crore and consumption expenditure is ₹ 96 crore, find out the average propensity to save. When income rises to ₹ 160 crore and consumption expenditure to ₹ 120 crore, what will be the average propensity to consume and marginal propensity to consume?

Sol. Here, in first condition $Y =$ ₹ 120 crore

$C =$ ₹ 96 crore

Hence, $S = Y - C = 120 - 96 =$ ₹ 24 crore

Now, Average Propensity to Save

$$APS = \frac{S}{Y} = \frac{24}{120} = 0.2$$

Again when income and expenditure rise

$Y =$ ₹ 160 crore; $C =$ ₹ 120 crore

So, Average Propensity to Consume

$$APS = \frac{C}{Y} = \frac{120}{160} = 0.75$$

Here, $\Delta Y = 160 - 120 =$ ₹ 40 crore

$\Delta C = 120 - 96 =$ ₹ 24 crore

So, Marginal Propensity to Consume

$$MPC = \frac{\Delta C}{\Delta Y} = \frac{24}{40} = 0.6$$

Numerical 11

If national income is ₹ 80 crore and consumption expenditure is ₹ 72 crore, find out the average propensity to save. When income rises to ₹ 120 crore and consumption expenditure to ₹ 102 crore, what will be the marginal propensity to consume and marginal propensity to save?

Sol. Here in first condition $Y =$ ₹ 80 crore

$C =$ ₹ 72 crore

Hence, $S = Y - C = 80 - 72 =$ ₹ 8 crore

Average Propensity to Save (APS) $= \frac{S}{Y} = \frac{8}{80} = 0.1$

Again, when income and consumption expenditure rise

$Y = 120$ crore ; $C =$ ₹ 102 crore

$\Delta C = 102 - 72 =$ ₹ 30 crore

$\Delta Y = 120 - 80 =$ ₹ 40 crore

Marginal Propensity to Consume

$$MPC = \frac{\Delta C}{\Delta Y} = \frac{30}{40} = 0.75$$

Again, Marginal Propensity to Save (MPS)

$= 1 - MPC = 1 - 0.75 = 0.25$

Numerical 12

A household has an income of ₹ 8,000 and spends ₹ 6,000 on consumption. When their income increases to ₹ 10,000, they increase their spending to ₹ 7,500.

Find

(i) Marginal Propensity to Consume (MPC).

(ii) Average Propensity to Save (APS) at the higher income level.

Sol.

	Income (Y)	Consumption (C)	Saving ($S = Y - C$)
Initial	8,000	6,000	2,000
New	10,000	7,500	2,500

(i) MPC = $\Delta C / \Delta Y$

where, ΔC = New C – Initial C

= 7,500 – 6,000 = 1,500

ΔY = New Y – Initial Y

= 10,000 – 8,000 = 2,000

Now, substitute the values

$$MPC = \frac{1{,}500}{2{,}000} = 0.75$$

(ii) APS = S/Y

At higher income level $Y = 10{,}000$ and

Saving = 2,500 = 2,500/10,000 = 0.25

Numerical 13

In an economy, the ratio of average propensity to consume and average propensity to save is 3 : 2. The level of income is ₹ 10,000 crore. How much are the savings? Calculate.

Sol. $\frac{APC}{APS} = \frac{3}{2}$; given $Y =$ ₹ 10,000 crore

Now, as $APS = \frac{S}{Y}$; $APC = \frac{3}{5}$ and $APS = \frac{2}{5}$

Therefore, $APS = \frac{S}{Y} = \frac{2}{5}$

$\Rightarrow \frac{2}{5} = \frac{S}{10{,}000} \Rightarrow S = 10{,}000 \times \frac{2}{5} =$ ₹ 4,000 crore

Numerical 14

It is given for an economy that MPC is 2/3rd of MPS, while consumption at zero level of income is ₹ 200 crore. Derive the consumption and saving functions.

What do you suggest about this economy?

Sol. Given, $MPC = \frac{2}{3}$ MPS ; $\overline{C} =$ ₹ 200 crore

$MPC + MPS = 1 \Rightarrow \frac{2}{3} MPS + MPS = 1$

$MPS = \frac{3}{5} = 0.6 = s$

b or $MPC = \frac{2}{3} MPS = \frac{2}{3} \times 0.6 = 0.4$

Consumption Function $(C) = (\overline{C}) + bY = 200 + 0.4Y$

We also know that $-s$, the negative of $\overline{C}$

Saving Function $(S) = -\overline{S} + sY = -200 + 0.6Y$

The economy suggests that people consume less and save more out of additional income.

Numerical 15

The saving curve of an economy makes an intercept on negative axis at ₹ 10 crore and 25% of additional income is saved. Find out the consumption function.

Sol. MPS = 25% *or* 0.25

b or $MPC = 1 - MPS = 1 - 0.25 = 0.75$

Intercept $- S = -10$

Hence, $\overline{C} = -(-10) = 10$

Therefore, Consumption function $(C) = \overline{C} + bY$

$= 10 + 0.75Y$

Numerical 16

If marginal propensity to save is 40% and is constant at all levels of income and the autonomous consumption is ₹ 100 crore, find consumption function of the given hypothetical economy.

Sol. Given, Marginal Propensity to Save (MPS) = 40% = 0.4

MPC = 1 – MPS = 1 – 0.4 = 0.6

Autonomous Consumption $(\overline{C})$ = ₹ 100 crore

Consumption function would be

$$C = \overline{C} + MPC\ (Y)$$

$$= 100 + 0.6Y$$

Numerical 17

The consumption function of an economy is $C = 140 + 0.8Y$ (amount in ₹ crore). Determine that level of income where average propensity to consume will be one.

Sol. Given, $C = 140 + 0.8Y$

Average Propensity to Consume (APC = C/Y) will be one when

$$Y = C$$
$$Y = 140 + 0.8Y$$
$$Y - 0.8Y = 140$$
$$0.2Y = 140$$
$$Y = 700$$

Average propensity to consume will be one when the level of income = ₹ 700 crore.

Numerical 18

You are given the consumption function of an imaginary economy, $C = 100 + 0.8Y$, where C = Consumption and Y = Income. **CBSE Term II 2022**

Calculate

(i) Then value of Marginal Propensity to Save (MPS).

(ii) The level of income at break-even point.

Sol. (i) Given, $C = 100 + 0.8Y$

MPC = 0.8

MPC + MPS = 1

MPS = 1 − MPC = 1 − 0.8 = 0.2

(ii) As we know, at break-even point

$$Y = C$$
$$Y = 100 + 0.8Y$$
$$0.2Y = 100$$
$$Y = 500$$

Numerical 19

If in an economy saving function is given by $S = (-)\ 50 + 0.2\ Y$ and Y = ₹ 2,000 crore, consumption expenditure for the economy would be ₹ 1,650 crore, the autonomous investment is ₹ 50 crore and the marginal propensity to consume is 0.8. True or False? Justify your answer with proper calculations.

Sol. True.

Given, $S = (-)\ 50 + 0.2\ Y$, Y = ₹ 2,000 crore,

Consumption Expenditure = ₹ 1,650 crore and

Autonomous Investment = ₹ 50 crore

Now, $S = (-)\ 50 + 0.2\ (2{,}000)$

$= -\ 50 + 400$ = ₹ 350 crore

At equilibrium level of income,

$$Y = C + S$$
$$2{,}000 = C + 350$$
$$C = 2{,}000 - 350 = ₹\ 1{,}650 \text{ crore}$$

As given in equation,

MPS = 0.2

MPC + MPS = 1

MPC + 0.2 = 1

MPC = (1 − 0.2) = 0.8

So, all the given values are correct.

Numerical 20

With the help of consumption function $C = 20 + 0.8Y$, calculate savings at an income level of ₹ 500 crore.

Sol. $C = 20 + 0.8Y$

Savings = Income − Consumption

$= Y - (20 + 0.80Y) = Y - 20 - 0.80Y$

$S = -20 + 0.20Y$

As, $Y = 500$

$S = -20 + 0.20\ (500) = -20 + 100 = 80$ crore

Numerical 21

Estimate the value of aggregate demand in an imaginary economy

(i) Autonomous Investment (I_0) = ₹ 100 crore

(ii) Marginal Propensity to Save (MPS) = 0.2

(iii) Level of income (Y) = ₹ 4,000 crore

(iv) Autonomous Consumption Expenditure ($\overline{C}$) = ₹ 50 crore **CBSE 2025, SQP 2019**

Sol. Given, autonomous investment = ₹ 100 crore

Marginal Propensity to Save (MPS) = 0.2

Level of Income (Y) = ₹ 4,000 crore

Autonomous Consumption Expenditure ($\overline{C}$) = ₹ 50 crore

Marginal Propensity to Consume (MPC)

= 1 − MPS = 1 − 0.2 = 0.8

We know that,

or $AD = C + I$

$AD = \overline{C} + MPC\ (Y) + I_0$

$= 50 + 0.8\ (4{,}000) + 100$

$= 50 + 3{,}200 + 100$ = ₹ 3,350 crore

Numerical 22

Find investment expenditure from the following

National Income = ₹ 1,000.

Autonomous Consumption = ₹ 250.

Marginal Propensity to Consume = 0.7

Sol. Given, National Income (Y) = ₹ 1,000

Autonomous Consumption ($\overline{C}$) = ₹ 250

Marginal Propensity to Consume (MPC) = 0.7

We know that, $Y = C + I$

$$Y = \overline{C} + \text{MPC}(Y) + \text{I}$$

$$I = Y - \overline{C} - \text{MPC}(Y) = 1{,}000 - 250 - 0.7(1{,}000)$$

$$= 1{,}000 - 250 - 700 = 1{,}000 - 950 = 50$$

Investment expenditure = ₹ 50

Numerical 23

State whether the following statements are true or false. Give reasons for your answer.

(i) When marginal propensity to consume is greater than marginal propensity to save, the value of investment multiplier will be greater than 5.

(ii) The value of marginal propensity to save can never be negative.

Sol. (i) No, the statement is false. This can be understood by an example. Suppose, the value of MPC = 0.6, hence, MPS = 0.4 (as MPS = 1 − MPC).

Here, MPC > MPS

Now, $K = \frac{1}{1-\text{MPC}} = \frac{1}{1-0.6}$ *or* $= \frac{1}{0.4} = 2.5$

So, $K < 5$ even if MPC > MPS.

(ii) Yes, the statement is true. As MPS tells about the change in savings due to change in income and even if the entire income is consumed, savings can be at most zero, so MPS can never be negative.

Numerical 24

For two hypothetical economies A and B, the value of Marginal Propensity to Consume (MPC) stands at 0.6 and 0.8 respectively. Assuming for both the economies, Autonomous Consumption ($\overline{C}$) to be ₹ 40 crore and Investment Expenditure (I) to be ₹ 100 crore.

Calculate **CBSE SQP 2025**

(i) Break-even level of income for economy A.

(ii) Equilibrium level of income for economy B.

Sol. Break-even level of income $Y = \frac{\overline{C}}{1-\text{MPC}}$

Equilibrium level of income $Y = \frac{\overline{C} + I}{1-\text{MPC}}$

$$Y = \frac{C}{1-\text{MPC}} \Rightarrow Y = \frac{40}{1-0.6} = \frac{40}{0.4} = 100 \text{ crore}$$

$$Y = \frac{\overline{C}+I}{1-\text{MPC}} \Rightarrow Y = \frac{40+100}{1-0.8} = \frac{140}{0.2} = 700 \text{ crore}$$

(i) Break-even level of income for economy A ₹ 100 crore

(ii) Equilibrium level of income for economy B ₹ 700 crore

Numerical 25

In an economy, investment is invested by ₹ 1,000 crore. Calculate the change in total income, if marginal propensity to consume is 0.6.

Sol. Here, MPC = 0.6; ΔI = ₹ 1,000 crore

We know that MPC + MPS = 1

$$\text{MPS} = 1 - \text{MPC} = 1 - 0.6 = 0.4$$

Again we know that

$$K = \frac{1}{\text{MPS}} = \frac{1}{0.4} = 2.5$$

Again $K = \frac{\Delta Y}{\Delta I} \Rightarrow 2.5 = \frac{\Delta Y}{1{,}000}$

$\Rightarrow \Delta Y$ = ₹ 2,500 crore

Numerical 26

If in an economy

Change in initial investment (ΔI) = ₹ 1,000 crore

Marginal Propensity to Save (MPS) = 0.2.

Find the value of the following

(i) Investment multiplier (K)

(ii) Change in final income (ΔY) **CBSE 2020**

Sol. Given, change in initial investment (ΔI) = ₹ 1,000 crore

Marginal Propensity to Save (MPS) = 0.2

(i) Investment Multiplier (K) = 1/ MPS = 1/0.2 = 5

(ii) We also know that,

Investment Multiplier (K) = $\Delta Y / \Delta I$

Increase in Income (ΔY) = $K \times \Delta I$

= 5 × 1,000 = ₹ 5,000

Numerical 27

As a result of increase in investment by ₹ 60 crore, national income rises by ₹ 420 crore. Calculate MPC.

Sol. Here, ΔI = ₹ 60 crore

ΔY = ₹ 420 crore

$$K = \frac{\Delta Y}{\Delta I} = \frac{420}{60} = 7$$

Now, $K = \frac{1}{1-\text{MPC}}$

$$\Rightarrow \quad 7 = \frac{1}{1-\text{MPC}}$$

$$7(1-\text{MPC}) = 1$$

$$7 - 7\text{ MPC} = 1$$

$$7 - 1 = 7\text{MPC}$$

$$\frac{6}{7} = \text{MPC}$$

$$0.85 = \text{MPC}$$

Numerical 28

In an economy, everytime income rises, 75% of the rise in income is spent on consumption. Now, suppose in the same economy, investment rises by ₹ 750 crore.

Calculate the following

(i) Change in income (ii) MPS

Sol. (i) Here, MPC = 0.75; $\Delta I =$ ₹ 750 crore

Now, $K = \dfrac{1}{1 - \text{MPC}}$

$\therefore \quad K = \dfrac{1}{1-0.75} = \dfrac{1}{0.25} = 4$

Again, $K = \dfrac{\Delta Y}{\Delta I}$ or $4 = \dfrac{\Delta Y}{750}$

$\therefore \Delta Y = 750 \times 4$

$\Delta Y =$ ₹ 3,000 crore

(ii) MPS = 1 − MPC = 1 − 0.75 = 0.25

Numerical 29

In an economy, the equilibrium level of income is ₹ 12,000 crore. The ratio of marginal propensity to consume and marginal propensity to save is 3 : 1. Calculate the additional investment needed to reach new equilibrium level of income of ₹ 20,000 crore.

Sol. Here, $\Delta Y = 20{,}000 - 12{,}000$

or $\Delta Y =$ ₹ 8,000 crore

$\text{MPC} = \dfrac{3}{4}$ as $\left(\dfrac{\text{MPC}}{\text{MPS}} = \dfrac{3}{1}\right)$

Hence, $K = \dfrac{1}{1 - \text{MPC}} \Rightarrow K = \dfrac{1}{1 - \frac{3}{4}}$

$\Rightarrow \quad K = \dfrac{1}{1-0.75}$

$\Rightarrow \quad K = \dfrac{1}{0.25} = 4$

Again, $K = \dfrac{\Delta Y}{\Delta I}$

or $4 = \dfrac{8{,}000}{\Delta I}$

or $\Delta I = \dfrac{8{,}000}{4} = 2{,}000$

$\therefore$ Additional investment required = ₹ 2,000 crore

Numerical 30

In an economy, investment increases by ₹ 1,000 crore and marginal propensity to save is 0.25.

Calculate

(i) Investment Multiplier (K)

(ii) Total Increase in Income (ΔY) **CBSE 2021 C**

Sol. Given that

MPS = 0.25 and $\Delta I = \Delta$ 1,000 crore

(i) Investment Multiplier (K)

= 1/MPS = 1/0.25 = 4

(ii) Total increase in income (ΔY)

$K = \Delta Y / \Delta I$

$4 = \Delta Y / 1{,}000$

$\Delta Y =$ ₹ 4,000 crore

Numerical 31

If an economy plans to increase its income by ₹ 2,000 crore and the marginal propensity to consume is 75%. Estimate the increase in investment required to achieve the targeted increase in income. **CBSE SQP 2023**

Ans. Given, MPC = 0.75, ΔY = ₹ 2,000 crore

K = 1/1 − MPC

=1/1 − 0.75 =1/0.25 = 4

According to the question

$K = \Delta Y / \Delta I$

$4 = 2{,}000 / \Delta I$

$\Delta I = 2{,}000/4 =$ ₹ 500 crore

Therefore, increase in investment (ΔI) required

= ₹ 500 crore

Numerical 32

For a hypothetical economy, the government incurs an investment expenditure of ₹ 1,000 crore. If the value of Marginal Propensity to Save (MPS) falls from 0.25 to 0.10, calculate the value increase in income due to change in the value of marginal propensity to save. **CBSE SQP 2024**

Sol. Given, Change in Investment (ΔI) = ₹ 1,000 crore

MPS	Investment Multiplier $K = \dfrac{1}{\text{MPS}}$	Change in Income (ΔY) $\Delta Y = K \times \Delta I$ (₹ in crore)
0.25	$\dfrac{1}{0.25} = 4$	$4 \times 1{,}000 = 4{,}000$
0.10	$\dfrac{1}{0.10} = 10$	$10 \times 1{,}000 = 10{,}000$

Increase in Income (ΔY) = 10,000 − 4,000 = ₹ 6,000 crore

Numerical 33

In an economy, investment expenditure is increased by ₹ 600 crore and marginal propensity to consume is 0.6. Calculate the total increase in income and saving.

Sol. Given, increase in investment expenditure

(ΔI) = ₹ 600 crore

Marginal Propensity to Consume (MPC) = 0.6

We know that,

Multiplier (K) $=1/\ 1-\text{MPC} = 1/1-0.6 = 2.5$

$\text{MPS} = 1-\text{MPC} = 1-0.6 = 0.4$

Increase in Income $= K \times \Delta I = 2.5 \times 600 = 1{,}500$

Increase in Saving $= \text{MPS} \times \Delta Y = 0.4 \times 1{,}500 = 600$

Increase in Income = ₹ 1,500 crore

Increase in Saving = ₹ 600 crore

Numerical 34

An increase in investment by ₹ 800 crore leads to increase in national income by ₹ 3,200 crore. Calculate marginal propensity to consume and marginal propensity to save.

Sol. Given, increase in investment (ΔI) = ₹ 800 crore

Increase in national income (ΔY) = ₹ 3,200 crore

Multiplier (K) $= \Delta Y/\Delta I$

$$K = 3{,}200/800 = 4$$

We know, $K = 1/1-\text{MPC}$

$$4 = 1/1 - \text{MPC}$$

$$1-\text{MPC} = 0.25$$

$$\text{MPC} = 1-0.25$$

$$\text{MPC} = 0.75$$

We also know that,

$$\text{MPC} + \text{MPS} = 1$$

$$\text{MPS} = 1-\text{MPC}$$

$$1-0.75 = 0.25$$

Marginal propensity to consume = 0.75

Marginal propensity to save = 0.25

Numerical 35

In an economy, an increase in investment leads to increase in national income which is four times the increase in investment. Calculate marginal propensity to consume.

Sol. Here, $K = 4$ *or* $\dfrac{\Delta Y}{\Delta I} = 4$

Now, $K = \dfrac{1}{\text{MPS}} = \dfrac{1}{1-\text{MPC}} \Rightarrow 4 = \dfrac{1}{1-\text{MPC}}$

$$1-\text{MPC} = \frac{1}{4} \Rightarrow \text{MPC} = 1 = \frac{1}{4}$$

$$\Rightarrow \quad \text{MPC} = \frac{3}{4} = 0.75$$

Numerical 36

In an economy, the equilibrium level of income is ₹ 10,000 crore. The ratio of marginal propensity to consume and marginal propensity to save is 3:2.

Calculate the additional investment required to reach the equilibrium level income of ₹ 20,000 crore.

Sol. Here $\Delta Y = 20{,}000 - 10{,}000 =$ ₹ 10,000 crore

$$\frac{\text{MPC}}{\text{MPS}} = \frac{3}{2}$$

So, $\text{MPC} = \dfrac{3}{5}$

Hence,

$$K = \frac{1}{1-\text{MPC}} = \frac{1}{1-\frac{3}{5}} = \frac{1}{0.4}$$

$$\Rightarrow \quad K = 2.5$$

Again, $K = \dfrac{\Delta Y}{\Delta I}$

$$\Rightarrow \quad 2.5 = \frac{10{,}000}{\Delta I}$$

$$\Rightarrow \quad \Delta I = \frac{10{,}000}{2.5}$$

= ₹ 4,000 crore

∴ Additional investment required = ₹ 4,000 crore

SELF ASSESSMENT TEST

Objective Type Questions

1. There is a direct relationship between induced investment and income, therefore, induced investment curve is
   (a) positively sloped upward
   (b) negatively sloped downward
   (c) parallel to X-axis
   (d) parallel to Y-axis
2. In the two-sector model, the slope of the consumption function curve depends on
   (a) government spending
   (b) Marginal Propensity to Consume (MPC)
   (c) Marginal Propensity to Save (MPS)
   (d) Both MPC and MPS
3. Maximum value MPC is
   (a) 1 (b) 2
   (c) 5 (d) Infinity
4. What is the formula of APS?
   (a) APS $=\frac{\Delta C}{\Delta Y}$ (b) APS $=\frac{\Delta S}{\Delta Y}$
   (c) APS $=\frac{Y}{S}$ (d) APS $=\frac{S}{Y}$
5. When the Marginal Propensity to Consume (MPC) increases, the value of the multiplier
   (a) decreases (b) increases
   (c) remains the same (c) becomes zero
6. Which of the following statements is/are correct?
   I. Marginal propensity to consume can never be zero.
   II. Investment multiplier can work forward as well as backward.

   Codes
   (a) Only I (b) Only II
   (c) Both I and II (d) None of these

Answers 1. (a) 2. (b) 3. (a) 4. (d) 5. (b) 6. (b)

Short Answer Type Questions

7. Explain the difference between aggregate demand and aggregate supply.
8. Given Keynes's assertion that 'consumption includes an autonomous component', how does this explain the consumption curve's deviation from the origin in standard economic models?
9. Differentiate between average propensity to consume and average propensity to save.
10. What are ex-ante measures?
11. Briefly explain the components of aggregate supply.

Long Answer Type Questions

12. Explain the working of multiplier.
13. Using suitable numerical example, explain the derivation of saving function from consumption function.

Numerical Questions

14. In an economy, total savings are ₹ 2,000 crore and the ratio of average propensity to save and average propensity to consume is 2 : 7. Calculate the level of income in an economy.

Ans. ₹ 9,000 crore

15. In an economy investment is increased by ₹ 300 crore. If marginal propensity to consume is 2/3, calculate increase in national income.

Ans. National income increases by ₹ 900 crore

16. Complete the following table

Income (₹)	Saving (₹)	Average Propensity to Consume	Marginal Propensity to Consume
0	– 40	–	–
50	– 20	...	...
100	0	...	0.6
150	30	0.8	...
200	50	...	...

17. In an economy, the initial income was ₹ 1,000 crore which increased by ₹ 2,500 crore.
    Given MPS = 0.3 ; $\overline{C}$ = ₹ 500
    Calculate the investment expenditure at the increased level of income.

Ans. I =₹ 550 crore

05

CHAPTER

Equilibrium in an economy reflects a state where market forces balance, resulting in stable prices and optimal resource allocation. Disequilibrium, however, disrupts this harmony, leading to fluctuations in prices, output and employment.

YOUR STUDY GOALS

- 5.1 Short-run Equilibrium in the Economy
- 5.2 Equilibrium Level
- 5.3 Disequilibrium in the Economy
  - Excess Demand
  - Deficient Demand

YOUR PRACTICE GOAL

- Objective Type Questions (70 Qs ; MCQs, A-R, Statements, Matching, Concept Identification)
- Subjective Questions (26 SAs, 10 LAs)
- 24 Numerical Questions
- Self Assessment Test (8 MCQs, 6 SAs, 3 LAs, 4 Numerical)

Equilibrium and Disequilibrium in the Economy

5.1 Short-run Equilibrium in the Economy

In macroeconomics, short-run may be defined as a period of time when 'technology' as a factor remains constant.

It can also be defined as the period of time during which, level of output is determined only by the level of employment.

$$\boxed{\uparrow \text{level of employment} \Rightarrow \uparrow \text{level of output}}$$

So, if income remains unchanged, then economy is said to be in short-run equilibrium.

Equilibrium Output

Equilibrium output refers to a situation, where

$$\boxed{\text{Aggregate Demand (AD)} = \text{Aggregate Supply (AS)}}$$

Since, Aggregate Demand = Consumption + Investment

or $\boxed{AD = C + I}$

and Aggregate Supply = Consumption + Saving

or $\boxed{AS = C + S}$

We can write the equation of equilibrium output as under

Equilibrium Output = AS = AD

$\Rightarrow$ $C + S = C + I$ *or* $S = I$

Thus, equilibrium output is also achieved when,

Saving = Investment $\Rightarrow$ $\boxed{S = I}$

Note Here, all the aggregates i.e. AD, AS, S and I are in ex-ante sense.

Approaches to Determine Short-run Equilibrium

There are two approaches to determine short-run equilibrium, which are as follows

- AD = AS Approach
- $S = I$ Approach

Assumptions of Equilibrium

Following assumptions are required while determining equilibrium output

- The determination of equilibrium income is to be studied with respect to a two-sector closed economic model comprising households and firms.
- Investment expenditure by the firms is assumed to be constant or autonomous.
- General price level in the economy remains constant.
- Equilibrium level of income and employment is to be determined in context of short-run.

I. Aggregate Demand (AD) = Aggregate Supply (AS) Approach

According to Keynesian theory of income determination, the equilibrium level of income and employment is determined at a point where aggregate demand in an economy becomes equal to aggregate supply or total output at a given point of time.

It can be illustrated with the help of schedule and diagram given below

Income (Y) (₹ in crores)	**Consumption** (C) (₹ in crores)	**Savings** (S) (₹ in crores)	**Investment** (I) (₹ in crores)	**AD** ($C+I$)	**AS** ($C+S$)	**Remark**
0	200	−200	200	400	0	AD > AS
500	600	−100	200	800	500	AD > AS
1,000	1,000	0	200	1,200	1,000	AD > AS
1,500	1,400	100	200	1,600	1,500	AD > AS
2,000	1,800	200	200	2,000	2,000	AD = AS
2,500	2,200	300	200	2,400	2,500	AD < AS
3,000	2,600	400	200	2,800	3,000	AD < AS

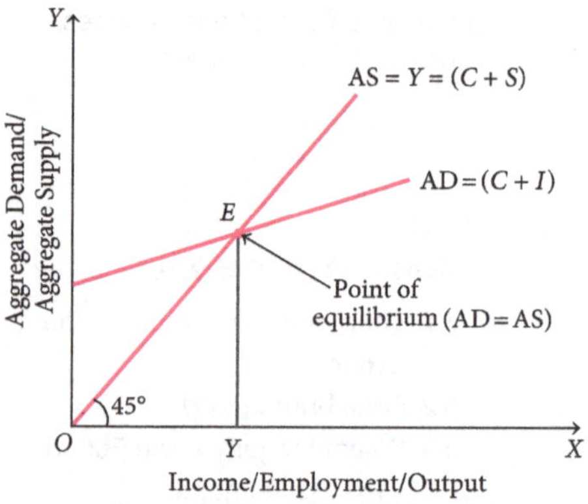

Determination of Equilibrium Output

In the graph, E is the point of equilibrium because at this point AD = AS and OY is the equilibrium level of output/income/employment. The given situation where AD=AS, is referred to as **effective demand.**

When AS>AD

- Flow of goods and services tends to exceed their demand.
- As a result, some goods remain unsold.
- To clear unwanted stock, the producers would plan to cut down in production by decreasing employment and output.
- Consequently, AS would reduce to become equal to AD.

When AD>AS

- Flow of goods and services tends to be less than their demand.
- As a result, existing stocks of the producers would fall below the desired level.
- To rebuild desired stock, the producers would plan for greater production by increasing employment and output.
- Consequently, AS would increase to become equal to AD.

II. Savings (S) = Investment (I) Approach

According to this approach, equilibrium level of income/output is determined at a point where planned or ex-ante saving is equal to planned or ex-ante investment.

This can be illustrated with the help of the following schedule and diagram.

Equilibrium by Saving and Investment Approach

Income (*Y*) (₹ in crores)	Consumption (*C*) (₹ in crores)	Savings (*S*) (₹ in crores)	Investment (*I*) (₹ in crores)	Remarks
0	200	−200	200	S < I
500	600	−100	200	S < I
1,000	1,000	0	200	S < I
1,500	1,400	100	200	S < I
2,000	1,800	200	200	S = I (*E*)
2,500	2,200	300	200	S > I
3,000	2,600	400	200	S > I

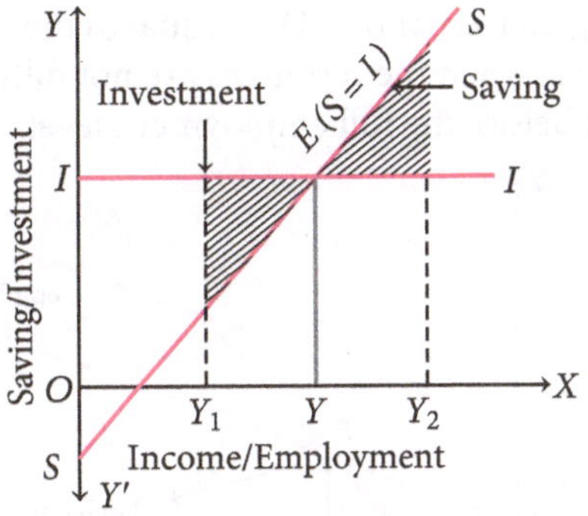

Determination of Equilibrium Output

In the graph, *SS* curve is the saving curve and *II* is the investment curve representing autonomous investment. Equilibrium occurs at point *E*, where *SS* curve and *II* curve intersect and *OY* is the equilibrium level of output.

When S > I

- It means that households are not consuming as much as firms expected them to.
- As a result, the inventory rises above the desired level.
- Thus, firms will cut production, leading to fall in income and savings.
- This will continue till economy moves back to equilibrium at point *E*.

When S < I

- It means that households are consuming more and saving less than the firms expected them to.
- As a result, the inventory would fall below the desired level.
- Thus, firms will increase production, leading to rise in income and savings.
- This will continue till economy moves back to equilibrium at point *E*.

5.2 Equilibrium Level

According to Keynes, equilibrium level can be achieved at

- Full employment level
- Underemployment level
- Over full employment level

Full Employment Equilibrium

Full employment refers to a situation where all those who are able to work and are willing to work, are getting work.

Full employment equilibrium is a situation when the Aggregate Demand (AD) is equal to the Aggregate Supply (AS) at full employment level.

In the graph given,

- Point '*E*' represents full employment equilibrium level.
- At this level of output/income/employment, no one is involuntarily unemployed.

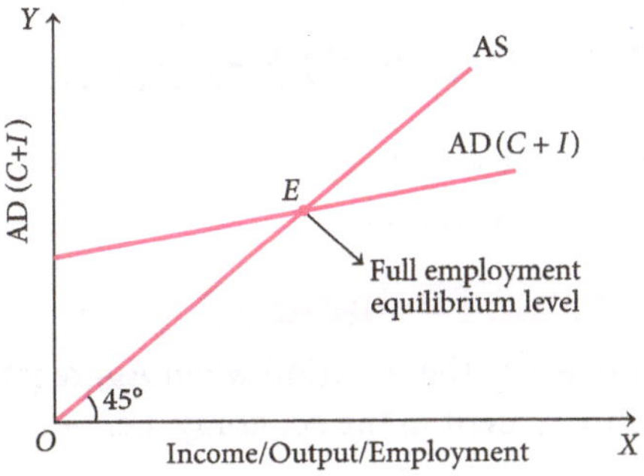

Under Employment Equilibrium

Under employment refers to a situation when all those who are able to work at existing wage rates, are not getting jobs. It is called **involuntary unemployment**.

Under employment equilibrium is a situation where the Aggregate Demand (AD) is equal to the Aggregate Supply (AS), but when the resources are not fully employed. It occurs before the full employment level.

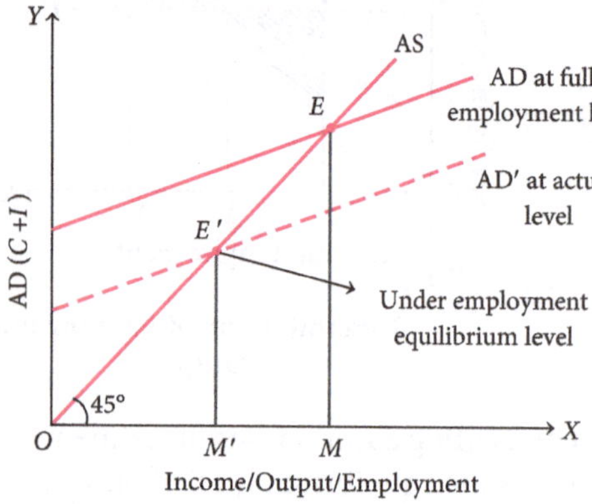

In the graph given,

- AD′ = AS at point E′ which is lower than full employment level.
- Point E′ shows under employment equilibrium.

Over Full Employment Equilibrium

It refers to the situation in which AD = AS, but beyond the full employment level. It means that actual (ex-post) Aggregate Demand (AD) tends to be higher than what is required to maintain full employment. As the economy has already achieved full employment and there is no idle capacity, hence AD cannot be increased further. As a result, it will end up creating excess demand.

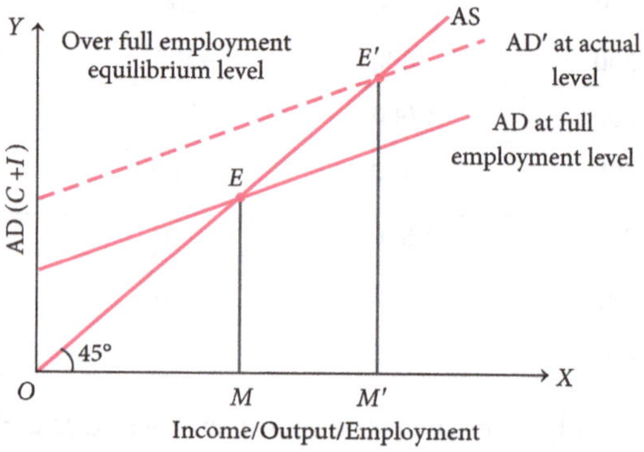

In the above graph

- AD′= AS at point E′ which is higher than full employment level of equilibrium.
- Point E′ depicts a condition of over full employment equilibrium.

Types of Unemployment

- **Voluntary Unemployment** It refers to the situation when some people are not willing to work at the existing wage rate.
- **Involuntary Unemployment** It refers to the situation where some people are not getting work, even when they are willing to work at the existing wage rate.
- **Frictional Unemployment** It refers to temporary unemployment due to changing of jobs in a dynamic economy.
- **Structural Unemployment** It refers to unemployment caused by progressive decline of an industry over a long period.

5.3 Disequilibrium in the Economy

There are two disequilibrium situations, i.e.

- Excess demand
- Deficient demand

Excess Demand

It refers to the situation when Aggregate Demand (AD) is greater than Aggregate Supply (AS) corresponding to full employment in the economy, i.e.

$$AD > AS$$

Excess demand gives rise to an inflationary gap or inflation.

Inflationary Gap

The extent to which actual aggregate demand exceeds the aggregate demand required for full employment, it is termed as inflationary gap.

It is equal to the difference between the actual level of aggregate demand and the level of the aggregate demand required to establish full employment equilibrium. It measures the size of excess demand.

It is depicted in the graph below

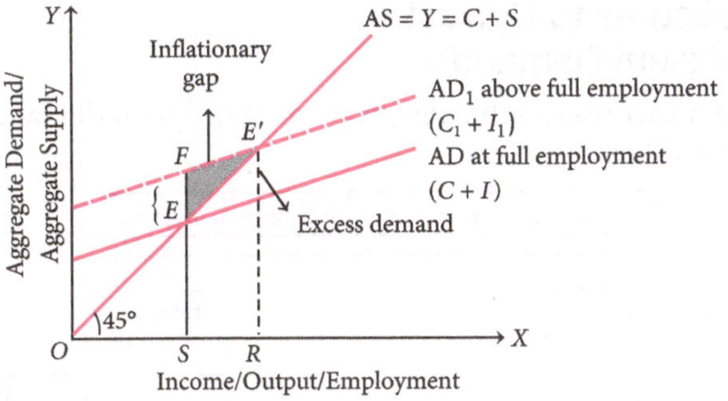

Causes of Excess Demand and Inflationary Gap

The main causes of excess demand is the increase in money supply in the economy which is due to

- Increase in investment demand
- Increase in consumption demand
- Increase in export demand
- Increase in disposable income
- Increase in money supply due to deficit financing
- Increase in the government demand for goods and services
- Increase in private demand
- Reduction in taxes
- Fall in imports

Consequences of Excess Demand and Inflationary Gap

- When AD increases beyond its full employment level, output remains constant, because output cannot exceed full employment level.
- Flow of goods and services remaining constant, excess demand implies excess pressure of demand on the existing output.
- Inflationary gap causes a rise in price level or inflation because full employment has already been attained, hence output and income level cannot be increased.
- Inflation causes an increase in cost of production.
- The fluctuations in business cycle are influenced mainly by the changes in the aggregate demand.

It is the deficiency or excess of aggregate demand that a effects output, employment and prices in the economy. Consequently, economy faces economic fluctuations like boom, recession, recovery, etc.

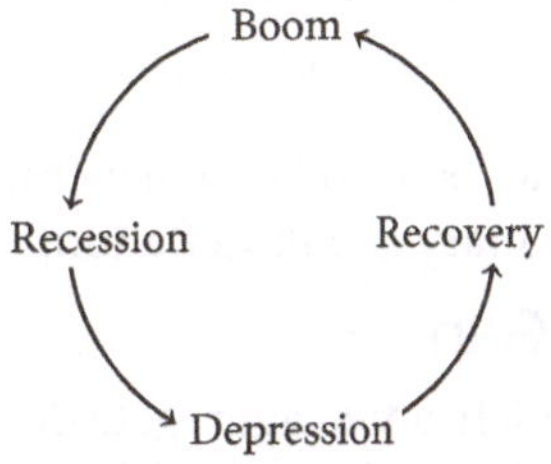

Business Cycle

Measures to Correct Excess Demand

The measures to address the problem of excess demand are as follows

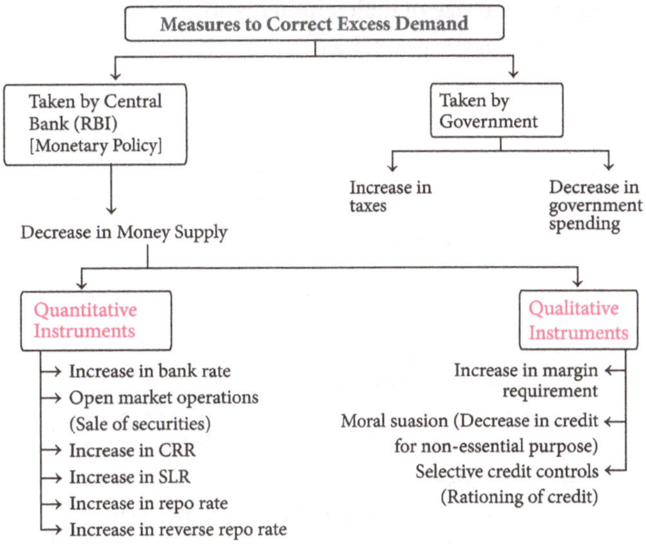

Note For working of quantitative and qualitative instruments, refer to topic 'Credit Control Policy of Central Bank' in Chapter-3.

Increase in Taxes

In a situation of excess demand, the government raises taxes. It will decrease disposable income of buyers as well as their purchasing power and they will spend less on consumption of goods and services. Thus, aggregate demand will fall.

Decrease in Government Spending

In a situation of excess demand, the government reduces its expenditure on public works like construction of roads, buildings, etc. This will decrease the level of employment. It will in turn, decrease the wages and the purchasing power. Thus, aggregate demand will fall.

Deficient Demand

It refers to the situation when Aggregate Supply (AS) is greater than Aggregate Demand (AD) corresponding to full employment in the economy, i.e.

AS > AD

Deficient demand leads to fall in general price level and results in deflationary gap or deflation.

Deflationary Gap

The extent to which actual aggregate demand falls short of the aggregate demand required for full employment level, is termed as deflationary gap.

It is equal to the difference between the actual level of aggregate demand and the level of aggregate demand required to establish full employment equilibrium.

It measures the size of deficient demand.

It is depicted in the graph below

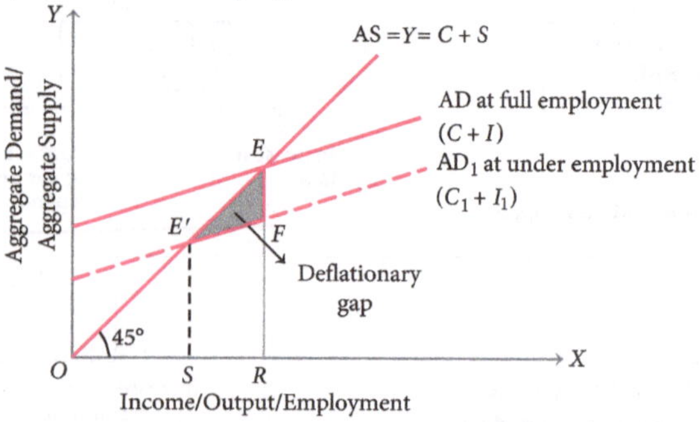

Causes of Deficient Demand and Deflationary Gap

The main cause of deficient demand is the decrease in money supply in the economy which is due to

- Decrease in investment demand
- Decrease in public expenditure
- Decrease in export demand
- Decrease in consumption demand
- Decrease in disposable income
- Decrease in supply of money
- Decrease in credit creation
- Increase in taxes
- Rise in imports

Consequences of Deficient Demand and Deflationary Gap

- When AD fails to cope with fuller employment of the factors, producers tend to build up unwanted inventory stock.

Actual Stocks > Desired Stocks

- Idle inventory stocks would force the producers to plan lower production, implying a cut in planned AS, i.e. a reduction in the level of planned output.
- Reduction in the level of planned output causes a situation of reduction in employment.
- Deflationary gap causes the economy's income, output, employment and prices to decline, hence pushing the economy into under employment equilibrium.

Measures to Correct Deficient Demand

The measures to solve the problem of deficient demand are as follows

Measures to Correct Deficient Demand

- Taken by Central Bank (RBI) [Monetary Policy]
  - Increase in Money Supply
    - Quantitative Instruments
      - Decrease in bank rate
      - Open market operations (Purchase of securities)
      - Decrease in CRR
      - Decrease in SLR
      - Decrease in repo rate
      - Decrease in reverse repo rate
    - Qualitative Instruments
      - Decrease in margin requirement
      - Moral suasion (Increase in credit for non-essential purpose)
      - Selective credit controls (Withdrawl of rationing of credit)
- Taken by Government
  - Decrease in taxes
  - Increase in government spending

Note For working of quantitative and qualitative instruments, refer to topic 'Credit Control Policy of Central Bank' in Chapter-3.

Decrease in Taxes

In a situation of deficient demand, government reduces the rates of all taxes. This increases the purchasing power of the people and increases both consumption and investment expenditures.

Increase in Government Spending

In a situation of deficient demand, government increases its expenditure on public works like construction of roads, buildings, etc.

It will result in rise in demand for goods and services. The rise in government expenditures should be equal to the deflationary gap.

Mind Map

1 Short-run Equilibrium in the Economy

Short-run can be defined as the period of time during which level of output is determined only by the level of employment.

↑ Level of employment ⇒ ↑ Level of output

Equilibrium Output

Equilibrium output refers to a situation, where Aggregate Demand (AD) = Aggregate Supply (AS)

Equilibrium Output = AS = AD

$$C + S = C + I \text{ or } S = I$$

Equilibrium output is also achieved when S = I

2 Aggregate Demand (AD) = Aggregate Supply (AS) Approach

According to Keynesian theory of income determination, the equilibrium level of income and employment is determined at a point where aggregate demand in an economy becomes equal to aggregate supply or total output at a given point of time.

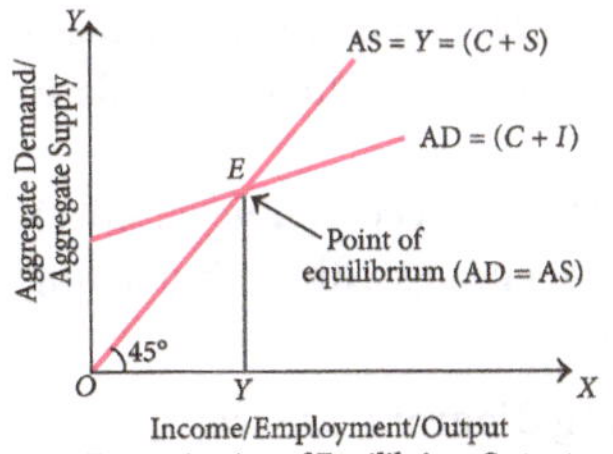

Determination of Equilibrium Output

In the graph, *E* is the point of equilibrium because at this point AD = AS and *OY* is the equilibrium level of output. The given situation where AD = AS, is referred to as **effective demand**.

3 Savings (S) = Investment (I) Approach

According to this approach, equilibrium level of income/output is determined at a point where planned or ex-ante saving is equal to planned or ex-ante investment.

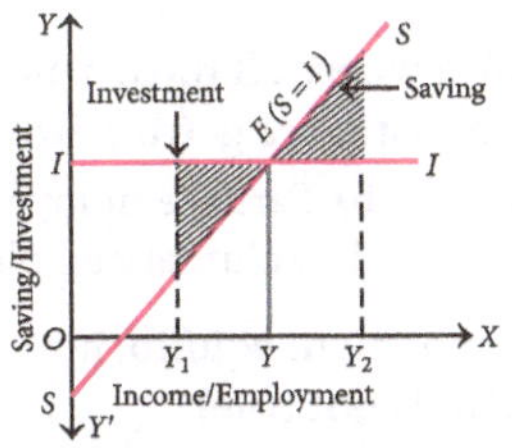

Determination of Equilibrium Output

In the graph, *SS* curve is the saving curve and *II* is the investment curve representing autonomous investment. Equilibrium occurs at point *E*, where *SS* curve and *II* curve intersect and *OY* is the equilibrium level of output.

EQUILIBRIUM AND DISEQUILIBRIUM IN THE ECONOMY

4 Equilibrium Level

Equilibrium level can be achieved at full employment, underemployment and over full employment level.

Under Employment Equilibrium

Under employment refers to a situation, when all those who are able to work at existing wage rates, are not getting jobs. It is called **involuntary unemployment**.

Full Employment Equilibrium

Full employment refers to a situation where all those who are able to work and are willing to work, are getting work. Full employment equilibrium is a situation when the Aggregate Demand (AD) is equal to the Aggregate Supply (AS) at full employment level. At this level of output/income/employment, no one is involuntarily unemployed.

Over Full Employment Equilibrium

It refers to the situation in which AD = AS, but beyond the full employment level. It means that actual (ex-post) Aggregate Demand (AD), tends to be higher than what is required to maintain full employment.

5 Disequilibrium in the Economy

There are two disequilibrium situations, i.e. excess demand and deficient demand.

Excess Demand

It refers to the situation when Aggregate Demand (AD) is greater than Aggregate Supply (AS) corresponding to full employment in the economy. Excess demand gives rise to inflationary gap or inflation.

Inflationary Gap The extent to which actual aggregate demand becomes higher than the aggregate demand required for full employment, it is termed as inflationary gap.

Measures to Correct Excess Demand

- Increase in taxes
- Decrease in government spending
- Decrease in money supply through quantitative and qualitative instruments

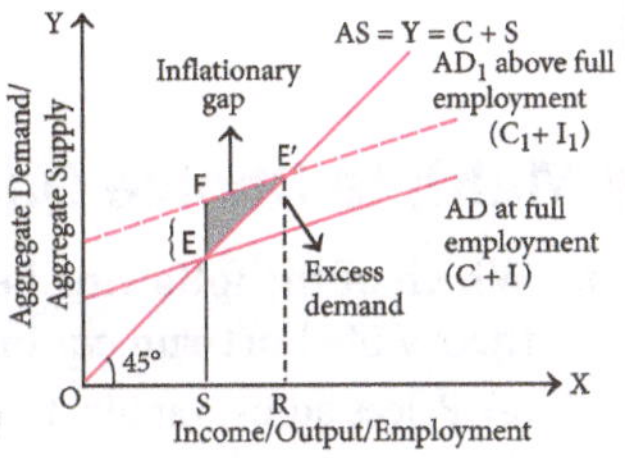

Deficient Demand

It refers to the situation when Aggregate Supply (AS) is greater than Aggregate Demand (AD) corresponding to full employment in the economy. Deficient demand leads to fall in general price level and results in deflationary gap or deflation.

Deflationary Gap It is the extent to which actual aggregate demand falls short of the aggregate demand required for full employment level.

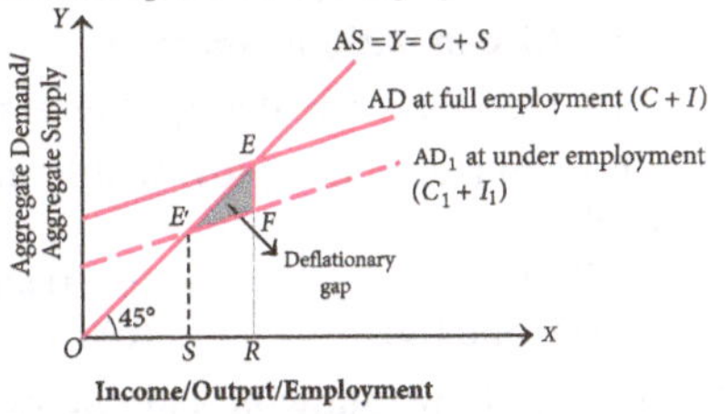

Measures to Correct Deficient Demand

- Decrease in taxes
- Increase in government spending
- Increase in money supply through quantitative and qualitative instruments

EXAM PATTERN QUESTIONS

Objective Type Questions

Multiple Choice Questions (MCQs)

1. Which of the following best describes the Keynesian theory of short-run equilibrium?

(a) Prices adjust rapidly to restore equilibrium
(b) Aggregate demand determines output and employment levels
(c) Government intervention is unnecessary in stabilising the economy
(d) Long-run equilibrium is achieved through flexible wages and prices

2. Suppose in an economy, planned spendings are greater than planned outputs.

Identify the correct option with respect to effects on the economy CBSE 2025

(i) Decrease in planned inventories in the economy
(ii) Rise in national income
(iii) Decrease in real output level in the economy
(iv) Decrease in employment level in the economy

Codes

(a) Only (i) (b) (i) and (ii)
(c) (iii) and (iv) (d) (ii), (iii) and (iv)

3. Which of the following statements is incorrect when the economy is in equilibrium?

(a) $S = I$ (b) AD = AS
(c) Actual savings = Actual investment
(d) Planned savings ≠ Planned investment

4. Suppose the Aggregate Demand (AD) in an economy is given by AD = 200 + 0.75*Y*. If the Aggregate Supply (AS) is represented by national income *Y*, find the equilibrium level of output. Competency Based Que

(a) ₹ 800 crore (b) ₹ 400 crore
(c) ₹ 600 crore (d) ₹ 1,000 crore

5. Given that the equilibrium income (*Y*) is ₹ 2,400, autonomous expenditure is ₹ 200 and the consumption (*C*) at equilibrium is ₹ 1,800, calculate the Marginal Propensity to Consume (MPC). Competency Based Que

(a) 0.78 (b) 0.66 (c) 0.33 (d) 0.45

6. In a closed economy, if saving is given by $S = -50 + 0.2Y$ and investment is ₹ 150 crore, what is the equilibrium level of income? Competency Based Que

(a) ₹ 500 crore (b) ₹ 800 crore
(c) ₹ 1,000 crore (d) ₹ 1,500 crore

7. If Savings (*S*) < Investment (*I*) in an economy, what is the likely impact on business inventories?

(a) Inventories will increase, indicating a surplus of goods
(b) Inventories will decrease, indicating a shortage of goods
(c) Inventories will remain unchanged, indicating equilibrium
(d) There will be no impact on inventories

8. The Economic Times–May, 2024: "Share of consumer spend on health, transport, education up by record 26.9%."

An increase in the share of consumer spending on transport, health and education to 26.9% of private final consumption expenditure indicates Competency Based Que

(a) a potential inflationary pressure if supply in these sectors does not keep pace with increased demand
(b) a reduction in overall demand leading to a deflationary gap
(c) a state of full employment and economic equilibrium
(d) a shift in government spending without impacting private consumption

9. On the basis of following diagram, answer the following question

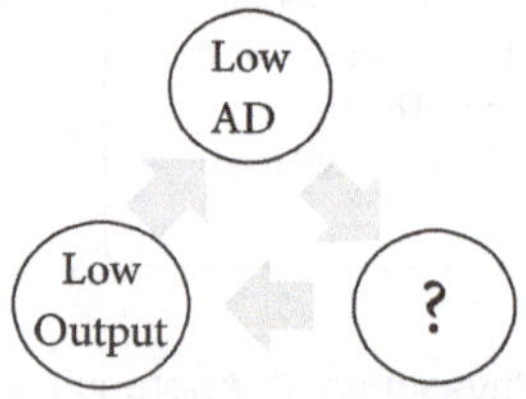

Choose the correct alternative to complete the cycle.

(a) Low saving (b) Low profit
(c) Low investment (d) Low rate of return

10. ...... refers to a situation where all those who are able to work and are willing to work, are getting work.

(a) Under employment (b) Partial employment
(c) Full employment (d) Voluntary employment

11. In case of an underemployment equilibrium, which of the following alternative is not true? CBSE 2020

(a) Aggregate demand is equal to aggregate supply
(b) There exist excess production capacity in the economy
(c) Resources are not fully and efficiently utilised
(d) Resources are fully and efficiently utilised

12. **When the economy is operating above the full employment equilibrium level, it leads to**
(a) excess supply of goods and services
(b) increased unemployment
(c) excess demand for goods and services
(d) stable prices with no inflationary pressure

13. **A situation when people are willing to work at given wage rates but do not get jobs is known as**
(a) full employment (b) involuntary unemployment
(c) underemployment (d) overemployment

14. **...... is equal to the difference between 'AD beyond full employment' and 'AD at full employment'.**
(a) Recession (b) Inflationary gap
(c) Deflationary gap (d) None of these

15.

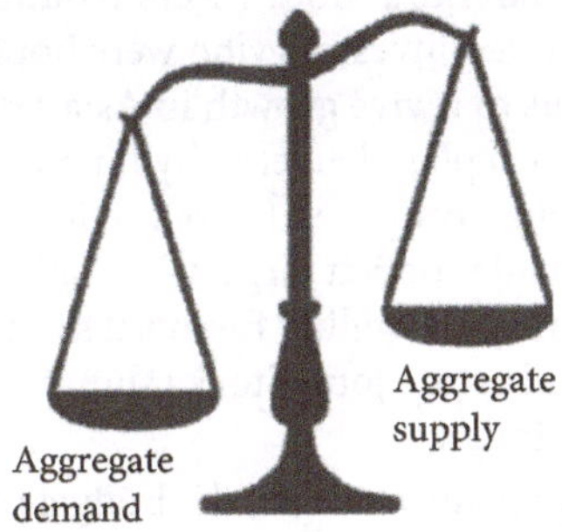

Interpret the image given above and identify the situation represented here.
(a) Situation of effective demand
(b) Situation of excess demand
(c) Situation of deficient demand
(d) Situation of underemployment equilibrium

16. **Which of the following is the cause of inflation?** **NCERT (QR)**
(a) Fall in loans
(b) Deficit financing
(c) An increase in CRR (d) Unfavourable BoP

17. **Consider the diagram below**

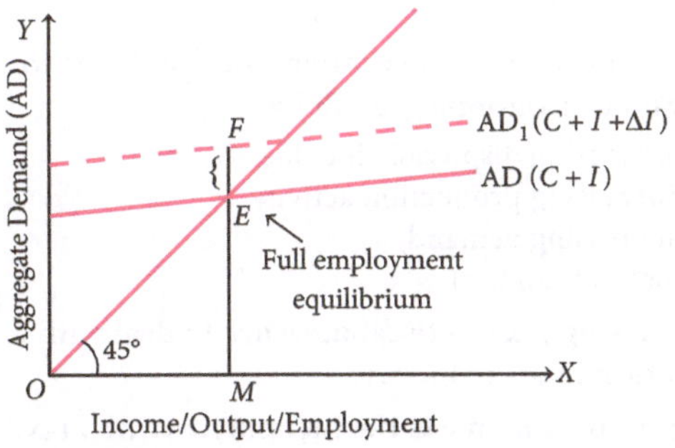

In the above diagram, *EF* represents
(a) excess demand (b) deficient demand
(c) effective demand (d) aggregate demand

18. **On the basis of following diagram, answer the following question**

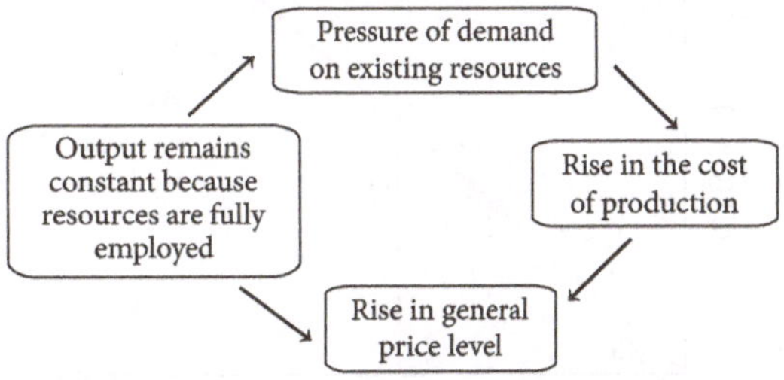

Considering the given cycle, the economy will slip into
(a) excess demand and deflationary spiral
(b) excess demand and inflationary gap
(c) deficient demand and deflationary spiral
(d) deficient demand and inflationary gap

19. **Arrange the following in the correct sequential order, if the government of a nation is trying to curtail the situation of inflationary gap.**
CBSE 2024; Competency Based Que

(i) Decrease in disposable income
(ii) Increase in taxes
(iii) Decrease in aggregate demand

Codes
(a) (i), (ii), (iii) (b) (iii), (ii), (i)
(c) (ii), (iii), (i) (d) (ii), (i), (iii)

20. **Of the following, which policy is wrong to adopt when the economy is having excess demand?**
(a) Increase in bank rate
(b) Buying of securities by central bank
(c) Increasing the legal reserves
(d) Increase in margin requirements

21. **The South African Reserve Bank (Sarb) has raised interest rates by a cumulative 350 basis points (bps) since the end of November 2021, taking the prime lending rate to the current 7% – higher than pre-pandemic levels.**

Source *https://www.moneyweb.co.za/news/economy/to-hike-repo-rate-by-50bps-or-25bps-that-is-the-question/*

The above action taken by the central bank is expected to **Competency Based Que**
(a) increase inflation in the economy
(b) curb inflation in the economy
(c) increase economic growth
(d) Both (a) and (c)

22. **When does a situation of deficient demand arise in an economy?**
(a) AD > AS (b) S > I
(c) AD < AS (d) S < I

23. Consider the diagram given below

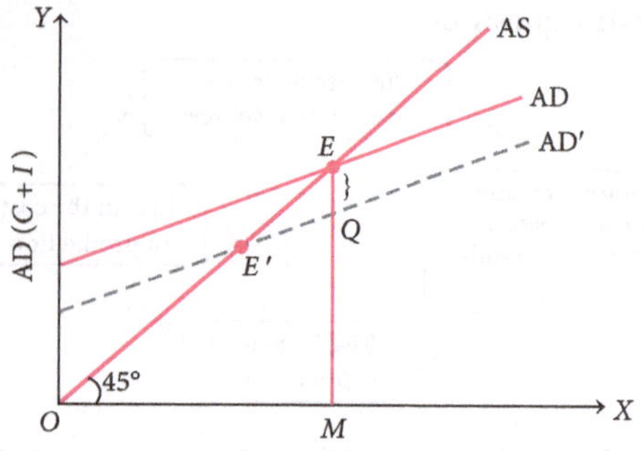

In the above diagram, EQ represents

(a) inflationary gap
(b) deflationary gap
(c) Both (a) and (b)
(d) None of these

24. "Interim Budget 2024 focuses on boosting rural consumption to stimulate demand."
This headline suggests that the government is concerned about **Competency Based Que**

(a) deficient demand
(b) excess demand
(c) balanced demand
(d) aggregate supply

25. If GDP is falling and unemployment rate is rising, which of the following fiscal policy measures should government take? **NCERT (QR)**

(a) To decrease spending
(b) To increase money supply
(c) To decrease taxes
(d) To decrease reserve requirement

26. The main causes of deficit demand are

(i) Decrease in money supply
(ii) Increase in public expenditure
(iii) Decrease in investment demand
(iv) Increase in export demand **Competency Based Que**

Codes

(a) (iii) and (iv)
(b) (i) and (iii)
(c) (ii) and (iii)
(d) (i) and (iv)

27. An economy is in a state of equilibrium with a deflationary gap. Which of the following combinations of fiscal and monetary policies would most likely help the economy return to full employment without inflation? **Competency Based Que**

(a) Contractionary fiscal policy and expansionary monetary policy
(b) Expansionary fiscal policy and contractionary monetary policy
(c) Contractionary fiscal policy and contractionary monetary policy
(d) Expansionary fiscal policy and expansionary monetary policy

28. The Economic Times, 1st February: "Budget 2024: Budget raises capex target by 11.1% to ₹ 11.11 lakh crore to steer India's economy to third largest spot."
Finance Minister Nirmala Sitharaman announced an 11.1% increase in capital expenditure (capex) outlay for the financial year 2024-25, raising the provision to ₹ 11.11 lakh crore, which represents 3.4% of GDP. This move is likely to **Competency Based Que**

(a) increase deficient demand in the economy
(b) reduce deficient demand in the economy
(c) have no impact on deficient demand
(d) lead to excess demand in the economy

Direction *Read the case study and answer the questions 29 to 32 on the basis of the same*

Prime Minister Narendra Modi's second budget in seven months disappointed investors who were hoping for big-bang stimulus to revive growth in Asia's third largest economy. The fiscal plan delivered by Finance Minister Nirmala Sitharaman proposed tax reductions for individuals and wider deficit targets, but failed to provide specific steps to fix a struggling financial sector, improve infrastructure and create jobs. Stocks slumped, reflecting the subdued sentiment.

"Far from being a game changer, the budget provides little in terms of short-term growth stimulus," said Priyanka Kishore, head of India and South-East Asia economics at Oxford Economics Ltd. in Singapore.

"While income tax cuts will provide some relief on the consumption front, the multiplier effect is low and the overall stance of the budget is not expansionary."

The focus now shifts to the Reserve Bank of India's interest rate decision on 6th February, 2020. However, having already cut interest rates five times last year and with inflation exceeding 7 percent, well above the central bank's target, there's limited scope for Governor Shaktikanta Das to ease more.

Source *NDTV Budget, 2020*

29. A direct tax cut in government budget helps to stimulate economic growth by

(a) increasing disposable income
(b) increasing production activity
(c) increasing demand
(d) Both (a) and (c)

30. Decreasing tax is a fiscal measure to deal with ……… situation in an economy.

31. Disposable income is the income ………… tax.

32. The above paragraph indicates which of the following economic situation?

(a) Recession
(b) Boom
(c) Depression
(d) None of these

Direction *Read the case study and answer the questions 33 to 36 on the basis of the same*

Smart City Project There was a time when India was used to be known as the country of Nagas and beggars. But now the demography has changed, India is world's 6th largest economy. But some areas are still a cause of concern for the government.

As per the census 2011, the slum population in India is 17.36% as percentage of urban population. Now, the government is trying to fetch out more and more people from the clutch of the poverty and slums. Hence the launch of the Smart City Project is a good step in this direction. The Smart Cities Mission (SCM) is a holistic city rejuvenation programme for 100 cities in India launched on 25th June, 2015.

The objective of the Smart Cities Mission is to promote cities that provide core infrastructure and give a decent quality of life to its citizens, a clean and sustainable environment and application of 'Smart' Solutions.

33. Under Smart City Project, Government of India is spending a lot of money on infrastructure development, resulting in .... in the level of aggregate demand.

34. Under Smart City Project, government is trying to fetch out more and more people from the clutch of the poverty and slums. This step of government indicates that India is trying to minimise .... unemployment.

35. Due to the Smart City Project, the government is increasing its spending on infrastructure. This type of government action indicates

(a) fiscal policy (b) monetary policy
(c) combination of both (d) None of these

36. Smart City Project of government is focusing on infrastructure development and increasing purchasing power of people through investment multiplier effect, as a result it will lead to

(a) inflation in economy (b) deflation in economy
(c) increase in level of employment and reduction in idle capacity of economy
(d) overutilisation of idle capacity of economy

Direction *Read the news report and answer the questions 37 to 40 on the basis of the same*

The Reserve Bank of India (RBI)cut repo rate to 4.4 percent. The lowest in the recent 15 years, so also it reduces CRR for all banks cut by the 100 basis point to release ₹ 1.37 lakh crore across the overall banking system.

RBI governor Dr. R Shaktikant Das adopted a big global recession and said India will not be immune; it all depends how India respond to the situation and it will aggregate demand will weaken and ease core inflation.

Source *Economic Survey 2012-13, p.100-101.* **CBSE SQP 2021**

37. Cut in repo rate by RBI is likely to .... the demand of goods and services in the economy.

(a) increase
(b) decrease
(c) keep same
(d) have uncertain effect on

38. Decrease in CRR will lead to

(a) fall in aggregate demand
(b) rise in aggregate demand
(c) no change in aggregate demand
(d) fall in general price level

39. The difference by which actual aggregate demand exceeds the aggregate demand requires to stabilise full employment equilibrium is known as ....

40. The impact of the excess demand according to Keynesian theory of income and employment in an economy.

(a) Decrease in income, employment and general price level
(b) Decrease in nominal income but no change in real output
(c) Increase in income, employment and general price level
(d) No change in income, employment but increase in general price level

Assertion-Reason

Direction *(Q.No. 41 to 50) Read the following Assertion (A) and Reason (R) and choose the correct alternative from the following*

Alternatives

(a) Both Assertion (A) and Reason (R) are true and Reason (R) is the correct explanation of Assertion (A)
(b) Both Assertion (A) and Reason (R) are true, but Reason (R) is not the correct explanation of Assertion (A)
(c) Assertion (A) is true, but Reason (R) is false
(d) Both Assertion (A) and Reason (R) are false

41. **Assertion** (A) Effective demand refers to the level of AD at a point when it is equal to AS.

Reason (R) It is that part of AD which is achievable.

42. **Assertion** (A) When planned saving is more than planned investment, firms would plan to reduce production.

Reason (R) Reducing production helps firms lower inventory levels when aggregate demand is insufficient to absorb the current level of goods produced.

43. **Assertion** (A) Full employment refers to absence of involuntary unemployment.

Reason (R) Under full employment situation, all willing and able bodied people get employment at prevailing wage rate. **CBSE 2023**

44. **Assertion** (A) Full employment is the economic state in which AS equals AD and resources are fully utilised. However, this does not imply a scenario of zero unemployment in the economy.

Reason (R) Full employment refers to the absence of unemployment in the economy.

45. **Assertion** (A) Disequilibrium in an economy can result in either surplus or shortage of goods.

Reason (R) Disequilibrium occurs when there is a mismatch between planned savings and planned investments.

46. **Assertion** (A) Excess demand does not lead to any increase in the level of output.

Reason (R) Excess demand gives rise to an inflationary gap.

47. **Assertion** (A) Implementing contractionary fiscal policy by reducing government expenditure is an effective measure to correct excess demand in an economy.

Reason (R) Reducing government expenditure decreases aggregate demand directly, which can help in controlling inflationary pressures associated with excess demand.

48. **Assertion** (A) At full employment, an inflationary gap is defined as the difference between aggregate demand and supply.

Reason (R) Inflation is the general price level increase caused by the inflationary gap.

49. **Assertion** (A) Deficiency of demand leads to reduction in employment and loss in profits to producers.

Reason (R) In this situation, producers tend to reduce their production capacity to meet the reduced demand.

50. **Assertion** (A) Lowering the reserve ratio requirement for banks is an effective measure to correct deficient demand in an economy.

Reason (R) Reducing the reserve ratio requirement increases the amount of money banks can lend, thereby increasing the money supply and stimulating economic activity.

Two Statements Based MCQs

Direction (Q.No. 51 to 60) *Read the following statements carefully and choose the correct alternative*

Alternatives

(a) Statement I is correct and Statement II is incorrect
(b) Statement II is correct and Statement I is incorrect
(c) Both the statements are correct
(d) Both the statements are incorrect

51. **Statement I** At the point of equilibrium where AD and AS are equal, S and I must be equal as well.

Statement II In an economy, ex-ante savings may not always be equal to ex-post savings.

52. **Statement I** If investment exceeds savings, the economy will experience a rise in national income until the excess investment is absorbed, bringing savings and investment back into balance.

Statement II At equilibrium, the level of investment is determined solely by the level of savings and is unaffected by external factors such as interest rates or business expectations.

53. **Statement I** If the economy is operating below full employment, an increase in aggregate demand will lead to an increase in both output and employment.

Statement II At full employment, any increase in aggregate demand will only cause inflation, not an increase in output.

54. **Statement I** Cyclical unemployment is typically more prevalent during periods of economic expansion.

Statement II Frictional unemployment may be considered beneficial for the economy as it allows for better job matches and improves overall efficiency.

55. **Statement I** Structural unemployment can result from changes in consumer preferences or shifts in global trade patterns.

Statement II Technological unemployment is a temporary phenomenon and does not have long-term effects on the labour market.

56. **Statement I** Inflationary gap is easier to handle for government than deflationary gap.

Statement II During deflationary gap, the government is required to infuse more funds in the economy and increase its spending.

57. **Statement I** Excess demand creates more employment opportunities.

Statement II Excess demand tends to occur when there is high liquidity in the market.

58. **Statement I** Deficit demand always leads to deflationary gap in an economy.

Statement II At the time of deficit demand, government must increase the rate of taxation on higher income groups.

59. **Statement I** During periods of economic depression, economy is caught in a low level equilibrium trap.

Statement II During economic depression, the unemployment rates rise and consumer confidence suffer.

60. **Statement I** Implementing higher taxes on consumption can be an effective measure to address excess demand.

Statement II Reducing interest rates during a period of deficient demand can help stimulate economic activity by making borrowing cheaper.

Matching

61. Match the statements given under Column I with the correct options given Column II

Column I	Column II
A. Inventory above target level	(i) S < I
B. Inflationary gap	(ii) AD < AS
C. Recessionary gap	(iii) AD > AS
D. Inventory below target level	(iv) S > I

Codes

	A	B	C	D		A	B	C	D
(a)	(i)	(iii)	(ii)	(iv)	(b)	(iv)	(iii)	(ii)	(i)
(c)	(ii)	(i)	(iii)	(iv)	(d)	(iii)	(ii)	(i)	(iv)

62. Match the statements given Column I with the correct options given Column II **Competency Based Que**

Column I	Column II
A. Quantitative instruments	(i) When AD>AS corresponding to full employment level of output in economy
B. Legal reserve requirements	(ii) Fiscal measure during excess demand
C. Excess demand	(iii) Aim to influence the total volume of credit in circulation
D. Decrease in government spending	(iv) Cash reserve ratio and statutory liquidity ratio

Codes

	A	B	C	D		A	B	C	D
(a)	(i)	(ii)	(iii)	(iv)	(b)	(ii)	(iii)	(i)	(iv)
(c)	(iii)	(iv)	(i)	(ii)	(d)	(iii)	(ii)	(iv)	(i)

63. Match Column I (Type of Unemployment) with Column II (Characteristics) and select the correct answer using the codes given below

Column I (Type of Unemployment)	Column II (Characteristics)
A. Involuntary unemployment	(i) A situation when a people choose to remain unemployed.
B. Frictional unemployment	(ii) Occurs during boom or recession in the economy.
C. Voluntary unemployment	(iii) Occurs when moving from one job to another.
D. Structural unemployment	(iv) An absence of demand for a certain type of workers.

Codes

(a) A-(i) (b) B-(ii) (c) C-(iii) (d) D-(iv)

64. Match Column I with Column II and select the correct answer using the codes given below

Column I	Column II
A. Excess demand	(i) Unsold inventories
B. Revenue and expenditure policy of government	(ii) Fiscal policy
C. Moral pressure and suasion	(iii) Banking Regulation Act
D. Correction of inflationary gap	(iv) Government expenditure on welfare

Codes

(a) A-(i) (b) B-(ii) (c) C-(iii) (d) D-(iv)

65. Match the statements given Column I with the correct options given Column II **Competency Based Que**

Column I (Phase of the Business Cycle)	Column II (Characteristics)
A. Expansion	(i) High unemployment and low consumer spending
B. Peak	(ii) Rising employment and increasing production
C. Contraction	(iii) Maximum economic output, with possible inflation
D. Trough/ Economic Low	(iv) Decreasing production and falling GDP

Codes

	A	B	C	D		A	B	C	D
(a)	(ii)	(iii)	(iv)	(i)	(b)	(iii)	(ii)	(iv)	(i)
(c)	(iv)	(i)	(iii)	(ii)	(d)	(ii)	(iv)	(iii)	(i)

Concept Identification

66. Situation in which all those who are able to work and are willing to work at the existing wage rate get work. **CBSE 2020**

67. The minimum rate of unemployment that must exist in the economy even when the labour market is in a state of equilibrium.

68. A situation when aggregate demand is in excess of aggregate supply crossponding to full employment in the economy.

69. The excess of available supply of output over the anticipated expenditure at constant prices of base period.

70. The rate of interest which is charged by a central bank while lending loans to a commercial bank.

Answers

1. (b) Aggregate demand determines output and employment levels
2. (b) (i) and (ii)
3. (d) Planned savings ≠ Planned investment
4. (a) AD=AS $\Rightarrow$ $200 + 0.75Y = Y$
   $\Rightarrow 0.25Y = 200 \Rightarrow Y = 200/0.25 =$ ₹ 800 crore
5. (b) $C = \bar{c} + bY \Rightarrow 1{,}800 = 200 + b\,(2{,}400)$
   $b = 1{,}600/2{,}400 = 0.66$
6. (c) $S = I \Rightarrow -50 + 0.2Y = 150$
   $0.2Y = 200 \Rightarrow Y = 200/0.2 =$ ₹ 1,000 crore
7. (b) Inventories will decrease, indicating a shortage of goods
8. (a) potential inflationary pressure if supply in these sectors does not keep pace with increased demand
9. (c) Low investment
10. (c) Full employment
11. (d) Resources are fully and efficiently utilised
12. (c) excess demand for goods and services
13. (b) involuntary unemployment
14. (b) Inflationary gap
15. (b) Situation of excess demand
16. (b) Deficit financing
17. (a) excess demand
18. (b) excess demand and inflationary gap
19. (d) (ii), (i), (iii)
20. (b) Buying of securities by central bank
21. (b) curb inflation in the economy
22. (c) Deficient demand arises when AD is short of AS corresponding to full employment in the economy.
23. (b) deflationary gap
24. (a) This implies that the government is concerned about a lack of demand.
25. (c) To decrease taxes
26. (b) (i) and (iii)
27. (d) Expansionary fiscal policy and expansionary monetary policy
28. (b) Government may tackle this deficient demand by increasing its spending.
29. (d) Both (a) and (c)
30. deflationary gap
31. after
32. (a) Recession
33. increase
34. involuntary
35. (a) Increased government spending, especially on infrastructure projects, is an example of fiscal policy, as it involves direct government expenditure to influence economic activity.
36. (c) increase in level of employment and reduction in idle capacity of economy
37. (a) increase
38. (b) rise in aggregate demand
39. inflationary gap
40. (d) No change in income, employment but increase in general price level
41. (a) Both Assertion (A) and Reason (R) are true and Reason (R) is the correct explanation of Assertion (A)
42. (a) Both Assertion (A) and Reason (R) are true and Reason (R) is the correct explanation of Assertion (A)
43. (a) Both Assertion (A) and Reason (R) are true and Reason (R) is the correct explanation of Assertion (A)
44. (c) Assertion (A) is true, but Reason (R) is false
45. (b) Both Assertion (A) and Reason (R) are true, but Reason (R) is not the correct explanation of Assertion (A)
46. (b) Since, the production is already at full capacity the increased demand does not lead to any increase in the level of output.
47. (a) Both Assertion (A) and Reason (R) are true and Reason (R) is the correct explanation of Assertion (A)
48. (b) Both Assertion (A) and Reason (R) are true, but Reason (R) is not the correct explanation of Assertion (A)
49. (a) Both Assertion (A) and Reason (R) are true and Reason (R) is the correct explanation of Assertion (A)
50. (a) Both Assertion (A) and Reason (R) are true and Reason (R) is the correct explanation of Assertion (A)
51. (c) Both the statements are correct
52. (a) Investment is influenced by various factors beyond savigs, such as interest rates, business expectations and economic policies. These play a crucial role in determining investment levels.
53. (c) Both the statements are correct
54. (b) Cyclical unemployment is actually more prevalent during economic downturns, such as recessions, when overall economic activity and demand for goods and services decrease, leading to layoffs and job losses.
55. (a) Technological unemployment may be temporary for some individuals as they transition to new types of work, it can have long-term effects on the labour market, especially if certain industries or occupations become obsolete due to automation or technological progress.
56. (c) Both the statements are correct
57. (b) Excess demand occurs when economy is at full employment level.
58. (a) At the time of deficit demand, government must reduce the taxes to allow disposable income to increase.
59. (c) Both the statements are correct
60. (c) Both the statements are correct
61. (b) (iv) (iii) (ii) (i)
62. (c) (iii) (iv) (i) (ii)
63. (d) D-(iv)
64. (b) B-(ii)
65. (a) (ii) (iii) (iv) (i)
66. Full employment
67. Natural rate of unemployment
68. Excess demand
69. Deflationary gap
70. Bank rate

Subjective Questions

Short Answer Type Questions

1. What are the basic assumptions related to Keynes theory?

Ans. Three basic assumptions of the Keynesian theory are

(i) **Short Period Analysis**
Equilibrium GDP, according to Keynesian theory, is discussed only with reference to short period of time.

(ii) **Closed Economy**
Keynes discuss the theory of equilibrium GDP in the context of a closed economy. This is an economy which has no economic relations with the rest of the world, there are no imports or exports, so that $AD = C + I$.

(iii) **AS is Perfectly Elastic**
Keynes assumes that AS is perfectly elastic. It means that we are studying an economy in which there is an excess capacity.

2. Discuss the significance of 45° line in Keynesian economics. CBSE SQP 2018

Or **"The 45° line in Keynesian economics plays a crucial role in aggregate supply analysis." Explain its significance in the context of consumption and income equilibrium.** Competency Based Que

Ans. Aggregate supply is obtained by adding consumption and saving schedules. The straight line obtained which will originate from point of origin will form a 45° angle there by establishing the relation of $Y = C + S$.

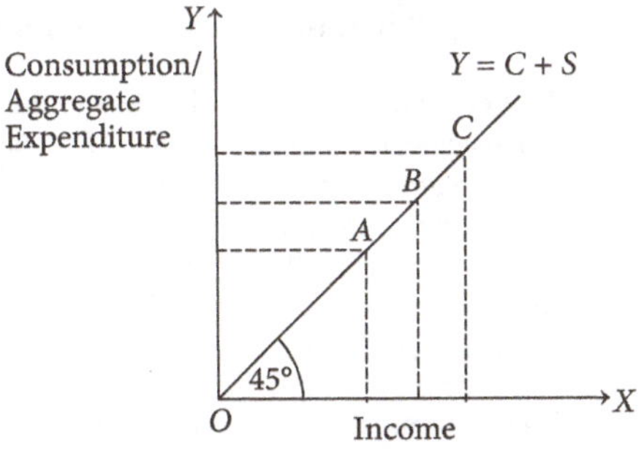

At all points on 45° line, consumption is equal to income. It helps under the Keynesian economic analysis. Since the two variables (consumption/aggregate expenditure and income) are measured in the same units, the 45° line has a slope of one and it bisects the 90° angle formed by the two axis.

3. "In an economy, ex-ante aggregate demand is more than ex-ante aggregate supply." Elaborate the possible impact of the same, on the level of output, income and employment. CBSE SQP 2024; Competency Based Que

Ans. When ex-ante aggregate demand is more than ex-ante aggregate supply, it means that households are planning to consume more than what the firms expect them to. This will lead to unintended fall in inventories.

To restore the desired/intended level of inventories, producers may expand production. As a result, there may be an increase in the level of output, employment and income in the economy. For bringing back the inventory to the desired level, the firms would resort to increase in employment and output until the economy gets back at output level *OY*, where AD ultimately becomes equal to AS and there is no more tendency to change.

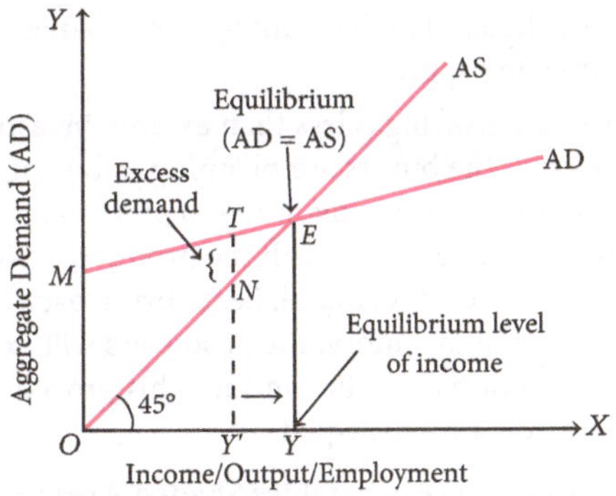

4. If ex-ante Aggregate Demand (AD) is lesser than ex-ante Aggregate Supply (AS), examine how effective demand might be restored.

Ans. When aggregate demand is less than aggregate supply in an economy, it creates a deflationary gap and the price levels tend to fall.

Deflationary gap discourages the producers to increase output due to increase in inventory levels. It leads to gradual decrease in aggregate supply and the economy attains equilibrium where, AD=AS.

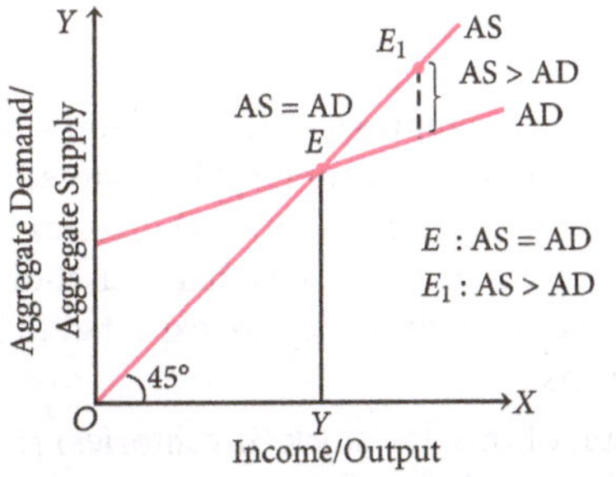

For bringing back the inventory to the desired level and clear the unwanted increase in inventory, the firms would resort to reduction in employment and output until the economy gets back at output level *OY*, where AD ultimately becomes equal to AS and there is no more tendency to change.

5. "Savings and investment are always equal." Discuss. Competency Based Que

Ans. S and I can be realised (ex-post) or planned (ex-ante). Planned S and planned I are equal only at equilibrium level. Realised S and realised I are always equal. The equality is derived as,

$$Y = C + S \text{ and } Y = C + I$$

Hence, $S = I$

So, in ex-ante sense, saving and investment may or may not be equal, but in ex-post sense, saving and investment are always equal.

6. If ex-ante investment exceeds ex-ante saving, explain how effective demand can be retrieved?

Ans. Effective demand is that level of output where the aggregate demand of the commodities is equal to the aggregate supply.

When ex-ante saving is less than ex-ante investment, it means that the buyers are planning to buy more than what the producers are planning to produce, resulting in a shortage of inventories with the producers. Now, to restore the effective demand, i.e. to bring back the desired level of inventory, the producers will expand their production and will continue this procedure until the two forces become equal.

7. In the given figure, what does Shaded Area (SA) represent? Explain its consequence on the economy. Competency Based Que

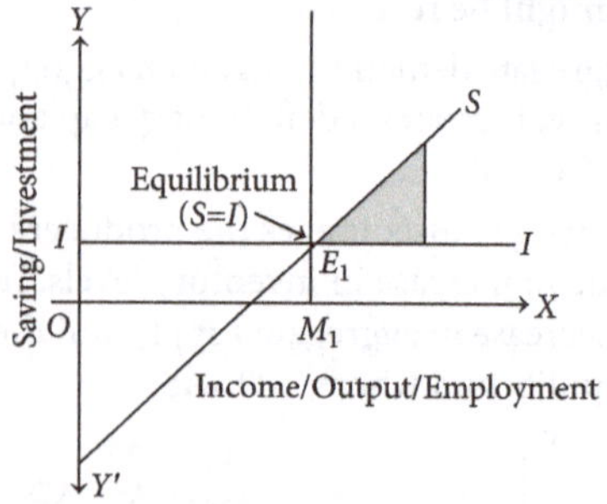

Ans. The shaded area represents the situation when Saving (S) is greater than Investment (I). The planned (ex-ante) savings exceeds planned (ex-post) investment (to the right of point E_1), it indicates that households are not consuming as much as they are expected to be consumed by the firms.

As a result of this, the stock (inventories) rises above the desired level and thus, firms will cut production, leading to fall in income and savings. This will continue till the economy moves back to the equilibrium at point E_1.

8. Explain the meaning of equilibrium level of income. Can there be unemployment in the economy at equilibrium level of income? Explain.

Ans. Equilibrium level of income is the level of income/output where the aggregate demand is equal to aggregate supply in an economy, i.e. AD = AS.

In other words, when desired output/income equals to desired expenditure, equilibrium output is struck.

There can be unemployment even if the economy is at equilibrium at AS = AD corresponding to the situation of less than full employment.

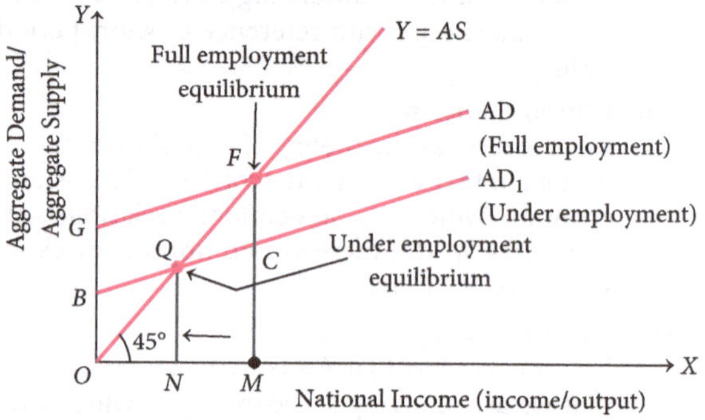

In the diagram, AD is the Aggregate Demand corresponding to full employment level at F. However, AD_1 is Aggregate Demand corresponding to under full employment equilibrium of point Q. Even at this point of equilibrium, the economy may face the problem of unemployment.

9. Differentiate between full employment and underemployment equilibrium.

Ans. Differences between full employment and underemployment equilibrium are

Basis	Full Employment Equilibrium	Underemployment Equilibrium
Meaning	It refers to the situation when aggregate demand equals aggregate supply and all those who are able to work and willing to work (at the existing wage rate), get work.	It refers to the situation when AD equals to AS, but all those who are able to work and willing to work (at the existing wage rate), do not get work.
Equivalent	It corresponds to the highest possible level of output in the economy under the given circumstances.	It does not correspond to the highest possible level of output in the economy.
Inflationary Gap	Attempt to increase production beyond full employment equilibrium causes inflationary gap.	Attempt to increase production beyond under employment equilibrium does not cause inflation.

10. Distinguish between frictional unemployment and structural unemployment.

Ans. Differences between frictional unemployment and structural unemployment are

Basis	Frictional Unemployment	Structural Unemployment
Meaning	It takes place when due to the frictions in the industry, some workers are removed from jobs.	It takes place due to the structural changes in the economic organisations.
Reason	It is the result of a shortage of raw materials, strikes, power failure, etc.	It is the result of a change in the production process, shifting the industry from one region to another, technological changes, etc.
Nature	It is temporary unemployment.	It may be long-term unemployment.

11. What makes voluntary unemployment different from involuntary unemployment?

Ans. Differences between voluntary unemployment and involuntary unemployment are

Basis	Voluntary Unemployment	Involuntary Unemployment
Meaning	It is a situation where those who are not willing to do work although suitable work is available to them i.e. they are unemployed of their own will.	It is a situation where people are eligible and willing to work but fail to find work.
Reason	These people are not included in the workforce of the country.	These people are included in the workforce of the country.
Nature	Housewives.	Person having engineering and still unemployed.

12. What is meant by inflationary gap? State three measures to reduce this gap. **CBSE 2018**

Ans. The extent to which current aggregate demand becomes higher than the aggregate demand required for full employment, is termed as inflationary gap.

Three measures to reduce inflationary gap are

(i) Reduction in government expenditure on public works, public welfare and defence, etc.

(ii) Reduction in public expenditure on transfer payments and subsidies.

(iii) Increase in taxes to lower the disposable income with the people.

13. Explain how increase in money supply causes inflation.

Ans. Money is controlled by the central bank of the country as RBI in India. Increase in money supply by the central bank leads to increase in liquidity in the economy.

Increased liquidity causes excess demand for goods and services and if the economy is already operating to its full potential, then it would result in causing inflation.

14. In the given figure, what does the gap 'KT' represent? State any two fiscal measures to correct the situation.
CBSE 2020, 19; Competency Based Que

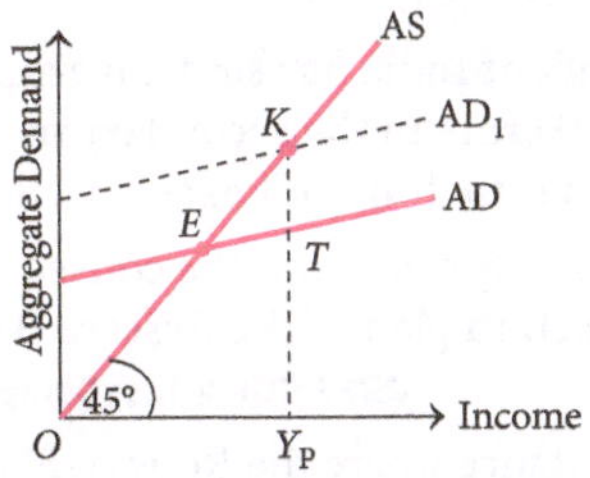

Full employment level of income

Ans. In the given figure, the gap KT represents inflationary gap. AD and AS represents aggregate demand and aggregate supply respectively at full employment level and 'E' is the point of equilibrium.

AD represents actual aggregate demand which exceed aggregate demand at the point of equilibrium. This will create inflationary pressures in the economy.

Two fiscal measures to correct the situation are as follows

(i) **Decrease in Government Expenditure**
It is necessary that government's expenditure should be less than its income, in order to correct the situation of excess demand.

(ii) **Increase in Taxes**
The government should levy new taxes and enhance the rate of the existing ones. This will reduce disposable income of the people and hence, lead to reduction in aggregate demand.

15. In India, inflation is rising day-by-day, it is the matter of concern for the government. Explain how RBI helps in controlling inflation.

Ans. At the time of inflation, RBI controls the supply of credit in the economy by using quantitative and qualitative instruments.

It implies increase or decrease in the supply of money by regulating the credit creation by the commercial banks.

Quantitative Instruments

(i) **Bank Rate Policy** In case of excess demand, the RBI increases the bank rate or interest rate which makes the credit dear.

(ii) **Open Market Operations** In a situation of excess demand, RBI sells the eligible securities in its possession to commercial banks.

Qualitative Instuments

(i) **Marginal Requirement** Marginal requirement is raised to correct the situation of excess demand.

(ii) **Moral Suasion** In situation of excess demand, RBI imposes restrictions on commercial banks on granting loans.

16. Following news published in The Economic Times on 26th December 2021

"Reserve Bank of India has sold government securities worth ₹ 8,710 crore in the secondary market, over the last four weeks, to drain out excessive liquidity."

Identify the likely cause and the consequences behind this type of action plan of the Reserve Bank.

CBSE SQP 2023; Competency Based Que

Ans. The given instance where the Reserve Bank of India has sold government securities in the secondary market indicates inflation as a possible cause behind the action taken by RBI.

By selling off the government securities, RBI withdraws money from circulation, thereby reducing the lending capacity of the commercial banks. In this process, the economy will experience a contraction of credit, leading to a reduction in consumption and investment demand. Consequently, the inflationary pressure in the economy will get eased out.

17. Explain, how the reverse repo rate helps in correcting excess demand in an economy? **CBSE 2020**

Ans. Reverse repo rate is the rate at which commercial banks deposit their excess funds with the central bank or in other words, the rate at which central bank borrows from commercial banks. In the situation of excess demand, central bank raises the 'reverse repo rate' which locks the excess liquidity of commercial banks with central bank, hence it causes a fall in aggregate demand to attain the full employment equilibrium.

18. "An economy is operating at underemployment level of income." What does this situation indicate? Discuss any one fiscal measure to tackle this situation.

CBSE 2025; Competency Based Que

Ans. The situation indicates that the economy is facing 'deficient demand'. Deficient demand occurs when aggregate demand is less than aggregate supply. It is shown in the diagram.

In the diagram, full employment level of demand is indicated by AD_1.

If demand level happens to be AD_2, the gap between AD_1 and AD_2 is equal to *ab*. Deficient Demand is indicated by *abc*.

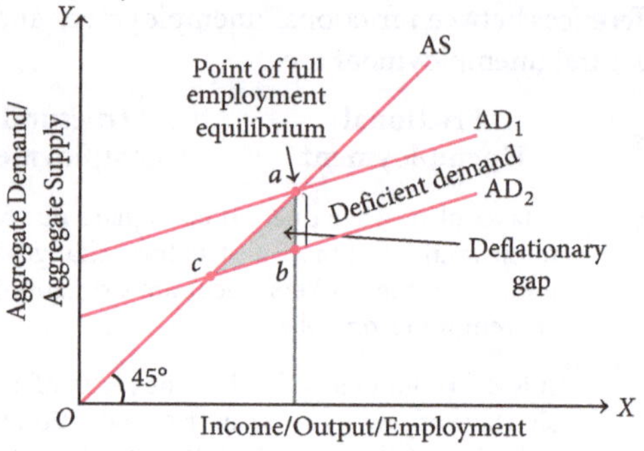

One effective fiscal measure to address this issue is increasing government expenditure.

19. In the given figure, what does *EQ* represent? Explain its impact on the economy. **Competency Based Que**

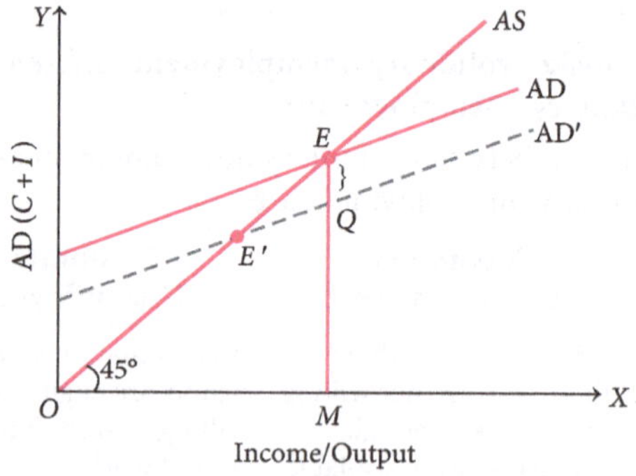

Ans. '*EQ*' represents the situation of 'deficient demand'. Deficient demand refers to a situation wherein aggregate demand in the economy falls short of aggregate supply of goods and services at full employment. As a result, resources of the economy remain partly utilised indicating underemployment.

Impacts

(i) **Effect on General Price Level**
Deficient demand causes the general price level to fall because it arises when aggregate demand is less than aggregate supply at full employment level. This leads to deflation in an economy, creating deflationary gap.

(ii) **Effect on Employment**
Due to deficient demand, investment level is reduced, which causes involuntary unemployment in the economy due to fall in the planned output.

(iii) **Effect on Output**
Low level of investment and employment implies low level of output.

20. "Taxes help to curb deflationary situation in the economy." Comment.

CBSE Term II 2022; Competency Based Que

Ans. The given statement is correct as under the situation of deficient demand, government generally reduces tax rates.

This leads to higher disposable income in the hands of people. As a result, people will be able to spend more on consumption and investment expenditure. This step taken by government ultimately raises the level of aggregate demand and helps to tackle the situation of deficient demand prevailing in the economy.

21. **"The government has raised the exemption limit for the payment of income tax from ₹ 2 lakh to ₹ 2.5 lakh."**
If the situation of deficient demand is prevailing in the economy, what will be the impact of this action taken by the government?
CBSE Term II 2022; Competency Based Que

Ans. Deficient demand refers to the situation when Aggregate Demand (AD) is less than the Aggregate Supply (AS) in an economy, corresponding to full employment in the economy. Here, government has raised exemption limit for the payment of income tax. This will increase the purchasing power of the people and will increase both consumption and investment expenditures.

This rise in consumption and investment expenditures will increase the level of Aggregate Demand (AD) and will help to check the problem of deficient demand.

22. **"To boost the falling demand in the economy, the Reserve Bank of India recently reduced the repo rate." Elaborate the rationale behind the steps taken by the central bank.** **CBSE 2020; Competency Based Que**

Ans. Repo rate is the rate at which the Reserve Bank of India lends money to the commercial banks.

To boost the falling demand in the economy, repo rate is decreased. As a follow-up action, the commercial banks lower the market rate of interest (the rate at which commercial banks lend money to consumers and investors). This increases demand for credit.

Consequently, consumption expenditure and investment expenditure are increased. Implying an increase in aggregate demand, as required to boost falling demand in the economy.

23. **Analyse the role of government spending in correcting the situation of deficient demand and excess demand.**
CBSE Term II 2022

Ans. **Deficient Demand**
The government may plan to increase its spending, to correct deficient demand. This will lead to an increase in disposable income (purchasing power) in the hands of the general public. Thus, aggregate demand will rise and deficient demand will be managed accordingly.

Excess Demand
Government should reduce its spending. It leads to fall in the income in the hands of public and consequently the purchasing power reduces. Thus, it will help to correct the situation of excess demand.

24. **"India has been dealing with the problem of deficient demand since the imposition of the Covid lockdown in March 2020."**
State and discuss any two monetary policy measures to combat the situation of deficient demand in India.
CBSE 2021; Competency Based Que

Ans. A situation when aggregate demand falls short of aggregate supply at the full employment level of equilibrium is called deficient demand.

Two monetary measures undertaken to solve the problem of deficient demand in India are as follows

(i) When there is a situation of deficient demand, the bank rate may be reduced by the central bank, which would further decrease the lending rate for commercial banks. This pushes the public to borrow more funds and would lead to an increase in aggregate demand.

(ii) In the situation of deficient demand, the central bank purchases securities from the open market. This will lead to an increase in the money supply for the public and enhance the purchasing power and in the end, increase the levels of aggregate demand in the economy.

25. **What is monetary policy? Explain the bank rate and margin requirements in influencing the availability of credit in an economy.**

Ans. Monetary policy refers to the regulation of the money supply, interest rates, and credit availability by the central bank to manage inflationary or deflationary gaps in the economy.

Bank rate is the rate at which the central bank offers loan to the commercial banks as 'lender of last resort'. During inflation, bank rate is increased to reduce the money supply in the economy because commercial banks will also increase the interest rates accordingly.

It will imply a check on the borrowing from commercial banks. Thus, overall supply of money/credit is reduced in the economy. During deflation, bank rate is lowered leading to increase in supply of money/credit.

Margin requirements refer to the difference between market value of the security offered for loan and the amount of loan offered by the commercial bank.

During inflation, supply of money/credit is reduced by raising the requirement of margin and *vice-versa*.

26. Explain the role of repo rate and reverse repo rate in correcting deflationary gap in an economy.

Ans. Repo rate is the interest rate at which commercial banks borrow money from the central bank in exchange for securities with the promise to buy them back after a set period of time.

Similarly, the reverse repo rate is the interest rate at which commercial banks lend to the central bank.

The reverse repo rate is always a few basis points lower than the repo rate.

When the repo rate falls, commercial banks can borrow at lower cost. This leads to lowering of interest rates on loans to the general public. The decrease in interest rates increases the demand for loans for both investment and consumption purposes.

As a result, aggregate demand increases. Similarly, when the reverse repo rate is lower than the repo rate, banks prefer to park their funds with the central bank and use that fund to make loans to the general public, thus also expanding credit. This has a positive effect on aggregate demand by closing the deflationary gap.

Long Answer Type Questions

27. With the use of the aggregate supply and demand curves, describe the theory underlying the calculation of income and employment. Competency Based Que

Ans. In an economy, equilibrium level of income and employment is determined when AD (Aggregate Demand) is equal to AS (Aggregate Supply).

According to Keynes, AS may be assumed to be elastic in an economy where full employment (of resources) is yet to be achieved. Accordingly, AD becomes the principal determinant of equilibrium level of income. It can be explained through the following diagram

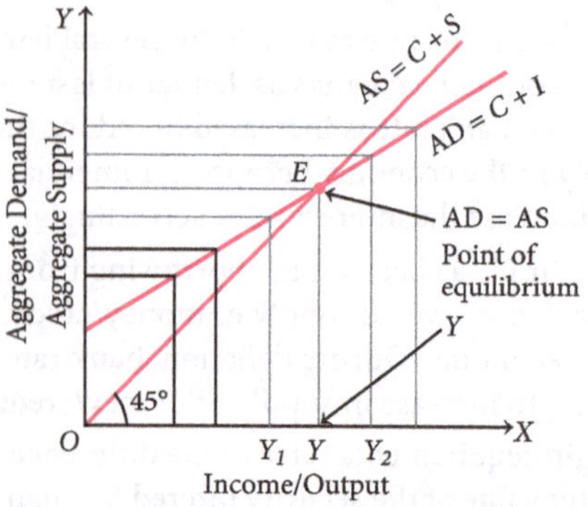

In the above diagram, AD represents aggregate demand curve and 45° line is the line of reference, where AS = Y. Equilibrium level of income Y is determined at point E, where AD = AS.

Prior to point E, when AD > AS; firms experience unplanned inventory depletion, leading to higher production, employment and income.

Beyond point E, when AS > AD; firms accumulate unsold goods, leading to reduced production and layoffs, causing income to decline.

It is only when AS = AD, that the equilibrium is struck. Because the equality between AS and AD implies that the desired level of output in the economy (as indicated by AS) is exactly equal to the desired level of expenditure (indicated by AD) in the economy.

So that the entire output as planned by the producers (during an accounting year) is purchased by the buyers.

There are no undesired or unwanted inventories (stock of goods) with the producers.

28. Explain determination of equilibrium level of income using consumption plus investment ($C + I$) approach. Use diagram.

Ans. Equilibrium level of income is the point where aggregate demand equals to aggregate supply in an economy.

It can be explained with the help of schedule and diagram given below

Y	C	I	AD (C+I)	AS (Y)	
0	500	1,000	1,500	0	
1,000	1,000	1,000	2,000	1,000	AD > AS
2,000	1,500	1,000	2,500	2,000	
3,000	2,000	1,000	3,000	3,000	AD = AS (Equilibrium)
4,000	2,500	1,000	3,500	4,000	AD < AS
5,000	3,000	1,000	4,000	5,000	

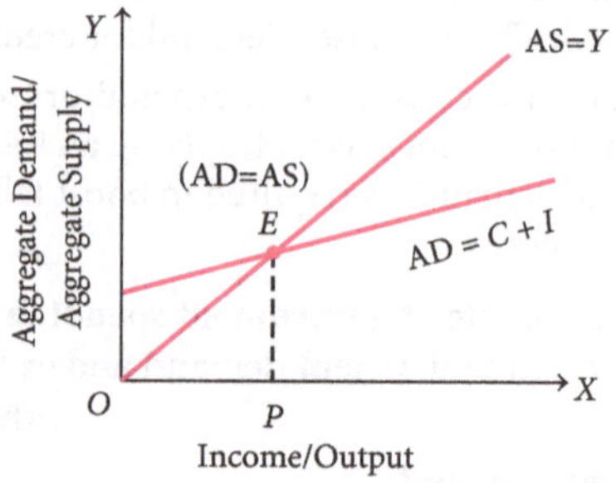

E represents the equilibrium point and OP represents the equilibrium level of national income, where AD = AS.

29. Using the functions of investment and saving, explain the equilibrium of economy. Include an explanation and diagram of the alterations that occur in an economy when it is out of balance.

Ans. Equilibrium level of income is determined at a point where ex-ante or planned saving is equal to planned investment.

This is because, in equilibrium,

AS = AD *or* $C + S = C + I$ *or* $S = I$.

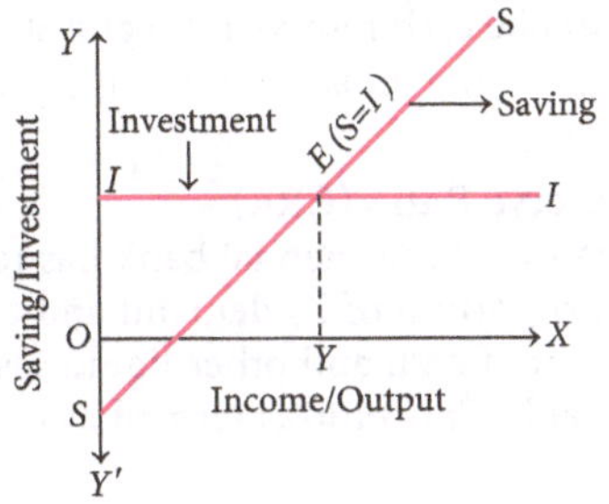

In the diagram above, E is the point where $S = I$, hence, the point at which the economy is in equilibrium. OY is the equilibrium level of national income.

(i) **When Savings > Investment** (AD < AS)

- When savings are greater than investment in an economy, it refers to AD < AS. There will be a rise in inventory stock and prices will start to fall.
- To clear their stocks, producers will now plan lesser output, leading to lower income in the economy. Lower income implies lower savings. The process will continue until $S = I$ is restored.

(ii) **When Savings < Investment** (AD > AS)

- When savings are less than investment, it implies a situation where the withdrawal of expenditure (S) is less than the injection of expenditure (I) into the circular flow of income.
- Accordingly, overall expenditure in the economy would exceed the amount required to buy the planned output. This leads to a situation of higher AD than AS.
- To cope with this, producers will now plan higher output, leading to higher income and higher savings. The process will continue until $S = I$ is restored.

30. What changes will take place to bring an economy in equilibrium if **Competency Based Que**

(i) planned savings are greater than planned investment?

(ii) planned savings are less than planned investment?

Or

If planned savings exceeds planned investments in an economy, explain its likely impact on income, output and employment. **CBSE 2023**

Or

Discuss the working of the adjustment mechanism, if ex-ante investments are less than ex-ante savings. **CBSE 2020**

Ans. The situation when $S > I$ or when $S < I$, is explained with the help of following diagram

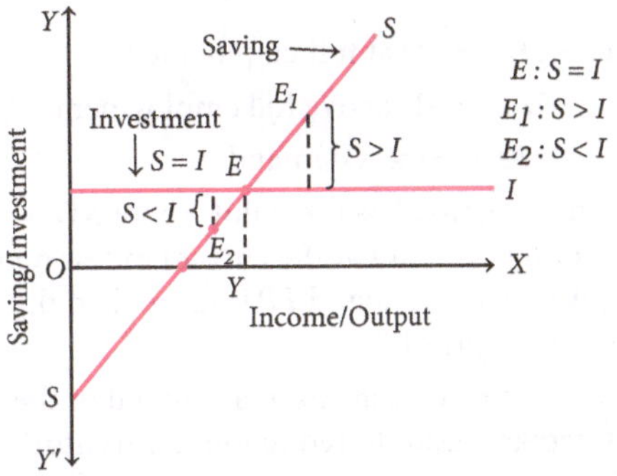

In the above diagram, equilibrium is struck at point E, when $S = I$.

Equilibrium level of income $= OY$.

(i) $S > I$ at point E_1. It is a situation when AD < AS. In such a situation, the following changes will occur

- Stocks of the producers would be in excess of the desired limit.
- Profits will start shrinking.
- Desired level of output for the subsequent year will face a decrease.
- Levels of income and employment will tend to shrink to the point where $S = I$, corresponding to point E in the diagram.

(ii) $S < I$ at point E_2. It is a situation when AD > AS. In such a situation, the following changes will occur

- Existing stocks of the producers will not be enough to cope with the level of AD.
- Profits may increase due to higher demand.
- Producers will plan higher level of output for the subsequent years.
- Level of output and employment will rise or drive the economy to the point of equilibrium at point E.

31. In macroeconomics, what does the concept of excess demand mean? Describe how the open market mechanism works to rectify it.

Ans. The situation in an economy, when aggregate demand is more than the aggregate supply corresponding to full employment, is termed as excess demand situation.

In other words, the level of aggregate demand exceeds the level of aggregate supply, even when there is full capacity production in the economy.

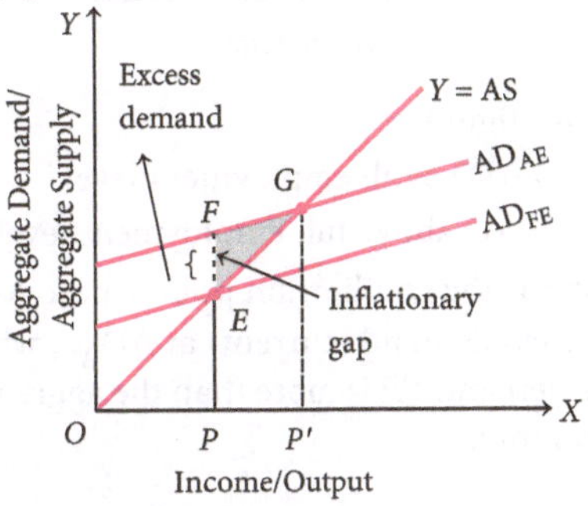

Where, AD_{FE} = AD at full employment
AD_{AE} = AD above full employment
EF = Excess demand

In the above figure, E is the point where AD = AS, i.e. equilibrium point. But at the current excess demand of AD_{AE}, Aggregate Demand FP is more than the Aggregate Supply of EP.

Hence, EF represents the excess demand in the economy. Excess demand leads to reduction in inventories and inflation in the economy.

High prices encourage producers to produce more to reach the desired level of stock. Hence, the AS will also rise and economy will attain a new equilibrium at point G with national income OP.

Open market operations refer to sale and purchase of securities by the central bank on behalf of government in the open market. It directly affects the supply of money in the hands of citizens of the country. In case of excess demand, the central bank sells its securities to common public and financial institutions. It reduces the supply of money in the economy and reduces the money/credit creation power of commercial banks. Thus, the aggregate demand comes down and the economy attains equilibrium.

32. Describe the fundamental concept of the inflationary gap. Elaborate on how legal reserves help to mitigate it.

Ans. Inflationary gap occurs when aggregate demand is greater than aggregate supply corresponding to full employment level.

This inflationary gap, i.e. excess of aggregate demand causes inflation in the economy and price levels tend to rise.

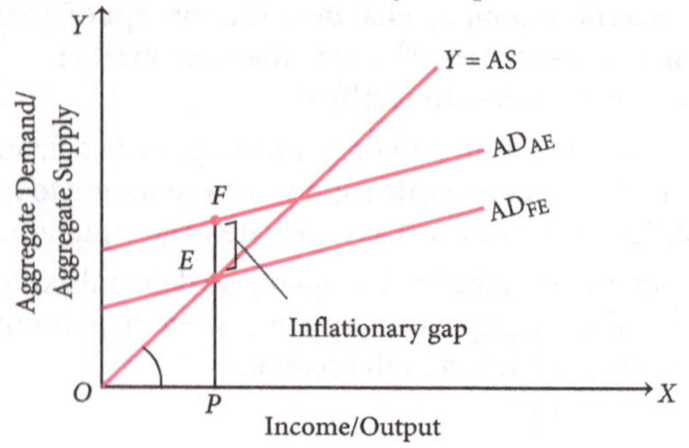

In the above figure,

AD_{FE} = AD at full employment level
AD_{AE} = AD above full employment level

The point E is the equilibrium point where AD = AS. But there is excess demand (current) at AD_{AE}, where aggregate demand FP is more than the aggregate supply in the economy.

This difference of actual aggregate demand and supply, i.e. EF is the inflationary gap.

Inflationary Gap = Excess Demand

$$= AD_{AE} - AD_{FE} = EF$$

Legal reserves like cash reserve ratio and statutory liquidity ratio are the tools to correct the problem of inflationary gap

(i) **Cash Reserve Ratio** (CRR)

Each and every commercial bank has to keep a certain proportion of its demand and time deposits in the form of cash and other liquid assets with the central bank. This ratio is termed as cash reserve ratio.

To correct the problem of inflationary gap, the central bank increases the CRR. It reduces the supply of money and credit creation capabilities of commercial banks.

Due to lesser supply of money, the aggregate demand comes down and the economy attains equilibrium situation.

(ii) **Statutory Liquidity Ratio** (SLR)

It refers to a fixed percentage of the total assets of a bank in the form of cash or other liquid assets that is required to be maintained by the bank.

During the situation of inflationary gap, SLR is increased. This reduces the credit creation capacity of commercial banks and reduces the flow of money in the economy.

As a result of that, the aggregate demand comes down and ultimately, the economy attains equilibrium.

33. Distinguish between inflationary gap and deflationary gap. State one measure for each, by which these can be corrected.

Ans. Differences between inflationary gap and deflationary gap are

Basis	Inflationary Gap	Deflationary Gap
Meaning	The excess of aggregate demand above the level required to maintain equilibrium in full employment situation in an economy, is termed as inflationary gap.	When there is involuntary unemployment in the economy, there is a short fall in aggregate demand from the level required to maintain a full employment equilibrium. This short fall is termed as deflationary gap.
Effect on Price Level	It causes inflation and increases price levels in an economy.	It causes reduction in prices in the economy.

Inflationary and deflationary gap can be corrected by opting following means

(i) To correct the inflationary gap, government should form fiscal and monetary policy to close the gap. Monetary policy can be used in such a manner that it will contract the money supply in the economy by raising interest rates and opts the method of progressive taxation as a fiscal policy measure.

(ii) To correct the deflationary gap, government should stood doing the additional expenditure equal to deflationary gap, so that deflationary gap is wiped out.

34. Define deflationary gap. Elucidate how the marginal requirement helps to lower it.

Ans. When there is involuntary unemployment in the economy, there is a short fall in aggregate demand from the level that is required to maintain a full employment equilibrium. This short fall is termed as deflationary gap. In the given figure, AD_{FE} = AD at full employment level and AD_{IU} = AD at involuntary unemployment level The point *E* is the equilibrium point, where AD = AS. But at the current deficient demand situation (due to involuntary unemployment) of AD_{IU}, the aggregate demand *FP* is less than the actual supply *EP* in the economy. Hence, *EF* is the deflationary gap.

Deflationary Gap = Deficient Demand

$$= AD_{FE} - AD_{IU} = EF$$

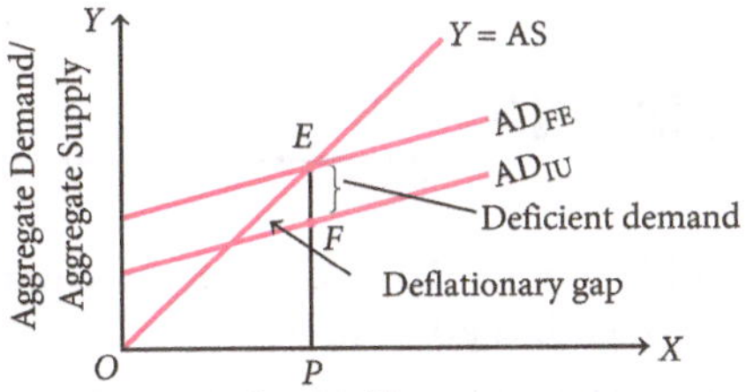

Marginal requirement refers to the difference between the amount of loan granted and the current value of security offered for loans.

In case of deflationary gap, the marginal requirements are lowered to increase the flow of credit by encouraging people to borrow. As a result of that, the aggregate demand increases and ultimately, the economy attains equilibrium.

35. Explain the role of the following in correcting 'deficient' demand in an economy

(i) Open market operations

(ii) Bank rate **(iii) Reverse repo rate**

Ans. Deficient demand refers to the situation when aggregate demand is short of aggregate supply corresponding.

Role of following in correcting deficient demand is as follows

(i) **Open Market Operations**

The selling and buying of securities by the central bank is referred to as 'open market operations.' When there is deficient demand, the central bank purchases securities on the open market and pays the sellers.

The money leaves the central bank and eventually finds its way into the commercial banks as deposits. As a result, the banks' ability to lend money increases. More loans are available to people, which will increase aggregate demand.

(ii) **Bank Rate**

The interest rate that the central bank charges commercial banks for extending credit to them is known as the 'bank rate.' However, there is an inverse link between the demand for loans and the interest rate. As a result, when bank rates rise, interest rates rise and loan demand declines. Therefore, the bank rate ought to be decreased when there is insufficient demand. This will cause the interest rate to decline, which will ultimately raise loan demand. Thus, aggregate demand will rise as a result.

(iii) **Reverse Repo Rate**

Reverse repo rate is the rate at which RBI borrows money from commercial banks. To correct deficient demand, the reverse repo rate should be lowered. A lower reverse repo rate makes it less attractive for banks to park their funds with the RBI. As a result, banks lend more to businesses and consumers, increasing the money supply in the economy. This leads to higher aggregate demand, helping to correct the situation of deficient demand.

36. The Aggregate Supply/Aggregate Demand (AD/AS) model is useful for evaluating the conditions and factors that affect the level of Gross Domestic Product (GDP) and inflation.

The factors affecting aggregate demand include level of income, wealth, population, interest rates, credit availability, government demand, taxation, investments, etc. Those that affect aggregate supply are costs, labour wages, recourses available, productivity and expectations like profits, inflationary and interest rates.

According to Keynesian economics, not all GDP investment sums as part of aggregate demand, thus there would be reduced national output and income when there is unplanned investment.

Production process sometimes produces excess goods that result in reduction in prices or demand.

So, when aggregate expenditures are not equal to aggregate production, this results in changes in prices. This situation is where buyers and the sellers are out of balance. The household and government are unable to purchase all the real production that the producers have and are unable to sell.

Disequilibrium simply means an imbalance between total demand and total supply in production.

Equilibrium aggregate market is the state where the real aggregate expenditures are equal to real production. This implies that real expenditures and/or production do not change, i.e. the opposing forces of aggregate demand and aggregate supply are in balance.

(i) What happens when aggregate demand is not equal to aggregate production?

(ii) Briefly explain the impact of macroeconomic disequilibrium using a suitable example.

Competency Based Que

Ans. (i) Aggregate production indicates aggregate supply in the economy. When aggregate demand and supply are not equal there are broadly two situations which are explained below

- When AD > AS, it means that the buyers are planning to buy more goods and services than the producers are planning to produce or supply. In this situation, inventories start falling and come below the desired level, thus producers expand their production. This raises the income level, which keeps rising till AD and AS are equal again.
- When AD < AS, it means that the buyers are planning to buy fewer goods and services than the producers are planning to produce or supply. In this situation, inventories start rising and move above the desired level. So, the producers curtail the production and retrench the workers and unemployment prevails. This reduces the income level, which keeps on falling till AD and AS become equal again.

(ii) Macroeconomic equilibrium is a condition in the economy in which the quantity of aggregate demand equals the quantity of aggregate supply. If there are changes in either aggregate demand or aggregate supply, you could also see a change in price, unemployment and inflation.

e.g. If the aggregate demand for your lemonade is too low, then your new business venture won't need to keep making as much lemonade and if you hired any friend(s) to help you run your lemonade stand, you may have to let them go. This is because if customers are not buying lemonade, you won't be making money, which means you won't be able to pay any of your friends. When this happens in large companies, workers are often laid off, which ultimately causes the unemployment rate to increase.

Numerical Questions

Numerical 1

Measure the level of ex-ante aggregate demand when autonomous investment and consumption expenditure (A) is ₹ 50 crore and MPS is 0.2 and level of income (Y) is ₹ 4,000 crore. State whether the economy is in equilibrium or not (cite reasons). **NCERT**

Sol. $A =$ ₹ 50 crore; MPS $= 0.2$; $Y =$ ₹ 4,000 crore

$AD = A + cY = 50 + (1-0.2) \times 4{,}000$

[Putting the values of A, Y and c, $c = 1 - \text{MPS}$]

$= 50 + 0.8 \times 4{,}000 = 50 + 3{,}200 =$ ₹ 3,250 crore

₹ 3,250 crore < ₹ 4,000 crore. So, $AD < Y$

Hence, economy is not in equilibrium. There is the situation of excess supply or deficient demand.

Numerical 2

The given income ₹ 1,500 crore is greater than equilibrium level of income ₹ 1,200 crore. Therefore, the economy is not in equilibrium.

Calculate equilibrium level of income for a hypothetical economy, for which it is given that

Autonomous Investments = ₹ 500 crore; Consumption Function, $C = 100 + 0.80Y$

Sol. Given Consumption function is,

$C = 100 + 0.8Y$

Autonomous investments = ₹ 500 crore

We know, at equilibrium level

$Y = C + I \Rightarrow Y = 100 + 0.8Y + 500$

$Y - 0.8Y = 600 \Rightarrow 0.2Y = 600$

$Y =$ ₹ 3,000 crore

Numerical 3

Calculate autonomous consumption expenditure from the following data about an economy which is in equilibrium

National Income = ₹ 500

Marginal Propensity to Save = 0.30

Investment Expenditure = 100

Sol. Given, $Y = ₹\,500$; MPS $= 0.30$; $I = 100$; $\overline{C} = ?$

b or MPC $= 1 - \text{MPS} = 1 - 0.30 = 0.70$

$$Y = C + I \text{ or } Y = \overline{C} + bY + I$$
$$500 = \overline{C} + 0.70 \times 500 + 100$$
$$500 = \overline{C} + 350 + 100$$
$$\overline{C} = 500 - 450 = 50$$

$\therefore$ Autonomous consumption $(\overline{C}) = 50$

Numerical 4

An economy is in equilibrium. From the following data about an economy. Calculate autonomous consumption

(i) Income = ₹ 15,000 **(ii) MPS = 0.3**

(iii) Investment Expenditure = ₹ 800

Sol. Given, $Y = ₹\,15{,}000$; MPS $= 0.3$; $I = ₹\,800$

We know,

MPC + MPS $= 1$; MPC $= 1 - 0.3 = 0.7$

We know at equilibrium level,

$$S = I$$
$$\therefore \quad S = ₹\,800$$

Now, $Y = C + I$ or $Y = C + S$

$$15{,}000 = (\overline{C} + bY) + S$$
$$15{,}000 = \overline{C} + 0.7(15{,}000) + 800$$
$$15{,}000 = (\overline{C} + 10{,}500) + 800$$
$$10{,}000 - 800 = \overline{C} + 10{,}500$$
$$14{,}200 = \overline{C} + 10{,}500$$
$$14{,}200 - 10{,}500 = \overline{C}$$
$$₹\,3{,}700 = \overline{C}$$

Numerical 5

An economy is in equilibrium. From the following data about an economy calculate autonomous consumption.

(i) Income = ₹ 5,000

(ii) Marginal Propensity to Save = 0.2

(iii) Investment Expenditure = ₹ 800

Sol. Given, Income $(Y) = ₹\,5{,}000$

Marginal Propensity to Save (MPS) $= 0.2$ and Investment Expenditure $= ₹\,800$

We know that,

$$\text{MPS} + \text{MPC} = 1$$

On substituting MPS $= 0.2$, we get

$$\text{MPC } (b) = 1 - 0.2 = 0.8$$

We also know that at the point of equilibrium,

Savings = Investment

$\therefore$ Savings = ₹ 800

Now, Income = Consumption + Savings

$5{,}000 = \overline{C} + b.\ (5{,}000) + 800$, where

$\overline{C}$ = Autonomous consumption and b = MPC

$\therefore 5{,}000 - 800 = \overline{C} + 0.8 \times 5{,}000 \Rightarrow 4{,}200 = \overline{C} + 4{,}000$

$\therefore \quad \overline{C} = 4{,}200 - 4{,}000 = ₹\,200$

$\therefore$ Autonomous consumption in the economy = ₹ 200

Numerical 6

Find investment from the following

National Income = ₹ 800

Autonomous Consumption = ₹ 300

Marginal Propensity to Consume = 0.60

Sol. Here, $Y = ₹\,800$; $\overline{C} = ₹\,300$; MPC or $b = 0.60$

We know,

$$Y = C + S \Rightarrow Y - C = S$$

or $\quad S = Y - (\overline{C} + bY) = 800 - [300 + 0.60\,(800)]$

$$= 800 - (300 + 480) = 800 - (780) = ₹\,20$$

At equilibrium level of income, $S = I$

Hence, investment = ₹ 20

Numerical 7

Suppose an economy is in equilibrium. From the following data, calculate investment expenditure in the economy

(i) National Income = ₹ 40,000 crore

(ii) Marginal Propensity to Consume (MPC) = 0.8

(iii) Autonomous Consumption $(\overline{C})$ = ₹ 100 crore **CBSE 2024**

Sol. Here, $Y = ₹\,40{,}000$; $\overline{C} = ₹\,100$; MPC $= 0.8$

We know that,

$$Y = C + S$$
$$Y = (\overline{C} + bY) + S$$
$$40{,}000 = [100 + 0.8(40{,}000)] + S$$
$$40{,}000 = [100 + 32{,}000] + S$$
$$40{,}000 - 32{,}100 = S$$
$$S = ₹\,7{,}900$$

At equilibrium level, $I = S$

$\therefore$ Investment = ₹ 7,900

Numerical 8

Calculate investment expenditure from the following data about an economy which is in equilibrium

National Income = ₹ 1,000

Marginal Propensity to Save = 0.20

Autonomous Consumption Expenditure = ₹ 100

Sol. Given, $Y = ₹\,1{,}000$; MPS $= 0.20$; $\overline{C} = ₹\,100$; $I = ?$

b or MPC $= 1 - \text{MPS} = 1 - 0.20 = 0.80$

$$Y = C + I$$

or $\quad Y = \overline{C} + bY + I$

$$1{,}000 = 100 + 0.80 \times 1{,}000 + I$$
$$I = 1{,}000 - 900, \quad I = 100$$

Numerical 9

An economy is in equilibrium, calculate the Marginal Propensity to Save (MPS) from the following

(i) National Income (Y) ₹ 4,400

(ii) Autonomous Consumption ($\overline{C}$) = ₹ 1,000

(iii) Investment Expenditure (I) = ₹ 70 **CBSE Term II 2022**

Sol. Consumption function is $C = a + by$, where a is autonomus consumption, b is MPC and y is income in economy.

$$AD = AS$$
$$Y = C + I$$
$$4{,}400 = 1{,}000 + b \times 4{,}400 + 70$$
$$4{,}400 - 1{,}000 = 4{,}400b + 70$$
$$3{,}400 - 70 = 4{,}400b$$
$$3{,}330 = 4{,}400b$$
$$b = \frac{3{,}330}{4{,}400} = 0.75$$
$$MPS + MPC = 1$$
$$MPS + 0.75 = 1$$
$$MPS = 1 - 0.75 = 0.25$$

Numerical 10

Calculate Marginal Propensity to Consume (MPC) from the following data about an economy which is in equilibrium

National Income = ₹ 2,000

Autonomous Consumption Expenditure = ₹ 200

Investment Expenditure = 100

Sol. Given, $Y = ₹\,2{,}000;\quad \overline{C} = ₹\,200;\quad I = 100$

We know, $Y = C + I,\; C = \overline{C} + bY$

$$Y = \overline{C} + bY + I$$

For calculating MPC, we use following equation

$$Y = \overline{C} + bY + I$$
$$b = MPC$$
$$2{,}000 = 200 + 2{,}000\,b + 100$$
$$b = \frac{2{,}000 - 300}{2{,}000} = \frac{1{,}700}{2{,}000} = 0.85$$

Thus, MPC = 0.85

Numerical 11

An economy is in equilibrium. Calculate Marginal Propensity to Consume

National Income = ₹ 1,000

Autonomous Consumption Expenditure = ₹ 200

Investment Expenditure = ₹ 100

Sol. Given, National Income (Y) = ₹ 1,000

Autonomous Consumption Expenditure ($\overline{C}$) = ₹ 200

Investment Expenditure (I) = ₹ 100

Marginal Propensity to Consume (MPC/b) = ?

We know that at the equilibrium level,

Savings = Investment

So, Income (Y) = Consumption Expenditure (C) + Investment (I)

Also, Consumption Expenditure (C) = $\overline{C} + bY$

So, it follows that,

$$Y = \overline{C} + bY + I$$

On substituting the given variables, we get

$$1{,}000 = 200 + b\,(1{,}000) + 100$$

or $1{,}000 = 300 + 1{,}000b$

or $700 = 1{,}000b$

or $b = \frac{700}{1{,}000} = 0.7$

or Marginal Propensity to Consume (MPC) = 0.7

Numerical 12

"In an economy, the autonomous consumption is ₹ 100 and Marginal Propensity to Consume (MPC) is 0.6. If the equilibrium level of income is ₹ 2,000, then the autonomous investment is ₹ 300." Justify the statement with valid calculation. **CBSE Term II 2022**

Sol. Consumption function is $C = a + by$, where a is autonomous consumption, b is MPC and Y is the level of income in the economy. At equilibrium level of income

$$AS = AD$$
$$Y = C + I \Rightarrow 2{,}000 = 100 + 0.6(2{,}000) + I$$
$$\Rightarrow 2{,}000 = 100 + 1{,}200 + I$$
$$\Rightarrow I = 2{,}000 - 1{,}300 = ₹\,700$$

Therefore, if equilibrium income is ₹ 2,000, then investment should be ₹ 700.

Numercial 13

In an economy, C = 200 + 0.5Y is the consumption function where C is the consumption expenditure and Y is the national income. Investment expenditure is ₹ 400 crore.

Is the economy in equilibrium at an income level ₹ 1,500 crore? Justify your answer. **CBSE SQP 2021**

Sol. Given

Consumption function (C) = 200 + 0.5Y

Investment (I) = 400

Level of income (Y) = ₹ 1,500

At equilibrium level, AD = AS

$$Y = C + I$$

Thus, $Y = (200 + 0.5Y) + 400$

$Y - 0.5\,Y = 600$

$Y = 600/0.5 =$ ₹ 1,200 crore

The equilibrium level of income = ₹ 1,200 crore

The given income (₹ 1,500 crore) is greater than equilibrium level of income (₹ 1,200 crore). Therefore, the economy is not in equilibrium.

Numerical 14

On the basis of following information, identify whether the economy is in equilibrium or not

(i) Autonomous consumption and investment expenditure ($\bar{A}$) ₹ 500 crore

(ii) Marginal Propensity to Save (MPS) = 0.2

(iii) National Income = ₹ 4,000 crore **CBSE 2020**

Sol. Given, autonomous consumption and investment expenditure ($\bar{A}$) = ₹ 500 crore

Marginal Propensity to Save (MPS) = 0.2

National income (Y) = ₹ 4,000 crore

We know,

National income = AS = ₹ 4,000 crore

$$\text{AD} = \bar{A} + cY$$
$$= \bar{A} + 1 - \text{MPS}\,(Y)$$
$$= 500 + 1 - 0.2\,(4{,}000) = 500 + 0.8\,(4{,}000)$$
$$= 500 + 3{,}200 = 3{,}700$$

Since, AS (4,000) > AD (3,700)

$\text{AS} \neq \text{AD}$

Thus, the economy is not in a state of equilibrium.

Numerical 15

Assume the following for a hypothetical economy **CBSE 2024 C**

(i) Autonomous Consumption Expenditure ($\bar{C}$) = ₹ 25 crore

(ii) Marginal Propensity to Save (MPS) = 0.1

(iii) Level of Income (Y) = ₹ 2,000 crore

(iv) Autonomous Investment (I) = ₹ 25 crore

Is the economy in equilibrium situation? Justify your answer with valid calculations.

Sol. The equilibrium condition is when Aggregate Demand (AD) = Aggregate Supply (AS) *or* AD = Y.

The formula for AD is

AD = Consumption (C) + Investment (I)

Consumption Function C = C + MPC × Y

Here, MPC = 1 – MPS = 1 – 0.1 = 0.9

C = 25 + 0.9 × 2,000 = 25 + 1,800 = 1,825 crore

Given I = 25 crore

AD = $C + I$ = 1,825 + 25 = 1,850 crore

Aggregate Supply (AS) = Y = 2,000 crore

Since AD = 1,850 crore and AS = 2,000 crore, the economy is not in equilibrium. The economy is not in equilibrium because aggregate demand (₹ 1,850 crore) is less than aggregate supply (₹ 2,000 crore). This indicates a deflationary gap, where the economy is producing more than what is being demanded.

Numerical 16

An economy is in equilibrium. Calculate National Income from the following

Autonomous Consumption = ₹ 100

Marginal Propensity to Save = 0.2

Investment Expenditure = ₹ 200

Sol. Autonomous Consumption ($\bar{C}$) = ₹ 100

Marginal Propensity to Save (MPS) = 0.2

Investment Expenditure (I) = ₹ 200

∴ Marginal Propensity to Consume

(MPC) = 1 – MPS = 1 – 0.2 = 0.8

As the economy is in equilibrium,

$$Y = C + I$$
$$Y = \bar{C} + bY + I \qquad [b = \text{MPC}]$$
$$Y = 100 + 0.8Y + 200$$
$$Y - 0.8Y = 300$$
$$Y = \frac{300}{0.2} = ₹\ 1{,}500$$

Numerical 17

Answer the following questions based on the data given below

(i) Planned Investments = ₹ 100 crore

(ii) $C = 50 + 0.50Y$

(a) Determine the equilibrium level of income.

(b) Calculate the value of savings at equilibrium level of national income.

(c) Calculate the value of investment multiplier. **CBSE 2020**

Sol. (a) Equilibrium level of income = $C + S$

where, C = Consumption Expenditure and

S = Savings

Also, we know that at equilibrium level,

Planned Savings = Planned Investments

So,
$$Y = C + I$$
$$Y = 50 + 0.50Y + 100$$
$$Y - 0.50Y = 150$$
$$0.50Y = 150$$
$$\therefore \quad Y = \frac{150}{0.5}$$
$$= ₹\ 300 \text{ crore}$$

(b) We know that,

$$Y = C + S$$
$$300 = 50 + 0.50Y + S$$
$$300 = 50 + 0.50 \times 300 + S$$
$$300 = 50 + 150 + S$$
$$300 = 200 + S$$
$$\therefore \quad S = ₹\ 100 \text{ crore}$$

(c) Investment Multiplier $(K) = \frac{1}{1 - \text{MPC}}$, where

MPC = Marginal Propensity to Consume = 0.5

(The coefficient of Y in the consumption function represents MPC)

So, $K = \frac{1}{1-0.5} = \frac{1}{0.5} = 2$

Numerical 18

The saving function of an economy is given as $S = -25 + 0.25Y$

If the planned investment is ₹ 200 crore, calculate the following

(i) Equilibrium level of income in the economy.

(ii) Aggregate demand at income of ₹ 500 crore. **CBSE 2019**

Sol. Given, $S = -25 + 0.25Y$

Planned investment (I) = ₹ 200 crore

At equilibrium,

$$S = I \Rightarrow -25 + 0.25Y = 200$$

$0.25Y = 200 + 25$; $0.25Y = 225$

$$Y = 225/0.25 = 900$$

We know at equilibrium,

$$\text{AD} = C + I = 25 + (1 - 0.25)\ Y + 200$$
$$= 25 + 0.75\ (500) + 200$$
$$= 25 + 375 + 200 = ₹\ 600 \text{ crore}$$

So,

(i) Equilibrium level of income in the economy = ₹ 900 crore.

(ii) Aggregate demand at income of ₹ 500 crore = ₹ 600 crore.

Numerical 19

The saving function of an economy is given as $S = (-)\ 10 + 0.20Y$

If the ex-ante investments are ₹ 240 crore, calculate the following

(i) Equilibrium level of income in the economy.

(ii) Additional investments which will be needed to double the present level of equilibrium income. **CBSE 2019**

Sol. Given,

$S = -10 + 0.20Y$

Ex-ante investments (I) = ₹ 240 crore

At equilibrium,

$$S = I$$
$$-10 + 0.20Y = 240$$
$$0.20Y = 240 + 10$$
$$0.20Y = 250$$
$$Y = 250/0.20 = 1{,}250$$
$$K = 1/\text{MPS} = 1/0.20 = 5$$
$$\text{Multiplier } (K) = \Delta Y/\Delta I$$
$$5 = 1{,}250/\Delta I$$
$$\Delta I = 250$$

Thus,

(i) Equilibrium level of income in the economy = ₹ 1,250 crore.

(ii) Additional investments needed to double the present level of equilibrium income = ₹ 250 crore.

Numerical 20

The saving function of an economy is $S = -600 + 0.25Y$. The economy is in equilibrium when income is equal to ₹ 5,000.

Calculate

(i) Investment expenditure at equilibrium level of income.

(ii) Investment multiplier.

Sol. (i) Given, $S = -600 + 0.25Y$

Income (Y) = ₹ 5,000

At the equilibrium level,

$$S = I \Rightarrow -600 + 0.25Y = I$$
$$I = -600 + 0.25(5{,}000) = -600 + 1{,}250 = 650$$

(ii) $K = 1/1 - \text{MPC} = 1/\text{MPS}$

From saving function,

MPS = 0.25 = 1/0.25 = 4

So,

(a) Investment expenditure at equilibrium level of income = ₹ 650

(b) Investment multiplier = 4

Numerical 21

The saving function of an economy is $S = -200 + 0.25Y$. The economy is in equilibrium when income is equal to ₹ 2,000. Calculate

(i) Investment expenditure at equilibrium level of income.

(i) Autonomous consumption.

(iii) Investment multiplier.

Sol. (i) Given, $S = -200 + 0.25Y$

Income (Y) = ₹ 2,000

At the equilibrium level,

$$S = I$$

$$-200 + 0.25Y = I$$

$$I = -200 + 0.25\,(2{,}000)$$

$$I = -200 + 500 = 300$$

$$S = -200 + 0.25\,(0) = -200$$

(ii) At $Y = 0$,

Autonomous Consumption $(\bar{C}) = -(\bar{S})$

$$= -(-200) = 200$$

(iii) Investment Multiplier $(\bar{K}) = \dfrac{1}{1-\text{MPC}} = \dfrac{1}{\text{MPS}}$

$$K = \frac{1}{0.25} = 4$$

Numerical 22

In an economy, $S = -350 + 0.4Y$ is the saving function, where S is saving and Y is national income. If investment expenditure is ₹ 1,100.

Calculate

(i) Equilibrium level of national income.

(ii) Consumption expenditure at equilibrium.

Sol. $S = -350 + 0.4Y$; $I =$ ₹ 1,100

(i) At equilibrium level of national income

$$S = I$$

$$-350 + 0.4Y = 1{,}100$$

$$0.4Y = 1{,}100 + 350$$

$$0.4Y = 1{,}450$$

$$Y = \frac{1{,}450}{0.4} = 3{,}625$$

$Y =$ ₹ 3,625

(ii) Consumption $= Y = C + I$

$$3{,}625 = C + 1{,}100$$

$$3{,}625 - 1{,}100 = C$$

₹ 2,525 $= C$

Numerical 23

In an economy, $C = 300 + 0.5Y$ and $I =$ ₹ 600 (where, C = Consumption, Y = Income, I = Investment). Calculate the following

(i) Equilibrium level of income.

(ii) Consumption expenditure at equilibrium level of income.

Sol. (i) Here, $I =$ ₹ 600 and $C = 300 + 0.5Y$

Now, we know that, $Y = C + I$

$\Rightarrow \quad Y = 300 + 0.5Y + 600$

or $\quad Y - 0.5Y = 900$

or $\quad 0.5Y = 900$

So, $\quad Y = \dfrac{900}{0.5} =$ ₹ 1,800

(ii) Again, $\quad Y = C + I \Rightarrow 1{,}800 = C + 600$

So, $\quad C = 1{,}800 - 600 =$ ₹ 1,200

Numerical 24

In an economy, the saving function is $S = -800 + 0.4Y$ where S is saving and Y is income.

Calculate the equilibrium level of income and consumption expenditure when investment expenditure is ₹ 1,000.

Sol. Given, $S = -800 + 0.4Y$

Investment expenditure (I) = ₹ 1,000

At equilibrium,

$S = I \quad \Rightarrow -800 + 0.4Y = 1{,}000$

$0.4Y = 1000 + 800$

$0.4Y = 1{,}800$

$Y = 1{,}800/0.4 = 4{,}500$

When $Y = 4{,}500$

We know that,

$S = -800 + 0.4\,(4{,}500) = -800 + 1{,}800 =$ ₹ 1,000

Consumption $(C) = Y - S = 4{,}500 - 1{,}000 = 3{,}500$

So, Equilibrium level of income = ₹ 4,500

Equilibrium level of consumption expenditure = ₹ 3,500

SELF ASSESSMENT TEST

Objective Type Questions

1. Actual level of aggregate demand is known as
(a) effective demand
(b) ex-ante AD
(c) ex-post AD
(d) planned AD

2. If aggregate demand exceeds aggregate supply, it may result in
(a) inflation
(b) deflation
(c) recession
(d) No change in price level

3. When savings are greater than investment in an economy, it is likely to lead to
(a) an increase in aggregate demand
(b) inflationary pressure
(c) a rise in consumer spending
(d) unemployment and recession

4. Which of the following measures is used by the Reserve Bank of India (RBI) to control inflation?
(a) Reducing the Cash Reserve Ratio (CRR)
(b) Increasing the repo rate
(c) Providing more liquidity to banks
(d) Reducing the Statutory Liquidity Ratio (SLR)

5. Deficient demand is associated with
(a) high inflation rates
(b) low levels of aggregate demand
(c) excessive exports over imports
(d) overproduction in the economy

6. When the RBI sells government securities in the open market, it aims to
(a) increase the money supply and encourage lending in the economy.
(b) reduce the money supply and control inflation.
(c) increase the foreign exchange reserves.
(d) reduce the interest rates to promote economic growth.

7. Which of the following statements is/are correct?
I. At full employment level employment increases.
II. Increse in imports increases AD.

Codes
(a) Only I
(b) Only II
(c) Both I and II
(d) None of the above

8. **Statement I** Inflationary gap arises when aggregate demand exceeds aggregate supply at full employment level.

Statement II Inflationary gap leads to a decrease in general price level.

Alternatives
(a) Statement I is correct and Statement II is incorrect
(b) Statement II is correct and Statement I is incorrect
(c) Both the statements are correct
(d) Both the statements are incorrect

Answers 1. (c) 2. (a) 3. (d) 4. (b) 5. (b) 6. (b) 7. (d) 8. (a)

Short Answer Type Questions

9. What happens if AD<AS prior to full employment level of output?

10. Can an economy be in a state of over full employment equilibrium? Explain with the help of a diagram.

11. What changes will take place to bring an economy in equilibrium if savings are less than investment?

12. Draw a diagram showing inflationary gap.

13. Mention the activities performed in open market operations.

14. "In recent policy announcements, the Reserve Bank of India highlighted adjustments in interest rates and liquidity management operations, aiming to achieve a balanced economic environment.

Such measures are crucial to ensure that economic growth does not come at the cost of rising prices, maintaining purchasing power and economic stability."

— RBI Policy Release

Based on the statement above, discuss how the RBI might approach inflation control in the economy.

Long Answer Type Questions

15. How excess demand affects developed economies?
16. Explain determination of equilibrium level of income using consumption plus investment ($C+I$) approach. Use diagram.
17. "An economy is operating at underemployment level of income." What is meant by the given statement? Discuss one fiscal measure and one monetary measure to tackle the situation.

Numerical Questions

18. Find consumption expenditure from the following
    Autonomous Consumption = ₹ 100
    Marginal Propensity to Consume = 0.70
    National Income = ₹ 1,000

Ans. ₹ 800

19. Find national income from the following
    Autonomous Consumption = ₹ 100
    Marginal Propensity to Consume = 0.60
    Investment = ₹ 200

Ans. ₹ 750

20. In an economy, $C = 200 + 0.9\,Y$ is the consumption function (where, C = Consumption expenditure and Y = National income) and investment expenditure is ₹ 3,000. Calculate
    (i) Equilibrium level of national income
    (ii) Consumption expenditure at equilibrium level of national income.

Ans. (i) Y = ₹ 32,000
(ii) C = ₹ 29,000

21. An economy is in equilibrium.
    Find Marginal Propensity to Consume from the following
    National Income = ₹ 2,000
    Autonomous Consumption = ₹ 400
    Investment Expenditure = ₹ 200

Ans. 0.7

06

CHAPTER

Government Budget and the Economy

A government budget is a forecast of a government's expenditures and revenues for a specific period, typically a year, known as a financial or fiscal year. It is a crucial financial document outlining a nation's economic priorities and policy plans for a fiscal year.

▼ YOUR STUDY GOALS

6.1 Concept of Government Budget
6.2 Components of Government Budget
 – Revenue Budget
 – Capital Budget
6.3 Measures of Budget Deficit

▼ YOUR PRACTICE GOAL

- Objective Type Questions (65 Qs ; MCQs, A-R, Statements, Matching, Concept Identification)
- Subjective Questions (25 SAs, 10 LAs)
- 11 Numerical Questions
- Self Assessment Test (6 MCQs, 5 SAs, 2 LAs, 3 Numerical)

6.1 Concept of Government Budget

Government budget is a statement of estimates of the government's expected receipts and expenditure during the financial year or fiscal year which is taken from 1st April to 31st March. As per Article 112, it is a constitutional requirement in India.

In India, the finance minister presents annual budget of the government for its approval on 1st of February every year.

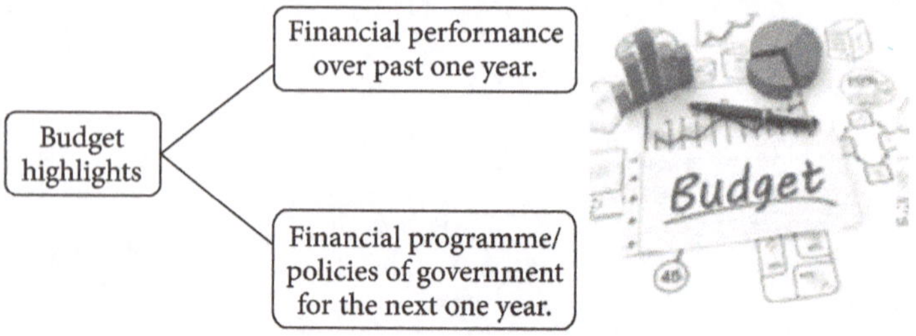

The programmes and policies of the government (as presented in the budget) are known as 'budgetary policy' or 'fiscal policy' of the government.

Objectives of Government Budget

Objectives of government budget include the following

Objectives	Explanation
Redistribution of Income and Wealth	Government aims to improve the distribution of income and wealth in an economy, through its budgetary policy. For this purpose, it uses fiscal tools of taxation and subsidies to bring fair or equitable distribution of income.
Reallocation of Resources	The government of a country, through its budgetary policy, directs the allocation of resources in a manner such that there is a balance between the goals of profit maximisation and social welfare. It is achieved in the following manner • Providing tax concessions and subsidies to the producers to encourage domestic production. e.g. Make in India scheme. • Government provides public goods. These goods promote social welfare. The public goods are non-rivalrous and non-excludable in nature.
Economic Growth	The growth rate of a country depends on the rate of savings and investment. Therefore, budgetary policy in this regard tries to create conditions conducive for increase in savings and investment. Government tries to achieve this through tax rebates, giving incentives to producers, etc.
Generation of Employment	Government promotes labour intensive technology, undertakes public works programmes like construction of roads, dams, canals, bridges, etc. to promote employment generation in the economy. Several programmes are initiated through budget to reduce the problem of poverty and unemployment like MGNREGA.
Economic Stability	Government tries to establish economic stability in the country through its budgetary policy. Government can do so in the following manner • During the boom period, rate of inflation rises, so, government reduces its expenditure to reduce the level of aggregate demand. • During recession and depression, there is situation of deflation. So, government increases its expenditure and reduces the taxes to increase aggregate demand.
Management of Public Enterprise	Public Sector Units (PSUs) are established with an aim of social welfare of public. Government, through budgetary policy, tries to manage the expenditure and revenue of these PSUs. Examples of PSUs are BHEL, ONGC, etc.

6.2 Components of Government Budget

The budget of the Central Government has two components. It can be easily understood with the help of following flow chart

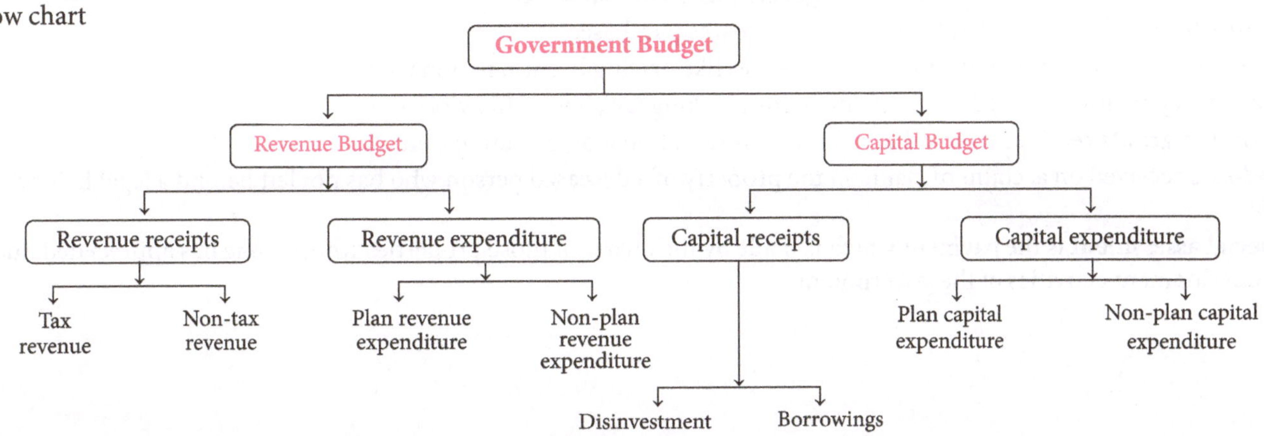

Revenue Budget

The revenue budget shows the expected revenue receipts of the government and the expected revenue expenditure that can be met from these receipts.

These components are explained as follows

1. Revenue Receipts

Receipts which do not create a liability for the government or do not lead to reduction in assets for the government are known as revenue receipts. e.g. Tax levied by government is revenue receipt as it does not create any liability.

These revenue receipts are classified into two heads

(i) Tax Revenue/Receipt

It consists of the proceeds of taxes and other duties levied by the Central Government. A tax is a legally compulsory payment imposed by the government on the households and producers.

Tax revenue comprises direct taxes and indirect taxes.

Direct Tax	Indirect Tax
It is a tax levied on the income of household and firms.	It is a tax levied on goods and services.
Its final burden cannot be shifted onto others. e.g. Income tax, wealth tax.	Its final burden can be shifted to others. e.g. Excise tax, GST.

Different Tax Systems

- **Progressive Tax System** It is a tax system that causes relatively less burden on the poor and more on the rich, i.e. tax rate rises with rise in income.
- **Regressive Tax System** It is a tax system that causes relatively more burden on the poor and less on the rich, i.e. tax rate falls with rise in income.
- **Proportional Tax System** It is a tax system in which the rate of taxation remains constant with increase or decrease in income.
- **Lumpsum Tax System** It is a tax system that does not depend on income. Property tax is a lumpsum tax.

(ii) Non-tax Revenue/Receipt

Revenue received by the government from sources other than taxes are referred to as non-tax revenue.

Following are the sources of non-tax revenue

- **Interest income** from loans given to state government, companies, etc.
- **Profits** from PSU and dividends received from shares purchased.
- **Fees** like registration fee, import fee or license fees like driving licence, national permit license.
- **Fines and penalties** charged by government for breaking law, like traffic violation.
- **Gifts and grants** received from other countries, international organisations, etc.
- **Escheats** received on account of claim on the property of a deceased person who has not left behind a legal heir or a will.
- **Special assessment** is the payment which is made by the owner of those properties whose value has appreciated due to development activities of the government.

2. Revenue Expenditure

These are those expenditures which neither create any asset nor reduce liabilities of the government. These are recurring in nature. These expenditures are incurred for smooth functioning of government departments and for meeting day-to-day expenses of the government.
e.g. Payment of salaries and pensions, interest payments, subsidies, etc.

Capital Budget

The capital budget is an account of the assets as well as the liabilities of the Central Government, which takes into consideration changes in capital.

Capital budget is the statement of estimated capital receipts and estimated capital expenditure during a fiscal year.

These components are explained as follows

1. Capital Receipts

All those receipts of the government which create liabilities for the government or reduce assets of the government, are termed as capital receipts.

Capital receipts are obtained by the government by raising funds through borrowings, recoveries of loans and disposing of assets.

Sources of Capital Receipts

- **Disinvestment** It refers to withdrawal of existing investment, i.e. when government sells its shares of Public Sector Undertakings (PSUs) to private sector. e.g. The Government of India sold its shares in Maruti Udyog.
- **Borrowings** It creates liability for the government. Accordingly, borrowings are to be treated as capital receipts.
- **Recovery of Loans** When entities like state governments, union territories, etc. repay the loan, then it is treated as capital receipt because it reduces the assets of the government.
- **Small Savings** The government raises funds from the public by issuing National Savings Certificates (NSCs), post office deposits, etc.

2. Capital Expenditure

Capital expenditure is the expenditure of the government which either create assets for the government or reduces liabilities of the government.

This includes expenditure on the acquisition of land, building, machinery, equipment, investment in shares, loans and advances by the Central Government to state and union territory governments, PSUs and other entities.

Types of Expenditure

Expenditure can be categorised as follows

Type	Explanation
Plan Expenditure	It is related to the five year plans and central assistance for state and union territory plans. It includes both revenue and capital expenditure.
Non-plan Expenditure	It refers to the expenditure which is not related to five year plans. It covers various general, social and economic services provided by the government. e.g. Expenditure as a relief to the earthquake victims.
Developmental Expenditure	It relates to the growth and development activities of the government. e.g. Expenditure incurred on construction of Metro Rail.
Non-developmental Expenditure	It relates to non-development activities like payment of pensions, interest on loan, etc. of the government.

Types of Budget

There are three types of budget which are as follows

Balanced Budget	Surplus Budget	Deficit Budget
Budget in which government's estimated receipts (both capital and revenue) are equal to government's estimated expenditure (both capital and revenue).	Budget in which government's estimated receipts (both capital and revenue) are more than government's estimated expenditure (both capital and revenue).	Budget in which government's estimated receipts (both capital and revenue) are less than government's estimated expenditure (both capital and revenue).
Budget Receipts = Budget Expenditure	Budget Receipts > Budget Expenditure	Budget Receipts < Budget Expenditure

6.3 Measures of Budget Deficit

Budgetary deficit is the overall deficit of the government budget. It is calculated as the difference between total expenditures and total receipts.

Budget Deficit = Total Expenditure – Total Receipts

There are three measures of budget deficit and they have their own implications for the economy. These measures are as follows

1. Revenue Deficit

It is defined as the excess of government's revenue expenditure over revenue receipts during a given fiscal year.

Revenue deficit includes only such transactions that affect the current income and expenditure of the government. It is calculated as

Revenue Deficit = Revenue Expenditure – Revenue Receipts

Implications and Measures related to Revenue Deficit

Implications of Revenue Deficit	Measures to Reduce Revenue Deficit
• Warning to government either to reduce government expenditure or increase its revenue. • Leads to disinvestment, creates inflationary situation. • Increases borrowing to meet consumption requirements. • Reduction in productive capital expenditure or welfare expenditure. • Shows inefficiency of government, lead to debt-interest build-up.	• Reduction in government's expenditure. • Increase in government's revenue.

2. Fiscal Deficit

Fiscal deficit is the difference between the government's total expenditure and total receipts (excluding borrowings) during a given fiscal year.

It is calculated as

Fiscal Deficit = Total Budget Expenditure – Total Budget Receipts (Excluding borrowings)

or = Total Budget Expenditure – (Revenue Receipts + Non-debt Creating Capital Receipts)

or = Revenue Deficit + Capital Expenditure – Non-debt Creating Capital Receipts

or = Borrowings

Where, non-debt creating capital receipts are those receipts which are not borrowings and therefore, do not give rise to debt. Also, revenue deficit is a part of fiscal deficit.

Implications and Measures related to Fiscal Deficit

Implications of Fiscal Deficit	Measures to Reduce Fiscal Deficit
• Affects future economic growth of country • Increases foreign dependence • Increases liability • A fiscal deficit reflects the government's total borrowing needs, leading to interest payments that raise revenue expenditure and cause revenue deficits. This will create a **debt trap**.	• Reduction in public expenditure by (a) Reducing subsidies (b) Reducing non-developmental expenditure • Steps to increase revenue by (a) Increasing the incidence and burden of tax (b) Increasing the profitability of PSUs (c) Controlling tax evasion

3. Primary Deficit

Primary deficit is the difference between fiscal deficit and interest payments.

It is calculated as

$$\text{Primary Deficit} = \text{Fiscal Deficit} - \text{Interest Payments}$$

Implications and Measures related to Primary Deficit

Implications of Primary Deficit	Measures to Reduce Primary Deficit
• Indicates borrowing requirements of the government to meet fiscal deficit net of interest payment. • Zero primary deficit, i.e. the government has to resort to borrowings only to make interest payment.	• Efforts should be made to reduce fiscal deficit. • Early repayment of loans should be encouraged.

How can Deficits be Financed?

Deficits, occurring in the government budget, can be financed in the following ways

Revenue Deficit	• Increase in taxes • Disinvestment • Reduction in expenditure
Fiscal Deficit	• Borrowings • Deficit financing

1. **Increase in Taxation** Government can impose higher tax rates to generate high revenue.
2. **Disinvestment** Government can disinvest non-profitable and sick PSUs to increase capital receipts and reduce expenditure.
3. **Reduction in Expenditure** Non-development expenditures should be reduced to avoid deficit generation.
4. **Borrowings** Government can borrow from internal and external sources to finance deficit.
5. **Deficit Financing** RBI prints new currency and advances loans to government against approved securities, leading to inflation.

Important Formulae

1. Budgetary Deficit = Total Budget Expenditure – Total Budget Receipts
2. Revenue Deficit = Revenue Expenditure – Revenue Receipts
3. Fiscal Deficit = Total Budget Expenditure – Total Budget Receipts (Excluding Borrowings)
4. Primary Deficit = Fiscal Deficit – Interest Payments

Mind Map

1 Concept of Government Budget

Government budget is a statement of estimates of the government's expected receipts and government's expected expenditure during the financial year or fiscal year. The programmes and policies of the government are known as budgetary policy or fiscal policy of the government.

2 Objectives of Government Budget

- **Redistribution of Income and Wealth** Government aims to improve the distribution of income and wealth in an economy.
- **Reallocation of Resources** The government directs the allocation of resources in a manner such that there is a balance between the goals of profit maximisation and social welfare.
- **Economic Growth** Budgetary policy tries to create conditions conducive for increase in savings and investment.
- **Generation of Employment** Government undertakes various programmes to promote employment generation.
- **Economic Stability** Government tries to establish economic stability in the country through its budgetary policy.
- **Management of Public Enterprise** Public sector units are established with an aim of social welfare of public.

3 Components of Government Budget

The budget of the Central Government has two components, i.e. revenue budget and capital budget.

Capital Budget
It is an account of the assets as well as the liabilities of the Central Government, which takes into consideration changes in capital. The components of capital budget are

1. **Capital Receipts** All those receipts of the government which create liabilities for the government or reduce assets of the government, are termed as capital receipts. Sources include disinvestment, borrowings, recovery of loans and small savings.
2. **Capital Expenditure** It is the expenditure of the government which either create assets for the government or reduces liabilities of the government. Types of expenditure include plan expenditure, non-plan expenditure, developmental expenditure and non-developmental expenditure.

Revenue Budget
It shows the expected revenue receipts of the government and the expected revenue expenditure that can be met from these receipts. It includes

1. **Revenue Receipts** These receipts do not create a liability for the government or do not lead to reduction in assets for the government.
   These can be classified into two heads
   - **Tax Revenue/Receipt** It consists of the proceeds of taxes and other duties levied by the Central Government. It comprises of direct and indirect taxes.
   - **Non-tax Revenue/Receipt** It is a revenue received by the government from sources other than taxes. Following are the sources
     – Interest income–Profits–Fees
     – Fines and penalties –Gifts and grants–Escheats
     – Special assessment
2. **Revenue Expenditure** They neither create any asset nor reduce liabilities of the government.

GOVERNMENT BUDGET AND THE ECONOMY

6 How can Deficits be Financed?

Deficits, occurring in the government budget, can be financed in the following ways

- **Increase in Taxation** Government can impose higher tax rates to generate high revenue.
- **Disinvestment** Government can disinvest non-profitable and sick PSUs to increase capital receipts and reduce expenditure.
- **Reduction in Expenditure** Non-development expenditures should be reduced to avoid deficit generation.
- **Borrowings** Government can borrow from internal and external sources to finance deficit.
- **Deficit Financing** RBI prints new currency and advances loans to government against approved securities, leading to inflation.

5 Measures of Budget Deficit

Budgetary deficit is overall deficit of the government budget. It is calculated as
Budget Deficit = Total Expenditure–Total Receipts
There are three measures of budget deficit, i.e. revenue deficit, fiscal deficit, primary deficit.

Primary Deficit
It is the difference between fiscal deficit and interest payments. It is calculated as
Primary Deficit = Fiscal Deficit– Interest Payments

Revenue Deficit
It is defined as excess of government's revenue expenditure over revenue receipts during the given fiscal year. Revenue deficit includes only such transactions that affect the current income and expenditure of the government. It is calculated as
Revenue Deficit = Revenue Expenditure – Revenue Receipts

Fiscal Deficit
It is the difference between the government's total expenditure and total receipts, excluding borrowings, during a given fiscal year.
It is calculated as
Fiscal Deficit = Total Budget Expenditure – Total Budget Receipts (Excluding borrowings)
or = Total Budget Expenditure – (Revenue Receipts + Non-debt Creating Capital Receipts)
or = Revenue Deficit + Capital Expenditure – Non-debt Creating Capital Receipts
or = Borrowings

4 Types of Budget

- **Balanced Budget** Budget in which the government's estimated receipts are equal to government's estimated expenditure.
- **Surplus Budget** Budget in which the government's estimated receipts are more than government's estimated expenditure.
- **Deficit Budget** Budget in which government's estimated receipts are less than government's estimated expenditure.

EXAM PATTERN QUESTIONS

Objective Type Questions

Multiple Choice Questions (MCQs)

1. **What will be the impact on government revenue when the cigarette prices are increased, assuming demand for cigarettes is inelastic?** **NCERT (QR); Competency Based Que**

(a) Government revenue will increase
(b) Government revenue will decrease
(c) No effect on government revenue
(d) None of the above

2. **The government introduces a progressive tax policy, increasing tax rates for higher income brackets while providing subsidies for essential goods to the lower income groups. This measure most likely aims to achieve which objective of the budget?** **Competency Based Que**

(a) Allocation of resources
(b) Economic growth
(c) Redistribution of income
(d) Economic stability

3. **Since Q_2 :2024-25, the government is implementing measures to reduce inflation by cutting down on public expenditure and increasing taxes. This move is primarily aimed at which objective of the government budget?** **Competency Based Que**

(a) Redistribution of income
(b) Allocation of resources
(c) Economic growth
(d) Economic stability

4. **"Budget is used as an important policy instrument to combat fluctuations in an economy." In the light of above lines, identify the related objective of government budget.** **CBSE Term I 2021; Competency Based Que**

(a) Allocation of resources
(b) Stabilisation of price
(c) Growth of the economy
(d) Redistribution of income

5. **Government provides various goods like roads, parks, street light and defence services, etc. to general public through budgetary provisions. These goods are called ....**

(a) budgetary goods
(b) government goods
(c) public goods
(d) private goods

6. **Economic growth means increasing per capita income over a period of time. Economic growth objective of the government budget depends on** **Competency Based Que**

(a) profit maximisation
(b) rate of savings and investment
(c) fair distribution of income
(d) removal of poverty

7. **Study the given chart carefully and answer the question that follows**

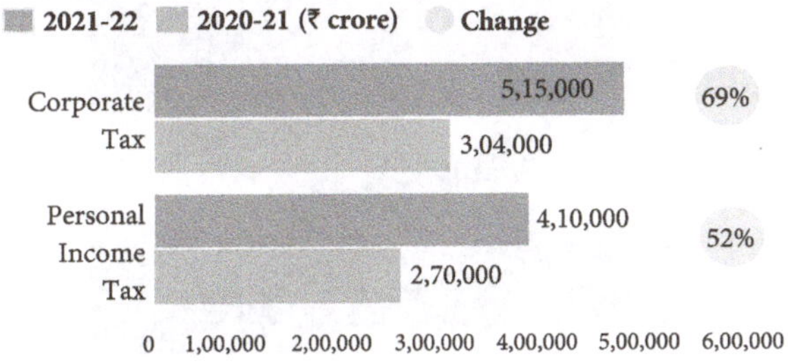

Source *Govtofficial*

The graph shows the comparative study of revenue collection under which category of tax?

(a) Indirect tax
(b) Direct tax
(c) Capital tax
(d) Excise duty

8. **Complete the given flow chart.**

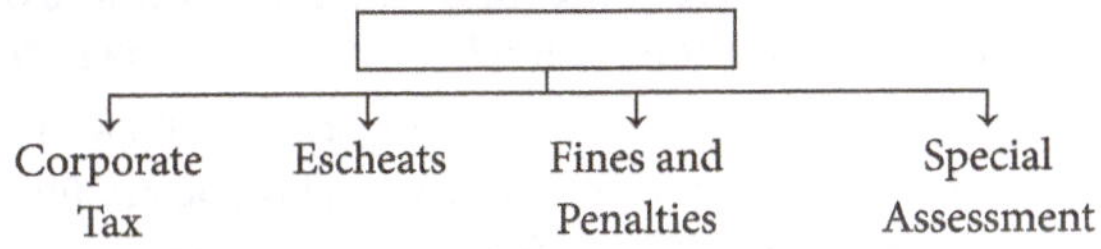

(a) Revenue Receipts
(b) Capital Receipts
(c) Non-tax Revenue
(d) Tax Revenue

9. **Dividends received from Public Sector Undertakings (PSUs) are a part of the government's ....** **CBSE SQP 2024**

(a) non-tax revenue receipts
(b) tax receipts
(c) capital receipts
(d) capital expenditure

10. **Identify the non-tax revenue from the following statement.**
"It refers to the claim of the government on the property of a person who dies without leaving behind any legal heir or a will." **Competency Based Que**

(a) Special assessment
(b) Escheats
(c) Forfeitures
(d) Fees

11. **"The Cabinet led by Prime Minister has decided that the Central Government will provide free foodgrains to 81.35 crore (approx.) beneficiaries under the Pradhan Mantri Garib Kalyan Anna Yojana (PMGKAY) for a period of five years with effect from 1st January, 2024."**
Source *https://pib.gov.in/PressReleaseIframePage.aspx?PRID=1980689*
Based on the aforesaid statement, identify the budgetary objective the government is trying to achieve and choose the correct option. **CBSE SQP 2025; Competency Based Que**
(a) Reallocation of resources
(b) Economic stability
(c) Redistribution of income
(d) Economic instability

12.

Which type of government expenditure is represented by the picture above?
(a) Revenue expenditure
(b) Capital expenditure
(c) Transfer payments
(d) Subsidies

13. **Identify which of the following is an example of non-debt capital receipt?** **CBSE Term I 2021**
(a) Financial aid from MNC for victims in flood affected area
(b) Borrowings from International Monetary Fund (IMF)
(c) Recovery of loans from state governments
(d) Dividend paid by State Bank of India (SBI) to the government

14. **The government of a country decides to reduce its public debt by using excess funds available after covering all its expenditures for the fiscal year. Which term best describes this situation?**
(a) Budget deficit (b) Budget surplus
(c) Fiscal deficit (d) Revenue deficit

15. **The government budget has a revenue deficit. This gets financed by** **Competency Based Que**
(i) Borrowing **(ii) Disinvestment**
(iii) Tax revenue **(iv) Indirect taxes**
Codes
(a) (i) and (iv) (b) (iii) and (iv)
(c) (i) and (ii) (d) (iii) and (ii)

16. **Approximately how much more were the budgeted disinvestments than the actual disinvestments in 2020-21?**

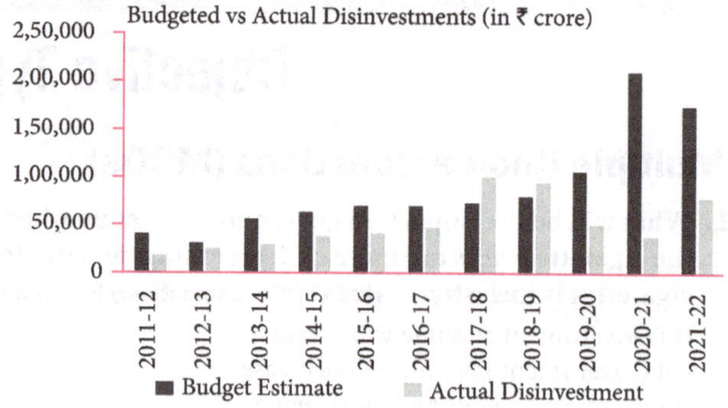

Note Actual data for 2021-22 is revised estimate.
Source *Union Budget documents (various years) : PRS*
(a) ₹ 50,000 crore (b) ₹ 1,00,000 crore
(c) ₹ 1,50,000 crore (d) ₹ 2,00,000 crore

17. **According to the Union Budget 2024-25, the government is targeting a revenue deficit of 1.8% of GDP.**
Source *Union Budget 2024-25 Analysis, PRS Legislative Research*
Which of the following statements accurately reflects the relationship between the revenue deficit and fiscal deficit?
(a) Revenue deficit is higher than fiscal deficit
(b) Fiscal deficit includes revenue deficit and capital expenditure
(c) Revenue deficit does not contribute to fiscal deficit
(d) Fiscal deficit is based only on revenue deficit

18. **High ...... gives a warning to the government either to cut its expenditure or increase its tax receipts.**
(a) budget (b) revenue deficit
(c) primary deficit (d) fiscal deficit

19. **Which of the following statements is true?**
(a) Loan from IMF is a revenue receipt
(b) Higher revenue deficit necessarily leads to higher fiscal deficit
(c) Borrowings by a government represents a situation of fiscal deficit
(d) Revenue deficit is the example of capital receipts over the revenue receipts

20. **If revenue expenditure is ₹ 500 crore and revenue deficit is ₹ 100 crore, what is revenue receipt?**
(a) ₹ 400 crore (b) ₹ 600 crore
(c) ₹ 450 crore (d) ₹ 550 crore

21. **A government's revenue receipts are ₹ 12,000 crore and revenue expenditure is 1.5 times the revenue receipts. What is the revenue deficit?**
(a) ₹ 18,000 crore (b) ₹ 6,000 crore
(c) ₹ 8,000 crore (d) ₹ 10,000 crore

22. **As per the data presented in the Union Budget 2023-24, the total receipts of the government other than borrowings and the total expenditure are estimated at ₹ 27.2 lakh crore and ₹ 45 lakh crore respectively. The value of the .... deficit would be ₹ 17.8 lakh crore.**

CBSE SQP 2025; Competency Based Que

(a) revenue (b) fiscal
(c) budgetary (d) primary

23. **Find fiscal deficit from the information given below**

S.No.	Items	₹ (in lakhs)
(i)	Borrowing by the Government	600
(ii)	Revenue Receipts	100
(iii)	Capital Receipts	750
(iv)	Interest Payment	150

(a) ₹ 100 (b) ₹ 250 (c) ₹ 600 (d) ₹ 800

24. **If the budgetary deficit of the government is ₹ 25,000 crore and the borrowings and other liabilities are ₹ 7,000 crore, how much will be the fiscal deficit?**

Competency Based Que

(a) ₹ 25,000 crore (b) ₹ 32,000 crore
(c) ₹ 18,000 crore (d) ₹ 7,000 crore

25.

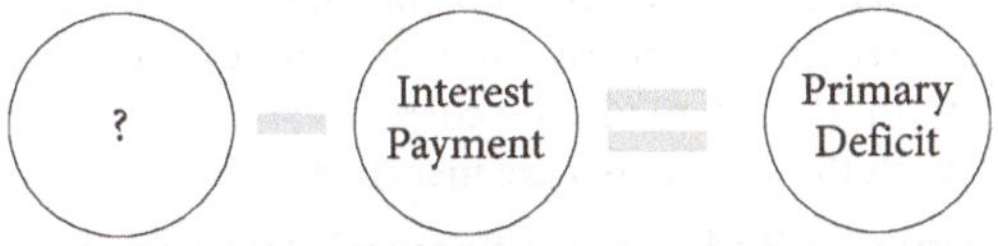

On the basis of the above image, complete the equation by choosing correct alternative.

(a) Budgetary Deficit (b) Revenue Deficit
(c) Fiscal Deficit (d) Balanced Budget

26. **Zero .... means that the government has to resort to borrowings only to make interest payments.**

(a) budget deficit (b) fiscal deficit
(c) primary deficit (d) revenue deficit

27. **The initial fiscal deficit is ₹ 20,000 crore and the initial primary deficit is ₹ 6,000 crore. If the interest payments increase by 35%, what are the new interest payments?**

Competency Based Que

(a) ₹ 14,000 crore (b) ₹ 8,100 crore
(c) ₹ 18,900 crore (d) ₹ 9,000 crore

Direction *Read the case study and answer the questions 28 to 31 on the basis of the same*

Budgetary deficits must be financed by either taxation, borrowing or printing money. Governments have mostly relied on borrowing, giving rise to what is called government debt. If the government continues to borrow year after year, then interest payments increase and these further increase the debt.

Also, government borrowings from the people reduces the savings available to the private sector. This reduces capital formation and growth. These debts increases the burden on future generations as the debts raised today are required to be paid-off in future.

28. **Budgetary deficits can be financed by**

(a) taxation (b) borrowings
(c) printing money (d) All of these

29. **If the government borrows year after year, then this .... interest payments.**

30. **Government borrowing reduces the .... available to the private sector.**

31. **Government borrowings increases the burden on future generations.**

(a) True (b) False
(c) Partially true (d) Can't say

Direction *Read the case study and answer the questions 32 to 35 on the basis of the same*

State of the Economy 2022-23: Recovery Complete-Chapter 1

A capex thrust in the last two budgets of the Government of India was not an isolated initiative meant only to address the infrastructure gaps in the country. It was part of a strategic package aimed at crowding in private investment into an economic landscape broadened by the vacation of non-strategic PSEs (disinvestment) and idling public sector assets.

Three developments support this. First, the significant increase in the capex budget in FY23, as well as its high rate of spending. Second, direct tax revenue collections have been highly buoyant and so have GST collections, which should ensure the full expending of the capex budget within the budgeted fiscal deficit. The growth in revenue expenditure has also been limited to pave the way for higher growth in capex.

Third, the pick-up in private sector investment since the January-March quarter of 2022. Evidence shows an increasing trend in announced projects and capex spending by the private players. Surveys of leading industry CEOs also reveal their plans and commitment to increasing capex.

32. **The recent increase in capex spending by the Indian government is primarily intended to**

(a) address infrastructure gaps alone
(b) attract private investment and broaden the economy
(c) reduce public sector debt
(d) stimulate immediate economic growth

33. **To pave the way for higher capex growth, the growth in .... expenditure has been limited.**

34. **The vacation of non-strategic PSEs and focus on idling assets is meant to .... the economic landscape for private participation.**
(a) narrow
(b) unchange
(c) broaden
(d) specialise

35. **The high capex spending rate in FY23 and buoyant revenue collections, especially of .... and ....**

Assertion-Reason

Direction (Q.No. 36 to 45) *Read the following Assertion (A) and Reason (R) and choose the correct alternative from the following*

Alternatives

(a) Both Assertion (A) and Reason (R) are true and Reason (R) is the correct explanation of Assertion (A)
(b) Both Assertion (A) and Reason (R) are true, but Reason (R) is not the correct explanation of Assertion (A)
(c) Assertion (A) is true, but Reason (R) is false
(d) Both Assertion (A) and Reason (R) are false

36. **Assertion** (A) Public goods are non-rivalrous.

Reason (R) The benefits of such goods can be enjoyed by all and are not restricted to any one person.

37. **Assertion** (A) Government imposes heavy taxes on alcohol and gives subsidy on LPG gas.

Reason (R) The government undertakes such a measure to ensure economic stability in the country.

38. **Assertion** (A) The government has allocated extra money in budget 2021 to provide safe drinking water facilities and sanitation to the people.

Reason (R) The government does it because sanitation and providing drinking water are public goods.

39. **Assertion** (A) Capital gain tax is an indirect tax.

Reason (R) Its burden can be shifted, i.e. its impact and incidence lies on different people.

40. **Assertion** (A) Under regressive taxation, the average tax rate decreases as the taxable amount increases.

Reason (R) Regressive taxation places a heavier burden on lower income individuals compared to higher income individuals.

41. **Assertion** (A) The impact and incidence of indirect tax lie on different persons.

Reason (R) Indirect taxes can be avoided by not entering into those transactions, which call for such taxes.

42. **Assertion** (A) A developing country like India prepares a deficit budget, i.e. its expenditure is more than its receipts.

Reason (R) A developing country generally has to spend more on infrastructural projects.

43. **Assertion** (A) Public debt is not necessarily harmful to an economy.

Reason (R) Borrowing to finance productive expenditure can stimulate economic growth and enhance the government's ability to repay its debts in the future.

44. **Assertion** (A) A higher fiscal deficit can lead to inflationary pressures in the economy.

Reason (R) The government often resorts to borrowing from the Reserve Bank of India (RBI) to finance its fiscal deficit, increasing the money supply in the economy.

45. **Assertion** (A) A higher primary deficit is beneficial for the economy.

Reason (R) A higher primary deficit suggests that the government is borrowing extensively to finance its current expenditure, even after covering the interest on previous debt, which could stimulate economic growth.

Two Statements Based MCQs

Direction (Q.No. 46 to 55) *Read the following statements carefully and choose the correct alternative*

Alternatives

(a) Statement I is correct and Statement II is incorrect
(b) Statement II is correct and Statement I is incorrect
(c) Both the statements are correct
(d) Both the statements are incorrect

46. **Statement I** Budget is the financial statement of government's profit and loss during a year.

Statement II Budget is prepared at all levels of government.

47. **Statement I** Public goods are non-excludable.

Statement II Consumption of public goods by people is of rivalrous nature. **CBSE Term I 2021**

48. **Statement I** Government budget is an accounting statement showing actual receipts and expenditure of the government during a fiscal year.

Statement II Two main components of government budget are revenue budget and capital budget. **CBSE Term I 2021**

49. **Statement I** The primary objective of the government budget is to ensure the equitable distribution of income and wealth within the economy.

Statement II A fiscal deficit necessarily implies that the government is overspending and mismanaging its resources.

50. **Statement I** Proportional tax system imposes the same tax rate on all income levels.

Statement II Progressive tax system is more beneficial for lower income individuals.

51. **Statement I** GST can be both direct tax and indirect tax.
Statement II Payment of indirect taxes is shifted to consumers by businesses.

52. **Statement I** Foreign grants-in-aid receipts do not lead to any claim on the government.
Statement II Disposal of equity by the public sector undertakings in the market may lead to a decrease in the assets of the government. **CBSE SQP 2025**

53. **Statement I** A balanced budget occurs when government expenditure exceeds government revenue.
Statement II A budget deficit occurs when government expenditure exceeds government revenue.

54. **Statement I** The government's decision to increase capital expenditure, even if it leads to a higher fiscal deficit, is often seen as a measure to boost long-term economic growth.
Statement II A revenue deficit implies that the government is borrowing money to finance its routine operational expenses, which can lead to crowding out of private investment.

55. **Statement I** Fiscal deficit is always greater than primary deficit.
Statement II Fiscal deficit indicates borrowing requirements of the government. **CBSE Term I 2021**

Matching

56. Match the following **NCERT (QR)**

	Column I		Column II
A.	Pradhan Mantri Awas Yojana	(i)	2015
B.	Implementation of GST	(ii)	2016
C.	Make in India	(iii)	2014
D.	Demonetisation	(iv)	2017

Codes

	A	B	C	D		A	B	C	D
(a)	(i)	(iv)	(iii)	(ii)	(b)	(ii)	(iii)	(i)	(iv)
(c)	(iii)	(ii)	(iv)	(i)	(d)	(iv)	(i)	(ii)	(iii)

57. **Match the options of Column I with their correct options in Column II** **Competency Based Que**

	Column I		Column II
A.	Provision of public goods by the government	(i)	Reducing inequalities in income
B.	The government imposes a cess of 2% on tax payers whose income exceed ₹ 10 crore	(ii)	Management of PSUs
C.	Government gives tax rebate to industries established in backward regions	(iii)	Reallocation of resoures
D.	PSUs are operated and managed to promote social welfare	(iv)	Reducing regional disparities

Codes

	A	B	C	D		A	B	C	D
(a)	(i)	(ii)	(iii)	(iv)	(b)	(ii)	(iv)	(i)	(iii)
(c)	(iii)	(i)	(iv)	(ii)	(d)	(iv)	(iii)	(ii)	(i)

58. **Match the options of Column I with their correct options in Column II** **Competency Based Que**

	Column I		Column II
A.	Corporation tax	(i)	Capital receipt
B.	Special assessment	(ii)	Tax revenue
C.	Sale of shares of Maruti by government	(iii)	Capital expenditure
D.	Purchase of land for constructing express way	(iv)	Non-tax revenue

Codes

	A	B	C	D		A	B	C	D
(a)	(i)	(ii)	(iii)	(iv)	(b)	(ii)	(iv)	(i)	(iii)
(c)	(iii)	(i)	(iv)	(ii)	(d)	(iv)	(iii)	(ii)	(i)

59. **Identify the correct pair**

	Column I		Column II
A.	Revenue deficit	(i)	Total Expenditure – Revenue Receipts
B.	Fiscal deficit	(ii)	Total Expenditure – Total Receipts (including borrowings)
C.	Primary deficit	(iii)	Fiscal Deficit – Interest Payments

Codes
(a) A-(i) (b) B-(ii)
(c) C-(iii) (d) None of these

60. **Choose the correct pair**

	Column I		Column II
A.	Progressive tax	(i)	Tax rate rises with rise in income
B.	Regressive tax	(ii)	It causes more burden on the rich
C.	Proportional tax	(iii)	Rate of taxation is constantly changing
D.	Indirect tax	(iv)	Burden of tax cannot be shifted

Codes
(a) A-(i) (b) B-(ii)
(c) C-(iii) (d) D-(iv)

Concept Identification

61. The goods which satisfy collective needs of the people. These goods promote social welfare. **CBSE 2020**

62. The expenditure of the government which neither creates assets nor causes a reduction in liabilities of the government. **CBSE 2020**

63. The expenditure which is not related to any specified plan for the year.

64. The statement of estimated capital receipts and estimated capital expenditure during a fiscal year.

65. (Revenue Expenditure + Capital Expenditure) – (Revenue receipts + Capital receipt other than Borrowing) = ...

Answers

1. (a) Government revenue will increase
2. (c) Progressive taxation and subsidies for the poor are used to reduce income inequalities by transferring income from high income groups to lower income groups.
3. (d) Reducing public expenditure and increasing taxes can curb excessive demand in the economy, helping to control inflation and maintain price stability.
4. (b) Stablisation of price
5. (c) public goods
6. (b) Growth rate of a country depends on the rate of savings and investment. Budgetary policy creates conditions conductive for increase in savings and investment.
7. (b) Direct tax
8. (c) Non-tax revenue
9. (a) non-tax revenue receipts
10. (b) Escheats
11. (c) Redistribution of income
12. (b) Capital expenditure
13. (c) Recovery of loans from state governments
14. (b) Budget surplus
15. (c) (i) and (ii)
16. (c) Budgeted – Actual Disinvestment = 2,00,000 – 50,000 = ₹ 1,50,000 crore
17. (b) Fiscal deficit includes revenue deficit and capital expenditure
18. (b) revenue deficit
19. (c) Borrowings by a government represents a situation of fiscal deficit
20. (a) Revenue Deficit = Revenue Expenditure – Revenue Receipt = 500 – 100 = ₹ 400 crore
21. (b) Revenue Expenditure = 1.5 × 12,000 = ₹ 18,000 crore
    Revenue Deficit = 18,000 – 12,000 = ₹ 6,000 crore
22. (b) fiscal
23. (c) Fiscal Deficit = Borrowings = ₹ 600 lakh
24. (b) Fiscal Deficit = Budgetary Deficit of the Government + Borrowings and Other Liabilities = 25,000 + 7,000 = ₹ 32,000 crore
25. (c) Fiscal Deficit
26. (c) primary deficit
27. (c) Initial Interest Payments = Fiscal Deficit– Primary Deficit = 20,000 – 6,000 = ₹ 14,000 crore
    New Interest Payments = 14,000 + 35% of ₹ 14,000 = ₹ 18,900 crore
28. (d) All of these
29. increases
30. savings
31. (a) True
32. (b) attract private investment and broaden the economy
33. revenue
34. (c) broaden
35. direct tax, GST
36. (a) Both Assertion (A) and Reason (R) are true and Reason (R) is the correct explanation of Assertion (A)
37. (c) Government undertakes such measures to reallocate resources.
38. (a) Both Assertion (A) and Reason (R) are true and Reason (R) is the correct explanation of Assertion (A)
39. (d) Capital gain tax is direct tax as its burden cannot be shifted onto other person.
40. (b) Both Assertion (A) and Reason (R) are true, but Reason (R) is not the correct explanation of Assertion (A)
41. (b) Both Assertion (A) and Reason (R) are true, but Reason (R) is not the correct explanation of Assertion (A)
42. (a) Both Assertion (A) and Reason (R) are true and Reason (R) is the correct explanation of Assertion (A)
43. (a) Both Assertion (A) and Reason (R) are true and Reason (R) is the correct explanation of Assertion (A)
44. (a) Both Assertion (A) and Reason (R) are true and Reason (R) is the correct explanation of Assertion (A)
45. (d) A higher primary deficit signals excessive borrowing, causing fiscal instability. While borrowing may boost growth if invested, it often funds current expenses, making it unsustainable.
46. (b) Budget is an annual estimated statement of government's receipts and expenditures during a fiscal year.
47. (a) Consumption of public goods is non-rivalrous, i.e. one person's consumption does not reduce the availability for others.

48. (b) Government budget is a statement of estimated receipts and expenditure of the government for the fiscal year which is to begin.

49. (a) A fiscal deficit does not necessarily indicate mismanagement.

It can occur due to government spending on long-term growth projects or during periods of economic downturns to stimulate the economy.

50. (c) Both the statements are correct

51. (b) GST is a form of indirect tax.

52. (c) Both the statements are correct

53. (b) A balanced budget occurs when government expenditure equals government revenue. Therefore, if government expenditure exceeds government revenue, the budget would not be balanced.

54. (c) Both the statements are correct

55. (b) Fiscal Deficit = Primary Deficit + Interest Payment. If interest payment is nil, they are equal.

56. (a) (i) (iv) (iii) (ii)
57. (c) (iii) (i) (iv) (ii)
58. (b) (ii) (iv) (i) (iii)
59. (c) C-(iii)
60. (a) A-(i)
61. Public goods
62. Revenue expenditure
63. Non-plan expenditure
64. Capital budget
65. Fiscal Deficit

Subjective Questions

Short Answer Type Questions

1. Discuss any three objectives of a government budget.

Ans. Government budget is an annual financial statement of estimated receipts and expenditure of the government during a fiscal year, as recorded in Article 112 of the Indian Constitution.

Objectives of government budget are as follows

(i) **Economic Growth**
The overall economic growth of a nation relies on savings and investments. Budgetary policies are hence introduced to infuse enough resources in different public sectors.

(ii) **Reallocation of Resources**
Through a budget, the government endeavours to equally allocate resources and wealth. They encourage small industries like 'Khadi' to flourish by allowing subsidised loans and reduced taxes on raw material, needed for production.

(iii) **Redistribution of Income**
To close the income gap between rich and poor, several budgetary schemes are launched from the government's end. Fiscal instruments like subsidies, taxations, etc. are effectively used to achieve this goal.

2. Explain, why public goods must be provided by the government? NCERT

Ans. Public goods such as parks, roads, water supply, bridges, national defence, etc. are the goods which people urgently need for their day-to-day living, but market mechanism cannot produce these goods in sufficient quantities, due to its features of non-rivalrous and non-excludable in consumption. Therefore, these goods need to be provided by the government.

3. "Spending by the government on creating public goods is increased." Explain the corresponding economic value. Competency Based Que

Ans. The economic value that is reflected in the rise in the production of public goods is the value of 'social welfare'. The major objective of the budgetary policy of the government is to enhance the welfare of the society at large.

For this, it performs the allocative function. The allocative function is concerned with allocating the resources between private and public sectors.

As the public goods cannot be provided by the private sectors through market mechanism, hence the need for providing such goods is to be fulfilled by the government.

In addition to this, private goods cannot be afforded by all, i.e. only those who can pay for these goods can avail the benefits of such goods. Since public goods are essential for overall welfare and are required by all, thus, government provides these goods.

4. Government has started spending more or providing free services like education and health to the poor. Explain the economic value it reflects. Competency Based Que

Ans. The economic value reflected by the above act of the government is 'promoting social justice'. The government uses the fiscal instruments of subsidies and taxation to improve the distribution of income and wealth in the economy.

By spending more on provision of free services like education and health, government is trying to promote social justice. Social justice is the principal objective of annual budget of a developing country like India. It leads to fair and equitable distribution of income in an economy.

5. Elaborate on how the government budget can contribute to economic stabilisation?

Ans. Government budget can be helpful in bringing economic stabilisation in the economy by checking inflationary and deflationary tendencies. To curb the inflationary tendency, the government can prepare a surplus budget. Such a budget reduces the money supply in the economy, leading to a fall in the level of aggregate demand. As aggregate demand falls, the price level or the rate of inflation also falls. To curb the deflationary tendency, the government can prepare a deficit budget. Such a budget increases the money supply in the economy, leading to an increase in the level of aggregate demand. As aggregate demand rises, the price level also rises and rate of deflation begins to fall.

6. "Government budget can be a useful instrument in reducing inequalities in the distribution of income and wealth in an economy."

Do you agree with the given statement? Present valid arguments in favour of your answer. CBSE 2024; Competency Based Que

Or **"Taxation is an effective tool to reduce the inequalities of income." Justify the given statement with valid reasons.** All India 2020

Ans. A budget can be used as an instrument to reduce the inequalities in the distribution of income and wealth in the following ways

(i) Tax rates should be made progressive, i.e. rate of tax should increase with increase in income.

(ii) Increasing government expenditure by providing free services to the poor like education, medical facilities, etc. This will raise the disposable income of the poor.

(iii) The amount collected through tax is given to the poor in the form of subsidies. Thus, the gap between rich and poor can be reduced.

(iv) Strict measures should be adopted to check tax evasion by the rich people.

7. How are the capital receipts different from revenue receipts?

Ans. Differences between capital receipts and revenue receipts are

Basis	Capital Receipts	Revenue Receipts
Meaning	It refers to those related to the capital transactions of an organisation or a government.	It refers to those related to the day-to-day operations of an organisation or a government.
Sources	They come from sources such as the sale of assets, borrowing and capital grants.	They come from taxes, fees and fines.
Purpose	These are used for long-term investments, such as building infrastructure or acquiring fixed assets.	These are used for recurring expenses, such as salaries, maintenance and services.
Duration	They have a long-term impact on an organisation's finances.	They have a short-term impact.

8. Study the given picture carefully.

Sources of state and local government tax revenues for a financial year

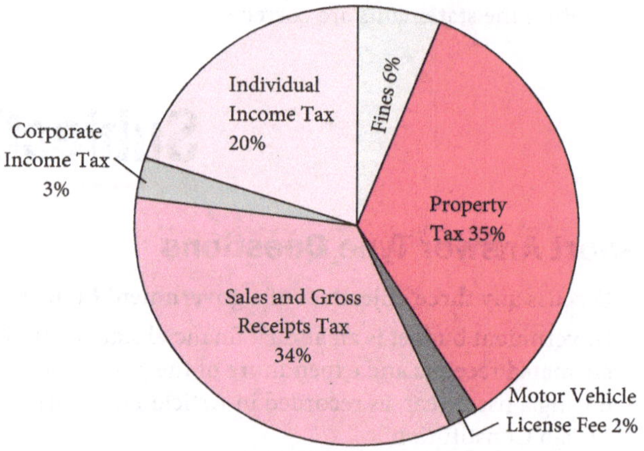

Answer the following questions based on common knowledge and picture.

(i) Categorise the given items in the picture into tax/non-tax receipts.

(ii) Should national parks and highways, often funded through taxes like those in the chart, be treated as public goods funded by taxpayers or as private goods supported by user fees? Explain your reasoning. Competency Based Que

Ans. (i) **Tax Receipts**

Individual income tax, property tax, sales and gross receipts tax, corporate income tax.

Non-tax Receipts

Fines, motor vehicle licence fee.

(ii) National parks and highways are often considered public goods because they are non-excludable and non-rivalrous. As a public good, they provide widespread benefits, such as environmental conservation and improved transportation, which are accessible to all.

Funding them through taxes ensures equitable access for everyone, regardless of income. However, incorporating user fees for specific services (like tolls or park entry) can help cover maintenance costs and ensure responsible usage.

A balanced approach combining both methods is often ideal.

9. Identify the type of budget receipt shown in the image below and explain other types of receipts under this category. **Competency Based Que**

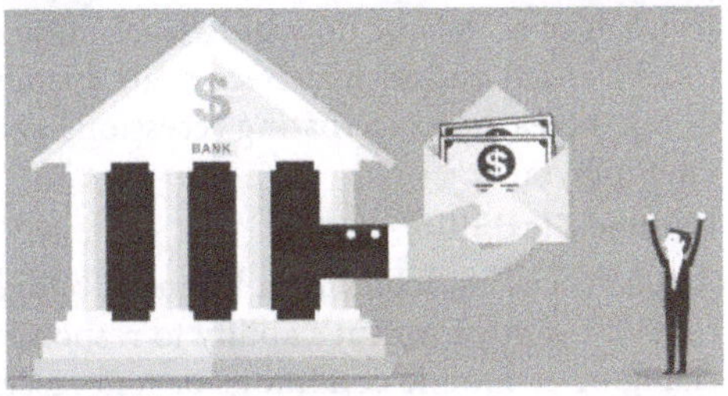

Ans. The above image is showing 'borrowing by the government from the banks'. This is a type of capital receipt.

Other types of capital receipts include the following

(i) **Disinvestment**

At the point when the government raises assets by selling its equity shares holding, it is called disinvestment. It prompts a decrease in the resources held by the public authority.

(ii) **Recovery of Loans**

The local government awards credits to state legislatures, association region states and different gatherings. Granting loans increases the financial assets of the government. When the government recovers these credits from its borrowers, it is treated as capital receipts. It prompts a decrease in the monetary resources of the public authority.

10. Distinguish between revenue and capital expenditure. **NCERT**

Ans. Differences between revenue expenditure and capital expenditure are

Basis	Revenue Expenditure	Capital Expenditure
Meaning	These are those expenditure of government which neither cause increase in government assets nor cause any reduction in government liabilities.	It is the expenditure of government which leads to either increase in government assets or reduction in government liabilities.
Purpose	It is spent on normal functioning of government departments and various provisions.	It is spent on acquisition of assets, repayment of borrowings and granting of loans and advances.
Nature	It is a recurring expenditure.	It is non-recurring expenditure.
Example	Expenditure on old age pensions, expense on administrative services, expense on national security, expense on health and education, etc.	Expenditure on the construction of national highways, repayment of government loans, establishment of factories, etc.

11. Is the following, a revenue expenditure or capital expenditure in the context of government budget? Give reason. **Competency Based Que**

(i) Expenditure on collection of taxes.

(ii) Expenditure on purchasing computers.

Ans. (i) **Expenditure on Collection of Taxes**

It is a revenue expenditure, as it does not reduce any government liability nor increases government asset.

(ii) **Expenditure on Purchasing Computers**

It is a capital expenditure, as it creates physical assets for the government.

12. Classify the following statements as revenue receipts or capital receipts. Give valid reasons in support of your answer

(i) Financial help from a multinational corporation for victims in a flood affected area.

(ii) Sale of shares of a Public Sector Undertaking (PSU) to a private company, Y Pvt. Ltd .

(iii) Dividend paid to the government by the State Bank of India.

(iv) Borrowings from International Monetary Fund (IMF). **Competency Based Que**

Ans. (i) Revenue receipt as it neither impacts assets nor liabilities of the government.

(ii) Capital receipt as it reduces assets of the government.

(iii) Revenue receipt as there was no impact on assets or liabilities.

(iv) Capital receipt as it increases liabilities.

13. Classify the following receipts into revenue receipts and capital receipts. Give reason in support of your answer.

(i) Debt cleared by Sri Lanka Government to the Indian Government.

(ii) Interest received on loans.

(iii) Dividend received from public enterprises.

(iv) Grants from foreign government.

CBSE 2024; Competency Based Que

Ans. (i) Recovery of loans is a capital receipt as it will lead to decline in financial assets of the government.

(ii) Interest received on loans is a revenue receipt as it neither create liability nor reduce the assets of the government.

(iii) Dividend received from public enterprises is a revenue receipt as it neither create a liability nor reduce the assets of the government.

(iv) Grants from foreign government is a revenue receipt as it neither create liability nor reduce assets of the government.

14. **"A budget can be deficit, surplus or balanced." Do you agree with the given statement? Give valid reasons in support of your answer.**
CBSE 2024 C; Competency Based Que

Ans. Yes, I agree. A deficit budget occurs when government expenditure exceeds revenue. It is often used to fund development projects by borrowing or printing money. A surplus budget happens when revenue exceeds expenditure, typically used to repay debt or save for future needs. A balanced budget occurs when expenditure equals revenue, promoting fiscal discipline but limiting growth stimulation. The type of budget depends on the government's economic priorities and policies.

15. **Differentiate between balanced budget and surplus budget.**

Ans. Differences between balanced budget and surplus budget are

Basis	Balanced Budget	Surplus Budget
Meaning	It is a type of budget in which the estimated revenue of the government is equal to estimated expenditure of the government.	It is that type of budget in which the estimated revenue is greater than the estimated expenditure.
Relation with AD	It would not affect the aggregate demand in the economy.	It would lead to reduction in aggregate demand.
Impact on Economy	The balanced budget policy is called 'sound finance' where the government performs only minimum function.	The policy of surplus budget would lead to unemployment and recession in the economy.

16. **"A balanced budget is often seen as a hallmark of fiscal responsibility for governments." Discuss the importance of maintaining a balanced budget and analyse the potential drawbacks associated with this approach.**
Competency Based Que

Ans. Maintaining a balanced budget is indeed regarded as a crucial aspect of fiscal responsibility for governments. It's importance is as follows

(i) **Fiscal Discipline**
A balanced budget reflects prudent financial management and discipline within the government, ensuring that expenditures do not exceed revenues.

(ii) **Economic Stability**
It helps in stabilising the economy by preventing excessive borrowing, which can lead to inflationary pressures and financial instability.

Drawbacks of a balanced budget are

(i) **Contractionary Fiscal Policy**
In times of economic downturns, adhering strictly to a balanced budget may necessitate spending cuts or tax increases, exacerbating recessions and unemployment.

(ii) **Limited Flexibility**
A rigid focus on achieving a balanced budget may restrict the government's ability to respond to changing economic conditions or unforeseen emergencies.

17. **In reference to picture, identify the concept it represents and discuss its types.** Competency Based Que

Ans. Budgetary deficit is represented in the picture.

A budgetary deficit is referred to as the situation in which the expenditure is more than the revenues.

There are three types of budget deficit. They are explained follows

(i) **Fiscal Deficit**
Fiscal deficit refers to a situation, wherein, a government's total expenditure exceeds its total receipts, minus the borrowings within a financial year.

It serves as a measure of the amount of money that the government needs to borrow to meet its expenses, especially at a time when its resources are insufficient.

It can be expressed as

Gross Fiscal Deficit = Total Expenditure − (Revenue Earning +Non-debt Creating Receipts)

(ii) **Revenue Deficit**
Revenue deficit can be defined as the excess of revenue expenditure over revenue receipts.

Revenue Deficit = Revenue Expenses − Revenue Receipts

(iii) **Primary Deficit**

It can be explained as the fiscal deficit of a given year without the payment of interest on previous borrowings.

Primary Deficit = Fiscal Deficit − Loan Interest Payments

18. Give the relationship between revenue deficit and the fiscal deficit. NCERT

Ans. Fiscal deficit refers to the situation of excess of total expenditure over total receipts (excluding borrowings), where total expenditure and receipts includes both revenue as well as capital, hence it can be said that, revenue deficit is a part of fiscal deficit, wherein fiscal deficit is a broader concept.

19. What is debt trap? Suggest measures to control such situation.

Ans. Debt trap refers to a situation in which government borrows new funds to pay previous loan or to pay interest on previous loans. This creates a trap for the government, increasing the burden of future payments.

In order to solve this problem, government may resort to disinvestment or may reduce wasteful expenditures like unnecessary subsidies, etc.

20. Is deficit budget a sign of government inefficiency? Competency Based Que

Ans. No, a deficit budget is not a sign of government inefficiency. In fact, budgetary deficit may be a planned strategy of the government during periods of depression, when the government needs to accelerate the pace of expenditure in the economy and hence pace of economic growth.

21. Can there be a fiscal deficit without a revenue deficit? Competency Based Que

Ans. Yes, there can be a fiscal deficit without a revenue deficit. This situation can arise when the capital expenditure of the budget exceed the capital receipts other than borrowings.

In other words, when capital budget deficit exceeds revenue budget surplus.

22. Distinguish between fiscal deficit and revenue deficit.

Ans. Differences between fiscal deficit and revenue deficit are

Basis	Fiscal Deficit	Revenue Deficit
Meaning	A fiscal deficit is the excess of budget expenditure over budget receipts other than borrowings.	A revenue deficit is the surplus of revenue expenditure over revenue receipts.
Significance	It reflects the total government borrowings during a fiscal year.	It reflects the inefficiency of the government to reach its regular or recurring expenditure.
Formula	Total Budget Expenditure − Total Budget Receipt (excluding borrowings)	Revenue Expenditure − Revenue Receipts

23. "Tax revenue collection of the government may be categorised under two heads." State and explain the two heads of tax revenue. CBSE SQP 2025

Ans. Tax revenue of the government is categorised into two heads

(i) **Direct Taxes**

These are taxes directly levied on individuals or organisations and cannot be shifted to others. Examples include income tax, corporate tax, etc.

(ii) **Indirect Taxes**

These are taxes levied on goods and services and are paid indirectly by consumers. Examples include GST (Goods and Services Tax), etc.

24. What do you mean by primary deficit? Explain its implications.

Ans. Primary deficit is equal to fiscal deficit less of interest payments.

Primary Deficit = Fiscal Deficit − Interest Payments

Implications of primary deficit are

(i) It indicates borrowing requirements of the government to meet fiscal deficit net of interest payments.

(ii) It enables us to see the way, the government is currently conducting its financial affairs.

25. Compare the trends depicted in the figures given below. CBSE SQP 2023; Competency Based Que

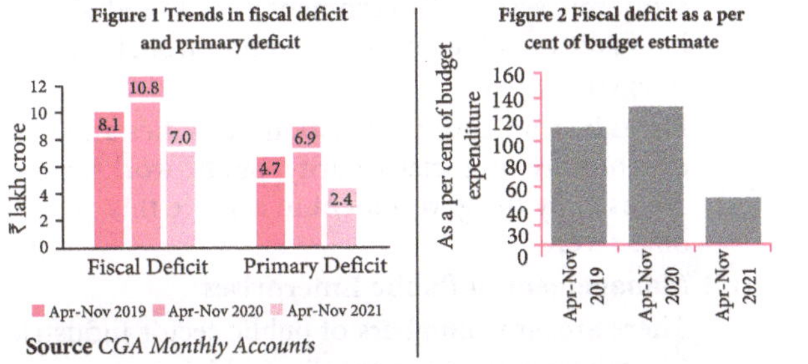

Source *CGA Monthly Accounts*

Ans. Considering the data represented in the given diagram, trend of year-on-year deficit (reporting for April to November) may be stated as follows

(i) Fiscal deficit in 2020 increased to 10.8 lakh crore from 8.1 lakh crore in 2019. In 2021 it has gone down to 7 lakh crore.

(ii) Primary deficit in 2020 increased to 6.9 lakh crore from 4.7 lakh crore in 2019. In 2021 it has gone down to 2.4 lakh crore.

(iii) Fiscal deficit in 2020 increased to 135.1% of budget expenditure from 114.8% in 2019. In year 2021, it is 46.2% of budget expenditure.

Long Answer Type Questions

26. Define government budget. Explain the objectives of budget in detail.

Ans. Government budget is a statement of estimates of the government's expected receipts and government's expected expenditure during the financial year or fiscal year which is taken from 1st April to 31st March.

In India, Article 112 of the Constitution and Article 202 of the Constitution requires to prepare 'annual budget' for central government and every state government respectively. Finance Minister presents annual budget of the government for its approval on every 1st February.

Objectives of Government Budget

Government prepares the budget for fulfilling certain objectives. These objectives are the direct outcome of government's economic, social and political policies. The various objectives of government budget are

(i) **Reallocation of Resources**

Through the budgetary policy, government aims to reallocate resources in accordance with the economic (profit maximisation) and social (public welfare) priorities of the country. e.g. Government discourages the production of harmful consumption goods (like liquor, cigarettes, etc.) through heavy taxes and encourages the use of 'khadi products' by providing subsidies.

(ii) **Redistribution of Income and Wealth**

Economic inequality is an inherent part of every economic system. Government aims to reduce such inequalities of income and wealth, through its budgetary policy.

Fiscal instruments like taxation, subsidies and expenditure on social security, public works, etc. are used by the government to achieve this objective.

(iii) **Management of Public Enterprises**

There are large numbers of public sector industries (especially natural monopolies) which are established and managed for social welfare of the public.

Budget is prepared with the objective of making various provisions for managing such enterprises and providing them financial help.

(iv) **Economic Stability**

Government budget is used to prevent business fluctuations of inflation or deflation and to maintain economic stability.

The government aims to control the different phases of business fluctuations through it budgetary policy. Policies of surplus budget during inflation and deficit budget during deflation are adopted to achieve stability in the economy.

(v) **Economic Growth**

Economic growth has been the main objective of every economy at all times. The growth rate of a country depends on rate of saving and investment. For this purpose, budgetary policy aims to mobilise sufficient resources for investment in the public sector.

Therefore, the government makes various provisions in the budget to raise overall rate of savings and investments in the economy.

27. Elaborate the objective of 'allocation of resources' in the government budget. Delhi 2020

Ans. Budget refers to the annual financial statement of estimated revenue and estimated expenditure of the government, during a fiscal year (1st April to 31st March).

Allocation of resources is one of the major objective of government budget. Government through its budget reallocates resources so that social and economic objectives can be met.

In other words, the government through its budgetary policy, directs the allocation of resources in a manner such that there is a balance between the goals of profit maximisation and social welfare.

Private enterprises work only with profit motive, however government pursues both the goals of profit and welfare side by side. Government tries to discourage production of goods through heavy taxation which are socially undesirable (like alcohol, tobacco).

On the other hand, production of socially desirable goods is encouraged through subsidies (like LPG). Also in many areas where goods cannot be provided through market mechanism, government undertakes production on its own like public parks, provision of good sanitation, etc.

28. (i) **"Through its budgetary policy, the government allocates resources as per the requirements of the country." Do you agree with the given statement? Support your answer with the valid reasons.** Competency Based Que

(ii) **Define 'direct tax'.**

Ans. (i) Yes, I agree with the statement that through its budgetary policy, the government allocates resources as per the requirements of the country.

The government may influence the allocation of resources through

- Policy heavy taxes may be imposed on harmful products to discourage their production and subsidies may be provided on the production of socially useful products to encourage their production.
- Government may directly undertake production of certain goods and services in the areas where the private sector may not be willing to participate in production activities.

(ii) Direct tax is a tax in which the incidence and impact of tax payment falls on the same entity, i.e. the burden of payment can't be shifted by the tax payer. e.g. Income tax.

29. (i) **Explain the economic stability objective of government budget.**

(ii) **"Under the Ayushmaan Bharat Scheme, the government provides free medicines to the economically backward section of the society." Identify and discuss the nature of the government expenditure indicated in the given statement.**

CBSE SQP 2024; Competency Based Que

Ans. (i) Government budget is set to achieve and attain various social and economic objectives in the nation. One such objective is to maintain the economic stability. Economic stability refers to a condition where the economy is free of fluctuations and the price level is stable. It can be achieved by correcting the situations of deficient and excess demand in the economy.

Inflationary gap or excess demand is corrected by reducing government expenditure and increasing the revenue. Whereas, deflationary gap or deficient gap is corrected by increasing the government expenditure and reducing the revenue.

(ii) Under the Ayushmaan Bharat Scheme, the government expenditure indicated is social expenditure, which is classified as revenue expenditure. Revenue expenditure refers to recurring expenses incurred by the government that do not create long-term assets but are essential for day-to-day functioning and welfare initiatives.

This expenditure focuses on providing free medicines to the economically weaker sections of society, aiming to improve public health and reduce financial stress on the underprivileged. The objective of this expenditure is to promote inclusive development by enhancing access to essential healthcare services for the economically backward population.

30. What do you understand by GST? How good is the system of GST as compared to the old tax system? State its categories. **NCERT**

Ans. Goods and Services Tax (GST) is the single comprehensive indirect tax, operational from 1st July, 2017, on supply of goods and services, right from the manufacturer/service provider to the consumer.

It is a destination based consumption tax with facility of input tax credit in the supply chain. It is applicable throughout the country with one rate for one type of good/service.

It has replaced large number of taxes on goods and services levied on production/sale of goods or provision of services, such as Central Excise Duty, Service Tax, Central Sales Tax, VAT/Sales Tax, etc.

In the old tax regime, taxes were imposed on the value added at each stage, as well as, on the total value. This escalated the price.

The GST regime is superior in the following aspects

(i) GST has simplified the multiplicity of taxes on goods and services.

(ii) The laws and rates of taxes across the country are standardised.

(iii) It has facilitated the freedom of movement of goods and services and created a common market in the country.

(iv) It is aimed at reducing the cost of business operations and cascading effect of various taxes on consumers. It has also reduced the overall cost of production which will make Indian products/services more competitive in the domestic and international markets.

(v) It will also result into higher economic growth.

(vi) Compliance will also be easier as all tax payment related services like registration, returns, payments are available online through a common portal www.gst.gov.in.

(vii) It has expanded the tax base, introduced higher transparency in the taxation system, reduced human interface between taxpayer and government and is furthering ease of doing business.

The following are its categories

(i) Central GST (CGST)

(ii) State GST (SGST)

(iii) Union Territory GST (UTGST)

31. Define revenue receipts in a government budget. Explain how government budget can be used to bring in price stability in the economy?

Ans. Receipts which do not create a liability for the government or do not lead to reduction in assets, are known as revenue receipts.

Revenue receipts are receipts of the government which are non-redeemable, i.e. they cannot be re-claimed from the government.

These are divided into tax and non-tax revenues

(i) **Tax Revenue**

It consists of the proceeds of taxes and other duties levied by the central and the state governments. Tax revenues comprise of direct taxes and indirect taxes.

(ii) **Non-tax Revenue**

Non-tax revenue of the government mainly consists of interest receipts on account of loans by the government, dividends and profits on investments made by the government, fees and other receipts for services rendered by the government.

Grants-in-aid from foreign countries and international organisations are also a part of non-tax revenue.

The government budget is a statement of estimated receipts and expenditures of the government during the financial year. One of the objectives of the government budget is to achieve 'economic stability'.

Government tries to establish economic stability by its budgetary policies related to income and expenditure. Economic stability refers to a situation without fluctuations in price levels and stability of exchange rate in an economy.

Economic stability is achieved by protecting the economy from harmful effects of various trade cycles and its phases, i.e. boom, recession, depression and recovery.

32. (i) **Elaborate the concept of following**

- **Fiscal deficit**
- **Revenue deficit**
- **Primary deficit**

(ii) **What does a zero primary deficit indicates?**

Ans. (i)

- A fiscal deficit is the distinction between the government's total expenditure and its total receipts, which excludes borrowing.
  Gross Fiscal Deficit = Total Expenditure – (Revenue Receipts + Non-debt Creating Capital Receipts)
- A revenue deficit refers to the excess of the government's revenue expenditure over the revenue receipts.
  Revenue Deficit = Revenue Expenditure – Revenue Receipts
  This deficit only incorporates current income and current expenses. A high degree of deficit symbolises that the government should reduce its expenses.
- Primary deficit refers to fiscal deficit minus interest payments. It represents the borrowing requirement of the government excluding interest obligations.
  Gross Primary Deficit = Gross Fiscal Deficit – Net Interest Liabilities

(ii) A zero primary deficit means fiscal deficit is equal to interest payments. This indicates that government is paying its interest commitments by the way of borrowings, which is not a good sign as borrowings further increases future liabilities.

33. (i) **"The Union Budget 2023-24 had proposed an allocation of ₹ 22,138 crore to the Micro, Small and Medium Enterprise (MSME) Ministry." Identify and explain the objective that the government is trying to achieve with the proposed expenditure.**

(ii) **State the formulae for calculating fiscal deficit and revenue deficit.** CBSE 2024 C

Ans. (i) The proposed allocation of ₹ 22,138 crore to the MSME Ministry aims to

- **Promote Economic Growth**
  Support MSMEs as they contribute significantly to GDP and employment generation.
- **Job Creation**
  Boost small businesses to provide more employment opportunities.
- **Encourage Innovation and Competitiveness**
  Facilitate technology up gradation and innovation in MSMEs.
- **Reduce Regional Disparities**
  Support MSMEs in rural and semi-urban areas to ensure balanced development.

(ii) **Fiscal Deficit**

Fiscal Deficit = Total Expenditure – Total Receipts (excluding borrowings).

Revenue Deficit

Revenue Deficit = Revenue Expenditure – Revenue Receipts.

34. **"Governments across nations are too much worried about the term fiscal deficit." Do you think that fiscal deficit is necessarily inflationary in nature? Support your answer with valid reasons.**

Or **"Fiscal deficit is necessarily inflationary in nature." Do you agree? Support your answer with valid reasons.**

CBSE SQP 2018; Competency Based Que

Ans. No, I do not agree with the statement. Fiscal deficit represents the government's borrowings, with borrowing from the RBI being a significant component. Such borrowing increases the money supply in the economy, which in turn raises the general price level.

A sustained rise in the general price level over time results in an inflationary spiral, which is why governments worldwide are concerned about high fiscal deficits. However, Keynes challenged the view that fiscal deficits always lead to inflationary spirals.

On the contrary, he advocated using fiscal deficits as a critical policy tool to address economic depression. According to Keynes, depression is a phase marked by low investment due to inadequate Aggregate Demand (AD).

As a result, output levels (and consequently income levels) remain low, resources are underutilised and unemployment becomes a significant issue.

In such circumstances, a deficit budget can be an effective policy measure, as an increase in money supply through borrowing boosts aggregate demand in two ways

(i) Directly, by increasing government expenditure.

(ii) Indirectly, by encouraging higher consumption and investment spending by individuals.

Therefore, it is concluded that fiscal deficits are not always inflationary in nature.

35. **Government provides certain goods and services which cannot be provided by the market mechanism. Examples of such goods are national defence, roads, government administration, etc. which are referred to as public goods.**

There are two major differences between public and private goods. One, the benefits of public goods are available to all and are not only restricted to one particular consumer. e.g. If a person wears a shirt, it will not be available to others. It is said that this person's consumption stands in rival relationship to the consumption of others. However, if we consider a public park or measures to reduce air pollution, the benefits will be available to all. One person's consumption of a good does not reduce the amount available for consumption for others and so several people can enjoy the benefits, that is, the consumption of many people is not 'rivalrous'.

Two, in case of private goods, anyone who does not pay for the goods can be excluded from enjoying its benefits. If you do not buy a ticket, you will not be allowed to watch a movie at a local cinema hall. However, in case of public goods, there is no feasible way of excluding anyone from enjoying the benefits of the good. That is why public goods are called non-excludable. Even if some users do not pay, it is difficult and sometimes impossible to collect fees for the public good. These non-paying users are known as 'free-riders'. Consumers will not voluntarily pay for what they can get for free and for which there is no exclusive title to the property being enjoyed. The link between the producer and consumer which occurs through the payment process is broken and the government must step in to provide for such goods.

On the basis of the given text and common understanding, answer the following questions

CBSE 2025; Competency Based Que

(i) Describe how the government's role in providing public goods impacts community welfare.

(ii) Define free-riders. Explain the challenges posed by the free-riders in the context of public goods.

Ans. (i) The government plays a crucial role in providing public goods, which significantly enhances community welfare in the following ways

- **Ensuring Availability for All**
  Public goods like roads, national defence and pollution control benefit everyone equally. Since they are non-rivalrous, one person's use does not reduce availability for others.
- **Addressing Market Failure**
  Due to the free-rider problem, private firms may not supply these goods, as people can benefit without paying. The government ensures their provision, preventing market failure and maintaining essential services.
- **Enhancing Quality of Life**
  Public goods improve safety, infrastructure, and environmental conditions, fostering economic growth and overall well-being. This leads to a more stable and prosperous society.

By providing public goods, the government ensures fairness, accessibility and long-term community welfare.

(ii) Free-riders are individuals who benefit from a public good without contributing to its cost. Since public goods are non-excludable, people may choose not to pay, knowing they cannot be denied access.

This creates several challenges

- **Underfunding of Public Goods**
  If many people avoid paying, the government may struggle to raise enough resources to maintain or improve public goods.
- **Overuse and Degradation**
  Since individuals do not bear direct costs, public goods like parks or roads may be overused, leading to congestion or depletion.
- **Burden on the Government**
  The government must use tax revenue or public funds to finance these goods, which can strain financial resources.

To address the free-rider problem, the government uses taxation and regulations to ensure that public goods are funded and accessible to all.

Numerical Questions

Numerical 1

Calculate budgetary deficit from the following data

S.No.	Items	₹ (in crores)
(i)	Total Expenditure	1,00,000
(ii)	Total Receipts	88,000

Sol. Budgetary Deficit = Total Expenditure − Total Receipts

= 1,00,000 − 88,000 = ₹ 12,000 crore

Numerical 2

Calculate revenue deficit from the following data

S.No.	Items	₹ (in crores)
(i)	Revenue Receipts	50,000
(ii)	Revenue Expenditure	60,000

Sol. Revenue Deficit

= Revenue Expenditure − Revenue Receipts

= 60,000 − 50,000 = ₹ 10,000 crore

Numerical 3

A government budget shows a primary deficit of ₹ 6,500 crore. The revenue expenditure on interest payment is ₹ 400 crore. How much is the fiscal deficit?

Sol. Fiscal Deficit = Primary Deficit + Interest Payment

= 6,500 + 400 = ₹ 6,900 crore

Numerical 4

Calculate fiscal deficit.

S.No.	Items	₹ (in crores)
(i)	Borrowings	9,000
(ii)	Interest	200

Sol. Fiscal Deficit = Borrowings

Thus, fiscal deficit = ₹ 9,000 crore

Numerical 5

As per the government budget, the interests payments are estimated at ₹ 2,000 crore, which is 20% of primary deficit. Calculate the fiscal deficit.

Sol. Interest payment = 20% of primary deficit

Primary Deficit = $\frac{100}{20} \times 2{,}000$ = ₹ 10,000 crore

Fiscal Deficit = Primary Deficit + Interest Payment

= 10,000 + 2,000 = ₹ 12,000 crore

Numerical 6

Calculate primary deficit.

S.No.	Items	₹ (in crores)
(i)	Fiscal Deficit	9,000
(ii)	Interest Payment by Government	400

Sol. Primary Deficit = Fiscal Deficit − Interest Payment by Government

= 9,000 − 400 = ₹ 8,600 crore

Numerical 7

Calculate revenue, fiscal and primary deficits.

S.No.	Items		₹ (in crores)
(i)	Revenue Receipts		19,000
(ii)	Capital Receipts		
	(a) Recovery of Loan	1,200	
	(b) Borrowings	7,000	8,200
(iii)	Total Receipts		27,200
(iv)	Total Expenditure		
	(a) Revenue (including interest payment of ₹ 6,000 crore)	24,000	
	(b) Capital	33,000	57,000

Sol. Revenue Deficit

= Revenue Expenditure − Revenue Receipts

= 24,000 − 19,000 = ₹ 5,000 crore

Fiscal Deficit = Total Expenditure − Total Receipts (excluding Borrowings)

= 57,000 − 1,200 = ₹ 55,800 crore

Primary Deficit = Fiscal Deficit − Interest Payments

= 55,800 − 6,000 = ₹ 49,800 crore

Numerical 8

Find fiscal deficit and primary deficit from the following

S.No.	Items	₹ (in crores)
(i)	Revenue Expenditure	70,000
(ii)	Borrowings	15,000
(iii)	Revenue Receipts	50,000
(iv)	Interest Payments	25% of Revenue Deficit

Sol. Fiscal Deficit = Borrowings = ₹ 15,000 crore

Primary Deficit = Fiscal Deficit − Interest Payments

Here, Fiscal Deficit = ₹ 15,000 crore

Interest Payments = 25% of Revenue Deficit

= 25% × (70,000 − 50,000)

= 25% × 20,000 = ₹ 5,000 crore

On substituting,

Primary Deficit = 15,000 − 5,000 = ₹ 10,000 crore

Numerical 9

On the basis of the given information, calculate the value of **CBSE SQP 2024**

(i) Fiscal deficit (ii) Primary deficit

S.No.	Items	2021-22 ₹ (in crores)
(i)	Revenue Receipts	20
(ii)	Capital Expenditure	15
(iii)	Revenue Deficit	10
(iv)	Non-debt creating Capital Receipts	50% of Revenue Receipts
(v)	Interest Payments	4

Sol. (i) Fiscal Deficit = Revenue Deficit + Capital Expenditure − Non-debt Creating Capital Receipts

= 10 + 15 − (50/100 × 20) = ₹ 15 crore

(ii) Primary Deficit = Fiscal Deficit − Interest Payments

= 15 − 4 = ₹ 11 crore

Numerical 10

From the following data, calculate

(i) Revenue deficit and (ii) Fiscal deficit **CBSE 2020**

S. No.	Items	₹ (in crores)
(i)	Tax Revenue	1,200
(ii)	Revenue Expenditure	3,700
(iii)	Non-tax Revenue	2,000
(iv)	Recovery of Loans	145
(v)	Capital Expenditure	500
(vi)	Disinvestment	120
(vii)	Interest Payments	1,070

Sol. (i) Revenue Deficit = Revenue Expenditure − Revenue Receipts (Tax Revenue + Non-tax Revenue)

= 3,700 − (1,200 + 2,000)

= 3,700 − 3,200

= ₹ 500 crore

(ii) Fiscal Deficit = Revenue Expenditure + Capital Expenditure − Revenue Receipts (Tax Revenue + Non-tax Revenue) − Capital Receipts + Net of Borrowing Recovery of Loans + Disinvestment)

= 3,700 + 500 − 1,200 + 2,000) − 145 + 120

= 3,700 + 500 − 3,200 − 265

= 4,200 − 3,465

= ₹ 735 crore

Numerical 11

From the following information, determine

(i) Capital expenditure

(ii) Total expenditure

(iii) Interest payments

S. No.	Items	₹ (in crores)
(i)	Fiscal Deficit	2,400
(ii)	Revenue Deficit	1,800
(iii)	Primary Deficit	10,000
(iv)	Revenue Receipts	12,000
(v)	Non-debt creating Capital Receipts	20,000

Sol. (i) Fiscal Deficit = Revenue Deficit + (Capital Expenditure − Non-debt creating Capital Receipts)

24,000 = 18,000 + (Capital Expenditure − 20,000)

Capital Expenditure = 24,000 − 18,000 + 20,000

= ₹ 26,000 crore

(ii) Total Expenditure = Revenue Expenditure + Capital Expenditure

Revenue Expenditure = Revenue Deficit + Revenue Receipts

= 18,000 + 12,000

= ₹ 30,000 crore

(iii) Primary Deficit = Fiscal Deficit − Interest Payments

10,000 = 24,000 − Interest Payments

Interest Payment = 24,000 − 10,000

= ₹ 14,000 crore

SELF ASSESSMENT TEST

Objective Type Questions

1. The government of a country has announced an increase in public expenditure to build new infrastructure projects, such as highways and hospitals. Which of the following objectives of the government budget does this decision primarily align with?
   (a) Reducing regional disparities
   (b) Economic stability
   (c) Redistribution of income
   (d) Economic growth

2. Indirect taxes are ……… in nature.
   (a) proportional (b) flexible
   (c) artificial (d) None of these

3. Expenditure by the government on the construction of a hospital building will be taken as ……… only as long as the hospital project is not completed.
   (a) plan revenue expenditure
   (b) plan capital expenditure
   (c) non-plan revenue expenditure
   (d) non-plan capital expenditure

4. If revenue expenditure is ₹ 980 crore, tax revenue is ₹ 410 crore and non-tax revenue is ₹ 365 crore, then find revenue deficit.
   (a) ₹ 615 crore (b) ₹ 205 crore
   (c) ₹ 765 crore (d) ₹ 570 crore

5. If total expenditure is ₹ 250 crore, revenue receipt is ₹ 180 crore and capital receipt is ₹ 30 crore, then budget deficit would be
   (a) ₹ 220 crore (b) ₹ 210 crore
   (c) ₹ 40 crore (d) ₹ 70 crore

6. Which of the following statements is/are correct?
   I. Private goods are non-excludable.
   II. No indirect tax is levied on Khadi items.
   Codes
   (a) Only I (b) Only II
   (c) Both I and II (d) None of these

Answers 1. (d) 2. (a) 3. (b) 4. (b) 5. (c) 6. (b)

Short Answer Type Questions

7. Give a brief note, why Goods and Services Tax (GST) is considered an indirect tax?

8. Discuss the difference between plan and non-plan expenditure of the government.

9. How can a deficit be financed?

10. Explain the different taxes levied by the State Government.

11. "The Union Budget often garners significant public and expert attention as it lays the foundation for the nation's economic priorities and strategies." Do you agree with the given statement? Support your answer with valid reasons.

Long Answer Type Questions

12. What is the significance of fiscal deficit?

13. Does public debt impose a burden? Comment.

Numerical Questions

14. Find borrowing by the government if payment of interest is estimated to be of ₹ 10,000 crore which is 25% of primary deficit.

Ans. ₹ 35,000 crore

15. From the following data about a government budget, find out the following
   (i) Revenue deficit (ii) Fiscal deficit
   (iii) Primary deficit

S.No.	Items	₹ (in arab)
(a)	Capital Receipts Net of Borrowings	95
(b)	Revenue Expenditure	100
(c)	Interest Payments	10
(d)	Revenue Receipts	80
(e)	Capital Expenditure	110

Ans. (i) ₹ 20 arab (ii) ₹ 35 arab (iii) ₹ 25 arab

16. From the following data about a government budget, find
   (i) Revenue deficit (ii) Fiscal deficit
   (iii) Primary deficit

S.No.	Items	₹ (in arab)
(a)	Tax Revenue	47
(b)	Capital Receipts	34
(c)	Non-tax Revenue	10
(d)	Borrowings	32
(e)	Revenue Expenditures	80
(f)	Interest Payments	20

Ans. (i) ₹ 23 arab (ii) ₹ 32 arab (iii) ₹ 12 arab

07 CHAPTER

Foreign exchange refers to the reserve of foreign currencies in the domestic country, like currency of US (Dollars) and UK (Pounds) are the foreign exchanges for India.

Foreign Exchange Rate

YOUR STUDY GOALS

7.1 Meaning of Foreign Exchange Rate
- Fixed Exchange Rate System
- Flexible Exchange Rate System
- Managed Floating Exchange Rate System

7.2 Foreign Exchange Market

YOUR PRACTICE GOAL

- Objective Type Questions (58 Qs ; MCQs, A-R, Statements, Matching, Concept Identification)
- Subjective Questions (26 SAs, 8 LAs)
- Self Assessment Test (7 MCQs, 8 SAs, 2 LAs)

7.1 Meaning of Foreign Exchange Rate

Foreign exchange rate refers to the rate at which one unit of domestic currency is exchanged with the number of units of currency of another country. It is also referred to as **external value of the domestic currency**.

According to **Crowther**, "The rate of exchange measures number of units of one currency which is exchanged in the foreign market for one unit another."

Types of Foreign Exchange Rate

There are three important methods for determination of foreign exchange rate

- Fixed exchange rate system
- Flexible exchange rate system
- Managed floating exchange rate system

Fixed Exchange Rate System

Under this system, exchange rate is determined or fixed by the government of a country and the changes can be made by the government only. It is also known as **pegged exchange rate system**.

The government tries to stabilise the exchange rate under this method by fixing it at a particular level. In the figure given, the market determined exchange rate is e.

If government wants to encourage exports, it would make rupee cheaper by fixing higher exchange rate.

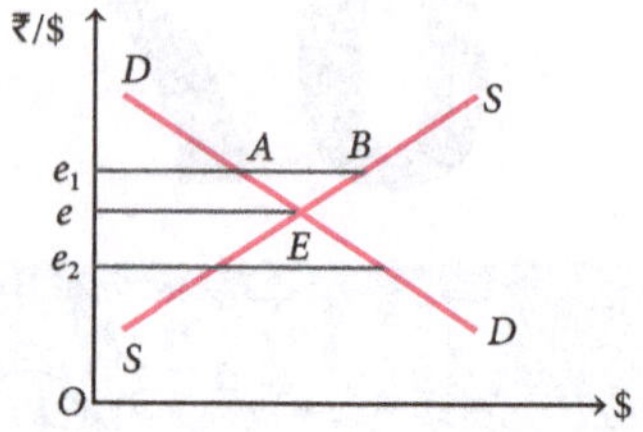

Thus, the new exchange rate set by the government is e_1, (above the market equilibrium in the figure), where $e_1 > e$ (original exchange rate).

- At this exchange rate (point e_1), the supply of dollars exceeds the demand for dollars. The RBI intervenes in the foreign exchange market to absorb excess supply of dollars, allowing the government to maintain any exchange rate in the economy. However, this intervention accumulates more foreign exchange.
- If the exchange rate is set below market equilibrium (point e_2), it leads to an excess demand for dollars, requiring the government to sell foreign exchange reserves to meet excess demand.

Devaluation and Revaluation

In fixed exchange rate system, when some government action increases the exchange rate (thereby, making domestic currency cheaper), it is called **devaluation**.

On the other hand, a **revaluation** is said to occur, when the government decreases the exchange rate (thereby, making domestic currency costlier) under their system.

Under fixed exchange rate system, the government fixes the value of its currency in terms of an '*external standard*.' It can be done using following systems/standards

1. **Gold Standard System of Exchange Rate** According to this system, gold was taken as the common unit of parity between currencies of different countries in circulation. Each country is to define the value of its currency in terms of gold.
2. **The Bretton Woods System of Exchange Rate** The Bretton Woods Conference in 1944, re-established a fixed exchange rate system by setting up International Monetary Fund (IMF) and World Bank. This system differed from the gold standard in currency conversion options. This system requires countries to fix their currency against the US dollar.

Merits of Fixed Exchange Rate System
- Promotion of international trade through stability in exchange rate.
- Acceleration in capital formation.
- Helpful in maintaining favourable balance of payments.
- Helpful to check domestic inflation.
- Helpful to prevent speculation in foreign exchange market.

Demerits of Fixed Exchange Rate System
- Requires high reserves of gold and foreign exchange.
- Control over various sectors.
- High fluctuation in exchange rates may result in undervaluation or overvaluation of currency.
- Constant intervention of central bank.

Flexible Exchange Rate System

It is that rate which is determined by market forces of demand and supply, without direct government intervention.

In other words, it is the rate determined by the demand for and the supply of different currencies in the foreign exchange market. It is also known as **floating exchange rate system**.

Demand and Supply of Foreign Exchange

Demand for Foreign Exchange	Supply of Foreign Exchange
Domestic residents and government of country demand foreign exchange for following purposes • Purchase of foreign goods. • Gifts and grants to the rest of the world. • Repayment of international loans. • To purchase financial assets in a foreign country. • To invest directly in shops, factories, buildings in foreign countries. • To speculate on the value of foreign currency.	Domestic residents and government of country may get supply of foreign exchange for following sources • Foreign Direct Investment (FDI). • Speculative purchase of foreign exchange. • Expenditure on tourism by foreign residents. • Purchase of domestic goods by foreigners. • Transfer of foreign exchange by residents.
Demand Curve The demand of foreign exchange has an inverse relation with foreign exchange rate, thus, it is negatively sloped. 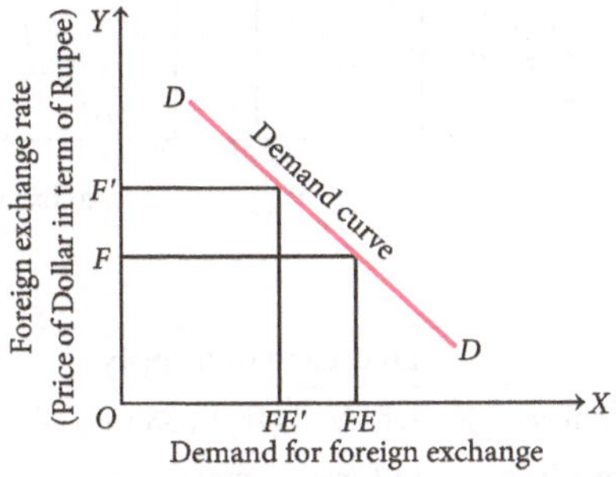	**Supply Curve** The supply of foreign exchange has positive relation with foreign exchange rate, thus it is positively sloped. 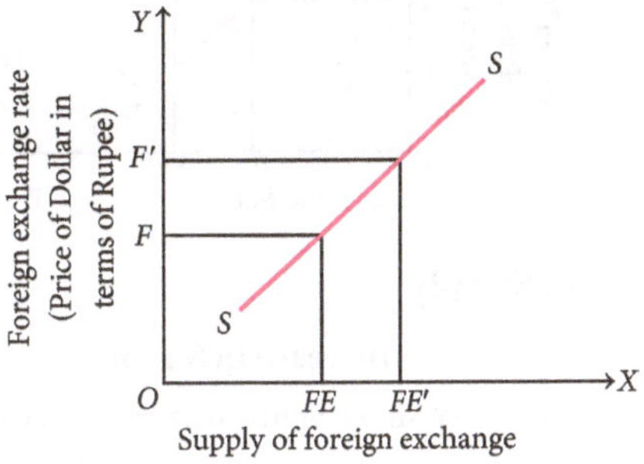

Demand curve figure text:

Supply curve figure text:

Determination of Flexible Foreign Exchange Rate

Flexible foreign exchange rate is determined when the demand for a currency in terms of another currency is equal to its supply.

In the given figure, line *SS* shows the supply of foreign currency. Line *DD* shows the demand for foreign currency. The point *E*, at which *DD* equals to *SS*, represents the **equilibrium rate of exchange**.

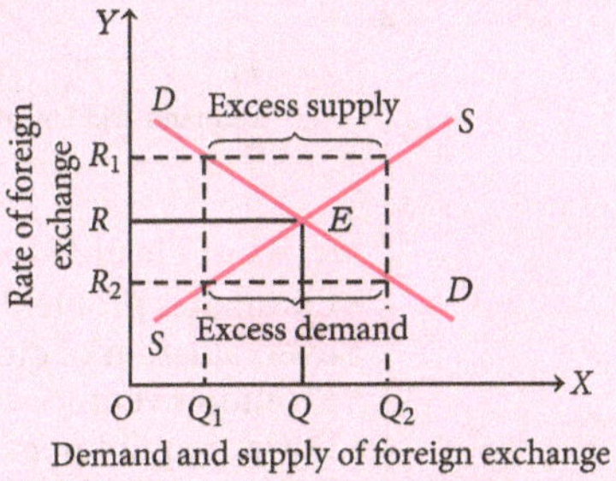

- If the exchange rate becomes R_1, there will be excess supply (OQ_2) as at a higher exchange rate, there will be more supply of foreign exchange compared with demand (OQ_1).
  This will push foreign exchange rate down and gap will shrink, this process will continue till market reach the equilibrium.
- If the exchange rate becomes R_2, there will be excess demand (OQ_2) as at a lower exchange rate, there will be more demand for foreign exchange compared with supply (OQ_1).
  This will push the foreign exchange rate up and the gap will shrink, this process will continue till market reach the equilibrium.

Effect of Change in Demand and Supply

The exchange rate will be affected if there are changes in demand and supply of foreign exchange. In such a situation, a new exchange rate will be determined.

The different conditions are discussed below

1. **Change in Demand**

Increase in Demand

- Supply curve shifts rightwards from *DD* to *D′D′*.
- It will result in rise in foreign exchange rate.

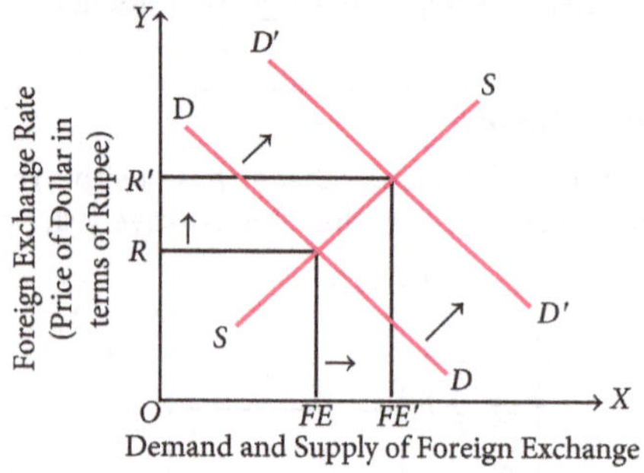

Decrease in Demand

- Demand curve shifts leftwards from *DD* to *D′D′*.
- It will result in fall in foreign exchange rate.

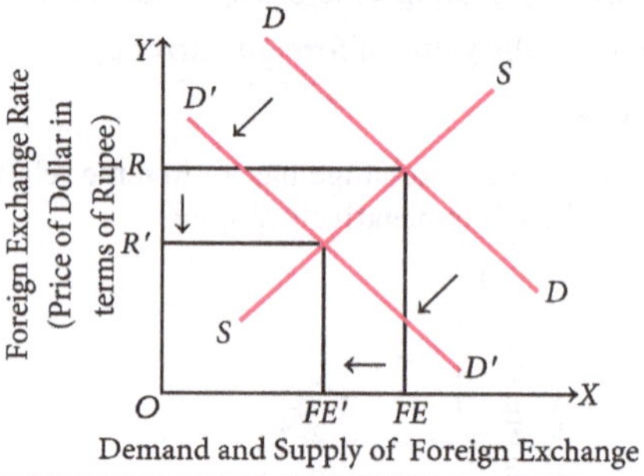

2. **Change in Supply**

Increase in Supply

- Supply and curve shifts rightwards from *SS* to *S′ S′*.
- It will result in fall in foreign exchange rate.

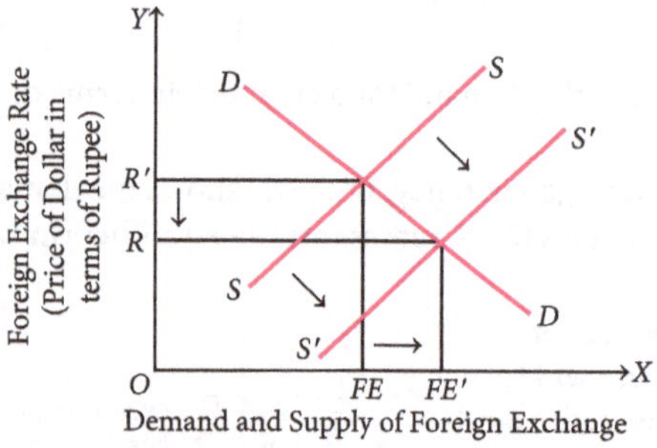

Decrease in Supply

- Supply curve shifts leftwards from *SS* to *S′ S′*.
- It will result in rise in foreign exchange rate.

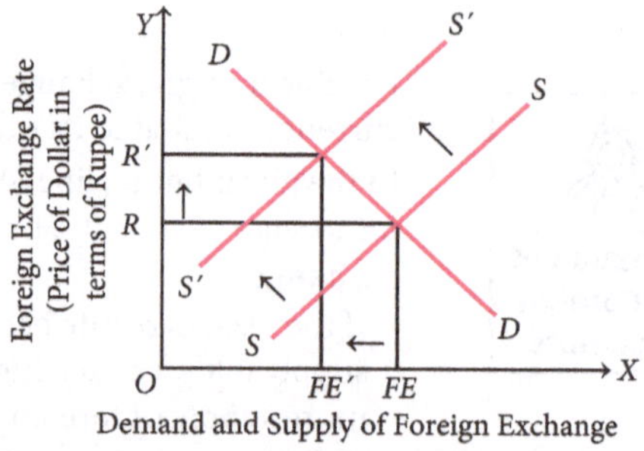

Merits of Flexible Exchange Rate System

- Eliminates problems of undervaluation or overvaluation of currency.
- Promotes venture capital.
- Lower requirement of reserve funds.
- Efficient utilisation of resources.

Demerits of Flexible Exchange Rate System

- Causes market instability.
- Creates uncertainty due to currency fluctuation.
- Instability in international trade.
- Encourages speculation.

Managed Floating Exchange Rate System

In this system, the exchange rate is determined in the foreign exchange market freely by the market forces. However, excessive fluctuations in the exchange rate are checked by the central bank.

It is a mixture of a flexible exchange rate system (the float part) and a fixed exchange rate system (the managed part).

Managed floating is also known as **dirty floating**, if a country manipulates the exchange rate for trade advantage rather than stabilising market fluctuations.

Currency Depreciation and Currency Appreciation

The value of currency may appreciate or depreciate under flexible and managed floating exchange rate systems.

Currency Depreciation	Currency Appreciation
• It refers to the decrease in the value of domestic currency in relation to the value of other currencies in foreign exchange market. • Demand for foreign exchange ↑ or ⇒ Exchange rate ↑ Supply for foreign exchange ↓ This implies domestic currency depreciation. • **Effects** of depreciation of currency – Encourages exports from a country. – Discourages imports from rest of the world.	• It refers to the rise in the value of domestic currency in relation to the value of other currencies in foreign exchange market. • Supply of foreign exchange ↑ or ⇒ Exchange rate ↓ Demand for foreign exchange ↓ This implies domestic currency appreciation. • **Effects** of appreciation of currency – Imports will rise. – Exports will fall.

7.2 Foreign Exchange Market

It is the market in which foreign currencies are traded, i.e. are bought and sold. The major participants in this market are commercial banks, foreign exchange brokers, other authorised dealers, central bank, etc.

There are two **types** of foreign exchange market

Basis	Spot Market	Forward Market
Meaning	It handles only spot or current transactions of foreign exchanges.	It deals with the purchase and sale of foreign exchange that are contracted today, but are implemented in future.
Transaction Settlement	Payment is made and received on the spot. In case of payment through cheque, two business days window is given for settlement.	Foreign currency is to be bought or sold on a specified date in future on the rate settled upon today.
Nature of Exchange Rate	The rate at which transactions in spot market takes place is referred to as spot exchange rate or current rate of exchange.	The rate at which transactions are settled upon is referred to as forward exchange rate.
Hedging	It does not allow hedging.	It allows hedging.

Functions of Foreign Exchange Market

Function	Explanation
Transfer Function	It facilitates transfer of purchasing power across different countries of the world. This function is performed using credit instruments such as bills of foreign exchange, bank drafts, etc.
Credit Function	It facilitates credit for international trade. e.g. Generally, bills of exchange with a maturity period of three months is used for making international payments.
Hedging Function	It facilitates protection against risks of foreign exchange fluctuations, etc.

Mind Map

FOREIGN EXCHANGE RATE

1 Meaning of Foreign Exchange Rate

Foreign exchange rate refers to the rate at which one unit of domestic currency is exchanged with the number of units of currency of another country.

2 Fixed Exchange Rate System

Exchange rate is determined or fixed by the government of a country and the changes can be made by the government only.
It is also known as pegged exchange rate system.
The government tries to stabilise the exchange rate under this method by fixing it at a particular level. In the figure given, the market determined exchange rate is e. If government wants to encourage exports, it would make rupee cheaper by fixing higher exchange rate.
The new exchange rate set by the government is e_1, (above the market equilibrium in the figure), where $e_1 > e$ (original exchange rate). If the exchange rate is set below market equilibrium (point e_2), it leads to an excess demand for dollars, requiring the government to withdraw dollars from its past holdings

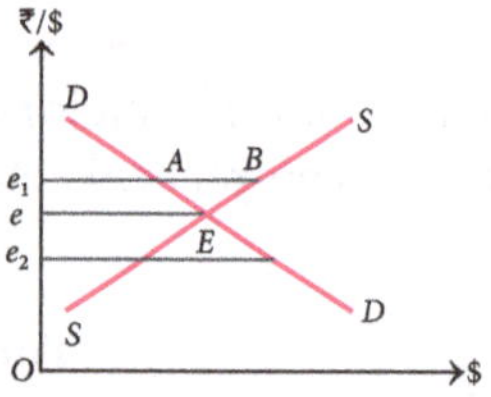

Under fixed exchange rate system, the government fixes the value of its currency in terms of an 'external standard'. It can be done using following systems

1. **Gold Standard System of Exchange Rate** According to this system, gold was taken as the common unit of parity between currencies of different countries in circulation.
2. **The Bretton Woods System of Exchange Rate** The Bretton Woods Conference in 1944, re-established a fixed exchange rate system by setting up International Monetary Fund (IMF) and World Bank, differing from the gold standard in currency conversion options.

3 Flexible Exchange Rate System

It is that rate which is determined by market forces of demand and supply. It is also known as floating exchange rate system.

Demand and Supply of Foreign Exchange

- The demand of foreign exchange has inverse relation with foreign exchange rate, thus it is negatively sloped.

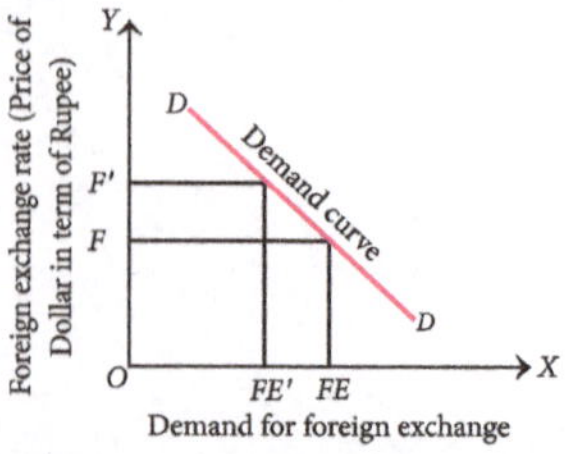

- The supply of foreign exchange has positive relation with foreign exchange rate, thus it is positively sloped.

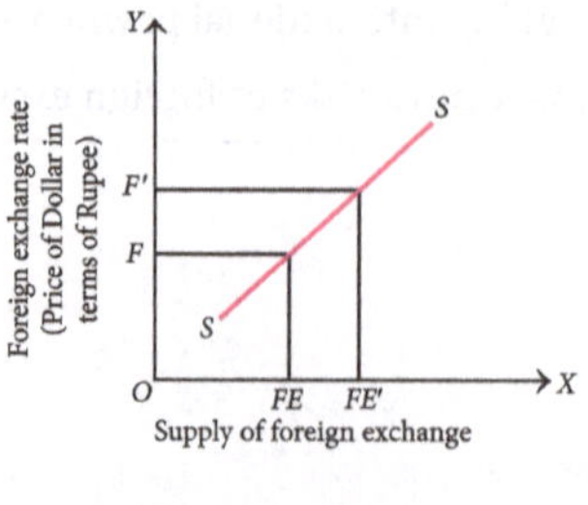

Determination of Flexible Rate

In the given figure, line *SS* shows the supply of foreign currency. Line *DD* shows the demand for foreign currency. The point *E*, at which *DD* equals to *SS*, represents the **equilibrium rate of exchange.**

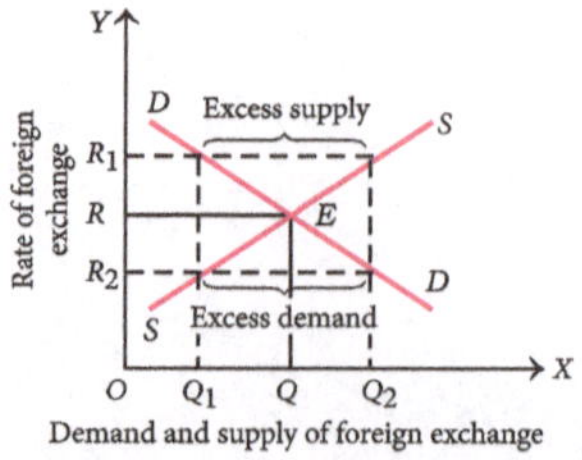

4 Managed Floating Exchange Rate System

The exchange rate is determined in the foreign exchange market freely by the market forces. However, excessive fluctuations in the exchange rate are checked by the central bank. It is also known as dirty floating, if a country manipulates the exchange rate by not following rules and regulations.

Currency Depreciation and Currency Appreciation

The value of currency may appreciate or depreciate under flexible and managed floating systems.

- **Currency Depreciation** It refers to the decrease in the value of domestic currency in relation to the value of other currencies in foreign exchange market.
- **Currency Appreciation** It refers to the rise in the value of domestic currency in relation to the value of other currencies in foreign exchange market.

5 Foreign Exchange Market

It is the market in which foreign currencies are traded, i.e. bought and sold. Major participants are commercial banks, foreign exchange brokers, other authorised dealers, etc.

Types

- **Spot Market** It handles only spot or current transactions of foreign exchanges.
- **Forward Market** It deals with the purchase and sale of foreign exchange that are contracted today, but are implemented in future.

Functions

- **Transfer Function** It facilitates transfer of purchasing power across different countries of the world.
- **Credit Function** It facilitates credit for international trade.
- **Hedging Function** It facilitates protection against risks of foreign exchange fluctuations, etc.

EXAM PATTERN QUESTIONS

Objective Type Questions

Multiple Choice Questions (MCQs)

1. Price of one currency in relation to another currency, determined by the free market forces, is known as ……… . **CBSE Term I 2021**

(a) equilibrium price (b) fixed exchange rate
(c) foreign exchange rate (d) flexible exchange rate

2. Countries often impose restrictions on free foreign trade **NCERT (QR)**

(a) to protect domestic consumers
(b) to protect foreign consumer
(c) to protect foreign producer
(d) to protect domestic producer

3. In international trade, if the domestic price of goods is more than the world price **NCERT (QR)**

(a) the country will neither import nor export
(b) the country will become an exporter of the goods
(c) the country will become an importer of the goods
(d) additional information is required

4. The image given below is indicating which type of exchange rate regime?

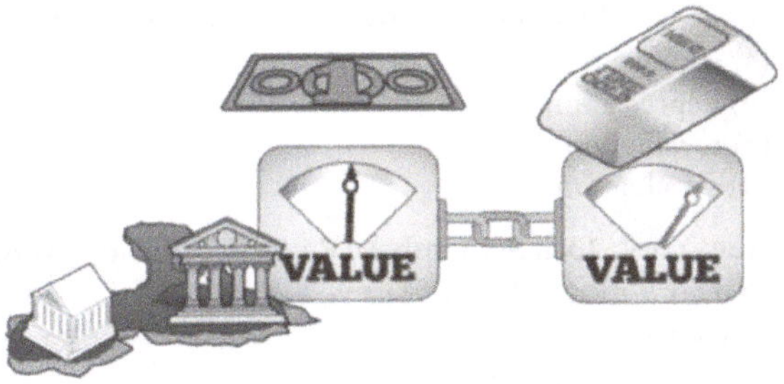

(a) Fixed exchange rate (b) Floating exchange rate
(c) Managed floating exchange rate
(d) None of the above

5. Which of the following is a potential advantage of a fixed exchange rate system?

(a) Flexibility to adjust to economic shocks
(b) Stable and predictable exchange rates
(c) Speculative attacks are impossible
(d) Increased competitiveness in international trade

6. When a country's currency is revalued, it will likely result in

(a) an increase in the demand for domestic goods abroad
(b) a reduction in the cost of imports
(c) higher inflation due to increased import costs
(d) an increase in domestic demand for foreign goods

7. Under the ……… exchange rate system, market forces automatically adjust the surplus and deficit in the balance of payments account. **CBSE SQP 2025**

(a) fixed (b) flexible
(c) managed floating (d) dirty floating

8. Under ……… exchange rate system, the Central Bank and government of the country do not have any authority to interfere in the exchange rate determination. **CBSE 2024 C**

(a) fixed (b) floating
(c) managed floating (d) gold standard

9. Identify the correct reason(s) that may affect the demand for foreign exchange in an economy. **CBSE SQP 2024; Competency Based Que**

I. Imports of visibles II. Exports of invisibles
III. Remittances by residents working abroad
IV. Purchase of assets abroad

Codes
(a) I and II (b) II and III (c) III and IV (d) I and IV

10. Identify, which of the following is not a source of demand for foreign exchange. **CBSE 2025, 24; Competency Based Que**

(a) Import of goods and services
(b) Gifts by Indians to their families living abroad
(c) Indian tourists visiting foreign countries
(d) Loans from Rest of the World (RoW)

11. Exports of Covid-19 vaccines manufactured in India has led to **CBSE Term I 2021; Competency Based Que**

(a) inflow of Indian currency
(b) outflow of foreign currency
(c) inflow of foreign currency and employment generation
(d) outflow of foreign currency and employment generation

12. "Foreign exchange supply is influenced by various transactions and activities that bring foreign currency into the domestic economy."

Identify the item that increases the supply of foreign exchange. **Competency Based Que**

(a) Import of goods from China
(b) Indian students going to USA for MBA
(c) Donation of $ 50 million received from Microsoft
(d) Purchase of land in England

13. Which of the following is a disadvantage of a flexible exchange rate system?
(a) It eliminates the need for central bank intervention
(b) It may lead to currency manipulation by governments
(c) It promotes stability in international trade
(d) It encourages speculation in the foreign exchange market

14. Dr. Deepa delivered a lecture on different types of foreign exchange rate systems. She stated that, in a particular exchange rate system, to keep the foreign exchange rate within certain limits the central bank maintains huge foreign exchange reserves.
Identify the type of exchange rate system Dr. Deepa referred to **CBSE Term I 2021; Competency Based Que**
(a) fixed exchange rate system
(b) flexible exchange rate system
(c) managed floating exchange rate system
(d) gold exchange rate system

15. Under the .... exchange rate system, the central bank can control the rise/fall of foreign exchange rate in a range bound manners. **CBSE 2024**
(a) fixed (b) flexible
(c) managed floating
(d) gold standard

16. Identify which of the following statements is true?
(a) The flexible exchange rate system gives the government more flexibility to maintain large stocks of foreign exchange reserves
(b) In the managed floating exchange rate system, the government intervenes to buy and sell foreign currencies
(c) Under managed floating exchange rate system, considering the depreciation of Indian currency, the Reserve Bank of India has decided to purchase Indian currency in the open market
(d) In the fixed exchange rate system, market forces fix the exchange rate

17.

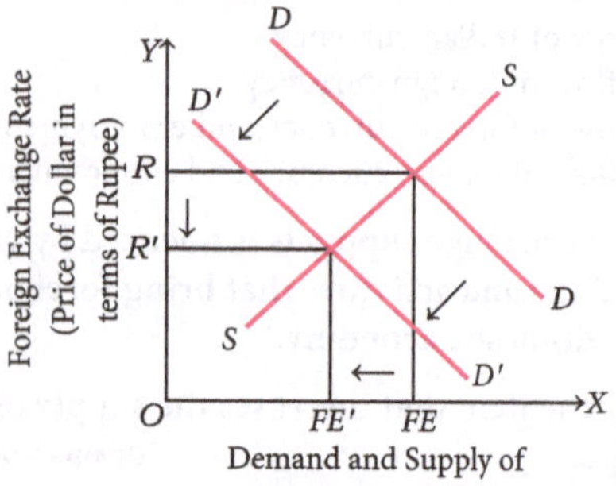

Demand and Supply of Foreign Exchange

On the basis of above diagram, which type of shifting of demand curve from *DD* to *D'D'* indicates?
(a) Appreciation of domestic currency
(b) Depreciation of domestic currency
(c) Depreciation of foreign currency
(d) Revaluation of domestic currency

18. Mumbai, 19th January (PTI) The rupee depreciated 15 paise to 81.45 against the US dollar in early trade on Thursday, weighed down by a muted trend in domestic equities and foreign fund outflows. At the interbank foreign exchange, the domestic unit opened weak at 81.45 against the dollar, registering a decline of 15 paise over its last close.

Source *https://economictimes.indiatimes.com/markets/forex/rupee-falls-15-paise-to-81-45-against-us-dollar/articleshow/97116879.cms*

How the above new unit impacts the exports from India? **Competency Based Que**
(a) Increase
(b) Decrease
(c) Remain constant
(d) Either (a) or (b)

19. Exchange rate between Indian Rupee and US Dollar has changed from 71.49 (November, 2020) to 72.82 (January, 2021) through changes to market forces of demand and supply. Therefore, it is believed that India's balance of payments this year going to be 'very-very strong', Commerce and Industry Minister Piyush Goyal said on Monday.
Here, change from 1$ = ₹ 71.49 to ₹ 72.82 is called as .... of Indian currency. **Competency Based Que**
(a) appreciation
(b) depreciation
(c) revaluation
(d) devaluation

20. New York, 13th September (Reuters) : "US dollar drops to near 9 month low versus yen amid talk of larger fed rate cut."

Source *https://www.reuters.com/markets/currencies/dollar-weak-traders-add-wagers-big-rate-cut-fed-2024-09-13/*

How would a potential rate cut by the Federal Reserve likely impact the attractiveness of the US dollar to investors? **Competency Based Que**
(a) The US dollar would become more attractive to investors due to higher interest rates
(b) The US dollar's attractiveness to investors would remain unchanged despite the rate cut
(c) The US dollar could become less attractive to investors as other currencies might offer higher returns
(d) The US dollar's attractiveness would improve because of increased investor confidence in the US economy

21. **The image given below is depicting which type of foreign exchange market?**

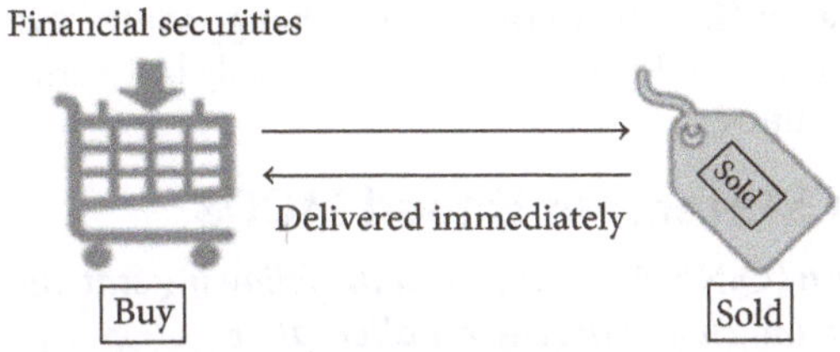

(a) An over-the-counter market for foreign exchange
(b) A spot market for foreign exchange
(c) A forward market for foreign exchange
(d) A futures market for foreign exchange

22. **The spot market is characterised by the following**

I. Only handling current transactions
II. Determining the forward rate of exchange
III. Determining the immediate rate of exchange

Competency Based Que

Codes

(a) I, II and III (b) I and II
(c) II and III (d) I and III

23. **The forward market is the one that**

(a) deals with foreign exchange transactions intended for delivery in the future
(b) manages on-the-spot transactions
(c) manages both present and upcoming transactions
(d) Not one of these

24. **Hedging is possible in**

(a) spot market (b) forward market
(c) managed floating system (d) None of these

Direction *Read the case study and answer the questions 25 to 28 on the basis of the same*

Indian's exchange rate policy has evolved in line with international and domestic developments. Post-independence, in view of the prevailing Bretton Woods system, the Indian rupee was pegged to the Pound sterling. With the breakdown of the Bretton Woods system and also the declining share of UK in India's trade, the rupee was delinked from the Pound sterling in September, 1975.

During the period between 1975 to 1992, the exchange rate was officially determined by the RBI within nominal band of plus or minus 5 percent of the weighted basket of currencies of India's major trading partners. This exchange rate was referred to as 'adjustable nominal peg with a band'.

25. **Post-independence, the exchange rate was determined under**

(a) fixed exchange rate system
(b) flexible exchange rate system
(c) managed floating exchange rate system
(d) None of the above

26. **Immediately after independence, India rupee was pegged to the ....**

27. **The rupee was delinked from the Pound sterling in .... .**

28. **The rupee was delinked from Pound sterling in 1975 because**

(a) the Bretton Woods system broke down
(b) UK's share was declining in India's trade
(c) Both (a) and (b) (d) None of the above

Direction *Read the case study and answer the questions 29 to 32 on the basis of the same*

Each nation has its own currency when monetary transactions are conducted within the national borders, payments are made in the currency of that country for example Indian currency is called rupee. To be more exact it is called Indian rupee payments within the national borders of India are made in Indian rupees.

Similarly, each other nation has its own currency for example Pakistan currency is called Pakistani rupee, USA currency US dollar, Kuwait currency Kuwaiti Dinar, UAE currency dirham and so on. Payments within the nation borders of Pakistan are made in Pakistani rupees, payment within the national border of USA is USA dollars, etc.

When transactions are conducted across National borders one currency must be converted into another. Conversion rate between two currencies is decided by two ways first fixed exchange rate second floating or flexible exchange rate.

29. **Which of the following statements accurately defines the function of exchange rates in international economics?**

(a) Exchange rates determine the price at which goods are traded across international markets
(b) Exchange rates are the value at which one currency can be exchanged for another
(c) Exchange rates set the terms for international service agreements
(d) Exchange rates influence the price of both goods and services domestically

30. **The exchange rate system where the value of the currency is determined by the market forces is known as the .... exchange rate system.**

31. **A depreciation of the domestic currency generally makes .... more expensive and .... cheaper.**

32. **If India and the USA, both adopt a floating exchange rate system, which factor is most likely to directly affect the exchange rate between the Indian Rupee (INR) and the US Dollar (USD)?**

(a) The inflation rate in both countries
(b) The fixed government determined exchange rate
(c) The economic performance of other countries
(d) The central bank's intervention in international trade

Assertion-Reason

Direction (Q.No. 33 to 40) *Read the following Assertion (A) and Reason (R) and choose the correct alternative from the following*

Alternatives

(a) Both Assertion (A) and Reason (R) are true and Reason (R) is the correct explanation of Assertion (A)
(b) Both Assertion (A) and Reason (R) are true, but Reason (R) is not the correct explanation of Assertion (A)
(c) Assertion (A) is true, but Reason (R) is false
(d) Assertion (A) is false, but Reason (R) is true

33. **Assertion** (A) When the price of foreign exchange rises, the demand for foreign currency will fall.

Reason (R) There exists an inverse relation between foreign exchange rate and demand for foreign currency.

34. **Assertion** (A) Foreign exchange rate supports the comparison of international costs and prices.

Reason (R) Foreign exchange rate is the price of one currency in terms of another commodities. **CBSE Term I 2021**

35. **Assertion** (A) Fixed exchange rate system involves active involvement of central bank/government of the respective countries.

Reason (R) In fixed exchange rate system, once the exchange rate is decided it is usually kept as fixed in order to maintain the stability in economic transactions.

36. **Assertion** (A) Under the gold standard system, the value of a country's currency was directly linked to the quantity of gold held by that country's central bank.

Reason (R) Countries adhering to the gold standard system agreed to convert their currency into a fixed amount of gold, providing stability to exchange rates.

37. **Assertion** (A) Other things remaining constant, devaluation of domestic currency may lead to rise in national income of the nation.

Reason (R) Devaluation of domestic currency refers to reduction in the value of domestic currency by the government with respect to foreign currency under the fixed exchange rate system. **CBSE 2025**

38. **Assertion** (A) Demand for foreign exchange leads to inflow of foreign exchange.

Reason (R) Investment made by foreigners for purchasing financial and physical assets causes inflow for foreign exchange.

39. **Assertion** (A) Managed floating exchange rate system is an amalgamation of fixed exchange rate and flexible exchange rate.

Reason (R) Central bank can manipulate the flexible exchange rate system.

40. **Assertion** (A) A contractual rate of exchange is the forward rate of exchange.

Reason (R) A forward rate of exchange contract is one that is signed now but may occasionally be honoured in the future.

Two Statement Based MCQs

Direction (Q.No. 41 to 48) *Read the following statements carefully and choose the correct alternative*

Alternatives

(a) Statement I is correct and Statement II is incorrect
(b) Statement II is correct and Statement I is incorrect
(c) Both the statements are correct
(d) Both the statements are incorrect

41. **Statement I** The foreign exchange rate is determined solely by the demand and supply of a country's currency in the foreign exchange market.

Statement II A decrease in a country's interest rates relative to other countries can lead to a depreciation of its currency.

42. **Statement I** A flexible exchange rate system allows a country to absorb external shocks more effectively by automatically adjusting the currency value based on market forces.

Statement II A flexible exchange rate system eliminates the uncertainty in the foreign exchange market, making it stable for foreign investment.

43. **Statement I** The price of a given currency in terms of another is known as bank rate.

Statement II Demand curve for foreign exchange is a downward sloping curve. **CBSE 2025**

44. **Statement I** Under managed floating exchange rate, exchange rate is fixed by the government.

Statement II Excessive fluctuation under managed floating is managed by the central bank.

45. **Statement I** To restore the value of depreciating domestic currency, central bank will buy the foreign currency in the international market.

Statement II Depreciation of currency has same effect on exports as devaluation of currency.

46. **Statement I** Revaluation and appreciation of currency are same concept.

Statement II Appreciation of foreign currency implies depreciation of the domestic currency.

47. **Statement I** Spot market handles current transactions.

Statement II Spot exchange rate is that exchange rate at which forward transactions are to be honoured.

48. **Statement I** Forward market contracts are primarily used for speculative purposes, allowing traders to bet on future price movements rather than to manage price risk.

Statement II Forward market transactions are contracted to hedge against the risk of price fluctuations in the future, allowing businesses to lock in prices and avoid uncertainty.

Matching

49. Match the options of Column I with correct options in Column II

Column I		Column II
A. Flexible exchange rate system	(i)	The government is the controlling authority
B. Managed floating exchange rate system	(ii)	Market forces of demand and supply
C. Fixed exchange rate system	(iii)	Hybrid system

Codes

	A	B	C		A	B	C
(a)	(i)	(ii)	(iii)	(b)	(ii)	(iii)	(i)
(c)	(iii)	(ii)	(i)	(d)	(iii)	(i)	(ii)

50. Match the options of Column I with correct options in Column II

Column I		Column II
A. Rupee-Pound exchange rate changes from ₹ 95 - £ 1 to ₹ 65 - £ 1	(i)	Rupee is appreciating
B. Rupee-Pound exchange rate changes from ₹ 65 - £1 to ₹ 95 - £1	(ii)	Rupee is depreciating
C. Rupee-Pound exchange rate increased by the central bank	(iii)	Rupee is devalued

Codes

	A	B	C		A	B	C
(a)	(i)	(ii)	(iii)	(b)	(iii)	(ii)	(i)
(c)	(ii)	(i)	(iii)	(d)	(ii)	(iii)	(i)

51. Choose the correctly matched pair from the following

Column I		Column II
A. Demand of foreign exchange	(i)	Inflow of foreign exchange
B. Supply of foreign exchange	(ii)	Outflow of foreign exchange
C. Excess demand	(iii)	Exchange rate < Price of foreign currency
D. Excess supply	(iv)	Receipts from export of goods and services

Codes

(a) A-(i) (b) B-(ii)
(c) C-(iii) (d) D-(iv)

52. Choose the correctly matched pair from the following

Column I		Column II
A. Gold standard system of exchange rate	(i)	An old variant of fixed exchange rate system
B. Spot market	(ii)	Allow hedging
C. Par exchange rate	(iii)	More rupee are needed to buy one US $
D. Degree of speculation	(iv)	Very high in the fixed exchange rate system

Codes

(a) A-(i) (b) B-(ii)
(c) C-(iii) (d) D-(iv)

53. Match the options of Column I with correct options in Column II **Competency Based Que**

Column I		Column II
A. Increase in demand for foreign exchange	(i)	Improvement in the domestic trade balance
B. Increase in supply of foreign exchange	(ii)	Increased foreign investment in the domestic country
C. Decrease in demand for foreign exchange	(iii)	Imposition of import restrictions or tariffs
D. Decrease in supply of foreign exchange	(iv)	Political instability in the domestic country

Codes

	A	B	C	D
(a)	(iii)	(ii)	(iv)	(i)
(b)	(iv)	(ii)	(i)	(iii)
(c)	(iv)	(iii)	(i)	(ii)
(d)	(i)	(ii)	(iii)	(iv)

Concept Identification

54. The point where demand for foreign currency and supply of foreign currency are equal to each other.

55. A rise in the value of domestic currency in relation to a foreign currency.

56. Protection against the risk related to variations in foreign exchange rate.

57. The exchange rate which prevails in the market when transactions are made.

58. A sort of 'contracted' exchange rate to be applicable for the transactions which are signed today but are to be honoured sometimes in the future.

Answers

1. (c) foreign exchange rate
2. (d) to protect domestic producer
3. (c) the country will become an importer of the goods
4. (a) Fixed exchange rate
5. (b) Stable and predictable exchange rates
6. (b) a reduction in the cost of imports
7. (b) flexible
8. (b) floating
9. (d) I and IV
10. (d) Loans from Rest of the World (RoW)
11. (c) inflow of foreign currency and employment generation
12. (c) Donation of $ 50 million received from Microsoft
13. (d) It encourages speculation in the foreign exchange market
14. (c) managed floating exchange rate system
15. (c) managed floating
16. (c) Under managed floating exchange rate system, considering the depreciation of Indian currency, the Reserve Bank of India has decided to purchase Indian currency in the open market
17. (a) Appreciation of domestic currency
18. (a) Increase
19. (b) depreciation
20. (c) The US dollar could become less attractive to investors as other currencies might offer higher returns
21. (b) A spot market for foreign exchange
22. (d) I and III
23. (a) deals with foreign exchange transactions intended for delivery in the future
24. (b) forward market
25. (a) fixed exchange rate system
26. Pound sterling
27. September, 1975
28. (c) Both (a) and (b)
29. (b) Exchange rates are the value at which one currency can be exchanged for another
30. floating (or flexible)
31. imports, exports
32. (a) The inflation rate in both countries
33. (a) Both Assertion (A) and Reason (R) are true and Reason (R) is the correct explanation of Assertion (A)
34. (b) Both Assertion (A) and Reason (R) are true, but Reason (R) is not the correct explanation of Assertion (A)
35. (b) Both Assertion (A) and Reason (R) are true, but Reason (R) is not the correct explanation of Assertion (A)
36. (a) Both Assertion (A) and Reason (R) are true and Reason (R) is the correct explanation of Assertion (A)
37. (b) Both Assertion (A) and Reason (R) are true, but Reason (R) is not the correct explanation of Assertion (A)
38. (a) Both Assertion (A) and Reason (R) are true and Reason (R) is the correct explanation of Assertion (A)
39. (c) There is no central bank intervention. If manipulated, it becomes managed floating exchange rate system.
40. (a) Both Assertion (A) and Reason (R) are true and Reason (R) is the correct explanation of Assertion (A)
41. (b) While demand and supply play a significant role in determining exchange rates, they are not the sole factors. Other factors such as interest rates, inflation, government intervention, and economic indicators also influence exchange rates.
42. (a) A flexible exchange rate system can actually introduce more uncertainty in the foreign exchange market, as currency values fluctuate frequently with changes in market sentiment, economic data and other external factors.
43. (b) The price of a given currency in terms of another is called the exchange rate.
44. (b) Under managed floating exchange rate, exchange rate is determined by market forces.
45. (b) To restore the value of depreciating domestic currency, central bank will sell the foreign currency in the international market.
46. (b) Revaluation is an increase in the value of a country's currency as a result of a government or central bank's decision under a fixed exchange rate system. Appreciation is an increase in a currency's value due to market forces, such as higher demand for that currency, in a flexible or floating exchange rate system. While both terms involve an increase in currency value, they occur under different systems and mechanisms, so they are not the same concept.
47. (a) The spot exchange rate is the current exchange rate for immediate transactions, not for forward transactions. Forward transactions are conducted at a forward exchange rate, which is agreed upon today for delivery at a future date.
48. (b) Some participants in the forward market may use contracts for speculative purposes, but this is not the primary reason for the existence of forward markets. The core purpose of forward markets is to manage and mitigate price risk rather than to speculate on future price movements.
49. (b) (ii) (iii) (i)
50. (a) (i) (ii) (iii)
51. (c) C-(iii)
52. (a) A-(i)
53. (b) (iv) (ii) (i) (iii)
54. Equilibrium exchange rate
55. Currency appreciation
56. Hedging
57. Spot exchange rate
58. Forward exchange rate

Subjective Questions

Short Answer Type Questions

1. Discuss some of the exchange rate arrangements that countries have entered into to bring about stability in their external accounts. NCERT

Ans. The exchange rate arrangements that countries have entered into brings about stability in their external accounts, these are flexible exchange rates, fixed exchange rates and managed floating exchange rates.

The fixed exchange rate is what is fixed and is declared by the government. The flexible exchange rates are which is established by the demand and supply of various currencies in the international market.

The managed floating exchange rate is when the central bank allows the market forces to determine the exchange rate.

2. According to a report in The Economic Times, "An increase in the exchange rate can influence a country's economic indicators like national income." Do you agree with statement? Support your answer with valid argument. Competency Based Que

Ans. Yes, I agree with the statement that an increase in the exchange rate can influence a country's economic indicators like GDP growth.

The national income will increase when there is rise in exchange rate. Domestic currency depreciates when there is a rise in foreign exchange rate.

The foreign countries can now purchase more quantity of goods and services from the same amount of foreign currency from the domestic country. As a result, exports will rise and imports will fall. A rise in the export raises the level of aggregate demand which further raises the level of output and income.

Hence, as the domestic currency depreciates an economy experiences trade surplus. This in turn boosts the national income.

3. How fixed rate of exchange is determined?

Ans. A fixed rate is determined by the government through its central bank. To maintain its exchange rate, the government will buy and sell its own currency against the currency to which it is fixed. Such a rate of exchange has been associated with Gold Standard System during 1830-1918.

According to this system, value of every currency is determined in terms of gold. Accordingly, ratio between gold value of the two currencies was fixed as exchange rate between those currencies.

4. Examine two benefits and drawbacks of a fixed exchange rate system.

Ans. Benefits of fixed exchange rate are as follows

(i) It ensures stability in the international money market.

(ii) It encourages international trade.

The drawbacks of a fixed exchange rate include

(i) Preventing adjustments for currencies that become under or overvalued.

(ii) Fixed exchange rate discourages venture capital in the international money market.

5. Analyse the diagram given below and explain the mechanism of determining the exchange rate. Competency Based Que

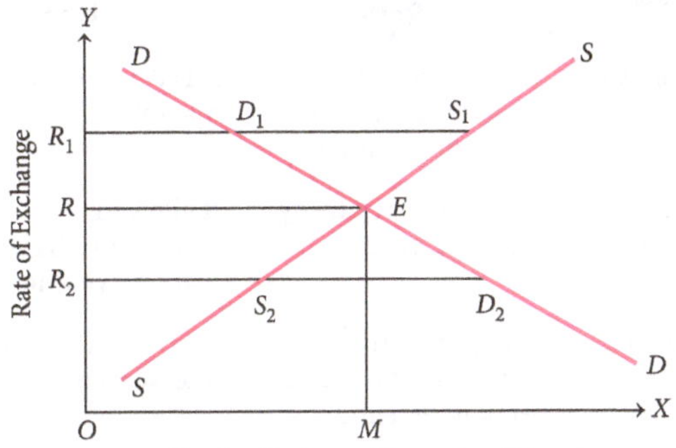

Or **How is exchange rate determined under a flexible exchange rate regime?** NCERT

Ans. In the figure, X-axis represents demand for and supply of foreign currency and Y-axis represents the exchange rate.

DD is the demand curve that is downward slopping, showing an inverse relationship between the rate of exchange and demand for foreign currency.

Whereas, the supply curve is upward sloping, showing positive relationship between the rate of exchange and the supply of foreign currency.

'*E*' is the equilibrium rate of exchange, where the demand equates the supply of foreign exchange (*OR*).

Now, if the exchange rate rises to OR_1, then the supply exceeds the demand, forcing the exchange rate to fall back to *OR*.

On the contrary, if the exchange rate falls to OR_2, there is excess demand over supply. Hence, the rate of exchange rises from R_2 to *R*. Hence, the equilibrium exchange rate (*OR*) is determined by demand and supply of foreign currency.

6. Identify two factors each contributing to the demand and supply of foreign exchange.

Ans. Factors contributing to demand of foreign exchange

(i) To purchase goods and services from other countries i.e. import.

(ii) To send a gift abroad.

Factors contributing to supply of foreign exchange

(i) Foreigners purchasing home countries goods and services through exports.

(ii) Foreign investment in home country through joint ventures and through financial market operation.

7. Distinguish between fixed and flexible foreign exchange rate.

Ans. Difference between fixed and flexible foreign exchange rate are

Basis	Fixed Exchange Rate	Flexible Exchange Rate
Determination	It is determined by government or central bank intervention.	It is determined by market forces.
Currency Valuation	It maintain relatively stable currency values.	It allow for fluctuations based on market dynamics.
Government Intervention	It require active government or central bank intervention.	It involve less frequent intervention.
Stability and Volatility	It offer stability but can be vulnerable to speculative attacks.	It introduce more volatility but provide resilience to external shocks.

8. Explain the relationship between a fall in the price of a foreign currency and the subsequent increase in demand for that currency. **Competency Based Que**

Ans. Foreign exchange rate has an inverse relationship with the demand for foreign currency. With a fall in the price of foreign exchange, the value of domestic currency increases and that of foreign currency falls.

It implies that foreign goods become cheaper and their domestic demand increases.

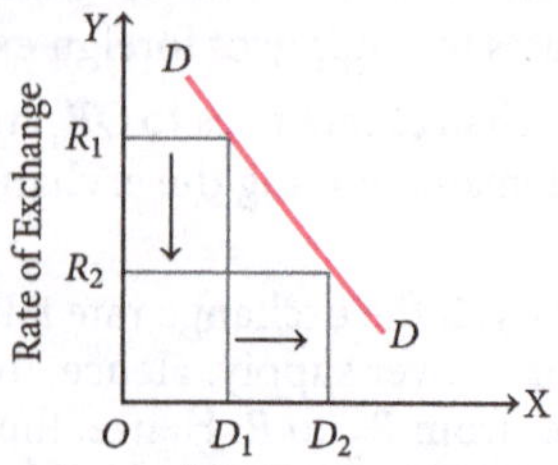

The rising domestic demand for foreign goods implies higher demand for foreign exchange which increases from OD_1 to OD_2, when exchange rate falls from OR_1 to OR_2, as shown in the figure.

9. Explain the effect of

(i) depreciation of domestic currency on exports.

(ii) appreciation of domestic currency on exports.

Ans. (i) Domestic currency depreciates when there is a rise in foreign exchange rate. The foreign countries can now purchase more quantity of goods and services from the same amount of foreign currency from the domestic country.

(ii) Domestic currency appreciates when there is a fall in foreign exchange rate. The domestic economy can now buy more quantity of goods and services from foreign countries for the less amount of domestic currency. As a result, export discourages and imports rises.

10. Explain the effect of

(i) appreciation of home currency on imports of the country.

(ii) depreciation of home currency on imports of the country.

Ans. (i) Home (domestic) currency appreciates when there is a fall in foreign exchange rate. The domestic economy can now buy more quantity of goods and services from foreign countries for the same amount of domestic currency. As a result, imports will rise and exports will fall.

(ii) Home (domestic) currency depreciates when there is a rise in foreign exchange rate. The domestic country can now buy less quantity of goods and services from foreign countries for the same amount of domestic currency. As a result, imports will fall and exports will rise.

11. Do you agree with the following statements? Give reason.

(i) "Less developed countries frequently engage in the devaluation of their currency."

(ii) "A fall in the value of domestic currency induces the private investment." **Competency Based Que**

Ans. (i) Yes, less developed countries often devalue their currency. This is because of the three principal reasons

- Devaluation, implying a planned fall in the value of the domestic currency is expected to raise the demand for the domestically produced goods and services. Accordingly, exports are expected to rise.
- Rise in exports is expected to increase the supply of foreign exchange into the domestic economy. This facilitates the import of essential goods from the rest of the world.

- A fall in the value of domestic currency induces private foreign investment. This is expected to promote GDP growth.

(ii) No, because a rise in exchange rate (currency depreciation) may not always lead to a rise in our export earnings.
A rise in exchange rate is beneficial only when elasticity of demand for our exports is greater than unity. Moreover, exports from domestic country are majorly dependent upon the demand for domestic goods in the international market.

12. "India is taking huge leaps in the index of ease of doing business, as a result, many MNCs are shifting their production base to India."
In the light of the above statement, comment upon the flow of foreign exchange and its likely impact on the Indian economy. **CBSE 2020; Competency Based Que**

Ans. The statement is correct that with improvements in the ease of doing business, India has the potential to attract more Multinational Corporations (MNCs) to establish their production bases and expand their activities in the country. As a result, this will lead to an increase in Foreign Direct Investment (FDI), which brings in more foreign exchange (such as US dollars) into the Indian economy. This inflow of foreign exchange will increase its supply in the market, which could lead to a decrease in the foreign exchange rate. In simpler terms, it means that the Indian Rupee (₹) may appreciate (₹).
Furthermore, the growth in MNC presence in India, driven by higher FDI, will not only boost production but also create more employment opportunities within the Indian economy, supporting overall economic growth.

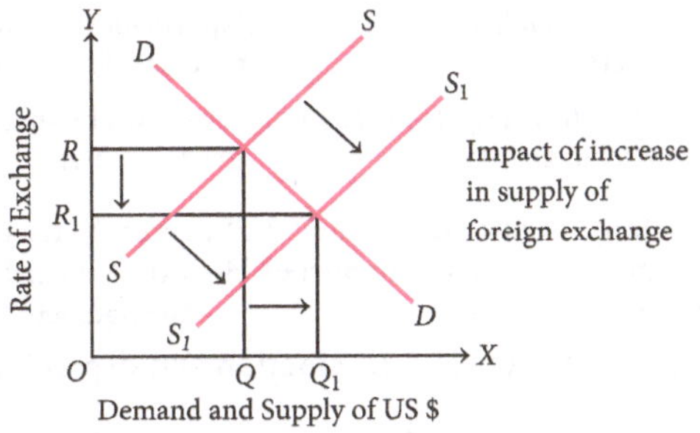

As the supply of foreign exchange increases, the exchange rate falls from OR to OR_1.

13. 7th August, 2024; Money Control : "Rupee plunges to record low of ₹ 83.9725 against US dollar ($)."
In the light of the above report, discuss the impact of the situation of Indian imports'. **Competency Based Que**

Ans. As the value of Indian rupees reached to its lowest, this shows that the value of Indian rupee is falling as compared with USD.
Also, due to depreciation of rupee, Indians will find imported goods costlier. So, our imports will decrease and at the same time, exports from India will become cheaper for foreigners, leading to increase in exports.

14. "US dollar has recorded a jump of 0·75 paise per dollar (p/$) in the last one month; this situation might bring smiles and sorrows to different types of traders (exporters and importers)." Justify the given statement. **Competency Based Que**

Ans. The statement suggests that the US dollar has increased in value by 0.75 paise per dollar in the last month. The given condition indicates to the situation of depreciation of home currency (₹) with respect to foreign currency (US $).
This implies that more units of Indian currency (₹) are to be paid to buy one unit of foreign currency (US $). This has both positive and negative effects on different types of traders.
This may lead to sorrows for importers, as they have to pay higher amount for their imports. Also, this may bring smiles for exporters, as they would be getting higher earnings for their exports.

15. "Foreign Institutional Investors (FIIs) remained net seller in the Indian capital markets over the last few weeks." – The Economic Times
State and discuss the likely effects of the given statement on foreign exchange rate with reference to the Indian economy. **CBSE SQP 2020; Competency Based Que**

Ans. Selling of securities by Foreign Institutional Investors (FII's) in Indian capital market will lead to fall in the supply of foreign currency in the economy. This situation might lead to excess demand of foreign currency at the prevailing foreign exchange rate.
As a result, a new equilibrium rate of foreign exchange will be determined which will be higher than the prevailing foreign exchange rate, leading to depreciation of domestic currency.

16. Explain the concept of a managed floating exchange rate system briefly.

Ans. It is a mixture of a flexible exchange rate system (the float Part) and a fixed exchange rate system (the managed part).
In this system, the exchange rate is determined in the foreign exchange market freely by the market forces. However, excessive fluctuations in the exchange rate are checked by the central bank.
Managed floating is also known as dirty floating, if a country manipulates the exchange rate by not following rules and regulations.

e.g. If the rupee-dollar exchange rate in the foreign exchange market changes from ₹ 70 to ₹ 90, then this comes under excessive fluctuation. In such a situation, the central bank will intervene by increasing the supply of dollar in the market.

17. Identify the type of exchange rate system shown in the image below and write any two advantages of this regime. Competency Based Que

Ans. The image given above is indicating managed floating exchange rate system.

Advantages of managed floating exchange rate system are

(i) **Enhances Market Efficiency**
The macroeconomics affects the exchange rate in international markets, which affects the share market of nations, forcing governments to perform better.

(ii) **Favourable Market Conditions for the Country**
It is determined by demand and supply. Hence, the exchange rate increases if market conditions are favourable to the country. Accordingly, the government gets the benefit of the same.

18. "A country deliberately keeps the value of its currency low under the managed floating system." Discuss briefly how it will affect the exports of the country. CBSE 2020 C; Competency Based Que

Ans. If a country deliberately keeps the value of its currency low under the managed floating system, it can have a positive effect on the exports of the country.

A low valued currency makes the country's exports cheaper in foreign markets, which can increase the demand for those exports. This is because foreign buyers can purchase more units of the country's exports for the same amount of their own currency, making the exports more attractive and competitive. As a result, the country's export revenues may increase, leading to economic growth and development.

On the other hand, a low valued currency can also make imports into the country more expensive, as it takes more units of the country's currency to purchase the same amount of foreign goods. This can lead to higher prices for imported goods, which may be passed on to consumers.

Overall, a country deliberately keeping the value of its currency low under the managed floating system can have both positive and negative effects on the country's trade balance.

19. Would the central bank need to intervene in managed floating system? Explain why? NCERT

Ans. Managed floating system is a hybrid system that combines the features of both systems of exchange, i.e. fixed exchange rate system and flexible exchange rate system. In this system, the central bank can intervene to purchase or sell foreign currencies in an effort to moderate exchange rate movements, whenever they feel such actions are appropriate.

20. Explain the relationship between fall in price of a US Dollar ($) and its demand. CBSE 2020

Ans. Fall in the price of a US Dollar ($) is a situation when less Indian rupees are needed to buy a unit of US Dollar ($). It leads to a rise in demand for foreign goods and services. Accordingly, demand for foreign currency tends to rise.

e.g. When the price of foreign currency falls, it becomes cheaper to go abroad for higher education. Number of students going abroad will rise, leading to a rise in demand for foreign currency.

21 Distinguish between appreciation of home currency and depreciation of home currency. CBSE 2019

Ans. Difference between appreciation of home currency and depreciation of home currency are

Basis	Appreciation of Home Currency	Depreciation of Home Currency
Meaning	It refers to increase in the value of domestic currency as compared with foreign currency due to changes in market forces of demand and supply.	If refers to decrease in the value of domestic currency as compared with foreign currency due to changes in the market forces of demand and supply.
Effect	Exports fall and imports increase.	Exports increase and imports fall.
Shown By	It is shown by decrease in exchange rate.	It is shown by increase in exchange rate.

22. "Devaluation and depreciation of currency are one and the same thing." Do you agree? How do they affect the exports of a country? Competency Based Que

Or **Differentiate between devaluation and depreciation.** NCERT

Ans. No, I do not agree with the given statement. Devaluation is the fall in the value of domestic currency in relation to foreign currency as planned by the government in a situation when exchange rate is not determined by the forces of demand and supply but is fixed by the government of different countries.

On the other hand, depreciation is the fall in the value of domestic currency in relation to foreign currency in a situation when exchange rate is determined by the forces of demand and supply in the international money market.

As a general phenomenon, any depreciation/devaluation of currency may result into increase in exports of the goods and services from the country since it would increase the global competitiveness of the goods.

23. **"Devaluation of currency and depreciation of currency have the same implications, but they originate from divergent sources."**

Do you agree with the given statement? Give valid reason in support of your answer.

CBSE 2024 C; Competency Based Que

Ans. Yes, I agree with the given statement. Devaluation and depreciation of currency may have the same implications such as making exports cheaper and imports costlier, which can boost a country's exports, however, they originate from different sources

(i) **Devaluation**
It is a deliberate decision by the government to lower the value of its currency in a fixed exchange rate system. It occurs due to policy actions taken by the central bank or the government to make exports competitive.

(ii) **Depreciation**
It occurs automatically due to market forces of demand and supply in a floating exchange rate system. Factors like inflation, interest rate differences or trade imbalances may lead to depreciation.

24. **Analyse the given image carefully and state the impact of Indian rupee depreciating on the economy.**

Competency Based Que

Measure – Indian Rupees per USD

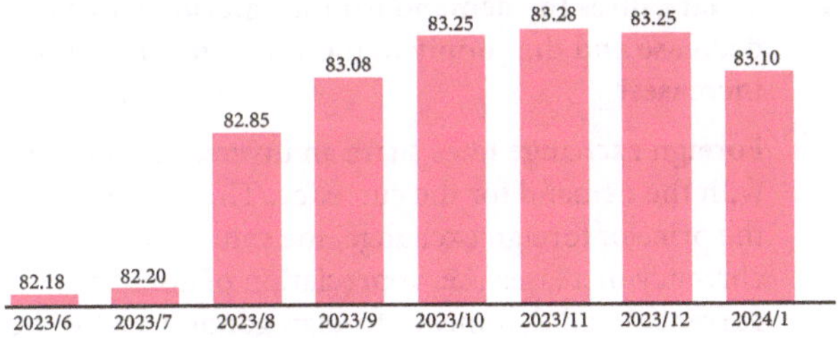

Source *Google Finance*

Ans. The currency chart for India shows data for the Indian rupees per USD exchange rate. An increase, means depreciation of Indian rupees against the USD. The series shown in graph from 2023 to January 2024 for India.

The most recent available data point is ₹ 83.10 Indian rupees per USD, a change of – 0.19% from the previous data point of ₹ 83.25 Indian rupees per USD.

Depreciation implies that goods from India become cheaper to export and it becomes cheaper for foreigners to visit India.

25. **According to the Financial Times, "The foreign exchange market plays a critical role in the global economy, influencing trade, investment and financial stability across borders."**

Based on this statement, explain the main functions of the foreign exchange market.

Ans. The foreign exchange market is essential to the global economy, performing several key functions that facilitate international economic activities.

The various functions are as follows

(i) **Transfer Function**
The basic and the most obvious function of the foreign exchange market is to transfer the funds or the foreign currencies from one country to another for settling their payments. The market basically converts one's currency to another.

(ii) **Credit Function**
The FOREX provides short-term credit to the importers in order to facilitate the smooth flow of goods and services from various countries. The importer can use his own credit to finance foreign purchases.

(iii) **Hedging Function**
The third function of a foreign exchange market is to hedge the foreign exchange risks. The parties in the foreign exchange are often afraid of the fluctuations in the exchange rates, which means the price of one currency in terms of another currency. This might result in a gain or loss to the party concerned.

26. Write short notes on

(i) Spot market (ii) Forward market

Ans. (i) **Spot Market**
The market which handles only spot or current transactions of foreign exchanges is termed as spot market or current market. In this market, payment is made and received on the spot.
However, a window of two business days is given to settle the transaction, in case the payment is being made through cheques. The rate at which transactions in spot market takes place is referred to as spot exchange rate or current rate of exchange.

(ii) **Forward Market**
The market which deals with the purchase and sale of foreign exchange that are contracted today, but are implemented in future is called forward market. In this market, foreign currency is to be bought or sold on a specified date in future on the rate settled upon today. The rate at which transactions are settled upon is referred to as forward exchange rate.

Long Answer Type Questions

27. Describe the merits and demerits of fixed exchange rate.

Ans. In a fixed exchange rate system, a country fixes its currency to another currency or a basket of currencies at a specific rate.

Merits of fixed exchange rate are as follows

(i) **Stability and Predictability**

Fixed exchange rates offer stability and predictability for businesses engaged in international trade.

(ii) **Inflation Control**

Fixed exchange rates can help control inflation.

(iii) **Exchange Rate Risk Mitigation**

Businesses and investors can hedge against exchange rate risk more effectively in a fixed exchange rate system because the rates are stable.

(iv) **Promotes Trade and Investment**

Fixed exchange rates can promote international trade and foreign direct investment by reducing currency risk for companies.

Demerits of fixed exchange rate are as follows

(i) **Limited Policy Autonomy**

Countries with fixed exchange rates have limited control over their domestic monetary policy. They must maintain currency reserves to defend the fixed rate.

(ii) **Vulnerability to Speculation**

Fixed exchange rates can make a country vulnerable to speculative attacks by investors who bet against the currency's fixed.

(iii) **External Shocks**

Fixed exchange rate systems can be vulnerable to external economic shocks.

(iv) **Imbalance in Trade**

Fixed exchange rates can lead to trade imbalances if the currency's value doesn't adjust to changes in the country's economic conditions. This can result in persistent trade deficits or surpluses.

28. Define foreign exchange and foreign exchange rate. Then, using explanations, clarify how the foreign exchange rate influences the demand for foreign exchange.

Ans. Foreign Exchange

It refers to the reserve of foreign currencies in the domestic country. Foreign exchange plays a key role in international transactions. For India, all the currencies other than Indian rupee are foreign exchange.

Foreign Exchange Rate

It is the rate at which one currency is exchanged for other currency in the foreign exchange market.

It is the rate at which one unit of a foreign currency is exchanged for domestic currency. e.g. If ₹ 50 is paid to buy one US dollar, then the exchange rate between the two currencies are 50 : 1 or $1 = ₹ 50.

Relation between Foreign Exchange Rate and Demand for Foreign Exchange

There is an inverse relationship between the foreign exchange rate and demand for foreign exchange.

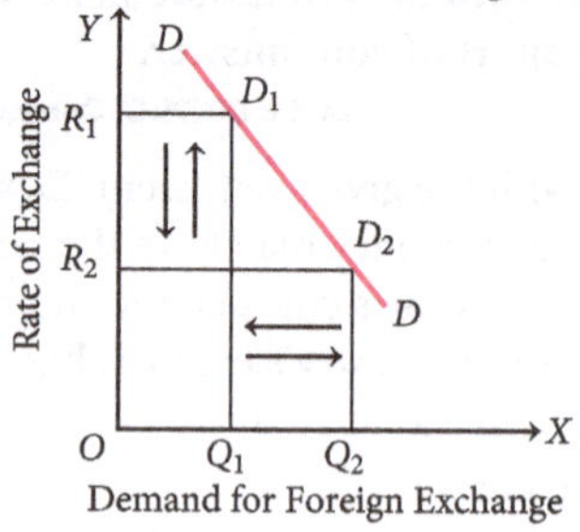

In the given figure, *DD* curve represents the demand for foreign currency. When exchange rate rises to R_1, demand for the foreign currency falls to Q_1.

On the other hand, when exchange rate falls to R_2, demand for the foreign currency rises to Q_2.

The demand curve for the foreign currency is always downward sloping and signifies an inverse relationship between demand and exchange rate.

A rise in exchange rate means that greater units of domestic currency is required to be paid for same unit of foreign currency. This makes import costlier. As a result, import falls leading to a fall in the demand for foreign exchange.

29. What causes the demand for foreign currency to decrease and the supply to increase when its price increases? **Competency Based Que**

Ans. Foreign exchange rates share an inverse relationship with the demand for the currency. Thus, with a fall in the price of foreign exchange, the value of domestic currency increases (i.e. appreciation of domestic currency) and that means foreign goods become cheaper and their domestic demand (i.e. imports) increases.

The rising domestic demand for foreign goods implies higher demand for foreign exchanges.

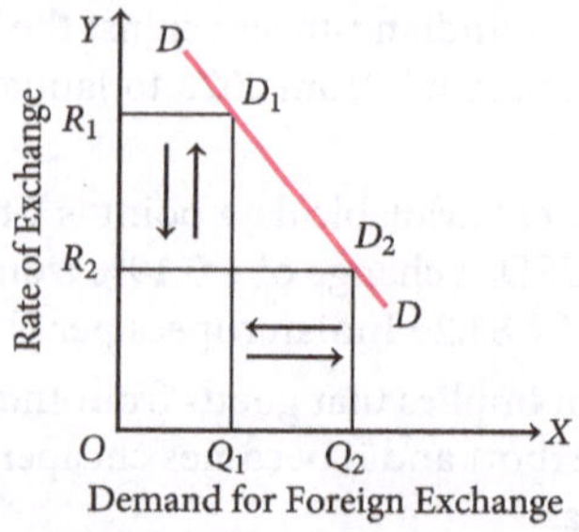

The supply of foreign currency is directly proportional to the price of foreign exchanges. When the price of a foreign currency falls, it leads to cheaper imports because it leads to appreciation of domestic currency. The exporters are discouraged due to costlier exports.

This results in lesser inflow or supply of foreign currency in the economy. As a result supply of foreign exchange decreases from OQ_2 to OQ_1 as shown in the figure.

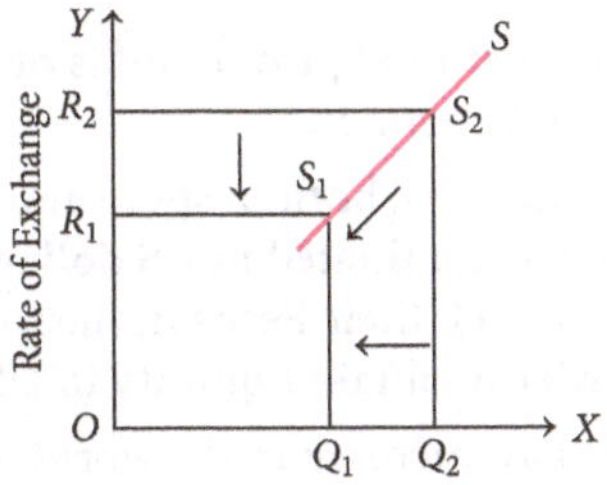

Supply of Foreign Currency

30. Describe the merits and demerits of flexible exchange rate.

Ans. The exchange rate for the currency is determined by the forces of demand and supply of different currencies in the foreign exchange market.

Merits of flexible exchange rate are as follows

(i) **Independent Monetary Policy**
Under flexible exchange rate system, a country is free to adopt an independent policy to conduct properly the domestic economic affairs.

(ii) **Shock Absorber**
A fluctuating exchange rate system protects the domestic economy from the shocks produced by the disturbances generated in other countries.
Thus, it acts as a shock absorber and saves the internal economy from the disturbing effects from abroad.

(iii) **Promotes Economic Development**
The flexible exchange rate system promotes economic development and helps to achieve full employment in the country.

(iv) **Solutions to Balance of Payment Problems**
The system of flexible exchange rates automatically removes the disequilibrium in the balance of payments.

Demerits of flexible exchange rate are as follows

(i) **Unstable Conditions**
Flexible exchange rates create conditions of instability and uncertainty which, in turn, tend to reduce the volume of international trade and foreign investment.

(ii) **Adverse Effect on Economic Structure**
The system of flexible exchange rates has serious repercussion on the economic structure of the economy. Fluctuating exchange rates cause changes in the price of imported and exported goods which, in turn, destabilise the economy of the country.

(iii) **Unnecessary Capital Movements**
The system of fluctuating exchange rates leads to unnecessary international capital movements. By encouraging speculative activities, such a system causes large-scale capital outflows and inflows, thus, seriously disturbing the economy of the country.

(iv) **Inflationary Effect**
Flexible exchange rate system involves greater possibility of inflationary effect of exchange depreciation on domestic price level of a country.

31. What will be its likely impact on foreign exchange rate and how? Competency Based Que

(i) Visits to foreign countries for sightseeing, etc. by the people of India is on the rise.

(ii) Giving incentives for exports.

(iii) Rise of foreign exchange rate in India.

Ans. (i) When there is a rise in the visit to foreign countries by the people in India, the demand for foreign currency increases.
With the supply of foreign currency remaining same, the foreign exchange rate rises, implying a depreciation of rupee.

(ii) The incentives for exports boost exports for the country. As a result of increase in exports, the supply of foreign currency in the country increases. With demand remaining the same, this results in a fall in the exchange rate, implying currency appreciation.

(iii) With the rise in foreign exchange rate in India, the demand for foreign currency increases. This rise in exchange rate implies depreciation in domestic currency. It encourages exports from a country and discourages imports from rest of the world.

32. Explain the difference managed floating exchange rate and flexible exchange rate.

Ans. Difference between managed floating exchange rate and flexible exchange rate are

Basis	Managed Floating Exchange Rate	Flexible exchange Rate
Determination	It is determined by forces of demand and supply with occasional government intervention.	It is determined by the demand and supply forces only.

Basis	Managed Floating Exchange Rate	Flexible exchange Rate
Name	It is also called dirty floating system.	It is also called free exchange rate system.
Fluctuations	Fluctuations are relatively less as government intervenes to ensure that the rate does not fluctuate much.	As it is determined by demand and supply forces, it is prone to more fluctuations.
Government Intervention	Government intervenes by selling or purchasing foreign currency in the international market.	No intervention.
Predictability of Trade	It is relatively more predictable as the variations in exchange rates are governed by the monetary authorities.	Unpredictable as the exchange rate is flexible in nature.

33. **"Recently, the rate of dollars has shot up and the Indian rupee has become very weak against dollars."**

What does this indicate? Also, explain its effect on the economy and balance of trade of the country. How will the RBI control this situation? Competency Based Que

Ans. When Indian rupee becomes weaker against US dollars, then it is known as domestic currency depreciation.

e.g. 1$ = ₹ 60 to 1$ = ₹ 65. This shows domestic currency depreciation i.e. now an Indian has to pay more rupees in order to buy 1$.

Currency depreciation has two major effects

(i) It will lead to an increase in exports because domestic goods are now cheaper.

(ii) It will also lead to a decrease in imports because foreign goods are now costlier.

So, the balance of trade will be on the surplus side since exports are increasing and imports are decreasing.

As far as the RBI is concerned, in order to reduce this high foreign exchange rate, it will increase the supply of foreign exchange by selling the foreign exchange from its reserves so as to bring down its value; through managed floating rate system.

34. **Oil imports represent a significant fraction of the trade balance for energy dependant economies. In the case of small open economies with floating exchange rates, the variability in oil prices is expected to have a large impact on the relative value of the currency.**

Since oil contracts are denominated in US dollars, changes in the price of oil have significant implications for the demand and supply of foreign exchange.

This relationship between the price of oil and the exchange rate has been established by the literature for oil producing countries but not for oil importing countries.

The case of the Dominican Republic, an energy dependant small open economy with a floating exchange rate is used to illustrate this connection.

In the case of the Dominican Republic, oil imports in 2003 represented 27 percent of total imports, which is up from 17 percent in 1994.

Thus, the international price of oil is of great relevance to the Dominican economy.

Because oil contracts, both in spot values and in future contracts, are denominated in US dollars, Dominican importers must sell their Pesos in the foreign exchange market in order to obtain liquidity in US dollars.

It follows that an increase in the world price of oil would place a depreciating pressure on the Dominican Peso, whereas a decrease in the world price of oil would allow for an appreciation of the Dominican currency.

The Dominican Republic needs of crude oil have been traditionally covered by Mexico, although in the last five years, Venezuela has increased its market quota.

Since the domestic refining capacity has not kept pace with the growing energy demands, the imports of refined gasoline have quickly surpassed those of crude oil. Therefore, the prices of Venezuelan Tia Juana, Mexican Isthmus and Mexican Mayan crude oils as well as the price of gasoline are relevant for this analysis. Both spot and future contract prices are considered.

(i) How does oil prices get affected by changes in exchange rate?

(ii) What is foreign exchange market and what are its functions? Competency Based Que

Ans. (i) Exchange rates can affect oil prices both directly and indirectly. This can occur through financial markets, portfolio rebalancing and hedging strategies. As oil prices are expressed in US dollars, oil futures may be a good hedge against an expected depreciation in the USD. Any change in the exchange rate (depreciation or appreciation of domestic currency) impacts the import bill for oil accordingly.

(ii) Foreign exchange market is a market where buyers and sellers trade foreign currencies.

Simply stated, a foreign exchange market is a market where various countries' currencies are bought and sold.

For functions of foreign exchange market, refer to Q.No. 25 of short answer type questions.

SELF ASSESSMENT TEST

Objective Type Questions

1. Gold standard system was part of .... exchange rate.
   (a) fixed (b) flexible
   (c) managed floating (d) None of these
2. Rise in exports leads to .... of foreign exchange.
   (a) outflow (b) inflow
   (c) no flow (d) None of these
3. In foreign exchange market, foreign exchange rate between Indian rupee and US dollar changes from ₹ 65/1$ to ₹ 60/1$. This refers to
   (a) appreciation of Indian currency
   (b) depreciation of US currency
   (c) appreciation of Indian currency and depreciation of US currency
   (d) depreciation of Indian currency and appreciation of US currency
4. What will be the effect of appreciation on domestic currency?
   (a) Imports will fall and exports will rise
   (b) Both exports and imports will fall
   (c) Imports will rise and exports will fall
   (d) Both exports and imports will rise
5. Buying and selling of foreign currencies take place at
   (a) goods market
   (b) gold market
   (c) foreign exchange market
   (d) All of the above
6. The forward market is primarily used by
   (a) individuals making small currency exchanges
   (b) businesses looking to hedge against currency fluctuations
   (c) tourists converting travel funds
   (d) local banks conducting domestic transactions
7. Which of the following statements is/are correct?
   I. Intentional increase in the price of exchange rate is a step under flexible exchange rate.
   II. Appreciation and depreciation of currency are also the components of managed floating exchange rate.

   Codes
   (a) Only I
   (b) Only II
   (c) Both I and II
   (d) None of the above

Answers 1. (a) 2. (b) 3. (c) 4. (c) 5. (c) 6. (b) 7. (b)

Short Answer Type Questions

8. "A fixed exchange rate system involves pegging a currency to another major currency or a basket of currencies. While it offers stability, it often limits a country's ability to adjust to economic changes and requires large foreign exchange reserves to maintain."
   In reference to above statement, discuss three demerits of a fixed foreign exchange rate system.
9. Distinguish between devaluation and depreciation of domestic currency.
10. Explain the effect of depreciation of domestic currency on imports.
11. Explain why there is inverse relationship between price of foreign currency and its demand?
12. When the price of a foreign currency falls, the supply of that foreign currency also falls. Explain, why?
13. "A managed floating rate system allows a currency to move with market forces, while the central bank may intervene to influence its value as needed."
    Based on the statement, explain the concept of a managed floating rate system.
14. Distinguish between spot market and forward market of domestic currency.
15. Enumerate the functions of foreign exchange market.

Long Answer Type Questions

16. How is exchange rate determined in the foreign exchange market? Explain the changes that takes place when supply of foreign exchange increases.
17. Explain three sources of demand for foreign exchange and three sources of supply of foreign exchange.

08

CHAPTER

> Balance of payments statistics systematically summarise the economic transactions of an economy with the rest of the world during a given period.
> — *Ministry of Statistics and Programme Implementation*

▼ **YOUR STUDY GOALS**

8.1 Meaning of Balance of Payments (BoP)
8.2 Components of Balance of Payments (BoP)
8.3 Equilibrium and Disequilibrium in BoP

▼ **YOUR PRACTICE GOAL**

- Objective Type Questions (66 Qs ; MCQs, A-R, Statements, Matching, Concept Identification)
- Subjective Questions (27 SAs, 8 LAs)
- 8 Numerical Questions
- Self Assessment Test (7 MCQs, 7 SAs, 3 LAs, 2 Numericals)

Balance of Payments

8.1 Meaning of Balance of Payments (BoP)

It is a systematic record of all **economic transactions** between the residents of a country and the rest of the world in a given period of time, usually one year.

It is prepared on the basis of double entry system of accounting and is a flow concept.

Economic Transactions Recorded in BoP

Transaction	Includes
Transaction involving visible items	All types of physical goods.
Transaction involving invisible items	Services like banking, insurance, etc.
Unilateral transactions (Unrequited transactions)	One-sided transaction like gifts, grants or donations.
Capital transfer transactions	Transactions involving capital receipts and capital payments.

Balance of Payments Structure

BoP account is prepared on a double entry basis, i.e. there are two sides of transactions.

Debit Side	Credit Side
Records transactions that result in the outflow of foreign currency.	Records transactions that result in the inflow of foreign currency.
Debit > Credit ⇒ BoP deficit.	Credit > Debit ⇒ BoP surplus.

8.2 Components of Balance of Payments (BoP)

The following are the two main components of BoP

- Current account
- Capital account

I. Current Account

Current account records the actual receipts and payments relating to export and import of goods and services and unilateral transfers during a given period of time, usually a financial year.

It shows the status of income and trade balance in the country. Also, these transactions do not impact the assets and liabilities of the country.

Components of Current Account

The main components of current account are

Component	Explanation	Adjustment (Recorded)
Export and Import of Visible Items/Goods	This includes export and import of visible items or goods like wheat, rice, machines, etc.	**Debit Side** (Negative side) Payment for import of goods. **Credit Side** (Positive side) Receipt from export of goods.
Export and Import of Invisible Items/Services	Current account also includes export and import of invisible items or services which are further categorised as **Transactions involving Factor Services** Compensation paid to employees, investment income like rent, interest or profit. **Transactions involving Non-factor Services** Transactions involve all services other than factor services like banking, insurance, etc.	**Debit Side** (Negative side) Payment made on account of factor and non-factor services. **Credit Side** (Positive side) Receipts on account of factor and non-factor services.
Unilateral Transfers/Current Transfers	These are the one-way transactions made by residents or non-residents settled abroad. They include gifts, donations and other remittances. In the BoP account, unilateral transfers are a part of 'invisibles'.	**Debit Side** (Negative side) Unilateral transfers made by residents to the rest of the world. **Credit Side** (Positive side) Unilateral transfers received by residents from the rest of the world.

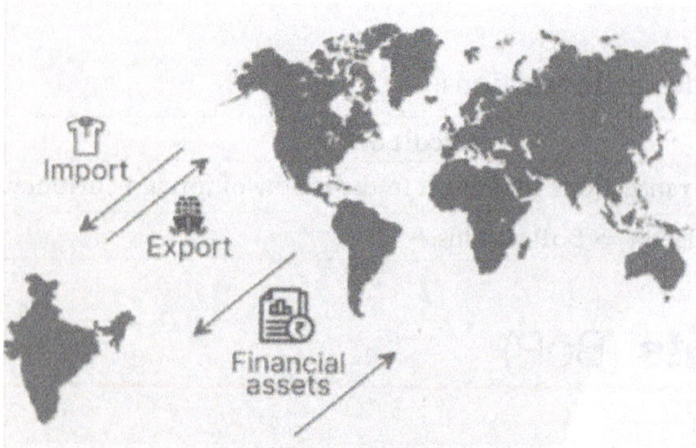

***Balance of Trade* (BoT)**

The term 'balance of trade' means the difference between value of exports and imports of visible goods in a given period of time. It is also known as 'balance of visible trade' or 'trade balance'.

$$BoT = V_x - V_m$$

Where, V_x = Value of goods exported

V_m = Value of goods imported

Deficit in the balance of trade occurs when value of exports of goods are less than value of imports of goods.

Surplus in the balance of trade occurs when value of exports of goods are more than value of imports of goods.

Balance on Current Account

The difference between total of debit and credit items shows the balance of current account.

It can show

Current Account Surplus	Current Account Deficit
It arises when the sum of credit items exceeds the sum of debit items.	It arises when the sum of debit items exceeds the sum of credit items.
It shows net inflow of foreign exchange.	It shows net outflow of foreign exchange.
It signifies that the nation is a lender to the rest of the world.	It signifies that the nation is a borrower from rest of the world.

Balance Related to Current Account

- **Trade Balance** It is the difference between export and import of goods.
- **Goods and Services Balance** It is computed in the following manner
  = Trade Balance + Balance of Non-factor Services
- **Invisibles Balance** It is computed in the following manner
  = Balance of Non-factor Services + Balance of Factor Services
  + Balance on Current Transfers
- **Current Account Balance** It is the sum of trade balance and invisibles' balance.

II. Capital Account

It records capital transactions between the residents of a country and the rest of the world. These transactions cause a change in the assets or liabilities of the residents of the country or its government during a financial year. It is used to finance deficit in current account and absorb surplus of current account.

Components of Capital Account

The main components of capital account are

Component	Explanation	Adjustment (Recorded)
Foreign Investment	It includes investment made by the residents of a country in rest of the world or by the residents of rest of the world in the domestic country. It includes **Foreign Direct Investment** (FDI) It is related to change in ownership status and allows direct control of purchaser over asset. **Foreign Portfolio Investment** (FPI) It refers to purchase of securities/financial assets by investors from another country.	**Debit Side** (Negative side) • Physical assets purchased by the residents of domestic country in rest of the world. • Financial assets purchased by the residents of domestic country in rest of the world. **Credit Side** (Positive side) • Physical assets purchased by the residents of rest of the world in the domestic country. • Financial assets purchased by the residents of rest of the world in the domestic country.

Component	Explanation	Adjustment (Recorded)
Borrowings	Borrowings to and from abroad also affect the assets and liabilities status of the country and are therefore recorded in capital account. It can be further categorised as **External Commercial Borrowing** It is available at market rate of interest in the international money market. **External Assistance** It is available at concessional rate of interest in the international money market.	**Debit Side** (Negative side) • Borrowings to abroad by private sector and government. • Repayment of loans taken from abroad by private sector and government. **Credit Side** (Positive side) • Borrowings from abroad by private sector and government. • Repayment of loans given to the rest of the world by private sector and government.
Other Components	• **NRI Deposits** It refers to deposits held by Non-Resident Indians (NRIs) in India. Here, only deposits held by NRIs in domestic economy are to be considered. • **Banking Capital** It refers to foreign assets held by the commercial banks. • **Short-term Trade Credit** It refers to purchases made in the international market without paying for them immediately.	

Official Reserves Account

This account shows the reserves of Foreign Exchange (FOREX) with the RBI. This account can be shown as a part of the capital account of BoP or as a separate account

- **As a part of Capital Account** In such a case, the BoP always balances.
- **As a Separate Account** In such a case, BoP may or may not balance.

The reserves in this account could be used by a country to balance any deficit in its BoP. The RBI sells foreign exchange when there is a deficit. On the other hand, net inflows or surplus in BoP helps in accumulating the official reserves that helps to cover the deficit, if arises.

Balance on Capital Account

The difference between debit and credit items shows the balance of capital account.

It can show

Capital Account Surplus	Capital Account Deficit
It arises when the sum of credit items exceeds the sum of debit items.	It arises when the sum of debit items exceeds the sum of credit items.
It shows net inflow of foreign exchange.	It shows net outflow of foreign exchange.

Errors and Omissions in BoP

- It is difficult to record all international transactions accurately. Thus, in addition to current account and capital account, there is one more element of BoP, called as errors and omissions.
- The net credit or net debit balance in actual balance of payments is often arises due to errors and omissions in statement compilation, which may be related to practical approximation to principles.
- In balance of payments, it is standard practice to display an item separately for net errors and omissions, also known as a statistical discrepancy or balancing item, to offset the overstatement or understatement of recorded components.

Autonomous and Accommodating Items of BoP

These items in BoP are classified as

Autonomous Items of BoP	Accommodating Items of BoP
• It refers to the international economic transactions which are made with a view to earn profit. • These transactions are independent of the state of BoP. • Autonomous items are called **above the line items** in BoP. • Main autonomous items include export/imports of goods/ services, unilateral transactions, capital transactions	• It refers to those transactions which are taken up by the government in order to keep the BoP balanced. • These transactions are based on the state of BoP and are not carried out with a view to earn profit. • Accommodating items are called **below the line items** in BoP. • Main accommodating items include borrowings from IMF, changes in foreign exchange reserves.

8.3 Equilibrium and Disequilibrium in BoP

BoP of a country can reflect the following two situations

BoP Situations

- **Disequilibrium in BoP**
  - **Surplus in BoP**
    - When the sum of the balance of the current account and capital account is positive.
    - There is inflow of foreign exchange leading to an increase in the official reserves account.
  - **Deficit in BoP**
    - When the sum of the balance of the current account and capital account is negative.
    - There is outflow of foreign exchange leading to decrease in official reserves account.
- **Equilibrium in BoP**
  - When the sum of the balances of the current and capital accounts equals to zero, BoP is said to be in equilibrium.

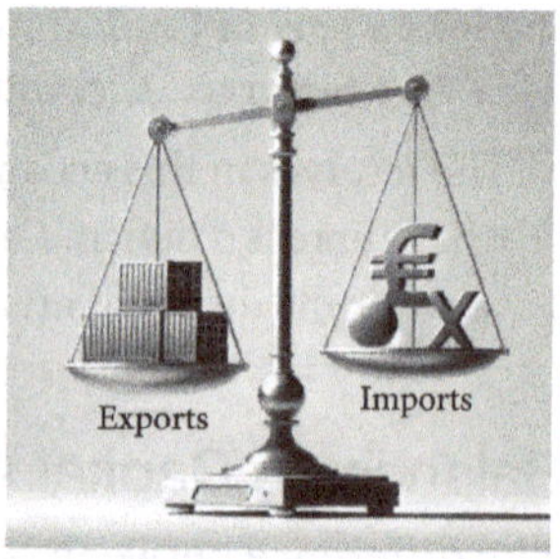

Causes for Surplus in BoP

Surplus in BoP can arise due to the following reasons

Cause	Explanation
Economic Growth	High economic growth leads to increased GDP, which will increase inflow of foreign exchange, resulting in surplus.
Low Level of Inflation	Low inflation in the domestic economy increases demand for domestic goods in international market, leading to increased exports and thus surplus in BoP.
Political Stability	Stable government policies attract foreign investment, further increasing BoP's surplus.

Causes for Deficit in BoP

Deficit in BoP can arise due to the following reasons

Category	Cause	Explanation
Economic Factors	**Inflation**	Increased prices due to higher wages and raw material prices makes export costlier and imports cheaper. This leads to a deficit in the balance of payments.
	Expenditure on Development Relations	Developing countries spend heavily on ambassadors and missions so as to develop relations with other countries negatively impacting the balance of payments.
	Fall in Demand	Fall in foreign market demand reduces exports, impacting balance of payments. e.g. Covid-19 outbreak led to decreased demand for Chinese goods.
	Import Services	Underdeveloped countries import capital and services from developed ones, causing a balance of payments deficit.
Political Factors	**Political Instability**	Instability in the domestic economy leads to foreign investors losing trust and a large outflow of foreign exchange due to preference of domestic investors investing abroad.
	Political Disturbances	Frequent changes in government, inadequate support to the government in Parliament also discourage inflows of capital. This leads to a deficit due to higher outflows than inflows.
Social Factors	**Demonstration Effect**	People of underdeveloped countries following the consumption pattern of developed countries leads to increased imports, resulting in a deficit in the Balance of Payments (BoP) account.
	Change in Tastes and Preferences	Unfavourable changes in consumer tastes and preferences towards domestic goods lead to a deficit in the BoP account.

Note Disequilibrium in balance of payments can be corrected by various methods like promoting exports, reducing imports, depreciation of currency and exercising foreign exchange control.

Effects of Deficit in BoP

Some of the effects of a deficit in BoP account are

- It reduces the foreign exchange reserves of a country.
- It slows the pace of economic development of the country.
- A country's economic credibility is hampered.
- A country's foreign dependence may take the form of political dependence.

Important Formulae

- Balance of Trade = Export of Goods – Import of Goods
- Current Account Balance = Trade Balance + Invisibles' Balance
- Invisibles Balance = Balance on Non-factor Services + Balance on Factor Services + Balance on Current Transfers
- Capital Account Balance = Capital Receipts – Capital Payments
- Overall Balance = Current Account Balance + Capital Account Balance + Errors and Omissions

When official reserves account is not a part of capital account

- BoP Surplus = Current Account Surplus + Capital Account Surplus
- BoP Deficit = Current Account Deficit + Capital Account Deficit

Mind Map

BALANCE OF PAYMENTS

1 Meaning of Balance of Payments (BoP)

It is a systematic record of all economic transactions between the residents of a country and the rest of the world in a given period of time, usually one year.
Economic transactions that are recorded in BoP include transactions involving visible items, invisible items, unilateral transactions and capital transfer transactions.

Balance of Payments Structure
BoP account is prepared on a double entry basis, i.e. there are two sides of transactions
- **Debit Side** Records transactions that result in the outflow of foreign currency.
- **Credit Side** Records transactions that result in the inflow of foreign currency.

2 Components of Balance of Payments (BoP)

There are two components of BoP, i.e. current account and capital account.

Current Account
It records the actual receipts and payments relating to export and import of goods and services and unilateral transfers during a given period of time, usually a financial year.

Components
- **Export and Import of Visible Items/Goods** Includes export and import of visible items or goods like wheat, rice etc.
- **Export and Import of Invisible Items/Services** Includes transactions involving factor services and transactions involving non-factor services.
- **Unilateral Transfers/Current Transfers** These are the one-way transactions made by residents or non-residents settled abroad.

Balance on Current Account
The difference between debit and credit items shows the balance of current account. It can show
- **Current Account Surplus** It arises when the sum of credit items exceeds the sum of debit items.
- **Current Account Deficit** It arises when the sum of debit items exceeds the sum of credit items.

Capital Account
It records capital transactions between the residents of country and rest of the world.

Components
- **Foreign Investment** It includes investment made by the residents of a country in rest of the world or by the residents of rest of the world in the domestic country. It includes foreign direct investment and foreign portfolio investment.
- **Borrowings** Borrowings to and from abroad also affect the assets and liabilities status of the country. It includes external commercial borrowing and external assistance.
- **Other Components** Includes NRI deposits, banking capital and short-term trade credit.

Balance on Capital Account
The difference between debit and credit items shows the balance of capital account. It can show
- **Capital Account Surplus** It arises when the sum of credit items exceeds the sum of debit items.
- **Capital Account Deficit** It arises when the sum of debit items exceeds the sum of credit items.

3 Errors and Omissions in BoP

- It is difficult to record all international transactions accurately. So, in addition to current account and capital account, there is one more element of BoP, called as errors and omissions.
- The net credit or net debit balance in actual balance of payments is often arises due to errors and omissions in statement compilation, which may be related to practical approximation to principles.
- In balance of payments, it is standard practice to display an item separately for net errors and omissions, also known as a statistical discrepancy or balancing item, to offset the overstatement or understatement of recorded components.

4 Autonomous and Accomodating Items of BoP

- **Autonomous Items of BoP** It refers to the international economic transactions which are made with a view to earn profit.
- **Accomodating Items of BoP** It refers to those transactions which are taken up by the government in order to keep the BoP balanced.

5 Equilibrium and Disequilibrium in BoP

BoP of a country can reflect the following two situations
1. **Disequilibrium in BoP** It occurs when there is
   - **Surplus in BoP** When the sum of the balance of the current account and capital account is positive.
   - **Deficit in BoP** When the sum of the balance of the current account and capital account is negative.
2. **Equilibrium in BoP** When the sum of the balances of the current and capital accounts equals to zero, BoP is said to be in equilibrium.

6 Causes for Surplus in BoP

Surplus in BoP can arise due to the following reasons
- **Economic Growth** High economic growth leads to increased GDP, which will increase inflow of foreign exchange, resulting in surplus.
- **Low Level of Inflation** Low inflation in the domestic economy increases demand for domestic goods in international market leading to increased exports.
- **Political Stability** Stable government policies attract foreign investment, further increasing BoP's surplus.

7 Causes for Deficit in BoP

Deficit in BoP can arise due to the following reasons

Economic Factors
- Inflation
- Fall in demand
- Import services
- Expenditure on development relations

Political Factors
- Political instability
- Political disturbances

Social Factors
- Demonstration effect
- Change in tastes and preferences

EXAM PATTERN QUESTIONS

Objective Type Questions

Multiple Choice Questions (MCQs)

1. **The balance of payments of an economy records the .... for a fiscal year.**

(a) income and expenditure of the government
(b) inflow and outflow of government funds
(c) inflow and outflow of foreign exchange to and from the economy
(d) inflow and outflow of capital to and from the rest of the world

2. **Which of the following is not a feature of Balance of Payments (BoP) account?**

(a) It includes economic transactions
(b) It has given period of time
(c) It records only capital transactions
(d) Trade between resident of a country and rest of the world

3. **Under the balance of payments structure of a nation, the two main categories of accounts for the classification of the transactions are .... and ....** **CBSE SQP 2022**

(i) current account
(ii) unilateral transfer account
(iii) capital account **(iv) loan account**

Identify the correct alternatives from the following.

(a) (i) and (ii) (b) (i) and (iii)
(c) (iii) and (iv) (d) (iv) and (i)

4. **The transaction shown below will be considered as which of the following trade?**

(a) Visible trade (b) Invisible trade
(c) Accommodating trade (d) None of these

5. **Which account has a direct impact on the income, output and employment?**

(a) Current account (b) Capital account
(c) Real account (d) Nominal account

6. **On the basis of the below chart, answer the following question.**

Choose the correct alternative to fill in the blank.

(a) Invisible Balance
(b) Visible Balance
(c) Capital Account Balance
(d) Error and Omissions

7. **"Interest on the deposit from a foreign bank is recorded in the current account." Choose the correct reason.** **Competency Based Que**

(a) It is visible good (b) It is invisible service
(c) Income from abroad (d) It is a transfer receipt

8. **Which of the following items will be entered on the credit side of current account in balance of payment of a country?**

(a) Borrowings from abroad
(b) Import of machinery
(c) Export of tea
(d) Foreign direct investment

9. **The .... account of balance of payments reflects the net changes in financial claims on the Rest of the World (RoW).** **CBSE 2024 C**

(a) trade (b) capital
(c) current (d) visible

10. **"The World Bank has been extending loans to Country X on favourable terms for infrastructure, poverty alleviation and rural development projects for four decades." Identify the reason for these loans to be listed as external assistance under the capital account of the balance of payments.** **CBSE SQP 2023; Competency Based Que**

(a) The loans have been taken from an entity outside the country
(b) The loans aim to improve the standard of living in the country
(c) The loans have crossed the three-decade period
(d) The loans can be paid-off over a longer period

11. **Read the following chart carefully and choose the correct alternative.**

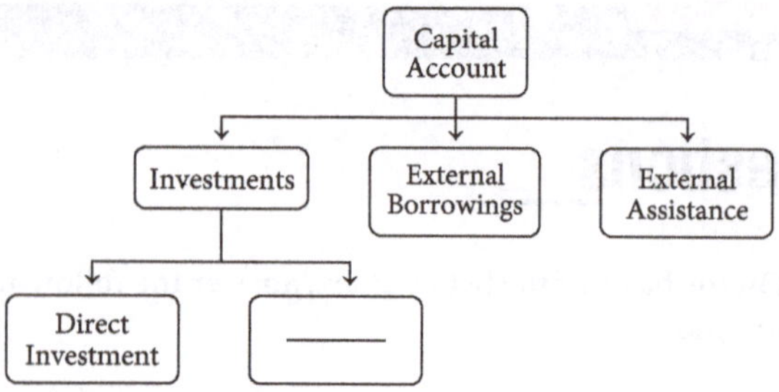

(a) Interest received on Loans
(b) Multilateral Loans
(c) Portfolio Investment (d) Government Aid

12. **"India has attracted total FDI inflow of US $ 22.53 billion between April 2021 to June 2021."**

This transaction will be recorded on .... side of .... account of balance of payments.

CBSE Term I 2021; Competency Based Que

(a) debit, current (b) credit, current
(c) credit, capital (d) debit, capital

13. **As per the Reserve Bank of India (RBI) press report, dated 29th December, 2022.**

"Net external commercial borrowings to India recorded an outflow of US$ 0.4 billion in the second quarter (2022-23)."

The above transaction will be recorded in the .... account on .... side of balance of payments account of India. **CBSE SQP 2024; Competency Based Que**

(a) current, credit (b) current, debit
(c) capital, credit (d) capital, debit

14. **Identify the incorrect statement with reference to balance of payments.** **CBSE 2022**

(a) Current account records export and import transactions of a nation
(b) Export of machinery is recorded in capital account
(c) Transfer of funds to the relatives abroad, entered on debit side of current account
(d) Current account records all such transactions, which do not impact asset or liability status of a country

15. **Which of the following statements is incorrect?** **CBSE Term I 2021**

(a) Balance of Payment (BoP) is a flow concept
(b) Balance of trade includes export and import of goods only
(c) Charity to foreign countries is recorded in capital account of BoP
(d) Balance of payment is broader concept than balance of trade

16. **Keeping all other factors constant, trade surplus may arise in the balance of payments of a nation because of ....** **CBSE 2024 C**

(a) rise in export of coffee to Japan
(b) fall in import of banking services
(c) fall in exports of cereals
(d) rise in remittances to abroad

17. **In a hypothetical economy, the following data is given.** **CBSE Term I 2021; Competency Based Que**

S.No.	Item	Amt (₹)
(i)	Merchandise Exports	100
(ii)	Merchandise Imports	90
(iii)	Tourism	70
(iv)	Net Remittances from Abroad	(–) 20

The value of balance on current account would be ₹ .... crore.

(a) 100 (b) 70 (c) 80 (d) 60

18. **Suppose that the Balance of Trade (BoT) of a nation exhibits a surplus of ₹ 20,000 crore. The import of merchandise of the nation is half of the exports of merchandise to the rest of the world.**

The value of exports would be ₹ .... crore.

CBSE SQP 2022; Competency Based Que

(a) 30,000 (b) 40,000 (c) 24,000 (d) 35,000

19. **When import is more than export, then .... occurs.** **NCERT (QR)**

(a) trade surplus (b) trade deficit
(c) excess supply (d) excess demand

20. **Trade surplus refers to ....**

(a) Export of goods and services > Import of goods and services
(b) Import of goods and services > Export of goods and services
(c) Export of invisible items > Import of invisible items
(d) Export of visible items > Import of visible items

21. **MANILA-The Philippines' Balance of Payment (BoP) position reversed to a surplus in December 2022 to USD 612 million and an economist forecasts further improvement in the coming months as structural US dollar inflows continue to increase.**

Data released by the Bangko Sentralng Pilipinas (BSP) on Thursday showed that the BoP position, which is the sum of a country's total trade with the rest of the world, last December is better than the previous month's USD 756 million deficit but is lower than year ago's USD 991 million surplus. The latest figures brought the end 2022 BoP position to a deficit of USD 7.26 billion, higher than the USD 1.35 billion deficits in end 2021.

Source *https://www.pna.gov.ph/articles/1193144*

Which of the following transactions is/are used to balance the BoP in accounting sense? Competency Based Que

(a) Autonomous items
(b) Accommodating items
(c) Official reserve transaction
(d) Both (b) and (c)

22. **In a recent economics seminar, Professor Sharma discussed various types of foreign exchange transactions. He mentioned that some transactions which are specifically undertaken by the central bank of a country with a view of correcting BoP imbalance and restoring BoP equilibrium.**

What type of foreign exchange transactions was Professor Sharma referring to? Competency Based Que

(a) Current account transactions
(b) Capital account transactions
(c) Autonomous transactions
(d) Accommodating transactions

23. **Foreign exchange transactions which are independent of other transactions in the balance of payments account are called**

(a) current transactions (b) capital transactions
(c) autonomous transactions
(d) accommodating transactions

24. **Which transactions are recorded in the balance of account with a profit maximisation motive?**

(a) Autonomous (b) Accommodating
(c) Compensatory (d) None of these

25. **Deficit in Balance of Payment (BoP) refers to the excess of ....** CBSE 2023

(a) current account payments over current account receipts
(b) capital account payments over capital account receipts
(c) autonomous payment over autonomous receipts
(d) accommodating payments over accommodating receipts

26. **Based on the given diagram, give answer for the following** CBSE SQP 2025

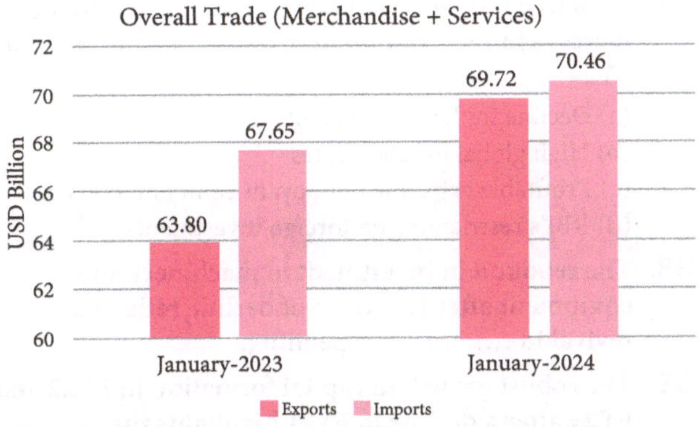

Source *https://commerce.gov.in/wp-content/uploads/2024/02/PIB-Press-Release-January-2024-1.pdf*

The trade under current account during January 2024 reflects a .... of USD .... billion.

(a) surplus, 0.74
(b) surplus, 3.85
(c) deficit, 0.74
(d) deficit, 3.85

27. **The following information is given for an imaginary country.** CBSE SQP 2023; Competency Based Que

Current Account	₹ (in crores'000)
Visible Exports	100
Visible Imports	150
Invisible Exports	70
Invisible Imports	30
Net Current transfer Balance	15

Balance on current account will be .... of ₹ .... thousand crore.

(a) deficit, 10 (b) surplus, 5
(c) deficit, 5 (d) surplus, 10

28. **Suppose, following data is presented, for an imaginary economy (all figures in ₹ '000 crore).** CBSE SQP 2023; Competency Based Que

Year	Visible Exports	Visible Imports
2010	280	240
2020	580	460

Identify, which of the statement about the period 2010 to 2020 is correct?

(a) Improvement in balance of trade
(b) Increase in trade deficit
(c) Improvement in balance in invisibles items
(d) Deterioration of balance of trade

29. **If the value of export of merchandise is ₹ 1,500 crore and imports of goods are 20 percent more than exports, the value of imports and trade deficit will be ... crore and ...... crore respectively.** Competency Based Que

(a) ₹ 1,800, ₹ 3,300
(b) ₹ 1,800, ₹ 300
(c) ₹ 1,200, ₹ 300
(d) ₹ 1,200, ₹ 3,300

30. **Which of the following can be a direct cause of a surplus in the balance of payments?**

(a) A decrease in remittances sent by expatriates
(b) An increase in foreign aid received by the government
(c) A significant increase in capital inflows through foreign investment
(d) A rise in domestic demand for foreign goods and services

31. A balance of payments deficit can arise due to which of the following?

(i) A decrease in domestic interest rates attracting foreign capital.
(ii) A rise in foreign debt repayments.
(iii) Devaluation of the domestic currency.
(iv) An increase in demand for imported luxury goods.

Competency Based Que

Codes

(a) (ii) and (iii) (b) (i) and (ii)
(c) (i) and (iv) (d) (ii) and (iv)

Direction *Read the case study and answer the questions 32 to 35 on the basis of the same*

India's current account balance posted a marginal surplus of USD 0.6 billion (0.1% of GDP) in the Jan-Mar quarter 2020, as against a deficit of USD 4.7 billion in Jan-Mar, 2019 and USD 2.6 billion in the previous quarter.

It is noteworthy that this is the first quarterly current account surplus since the Jan-Mar quarter of 2007. It is primarily on account of lower trade deficit at USD 35 billion and a rise in net invisible receipts (which includes services, primary and secondary income) at USD 35.6 billion.

The lower trade deficit is a result of the sharp decline in demand at both the national and international levels following the implementation of Covid-19 lockdowns and a fall in global crude oil prices since the beginning of this year.

In the financial account, net foreign direct investment at USD 12 billion was higher than USD 6.4 billion in Jan-March quarter 2019. On the portfolio investment side, there was a net outflow of USD 13.7 billion compared to USD 9.4 billion inflow the same quarter last year on account of money being pulled out from both debt and equity markets. A surplus at both current and capital account has resulted in a forex reserve accretion of USD 18.8 billion in the Jan-Mar quarter 2020.

32. Current account of BoP account records only exports and imports of goods and services. State true or false.

33. Current account surplus arises when credit items are .... debit items.

(a) less than (b) equal to
(c) more than (d) All of these

34. Foreign direct investment from abroad is recorded on the

(a) credit side of current account
(b) debit side of current account
(c) credit side of capital account
(d) debit side of capital account

35. Current account is a .... concept.

Direction *Read the case study and answer the questions 36 to 39 on the basis of the same*

National income data show that non-financial private sector capital formation, measured in current prices, expanded vigorously in FY22 and FY23 after a decline in FY21. However, investment in machinery and equipment declined for two consecutive years, FY20 and FY21, before rebounding strongly.

Early corporate sector data for FY24 suggest that capital formation in the private sector continued to expand but at a slower rate. Foreign direct investment, the subject of much analysis, has held up. RBI data on India's balance of payments shows us that the investment interest of external investors, measured in terms of dollar inflows of new capital, was USD 45.8 billion in FY24 compared to USD 47.6 billion in FY23.

This slight decline is in line with global trends. Reinvestment of earnings remained the same. Repatriation of investment was USD 29.3 billion in FY23 and USD 44.5 billion in FY24. Many private equity investors took advantage of buoyant equity markets in India and exited profitably.

It is a sign of a healthy market environment that offers profitable exits to investors, which will bring newer investments in the years to come. That said, the environment for foreign direct investment to grow in the coming years is not highly favourable for many reasons.

Source *https://www.indiabudget.gov.in/economicsurvey/doc/echapter.pdf-economic survey 2023-24*

36. What does the trend in FDI inflows in FY24 compared to FY23 suggest about external investor interest in India?

(a) Increased significantly
(b) Decreased slightly
(c) Remained unchanged
(d) Collapsed

37. Which of the following factors contributed to the increase in repatriation of investment from India in FY24?

(a) Decline in the Indian equity markets
(b) High global inflation rates
(c) Profitable exits due to buoyant equity markets in India
(d) RBI's restrictions on foreign investments

38. The rebound in investment in machinery and equipment after two years of decline reflects a revival in .... spending.

39. The robust growth in capital formation in FY22 and FY23 after a decline in FY21 highlights the .... nature of private sector investment.

Assertion-Reason

Direction (Q.No. 40 to 47) *Read the following Assertion (A) and Reason (R) and choose the correct alternative from the following*

Alternatives

(a) Both Assertion (A) and Reason (R) are true and Reason (R) is the correct explanation of Assertion (A)
(b) Both Assertion (A) and Reason (R) are true, but Reason (R) is not the correct explanation of Assertion (A)
(c) Assertion (A) is true, but Reason (R) is false
(d) Assertion (A) is false, but Reason (R) is true

40. **Assertion** (A) Imports of crude oil by India will have a favourable impact on balance of payment of India.

Reason (R) Imports of goods are recorded on the debit side of current account as it leads to outflow of foreign exchange. **CBSE Term I 2021**

41. **Assertion** (A) In both the accounting and the economic sense, balance of payments account is always in balance.

Reason (R) In accounting sense, balance of payment account is prepared on the basis of double entry system. **CBSE Term I 2021**

42. **Assertion** (A) India's Current Account Balance (CAB) recorded a surplus of US$ 19.8 billion (3.9% of GDP) in Q_1 of 2020-2021.

Reason (R) There has been a steeper decline in merchandise imports relative to exports in past few years.

43. **Assertion** (A) Unilateral transactions are an example of a current account component.

Reason (R) The capital account deals with transactions that are recurring in nature.

44. **Assertion** (A) If the receipts and payments on the current account are equal to each other, it depicts a situation of current account surplus.

Reason (R) A surplus current account means that the nation is a lender to other countries and a deficit current account means that the nation is a borrower from other countries.

45. **Assertion** (A) If official reserves are not shown as part of the capital account, they are presented separately and classified as 'below the line'.

Reason (R) Under such conditions, the combined current and capital accounts may exhibit a surplus or deficit in the Balance of Payments (BoP).

46. **Assertion** (A) Autonomous items may involve the movement of goods across the borders (like export and import of consumer goods or capital goods).

Reason (R) As a consequence, autonomous items lead to BoP imbalance.

47. **Assertion** (A) Accommodating transactions are undertaken to make equilibrium in BoP account.

Reason (R) In accounting sense, BoP account should always be balanced.

Two Statements Based MCQs

Direction (Q.No. 48 to 55) *Read the following statements carefully and choose the correct alternative*

Alternatives

(a) Statement I is correct and Statement II is incorrect
(b) Statement II is correct and Statement I is incorrect
(c) Both the statements are correct
(d) Both the statements are incorrect

48. **Statement I** Balance of payment is an accounting statement which records all the economic transactions that take place between the residents of a country during a given period of time.

Statement II Current account of balance of payment records all the transactions that relate to assets or liabilities. **CBSE Term I 2021**

49. **Statement I** Transfer payments are the receipts which the residents of a country get for free.

Statement II Transfer payments could be given by the government or by foreign citizens. **CBSE Term I 2021**

50. **Statement I** Borrowings from the rest of the world is a credit item of BoP.

Statement II All outflows of foreign currency are recorded on the debit of BoP.

51. **Statement I** Increase in foreign exchange reserves are debited in the capital account of BoP.

Statement II A surplus in BoT is sufficient to cover a deficit in BoP.

52. **Statement I** Export of financial services by India will be recorded on credit side of current account.

Statement II Foreign direct investments in India will be recorded on credit side of capital account. **CBSE SQP 2023**

53. **Statement I** A deficit in the balance of payments can be caused by a high level of imports relative to exports, leading to a negative trade balance.

Statement II A deficit in the balance of payments is solely caused by an increase in domestic savings rates, which reduces the need for foreign capital.

54. **Statement I** A surplus in the current account of the balance of payments occurs when a country's exports of goods and services exceed its imports.

Statement II A surplus in the capital account of the balance of payments implies that a country is experiencing a net outflow of foreign investment.

55. Statement I Autonomous transactions take place on both current and capital account.
Statement II Accommodating items are also known as 'above the line items'.

Matching

56. Match the following

	Column I		Column II
A.	Insurance services provided to an NRI	(i)	Credit side of capital account
B.	Toys imported from China	(ii)	Debit side of current account
C.	Borrowings from IMF	(iii)	Credit side of current account

Codes

	A	B	C		A	B	C
(a)	(i)	(ii)	(iii)	(b)	(ii)	(iii)	(i)
(c)	(iii)	(ii)	(i)	(d)	(iii)	(i)	(ii)

57. Match the following

	Column I		Column II
A.	Autonomous transaction	(i)	Gift of $1,000 from a relative living abroad
B.	Accommodating transaction	(ii)	Above the line transaction
C.	Invisibles	(iii)	Below the line transaction
D.	Unrequited transfers	(iv)	Rent received from a foreigner for property rented in Delhi

Codes

	A	B	C	D		A	B	C	D
(a)	(i)	(ii)	(iii)	(iv)	(b)	(ii)	(iii)	(iv)	(i)
(c)	(iv)	(i)	(ii)	(iii)	(d)	(iii)	(iv)	(i)	(ii)

58. Identify the correct pair

	Column I		Column II
A.	Autonomous Receipts > Autonomous Payments	(i)	Deficit in BoP
B.	Investment by Samsung company in India	(ii)	Credit side of capital account
C.	Unilateral transaction	(iii)	Export of handicraft goods to China

Codes
(a) A-(i) (b) B-(ii)
(c) C-(iii) (d) None of these

59. Identify the correct pair of formula from the following Column I and II **CBSE SQP 2021**

	Column I		Column II
A.	Capital account surplus	(i)	Receipts < Payments
B.	Current account surplus	(ii)	Receipts > Payments
C.	Balance current account	(iii)	Receipts ≠ Payments
D.	Current account deficit	(iv)	Receipts ≤ Payments

Codes
(a) A-(i) (b) B-(ii)
(c) C-(iii) (d) D-(iv)

60. From the following given sets of statements in Column I and II, choose the correct pair of statements **CBSE SQP 2022**

	Column I		Column II
A.	Exports of goods and services	(i)	Excess of exports of goods over the imports of goods
B.	Trade surplus	(ii)	An element of invisible items
C.	Current transfers to rest of the world	(iii)	Recorded as a positive item in the BoP account
D.	Portfolio Investments	(iv)	Foreign institutional investors

Codes
(a) A-(i) (b) B-(ii)
(c) C-(iii) (d) D-(iv)

Concept Identification

61. It records receipts and payments of foreign exchange of a country on account of such transactions which impact asset-liability status of a country in relation to rest of the world.

62. The items which cannot be seen, felt, touched or measured. e.g. Services of shipping, banking, insurance, etc.

63. Situation when total inflows on account of autonomous transactions are less than total outflows on account of such transactions.

64. The account indicating reserves of foreign exchange with the RBI.

65. The economic transactions in the current and capital account that are undertaken for certain economic or profit motive. These items are also known as 'above the line items'. **CBSE 2020**

66. The economic transactions that are undertaken by the RBI with a view to correcting imbalances in the country's BoP account. These items are also known as below the line items. **CBSE 2020**

Answers

1. (d) inflow and outflow of capital to and from the rest of the world
2. (c) BoP of a country is a systematic record of all the economic transactions between its residents and rest of the world in a given period of time, usually one year. It records both current and capital account transactions.
3. (b) (i) and (iii)
4. (a) Visible trade
5. (a) Current account
6. (a) Invisible Balance
7. (c) Income from abroad
8. (c) Export of tea
9. (b) capital
10. (b) The loans aim to improve the standard of living in the country
11. (c) Portfolio Investment
12. (c) credit, capital
13. (d) capital, debit
14. (b) Export of machinery is recorded in capital account
15. (c) Charity to a foreign country is recorded in the current account of the BoP because it's a transfer payment that leads to an outflow of foreign exchange.
16. (a) rise in export of coffee to Japan
17. (d) Current Account = (Export − Import) + Net Income + Net Current Transfer

    $= (100 - 90) + 70 - 20 = 10 + 50 = 60$
18. (b) Exports = E and Imports = M

    Balance of Trade Surplus = E − M = 20,000

    Here, M = 0.5E

    Now, $E - 0.5E = 20{,}000 \Rightarrow 0.5E = 20{,}000 \Rightarrow E = 40{,}000$
19. (b) trade deficit
20. (d) Export of visible items > Import of visible items
21. (d) Both (b) and (c)
22. (d) Accommodating transactions
23. (c) autonomous transactions
24. (a) Autonomous
25. (c) autonomous payment over autonomous receipts
26. (c) Current account is on deficit as Imports > Exports.

    Imports − Exports = 70.46 − 69.72 = 0.74
27. (b) Balance on Current Account

    = (Visible Exports − Visible Imports) + (Invisible Exports − Invisible Imports) + Net Current Transfer Balance

    = (100 − 150) + (70 − 30) + 15 = (−) 50 + 40 + 15 = 5
28. (a) Improvement in balance of trade
29. (b) Value of Imports = 1,500 × 120% = ₹ 1,800 crore
30. (c) A significant increase in capital inflows through foreign investment
31. (d) (ii) and (iv)
32. False. It also records unilateral receipts and payments.
33. (c) more than
34. (c) credit side of capital account
35. flow
36. (b) Decreased slightly
37. (c) Profitable exits due to buoyant equity markets in India
38. capital
39. cyclical
40. (d) Crude oil imports typically have an unfavourable impact on the balance of payments because they result in an outflow of foreign exchange, increasing the deficit on the current account. Importing crude oil involves significant expenditure in foreign currency.
41. (d) The balance of payments account is only in balance in the accounting sense. In the economic sense, it's not always in balance.
42. (a) Both Assertion (A) and Reason (R) are true and Reason (R) is the correct explanation of Assertion (A)
43. (c) The capital account deals with non-recurring transactions, such as investments, loans and the transfer of assets. These transactions are typically one-time events, unlike the current account, which deals with recurring transactions like exports, imports and unilateral transfers.
44. (d) If receipts and payments on the current account are equal, it means that the current account is balanced. A current account surplus occurs when receipts (exports, investment income, transfers, etc.) exceed payments (imports, transfers abroad, etc.), not when they are equal.
45. (b) Both Assertion (A) and Reason (R) are true, but Reason (R) is not the correct explanation of Assertion (A)
46. (b) Both Assertion (A) and Reason (R) are true, but Reason (R) is not the correct explanation of Assertion (A)
47. (a) Both Assertion (A) and Reason (R) are true and Reason (R) is the correct explanation of Assertion (A)
48. (d) BoP is a systematic statement of all economic transactions of a country with the rest of the world during a specific period, usually one year and current account of balance of payments account records only exports and imports of goods and services.
49. (c) Both the statements are correct
50. (c) Both the statements are correct

51. (a) A surplus in the Balance of Trade (BoT) is not necessarily sufficient to cover a deficit in the overall BoP. A BoP deficit can arise from various factors, including services, income and capital transactions and a surplus in the BoT may not be enough to offset these other deficits. Thus, the BoP balance needs to be considered as a whole, not just focusing on the trade balance.
52. (c) Both the statements are correct
53. (a) While changes in domestic savings rates can influence the balance of payments, they are not the sole cause of a deficit. An increase in domestic savings generally reduces the need for foreign capital, as more domestic funds are available for investment.
However, a balance of payments deficit can be caused by a variety of factors beyond domestic savings, such as high levels of imports, low levels of exports, capital flight or economic instability.
54. (a) A surplus in the capital account indicates that the country is experiencing a net inflow of foreign investment, not an outlfow.
55. (a) Accommodating items are also known as 'below the line items'.
56. (c) (iii) (ii) (i)
57. (b) (ii) (iii) (iv) (i)
58. (b) B-(ii)
59. (b) B-(ii)
60. (d) D-(iv)
61. Balance of payments on capital account
62. Invisible items
63. Deficit in balance of payments
64. Official reserves account
65. Autonomous items
66. Accommodating items

Subjective Questions

Short Answer Type Questions

1. Define the concept balance of payment. How does the 'borrowings from the rest of the world' are reflected in balance of payments and why?

Ans. Balance of payments account refers to the systematic record (official transaction book), which records all international transactions between residents of home country and the rest of the world. Balance of payments account is classified into current account and capital account.

Borrowings from abroad are recorded in the capital account of balance of payments as it is a foreign liability for the country.

2. Identify the following items as credit or debit transactions on balance of payments account. Exports, imports, borrowing from rest of the world, lending to the rest of the world, import of software services.

Ans. **Credit Side of BoP**

(i) Exports (Current account).
(ii) Borrowing from rest of the world (Capital account).

Debit Side of BoP

(i) Imports (Current account).
(ii) Lending to the rest of the world (Capital account).
(iii) Import of software services (Current account).

3. State on which side of capital account/current account, will the following transactions be recorded and why? CBSE 2019; Competency Based Que

(i) Interest on loan received from Nepal.
(ii) Import of mobile phones from China.

Ans. (i) It will be recorded in the credit side of current account of BoP, as it does not affect the assets or liabilities of the country.

(ii) It will be recorded in debit side of current account of BoP, as it leads to an outflow of foreign currency but does not affects assets or liabilities of the country.

4. State where following items are recorded in the balance of payment and why? Competency Based Que

(i) The sale of machinery to a German firm
(ii) India's humanitarian assistance to Africa

Ans. (i) It is recorded under trade balance in current account of BoP. All merchandise transactions are recorded as a trade balance in the current account on the credit side. It leads to inflow of foreign exchange.

(ii) It is recorded under invisible items of account BoP. All current transfers/transfer payment are recorded as an invisible balance in the current account BoP on the debit side. It leads to an outflow of foreign exchange.

5. **"Foreign Portfolio Investment (FPI) witnessed a sharp turnaround during 2023-24 with net FPI inflows of US$ 32.4 billion." In which sub-account and on which side of the balance of payments account, the above transaction will be recorded? Give reasons in support of your answer.** CBSE SQP 2025; Competency Based Que

Ans. Foreign portfolio investments in India in the fiscal year 2023-24 will be recorded on the credit side of the capital account of the Balance of Payments (BoP) account.

It is recorded on the credit side, as it results in the inflow of foreign exchange. Furthermore, such transactions are documented in the capital account as they reflect the change in the ownership of financial assets between the residents of a country and rest of the world.

6. **Differentiate between balance of trade and current account balance.** NCERT

Ans. Differences between balance of trade and current account balance are

Basis	Balance of Trade	Current Account Balance
Definition	It is a difference between exports and imports of goods only.	It is a sum of balance of trade, net income from abroad and net current transfers.
Components	It includes only visible items.	It includes both, visible and invisible items.
Concept	It is a narrow concept as it is a part of current account.	It is a broad concept as it includes balance of trade.

7. **(i) Differentiate between trade surplus and current account surplus.**

(ii) State the significance of current account surplus.

Ans. (i) Differences between trade surplus and current account surplus are

Basis	Trade Surplus	Current Account Surplus
Meaning	It is the situation where exports of goods are more than import of goods.	It is the situation where inflow from visible (BoT) and invisible items is more than outflow from visible and invisible items.
Includes	It is only one component of current account.	It includes other factors like the balance of visible trade, balance of unilateral transfers, etc.

(ii) Current account surplus signifies that the nation is a lender to the rest of the world.

8. **(i) Distinguish between 'trade deficit' and 'current account deficit'.** CBSE 2020, 19

(ii) State the significance of current account deficit.

Ans. (i) Differences between trade deficit and current account deficit are

Basis	Trade Deficit	Current Account Deficit
Meaning	Trade deficit is the situation where exports of goods are less than import of goods.	Deficit in current account is the situation where inflow from visible (BoT) and invisible items are less than outflow from visible and invisible items.
Includes	It is only one component of current account.	It includes other factors like balance on invisible trade and net current transfers.

(ii) Current account deficit signifies that the nation is a borrower from the rest of the world.

9. **Read the given figure carefully and compare the trends of overall exports and imports in India.** Competency Based Que

Overall Trade during December 2022*

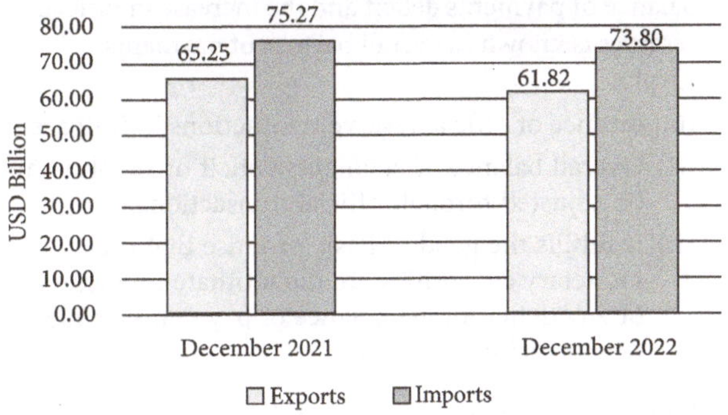

Source *Press release: 16th January, 2023; India's Foreign Trade: December 2022*

Ans. The graph shows a comparative analysis between 2021 and 2022 of India's foreign trade data. The graph illustrates that both exports and imports saw a decline in December 2022 compared to December 2021.

In December 2022, India's overall exports (combining merchandise and services) were estimated at USD 61.82 billion. This represented a decline of 5.26% compared to December 2021, indicating a year-on-year decrease in export activity.

Meanwhile, overall imports in December 2022 were estimated at USD 73.80 billion, showing a smaller negative growth of 1.95% over the same period last year.

This trend highlights a continued trade deficit, as imports exceeded exports and both exports and imports exhibited negative growth during this period.

10. Can there be a deficit in balance of trade without a deficit in balance of payments? Competency Based Que

Ans. Yes, there can be a deficit in balance of trade without a deficit in balance of payments.

BoT is only a component of current account of BoP, which includes only exports and imports of goods.

However, BoP includes both current as well as capital account, hence there is a much wider scope.

11. What are official reserve transactions? Explain their importance in the balance of payments. NCERT

Or **How official reserve transactions are helpful in maintaining balance in BoP?**

Ans. Financing the deficit by selling assets or by borrowing from abroad by monetary authorities of a domestic country is known as official reserve transactions. In other words, balancing the surplus by lending to abroad or purchasing assets from abroad by monetary authorities is called official reserves.

The decrease in official reserves is known as overall balance of payments deficit and the increase in official reserves is known as overall balance of payments surplus.

Importance of official reserve transactions in BoP are

(i) Overall balance of payments deficit or surplus can be adjusted through official transactions.

(ii) It fulfills the good of basic promise that the monetary authorities are the ultimate financiers of any deficit in the balance of payments or the receipts of any surplus.

12. Should a current account deficit be a cause for alarm? Explain. NCERT

Ans. A current account deficit means that the value of imports for goods and services are greater than the value of exports.

It leads to several negative effects which are

(i) Economic growth is not favourable.

(ii) Inflation and borrowings become major problems.

(iii) It also increases dependence on foreign country for borrowings, creating debt trap.

Thus, we can say that current account deficit is a cause for alarm because of the above stated negative effects on the country.

13. "Trade deficit must exist if a country is facing a situation of current account deficit." Defend or refute the statement, with valid argument. CBSE SQP 2021; Competency Based Que

Ans. The given statement is refuted as the Current Account Deficit (CAD) is a broader concept. CAD occurs when the foreign exchange payments on account of visible, invisibles and current transfers are in excess over the receipts of visible, invisibles and current transfers.

A country may face a situation of CAD, even if the country has trade surplus, with greater negative balances on account of services and unilateral transfers.

14. Madhavi Arora, lead economist at Edelweiss Securities, said FY 21 may see CAD improve to 0% as crude prices fall. 'We expect exports growth to remain fragile amid demand shock. Import growth may remain sluggish as well amid weak domestic demand.

Capital account may worsen in FY 21 as dollar funding could be a concern. BoP could remain in surplus of $32-35 billion, helped by lower current account despite weak FPI (Foreign Portfolio Investments) hot money appetite,' she added.

Source *Mint, 22nd June, 2020*

In this context, suggest various ways that can help to reduce current account deficit. Competency Based Que

Ans. A current account deficit occurs when the value of imports is greater than the value of exports. Policies to reduce current account deficit involve

(i) Devaluation of exchange rate (make exports cheaper – imports more expensive).

(ii) Reduce domestic consumption and spending on imports (e.g. Tight fiscal policy/higher taxes).

(iii) Supply side policies to improve the competitiveness of domestic industry and exports.

15. State whether the following statements are true or false. Give reasons for your answer.

(i) Difference between value of exports and imports of goods and services is called balance of trade.

(ii) External assistance is not recorded in balance of payments account.

(iii) Current account of balance of payments account records only export and import of goods and services.

(iv) Foreign investments are recorded in the capital account of balance of payments.

Competency Based Que

Ans. (i) False, because balance of trade only records the export and import of visible items, i.e. goods.

(ii) False, because external assistance is unilateral receipt which is included in the current account of balance of payments.

(iii) False, as current account of balance of payments account also records unilateral transfers.

(iv) True, as all kinds of foreign investments (foreign direct investments and portfolio investments) are included in the capital account of balance of payments.

16. **Distinguish between current account and capital account of balance of payments.**

Ans. Differences between current and capital account of Balance of Payments (BoP) are

Basis	Current Account of BoP	Capital Account of BoP
Nature of Transaction	These are the transactions which do not affect the assets or liabilities position of the country.	These are the transactions which affect assets or liabilities position of the country.
Concept	It is a flow concept.	It is a stock concept.
Formula/ Components	Current Account = Exports and Imports of Visible and Invisible Items + Unilateral Transactions + Income Received and Paid to Abroad	Capital Account = Borrowings and Lending from and to Abroad + Investment to and from Abroad + Change in the Reserve of Foreign Exchange

17. **What are the primary classifications of transactions that are recorded in the capital account of the balance of payments?**

Ans. The primary classifications of transactions (components) that are recorded in the capital account of the balance of payments are as follow

(i) **Foreign Investment**
It includes foreign direct investment and foreign institutional investment or portfolio investment by the residents of the country in abroad or by the rest of the world in domestic country.

(ii) **Borrowings**
It includes commercial borrowing by the government or private sector from rest of the world and external assistance to/by a country.

(iii) **Official International Reserve**
It includes the changes in gold and foreign exchange reserve with the Central Bank.

18. **"Capital account transactions lead to future claims." Defend or refute the given statement with valid arguments.** **Competency Based Que**

Ans. The given statement is defended. Capital account records all international transactions of assets, where assets are different forms of wealth holding instruments. e.g. Money, bonds, stocks, government debts, external borrowings, etc. All these instruments create future claims, one way or another. Thus, we may say that capital account transactions give rise to future claims.

19. **"In past decade, India has become a favourite outsourcing destination." In the light of the statement, state in which sub-account and on which side of balance of payments account will foreign investments in India be recorded? Give reasons.** **Competency Based Que**

Ans. Foreign investments in India will be recorded in the credit side of the capital account of the balance of payments accounts.
Capital account records the capital transactions such as loans and investments between India and the rest of the world, which causes a change in the assets and liabilities status of the residents of the country or the government. One of the component of capital account is 'foreign investment', which records Foreign Direct Investment (FDI), Foreign Institutional Investment (FII) or portfolio investment by the residents of India in abroad or by the rest of the world in the domestic territory.

So, foreign investments in India will be a part of this component and therefore will be recorded in the capital account. In the capital account, all transactions causing flow of foreign exchange in the country are recorded on the credit side.

Since investments from abroad will cause a flow of foreign exchange in the country, therefore it will be recorded on the credit side.

20. **"Current account deficit in an economy must be financed by a corresponding capital account surplus." Do you agree with the given statement? Give valid reason(s) in support of your answer.**
CBSE SQP 2024; Competency Based Que

Ans. Yes, the statement can be agreed upon.
Since, in accounting sense, Current Account + Capital Account = 0, if an economy is facing the situation of Current Account Deficit (CAD), the same must be financed through surplus in capital account.
CAD may be set-off through net capital inflows. Transactions like selling-off assets or borrowing from abroad, may be instrumental in balancing CAD in balance of payments account.

21. **"Government takes measures to restrict autonomous imports of gold." Explain the economic values desired to be achieved from this.** **Competency Based Que**

Ans. Restricting autonomous imports of gold will reduce the foreign exchange demand. It will reduce the foreign exchange payments. Since autonomous payments decline, BoP deficit will decline. This decline will reduce pressure of deficit and it is the economic value realised.

22. Distinguish between autonomous transactions and accommodating transactions in the balance of payments of the economy. CBSE 2025, SQP 2024

Ans. Differences between autonomous and accommodating transactions of balance of payments are as follows (any four)

Basis	Autonomous Transactions	Accommodating Transactions
Meaning	These transactions are those which are made with a view to earn profit.	These transactions are taken up by government to keep BoP balanced.
Recorded	These are recorded in both i.e. current and capital account of BoP.	These are recorded only in capital account of BoP.
Alternate Name	These are also known as above the line transactions.	These are also known as below the line transactions.
Undertaken By	These are undertaken by both government and private sector.	These are under-taken only by government sector.
Example	Export of intellectual property.	Receiving foreign aid, foreign exchange reserves accumulation.

23. Observe the image given below and explain what can be reflected? Competency Based Que

Ans. In the context of this chapter, the image given above highlights the situation of disequilibrium in BoP. Disequilibrium in BoP can be reflected in the following manner

(i) **Surplus in BoP**
When the sum of the balance of the current account and capital account is positive, then BoP account is said to be in surplus. In such a situation, there is inflow of foreign exchange leading to an increase in the official reserves account.

(ii) **Deficit in BoP**
When the sum of the balance of the current account and capital account is negative, then BoP account is said to be in deficit. In such a situation, there is outflow of foreign exchange leading to decrease in the official reserves account.

24. "Balance of payments always balances." Explain.

Ans. The statement means that the Balance of Payments (BoP) always comes to balance, even if there is a surplus or deficit in certain accounts.

When this happens, the following adjustment is made

(i) In the event of a surplus or a deficit, accommodating transactions are introduced in the BoP account.

(ii) These transactions are meant only to make such adjustments in the BoP account which eliminate the BoP surplus or deficit.

25. What is the concept and the significance of a deficit in balance of payments?

Or **State the meaning of 'balance of payments deficit'.** CBSE SQP 2025

Ans. Deficit in BoP refers to a situation when receipts of the country arising out of autonomous transactions are less than the corresponding payments to the rest of the world during the period of an accounting year. It highlights our net liabilities towards rest of the world.

Significance of Deficit in BoP

There is positive as well as negative significance of deficit in BoP. The positive significance is that, BoP deficit may be occurring on account of such capital imports which are essential to speed up the process of growth and development in the economy.
The negative significance is that it highlights our liabilities to the rest of the world. Greater the liability, greater is the strain on our GDP by the way of payments to the rest of the world.

26. Outline the meaning and reasons behind narrowing down of current account deficit. CBSE 2024 C

Ans. A Current Account Deficit (CAD) occurs when a country's imports of goods, services and transfers exceed its exports. It indicates that the country is spending more on foreign trade than it is earning.
Reasons for narrowing down CAD include

(i) **Increase in Exports**
Growth in exports boosts foreign earnings, reducing the trade gap.

(ii) **Decrease in Imports**
Lower demand for imports or reduced international prices of key imports (e.g. Crude oil).

(iii) **Remittances Growth**
Higher remittances from citizens working abroad improve the current account balance.

(iv) **Government Policies**
Policies like promoting domestic manufacturing or imposing tariffs reduce imports.

27. (i) **"However, a sharper decline in India's merchandise import growth, owing to declining commodity prices, resulted in a lower trade deficit in FY24."**
Analysis its impact on balance of payment and Indian economy. **Competency Based Que**
Source *https://www.indiabudget.gov.in/economic survey/doc/echapter.pdf Economic Survey 2023-24*

(ii) **Trade deficit is a component of current account or capital account.**

Ans. (i) A sharper decline in India's merchandise import growth due to falling commodity prices in FY24 led to a reduction in the trade deficit. This decrease in imports improves the current account of the Balance of Payments (BoP) by narrowing the gap between imports and exports.

As the trade deficit reduces, India's Current Account Deficit (CAD) improves, potentially leading to a surplus. Additionally, a lower trade deficit may boost investor confidence, increasing Foreign Direct Investment (FDI) and Foreign Portfolio Investment (FPI), which strengthens the capital account.

Overall, this can help stabilise the rupee and improve India's foreign exchange reserves, enhancing economic stability.

(ii) A trade deficit is a component of the current account, not the capital account. The current account records a country's transactions in goods, services, income and current transfers, while the trade balance (exports minus imports) is a major part of this account.

Long Answer Type Questions

28. What is balance of payments and discuss the detailed components that constitute it?

Ans. The balance of payments is a systematic record of all the economic/monetary transactions between the residents (all the units) of a country and the rest of the world in an accounting year.

There are two main accounts in the BoP

(i) **Current Account**

This account keeps record of all goods and services that come into and go out of the nation. This account is used to cover all payments for raw materials and finished items.

Tourism, engineering, stocks, commercial services, transportation and royalties from licenses and copyrights are among the various deliveries mentioned in this category. The sum of these elements determines a nation's BoP.

The components of current account are
- Export and import of goods.
- Export and import of services.
- Unilateral transfers to and from abroad.
- Income receipts and payments to and from abroad.

(ii) **Capital Account**

This account maintains records of capital transactions, like buying and selling real estate and other non-financial assets. Together with the purchase and sale of fixed assets by immigrants moving to a new country, this account also records the flow of taxes. The current account's surplus or deficit is governed by capital account financing and *vice-versa*.

Components of capital account are
- Foreign investments.
- Borrowings.
- Official foreign reserve.
- Other components.

29. What is meant by current account? Explain its various components.

Ans. Current account records the actual receipts and payments relating to export and import of goods and services and unilateral transfers during a given period of time, usually a financial year.

It shows the status of income and employment in the country. Also, these transactions do not impact the assets and liabilities of the country.

Components of current account are as follows

(i) **Export and Import of Visible Items/Goods**

Current account includes export and import of visible items or goods like wheat, rice, machine, etc. All payments for imports of goods are shown on debit side and receipts from exports of goods on credit side.

(ii) **Export and Import of Invisible Items/Services**

Current account also includes export and import of invisible items or services which are further categorised as factor services and non-factor services.

- **Transactions involving Factor Services** These transactions involve payments made to factors of production and involve the following
  (a) Compensation paid to employees.
  (b) Investment income involving payment received on account of rent, interest and profit.
- **Transactions involving Non-factor Services** These transactions involve all services other than factor services that involve the payments to factors of production. Examples of such services are banking, insurance, etc.

All payments made to factor and non-factor service are shown on debit side and receipts from factor and non-factor service shown on credit side.

(iii) **Unilateral Transfers/Current Transfers**

These are transfers made by residents or non-residents settled abroad in the form of gifts, donations, grants, remittances, etc. In the BoP account, unilateral transfers are a part of 'invisibles'. All unilateral transfers made by residents to rest of the world are shown on debit side and unilateral transfers received by residents from rest of the world shown on credit side.

30. "It records capital transactions between the residents of country and the rest of the world." Identify the account being highlighted in the given statement and state its components briefly. Competency Based Que

Ans. The capital account is being highlighted in the statement. It records capital transactions between the residents of country and the rest of the world. These transactions cause a change in the assets or liabilities of the residents of the country or its government during a financial year.

It is used to finance deficit in current account and absorb surplus of current account.

Components of capital account are as follows

(i) **Foreign Investment**

It includes investment made by the residents of a country in rest of the world or by the residents of rest of the world in the domestic country.

Foreign investment can be of the following types

- **Foreign Direct Investment** (FDI) It is related to change in the ownership status and allows direct control of the purchaser over the asset. e.g. Dominos opens its restaurants in India or Haldiram opens its restaurants in America.
- **Foreign Portfolio Investment** (FPI) It refers to the purchase of securities and other financial assets such as bonds, mutual funds, GDRs, etc. by investors from another country. It is same as Foreign Institutional Investors (FIIs).

All financial or physical assets purchase by residents in rest of the world are shown on debit side and financial or physical assets purchase by residents of rest of the world in the domestic country are shown on credit side.

(ii) **Borrowings**

Borrowings to and from abroad also affect the assets and liabilities status of the country and are therefore recorded in capital account.

Borrowings can be further categorised as follows

- **External Commercial Borrowing** It is available at market rate of interest in the international money market.
- **External Assistance** It is available at concessional rate of interest in the international money market.

(iii) **Other Components**

The other components of capital account include the following

- **NRI Deposits** It refers to deposits held by Non-Resident Indians (NRIs) in India. Deposits held by NRIs in the domestic economy only to be considered as a component of capital account.
- **Banking Capital** It refers to foreign assets held by the commercial banks.
- **Short-term Trade Credit** It refers to purchases made in the international market without paying for them immediately.

31. Trade balance and balance of payments are two most often used terms in economic sense. In the recent times, countries like India have started trading with other countries in a greater way.

In the light of the above statement, differentiate between the two concepts. Competency Based Que

Ans. Difference between balance of trade and balance of payment is as follows

Basis	Balance of Trade	Balance of Payment
Meaning	It is a statement that captures the country's export and import of goods with the remaining world.	It is a statement that keeps track of all economic transactions done by the country with the remaining world.
Records	Only goods related transactions are recorded.	Transactions related to both goods and services are recorded.
Capital Transfers	Not included in the balance of trade.	Included in balance of payment.
Use	It gives a partial view of the country's economic status.	It gives a clear view of the economic position of the country.
Result	It can be favourable, unfavourable or balanced.	Both the receipts and payment sides tallies.
Component	It is a component of current account of balance of payment.	Current account and capital account.

32. Explain in detail causes of deficit in balance of payments.

Ans. A deficit in BoP is the major cause of concern and its causes are as follows

(i) **Economic Factors**

- **Inflation** Increase in price of a good due to higher wages, higher prices of raw material, etc. makes export costlier and imports cheaper. This results in deficit in balance of payments.
- **Expenditure on Developing Relations** Developing countries, in order to develop relations with other countries, have to spend huge amount of money on ambassadors, missions, etc. This has adverse effect on balance of payments.
- **Fall in Demand** When the demand of the goods of a country falls in the foreign market, exports reduce and affect the balance of payments. e.g. Owing to the outbreak of Covid, the demand for Chinese goods has fallen in the international market.
- **Import of Services** Underdeveloped countries import capital and other services from developed countries. This results in deficit in BoP.

(ii) **Social Factors**

- **Demonstration Effect** When the people of underdeveloped countries follow the consumption pattern of the people of developed countries, this leads to an increase in the level of imports. This increase results in a deficit in the BoP account.
- **Change in Tastes, Preferences, Fashion and Trends** An unfavourable change in tastes and preferences of consumers towards domestic goods leads to a deficit in the BoP account.

(iii) **Political Factors**

- **Political Instability** Political instability of a country has an adverse effect on balance of payments of a country. In other words, when the government is instable in the domestic economy, foreign investors lose trust while domestic investors prefer to invest abroad. This results in huge outflow of foreign exchange.
- **Political Disturbances** Frequent changes in the government, inadequate support to the government in Parliament also discourage inflows of capital. This leads to a deficit due to higher outflows than inflows.

33. Indian investors lend abroad. Answer the following questions.

(i) In which sub-account and on which side of the balance of payments accounts such lending is recorded? Give reasons.

(ii) Explain the impact of this lending on market exchange rate. **Competency Based Que**

Ans. (i) Indian investors lend abroad. This will be recorded in the debit side of the capital account of the balance of payments accounts. Capital account records the capital transactions such as loans and investments between India and the rest of the world, which causes a change in the assets and liabilities status of the residents of the country or the government.

One of the components of capital account is 'foreign investment', which records Foreign Direct Investment (FDI), Foreign Institutional Investment (FII) or portfolio investment by the residents of India in abroad or by the rest of the world in the domestic territory.

So, lending by Indian investors will be a part of this component and therefore will be recorded in the capital account.

In the capital account, all transactions causing flow of foreign exchange out of the country are recorded in debit side.

Since, lending to abroad will cause a flow of foreign exchange out of the country, therefore it will be recorded in the debit side.

(ii) The market exchange rate will tend to rise due to this lending. The investors who want to lend abroad will demand foreign exchange.

As the demand for foreign exchange rises, with supply remaining the same, the market exchange rate will also rise.

34. The concepts of balance of trade and balance of payments are often misunderstood. Economists frequently say that while the balance of payments includes the balance of trade, the balance of trade does not include the balance of payments.

A country exports and imports many visible goods and invisible services. Invisible services include tourism, shipping and other transport services, banking, insurance services for whose exports and imports payments are made and received by the country in international trade.

A country's balance of trade refers to the value of imports and exports of commodities only. The balance of payments is, however, more comprehensive including as it does total debits and credits relating to all the items on account of which a country makes payments to and receives payments from the rest of the world.

In short, the balance of trade is only a part of the balance of payments. The balance of payments of a country is said to be in equilibrium when the demand for foreign exchange is exactly equivalent to the supply of it.

The balance of payments is in disequilibrium, when there is either a surplus or deficit in the balance of payments, the demand for foreign exchange exceeds the supply of it.

(i) Differentiate between visible trade and invisible trade.

(ii) Briefly explain the components of current account of BoP. Competency Based Que

Ans. (i) Visible trade, in economics, is the exchange of physically tangible goods between countries, involving the export, import and re-export of goods at various stages of production.

On the other hand, invisible trade involves the export and import of physically intangible items such as services.

(ii) Refer to Q. No. 29 of long answer type questions.

35. Read the following news report and answer the questions given below

India's balance of payments this year is going to be very very strong on the back of significant improvement in exports and a fall in imports, as stated by Commerce and Industry Minister Piyush Goyal.

"We are in July at about 91% export level of July 2019 figures. Imports are still at about 70-71% level of July 2019.

So, broadly, our balance of payments this year is going to be very, very strong which is why we feel confident that Indian industry will see opportunities for growth", he said country's trade turned surplus for the first time in 18 years as imports dropped by a steeper 47.59%.

The country posted a trade surplus of $0.79 billion in June. It is because of government's efforts to support and promote domestic manufacturing and industry.

(i) Discuss how a trade surplus impacts the current account of the balance of payments.

(ii) How do changes in exports and imports affect a country's current account balance in the balance of payments? Competency Based Que

Ans. (i) A trade surplus in the Balance of Payments (BoP) occurs when a country's exports of goods and services exceed its imports.

It can impact the economy in the following ways

- **Increased National Income** A trade surplus indicates higher exports, which boosts national income and economic growth.
- **Currency Appreciation** With more demand for the country's goods, the currency may appreciate, making imports cheaper but potentially reducing export competitiveness.
- **Foreign Exchange Reserves** A trade surplus strengthens foreign exchange reserves, providing a buffer for economic stability but may lead to reduced domestic consumption if over reliant on exports.

(ii) The current account in the Balance of Payments (BoP) reflects the difference between a country's exports and imports of goods and services. When exports exceed imports, the country runs a **current account surplus**, which strengthens the overall balance of payments.

This implies the country earns more from selling goods and services abroad than it is spending on imports. On the other hand, when imports exceed exports, a **current account deficit** occurs, weakening the BoP position. This means the country is spending more on foreign goods and services than it is earning from exports, which can lead to a depletion of foreign reserves or increased borrowing to finance the deficit.

Numerical Questions

Numerical 1

(i) Find the balance on the balance of payments account.

S. No.	Items	₹ (in lakhs)
(i)	Capital Account Balance	(– 400)
(ii)	Value of Imports	150
(iii)	Value of Exports	450
(iv)	Unilateral Transfers	100
(v)	Balance of Visible Trade	200

(ii) Is the overall balance of payments balanced?

Sol. (i) Balance on the Balance of Payments Account

= Value of Exports – Value of Imports + Unilateral Transfers + Capital Account Balance

= 450 – 150 + 100 + (– 400) = 0

(ii) Yes, balance of payment is balanced because balance of payment account is zero.

Numerical 2

Find current account balance from the following

S. No.	Items	₹ (in crores)
(i)	Capital Account Balance	80
(ii)	Export of Services	20

S. No.	Items	₹ (in crores)
(iii)	Balance of Visible Trade	50
(iv)	Transfers from One Country to Another Country	5

Sol. Current Account Balance = Balance of Visible Trade + Export of Services + Transfers from One Country to Another Country

= 50 + 20 + 5 = ₹ 75 crore

Numerical 3

In a hypothetical economy, the following data is given

S.No.	Items	₹ (in crores)
(i)	Merchandise Exports	100
(ii)	Merchandise Imports	90
(iii)	Tourism	70
(iv)	Net Remittances from Abroad	(–) 20

The value of balance on current account would be

Sol. Balance on Current Account = Merchandise Exports – Merchandise Imports + Tourism + Net Remittances from Abroad

= 100 – 90 + 70 + (–) 20 = ₹ 60 crore

Numerical 4

Find the balance on non-factor services from the following information

S. No.	Items	₹ (in crores)
(i)	Balance of Visible Trade	500
(ii)	Income	200
(iii)	Transfers	100
(iv)	Current Account Balance	900

Sol. Balance on Non-factor Services

= Current Account Balance – Balance of Visible Trade – Transfers – Income

= 900 – 500 – 100 – 200 = ₹ 100 crore

Numerical 5

What will be the value of imports, if the net imports are ₹ 160 crore and the value of exports is ₹ 400 crore?

Sol. Balance of Trade = Exports – Imports

Imports = Exports – Balance of Trade

= 400 – (–160) = ₹ 560 crore

or Imports = Exports + Net Imports

= 400 + 160 = ₹ 560 crore

Numerical 6

The balance of trade shows a deficit of ₹ 2,000 crore and the value of imports is ₹ 8,000 crore. What is the value of exports?

Sol. Given, Balance of trade = (–) ₹ 2,000 crore

Value of imports = ₹ 8,000 crore

Balance of Trade = Value of Exports – Value of Imports

or Value of Exports = Balance of Trade (Deficit) + Value of Imports

= (–) 2,000 + 8,000

= ₹ 6,000 crore

Numerical 7

If balance of payment of a country is ₹ (– 100) crore and total payment are ₹ 500 crore, find out its total receipts.

Sol. Balance of Payment = Total Receipts – Total Paymens

Total Receipts = Total Payment + BoP

= 500 + (–100) = 500 –100

= ₹ 400 crore

Numerical 8

The balance of trade shows a deficit of ₹ 10,000 crore and the exports of goods are half of imports of goods. Find out exports and imports.

Sol. Value of imports = M; Balance of trade = (–) 10,000

Exports = 1/2 (Imports) = 1/2 (M)

Balance of Trade = Exports – Imports

$$= \frac{1}{2}(M) - M$$

$$= \frac{M-2M}{2}$$

$$-10,000 = \frac{-M}{2}$$

So, Imports (M) = ₹ 20,000 crore

and Exports = $\frac{1}{2}$ (20,000) = ₹ 10,000 crore

SELF ASSESSMENT TEST

Objective Type Questions

1. Balance of payments of a country is a statement that records
   (a) sources of foreign exchange
   (b) uses of foreign exchange
   (c) Both (a) and (b) (d) None of the above
2. Trade deficit refers to ....
   (a) Export of visible items > Import of visible items
   (b) Import of goods and services > Export of goods and services
   (c) Export of goods and services > Import of goods and services
   (d) Import of visible items > Export of visible items
3. Which of the following is a stock concept?
   (a) Balance of payments (b) Current account
   (c) Capital account (d) Balance of trade
4. Unfavourable disequilibrium in BoP occurs when there is
   (a) balance of trade deficit
   (b) total exports are more than total imports
   (c) total imports are more than total exports
   (d) exports of goods and services are less than imports of goods and services
5. Invisible trade balance includes ....
   (a) goods (b) services
   (c) Both (a) and (b) (d) None of these
6. Suppose India is exporting goods more as compared to importing goods, this will lead to .... in balance of trade.
   (a) Either surplus or deficit (b) deficit
   (c) balanced (d) surplus
7. Which of the following statements is/are correct?
   I. Accommodating items are always recorded in capital account.
   II. Political instability has no impact on BoP.

   Codes
   (a) Only I (b) Only II
   (c) Both I and II (d) None of these

Answers 1. (c) 2. (d) 3. (c) 4. (c) 5. (b) 6. (d) 7. (a)

Short Answer Type Questions

8. What is meant by balance of trade?
9. Briefly discuss the components of the capital account of balance of payment.
10. What is meant by current account deficit and current account surplus? Discuss their significance.
11. How does the balance of payment reflect supply, demand status of foreign exchange for a country?
12. "According to the Reserve Bank of India's guidelines on the Balance of Payments (BoP), inflows under the capital account, such as Foreign Direct Investment (FDI) and Foreign Portfolio Investment (FPI), play a crucial role in bolstering a nation's economic strength."
    In the light of statement, discuss the economic value of these foreign exchange inflows within the capital account.
13. Government takes measures to restrict autonomous imports of gold. Explain the economic values desired to be achieved from this.
14. Identify the following items as credit or debit transactions on balance of payments account
    (i) Investment by Samsung in India.
    (ii) Export of software to France.

Long Answer Type Questions

15. Explain from your viewpoint, is the concept of demand for domestic goods and domestic demand for goods are one and the same thing?
16. Explain the components of BoP account in detail.
17. Explain the difference between autonomous and accommodating transactions in balance of payments. Also, explain the concept of balance of payment deficit in this context.

Numerical Questions

18. Find 'non-factor income from services' balance

Items	₹ (in crores)
Exports	100
Imports	150
Net Factor Payment	300
Net Transfer Payment	100
Current Account Balance	1,000

Ans. Non-factor income from services = ₹ 650 crore

19. Find current account balance from the following date

S. No.	Items	₹ (in crores)
(i)	Balance of Visible Trade	9,000
(ii)	Exports of Services	9,000
(iii)	Imports of Services	3,000

Ans. Current account balance = ₹ 15,000 crore

PART B
Indian Economic Development

01 CHAPTER

On the eve of independence, India's economy stood crippled by colonial exploitation, with stagnant agriculture and barely existent industries. Poverty was rampant and the country's infrastructure was underdeveloped.

Indian Economy on the Eve of Independence

▼ **YOUR STUDY GOALS**

1.1 Introduction
1.2 Sectors of Indian Economy on the Eve of Independence
1.3 Positive Effects of British Rule in India

▼ **YOUR PRACTICE GOAL**

- Objective Type Questions (54 Qs ; MCQs, A-R, Statements, Matching, Concept Identification)
- Subjective Questions (26 SAs, 10 LAs)
- Self Assessment Test (8 MCQs, 7 SAs, 3 LAs)

1.1 Introduction

The foundation of the Indian economy today is deeply connected with its colonial past, particularly during British rule. Britishers aimed to exploit India's natural resources for their own benefit, transforming the country into a raw material supplier for Britain's expanding industries. Understanding this exploitative relationship is crucial for assessing India's current level of development.

Indian Economy Before the British Rule

- Prior to British rule, India's economy was flourishing and developed.
- Bernier, a French explorer, described Bengal as 'richer than Egypt'.
- There were well-developed agricultural practices and self-sufficient villages.
- Indian handicrafts gained international recognition, such as the *Daccai Muslin* and was often referred as '*malmal khas*' or '*malmal shahi*' by foreigners.

Low Level of Economic Development under Colonial Rule

- India's independent economy, prior to British rule, was characterised by various kinds of manufacturing activities and agriculture as the main livelihood source.
- Handicraft industries were prominent in cotton, silk textiles, metal and precious stone works.
- British economic policies prioritised protecting and promoting their home country's economic interests over developing the Indian economy.
- These policies transformed India into a supplier of raw materials and consumer of finished industrial products from Britain.

Economic Growth under the British Rule

- There was no official estimate on **National Income** and **Per Capita Income** of India under the colonial rule because of lack of initiative shown by the British Government. Therefore, the level of economic growth cannot be predicted with accuracy.
- Some individuals, such as Dadabhai Naoroji, William Digby, Findlay Shirras, VKRV Rao and RC Desai made some attempts to study the level of growth during the colonial period.
- These studies produced inconsistent results. However, most of the studies did find that there was low level of economic growth during colonial rule.

State of Indian Economy on the Eve of Independence

Economy	Explanation
Colonial Economy	British colonial policies were concerned with economic interests of their home country over the development of India's economy.
Stagnant Economy	Stagnation is a prolonged period of little or no growth in an economy. The Indian economy experienced low growth rates, with a growth rate of less than 2% in the first half of the 20th century.
Backward Economy	Indian economy exhibited characteristics of a backward economy such as dependence on the agricultural sector, high birth and death rates, low literacy levels and low per capita income.
Semi-feudal Economy	Indian economy was a semi-feudal economy in which agricultural sector and modern industries existed side by side i.e. it had the mixture of feudalistic and capitalist modes of production with modern industries still in their formation stage.
Amputated Economy	India faced partition and the country witnessed large-scale religious riots. India faced the problem of rehabilitating the refugees as well as problem of shortage of jute and cotton as most of the area's growing these crops went to Pakistan.
Depleted Economy	It is an economy in which no efforts are made to replace the stock of capital assets which gets depreciated due to excessive use. Due to extensive exploitation by the colonial government, India's wealth was drained for the benefit of British economy. The British government used India's wealth for colonial staff salaries, war expenses, or other purposes.

1.2 Sectors of Indian Economy on the Eve of Independence

All the sectors of the economy *viz.* the agricultural sector, the industrial sector and foreign trade were badly hit by the colonial rule.

The critical indicators of change such as the demographic profile of the country, the occupational structure of people and the economic and social infrastructure indicated that the country was adversely affected by the colonial rule.

Agricultural Sector

On the eve of independence, around 85% of the country's population lived in villages and were dependent, either directly or indirectly on agriculture. However, despite being the occupation of such a large population, this sector was facing stagnation and constant deterioration due to the following reasons

Reason	Explanation
Low Level of Agricultural Productivity	Agricultural productivity was low as it was about 660 kg per hectare for wheat and 665 kg per hectare for rice. The following were its reasons • High degree of vulnerability. • Rift and turmoil between owners and tillers. • Uneconomic and fragmented landholdings. • Problem of unemployment and underemployment. • Use of primitive techniques of production.
Lack of Investment	India's agriculture faced challenges due to lack of investment in terracing, flood-control, drainage and soil desalination, affecting most of the tenants, small farmers and sharecroppers.
Exploitative Land Settlement System	The *zamindari* system in Bengal presidency led to agricultural stagnation in following ways • By granting profit to *zamindars* instead of cultivators in form of *lagaan.* • *Zamindars* interested in only collecting rent even in case of crop failures, causing social tension. • The system's changes were influenced by fixed **revenue settlement** terms, where *zamindars* need to deposit specified sum of revenue to avoid losing their rights.
Commercialisation of Agriculture	The Britishers encouraged commercialisation of agriculture which means that farmers were growing crops for sale in the market and not for self-consumption. This led to • An increase in indebtedness. • Economic conditions of farmers did not improve. • Due to fall in production of staple food crops, India faced frequent famines.

Industrial Sector

Prior to British rule in India, the country's economy was characterised by various kinds of manufacturing activities, particularly handicraft industries in the fields of cotton and silk textiles, metal and precious stone works, etc.

However, India could not develop a strong industrial base under the colonial rule. The following points discuss the state of the industrial sector on the eve of independence

Reason	Explanation
Systematic De-industrialisation (Decline of Handicraft Industry)	• British policy of systematic de-industrialisation led to the decline of the handicraft industry. • Unemployment increased as handicraft industries failed. • Indian goods made by hands could not compete with machine made cheap British goods. As demand for British goods increased, their imports also increased. • The two-fold motives (primary motive) for de-industrialisation was to export cheap raw materials from India, reducing India to a raw material exporter only and sell British manufactured goods in Indian market at higher prices. • The discriminatory tariff policy, introduced by Britishers, allowed free export of raw material and import of finished goods of British industries, but heavy duty was imposed on Indian handicraft exports.
Advent of Modern Industry	Indian Industrial Development during the second half of 19th century was as follows • Slow progress in modern industry establishment. • Indian cotton textile mills were established in Maharashtra and Gujarat. • British jute mills were established in Bengal. • Emergence of iron and steel industries in early 20th century. Tata Iron and Steel Company (TISCO) was incorporated in 1907. • Post-World War II, other industries in the fields of sugar, cement, paper, etc. were established.
Lack of Capital Goods Industries	India's industrialisation was hindered by the absence of a capital goods industry, which can produce machine tools used for producing articles for current consumption. Indians were dependent on Britain for machine and equipment supply.
Contribution towards GDP	Industrial sector's rate of growth and its contribution to Gross Domestic Product (GDP) remained very small.
Role of Public Sector	Public sector was operational in very small area. e.g. Railways, power generation, ports, etc.

Foreign Trade

India has been an important trading nation since ancient times. But when the restrictive policies of commodity production, trade and tariff were imposed by the colonial government, the structure, composition and volume of India's foreign trade was adversely affected.

Following points highlight the features of foreign trade during British rule

Feature	Explanation
Exporter of Primary Products	India became an exporter of primary products such as raw silk, cotton, wool, sugar, indigo, jute, etc.
Importer of Finished Goods	India became importer of finished consumer goods like cotton, silk and woollen clothes and capital goods like light machinery produced in the factories of Britain.
Monopoly Control on India's Foreign Trade	Britain maintained monopoly control over exports and imports in India. More than half of India's trade was restricted to Britain while the rest was allowed with few other countries such as China, Ceylon (Sri Lanka) and Persia (Iran). The opening of the **Suez Canal** further intensified British control over India's foreign trade.
Export Surplus	India generated an export surplus but it did not improved the economy of the country. The surplus was used to make payments for the administrative expenses of the British government, for war expenses and for import of invisible items. This led to drain of Indian wealth during British rule.
Scarcity of Essential Commodities	Several essential commodities such as foodgrains, clothes, kerosene, etc. were scarcely available in the domestic market as these were exported.

Trade through the Suez Canal

- Suez Canal is an artificial waterway running from North to South across the Isthmus of Suez North-Eastern Egypt.
- It was opened in 1869 and made access to the Indian market easier.
- The canal reduced the cost of transportation and provides a direct trade route for ships operating between European or American ports and ports located in South Asia, East Africa and Oceania.

Demographic Condition

It refers to various indicators related to the population of the country such as life expectancy, literacy rate, birth rate, etc. These parameters help to assess the quality of life of the population.

Before 1921, India was in the **first stage** of demographic transition. This stage was characterised by high birth and death rates.

After 1921, **second stage** of transition began from where death rate started to come down due to improved health facilities while birth rate remained high.

Some of the parameters reflecting the demographic condition after 1921 are given below

Parameters	Explanation
Low Life Expectancy	Life expectancy was very low at 32 years at the time of independence in contrast to the present expectancy of 69 years.
High Infant Mortality Rate	Infant mortality rate was quite high, about 218 per thousand in contrast to the present infant mortality rate of 33 per thousand.
Low Literacy Rate	On the eve of independence, the overall literacy rate was less than 16%. Female literacy level was at a negligible low level of 7%.
Increase in Population	India's population continued to grow post-1921, marking 1921 as the 'Year of Great Divide', which signifies that India has entered the second stage of demographic transition.
High Birth Rate and Death Rate	The birth rate and death rate were both high at 48 and 40 per thousand, respectively.
Poor Health Facilities	Public health facilities were either unavailable to a large population or highly inadequate when they were available.
Poverty	Extensive poverty prevailed in India during the colonial period.

Occupational Structure

It refers to the distribution of population across the different sectors *viz.* the primary, secondary and the tertiary sector.

Occupational Structure during Colonial Period

- Share of primary sector (70-75%)
- Share of secondary and tertiary sectors (10 and 15-20%)
- Regional variation

1. **Share of Primary Sector** The primary or agricultural sector accounted for the largest share of the workforce, i.e. 70-75% of the workforce.
2. **Share of Secondary and Tertiary Sectors** The secondary (manufacturing) and tertiary (services) sectors, accounted for only 10 and 15-20%, respectively.
3. **Regional Variation** There was a high degree of regional variation. Parts of Madras Presidency (comprising Tamil Nadu, Andhra Pradesh, Kerala and Karnataka), Bombay and Bengal witnessed a decline in the dependence of the workforce on the agricultural sector and increase in secondary and tertiary sectors.

   At the same time, Orissa, Rajasthan and Punjab witnessed an increase in the dependence of the workforce on the agricultural sector.

Infrastructure

Infrastructure comprises such industries which help in the growth of other industries. Under the colonial period, basic infrastructure industries such as railways, ports, water transport, posts and telegraphs developed. However, the real motive behind this development was not to provide basic amenities to the people but to fulfill various colonial interests.

The state of infrastructure under the colonial rule is discussed below

1. **Roads**
   - Roads were not suitable for modern transport.
   - Roads that were built primarily served the purposes of army mobilisation within India and raw material transportation to nearest railway station or port.
   - Acute shortage of all weather roads affected rural areas during rainy seasons. Therefore, people living in these areas suffered during natural calamities and famines.
2. **Railways**

   The British introduced railways in India in 1850. The railways affected the structure of the Indian economy positively as well as negatively in the following ways

Positive Impact of Railways	Negative Impact of Railways
• Enabled people to undertake long distance travel and thereby break geographical and cultural barriers. • Promoted commercialisation of Indian agriculture as agricultural produce could be sent to distant places. • Enabled the government to supply foodgrains fastly to famine affected areas.	• Enabled the goods from British factories to be transported to various parts of the country, thereby expanding their market. • Commercialisation of Indian agriculture adversely affected the self-sufficiency of the village economies in India.

3. **Water and Air Transport**
   - Colonial rulers failed to develop water transport due to uneconomical inland waterways.
   - The Coast Canal on Orissa coast was abandoned due to its inability to compete with railways.
   - The government established Tata Airlines in 1932 for air transport development.
4. **Communication**
   - Expensive system of electric graph was introduced in India for serving the purpose of maintaining law and order.
   - Postal services remained inadequate despite serving a useful public purpose.

1.3 Positive Effects of British Rule in India

Although the motive behind the British rule in India was colonial exploitation, but the means resulted in some positive effects which are as under

Positive Effect	Explanation
Political and Economic Unification of India	Prior to the British rule, the Indian sub-continent was divided into small and fragmented territories ruled by different dynasties. The British Government took over the control of these territories and unified the country politically and economically.
Development of Means of Transport	Although, the Britishers developed various means of transport, such as roads and railways for their personal benefit, yet these opened up new opportunities of growth and helped in the cultural unification of the country.
Growth of Monetary System	The colonial rule helped the country to shift from the barter system of exchange to a monetary system. This monetised system helped the country to benefit from large-scale production. 
Check over Famines	Roads and railways developed by Britishers worked as a great check on the occurrence and impact of famines. They helped in transporting food supplies to the affected areas in case of droughts.
Efficient System of Administration	The Britishers left behind an efficient system of administration. They also made exhaustive records of every plan, policy, agreement, etc. This system of administration and record keeping helped the independent Indian administration to efficiently manage the country.

Mind Map

INDIAN ECONOMY ON THE EVE OF INDEPENDENCE

1 Indian Economy Before the British Rule

- Prior to British rule, India's economy was flourishing and developed.
- Bernier, a French explorer, described Bengal as 'richer than Egypt'.
- There were well-developed agricultural practices and self-sufficient villages.
- Indian handicrafts gained international recognition, such as the *Daccai Muslin* and was often referred as '*malmal khas*' or '*malmal shahi*' by foreigners.

2 Low Level of Economic Development under Colonial Rule

- India's independent economy, prior to British rule, was characterised by various kinds of manufacturing activities and agriculture as the main livelihood source.
- Handicraft industries were prominent in cotton, silk textiles, metal and precious stone works.
- British economic policies prioritised protecting and promoting their home country's economic interests over developing the Indian economy.
- These policies transformed India into a supplier of raw materials and consumer of finished industrial products from Britain.

3 State of Indian Economy on the Eve of Independence

- **Colonial Economy** British colonial policies were concerned with economic interests of their home country over the development of India's economy.
- **Stagnant Economy** The Indian economy experienced low growth rates, with a growth rate of less than 2% in the first half of the 20th century.
- **Backward Economy** Indian economy exhibited characteristics of a backward economy such as dependence on the agricultural sector, high birth and death rates, low literacy levels and low per capita income.
- **Semi-feudal Economy** Indian economy was a semi-feudal economy in which agricultural sector and modern industries existed side by side.
- **Amputated Economy** India faced the problem of rehabilitating the refugees as well as problem of shortage of jute and cotton as most of the area's growing these crops went to Pakistan.
- **Depleted Economy** It is an economy in which no efforts are made to replace the stock of capital assets which gets depreciated due to excessive use.

4 Agricultural Sector

Despite being the occupation of such a large population, this sector was facing stagnation and constant deterioration because of the following reasons

- Low level of agricultural productivity
- Lack of investment
- Exploitative land settlement system
- Commercialisation of agriculture

5 Industrial Sector

India could not develop a strong industrial base under the colonial rule because of the following reasons

- Systematic de-industrialisation
- Advent of modern industry
- Lack of capital goods industry
- Contribution towards GDP
- Role of public sector

6 Foreign Trade

Restrictive policies of commodity production, trade and tariff were imposed by the colonial government, the structure, composition and volume of India's foreign trade was adversely affected. Features of foreign trade highlighted are

- Exporter of primary products
- Monopoly control on India's foreign trade
- Scarcity of essential commodities
- Importer of finished goods
- Export surplus

7 Demographic Condition

It refers to various indicators related to the population of the country. Parameters reflecting the demographic condition after 1921 include

- Low life expectancy
- Low literacy rate
- High birth rate and death rate
- Poverty
- High infant mortality rate
- Increase in population
- Poor health facilities

8 Occupational Structure

It refers to the distribution of population across the different sectors

- **Share of Primary Sector** The primary or agricultural sector accounted for the largest share of the workforce, i.e. 70-75% of the workforce.
- **Share of Secondary and Tertiary Sectors** The secondary (manufacturing) and tertiary (services) sectors accounted for only 10 and 15-20% respectively.
- **Regional Variation** There was a high degree of regional variation. Parts of Madras Presidency (comprising Tamil Nadu, Andhra Pradesh, Kerala and Karnataka), Bombay and Bengal witnessed a decline in the dependence of the workforce on the agricultural sector and increase in secondary and tertiary sectors.

9 Infrastructure

It comprises such industries which help in the growth of other industries. The state of infrastructure under the colonial rule is as follows

- **Roads** They were not suitable for modern transport.
- **Railways** It had both positive and negative impact.
- **Water and Air Transport** Colonial rulers failed to develop water transport. Government established Tata Airlines in 1932.
- **Communication** Postal services remained inadequate despite serving a useful public purpose.

10 Positive Effects of British Rule in India

- The British Government took over the control of the territories of Indian sub-continent and unified the country politically and economically.
- Although, the Britishers developed various means of transport, such as roads and railways for their personal benefit, yet these opened up new opportunities of growth and helped in the cultural unification of the country.
- The colonial rule helped the country to shift from the barter system of exchange to a monetary system. This monetised system helped the country to benefit from large-scale production.
- Roads and railways developed by Britishers worked as a great check on the occurrence and impact of famines. They helped in transporting food supplies to the affected areas in case of droughts.
- The system of administration and record keeping helped the independent Indian administration to efficiently manage the country.

EXAM PATTERN QUESTIONS

Objective Type Questions

Multiple Choice Questions (MCQs)

1. The Indian economy on the eve of independence was primarily an .... economy.

(a) industrialised (b) socialist
(c) agrarian (d) capitalist

2. Which of the following statements correctly describe the state of the Indian economy on the eve of independence? Competency Based Que

(a) High dependence on agriculture, with limited productivity and outdated methods
(b) Industrial growth was rapidly increasing, partly due to British policies that promoted modern industrial development
(c) The foreign trade sector was dominated by British exports, leading to a collection of wealth and diversification
(d) Although some infrastructure existed, it primarily served colonial interests, alongwith focus on domestic economic development

3. The colonial government made no sincere attempts to estimate India's national and per capita income, but most studies found that India's national income growth in the pre-independence era was .... and per capita income growth was .... CBSE QB; Competency Based Que

(a) close to 5 per cent, more than 2 per cent
(b) less than 3 per cent, more than 1 per cent
(c) close to half per cent, almost 0 per cent
(d) less than 2 per cent, close to half per cent

4. Which of the following statements correctly describe a stagnant economy? Competency Based Que

I. Little growth in income
II. High growth in income
III. Low level of productivity
IV. Voluntary unemployment

Codes
(a) I and III
(b) II and IV
(c) I and IV
(d) III and IV

5. Which of the following best describes the Indian economy on the eve of independence?

(a) Industrial economy (b) Urbanised economy
(c) Semi-feudal economy (d) Agricultural economy

6. "India's economic condition, on the eve of independence, was a result of systematic British exploitation." Which of the following best supports this statement? Competency Based Que

(a) India had a rapidly growing manufacturing sector
(b) The agricultural sector was thriving with sustainable farming practices
(c) British economic policies promoted the export of raw materials and the import of finished goods
(d) British policies led to the creation of significant infrastructure for India's future development

7. What was the main characteristic of Indian agriculture at the time of independence as depicted through image below?

(a) Highly industrialised
(b) Primitive techniques and low productivity
(c) Mechanised and capital intensive
(d) Dominated by plantation crops

8. Which of the following was a long-term consequence of the land revenue system implemented by the British, particularly the *zamindari* system, on Indian rural society?

(a) The empowerment of rural artisans
(b) The creation of a large class of indebted landless peasants
(c) Expansion of modern agricultural techniques
(d) Growth of cooperative farming communities

9. Which colonial policy had the greatest negative impact on Indian agriculture during British rule?

(a) Industrial Policy Resolution
(b) Commercialisation of agriculture
(c) Permanent Settlement Act (d) Nationalisation of land

10. Under the British rule, commercialisation of agriculture resulted in shifting of agricultural production from .... crops to .... crops. CBSE 2024

(a) cash, food (b) cotton, jute
(c) food, cash (d) jute, food

11. **Which sector saw minimal growth in employment opportunities during the British colonial period?**
(a) Service sector (b) Agricultural sector
(c) Industrial sector (d) Informal sector

12. **Which of the following industries in India faced significant decline due to colonial policies, severely impacting its traditional practices?**
(a) Sugar industry
(b) Handicraft industry
(c) Iron and steel industry
(d) Textile industry

13. **Britain maintained a monopoly control over India's exports and imports while the rest was allowed with a few other countries like ....** CBSE 2024 C

(i) China
(ii) Ceylon (Sri Lanka)
(iii) Persia (Iran)

Codes
(a) Only (i) (b) (i) and (ii)
(c) (ii) and (iii) (d) (i), (ii) and (iii)

14. **In 1945, a newspaper headline states, "Indian economy suffers from over-dependence on the British market." Which option best captures the implications of India's colonial trade dynamics?** Competency Based Que
(a) India maintained balanced trade relations globally, ensuring equitable exchanges
(b) India imported British machinery while exporting its raw materials, undermining local industry
(c) India had a trade surplus with Britain, fostering economic autonomy and reducing reliance on imports
(d) India's economy was structured to benefit British interests, exporting vital resources and importing finished goods, leading to industrial decline

15. **The major export commodity of India during the colonial period was ....**
(a) spices (b) textiles
(c) jute and cotton (d) iron ore

16. **In the 20th century, under British rule, India had an export surplus. Where was this surplus used?** CBSE QB; Competency Based Que
(a) To invest in capital goods industries in India
(b) To invest in capital goods industries in Britain
(c) To meet the official and war expenses of the British
(d) To pay the salaries of Indian government employees

17. **On the eve of India's independence in 1947, the Suez Canal played a pivotal role in shaping the country's economic landscape. As a crucial trade route, it facilitated the swift movement of goods between Europe and Asia, allowing British merchants to transport raw materials from India to Britain efficiently.**

This reliance on the canal not only boosted British trade interests but also influenced colonial policies in India, as the British sought to control resources and maintain economic dominance over the sub-continent.

On the basis of above lines, the reliance on the Suez Canal by British traders primarily led to which consequence for India's economy? Competency Based Que
(a) Diversification of agricultural products
(b) Strengthened local economies through reduced imports
(c) Heightened control over Indian resources by the British
(d) Increased foreign investment in Indian railways

18. **The image below shows a key maritime route that significantly impacted global trade during the colonial era. How did its construction benefit British control over the Indian economy?**

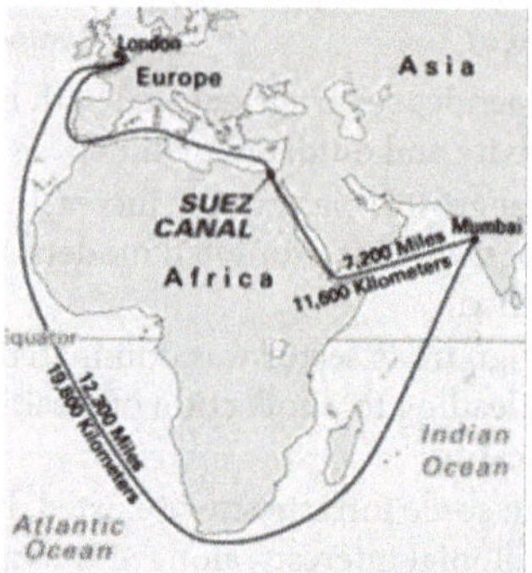

(a) It boosted Indian industries by improving exports
(b) It reduced the cost and time for transporting Indian raw materials to Britain
(c) It eliminated Indian competition in European markets
(d) It was built to increase India's trade with African colonies

19. **The life expectancy of the Indian population during British rule was approximately .... years.**
(a) 70 (b) 60
(c) 32 (d) 45

20. **Which of the following factors contributed most to the high infant mortality rate in India at the time of independence?**
(a) Advanced healthcare system
(b) Malnutrition and poor sanitation
(c) High literacy levels
(d) Access to clean drinking water

21. **What was the approximate proportion of the population working under tertiary sector on the eve of India's independence?**
(a) 10% (b) 75% (c) 20% (d) 26%

22. **During British rule, the introduction of .... led to the commercialisation of agriculture in India.**
(a) green revolution (b) Permanent Settlement Act
(c) railways (d) zamindari system

23.

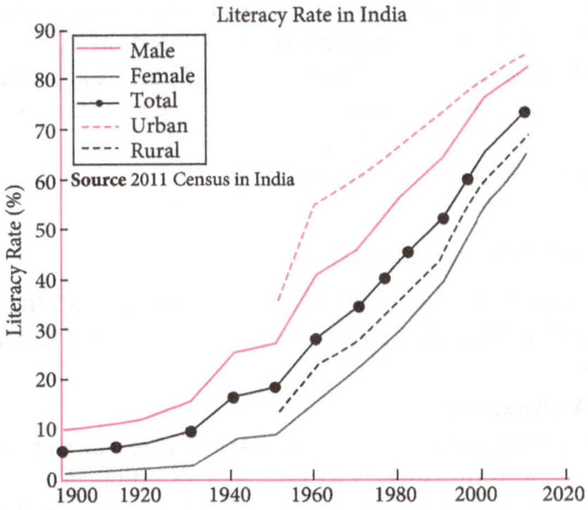

Analysing the literacy rates in India just before independence (as given in above graph), which of the following conclusions can be drawn about societal inequalities?

(a) Literacy was uniformly distributed across all regions and communities
(b) Education was primarily available to certain castes and classes
(c) Literacy rates were higher in rural areas compared to urban areas
(d) Women had equal access to education as men

24. How did the Britishers' focus on infrastructure for resource extraction impact India's economy after independence?

(a) It resulted in unbalanced regional development and economic disparities
(b) It helped India transition smoothly into a modern economy
(c) It left India with a well-developed industrial base
(d) It boosted Indian entrepreneurs to compete globally

Direction *Read the case study and answer the questions 25 to 28 on the basis of the same*

Before 1947, more than 90% of the national income relied on the Indian agriculture sector. A significant portion of the country's population resided in rural areas where agriculture was the primary source of livelihood. The pre-colonised India produced primary two crops, wheat and rice.

Even if it was only two types of crops, country's agriculture sector was sustainable and self-sufficient. The British invasion resulted in total commercialisation of India's agriculture industry.

On the eve of independence, the once most prominent sector of this country was known to be suffering from stagnation and constant degradation.

25. Commercialisation of agriculture means ....

26. Reasons for low productivity in agriculture sector was/were

(a) HYV seeds (b) low level of technology
(c) improved irrigation system
(d) All of the above

27. Which of the following statements is/are correct with reference to the *zamindari* system?

(i) The profit accruing out of the agriculture sector was proposed to go to the cultivators.

(ii) The main interest of the *zamindars* was only to collect rent regardless of the economic condition of the cultivators.

Codes

(a) Both are correct (b) Both are incorrect
(c) (i) correct, (ii) incorrect (d) (ii) correct, (i) incorrect

28. .... is reason for the stagnation in the agriculture sector under the British rule.

Direction *Read the case study and answer the questions 29 to 32 on the basis of the same*

How successful was this long phase of classical imperialism in British India, which lasted from the late 18th century until independence in 1947? The British claimed a huge set of achievements, including democracy, the rule of law, railways, the joint stock company and cricket, but the gap between theory and practice – with the exception of cricket – remained wide throughout the history of imperial relations between the two countries. Putting the tally together in the years of pre- independence assessment, it was easy to see how far short the achievements were compared with the rhetoric of accomplishment.

Alas, neither the stopping of famines nor the remedying of ill health was part of the high-performance achievements of British rule in India. Nothing could lead us away from the fact that life expectancy at birth in India as the empire ended was abysmally low: 32 years, at most.

The abstemiousness of colonial rule in neglecting basic education reflects the view taken by the dominant administrators of the needs of the subject nation. There was a huge asymmetry between the ruler and the ruled.

The British government became increasingly determined in the 19th century to achieve universal literacy for the native British population. In contrast, the literacy rates in India under the Raj were very low. When the empire ended, the adult literacy rate in India was barely 15%. The only regions in India with comparatively high literacy were the 'native kingdoms' of Travancore and Cochin (formally outside the British empire), which, since independence, have constituted the bulk of the state of Kerala.

These kingdoms, though dependent on the British administration for foreign policy and defence, had remained technically outside the empire and had considerable freedom in domestic policy, which they exercised in favour of more school education and public healthcare.

The 200 years of colonial rule were also a period of massive economic stagnation, with hardly any advance at all in real GNP per capita. These grim facts were much aired after independence in the newly liberated media, whose rich culture was in part – it must be acknowledged – an inheritance from British civil society.

Even though the Indian media was very often muzzled during the Raj – mostly to prohibit criticism of imperial rule, for example at the time of the Bengal famine of 1943 – the tradition of a free press, carefully cultivated in Britain, provided a good model for India to follow as the country achieved independence.

Source *https://www.theguardian.com/world/2021/june/29/british-empire-india-amartya-sen*

29. The passage discusses the legacy of the British Empire in India. Which statement best summarises this legacy?
(a) It was primarily one of prosperity and cultural exchange
(b) It was marked by significant advancements in education and health
(c) It resulted in lasting economic stagnation and social inequality
(d) It created a fully literate and healthy population

30. Which statement best reflects the gap between British claims of achievement and the reality of their rule in India?
(a) The British improved literacy rates and healthcare significantly
(b) British claims of advancements were often undermined by poor living conditions
(c) British policies led to economic prosperity and technological advancement in India
(d) British rule completely transformed Indian society for the better

31. British policies often resulted in a ...., leading to increased poverty and suffering among the Indian population.

32. **Assertion** (A) The adult literacy rate in India was very low under British rule.

Reason (R) The British prioritised education for their own population while neglecting the educational needs of Indians.

Alternatives
(a) Both Assertion (A) and Reason (R) are true and Reason (R) is the correct explanation of Assertion (A)
(b) Both Assertion (A) and Reason (R) are true, but Reason (R) is not the correct explanation of Assertion (A)
(c) Assertion (A) is false, but Reason (R) is true
(d) Both Assertion (A) and Reason (R) are false

Assertion-Reason

Direction (Q.No. 33 to 38) *Read the following Assertion (A) and Reason (R) and choose the correct alternative from the following*

Alternatives
(a) Both Assertion (A) and Reason (R) are true and Reason (R) is the correct explanation of Assertion (A)
(b) Both Assertion (A) and Reason (R) are true, but Reason (R) is not the correct explanation of Assertion (A)
(c) Assertion (A) is false, but Reason (R) is true
(d) Both Assertion (A) and Reason (R) are false

33. **Assertion** (A) The amputated economy led to long-term economic consequences for India.

Reason (R) The division of territories resulted in the separation of industries and agricultural resources.

34. **Assertion** (A) The British introduced cash crops in India to boost local agriculture.

Reason (R) Cash crops were necessary for the sustenance of the local economy.

35. **Assertion** (A) The *zamindari* system increased agricultural productivity in India.

Reason (R) *Zamindars* had a vested interest in improving land and production techniques.

36. **Assertion** (A) Commercialisation of agriculture helped the farmers.

Reason (R) Their financial status improved drastically.

37. **Assertion** (A) India developed a sound industrial base during the colonial rule.

Reason (R) The industrial sector was crying for modernisation, diversification, capacity building and increased public investment.

38. **Assertion** (A) The year 1921 is called as the year of great divide.

Reason (R) After the year 1921, India experienced a sharp rise in its population growth rate. **CBSE 2025**

Two Statements Based MCQs

Direction (Q.No. 39 to 45) *Read the following statements carefully and choose the correct alternative*

Alternatives

(a) Both the statements are correct
(b) Both the statements are incorrect
(c) Statement I is correct, but Statement II is incorrect
(d) Statement II is correct, but Statement I is incorrect

39. **Statement I** Agricultural productivity was very low during the British rule.

Statement II In absolute terms, there was growth in agricultural sector due to expansion of aggregate area under cultivation. **CBSE Term I 2021**

40. **Statement I** The decline of India's traditional handicrafts and industries was accelerated by British policies of high import tariffs on Indian goods.

Statement II India was the largest exporter of finished cotton goods to the world market on the eve of independence.

41. **Statement I** The British policies led to the collapse of India's world famous handicraft industries.

Statement II During the colonial rule in India, the contribution of the industrial sector to Gross Value Added (GVA) increased significantly. **CBSE SQP 2025**

42. **Statement I** The Indian economy witnessed rapid growth during British rule due to the establishment of various industries and modern infrastructure.

Statement II The British colonial policies caused stagnation in India's agricultural sector, leading to frequent famines and food shortages.

43. **Statement I** The services sector, including trade, transport and finance, employed a negligible portion of the Indian workforce on the eve of independence.

Statement II The dominance of agriculture in the occupational structure was partly due to the lack of industrialisation and modernisation during British rule.

44. **Statement I** The commercialisation of Indian agriculture was coercively introduced by the colonial government.

Statement II Britishers had a two-fold motive behind the enforcement of food crops production. **CBSE 2024 C**

45. **Statement I** The British introduced the telegraph system in India, which helped improve communication between different regions of the country and played a key role in administration and governance.

Statement II The telegraph system was widely accessible to the Indian population and contributed to the improvement of social and economic conditions across India.

Matching

46. Match the following

Column I	Column II
A. Stagnant economy	(i) Exploitation of resources
B. Semi-feudal economy	(ii) Low level of productivity
C. Colonial economy	(iii) Dominance of agricultural sector with few modern industries

Codes

	A	B	C		A	B	C
(a)	(i)	(ii)	(iii)	(b)	(ii)	(iii)	(i)
(c)	(iii)	(ii)	(i)	(d)	(iii)	(i)	(ii)

47. Match the following

Column I	Column II
A. First Census of India	(i) 1869
B. Opening of Suez Canal	(ii) 1850
C. Incorporation of TISCO	(iii) 1881
D. Introduction of Railways	(iv) 1907

Codes

	A	B	C	D		A	B	C	D
(a)	(i)	(ii)	(iii)	(iv)	(b)	(ii)	(iii)	(iv)	(i)
(c)	(iii)	(i)	(iv)	(ii)	(d)	(iii)	(iv)	(i)	(ii)

48. Match the following **Competency Based Que**

Column I	Column II
A. British monopoly of trade	(i) 1850-1920
B. Commercialisation of agriculture	(ii) Decline of traditional industries
C. De-industrialisation	(iii) Drain of wealth
D. Colonial impact on handicrafts	(iv) Cotton and jute export

Codes

	A	B	C	D		A	B	C	D
(a)	(iii)	(ii)	(iv)	(i)	(b)	(iii)	(iv)	(ii)	(i)
(c)	(iv)	(iii)	(ii)	(i)	(d)	(i)	(ii)	(iii)	(iv)

49. Choose the correct pair **Competency Based Que**

Column I	Column II
A. Urban centers	(i) Facilitated export of raw materials
B. Road development	(ii) Enabled military and administrative efficiency
C. Ports and harbors	(iii) Bombay, Calcutta and Madras
D. Communication networks	(iv) Limited access for rural areas

Codes

	A	B	C	D
(a)	(ii)	(iii)	(iv)	(i)
(b)	(iii)	(iv)	(ii)	(i)
(c)	(iv)	(i)	(iii)	(ii)
(d)	(iii)	(iv)	(i)	(ii)

Concept Identification

50. It refers to a shift from cultivation for self-consumption to cultivation for the market.

51. Policy where Indian handicrafts faced stiff competition from machine-made British goods.

52. A policy where Indian goods were taxed heavily, but British goods were given free entry into Indian markets.

53. It refers to the distribution of population across the different sectors *viz.* the primary, secondary and the tertiary sector.

54. The average number of years for which people are expected to live. **CBSE 2020**

Answers

1. (c) agrarian

2. (a) High dependence on agriculture, with limited productivity and outdated methods

3. (d) less than 2 per cent, close to half per cent

4. (a) I and III

5. (c) Semi-feudal economy

6. (c) British economic policies promoted the export of raw materials and the import of finished goods

7. (b) Primitive techniques and low productivity

8. (b) The creation of a large class of indebted landless peasants

9. (b) Commercialisation of agriculture

10. (c) food, cash

11. (c) Industrial sector

12. (b) Handicraft industry

13. (d) (i), (ii) and (iii)

14. (d) India's economy was structured to benefit British interests, exporting vital resources and importing finished goods, leading to industrial decline

15. (c) jute and cotton

16. (c) To meet the official and war expenses of the British

17. (c) Heightened control over Indian resources by the British

18. (b) It reduced the cost and time for transporting Indian raw materials to Britain

19. (c) 32

20. (b) Malnutrition and poor sanitation

21. (c) 20%

22. (c) railways

23. (b) Education was primarily available to certain castes and classes

24. (a) It resulted in unbalanced regional development and economic disparities

25. production of cash crops

26. (b) low level of technology

27. (d) (ii) correct, (i) incorrect

28. Land settlement systems

29. (c) It resulted in lasting economic stagnation and social inequality

30. (b) British claims of advancements were often undermined by poor living conditions

31. drain of resources

32. (a) Both Assertion (A) and Reason (R) are true and Reason (R) is the correct explanation of Assertion (A)

33. (a) Both Assertion (A) and Reason (R) are true and Reason (R) is the correct explanation of Assertion (A)

34. (d) There was an increase in the yield of cash crops, but it helped the farmers in no way.

Farmers were now mass producing cash crops instead of food crops, which were ultimately used for the benefit of British industries. Cash crops were promoted for the sustenance of the British economy not local economy.

35. (d) *Zamindari* system did not necessarily increase agricultural productivity. In many cases, it led to exploitation and neglect of agricultural improvement, as *zamindars* focused on collecting revenue rather than enhancing productivity.

36. (d) Due to commercialisation of agriculture, farmers were forced to produce cash crops leading to food insecurity.

37. (c) The industrial sector was in dismal state with hardly any capital goods industry and lack of support from the government.

38. (a) Both Assertion (A) and Reason (R) are true and Reason (R) is the correct explanation of Assertion (A)

39. (c) While the British did focus on expanding the area under cultivation to increase revenue, this did not result in 'growth' in the agricultural sector.

40. (c) By the time of independence, India had become a major exporter of raw materials like cotton, while the export of finished cotton goods had almost ceased due to the destruction of the Indian textile industry by British policies. British factories in Manchester and Lancashire dominated the cotton goods market.

41. (c) The industrial sector in India did not see a significant increase in its contribution to Gross Value Added (GVA) during colonial rule. In fact, colonial policies largely suppressed industrial growth in India, with the economy remaining predominantly agrarian.

42. (d) While the British did introduce infrastructure such as railways and roads, the Indian economy did not witness rapid growth. In fact, Indian industries were severely impacted by British policies, leading to deindustrialisation and the infrastructure was designed primarily for the benefit of British trade.

43. (a) Both the statements are correct

44. (a) Both the statements are correct

45. (c) The telegraph system was not widely accessible to the Indian population. It was mainly used by the British government for administrative control and military coordination rather than improving the social or economic conditions of the Indian masses.

46. (b) (ii) (iii) (i)

47. (c) (iii) (i) (iv) (ii)

48. (b) (iii) (iv) (ii) (i)

49. (d) (iii) (iv) (i) (ii)

50. Commercialisation of agriculture

51. De-industrialisation

52. Discriminatory tariff policy

53. Occupational structure

54. Life expectancy

Subjective Questions

Short Answer Type Questions

1. What was the focus of the economic policies pursued by the colonial government in India? What were the impacts of these policies? NCERT

Ans. The focus of economic policies pursued by the colonial government in India was to make India an exporter of raw material for the rapidly expanding modern industrial base and to target India as a market for its finished goods.

The British policies had the following impacts on India

(i) Agricultural sector had a lot of surplus labour and had extremely low productivity.

(ii) Industrial sector was backward and lacked diversification.

(iii) Poverty and unemployment were high.

(iv) Infrastructural facilities needed upgradation.

(v) Foreign trade was beneficial for the Britishers.

2. What do you understand by the drain of Indian wealth during the colonial period? NCERT

Ans. The Britishers exploited India in every possible way. Raw material from India was exported and expensive finished goods were imported to India. The heavy administrative costs (in the form of wages and salaries of the administrative staff) related to running of the colonial rule in India and the expenses incurred in fighting wars, were borne by revenues generated in India. All this led to drain of India's wealth.

3. Discuss briefly the estimates made by notable scholars regarding the national income and per capita income during the colonial rule in India. CBSE SQP 2025

Ans. Notable scholars like Dadabhai Naoroji, William Digby, Findlay Shirras and VKRV Rao attempted to estimate India's income during colonial rule. Their estimates revealed stagnation in India's economy

(i) National income growth was less than 2% per year.

(ii) Per capita income growth was close to 0.5% per year.

Conclusion

These estimates highlighted the exploitative nature of British policies and their failure to improve living standards in India.

4. Underscore some of India's most crucial economic challenges at the time of independence. NCERT

Ans. The Indian economy was a backward economy at the time of independence as over 70-75% of the population was engaged in agriculture.

There was a complete absence of any infrastructure for imparting knowledge on technical skills to the labourers.

The following were the economic challenges at the time of Independence

(i) Per capita income was low.

(ii) Large-scale unemployment and underemployment existed.

(iii) Agricultural sector and industrial sector both were in a dismal condition.

5. In the chapter, 'commercialisation of agriculture' has been cited as a reason for the dismal state of farmers at the time of independence. In context of the present time, do you think that such a concern over commercialisation of agriculture is justified? Competency Based Que

Ans. No, I do not think that concern over commercialisation of agriculture is justified in the present time.

Commercialisation of agriculture involves raising crops and livestock to sell for a profit. The goal of commercial agriculture is to make profits by maximising crop yields through labour-saving techniques, use of fertilisers, hybrid seeds and use of farming machinery.

Commercialisation of agriculture helps to increase the productivity. In the present context, it is of utmost importance that the productivity of agriculture has to be increased so as to feed the ever growing population. It is possible only by promoting commercial agriculture.

6. What were the main causes of India's agricultural stagnation during the colonial period? NCERT

Ans. The main causes of India's agricultural stagnation during the colonial period were

(i) **Land Revenue System under the British Rule**
The Britishers in India established the *zamindari* system. Under this system, the *zamindars* were the permanent owners of the land. For their ownership rights, they were required to pay a fixed sum to the government as land revenue and they were given full freedom to charge any revenue they wanted from the tillers. The *zamindars* had lavish and extravagant lifestyles and they mercilessly exploited the poor tillers and did nothing for their upliftment.

(ii) **Lack of Resources**
As the tillers had to pay huge amount of rent, referred to as '*Lagaan*', they were not left with any surplus to be able to provide for resources needed in agriculture in the form of fertilisers or providing for irrigation facilities. This further lowered the agricultural productivity.

(iii) **Commercialisation of Agriculture**
Instead of producing food crops, farmers were producing cash crops, which were ultimately used by British industries. This further compounded the plight of the tillers. Earlier they were growing crops to meet their family needs, but now they had to purchase from the market.
This led to an increase in indebtedness and they were constantly borrowing from moneylenders and landlords at very high rate of interests. Production of indigo is a good example of the same.

7. "Due to its quality, Indian indigo was in great demand in Britain. In 1810, almost 95% of the indigo imported into Britain was from India.

Indigo production became a very profitable business and many Britishers became indigo planters. They advanced loans to peasants at high rate and forced them to cultivate indigo in 25% of their land. They paid a low price for the indigo.

As the indigo plant had deep roots, it exhausted the soil fertility and the land was unfit for rice cultivation."

Do you think that the above practices of the British were justified? Competency Based Que

Ans. No, I do not think that the above practices are justified due to the following reasons

(i) The Britishers exploited Indian peasants by advancing them loans at a high rate of interest and by paying a low price for their produce.

(ii) The Britishers forced Indian peasants to cultivate indigo on 25% of their land holding. Since indigo plant exhausted the soil fertility, therefore the peasants had less land to cultivate in subsequent years.

8. "Although the *zamindari* system has been legally abolished in independent India, the agrarian sector remains underdeveloped."

What in your opinion, is the main cause for this persistent issue? Competency Based Que

Ans. Despite the abolition of the *zamindari* system, Indian agriculture remains backward due to two key reasons

(i) A significant portion of Indian farmers possess small and fragmented landholdings, which hinder economies of scale and the adoption of advanced agricultural techniques.

(ii) The institutional support in terms of credit, technology and infrastructure remains weak, with inefficient delivery systems failing to reach those most in need.

9. The Indian economy was an agro-based economy on the eve of independence. 75% of the Indian population was earning a livelihood from agriculture. Despite being a primary source of income for a major population, this sector faced a decline under the British rule.

In this context, how was the *zamindari* system of land settlement responsible for the stagnation of Indian agriculture? Competency Based Que

Ans. The *zamindars* were recognised as the permanent owners of land and were required to pay a fixed sum of money to the government on a specified day in lieu of this right.

If they defaulted on making payment, then this right was taken away from them. As a result of this, the *zamindars* charged huge rent from the tillers and even forced them to pay in case of crop failures. Inspite of charging a huge rent, they did nothing to improve the condition of agriculture.

As farmers had to pay huge amount of produce as rent, they were in no position to buy fertilisers and pesticides to increase the productivity of land. All this led to the stagnation of Indian agriculture.

10. Observe the picture given below and describe the state of Indian industries on the eve of independence. Competency Based Que

Ans. The industrial development pattern on the eve of independence was characterised by the following elements

(i) The public sector enterprises such as railways, power, post and telegraph were confined to areas which would enlarge the size of market for British products in India.

(ii) The industrial growth was lopsided, in the sense that consumer goods industry was not adequately supported by the capital goods industry.

(iii) No priority was given for the development of basic and heavy industries. Tata Iron and Steel Corporation (TISCO) established in 1907, was the only basic industry in India.

(iv) The pattern of development in the industrial sector was lopsided and was dominated by the presence of small industries and large industries, but very few medium industries.

11. "The economic policies imposed during the colonial period led to the marginalisation and eventual collapse of several local industries and crafts in colonised regions." Accept or deny the preceding assertion. Competency Based Que

Ans. The given assertion is accepted. It is a well acknowledged truth that the downfall of India's globally renowned handicraft industries occurred during the colonial era.

(i) India's reduction to the status of a mere raw material exporter was in the interests of the colonial rulers. This was practically demanded by Britain's emerging modern industries.

(ii) India was to serve as a ready market for these British businesses' imports, which were offered at lower prices. Thus, machine-made goods began to pose a threat to handicrafts.

(iii) The British did not take many steps to boost the handicraft industries' and its replacement by modern industrial base.

12. What was the effect of the systematic de-industrialisation policy followed by the British?

Ans. The effect of systematic de-industrialisation policy was as follows

(i) One of the outcomes of the British de-industrialisation policy was that it guaranteed the most possible profit to their own country by de-industrialising India.

(ii) India has a high rate of unemployment due to the collapse of the country's traditional handcraft industry.

(iii) To their considerable benefit, there was a demand for British goods imported as a result of the decline in the supply of locally produced items.

13. What was the two-fold motive behind the systematic de-industrialisation effected by the British in pre-independent India? NCERT

Or **State the two-fold motive for the systematic destabilisation of indigenous Indian industries in the British era.** All India 2020

Ans. The following are the two-fold motive behind the systematic de-industrialisation affected by the British

(i) **Making India a Supplier of Raw Materials**
The main motive of the British Government was to make India a mere supplier of cheap raw materials to feed its own rapidly expanding industrial base.

(ii) **Making India a Market for Finished Goods**
Another important objective of the British Government in de-industrialising Indian economy was to use India as a large and growing market to sell the finished goods produced by the British industries. So that their industries never face a demand shortage and could keep on flourishing.

14. Multinational Corporations (MNCs) have been dominating the Indian industrial landscape, posing a significant challenge to small-scale industries. How does this scenario compare to the period of British rule when Indian handicrafts faced severe competition from British machine-made goods? Competency Based Que

Ans. The challenges posed by Multinational Corporations (MNCs) to Indian small-scale industries in contemporary times bear some similarities to the period of British rule when Indian handicrafts faced stiff competition from British machine-made goods. Below is a comparative analysis

(i) Competition encourages the use of advanced technology, which can lead to growth for small-scale industries.

For small enterprises to grow, they need a fair environment. However, they lack access to low-cost funds compared to MNCs.

(ii) Small enterprises often struggle to upgrade their technology due to financial constraints, making them less competitive.

(iii) MNCs have more resources for advertising and market capture, whereas small businesses cannot spend as much on marketing.

(iv) Due to these disadvantages, the survival of small enterprises is uncertain in the face of competition from MNCs.

(v) This situation is similar to British rule when Indian handicrafts faced competition from machine-made British goods. During British rule, the decline of small industries was due to colonial exploitation. Today, the competition is driven by economic liberalisation, privatisation and globalisation under the New Economic Policy (NEP).

15. "During the British rule, contribution of industrial sector to the Gross Domestic Product (GDP) remained very low."

Justify the given statement with valid arguments in support of your answer. CBSE 2025; Competency Based Que

Or **Critically appraise some of the shortfalls of the industrial policy pursued by the British colonial administration.** NCERT

Ans. During British rule, the contribution of the industrial sector to India's Gross Domestic Product (GDP) remained very low due to the following reasons

(i) **De-industrialisation**
The British followed a policy of systematically destroying India's traditional handicraft industries by imposing heavy duties on Indian exports while allowing free imports of British manufactured goods. This led to a decline in indigenous industries.

(ii) **Lack of Modern Industries**
The British did not promote large-scale industrialisation in India. The limited industries that developed were mainly focused on raw material extraction for British industries, rather than manufacturing finished goods in India.

(iii) **Lack of Capital Goods Industries** The British did not establish capital goods industries such as iron and steel, which are essential for industrial development. As a result, India remained dependent on Britain for machinery and equipment, hindering industrial growth.

Due to these reasons, India's industrial sector remained underdeveloped, contributing minimally to GDP during British rule.

16. "Composition of foreign trade of any country tells us about the nature of commodities that are exported and imported."

What can you state about the composition of foreign trade at the time of independence? Competency Based Que

Ans. India's foreign trade at the time of independence is described as below

(i) The British followed a typical colonial pattern of trade in India, where it was made to serve their interests.

(ii) India exported raw materials to the home country of the British for their expanding industries.

(iii) India was also developed as a market for the finished goods of the British industries.

During the colonial period, Britain held a monopoly over India's imports and exports. Hence, the major part of foreign trade was restricted to Britain only, while the rest was permitted to trade with nations like Ceylon (Sri Lanka), Persia (Iran) and China. India was a massive exporter during the colonial period.

Thus, India was reduced to being a source of food for the British, a supplier of raw materials for the British industries and a market for their finished products.

17. Comment upon any two salient features of foreign trade policy of India on the eve of independence. CBSE 2020

Ans. Two salient features of foreign trade policy of India on the eve of independence are as under

(i) **Foreign Policy focused on the Export of Primary Products and Import of Finished Goods**
It was owing to colonial exploitation of the Indian economy, that India became net exporter of raw materials and primary products like raw silk, cotton, wool, jute, indigo, sugar, etc. and net importer of finished goods produced by the British industry like cotton, silk and woollen clothes, besides several types of capital goods produced in England.

(ii) **Monopoly Control of India's Foreign Trade**
During the British rule, exports and imports of the country came under monopoly control of the British government.
As a consequence

- More than 50 per cent of India's foreign trade was directed towards Great Britain.
- Exports of primary products (raw material) from India were directed to supply inputs to the British industry and imports of finished goods from Britain were directed to exploit the Indian market.

18. **"Opening up of Suez Canal helped in establishing the British monopoly control over India's foreign trade." Justify the given statement with valid arguments.** CBSE 2024; Competency Based Que

Ans. The given statement is true.

Suez Canal was opened in 1869 and is an artificial waterway running from North to South across the Isthmus of Suez in North-Eastern Egypt. It is one of the most important waterways in the world. The Suez Canal made it much easier for Britishers to transport goods to and from India.

It is the shortest trade link between Europe and countries on the Indian and Pacific Oceans. Because the majority of the world's goods are transported via sea, the Suez Canal greatly reduced the time and cost of transporting goods. This helped the colonial government the establish monopoly control over India's foreign trade.

19. **"During the colonial period, India's foreign trade was characterised by a large export surplus, however, this did not result in any flow of gold or silver into India." Justify the given statement with valid arguments.** CBSE SQP 2025; Competency Based Que

Ans. Throughout the colonial period, India's foreign trade was characterised by a significant export surplus. However, this surplus had detrimental consequences for the country's economy.

This export surplus did not bring gold or silver into India. Instead, it was used to cover expenses incurred by an office set-up by the colonial government in Britain, the expenses on the war fought by the British government and the import of invisible items, all contributed to the drain of India's wealth.

20. **Analyse the images given below and explain the demographic conditions under British rule in India?** Competency Based Que

Or **Enumerate any three demographic indicators under the colonial rule.** CBSE 2024 C

Ans. During the British raj era, the demographic conditions of India were as follows

(i) **Low Life Expectancy**
Life expectancy was very low at 32 years at the time of independence in contrast to the present expectancy of 69 years.

(ii) **High Infant Mortality Rate**
Infant mortality rate was quite high, about 218 per thousand in contrast to the present infant mortality rate of 33 per thousand.

(iii) **High Birth Rate and Death Rate**
The birth rate and death rate were both high at 48 and 40 per thousand, respectively.

(iv) **Poor Health Facilities**
Public health facilities were either unavailable to a large population or highly inadequate when they were available.

(v) **Poverty**
Extensive poverty prevailed in India during the colonial period.

21. **Give a quantitative appraisal of India's demographic profile during the colonial period.** NCERT

Ans. The first census in colonial India was conducted in 1881. It rose to 23.87 crore in 1891, but fell to 23.83 crore in 1901. It rose again in 1911 but again fell in 1921. From 1921 onwards, it has shown a consistent rise.

Therefore, 1921 is regarded as the defining year to mark demographic transition from first stage to second stage. The other demographic indicators related to social development were also not encouraging during the colonial period.

These were

(i) The overall literacy level was less than 16%.
(ii) Female literacy rate was about 7%.
(iii) Infant mortality rate was quite high at 218 per thousand births.
(iv) Life expectancy was also quite low at 32 years.

22. **Highlight the salient features of India's pre-independence occupational structure.** NCERT

Or **Discuss briefly any two salient features of India's pre-independence occupational structure.** All India 2020, Delhi 2020

Ans. The following are the salient features of India's pre-independence occupational structure

(i) **Predominance of Agriculture**
Under the colonial rule, India was basically an agrarian economy, with nearly 70-75% of its workforce engaged directly or indirectly in agriculture.

Due to massive poverty and widespread illiteracy during the colonial rule, a large proportion of the population was engaged in farming and related activities to earn their living.

(ii) **Lack of Opportunities in Industry**
Only a small proportion of population was employed in manufacturing sector. Only 10% of the total workforce was engaged in manufacturing and industrial sector.

(iii) **Unequal Distribution among Sectors**
There was unequal distribution of occupational structure amongst the primary (agriculture), secondary (manufacturing) and tertiary (service) sectors.

(iv) **Regional Imbalance**
There was regional variation in the occupational structure of India.

23. Enumerate any three infrastructural development activities undertaken by the colonial government in India. CBSE 2024 C

Ans. Three infrastructural development activities undertaken by the colonial government in India were

(i) **Construction of Railways**
The British built an extensive railway network to facilitate the transport of raw materials from production centers to ports for export and to bring finished goods from ports to the markets in the interior of the country.

(ii) **Development of Roads**
Roads were developed primarily to serve administrative and military purposes. They were also used to connect important towns with ports.

(iii) **Establishment of Postal and Telegraph Services**
The British introduced modern communication systems like the telegraph and postal services to improve administrative efficiency and maintain control over the vast territory.

24. "Development of railways during British rule encouraged colonial exploitation of the Indian resources." Justify the given statement with valid arguments. Competency Based Que

Ans. The opening of railways by the British government in India intensified colonial exploitation in several ways

(i) **Economic Exploitation**
The primary purpose of the railway system in India was to serve British economic interests. Railways were built to facilitate the movement of raw materials from the hinterlands to the ports for export to Britain and to enable the efficient transportation of British manufactured goods into India.

(ii) **Resource Extraction**
The railways played a crucial role in facilitating the extraction of resources from India's interior regions, such as coal, iron and other minerals, to feed the British industrial machine. This led to the depletion of India's natural resources without significant benefits for the Indian people.

(iii) **Market Manipulation**
The British used the railways to manipulate Indian markets in favour of British goods. The transportation infrastructure provided by the railways allowed British manufacturers to undersell Indian producers, thereby undermining indigenous industries and perpetuating India's economic dependence on Britain.

25. "The real motive behind infrastructural development under the British rule was not to provide basic amenities to the people of India but to subserve various colonial interests."

Do you agree with the given statement? Give valid reasons in support of your answer. CBSE 2025; Competency Based Que

Or **What objectives did the British intend to achieve through their policies of infrastructure development in India?** NCERT

Or **State and explain any two main causes behind infrastructural development by British rule.** CBSE 2023

Ans. Yes, the real motive behind infrastructural development under British rule was to serve colonial interests rather than to benefit the Indian people. The following reasons support this statement

(i) **Facilitating British Trade**
Railways, roads and ports were primarily developed to transport raw materials from different parts of India to ports for export to Britain and to distribute British manufactured goods within India. They were not meant to promote Indian industries.

(ii) **Strengthening British Control**
The British built railways and telegraph systems to improve communication and administration, enabling them to quickly suppress revolts and maintain effective control over India.

(iii) **Neglect of Social Infrastructure**
While transport infrastructure was developed, basic amenities like health, education and sanitation were largely ignored, proving that the British were not concerned with improving the standard of living of Indians.

Thus, infrastructural development under British rule was designed to serve their economic and political interests rather than to benefit the Indian population.

26. **In reference to the picture, analyse the positive impact of British rule on Indian economy?**

Ans. Although, the motive behind the British rule in India was colonial exploitation, but the means resulted in some positive effects which are as under

(i) **Political and Economic Unification of India**
Prior to the British rule, the Indian sub-continent was divided into small and fragmented territories ruled by different dynasties. The British Government took over the control of these territories and unified the country politically and economically.

(ii) **Development of Means of Transport**
Although, the Britishers developed various means of transport, such as roads and railways for their personal benefit, yet these opened up new opportunities of growth and helped in the cultural unification of the country.

(iii) **Growth of Monetary System**
The colonial rule helped the country to shift from the barter system of exchange to a monetary system. This monetised system helped the country to benefit from large-scale production.

Long Answer Type Questions

27. **Write a brief note on state of Indian economy on the eve of independence.**

Ans. Indian economy on the eve of independence, was characterised as (any four)

(i) **Colonial Economy**
India was a British colony and it faced colonial exploitation at the hands of Britishers. Britishers used policies that were concerned with the protection and promotion of the economic interest of their home country rather than with the development of Indian economy.

(ii) **Stagnant Economy**
Stagnation is a prolonged period of little or no growth in an economy. It is highlighted by periods of high unemployment and involuntary part time employment. The growth rate of Indian economy was low.
The country's growth of aggregate real output during the first half of the 20th century was less than 2% with a 0.5% growth in per capita output per year.

(iii) **Backward Economy**
Indian economy exhibited characteristics of a backward economy such as dependence on agricultural sector, high birth and death rate, low level of literacy, low per capita income, etc.

(iv) **Semi-feudal Economy**
Indian economy was a semi-feudal economy in which agricultural sector and modern industries existed side by side i.e. it had the mixture of feudalistic and capitalist modes of production. However, modern industries were in their formation stage.

(v) **Amputated Economy**
India faced partition and the country witnessed large-scale religious riots. India faced the problem of rehabilitating the refugees. It also faced the problem of shortage of jute and cotton as most of the area's growing these crops went to Pakistan.

28. **"The British Raj reversed the trajectory of India's economic growth and development." Do you agree with this view? Give reasons in support of your answer.**

Competency Based Que

Ans. Yes, the British Raj significantly reversed India's economic growth and development trajectory. The following points highlight the reasons for this reversal

(i) **Loss of Land Ownership**
Farmers were deprived of land ownership and exploitative systems like *zamindari* led to poverty and stagnation in agriculture.

(ii) **Decline of Handicrafts**
British tariff policies destroyed India's handicraft industries by favouring British industrial goods over Indian products.

(iii) **Shift in Trade Patterns**
India transitioned from exporting finished goods to exporting raw materials for British industries, while British goods dominated Indian markets.

(iv) **Economic Drain**
Wealth generated in India was not invested locally but transferred to Britain, depleting India's resources.

(v) **Neglect of Indigenous Industries**
The focus was on developing infrastructure to serve British interests, leaving Indian industries and economic systems to decline.

These factors collectively led to the reversal of India's economic growth during the British Raj.

29. "The traditional handicrafts industries were ruined under the British rule." Do you agree with this view? Give reasons in support of your answer. NCERT; Competency Based Que

Ans. Yes, the traditional handicrafts industries in India enjoyed worldwide reputation, but the British misrule in India led to the decline of Indian handicraft industry.

The Britishers adopted the following policies to systematically destroy the handicraft industry

(i) **Discriminatory Tariff Policy of the State**
The Britishers followed a discriminatory tariff policy by allowing tariff free exports of raw material from India (to provide for the requirements of their industries in Britain) and tariff free import of British industrial products (to promote British goods in India), but placed a heavy duty on the export of handicraft products. So, Indian handicraft products started losing their foreign as well as domestic markets.

(ii) **Competition with Machine-made Products**
Machine-made products from Britain were cheap and better in quality than the handicraft products. This competition forced many handicraftsmen to shut down their business.

(iii) **Introduction of Railways in India**
The Britishers introduced railways in India to expand the market of its low priced industrial products.
Consequently, the demand of high-priced handicraft products started to fall, thus leading to the downfall of handicraft industry.

(iv) **Disappearance of Princely Courts**
Prior to the British rule, *Rajas*, *Nawabs* and *Shehenshahs* ruled the different parts of our country and they were great patrons of the handicrafts. But, as the British Raj spread its tentacles, these princely courts declined and so did their patronage. This ultimately led to the decline of the handicrafts.

(v) **New Patterns of Demand**
As the British rule progressed in India, a new class emerged, which was keen to follow the British lifestyle. This changed the pattern of demand in favour of the British goods.

30. Briefly discuss the main features of international trade during the British rule.

Ans. The main features of international trade during the British rule are as follows

(i) **Exporter of Primary Products and Importer of Finished Goods**
Under the colonial rule, India became an exporter of primary products such as raw silk, cotton, wool, sugar, indigo, jute, etc. and an importer of finished consumer goods like cotton, silk and woollen clothes and capital goods like light machinery.

(ii) **Britain's Monopoly Control**
More than half of India's foreign trade was restricted to Britain. The opening of Suez Canal in 1869 further intensified British control over India's foreign trade.

(iii) **Surplus Trade but only to Benefit Britishers**
Due to huge exports of primary goods, our balance of trade showed a surplus. But the surplus so generated was not used as an investment for future growth, but was spent by the Britishers to fight wars to expand their territory. Accordingly, there was a huge drain of Indian wealth.

31. One of the reasons of high death rate and low life expectancy at the time of independence was the frequent outbreak of famines. What were the causes of outbreak of famines? Do you think that the Britishers were sensitive towards the plight of the starving Indians? Competency Based Que

Ans. Famines were a recurrent feature of the Indian economy in the pre-independence period. Famines in India resulted in many deaths over the course of the 18th, 19th and early 20th centuries. The last major famine was the Bengal famine of 1943.

Some of the causes of outbreaks of famine were

(i) In the pre-independent period, Indian agriculture was heavily dependent on monsoon. A bad monsoon led to the outbreak of famine.

(ii) Amartya Sen found that the famines during British rule were not due to lack of food but due to inequalities in the distribution of food.

(iii) Tirthankar Roy suggests that the famines in the British era were due to environmental factors inherent in Indian ecology.

No, I do not think that the Britishers were sensitive to the plight of the starving Indians. No policies or programmes were initiated by the government to reduce prices of food products or to provide relief of any kind.

32. (i) **State any one positive contribution made by the British in India.**

(ii) **Indicate the volume and direction of foreign trade of India at the time of independence.** CBSE 2020

Ans. (i) Construction of railways is a notable positive contribution by the British government. It served as a critical infrastructural facility in the Indian economy.

(ii)

- Owing to colonial exploitation of the Indian economy, India was a net exporter of raw materials and primary products such as raw silk, cotton, wool, jute, indigo, sugar, etc. and importer of finished goods produced by the British industry such as cotton, silk and woollen clothes, besides several types of capital goods produced in England.

- Despite the backwardness of the economy, our exports exceeded our imports. It was due to large-scale exports of raw material to Great Britain to cater to the industrial needs of that country.
- India's foreign trade was restricted to Britain while the rest was allowed with a few other countries like China, Ceylon (Sri Lanka) and Persia (Iran).

33. Analyse the key motivation behind developing railways in India as infrastructure initiative.

Ans. Railways were developed by the British Government to achieve the following objectives

(i) **To Promote the Commercial Interest of Britishers**
Industrialisation in Britain compelled the Britishers to look out for new markets for their finished goods and also identify the countries from where an interrupted supply of raw material could be ensured for their factories. To achieve these objectives, the Britishers introduced the railways in the country.

Railways connected the raw material producing areas to the port cities and also ensured that the goods imported from Britain were transported to every nook and corner of the country for sale.

(ii) **For Military Motives**
The Britishers established railways because they felt that it would help in faster movement of troops and supplies at the time of internal revolution or for defence against external aggression.

(iii) **Capital Investment**
Railways was quite successful in Britain and was earning substantial profits. Because of this, the British capitalists wanted to establish railways in India also, so that they would be able to earn profits on their investment.

(iv) **Political Interest**
The Britishers believed that the introduction of railways in India would provide political stability to the country.

34. Give the negative effects of the British rule in India.

Ans. The negative effects of British rule in India are as follows

(i) **Colonial Exploitation through Trade Malpractices**
The Britishers exploited India by following the given trade practices

- They collected raw material for British industries from India.
- They sold finished goods of British industries in India. To encourage the above trade, no duty was charged on imports from Britain and subsidy was given for exporting raw material to Britain.

(ii) **Use of British Capital to Exploit Country's Resources**
The Britishers used their capital and entrepreneurial skills to exploit India's natural resources and cheap labour resources.

The Britishers invested in mining and plantation industries and paid very low wages to the workers inspite of unsafe working conditions.

(iii) **Development of Industries which Complemented the British Industries**
The Britishers invested only in those industries which complemented the growth of their industries back home. So, they invested in developing railways, post and telegraphs, rubber, tea and coffee plantations, etc.

They totally neglected the development of key industries like iron and steel, machine-making industries, etc. Jute and cotton textile industries, were also discouraged as they could have been a threat for the textile factories of Britain.

(iv) **Partition of the Country**
The Britishers encouraged the Hindu-Muslim dispute for their own benefit, which led to the partition of the country.

35. The rule of the British in India is possibly the most controversial and the most hotly debated aspect of the history of the British Empire.

Admirers of British rule point to the economic developments, the legal and administrative system, and the fact that India became the centre of world politics.

Critics of British rule generally point out that all of these benefits went to a tiny British ruling class and the majority of Indians gained little.

Admirers of British rule counter this by saying that most Indians were poor and oppressed by their own leaders before the British arrived, and that British rule was less harsh on ordinary Indians than rule by Indian princes.

Perhaps the main reason why the arguments are so heated and so complex is that India was very different from the other territories that made up the empire. North America and Australia, for example, were sparsely populated and their populations were less economically developed than Britain. India, however, had a huge population and was just as developed as Britain in the 1700s when the British arrived.

The British were able to take control of India mainly because India was not united. The British signed treaties and made military and trading alliances with many of the independent states that made up India.

The British were very effective at infiltrating these states and gradually taking control of trade.

They often left the local princes in charge of the various parts of India. These local princes were effective at maintaining British rule and gained much from being loyal to the British. Competency Based Que

(i) **Mention some positive impacts of British rule except the ones mentioned in above case study.**

(ii) **"British rule was less harsh on ordinary Indians than rule by Indian princes." Do you agree with statement?**

Ans. (i) Some positive impacts of the British rule in India were the introduction of the railways, post and telegraph system for masses, introduction of Western sciences and the English language.

However, it is to be noted that the British introduced railways for its own benefits. Railways helped in the transportation of raw materials and finished goods from one part of the country to the other. Telegraph and railways also provided to the British a faster means of transport and communication respectively.

Western education was introduced to create a class of Indians who would be Indian in blood but English in manners. This was done to create a feeling of loyalty amongst the Indian masses.

(ii) No, because before the advent of the British, almost all the Indian states were self-sufficient. It may seem that the British rule in India transformed its society for the better. But upon closer examination, these benefits were purely coincidental, if not self-serving. Economic improvements were only enacted in order to better plunder the Indian economy. Even societal changes would have come out on their own without the need for British intervention. In the end, the negative effects of British Imperialism far outweigh the benefits.

36. **At the time of India's independence in 1947, the country's economy was primarily agrarian, with nearly 70-75% of its population depending on agriculture for their livelihood. Despite this heavy reliance on agriculture, the sector was in a dismal state, plagued by low productivity, outdated farming techniques and widespread poverty.**

The land tenure systems like Zamindari, Ryotwari and Mahalwari, implemented during British rule, had exploited farmers, leading to large-scale landlessness and tenant farming. Farmers were forced to cultivate cash crops like cotton, indigo and jute for the benefit of British industries, leading to a decline in the production of foodgrains. On the industrial front, India's traditional industries, particularly handicrafts and textile manufacturing, had been severely damaged by British colonial policies. Before British rule, India had a flourishing textile industry, renowned for products like Muslin of Dhaka and Kashmiri shawls.

However, with the imposition of heavy tariffs on Indian goods and the flood of cheap machine-made British textiles, India's handicraft industries collapsed. Industrialisation in India during British rule was minimal, with limited development of modern industries like iron, steel, and jute. The Tata Iron and Steel Company (TISCO) and a few jute mills were some of the few notable industrial enterprises in operation.

By 1947, the industrial sector contributed only about 10-12% to the country's GDP. India lacked a sound infrastructure and industrial growth was stunted due to the absence of capital investment and technological advancements. Additionally, the focus on export of raw materials and import of finished goods reduced the opportunity for industrial self-reliance.

(i) **Describe the condition of Indian agriculture on the eve of independence, mentioning the key reasons for its low productivity.**

(ii) **How did British colonial policies impact India's industrial sector? Cite any one example from the case study to explain.** Competency Based Que

Ans. (i) On the eve of independence, Indian agriculture was characterised by

- **Low Productivity**
  Agriculture was largely subsistence based, with outdated techniques and tools. There was little to no mechanisation or use of modern irrigation methods.
- **Land Tenure Systems**
  Systems like *zamindari*, Ryotwari and Mahalwari exploited farmers, often making them tenants or landless labourers. A large portion of the agricultural produce went to landowners and British administrators as taxes, leaving farmers with little income or incentives to improve their land.
- **Forced Cultivation of Cash Crops**
  Under British policies, farmers were forced to grow cash crops like indigo, cotton and jute for British industries, reducing food grain production, leading to frequent famines and food shortages.
- **Fragmented Landholdings**
  Farms were small and fragmented, making it difficult to adopt efficient farming practices.

(ii) British colonial policies had a devastating impact on India's industrial sector

- **Destruction of Handicraft Industry**
  Indian traditional industries, particularly the textile industry, suffered significantly. e.g. Muslin of Dhaka, once world renowned, saw a sharp decline as British policies imposed high tariffs on Indian textiles, while flooding the Indian market with cheap, machine-made British goods. This led to the collapse of India's once thriving handicraft industry.

SELF ASSESSMENT TEST

Objective Type Questions

1. Which of the following statements is/are true for estimation of India's national income and per capita income?
   (a) No sincere attempt was made by colonial government
   (b) Some individual attempt were made but they were not significant
   (c) Most studies by individual showed as GDP growth of about 0.5 per annum
   (d) All of the above

2. British pursued the .... policy which led to destruction of Indian handicrafts.
   (a) discriminatory tariff
   (b) bound tariffs
   (c) exploitative tariffs
   (d) None of the above

3. Which sector was the major contributor to GDP of the country as well as the biggest employer on the eve of independence?
   (a) Manufacturing (b) Services
   (c) Industry (d) Agriculture

4. The introduction of expensive mode of communication, i.e. telegraph serve the purpose of
   (a) maintaining law and order
   (b) maintaining trade
   (c) collect taxes
   (d) All of the above

5. During the British rule, island waterway proved to be uneconomical because
   (a) it was built at a high cost
   (b) of competition from railways
   (c) of easy access of airways
   (d) Both (a) and (b)

6. Railways enhanced commercialisation of Indian agriculture, however it leads to which of the following consequences?
   (a) Affected the self-sufficiency of villages
   (b) De-industrialisation of industries
   (c) Decline in foreign trade
   (d) All of the above

7. Which of the following statements is/are correct?
   (i) Colonial government took no initiative to invest in Indian industries.
   (ii) Low life expectancy during colonial rule was due to famines.

   Codes
   (a) Only I
   (b) Only II
   (c) Both I and II (d) None of these

8. **Statement I** The year 1921 is known as the 'Year of the Great Divide' in Indian demographic history.

   Statement II Prior to 1921, India's population growth was irregular and inconsistent.

   Alternatives
   (a) Both the statements are correct
   (b) Both the statements are incorrect
   (c) Statement I is correct, but Statement II is incorrect
   (d) Statement II is correct, but Statement I is incorrect

Answers 1. (d) 2. (a) 3. (d) 4. (a)
5. (d) 6. (a) 7. (c) 8. (a)

Short Answer Type Questions

9. Write a brief note on Indian economy prior to British rule.
10. What is meant by a stagnant economy? Was Indian economy stagnant under the British rule?
11. Explain the causes of downfall of the Indian handicrafts during the British rule.
12. In which areas was public sector operational during the colonial rule?
13. During British rule, India's foreign trade was heavily controlled and structured to benefit Britain. Discuss how this system affected the Indian economy and its role in the global trade network?
14. Examine the drawbacks of the *zamindari* system as described in historical accounts, focusing on its adverse effects on the economic and social structure of rural India under British rule.
15. Why was agriculture productivity low at the time of independence?

Long Answer Type Questions

16. Briefly describe the state of occupational structure at the time of independence.
17. Explain the state of India's demographic profile on the eve of independence.
18. Explain positive and negative contributions of colonial government on Indian economy.

02

CHAPTER

Between 1950 to 1990, India's economy underwent significant changes across various sectors, with a focus on industrialisation, agriculture and services. Government policies aimed at self-reliance, while challenges like poverty and inefficiency persisted.

YOUR STUDY GOALS

2.1 Indian Economy

2.2 Economic Planning in Independent India

2.3 Effect of FYPs on Different Sectors between 1950-1990

YOUR PRACTICE GOAL

- Objective Type Questions (65 Qs ; MCQs, A-R, Statements, Matching, Concept Identification)
- Subjective Questions (26 SAs, 12 LAs)
- Self Assessment Test (7 MCQs, 6 SAs, 3 LAs)

Indian Economy and Changes in Different Sectors [1950-1990]

2.1 Indian Economy

Economic system is a system through which central problems of economy can be solved.

An economic system is a type of social system that determines how resources are allocated and goods and services are produced, distributed as well as consumed. Every economic system must address three basic questions

- What to produce?
- How to produce?
- For whom to produce?

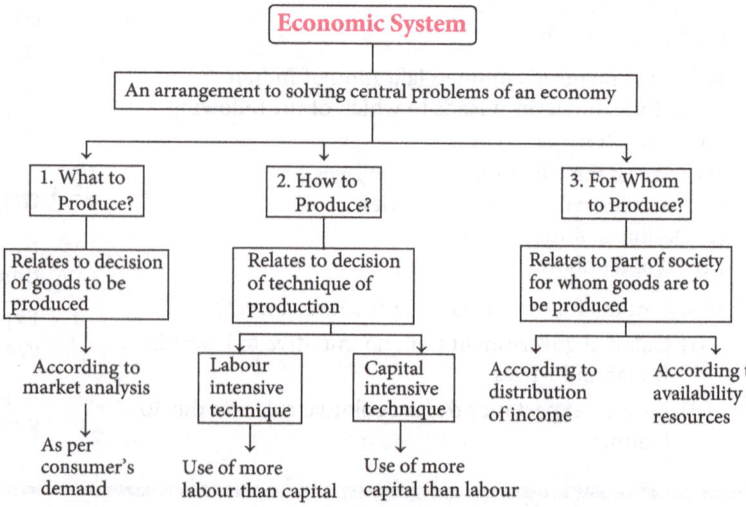

Types of Economic System

After independence, the leaders of independent India had the choice of the following three forms of economic system which can solve the central problems of economy

- Socialist economy
- Capitalist economy
- Mixed economy

Comparative Study of Socialist, Capitalist and Mixed Economy

Basis	Socialist Economy	Capitalist Economy	Mixed Economy
Meaning	It is an economic system in which all economic decisions are taken by the government.	In this economic system, government does not intervene in the market, so all the economic decisions are taken by private sector.	It is an economic system in which public sector and private sector have respective roles in the production and distribution of goods and services.
Ownership of Resources	Owned and controlled by the State.	Owned and controlled by private individuals or corporations.	Both private and public sectors own resources.
Economic Decisions	Made by the government.	Made by individuals and private businesses based on market forces.	Made by both government and private sector.
Profit Motive	Not prioritised; focus on welfare and equality.	Primary objective is profit maximisation.	Profit motive exists, but balanced with social welfare goals.
Means of Production	State-controlled.	Privately controlled.	Both state and private ownership exist.
Wealth Distribution	More equal; focus on reducing income inequality.	Unequal; income disparity is common.	Attempts to balance wealth distribution through taxation and welfare.
Competition	Absent or limited; government monopoly in most sectors.	Encouraged; market competition drives innovation and efficiency.	Exists in some sectors, while others may have government control.
Examples	Former Soviet Union, Cuba.	USA, Singapore.	India, UK, France.

Out of the three above discussed economies, the **leaders of India** decided to choose **mixed economy** because it was not possible for a country to change the ownership pattern of land and other properties, as in a socialist economy. Also, the capitalist economy system was not favoured by the then Prime Minister Jawaharlal Nehru.

2.2 Economic Planning in Independent India

After adopting for mixed economy, there was a need for a planned system that would help to achieve the objectives of **growth with stability** and **social justice**. Thus, economic planning was initiated in India.

Economic planning is a process in which a central authority of a country defines a set of goals to be achieved within a specified period and sets out a plan to achieve those goals, keeping in view the country's resources.

To facilitate economic planning, the following steps were initiated

- The **Planning Commission** was set-up in 1950 with Prime Minister as its chairman.
- The Planning Commission conducted a thorough assessment of human and physical resources, subsequently creating plans for optimal resource utilisation.
- The plans were formulated for a period of five years and thus came to be known as **Five Year Plans** (FYPs).
- The Industrial Policy Resolution, 1948 (IPR 1948) and directive principles significantly influenced the public sector's role in achieving economic planning objectives.
- The private sector was also encouraged to be a part of the planning process.
- The second five year plan, based on Prasanta Chandra Mahalanobis' ideas, laid out the fundamental goals of Indian planning.

NITI Aayog

The Government of India has constituted National Institution for Transforming India, also referred to as 'NITI Aayog' to replace the Planning Commission. It was formed via a resolution of the Union Cabinet on 1st January, 2015. It formulates strategic and long-term policies and programmes for the Government of India and provides relevant technical advice to the Centre and States.

The Goals of Five Year Plans

A plan illustrated the way in which the resources of a nation should be put to use. The five year plans were concerned with the removal of economic backwardness of the country and to make it a developed economy.

They were formulated to achieve certain common goals in the long-run, which are as follows

Goals of Five Year Plans
- Growth
- Modernisation
- Self-reliance
- Equity

1. Growth

It refers to increase in the country's capacity to produce goods and services within the country.

Growth implies
- either a larger stock of productive capital or
- a larger size of supporting services like transport and banking or
- an increase in the efficiency of productive capital and services.

Indicator of Economic Growth: Gross Domestic Product (GDP)

- A steady increase in GDP is a good indicator of economic growth.
- Growth in GDP can be achieved by ensuring sufficient resource supply and increasing productivity of factors of production.
- GDP is derived from three sectors of the economy i.e. primary sector (agriculture), secondary sector (industry) and tertiary sector (services).
- Structural composition of GDP
  - Contribution from primary, secondary and tertiary sectors.
  - In some countries, the primary sector contributes more to GDP growth, while in others, the tertiary sector drives growth.

2. Modernisation

To increase the production of goods and services, the producers have to **adopt new technology**. Adoption of new technology is known as modernisation.

e.g. A farmer using new seed varieties or a factory using new machines to boost output.

It involves changes in both production methods and social outlook, including granting equal status to women.

3. Self-reliance

It implies that a country should not be dependent on other countries to fulfil its basic needs.

The first seven five year plans gave importance to self-reliance by avoiding imports of those goods that could be produced in India itself.

This policy was considered a necessity due to following reasons
- To reduce India's dependence on foreign countries, especially for food.
- The government also feared that dependence on imported food supplies, foreign technology and foreign capital may increase the foreign interference in the policies of India.

4. Equity

It refers to reduction in disparity of income or wealth, by uplifting weaker sections of the society. It aims to distribute economic power equally. Every Indian should be able to meet his or her basic needs such as food, a decent house, education, healthcare, etc.

It is important to ensure that benefits of economic prosperity reach the poor sections instead of being enjoyed only by the rich.

Analysis of Five Year Plans in India

Achievements of Five Year Plans	Failures of Five Year Plans
• **Increase in National Income** Grew from 0.5% to 5% per annum. • **Increase in Per Capita Income** Increased at a rate of 2.9% per annum. • **Agriculture** Average growth rate was of 2.8% per annum. • **Industry** Growth rate of 7% per annum; self-sufficiency in consumer goods. • **Economic and Social Infrastructure** Significant improvements in transport, communication, irrigation facilities, banking, insurance, power, health and education. • **Employment** Targeted 58 million jobs in the eleventh plan, 70 million jobs in the twelfth plan. • **International Trade** Increased from ₹ 792 crore in 1948-49 to ₹ 38,11,422 crore in 2011-12.	• **Poverty** 21.9% of population lives below the poverty line. • **Inflation** Rising prices eroded purchasing power of money and increased wealth inequalities. • **Unemployment** 4 crore people were unemployed at the end of the eleventh plan. • **Inadequate Infrastructure** Poor transport as well as inadequate educational and medical facilities. • **Rising Inequalities** Wealth gap between rich and poor widened and got inadvertently promoted due to unequitable distribution of income.

2.3 Effect of FYPs on Different Sectors between 1950-1990

The first seven FYPs, covering the period between 1950-1990 had a considerable effect on the agriculture and industrial sector and also the foreign trade of the country.

The effect on these sectors have been discussed below

Agricultural Sector

The policy-makers of independent India addressed the issues of low agricultural productivity during colonial rule, through land reforms and promoting the use of High Yielding Variety (HYV) seeds. It resulted in green revolution in Indian agriculture.

To increase productivity, the government also gave subsidy to farmers.

Features (or Problems) of Agriculture

Feature	Explanation
Low Productivity	Low productivity of agricultural sector forced India to import food from the USA and Pakistan.
Dependence on Rainfall	Indian agriculture was mainly dependent upon monsoon which is uncertain, unreliable and irregular.
Subsistence Farming	Main objective of farmer was to secure subsistence for his family not to earn profit.
Traditional or Outdated Technology	Indian agriculture is still characterised by the use of orthodox farming techniques.
Small Holdings	Size of operational holdings has been declining year by year leading to increase in the number of marginal and small holdings and fall in the number of medium and large holdings.
Landlord Tenant Conflict	Insecurity of tenancy was a big problem for the tenants, particularly during the pre-independence period.
Disguised Unemployment	Agriculture being majorly a family occupation, there are usually more people engaged than required.

Land Reforms

Land reforms aim to change the ownership of landholdings for a rational distribution system and viable farming structure. Many underdeveloped and developing countries, including India, have initiated land reforms.

Key Steps of Land Reforms in India

Step	Explanation
Abolition of Intermediaries	• The zamindari system was abolished and ownership rights were transferred to the actual tillers (farmers) of land. • The policy of 'land to the tiller' was introduced to incentivise cultivators to invest in increasing output, as ownership would lead to profits from increased production. • About 200 lakh tenants came into direct contact with the government due to the abolition of intermediaries. **Challenges in Abolition of Intermediaries** • In some areas, former zamindars retained large areas of land by exploiting loopholes in the legislation. • Some tenants were evicted, with landowners falsely claiming self-cultivation to retain ownership of land. • The poorest agricultural labourers did not benefit from these reforms.
Land Ceiling	Land ceiling was imposed to limit the size of land an individual/family could own, to promote equitable distribution of landholdings. **Challenges in Land Ceiling** • Big landlords delayed implementation through court challenges. • Landholders evaded the law by registering land in relatives' names. • Loopholes in the legislation were exploited by large landowners to retain land.

New Agricultural Strategy : Green Revolution in India

It refers to the large increase in production of good grains through the use of High Yielding Variety (HYV) seeds.

Green revolution in India is marked by two distinct phases

Phase 1 (Mid-60s to Mid-70s) During this phase, (approximately mid 1960s up to mid 1970s), the use of HYV seeds was restricted to the more affluent States such as Punjab, Andhra Pradesh and Tamil Nadu. Further, the use of HYV seeds primarily benefitted the wheat growing regions only.

Phase 2 (Mid-70s to Mid-80s) During this phase, green revolution spread to almost the whole country and included more variety of crops.

> ***HYV Seeds***
>
> High Yielding Variety (HYV) seeds are better quality seeds which have a low maturity period, are highly productive and are disease resistant. The yield from these seeds exceeded 25 to 100% as compared to yields from normal seeds. Farmers require reliable irrigation facilities and financial resources for purchasing fertilisers and pesticides to get benefit from HYV seeds. Government encouraged the use of these seeds to increase crop productivity.

Analysis of Green Revolution

Effects of Green Revolution	Risk of Green Revolution
• **Marketable Surplus** Refers to the portion of agricultural produce that farmers sell after fulfilling their own consumption needs. The green revolution increased marketed surplus. • **Benefit to Low Income Groups** Green revolution increased agricultural output, causing foodgrain prices to drop, thus benefitting low income groups who spend more on food.	• **Inequality among Farmers** The green revolution risked widening the gap between small and big farmers, as only wealthy farmers could afford the new technology. However, the government addressed this risk by offering low interest loans and fertiliser subsidies to small farmers.

Effects of Green Revolution	Risk of Green Revolution
• **Self-sufficiency in Foodgrains** The green revolution made India self-sufficient in foodgrain production, ending the dependency on US imports. It also enabled the government to build a foodgrain stock for shortages.	• **Risk of Pest Attack** HYV crops were more vulnerable to pests, posing a risk to small farmers. This risk was reduced through government established research institutes offering pest control services.

Debate Over Subsidies

Subsidy It is basically a payment made by the government to the producers so that they charge less from the consumers. During the green revolution, subsidies were offered to farmers on purchase of HYV seeds and fertilisers. The debate over subsidies revolves around whether they should be continued or phased out.

Points for Subsidies (Defended)	**Points against Subsidies** (Opposed)
• Encourage farmers to adopt HYV technology. • Help farmers manage risks in a monsoon dependent agriculture. • Support poor farmers who can't afford inputs without subsidies. • Prevents widening inequality between rich and poor farmers.	• HYV technology is now widely accepted, so subsidies are no longer needed. • Benefits mostly the fertiliser industry. • Subsidy benefits large farmers in prosperous regions rather than small farmers. • Failed to benefit the target group (poor farmers), hence should be discontinued.

Conclusion While subsidies have helped promote the green revolution and support small farmers, there is growing concern that they disproportionately benefit big farmers and the fertiliser industry. Some economists suggest that instead of abolishing subsidies, reforms should ensure only poor farmers benefit. Others argue for phasing them out since their purpose has largely been served.

Industrial Sector

- Five year plans prioritised industrial development for stable employment and modernisation.
- At the time of independence, India's industrial base was weak, limited to cotton textiles and jute.
- Only two well-managed iron and steel industries existed *viz* one in Jamshedpur and other in Kolkata.
- The industrial sector contributed minimally to GDP and was dominated by the public sector.
- Small-scale industries were also encouraged within this sector.

Private and Public Sectors in Indian Industrial Development

Policy-makers debated the roles of government and private sector in industrial development. The government established Public Sector Undertakings (PSUs) to promote heavy industries and develop the infrastructure of the country.

Reasons for a Dominant Role of PSUs

Reasons	Explanation
Lack of Capital	The private sector lacked resources and capital to establish heavy industries, prompting government initiative.
Low Inducement to Invest	Low aggregate demand post-independence made private entrepreneurs hesitant to invest huge amount in new ventures, leading the government to initiate PSUs.
Promote Social Justice and Growth	To prevent income inequality, the government aimed for growth alongside social justice through PSUs. The government maintained control over vital industries, with private sector policies complementing public sector initiatives.

Industrial Policy Resolution (IPR),1956

Industrial policy is a set of standards or measures set by the government to boost the growth prospects of different industrial enterprises of the country.

Industrial policy resolution gave the leading role to the government in the process of industrialisation and laid the foundation for a socialistic pattern of society.

It's goal is to establish a leading government role in industrialisation and promote regional equality.

Principal Elements of IPR, 1956

Element	Details
Classification of Industries Based on Ownership	• **First Category** Exclusively owned by the government. • **Second Category** Private sector could supplement the efforts of state sector, with government's sole responsibility to initiate new units. • **Third Category** All other industries not specified above which were left for private sector.
Industrial Licensing	It is a written permission from the government to an industrial undertaking to manufacture specified goods. According to the Industries (Development and Regulation) Act, 1951, government can issue licenses for • New industry set-up • Expansion of existing industries • Product diversification

Industrial Licensing Motive

Industrial licensing was introduced for the following motives

- Industries in private sector could be established only after getting a license from the government.
- If an industrial unit was established in an economically backward area, then it was easier for it to obtain a license. These units were given concessions such as tax benefits and electricity at a lower tariff.
- An existing industry was also required to obtain a license for expanding its production. In this condition, the license was given if the government was convinced that the economy required larger quantity of goods.

Small Scale Industries

A Small-Scale Industry (SSI) is defined with reference to the maximum investment allowed on the assets of a unit. This limit has changed over a period of time. At the beginning of planning (1951), it was defined as the industry whose investment did not exceed ₹ 5 lakh. It is presently defined as the industry whose investment does not exceed ₹ 1 crore.

In 1955, the Village and Small-Scale Industries Committee or **Karve Committee**, recognised that it is possible to use small-scale industries for promoting industrial as well as rural development.

Role or Importance of SSI

Key Role	Explanation
Employment Generation	SSIs create more jobs than large industries due to being more labour intensive.
Protection from Large Firms	SSIs require protection from large firms to thrive, necessitating government support.
Government Support Measures	• **Reservation of Products** Certain products were reserved for SSIs based on their manufacturing capability. • **Concessions** Benefits like lower excise duty and bank loans at reduced interest rates were also given.

Foreign Trade

It refers to buying and selling of goods and services beyond the geographical boundaries of the country. In other words, it is the exchange of goods and services among different countries.

During the first seven FYPs, India's foreign trade was characterised by inward looking trade strategy. This strategy is called **import substitution.**

Import Substitution Policy

- This policy aimed at replacing imports with domestically produced goods.
- It's objective was to restrict imports and protect domestic industries from foreign competition.
- It is also called 'inward looking trade strategy'.
- e.g. Encouraging local production of vehicles instead of importing them.

Protection from Imports

- **Tariffs** are taxes on imported goods. They make imported goods more expensive and discourage their use.
- **Quotas** specify the maximum quantity of goods which can be imported.

Reasons for Adopting Import Substitution

Reason	Explanation
Competitive Position	Developing countries' industries need protection to compete with developed nations.
Foreign Exchange	Concerns about spending valuable foreign exchange on luxury imports.

Effects of Policies on Indian Economy

Policies on industrial development and foreign trade had both positive and negative impacts on Indian economy.

Positive Impacts	Negative Impacts
• Contribution of the industrial sector to GDP rose from 13% (1950-51) to 24.6% (1990-91). • Achieved a commendable 6% annual growth rate in the industrial sector. • Diversification of industries beyond cotton textiles and jute by 1990. • Growth of sunrise industries like electronics due to inward-looking trade strategy. • Protection to Small-Scale Industries (SSIs) increased investment opportunities and promoted self-employment. • Development of indigenous industries, especially in electronics and automobiles, due to protection from foreign competition.	• Protection of public sector industries led to growth of inefficient monopolies (e.g. Telecommunications, hotels). • Lack of modernisation in domestic production due to captive market dynamics. • Economic unviability led to shutdowns in private sector enterprises. • Misuse of license by industrial houses to prevent competition. • Government officials misused their power to grant licenses, further complicating the entrepreneurial landscape. Thus, whole system being referred to as **permit license raj.**

Conclusion

1. **Agricultural Sector** Achieved self-sufficiency in food due to the green revolution; abolition of zamindari system.
2. **Industrial Sector** Greater diversification in industries but excessive regulation hindered entrepreneurship as well as public sector dissatisfaction.
3. **Trade Sector** Inward-oriented policies limited quality improvements and failed to strengthen the export sector.

Thus, reform of economic policies was deemed necessary, leading to the 1991 New Economic Policy for increased efficiency.

Mind Map

INDIAN ECONOMY AND CHANGES IN DIFFERENT SECTORS [1950-1990]

1 Indian Economy

An economic system is a type of social system that determines how resources are allocated and goods and services are produced, distributed as well as consumed.

Types of Economic System

- **Socialist Economy** It is an economic system in which all economic decisions are taken by the government.
- **Capitalist Economy** In this economic system, government does not intervene in the market, so all the economic decisions are taken by private sector.
- **Mixed Economy** It is an economic system in which public sector and private sector have respective roles in the production and distribution of goods and services.

2 Economic Planning in Independent India

Economic planning is a process in which a central authority of a country defines a set of goals to be achieved within a specified period and sets out a plan to achieve those goals, keeping in view the country's resources.

To facilitate economic planning, the following steps were initiated

- The Planning Commission was set-up in 1950 with Prime Minister as its chairman.
- The Planning Commission conducted a thorough assessment of human and physical resources, subsequently creating plans for optimal resource utilisation.
- The plans were formulated for a period of five years and thus came to be known as Five Year Plans (FYPs).

3 Goals of Five Year Plans

- **Growth** It refers to increase in the country's capacity to produce goods and services within the country.
- **Modernisation** To increase the production of goods and services, the producers have to adopt new technology. Adoption of new technology is known as modernisation.
- **Self-reliance** It implies that a country should not be dependent on other countries to fulfill its basic needs.
- **Equity** It refers to reduction in disparity of income or wealth, by uplifting weaker sections of the society. It aims to distribute economic power equally.

Achievements of Five Year Plans

- Increase in national income
- Increase in per capita income
- Growth rate of 7% per annum in industry
- Significant improvements in economic and social infrastructure
- Increase in international trade
- Growth rate of 2.8% in agriculture
- Targeted 58 million jobs in the eleventh plan, 70 million jobs in the twelfth plan

Failures of Five Year Plans

- 21.9% of population lives below the poverty line.
- Rising prices eroded purchasing power of money and increased wealth inequalities.
- 4 crore people were unemployed at the end of the eleventh plan.
- Poor transport as well as inadequate educational and medical facilities.
- Wealth gap between rich and poor widened and got inadvertently promoted due to unequitable distribution of income.

4 Effect of FYPs on Different Sectors between 1950-1990

The first seven FYPs, covering the period between 1950-1990 had a considerable effect on the agriculture and industrial sector and also the foreign trade of the country.

Industrial Sector

- Five year plans prioritised industrial development.
- Government established Public Sector Undertakings (PSUs) to promote heavy industries and develop the infrastructure of country.
- Reasons for dominant role of PSUs included lack of capital, low inducement to invest and promote social justice and growth.

Industrial Policy Resolution (IPR), **1956**

Industrial policy is a set of standards or measures set by the government to boost the growth prospects of different industrial enterprises of the country. Principal elements included classification of industries based on ownership and industrial licensing.

Small-scale Industries

It is defined with reference to maximum investment allowed on the assets of a unit. It is defined as the industry whose investment does not exceed ₹ 1 crore. Role includes employment generation, protection from large firms and government support measures.

Agricultural Sector

Features or problems of agriculture are

- Low productivity
- Dependence on rainfall
- Subsistence farming, landlord tenant conflict
- Traditional or outdated technology
- Small holdings, disguised unemployment

Land Reforms These aim to change the ownership of landholdings for a rational distribution system and viable farming structure. Key steps include abolition of intermediaries and land ceiling.

New Agricultural Strategy: Green Revolution in India

It refers to the large increase in production of good grains through the use of High Yielding Variety seeds.

Subsidy It is basically a payment made by the government to the producers so that they charge less from the consumers.

Foreign Trade

It refers to buying and selling of goods and services beyond the geographical boundaries of the country. Import substitution policy aimed at replacing imports with domestically, produced goods. It is also called 'inward looking trade strategy'.

5 Effect of Policies on Indian Economy

Positive Impact

- Contribution of the industrial sector to GDP rose from 13% (1950-51) to 24.6% (1990-91).
- Achieved a commendable 6% annual growth rate in the industrial sector.
- Diversification of industries beyond cotton textiles and jute by 1990.
- Growth of sunrise industries like electronics due to inward-looking trade strategy.
- Protection to Small-Scale Industries (SSIs) increased investment opportunities and promoted self-employment.

Negative Impact

- Inefficient monopolies
- Lack of modernisation in domestic production
- Misuse of license
- Shutdowns in private sector
- Misuse of power by government officials

EXAM PATTERN QUESTIONS

Objective Type Questions

Multiple Choice Questions (MCQs)

1. Under which economy, the goods are distributed among people on the basis of demand and not on what people need?

(a) Capitalist economy
(b) Socialist economy
(c) Mixed economy
(d) Dual economy

2. Which of the following features is not associated with a socialist economy?

(a) The economy has no private property and everything is owned by the state
(b) The government decides what to produce, how to produce and for whom to produce
(c) Incomes are equitably distributed
(d) It is called a free market economy

3. Observe the image given below and identify the type of economic structure.

(a) Socialism (b) Capitalism
(c) Mixed economy (d) None of these

4. Which of the following statements is correct with reference to the mixed economy system in India? CBSE Term I 2021; Competency Based Que

(a) Pre-dominance of free market economic system over the government regulated economy
(b) Absence of economic planning
(c) Ownership of factors of production only to private
(d) Co-existence of public and private sector

5. When was planning initiated in India?

(a) In 1951 (b) In 1952
(c) In 1950 (d) In 1956

6. ……… is known as the Architect of Indian Planning. CBSE 2023; Term I 2021

(a) Jawaharlal Nehru
(b) PC Mahalanobis
(c) Dr. Manmohan Singh (d) Dr. Rajendra Prasad

7. Observe the image given below and identify the planning objective highlighted.

(a) Growth (b) Self-reliance
(c) Modernisation (d) Equality

8. Which of the following combinations accurately represent the components of modernisation as a planning objective? Competency Based Que

(i) Modernisation in technology
(ii) Modernisation in outlook
(iii) Modernisation in education
(iv) Modernisation in healthcare

Codes
(a) (i) and (ii) (b) (iii) and (iv)
(c) (i), (ii) and (iii) (d) (i), (ii), (iii) and (iv)

9. Identify the combination that lists achievements of the five year plans between 1950-1990. Competency Based Que

(i) Development of heavy Industry
(ii) Self-reliance in food production
(iii) Expansion of public sector
(iv) Surplus agricultural output
(v) Reduction of unemployment

Codes
(a) (i), (ii) and (iii)
(b) (i), (ii) and (iv)
(c) (ii), (iii) and (v)
(d) (i), (iii) and (iv)

10. Which of the following statements is true about the failure of the five year plans in India? **Competency Based Que**

(a) The five year plans successfully eradicated poverty across rural and urban areas
(b) Industrial development achieved during the plans led to balanced regional growth
(c) The agricultural sector lagged behind in growth despite initial focus, leading to rural distress
(d) All five year plans achieved their targeted economic growth rates without any discrepancies

11. The Planning Commission in India was replaced by the NITI Aayog in which year?

(a) 2012 (b) 2014
(c) 2015 (d) 2016

12. "Despite agricultural reforms, farmers struggle with fragmented landholdings and irrigation shortages."
– The Indian Express, 1982

Based on the headline, which of the following best describes a persistent problem in the agriculture sector of India between 1950 and 1990? **Competency Based Que**

(a) Large-scale consolidation of land improved farming efficiency
(b) Landholdings were often fragmented, making efficient farming difficult
(c) Irrigation infrastructure was sufficient, ensuring consistent water supply
(d) Agricultural production steadily increased without facing shortages

13. "The Indian government adopted a policy of fixing maximum land holding limit (ownership) for an individual."
It is commonly known as .... **CBSE 2025**

(a) green revolution (b) land ceiling
(c) marketable surplus (d) golden revolution

14. ...... is not a type of land reforms introduced by government of India after independence. **CBSE Term I 2021**

(a) Land ceiling
(b) Abolition of intermediaries
(c) Change in ownership of landholding
(d) Use of High Yielding Variety (HYV) seeds

15. "Green revolution brings agricultural boom, but small farmers left behind." **–The Times of India, 1975**

Which of the following describes a feature of India's agriculture sector (1950-1990)? **Competency Based Que**

(a) Mechanisation benefitted all farmers equally
(b) Large landowners benefitted more, increasing income disparity
(c) Farming remained mostly traditional with little technology
(d) Agricultural growth was uniform across all regions

16. In the first phase of green revolution, output was restricted mainly to .... **CBSE 2023**

(a) cereals and pulses (b) wheat and rice
(c) cotton and jute (d) jowar and bajra

17. Observe the table below and answer the question below.

Trend Growth Rates in GDP of various Sub-sectors in India at 1999-00 Prices, 1950-50 to 2010-11
(Per cent/Year)

Phase	All Sectors	Agriculture and Allied	Agriculture	Non-agriculture
Pre-green Revolution	3.71	2.00	1.97	5.42
Green Revolution	3.72	2.38	2.63	4.62
Period of Wider Dissemination	5.52	3.57	3.58	6.40
Post-reforms	6.01	2.08	2.04	7.23
Recovery	8.24	2.62	2.55	9.47

Source *https://www.mospi.gov.in/sites/default/files/Statistical_year_book_india_chapters/ch8.pdf*

During the post-reforms period, what was the approximate difference between the growth rates of the non-agriculture and agriculture and allied sectors? **Competency Based Que**

(a) 5.15 (b) 7.23 (c) 4.29 (d) 6.01

18. "In India, agricultural subsidies have always been a topic of debate among the economic thinkers."

Identify, which of the following statements is not an argument in favour of continuation of the agricultural subsidies in India? **CBSE Term I 2021; Competency Based Que**

(a) Subsidies encourage farmers to adopt newer technologies
(b) Subsidies help farmers to face the uncertainties of future
(c) Subsidies aim to reduce the inequalities between rich and poor farmers
(d) Subsidies mainly benefits the fertiliser industry and big farmers

19. .... is the portion of agricultural produce which is sold in the market by the farmers, after meeting their self-consumption requirements. **CBSE SQP Term I 2021**

(a) Trade surplus (b) Marketable surplus
(c) Producer surplus (d) Consumer surplus

20. The second phase of green revolution started in

(a) mid-60s (b) mid-70s
(c) mid-80s (d) mid-90s

21. In ...., first 'industrial policy resolution' of independent India was announced. **CBSE Term I 2021**

(a) 1947 (b) 1948 (c) 1951 (d) 1956

22. According to the Industrial Policy Resolution of 1956, under which category would this company be classified?

सेल SAIL

(a) First category (b) Second category
(c) Third category (d) Fourth category

23. Which of the following are characteristics of India's economic policies between 1950 and 1990?

I. Import substitution
II. Promotion of small-scale industries
III. Full liberalisation of trade
IV. Extensive public sector control

Codes **Competency Based Que**

(a) I and II (b) II and IV
(c) I, II and IV (d) I, III and IV

24. Which of the following is true for Small-Scale Industries (SSIs) in India? **Competency Based Que**

(a) SSIs require a minimum capital investment of ₹ 10 crores
(b) SSIs play a crucial role in generating employment and promoting balanced regional development
(c) SSIs are mainly focused on large-scale production for export markets
(d) SSIs do not contribute significantly to the country's GDP or industrial output

25. Identify the correct statement from the following. **CBSE 2024 C**

(a) India adopted the socialistic economic system after Independence
(b) Indian economic planning was implemented through Five Year Plans
(c) Land reforms under industrial sector were implemented by the Government of India
(d) Policy initiatives in the industrial sector were responsible for decline in Gross Domestic Product (GDP) in India

26. .... was the objective of import substitution policy in India. **CBSE Term I 2021**

(a) Production of high quality products
(b) Protection of domestic industries from foreign competition
(c) Promote imports (d) Promote privatisation

27. C Rajagopalachari, a founder of Swatantra Party, coined the term 'permit licence raj' to encapsulate the party's frustrations with Nehru's policies, writing in his magazine, "Swarajya : I want the corruptions of the permit/license raj to go... I want real, equal opportunities for all and no private monopolies created by the permit/licence raj." How were these private monopolies indulging in the corruption that C Rajagopalachari talks about? **CBSE SQP Term I 2021; Competency Based Que**

(a) They led to lobbying and personal benefits for big industrial houses
(b) They continued to function even when running into losses
(c) They exploited the people by grossly increasing prices
(d) They could not compete with international products

28. In the post-independence era, the policy-makers of India adopted an economic system that fundamentally implies the coexistence of ...... and .... **CBSE SQP 2025**

(a) small and large-scale industries
(b) small and medium-scale industries
(c) public and private sector
(d) private and foreign sector

Direction *Read the case study and answer the questions 29 to 32 on the basis of the same*

The performance of Indian economy during the period of first seven five year plans (1950-1990) was satisfactory if not very impressive. On the eve of independence, India was an industrially backward country, but during this period of first seven plans our industries became far more diversified, with the stress being laid on the public investments in the industrial sector.

The policy of import substitution led to protection of the domestic industries against the foreign producers but we failed to promote a strong export surplus. Although public sector expanded to a large extent but it could not bring desired level of improvement in the secondary sector.

Excessive government regulations prevented the natural trajectory of growth of entrepreneurship as there was no competition, no innovation and no modernisation on the front of the industrial sector. Many Public Sector Undertakings (PSU's) incurred huge losses due to operational inefficiencies, red-tapism, poor technology and other similar reasons. These PSU's continued to function because it was difficult to close a government undertaking even it is a drain on country's limited resources.

On the agricultural front, due to the measures taken under the green revolution, India more or less became self-sufficient in the production of foodgrains. So the needs for reform of economic policy was widely felt in the context of changing global economic scenario to achieve desired growth in the country. **CBSE QB**

29. **Which of the following was not a reason for the public sector to play a major role in the initial phase of Indian economic planning?**
(a) Private entrepreneurs lacked sufficient capital for investment
(b) Government aimed at social welfare
(c) The market was big enough to encourage private industrialists for investment
(d) The government wanted to protect the indigenous producers from the foreign competition

30. **Inward looking trade strategy aimed at ....**

31. **State whether the given statement is true or false.**
Mechanisation of the Indian agriculture was one of the cause of green revolution in India.

32. **Assertion** (A) Many public sector undertakings incurred huge losses due to operational inefficiencies.
Reason (R) Red-tapism was one of the reasons for continuation of such enterprises.
Alternatives
(a) Both Assertion (A) and Reason (R) are true
(b) Both Assertion (A) and Reason (R) are false

Direction *Read the case study and answer the questions 33 to 36 on the basis of the same*

The Industrial Policy Resolution of 1956 marked a significant step in the economic history of India, shaping the country's industrial development. It laid out the vision for a socialist pattern of society, where industries, especially those of strategic importance and public utility, were to be controlled by the state.

The government categorised industries into three groups. The first category included industries that were to be exclusively owned by the state. The second category comprised industries where the state would supplement private sector activity. The third category was left open for the private sector, though with government oversight and regulation through a licensing system.

The aim of this policy was to ensure that the government played a central role in industrial development, promoting self-reliance and fostering regional equality through the licensing system. It also laid the foundation for the development of Small-Scale Industries (SSIs) and the establishment of public sector enterprises.

Source *Industrial Policy Resolution, 1956*

33. **Which of the following industries were categorised to be exclusively owned by the State under the Industrial Policy Resolution of 1956?**
(a) Small-scale industries
(b) Consumer goods industries
(c) Strategic and essential industries
(d) Textile industries

34. **Which of the following was not a feature of the Industrial Policy Resolution of 1956?**
(a) The state had complete control over industries vital for national development
(b) License was required for the expansion of private industries
(c) Public sector industries were encouraged to foster regional balance
(d) Private industries were given full autonomy to expand without restrictions

35. **The .... Committee, set-up in 1955, recommended the development of Small-Scale Industries (SSIs) as a key strategy for industrial growth under the industrial policy resolution.**

36. **The Industrial Policy Resolution of 1956 formed the basis of the .... five year plan, which emphasised rapid industrialisation.**

Assertion-Reason

Direction (Q.No. 37 to 46) *Read the following Assertion (A) and Reason (R) and choose the correct alternative from the following*

Alternatives
(a) Both Assertion (A) and Reason (R) are true and Reason (R) is the correct explanation of Assertion (A)
(b) Both Assertion (A) and Reason (R) are true, but Reason (R) is not the correct explanation of Assertion (A)
(c) Assertion (A) is true, but Reason (R) is false
(d) Assertion (A) is false, but Reason (R) is true

37. **Assertion** (A) Socialism, as an economic system, appealed the most to Mr. Jawahar Lal Nehru but he did not adopt this economic system for India.
Reason (R) He was not in favour of the kind of socialism established in former Soviet Union where all means of production were owned by the government and there was no private property.

38. **Assertion** (A) The five year plans aimed to achieve economic growth while ensuring social justice and equitable distribution of resources.
Reason (R) This dual focus was designed to address both economic disparities and regional imbalances within the country.

39. **Assertion** (A) The introduction of the Land Ceiling Act in various States during the 1950s aimed to reduce disparities in land ownership.
Reason (R) The Land Ceiling Act was implemented to support large landholders in expanding their estates for commercial agriculture.

40. **Assertion** (A) The green revolution in the 1960s helped India achieve self-sufficiency in foodgrain production.

Reason (R) The green revolution focused on increasing agricultural production through the adoption of a High Yielding Variety (HYV) seeds, irrigation and chemical fertilisers.

41. **Assertion** (A) The purpose of license policy was to promote regional equalities.

Reason (R) The motive of licensing system was to monitor and control the industrial production. **CBSE Term I 2021**

42. **Assertion** (A) The public sector dominated India's industrial landscape during the period from 1950 to 1990.

Reason (R) The Industrial Policy Resolution of 1956 gave the private sector significant control over strategic industries such as defence, iron and steel and energy.

43. **Assertion** (A) The contribution of Small-Scale Industries (SSIs) to employment generation in India between 1950 and 1990 was marginal due to their limited production capacity.

Reason (R) Small-Scale Industries were labour-intensive and required low capital investment, making them well-suited for addressing India's unemployment problem during that period.

44. **Assertion** (A) The nationalisation of banks in 1969 led to a significant improvement in India's industrial growth during the 1970s.

Reason (R) The primary goal of nationalising banks was to ensure that banking facilities reached the rural and underdeveloped areas of India.

45. **Assertion** (A) During the period 1950-1990, India adopted an import substitution strategy to protect its domestic industries from foreign competition.

Reason (R) The success of import substitution was primarily due to the unrestricted import of capital goods, which significantly boosted local production capabilities.

46. **Assertion** (A) At higher levels of development, the share of agricultural sector towards GDP is the highest.

Reason (R) By 1990, the share of the service sector towards GDP was 40.59%.

Two Statements Based MCQs

Direction (Q.No. 47 to 56) *Read the following statements carefully and choose the correct alternative*

Alternatives

(a) Statement I is correct and Statement II is incorrect
(b) Statement II is correct and Statement I is incorrect
(c) Both the statements are correct
(d) Both the statements are incorrect

47. **Statement I** In a capitalist economy, the means of production are primarily owned and controlled by the government, which allocates resources based on central planning.

Statement II A key feature of a capitalist economy is that it promotes competition and consumer choice, with minimal government intervention in economic activities.

48. **Statement I** Economic development encompasses economic growth.

Statement II Economic development measures not only a sustained increase in GDP, but also a structural changes in the technical, economic and institutional spheres.

49. **Statement I** The five year plans included a comprehensive focus on social welfare programmes, with specific targets set for improving living standards and significantly reducing poverty rates in India through initiatives like the Integrated Rural Development Programmes (IRDP).

Statement II Despite the ambitious goals of these programmes, their effectiveness was often undermined by systemic bureaucratic inefficiencies, inadequate monitoring mechanisms and pervasive corruption, which limited the intended impact on the most vulnerable populations.

50. **Statement I** The five year plans emphasised the importance of balanced regional development, aiming to reduce disparities between different states in India.

Statement II In practice, however, the benefits of development were often concentrated in a few states, leading to increased regional inequalities.

51. **Statement I** Modernisation implies adoption of new technology along with a change in the social and economic outlook.

Statement II Over the years, there have been a reduction in the gender wage parity and in the female labour force participation rate.

52. **Statement I** The land reforms during the 1950-1990 period aimed at abolishing the zamindari system and redistributing land to landless farmers.

Statement II The success of land reforms was uneven, with landlessness persisting in many regions due to incomplete implementation.

53. **Statement I** The green revolution in India led to an increase in agricultural productivity, especially in food grains like wheat and rice during the 1960s.

Statement II The green revolution led to equitable distribution of wealth and benefitted all Indian farmers equally during 1950-1990.

54. **Statement I** During the 1950-1990 period, India's economic policy focused heavily on self-reliance, reducing foreign dependency by encouraging indigenous production.

Statement II This strategy of self-reliance led to rapid industrial modernisation and reduced inefficiencies in production across all sectors by 1990.

55. **Statement I** India's Industrial Policy Resolution of 1956 aimed at promoting heavy industries to make India self-reliant in capital goods production.

Statement II Between 1950 and 1990, India's small-scale industries grew at a faster rate compared to heavy industries, contributing more to industrial output.

56. **Statement I** India's economic strategy during 1950-1990 promoted exports and encouraging domestic production.

Statement II This import substitution policy made Indian industries globally competitive by the end of 1990, boosting exports in manufactured goods.

Matching

57. Match the following

Column I		Column II
A. Structural Composition	(i)	Implies a larger stock of productive capital
B. Growth as a FYP Goal	(ii)	Adoption of new technology
C. Modernisation	(iii)	Contribution made by each sector

Codes

	A	B	C		A	B	C
(a)	(i)	(ii)	(iii)	(b)	(iii)	(i)	(ii)
(c)	(ii)	(iii)	(i)	(d)	(iii)	(ii)	(i)

58. Match the following

Column I		Column II
A. Basis of IInd FYP	(i)	SSIs
B. Karve Committee	(ii)	Self-reliance
C. Basis of first seven FYPs	(iii)	IPR 1956

Codes

	A	B	C		A	B	C
(a)	(i)	(ii)	(iii)	(b)	(iii)	(i)	(ii)
(c)	(ii)	(iii)	(i)	(d)	(iii)	(ii)	(i)

59. Match the following

Column I (Concepts)		Column II (Descriptions)
A. Planning commission	(i)	A system of strict government control over industries through licensing
B. Green revolution	(ii)	A body responsible for formulating India's five year plans
C. Economic planning	(iii)	Government strategies to allocate resources efficiently for economic growth
D. License Raj	(iv)	Aimed to improve agricultural productivity through modern techniques

Codes

	A	B	C	D		A	B	C	D
(a)	(ii)	(iv)	(iii)	(i)	(b)	(iii)	(iv)	(ii)	(i)
(c)	(iv)	(iii)	(i)	(ii)	(d)	(i)	(ii)	(iii)	(iv)

60. Match the following

Column I (Concepts)		Column II (Descriptions)
A. Command economy	(i)	Focus on redistributing land to improve productivity and social equity.
B. Import substitution	(ii)	Focus on self-sufficiency and government control over resources.
C. Land reforms	(iii)	Promoted local production to reduce foreign dependency.
D. Mahalanobis strategy	(iv)	Strategy prioritising heavy industries and balanced economic growth.

Codes

	A	B	C	D		A	B	C	D
(a)	(ii)	(i)	(iii)	(iv)	(b)	(iii)	(iv)	(ii)	(i)
(c)	(iv)	(iii)	(i)	(ii)	(d)	(ii)	(iii)	(i)	(iv)

Concept Identification

61. An economy in which there is private as well as public ownership of the means of production. **CBSE 2020**

62. The distribution of income is in accordance with the abilities and efficiency of the people.

63. A strategy allocating country's scarce resources to different uses in a manner such that a given set of goals is achieved with in the specified period of time. **NCERT**

64. The state of non-dependence on rest of the world for the financial resources.

65. Surplus of farmer's output over and above his 'on-farm consumption'. **NCERT**

Answers

1. (a) Capitalist economy
2. (d) It is called a free market economy
3. (c) Mixed economy
4. (d) Co-existence of public and private sector
5. (c) In 1950
6. (b) PC Mahalanobis
7. (d) Equality
8. (a) (i) and (ii)
9. (a) (i), (ii) and (iii)
10. (c) The agricultural sector lagged behind in growth despite initial focus, leading to rural distress
11. (c) 2015
12. (b) Landholdings were often fragmented, making efficient farming difficult
13. (b) Land ceiling
14. (d) Use of High Yielding Variety (HYV) seeds
15. (b) Large landowners benefitted more, increasing income disparity
16. (b) wheat and rice
17. (a) 5.15 (7.23 – 2.08)
18. (d) Subsidies mainly benefits the fertiliser industry and big farmers
19. (b) Marketable surplus
20. (b) mid-70s
21. (b) 1948
22. (a) First category
23. (c) I, II and IV
24. (b) SSIs play a crucial role in generating employment and promoting balanced regional development
25. (b) Indian economic planning was implemented through Five Year Plans
26. (b) Protection of domestic industries from foreign competition
27. (a) They led to lobbying and personal benefits for big industrial houses
28. (c) public and private sector
29. (c) The market was big enough to encourage private industrialists for investment
30. protection of domestic industries
31. True
32. (a) Both Assertion (A) and Reason (R) are true
33. (c) Strategic and essential industries
34. (d) Private industries were given full autonomy to expand without restrictions
35. Karve
36. second
37. (a) Both Assertion (A) and Reason (R) are true and Reason (R) is the correct explanation of Assertion (A)
38. (a) Both Assertion (A) and Reason (R) are true and Reason (R) is the correct explanation of Assertion (A)
39. (c) The Land Ceiling Act was intended to limit the amount of land a person could own in order to distribute surplus land to landless farmers.
40. (a) Both Assertion (A) and Reason (R) are true and Reason (R) is the correct explanation of Assertion (A)
41. (b) Both Assertion (A) and Reason (R) are true, but Reason (R) is not the correct explanation of Assertion (A)
42. (c) The Industrial Policy Resolution of 1956 actually reserved strategic industries like defence, iron and steel, and energy for the public sector, not the private sector.
43. (d) SSIs actually contributed significantly to employment generation during this period because they were widespread and labour-intensive.
44. (b) Both Assertion (A) and Reason (R) are true, but Reason (R) is not the correct explanation of Assertion (A)
45. (c) The import substitution strategy involved imposing heavy tariffs and restrictions on foreign goods, not unrestricted imports of capital goods, which contradicts the essence of the strategy.
46. (d) As development progresses, agriculture's share declines while the service sector expands.
47. (b) In a capitalist economy, the means of production are owned and controlled by private individuals or corporations, not the government.
48. (c) Both the statements are correct
49. (c) Both the statements are correct
50. (c) Both the statements are correct
51. (a) The gender wage gap has reduced but there has been a substantial increase in the female labour force participation rate.
52. (c) Both the statements are correct
53. (a) The benefits of the green revolution were concentrated in regions with better irrigation facilities and wealth distribution was not equitable, with small and marginal farmers benefiting less.
54. (a) The strategy did not lead to rapid industrial modernisation and inefficiencies persisted in many sectors, partly due to protectionism and lack of competition.
55. (a) While small-scale industries did grow, heavy industries were the focus and dominated industrial output during this period.
56. (d) India's economic strategy during 1950-1990 primarily focused on import substitution rather than promoting exports.

The goal was to reduce foreign dependency by encouraging domestic production, not necessarily export promotion.

The import substitution policy led to inefficiencies and did not make Indian industries globally competitive by 1990. Exports in manufactured goods were not significantly boosted during this period.

57. (b) (iii) (i) (ii)
58. (b) (iii) (i) (ii)
59. (a) (ii) (iv) (iii) (i)
60. (d) (ii) (iii) (i) (iv)
61. Mixed economy
62. Equitable distribution
63. Plan
64. Self-reliance
65. Marketable surplus

Subjective Questions

Short Answer Type Questions

1. "In a command economy, resources are allocated by the government, often with the intention of achieving social equality, but critics argue that it leads to inefficiency and a lack of innovation." Competency Based Que

(i) Based on the statement, explain how a command economy allocates resources differently compared to a market economy.

(ii) Identify and discuss one major drawback of resource allocation in a command economy as mentioned in the statement.

Ans. (i) In a command economy, the government centrally plans and controls resource allocation, making decisions about production, distribution and consumption.

This contrasts with a market economy, where resource allocation is determined by the forces of supply and demand, with minimal government intervention.

(ii) One major drawback of resource allocation in a command economy is inefficiency. Because the government is responsible for all economic decisions, it may not respond effectively to changes in consumer preferences or market conditions. This can lead to mismatches between supply and demand, resulting in shortages of goods or surpluses of unwanted products.

2. Give two merits and demerits of mixed economic system.

Ans. The merits of mixed economic system are

(i) Mixed economy gives adequate scope to private individuals to co-exist and contribute towards economic development.

(ii) In this, planned economic development ensures stability and balanced development.

The demerits of mixed economic system are

(i) Mixed economy cannot effectively control the private sector industries which are outside the government purview.

(ii) It is characterised by red-tapism and high degree of corruption.

3. Why should plans have goals?

Ans. Every plan should have specified goals which it seeks to pursue. Goals are the ultimate targets; the achievement of which ensures the success of plans.

A plan specifies the means and ways to allocate scarce resources in an optimum manner to achieve these desired goals. Without specific goals, a plan would be directionless and resources would not be utilised in a proper manner without wastage. Therefore, every plan should have specific goals which it strives to achieve.

4. 'Economic growth' and 'economic development' means one and the same. Defend or refute the given statement. Do you think that India is economically developed? Why or why not? Competency Based Que

Ans. The given statement is refuted. Economic growth means that there is a continuous and sustained rise in the GDP of the country.

Economic development means that in addition to a continuous and sustained rise in the GDP, there is equitable distribution of income and changes in sectoral composition in favour of secondary and tertiary sectors.

The above interpretation of the two terms leads us to the conclusion that these terms do not convey the same meaning. Economic development is a wide term which includes economic growth within its purview.

No, I do not think that India is economically developed because income inequalities are continuously rising in our country. The rich are getting richer and the poor are getting poorer, thus defeating the value of social justice.

5. "The primary goal of the five year plans in India has been to achieve 'growth with equity,' focusing on sustained economic development while maintaining macroeconomic stability." Justify the statement with valid explanation. **Competency Based Que**

Ans. Both growth and equity are the two important objectives of Indian planning. While 'growth' refers to the increase in national income over a long period of time, 'equity' refers to an equitable distribution of this income so that the benefits of higher economic growth can be passed on to all sections of population to bring about social justice.

Growth is desirable but growth in itself does not guarantee the welfare of society. Growth is assessed by the market value of goods and services produced in the economy (GDP) and it does not guarantee an equitable distribution of income. In other words, the major share of Gross Domestic Product (GDP) might be owned by a small proportion of population, which may result in exploitation of weaker sections of society.

Hence, 'growth with equity' is a rational and desirable objective of planning. This objective ensures that the benefits of high growth are shared by all the people equally and hence, inequality of income is reduced alongwith growth in income.

6. Aatmanirbhar Bharat' had been at the roots of the Indian planning process in the form of 'self-reliance' as an objective of the planning process. Do you agree with the given statement? Justify the rationale of the given statement. **CBSE SQP 2020; Competency Based Que**

Or **Explain the rationale behind choosing 'self-reliance' as a central planning objective in India's development strategy.** **CBSE SQP 2025**

Ans. Yes, I agree with the given statement.

The concept of Aatmanirbhar Bharat (self-reliant India) aligns with the objective of self reliance that was emphasised in India's planning process, particularly in the early five year plans.

Post-independence, India aimed to reduce dependency on foreign aid and imports by promoting domestic industries and agriculture, a goal reflected in the green revolution and industrial policies. This laid the foundation for self-reliance as a national objective.

This initiative builds on the earlier goals of self-sufficiency but adapts to modern challenges, aiming for economic resilience, boosting domestic manufacturing and reducing dependence on imports, especially in strategic sectors.

Both past and current strategies aim to strengthen India's domestic capacity while integrating it with global markets, reflecting a sustained commitment to self-reliance in India's economic policy.

7. Does modernisation as a planning objective create contradiction in the light of employment generation? Explain.

Ans. No, modernisation as a planning objective does not contradict employment generation.

Modernisation refers to the use of new and modern technology in the production process. This may make some people lose their jobs in the initial stages, as machines take place of men.

But gradually, the use of modern technology and input will raise the productivity and the income of the people, that will further raise the demand for goods and services.

In order to fulfil this increased demand, more production output will be required and there will be more job opportunities, which will lead to higher employment in the economy. Even in the short-run, modernisation leads to creation of employment opportunities for skilled workers.

If proper training and vocational education is provided, it will lead to better employment in terms of quality of work and earnings.

Hence, both modernisation and employment generation are not contradictory but are complementary to each other.

8. Refer to the provided pictures and explain the various problems faced by the agriculture sector in India. **Competency Based Que**

Ans. Main problems of Indian agriculture highlighted in the images are as follows

(i) **Low Productivity**
The low productivity and production of agricultural sector forced India to import food from the USA and Pakistan.

(ii) **Dependence on Rainfall**
Indian agriculture was mainly dependent upon monsoon which is uncertain, unreliable and irregular.

(iii) **Traditional or Outdated Technology**
Indian agriculture is still characterised by the use of orthodox farming techniques.

(iv) **Small Holdings**
The size of operational holdings has been declining year-by-year leading to increase in the number of marginal and small holdings and fall in the number of medium and large holdings.

9. "The goal of equity was served by 'abolition of intermediaries' in agriculture in the post independence period."

Do you agree with the given statement? Support your answer with valid explanation.

CBSE 2025; Competency Based Que

Or **"Government's abolition of intermediaries: a promised empowerment for farmers or a failure in equitable land distribution." Critically analyse the outcomes and challenges of reform.**

Ans. No, I do not agree with the given statement.

The government's abolition of intermediaries, particularly the zamindari system, was heralded as a transformative reform aimed at empowering farmers by transferring land ownership directly to the tiller of land.

The policy of 'land to the tiller' was based on the idea that the cultivators will take more interest as they will have more incentive to invest in increasing output if they are the owners of the land.

On the positive side, the abolition intended to enhance agricultural productivity by motivating farmers to invest in their land, as they would directly benefit from any increased output.

However, the goal of equity was not fully served by abolition of intermediaries due to following reasons

(i) In some areas, the former zamindars continued to own large areas of land by making use of some loopholes in the legislation.

(ii) Even when the tillers got ownership of land, the poorest of the agricultural labourers did not benefit from land reforms.

In conclusion, while the abolition of intermediaries was framed as a progressive step toward achieving equitable land distribution, a critical analysis reveals that its implementation fell short of its ambitious goals.

10. "Land ceiling promotes equity." Support the given statement with valid reason.

CBSE SQP 2023; Competency Based Que

Ans. Land ceiling means fixing the maximum size of land which could be owned by an individual, beyond which it would be taken over by the government and would be allotted to landless and small farmers.

The purpose of land ceiling was to reduce the concentration of land ownership in few hands and hence promotes equity.

11. The land ceiling legislation also faced hurdles. The big landlords challenged the legislation in the courts, delaying its implementation. They used this delay to register their lands in the name of close relatives, thereby escaping from the legislation. The legislation also had a lot of loopholes which were exploited by the big landholders to retain their land. Land reforms were successful in Kerala and West Bengal because these states had governments committed to the policy of land to the tiller.

Unfortunately, other states did not have the same level of commitment and vast inequality in landholding continues to this day. In the light of the above mentioned information, mention the challenges faced by land ceiling legislation. **Competency Based Que**

Ans. Problems faced by land ceiling legislation are as follows

(i) Post-independence, India had more than 70 per cent of landholdings under 5 acres so the ceiling fixed on existing holdings by the states was very high.

(ii) In most states, the ceilings were imposed on individual and not family holdings, enabling landowners to divide up their holdings in the names of relatives or make Benami transfers merely to avoid the ceiling.

(iii) Further, in many states the ceiling could be raised if the size of the family of the landholder exceeded five.

(iv) Many exemptions to the ceiling limits were permitted by most states following the second plan recommendations that certain categories of land could be exempted from ceilings.

12. The percentage share of agricultural sector in the exports of the country declined in the period 1950-1990. Why?

Ans. The share of agricultural sector has fallen because of the reasons enumerated below

(i) During this period, there was substantial growth in Indian industrial sector. With growth in industrial sector, the domestic demand of agricultural products increased as they were being used as raw material in the factories.

(ii) During this period, there was a tremendous increase in the population of the country. As population grew, the domestic demand for agricultural products also grew.

13. **Look at the image given below.**

Based upon the image, explain the advantages of green revolution in India.

Ans. Advantages of green revolution are as follows

(i) It allows to create more food than conventional methods of growing.
(ii) It offers good yields in challenging conditions.
(iii) It allows a decline in food costs across the globe, making food economically sustainable.
(iv) It increases the per capita income of farmers by increasing the agricultural outputs.

14. **"Green revolution made India self-sufficient in food grains, but was criticised on ecological grounds." Do you agree with the given statement? Present valid reasons in support of your answer.** CBSE 2024 C

Ans. Yes, the green revolution made India self-sufficient in foodgrains by introducing High Yielding Variety (HYV) seeds, boosting productivity and reducing foodgrain prices.

However, it was criticised for

(i) **Environmental Damage**
Excessive use of chemical fertilisers and water led to soil degradation, groundwater depletion and pollution.

(ii) **Regional Inequality**
Benefits were limited to affluent states like Punjab and Haryana, widening regional disparities.

(iii) **Inequality among Farmers**
Wealthy farmers benefited more, while smaller farmers struggled to afford new technology.

(iv) **Loss of Biodiversity**
Focus on mono-cropping reduced genetic diversity.

15. **"Farm subsidies put a huge burden on the government finances, but are necessary for the poor and marginal farmers." Justify the given statement with valid explanation.** CBSE 2025, 24; Competency Based Que

Ans. Farm subsidies impose a significant financial burden on the government.

However, they are crucial for small and marginal farmers in India due to the following reasons

(i) **Financial Support**
Most Indian farmers have limited resources. Subsidies help them afford essential inputs like seeds and fertilisers, preventing financial distress.

(ii) **Risk Mitigation**
Agriculture is unpredictable due to monsoons and market fluctuations. Subsidies act as a safety net, ensuring stable livelihoods.

(iii) **Food Security**
Subsidies maintain agricultural production, preventing food shortages and price hikes.

(iv) **Preventing Rural Distress**
Without subsidies, farmers may quit agriculture, leading to migration and urban unemployment.

Thus, despite the financial burden, subsidies are crucial for sustaining small farmers and ensuring food security.

16. **"Direct and active participation of state was considered essential in industrial development process in period 1950-1990." Justify the given statement with valid explanation.** CBSE 2024; Competency Based Que

Ans. At the time of independence, Indian economic conditions were very poor and weak. There was neither private capital nor India have foreign investment credibility to attract foreign investment. Moreover, Indian planners did not want to be dependent on foreign capital for economic development. In such a situation, it seemed most rational that the public sector takes an active role.

Following are the reasons that explain the driving role of the public sector in industrial development

(i) **Lack of Capital with the Private Entrepreneurs**
At the time of independence, the requirement of capital for diversified industrial growth far exceeded its availability with private entrepreneurs. Accordingly, it became essential for the State to foster industrial growth through public sector undertakings.

(ii) **Lack of Incentives among the Private Entrepreneurs**
The private investors lacked the incentive to invest in large industries. Because of this reason, the public sector was forced to invest in the development of these industries.

(iii) **Socialistic Pattern of Society**
The government realised that a socialist society could be achieved only through direct participation of the State in the process of industrialisation because it requires an investment that generates employment rather than an investment that only maximises profit.

17. Differentiate between private sector and public sector. Give an example of each sector.

Ans. Differences between private sector and public sector are

Basis	Private Sector	Public Sector
Concept	Private sector is that part of the economy in which private entrepreneurs operate.	Public sector consists of industries owned and operated by the government.
Example	Reliance Industries.	Mahanagar Telephone Nigam Limited (MTNL).
Objective	The objective is to earn profits.	The objective is to do social welfare.

18. The Industrial Policy Resolution, 1956 has categorised industries on the basis of ownership. Discuss.

Ans. According to the Industrial Policy Resolution, 1956, industries were classified into three categories on the basis of ownership. These were as follows

(i) The first category consisted of industries which could be established and developed exclusively as public sector enterprises.

(ii) The second category consisted of industries in which public sector will be in the leading role while private sector will be in supportive role.

(iii) The third category consisted of all industries other than those specified in the above categories and was open for private sector.

19. Why was the 'policy of protection' considered necessary for industries?

Ans. The need for a 'policy of protection' in industries arose to support the growth of local industries. This policy shielded domestic industries from foreign competition through measures such as tariffs and quotas on imports. It was driven by the understanding that industries in developing nations were not yet equipped to compete with those in developed countries.

20. "Industrial licensing was used to promote regional equality." Discuss. Competency Based Que

Or **"Under the Industrial Policy Resolution (IPR) 1956 in India, the system of industrial licensing was introduced to promote regional equality." Justify the given statement with valid arguments.** CBSE SQP 2025

Ans. The licensing policy was introduced in the IPR of 1956 to promote regional equality.

As per this policy, private entrepreneurs were allowed to establish a new industry or to expand the productive capacity of the existing units only after obtaining license from the government.

Strict rules and regulations were required to be followed before a license was provided. However, if the new unit was proposed to be established in a backward region, then the license was provided on simpler terms. This promoted industrialists to establish new units in backward regions, thereby ensuring all-round development of the country.

21. Discuss briefly the role of small-scale industries in generating employment and equity in India under the planning period. CBSE 2025

Or **Discuss briefly the role of small-scale industries in the growth journey of India.** CBSE 2024

Ans. The roles of small-scale industries in India can be described as follows

(i) **Generation of Employment**
Small-scale industries serve as a significant employment generator in India. Employment is a crucial determinant of a nation's growth. Hence, the promotion and development of small-scale industries can lead to increased job opportunities, further promoting national growth.

(ii) **Lower Capital Requirement**
Unlike large-scale industries, small-scale industries require less capital. In countries like India, where capital is limited, small-scale industries can help to maintain a balance.

(iii) **Resource Utilisation and Entrepreneurial**
Skill development small-scale industries provide opportunities for entrepreneurial skill development, especially among the rural populace who do not have access to large-scale industries. These sectors also utilise resources available in rural areas, promoting rural development.

(iv) **Promotion of Equity**
Small-scale industries contribute to a more equitable distribution of income by providing employment in rural and semi-urban areas.

They help reduce regional disparities and uplift marginalised sections by fostering self-employment and inclusive growth.

22. In the small town of Kanha, Madhya Pradesh, India, a group of entrepreneurs decided to start various small-scale industries to boost local employment and produce goods tailored to the community's needs. Initially, their businesses thrived, attracting attention from nearby markets.

However, as time progressed, some entrepreneurs noticed that they were struggling to keep up with larger competitors who benefitted from economies of scale.

Additionally, they found it increasingly challenging to maintain a steady supply of quality raw materials at reasonable prices.

Despite their passion and commitment, several business owners began to feel overwhelmed by the growing complexities of managing finances, marketing their products and navigating regulatory requirements.

Based on the case, discuss the four primary problems faced by small-scale industries in India. Competency Based Que

Ans. Small-Scale Industries (SSIs) play a vital role in India's economic landscape by generating employment, promoting entrepreneurship and contributing to local development. However, these industries face several significant challenges as follows

(i) **Access to Capital**
Small-scale industries often struggle to secure financing from banks and financial institutions, impacting their ability to expand and improve operations.

(ii) **Infrastructure**
Poor infrastructure, such as inadequate roads and unreliable power supply, can impede production and distribution processes for SSIs in India.

(iii) **Demand Fluctuation**
Changes in consumer preferences and economic conditions can lead to unpredictable demand, affecting the sustainability of SSIs.

(iv) **Competition**
Larger firms, often with better resources and technology, may outcompete SSIs, making it challenging for them to thrive in the market.

23. "International trade allows countries to specialise, increases competition, lowers prices and provide consumers with more product variety, boosting economic efficiency and growth." Do you agree with the statement? Competency Based Que

Ans. Yes, I agree with statement because international or foreign trade have many benefits for the economy

(i) International trade encourages specialisation on the basis of comparative advantage. This enables a country to obtain foreign goods at a cheaper rate in context of the domestic resources used.

(ii) An increase in export trade widens the country's total market. Production of more goods will further lower the cost of production, leading to lower cost per unit.

(iii) It encourages competition, leads to innovation and increases capital flows.

(iv) It helps the country to earn valuable foreign exchange.

24. Explain how import substitution can protect domestic industry? NCERT

Ans. In the first seven five year plans, India followed an inward looking trade strategy.

This strategy aimed at replacing or substituting imports with domestic production i.e. instead of importing goods made in a foreign country, industries would be encouraged to produce them in India itself. This concept is referred to as import substitution.

Thus, the government protected the domestic industries from foreign competition through this policy.

Protection from imports took two forms

(i) Tariffs, i.e. a tax on imported goods to make imported goods more expensive and discourage their use.

(ii) Quotas specify the quantity of goods which can be imported.

The policy of import substitution provides protection to domestic industries from foreign competition. The rationale for this policy is that industries of developing countries like India are not in a position to compete against the goods produced by developed economies. It is assumed that if the domestic industries are protected in the formation stage, they will gain strength by being able to produce on large-scale and through experience they will be able to compete globally in the course of time.

25. What is sectoral composition of an economy? Is it necessary that the service sector should contribute maximum to GDP of an economy? Comment. NCERT; Competency Based Que

Ans. The sectoral composition of an economy is the proportionate contribution of different sectors to the Gross Domestic Product (GDP) of an economy during a year. It gives the share of agricultural sector, industrial sector and service sector in GDP. Yes, it is necessary that at the later stages of development, the service sector should contribute the maximum to the total GDP.

There exists a phenomenon called structural transformation which implies that as a country develops, gradually the country's dependence on the agricultural sector will shift from the maximum to minimum and at the same time, the share of industrial and service sector in the total GDP will increase.

In more developed countries, the share of the service sector is the maximum. Therefore, to ensure that a country is economically developed, the share of service sector should be the maximum.

26. Why, despite the implementation of green revolution, 65% of India's population continued to be engaged in the agriculture sector till 1990?

Ans. With the advent of green revolution, Indian agricultural production increased substantially that enabled India to attain the status of self-sufficiency in foodgrains.

However, India failed to achieve structural transformation associated with economic growth and development. The industrial sector's growth was not very significant during this period and thus, this sector could not provide employment opportunities to the surplus labour from agricultural sector.

The industrial sector in India failed to generate significant employment opportunities in order to attract and absorb excess agricultural labour.

This led to disguised unemployment in agriculture. The slow growth of secondary sector has been responsible for majority of population (approx 65%) to remain in agricultural occupation till 1990.

Long Answer Type Questions

27. "Mixed economy is the basic framework of planning in India." Justify the given statement.

Competency Based Que

Ans. Mixed economy is an economic system in which economic decisions are taken by the Central Government authority, as well as, some decisions are left to free play of the market. It is the basic framework of planning in India.

In this economy, the market will provide whatever goods and services it can produce economically and the government will provide essential goods and services which the market fails to provide.

The following features of Indian economy prove that mixed economy is the basic framework of planning in India

(i) In India, agriculture and most of the industrial and service sectors are in private hands.

(ii) Market forces of demand and supply have free role in determining prices in various markets, i.e. goods having higher demand will be highly priced and *vice-versa*.

(iii) Over the period of time, many big business houses have come into being and have been growing, such as Reliance, Infosys, Bajaj, etc.

(iv) After independence, the government recognised the need to provide infrastructure for the growth of the private sector. So, public sector was developed on a large-scale.

28. Give the achievements of five year plans in India.

Ans. Some major achievements of the five year plans are as follows

(i) **Increase in National Income**
Prior to planning, the national income of India increased at the rate of 0.5% per annum. During the period of planning, the average annual growth rate in India had been around 5%.

(ii) **Increase in Per Capita Income**
During the planning period, per capita income increased at the rate of 2.9% per annum.

(iii) **Institutional and Technical Changes**
In agriculture planning has contributed tremendously towards the development of agriculture in our country. During the period of planning, average growth rate of agricultural produce was 2.8% per annum.

(iv) **Growth and Diversification of Industry**
During the period of planning, the growth rate of industrial production has been around 7% per annum. Basic and capital goods industries have shown tremendous growth. In consumer goods industries, the country has become self-sufficient. Industrial sector has been diversified and modernised.

(v) **Economic and Social Infrastructure**
During the period of planning, economic infrastructure such as means of transport and communication, irrigation facilities and power, banking and insurance facilities have shown significant growth. Health and educational facilities have recorded a significant rise.

(vi) **Employment**
Concentrated efforts have been made to increase employment opportunities during the plan period. In the eleventh five year plan, the government fixed the target of creating 58 million jobs. The twelfth plan aimed at creating 70 million jobs.

29. Discuss the problems that the five year plans were unable to address.

Ans. The five year plans have not been able to address the following problems

(i) **Poverty**
The FYPs have failed to address the problem of poverty in our country. 21.9% of our population lives below poverty line and around 50% of the poor people of the world reside in India. The basic needs of food, shelter and clothing are not being fulfilled.

(ii) **Inflation**
The FYPs have also failed to check the problem of inflation in the country.
The continuously rising prices have eroded the purchasing power of money and increased the inequalities of wealth.

(iii) **Unemployment**
At the end of the eleventh plan, nearly 4 crore people were unemployed as the employment opportunities were not growing at the same rate in which the supply of labour was rising.

(iv) **Inadequate Infrastructure**
India has inadequate infrastructure. There is an acute shortage of public means of transport. Roads are in a pitiful condition, the cities are filthy and educational and medical facilities are highly inadequate.

(v) **Rising Inequalities**
The FYPs have failed to promote equitable distribution of income.
The rich people are getting richer and the poor people are getting poorer. The plans have in fact encouraged unequitable distribution of income.

30. Explain the importance of agricultural sector for the Indian economy.

Or

Why is agriculture sector deemed to be the backbone of Indian economy? Competency Based Que

Ans. The importance of agriculture in the Indian economy is evident by the following points

(i) **Employment**
In India, agriculture is the principal source of employment. Over 50% of working population is either directly or indirectly dependent on agriculture for means of their livelihood.

(ii) **Supplier of Raw Material for Industries**
Agriculture provides cotton for the textile industries, sugarcane for sugar industry, various seeds for oil industry and jute for gunnysack industry. The growth of the secondary sector is dependent on the primary sector.

(iii) **Contribution to International Trade**
Agriculture is the major contributor to external trade. India exports tea, jute, cashewnuts, tobacco, coffee, spices, etc. on a large-scale.

(iv) **Instrumental in the Growth of Transport Industry**
Both railways and roadways are the bulk carriers of agricultural products in India. Thus, agricultural sector is a major consumer of the transport services of our country.

(v) **Contribution to Wealth of Nation**
In terms of fixed assets, land occupies the highest rank in India.
In addition to it, a large amount is invested in irrigation projects. Thus, agricultural sector owns a large chunk of nation's wealth.

So, we can conclude that agriculture is not only an important component of the primary sector, but it also helps to sustain and develop both secondary as well as tertiary sector. Thus, it is the backbone of economy.

31. "Features of Indian agriculture themselves explain the story of its backwardness." Put out your views in the reference to this statement.

The government has initiated various policies to help the farmers. One such policy is 'loan waiver'. Briefly discuss this policy and identify the value promoted by the government. Competency Based Que

Ans. Indian agriculture is backward, despite the fact that it is of significant importance in the Indian economy. The main features of Indian agriculture are

(i) Agricultural output depends largely on rainfall and is affected by natural calamities like flood, drought, storm, etc.

(ii) The historical, social and cultural background of state affects agricultural output.

(iii) Over three-fourth of landholdings are of small size. Thus, agriculture is a source of livelihood for poor farmers.

(iv) Farming is a way of life rather than a commercial activity. Thus, production is mainly for self-consumption.

(v) There is little use of machinery.

The 'loan-waiver' policy has been implemented by the central, as well as state governments to waive-off the outstanding debt dues of the farmers in case of crop failure due to drought, excessive rainfall or any other natural calamity.

This policy aims to ease-off the burden of poor farmers in face of natural calamity. The value highlighted by the government is care and concern for the poor farmers of the country.

32. Explain the importance of industrial sector in the economy of a country.

Ans. Following points highlight the importance of industry in an economy

(i) **Structural Transformation**
Industrial development brings about structural transformation in the economy. It means that dependence of our economy on agriculture will be reduced.

(ii) **Source of Employment**
Indian economy has a very large skilled workforce which is still unemployed.
It is the establishment of industries only, which can generate employment opportunities on a large-scale.

(iii) **Enhancing further the Economic Growth**
As industrialisation progresses, the capital goods industry also starts to flourish. This helps in further economic growth and also helps an economy to attain self-sustaining development.

(iv) **Infrastructural Growth**
With the spread of industrialisation, the need for economic infrastructure such as roads, dams, banking, insurance and communication facilities also rises and this leads to their growth.

Also, with the improvement in quality of life, the demand for social infrastructure i.e. facilities related to health and education, also rise and leads to their development.

(v) **Strengthening the Economy**
Industries help to strengthen the economy in following ways

- With the growth of capital goods industry, the country is able to produce a number of goods in large quantities and at low cost.
- It helps in the establishment of infrastructure goods like dams, railways, etc. which cannot be imported.
- Industrialisation has helped our country to become self-reliant in defence goods.

33. Though public sector is very essential for industries, many public sector undertakings incur huge losses and are a drain on the economy's resources. Discuss the usefulness of public sector undertakings in the light of this fact. NCERT; Competency Based Que

Ans. The inefficiency and low productivity in Public Sector Undertakings (PSUs) may lead to wastage of scarce resources and result in huge losses forming a constraint on economic resources of the country, but they are still useful.

Public sector has been playing a very significant role in the economic development of India in the following ways

(i) **Creation of a Strong Industrial Base**
Public sector undertakings have contributed significantly towards the development of heavy and basic industries, thus creating a strong industrial base.

(ii) **Development of Infrastructure**
PSUs have helped in development of infrastructure of the country. A developed infrastructure boosted the progress of private sector in the country.

(iii) **Mobilisation of Savings**
Government companies formed under PSUs mobilise the savings of individuals through offer of shares and use these savings for the economic development of the country.

(iv) **Help to Earn Foreign Exchange**
Many PSUs produce goods which can be exported. The export earnings of PSUs such as HMT, STC, etc. have helped increase the flow of foreign exchange in the country.

Also, PSUs such as BHEL, ONGC, etc. helped the country to save on the import bill.

(v) **Development of Backward Areas**
PSUs are generally opened in backward areas so that these areas are also able to progress economically.

(vi) **Generation of Employment Opportunities**
PSUs have generated substantial employment opportunities and have helped to address the problem of poverty and unemployment.

(vii) **To Promote Equality**
PSUs check concentration of power in few hands and promote equality in the country.

34. Give the benefits of inward looking trade strategy.

Ans. The following benefits are credited to the country by following this trade policy

(i) **Increased Rate of Industrial Growth Leading to Structural Transformation**
This strategy, followed by the Indian government, helped the domestic industries to survive and expand their operations.

This resulted in an increased rate of industrial growth. The share of industrial sector towards the GDP of the country also increased.

(ii) **Diversification of Industrial Growth**
This strategy helped in diversifying the industrial activities in the country.

Till 1950, modern industries were merely confined to textile and jute industries, but the introduction of this policy helped in diversification of industries.

(iii) **Created Opportunities for Investment**
The policy of the government to protect small-scale industries induced the investors to invest in them.

These industries needed less capital and created opportunities for self-employment. The establishment of these industries promoted growth with equity and ensured that small savings are also channelised towards the economic growth of the country.

35. What are the drawbacks of inward looking trade strategy?

Ans. Inward looking trade strategy has the following drawbacks

(i) **Lack of Modernisation in the Industrial Sector**
This strategy protected the domestic industries from competition from foreign industries.

In the absence of any competition, domestic industries paid no attention to modernise their manufacturing facilities and supply superior quality products to consumers.

(ii) **Inefficient Utilisation of Resources**
This strategy encouraged the production of all the goods domestically.
This implied that the country should produce even those goods which it can import at a cheaper rate from foreign countries. This resulted in inefficient utilisation of scarce resources.

(iii) **Emergence of Black Market**
This strategy aimed to discourage imports by imposing high tariffs and quantitative restrictions.
This led to the emergence of a very strong black market where goods from foreign countries were smuggled into the India illegally. This led the economy to lose crores of rupees.

(iv) **Inadequate Flow of Foreign Capital**
This trade policy imposed several restrictions on flow of foreign capital. Foreign investors wanting to invest in India were required to comply with several rules and regulations. These formalities discouraged them from investing in India.

36. Critically assess the economic policy in place before 1991, focusing on its key achievements and shortcomings.

Ans. The economic policy prior to 1991 had several defining characteristics

(i) Economic growth was primarily pursued through five year plans.
(ii) Public enterprises were designated as crucial players in the economy.
(iii) Import substitution was the cornerstone of the industrialisation strategy.
(iv) Domestic industries were shielded from foreign competition.
(v) Development efforts were aimed at both large-scale and small-scale industries.

Achievements

(i) The policy facilitated economic growth, particularly through enhanced agricultural productivity, which subsequently led to increased industrial output.
(ii) The expansion of large-scale industries initiated a significant infrastructural transformation within the Indian economy. Meanwhile, small-scale industries made a noteworthy contribution towards realising growth objectives while promoting social equity.

Failures

(i) The public sector's persistent losses drained the nation's limited resources.
(ii) Many domestic industries struggled to meet international product quality standards.
(iii) Foreign exchange reserves dwindled to critically low levels, indicating a severe imbalance.

Overall, the growth process exhibited signs of stagnation, especially within the industrial sector. As a result, the government was compelled to transition to the New Economic Policy in 1991.

37. Some economists are of view that subsidies do not allow prices to indicate the supply of a good. When electricity and water are provided at a subsidised rate or free, they will be used wastefully without any concern for their scarcity.

Farmers will cultivate water intensive crops if water is supplied free, although the water resources in that region may be scarce and such crops further deplete. Also, if water is priced to reflect scarcity, farmers will cultivate crops according to region.

Fertiliser and pesticide subsidies can be harmful to environment. Subsidies provide an incentive for wasteful use of resources. Competency Based Que

(i) Apart from the negative effect of subsidies as discussed in the above para, highlight the basic advantages of providing subsidies.

(ii) How subsidies can be linked as threat to environment?

Ans. (i) Advantages of subsidies are as follows

- **Lowering Prices and Controlling Inflation**
They are especially applicable in the area of production cost inputs such as fuel prices, particularly when global crude oil prices are rising. Many countries subsidise fuel costs in order to keep prices from ballooning.
- **Preventing the Long-term Decline of Industries**
There are many industries that should be kept alive and functional, such as fishing and farming because they are essential to support a population.
Many new and fast growing industries may also benefit from being subsidised.
- **Greater Supply of Goods**
Governments want to increase the access of their population to goods and services such as water, food and education.
They therefore, provide an incentive that could be in the form of a tax credit or even straight-up cash. Markets that have positive externalities are usually the ones that receive such benefits.

(ii) Environmentally harmful subsidies cause polluters to pass on some of the costs of their production and consumption to the state and society, for example in the form of higher healthcare costs or costs to clean-up environmental damage which has been done.

Environmentally harmful subsidies also distort competition at the expense of environmentally sound technologies and products.

This blocks environmental protection efforts and slows down the shift to sustainable patterns of production and consumption.

To offset these disincentives, the state must give more support to environmentally sound technologies and products such as renewable energies. This is the only way they will have a fair chance of becoming established in the market.

38. **The green revolution, introduced in India during the 1960s, led to remarkable changes in agricultural practices, particularly in the production of wheat and rice. This period saw the introduction of high yielding variety seeds, chemical fertilisers and improved irrigation methods.**

While the green revolution significantly boosted food production, certain unforeseen challenges began to emerge over time in some regions.

Farmers who adopted these new technologies experienced rapid growth initially, but others, especially those without access to resources, faced hurdles.

As decades passed, some areas began witnessing shifts in soil health, water availability and crop diversity.

Based on the case study, discuss the following questions

(i) What was the primary goal of the green revolution in India?

(ii) Explain two significant contributions of the green revolution to Indian agriculture.

(iii) What possible issues might arise from the advancements of the green revolution in the long-term? **Competency Based Que**

Ans. (i) The primary goal of the green revolution in India was to increase agricultural production and ensure food security through the use of High Yielding Variety (HYV) seeds, improved irrigation, fertilisers and modern farming techniques.

(ii)
- **Increased Crop Yields**
  The green revolution introduced High Yielding Variety (HYV) seeds, which significantly boosted crop production, especially for staple foods like wheat and rice. This led to increased food availability and improved rural incomes.
- **Modernisation of Farming Techniques**
  The green revolution promoted the use of modern farming techniques, including advanced irrigation methods, chemical fertilisers and pesticides. This modernisation helped farmers increase productivity and efficiency in their agricultural practices.

(iii) The new agricultural strategy suffered from the following drawbacks
- **Confined to Food Crops**
  Green revolution was confined to the production of wheat and rice only. It did not cover pulses. Besides this, progress in major commercial crops like cotton, jute, oilseeds, etc. had been very slow.
- **Limited Coverage**
  Green revolution was practised only in few states of India, like Punjab, Haryana, Maharashtra, Tamil Nadu, Western Uttar Pradesh and in some selected districts of Andhra Pradesh. Thus, it widened regional inequalities.
- **Inequality among Farmers**
  Only big farmers benefitted from the application of new technology. This increased the inequality among farmers leading to the growth of capitalist farming in Indian agriculture.
- **Undesirable Social Effects**
  The increasing use of farm machinery created the problem of surplus labour in the agricultural sector. Besides this, the big farmers or landlords found it more profitable to cultivate land themselves. Therefore, some of landlords removed the landless farmers from their land. This led to a greater incidence of inequality among farmers, i.e. poor farmers became poorer.

SELF ASSESSMENT TEST

Objective Type Questions

1. ...... is an economy having elements of both capitalist and socialist economy.
   (a) Mixed economy (b) Socialist economy
   (c) Capitalist economy (d) None of these
2. Capitalist structure was not adopted by Indian economy due to
   (a) less scoper for improvement of quality of human life
   (b) more democratic structure was needed
   (c) there was a need to reduce role of public sector
   (d) None of the above
3. Which economic sector has the highest share in India's GDP?
   (a) Agriculture sector (b) Tertiary sector
   (c) Industrial sector (d) Export sector
4. Which of the following statement(s) is/are true for Indian agriculture for pre and post-colonial period?
   (a) Dependency of workforce in agriculture observed a gradual decline after colonial period
   (b) Land celling policy was a huge success leading to abolition of intermediaries completely
   (c) Green revolution benefitted to big farmer more than small and marginal farmers
   (d) All are true
5. Structural composition refers to the
   (a) number of people engaged in training
   (b) number of people engaged in different sectors
   (c) number of people engaged in tertiary sector
   (d) number of people facing unemployment
6. Which of the following is not true about agricultural subsidies?
   (a) They provide monetary assistance to enhance production activities in the economy
   (b) Eliminating subsidies could widen the gap between wealthy and poorer farmers
   (c) They contribute to inefficient or wasteful consumption in the economy
   (d) Subsidies always ensure equitable distribution of resources in agriculture
7. Which of the following statements is/are correct?
   (i) Under socialism, factors of production are owned by the society.
   (ii) Green revolution advocates use of HYV seeds and chemical based fertilisers.

   Codes
   (a) Only I
   (b) Only II
   (c) Both I and II
   (d) None of the above

Answers 1. (a) 2. (a) 3. (b) 4. (c) 5. (b) 6. (d) 7. (c)

Short Answer Type Questions

8. Briefly discuss the meaning of economic planning.
9. Radha, a farmer in Bihar, cannot afford HYV seeds and irrigation. Her yields are much lower than farmers in Punjab. Why did the green revolution benefit some regions more than others?
10. Trace the growth of industrial sector during the period 1950-51 to 1990-91.
11. "Green revolution in India is marked by two distinct phases." Elaborate.
12. To what extent, have the plans succeeded in accelerating the growth rate of Indian economy?
13. Rahul's grandfather worked in a textile mill during the 1970s. He recalls that strict industrial licensing policies and government controls often delayed business operations and limited the growth of industries. Many companies faced challenges like low productivity and lack of innovation.

    Discuss, how the industrial licensing policy (License Raj) hindered economic growth and industrial development in India during the 1950-1990 period?

Long Answer Type Questions

14. In the five year plans, why was more emphasise given towards public sectors?
15. Explain briefly the common goals of five year plans.
16. "While subsidies encourage farmers to use new technology, they are a huge burden on government finances." Discuss the usefulness of subsidies in the light of this fact.

03

CHAPTER

Liberalisation, Privatisation and Globalisation : An Appraisal

The Economic Policy of 1991 marked a turning point in India's economy, introducing liberalisation, privatisation and globalisation. These reforms dismantled restrictive regulations, boosted economic growth and integrated India into the global market.

YOUR STUDY GOALS

3.1 Economic Crisis of 1991
3.2 Liberalisation
3.3 Privatisation
3.4 Globalisation
3.5 Assessment or Appraisal of LPG Policies

YOUR PRACTICE GOAL

- Objective Type Questions (69 Qs ; MCQs, A-R, Statements, Matching, Concept Identification)
- Subjective Questions (25 SAs, 14 LAs)
- Self Assessment Test (7 MCQs, 7 SAs, 3 LAs)

3.1 Economic Crisis of 1991

Since independence, India adopted a mixed economy framework by combining advantages of capitalism and socialism to regulate the economy.

However, some scholars argue that excessive rules and regulations established due to this policy, hampered growth and development.

Other scholars highlight the role of the public sector in achieving growth in savings, developing industrial sector and expanding agriculture, ensuring food security.

In 1991, India faced an economic crisis relating to its external debt. Following points highlight the economic crisis of 1991

- Government was not able to repay its borrowings from abroad.
- Foreign exchange reserves could only cover two weeks of imports.
- Rising prices of essential goods.

To resolve the crisis, India introduced variety of policies under three heads, *viz.* Liberalisation, Privatisation and Globalisation (LPG).

Liberalisation Privatisation Globalisation

Causes Responsible for the Economic Crisis

Cause	Explanation
Rising Budget Deficit	Government spending exceeded revenue, leading to heavy borrowing. Deficit became unsustainable in the late 1980s, resulting increase in debt burden and depletion of foreign exchange reserves.
Unproductive Spendings	Large portion of revenue was spent on development programmes, social sectors and defense without generating returns. Rest of the revenue was also spent inefficiently.
Unproductive Use of Debt	The foreign exchange borrowed from other countries and international financial institutions was spent on meeting consumption needs rather than boosting exports or controlling imports.
Unproductive Public Sector	Government assigned an important role to public sector post-independence, however it performed poorly. Majority of PSUs incurred huge losses, which the government had to bear.
Rising Prices	General price level in the country was exhibiting inflationary pressure due to increased money supply and shortage of essential goods.
Inefficient Management	Poor economic management by the government which is evident from its unproductive spending, rising expenditure and inadequate revenue generation.

Emergence of NEP after Economic Crisis

- Indian government sought financial aid from the **International Bank for Reconstruction and Development** (IBRD, popularly known as **World Bank**) and **IMF** due to an economic crisis.
- The government received a $7 million loan to manage crisis, with the condition to liberalise the economy.
- India accepted IMF and World Bank conditions and introduced the **New Economic Policy** (NEP).
- NEP aimed to create a competitive economy and remove barriers for firms' entry and growth.
- Reform adopted in NEP are broadly classified as
  - (i) **Stabilisation Measures** Short-term measures to fix Balance of Payments (BoP) issues and control inflation.
  - (ii) **Structural Reform Measures** Long-term reforms to enhance economic efficiency and increase international competitiveness.

    The various structural reforms are categorised under liberalisation, privatisation and globalisation.

New Economic Policy : Structural Reforms

- **Liberalisation** (Introduced to put an end to the restrictions of entry and growth and open various sectors of the economy)
- **Privatisation** (Implies conversion of public sector companies into private sector companies)
- **Globalisation** (Means integration of country's economy with the world economy)

3.2 Liberalisation

Trade Liberalisation

It is defined as allowing the private sector companies to operate business transactions in a country with fewer restrictions. In developing countries, it also refers to opening the economy to multinationals and foreign investments.

The **objectives** of liberalisation are as follows

- To increase competition among domestic industries.
- To increase foreign capital formation and improve the technology.
- To decrease the debt of the country.
- To encourage cross border trade.
- To expand the size of the market.

Economic Reforms under Liberalisation

Reforms were initiated in the 1980s in areas of industrial licensing, export-import policy, technology, fiscal policy and foreign investment.

In 1991, broader reforms under liberalisation were implemented across various sectors, as discussed below

Industrial Sector Reforms

Reform	Explanation
Abolition of Industrial Licensing	Removed licensing requirements for all industries, except for a few sensitive sectors like alcohol, cigarettes, hazardous chemicals, explosives, electronics, aerospace, drugs and pharmaceuticals.
Contraction of Public Sector	The number of industries reserved for the public sector reduced to only three i.e. railways, atomic energy and defence.
Dereservation of Production of Goods	Removed restrictions on goods reserved for Small Scale Industries (SSIs), allowing any scale of businesses to participate.
Price Fixation and Distribution of Products	Allowed the market to determine prices for many industrial products.

Financial Sector Reforms

Reform	Explanation
Competition from Private Banks	Opened banking to private (domestic and foreign) banks, increasing competition and expansion of services for customers.
Change in Role of RBI	Role of RBI shifted from regulator to facilitator, allowing financial institutions more autonomy i.e. they can take decisions on certain matters without consulting RBI.
Increase in Foreign Investment Limit	Raised the limit on foreign investment in banks to 74%, enabling greater FII involvement in financial markets.

Fiscal/Tax Reforms

Reform	Explanation
Simplification of Direct Taxes	Lowered rate of income and corporate taxes, encouraging savings and voluntary income. Disclosure simplified many procedures for better compliance by tax payers.
Reduction of Indirect Tax Rates	Reduced rates on goods and services; introduced Goods and Services Tax (GST) in 2017 to unify tax system.

Foreign Exchange Reforms

Reform	Explanation
Devaluation of Rupee	Devaluation in 1991 led to increased foreign exchange inflow, helping to resolve the balance of payments crisis.
Market Forces determined Exchange Rate	After 1991, exchange rate in India was determined by market forces of demand and supply.

Trade and Investment Policy Reforms

- Aimed to liberalise foreign trade and promote technological efficiency.
- Abolished import quotas and reduced tariff rates.
- Import licensing policy abolished except for hazardous and environmentally sensitive industries.
- Export duties were eliminated to improve international competitiveness of Indian goods.
- Quantitative restrictions on imports of manufactured consumer goods and agricultural products was also removed.

Recent Reforms Introduced under Liberalisation

Recently the following reforms were introduced to encourage the process of liberalisation.

Demonetisation

It refers to the process where the government removes the status of a currency note as a legal tender, meaning it is no longer accepted for transactions in the market.

India has experienced demonetisation three times

- **1946** First demonetisation.
- **1978** Second demonetisation.
- **2016** Third demonetisation (on 8th November, 2016), when ₹ 500 and ₹ 1,000 currency notes were banned by Prime Minister Narendra Modi.

Objectives of Demonetisation

- To make India corruption free.
- To curb black money.
- To control escalating price rise.
- To stop fund flow to illegal activity.
- To make people accountable for every rupee they possess and pay income tax return.
- To make a cashless society and create a Digital India.

Effects of Demonetisation

- With banning of ₹ 500 and ₹ 1,000 notes, the country moved one step towards digitalisation. In the age where almost every person uses a mobile phone, the concept of online wallets came out to be very successful. Online wallet refers to an electronic device that allows an individual to make electronic transactions.
- The announcement of the demonetisation of the currency has caused huge inconvenience to the people.
- Cash crunch became a major problem due to the unavailability of small currency denominations of the last class cannot be determined.

Goods and Services Tax (GST)

The term GST has been defined in Article 366 (12A) to mean 'any tax on supply of goods or services or both except taxes on supply of the alcoholic liquor for human consumption.' It is a value added tax levied on most goods and services sold for domestic use.

It is a destination-based consumption tax, meaning the final seller passes the GST to the consumer, but businesses remit it to the government.

The purpose of GST is to generate revenue, reduce tax evasion and create a unified national market with a single tax structure 'one nation, one tax and one market'.

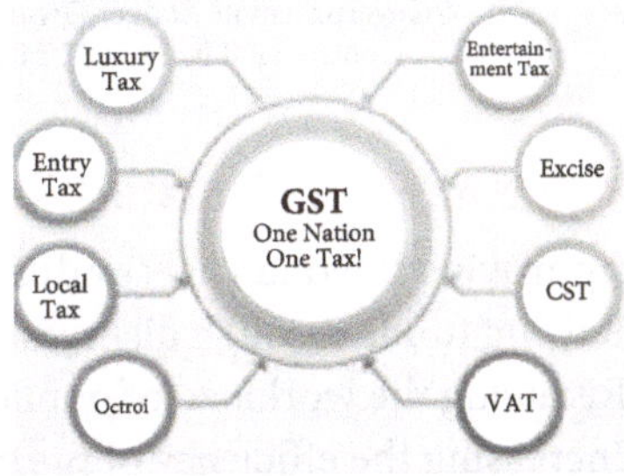

Objectives of GST

- To eliminate classification dispute between goods and services.
- To bring uniformity in tax rates and automated compliances.
- To ensure availability of input tax credit across the value chain and avoid cascading effect.
- To ensure simplification of registration, filing of return, tax administration and compliance.
- To harmonise tax base, laws and administration procedures across the country.

- To minimise tax rate slabs and prevent unhealthy competition among states.
- To ensure free movement of goods across the country without any additional tax.

Characteristics of GST

- Applicable to whole of India, including Jammu and Kashmir.
- Applies to the supply of goods and services, not on sale or production of goods and services.
- Based on destination-based consumption tax principle.
- Import of goods and services subject to IGST and custom duties.
- There are four tax slabs i.e. 5%, 12%, 18%, 28% and also, a zero-rated tax for SEZ areas.
- Mandatory GST registration for businesses with turnover exceeding ₹ 20 lakh (₹ 10 lakh for North-Eastern and hilly areas).
- Subsumed 17 indirect taxes and 23 cesses.
- Provides benefits of input tax credit, i.e. to subtract taxes paid on inputs from taxes paid on outputs.
- Includes anti-profiteering provisions enforced by the National Anti-Profiteering Authority (NAA).

Types of Taxes under GST

1. **Central Goods and Services Tax** (CGST) It is levied on intra-state transactions related to goods and services by the centre.
2. **State Goods and Services Tax** (SGST) It is levied on intra-state transactions related to goods and services by the states.
3. **Integrated Goods and Services Tax** (IGST) It is levied on inter-state transactions related to goods and services and is collected by the centre. It is equivalent to the sum total of CGST and SGST.

3.3 Privatisation

It is the process of transferring the ownership or management of the public sector units to the private sector.

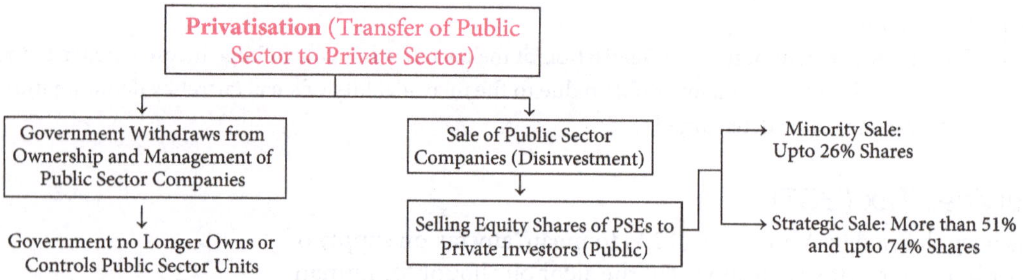

Objectives of Privatisation

- Improving the financial condition of the government.
- Raising funds through disinvestment.
- Reducing the workload of public sector.
- Increasing the efficiency of the government undertakings.
- Providing better goods and services to consumers.
- Encouraging healthy competition within an economy.
- Making way for Foreign Direct Investment (FDI).

3.4 Globalisation

It means integrating the domestic economy with the world economy.
It involves creation of network to link up economic, social and geographical boundaries of the world.

The **objectives** of globalisation are as follows
- To help the economy to adopt new and flexible methods of production.
- To increase the flow of foreign capital into the country.
- To improve the quality of goods produced in the economy.
- To improve the working of the banking and the foreign sector.
- To accelerate the rate of human development in the country.
- To enhance global integration and create a new world order which encourages free trade between nations.

Steps to Promote Globalisation

Steps	Explanation
I. **Increase in Equity Limit of Foreign Investment**	The general equity limit for Foreign Direct Investment (FDI) has been raised from 40% to 51%. In 47 high-priority industries and export trading houses, FDI is allowed up to 100%.
II. **Partial Convertibility**	It means sale and purchase of foreign currency at a price determined by the market forces of demand and supply. In India, there is partial convertibility as there are restrictions on capital account transactions, though the rupee is fully convertible in the current account.
III. **Liberal Foreign Trade Policy**	A long-term liberal foreign trade policy has been implemented which encourages free trade among countries.
IV. **Reduction in Tariffs**	Custom duties have been reduced drastically. Before 1991, custom duties were as high as 400%, but post 1991, maximum rate of duty is only 10%.

Outsourcing : An Outcome of Globalisation

- Outsourcing refers to contracting out some of its activities, which were earlier performed by an organisation, to a third party.
- Outsourcing involves hiring external sources for services previously provided internally, such as legal advice, computer services and advertising.
- The practice of outsourcing has increased due to advancements in communication and the growth of Information Technology (IT).
- Many services such as voice-based business processes (popularly known as BPO or call centres), record keeping, accountancy, banking services, music recording, film editing, book transcription, clinical advice or even teaching are being outsourced by companies in developed countries to India.
- Multinational corporations and even small companies prefer outsourcing their services to India because
  - Skilled workers are available at lower wage rates.
  - There has been significant growth in India's IT industry in India.

International Organisations Promoting Globalisation

The following international organisations play a crucial role in the process of globalisation

Organisation	Key Points
World Trade Organisation (WTO)	**Purpose** Only international organisation concerned with international trade laws. **Main Objective** Ensure smooth and free trade, promote multilateral trade agreements. **History** Founded in 1995, as the successor to General Agreement on Trade and Tariff (GATT, established in 1948). **Functions** Administers multilateral trade agreements, ensures equal opportunities in international markets. **Key Features** Establishes a rule-based trading regime; preventing arbitrary trade restrictions, ensures optimum utilisation of world resources.

Organisation	Key Points
International Monetary Fund (IMF)	**Foundation** Conceived at the Bretton Woods Conference (1944), established in 1946, began operations from March 1947. **Main Objective** Administer a code of conduct for international liquidity of its member countries, provide short-term loans to countries with temporary balance of payments deficits. **Functions** Monitors global economic stability, offers policy advice and financial assistance to member countries.
International Bank for Reconstruction and Development (IBRD)	**Foundation** Established in 1944 at the Bretton Woods Conference alongside the IMF. **Headquarters** Commonly known as the World Bank, located in Washington DC. **Membership** Comprises 188 member countries. **Main Focus** Provides loans to government to rebuild and develop essential infrastructure (railroads, highways, etc.).

3.5 Assessment or Appraisal of LPG Policies

The reform process has completed three decades since its introduction. Let us now look at the performance of the Indian economy during this period. LPG (Liberalisation, Privatisation and Globalisation) policies have had both positive and negative effects on the economy of India.

Positive Effects	Negative Effects
Vibrant Economy • Significant GDP growth from 5.6% (1980-91) to 8.2% (2007-12). • Strong growth in the services sector – 9.8% (2014-15).	**Neglect of Agriculture** – Decline in agricultural growth leading to rural distress. – Reduced public investment in agricultural infrastructure. – Increased costs for small farmers due to subsidy removal and international competition. – Rise in foodgrains prices due to shift from production for domestic market to production for export market.
Flow of Private Foreign Investment • Rise in foreign investment (FDI and FII) : from US $100 million (1990-91) to US $30 billion (2017-18).	**Uneven Growth in Industrial Sector** – Domestic manufacturers face competition from cheaper imports. – Inadequate investment in infrastructure hampers industrial growth.
Increase in Foreign Exchange Reserves • Reserves rose from about US $ 6 billion (1990-91) to US $ 413 billion (2018-19).	**Less Employment Opportunities** Despite GDP growth, job creation has not kept pace with economic expansion.
Stimulant to Industrial Production • Increased productivity and exports in sectors like auto parts, IT and textiles.	**Failure of Disinvestment Policies** – Disinvestment targets were not met and assets of PSEs were undervalued and sold to private sector. – Earnings from disinvestment used to cover revenue shortfalls rather than for development of PSEs.
Role of Private Sector • Enhanced participation of the private sector after abolishing industrial licensing.	**Failure of Fiscal Policies** – High tax evasion still persists and reduction in custom duties reduced revenue generation. – Tax incentives for foreign investors further diminish tax revenues.
	Concentration of Growth Process Growth concentrated only in selected areas in service sectors (telecommunications, IT, finance, etc).

Mind Map

LIBERALISATION, PRIVATISATION AND GLOBALISATION: AN APPRAISAL

1 Economic Crisis of 1991

During the economic crisis of 1991, government was not able to repay its borrowings from abroad and foreign exchange reserves could only cover two weeks of imports.

Causes Responsible for the Economic Crisis

- Rising budget deficit
- Unproductive use of debt
- Rising prices
- Unproductive spendings
- Unproductive public sector
- Inefficient management

2 Emergence of NEP after Economic Crisis

- Indian government sought financial aid from the International Bank for Reconstitution and Development (IBRD, popularly known as World Bank) and IMF due to an economic crisis.
- The government received a $7 million loan to manage crisis, with the condition to liberalise the economy.
- India accepted IMF and World Bank conditions and introduced the New Economic Policy (NEP).
- NEP aimed to create a competitive economy and remove barriers for firms' entry and growth. Reform adopted in NEP are broadly classified as stabilisation measures (Short-term measures) and structural reform measures (Long-term reforms).
- Various structural reforms are categorised under liberalisation, privatisation and globalisation.

3 Liberalisation

It is defined as allowing private sector companies to operate business in a country with fewer restrictions.

Objectives

- To increase competition among domestic industries
- To increase foreign capital formation and improve the technology
- To decrease the debt of the country and to encourage cross border trade
- To expand the size of the market

Economic Reforms under Liberalisation

Industrial Sector Reforms

- Abolition of industrial licensing
- Contraction of public sector
- De-reservation of production of goods
- Price fixation and distribution of products

Financial Sector Reforms

- Competition from private banks
- Change in role of RBI
- Increase in foreign investment limit

Fiscal/Tax Reforms

- Simplification of direct taxes
- Reduction of indirect tax rates

Foreign Exchange Reforms

- Devaluation of rupee
- Market forces determined exchange rate

Trade and Investment Policy Reforms

- Abolished import quotas, import licensing policy
- Elimination of export duties and liberalising foreign trade

Recent Reforms Introduced under Liberalisation

- **Demonetisation** It refers to the process where the government removes the status of a currency note as a legal tender, meaning it is no longer accepted for transactions in the market.
- **Goods and Services Tax** It has been defined in Article 366 (12A) to mean any tax on supply of goods or services or both except taxes on supply of the alcoholic liquor for human consumption.

4 Privatisation

It is the process of transferring the ownership or management of the public sector units to the private sector.

Objectives

- Improving the financial condition of the government.
- Raising funds through disinvestment.
- Reducing the workload of public sector.
- Increasing the efficiency of the government undertakings.
- Providing better goods and services to consumers.
- Encouraging healthy competition within an economy.
- Making way for Foreign Direct Investment (FDI).

5 Globalisation

It means integrating the domestic economy with the world economy.

Objectives

- To help the economy to adopt new and flexible methods of production.
- To increase the flow of foreign capital into the country.
- To improve the quality of goods produced in the economy.
- To improve the working of the banking and the foreign sector.
- To accelerate the rate of human development in the country.
- To enhance global integration and create a new world order which encourages free trade between nations.

Steps to Promote Globalisation

- Increase in equity limit of foreign investment
- Liberal foreign trade policy
- Partial convertability
- Reduction in tariffs

Outsourcing: An Outcome of Globalisation It refers to contracting out some of its activities, which were earlier performed by an organisation, to a third party.

6 Assessment or Appraisal of LPG Policies

Positive Effects

- **Vibrant Economy** Significant GDP growth from 5.6% (1980-91) to 8.2% (2007-12). Strong growth in the services sector – 9.8% (2014-15).
- **Flow of Private Foreign Investment** Rise in foreign investment (FDI and FII) : from US $100 million (1990-91) to US $30 billion (2017-18).
- **Increase in Foreign Exchange Reserves** Reserves rose from about US $ 6 billion (1990-91) to US $ 413 billion (2018-19).
- **Stimulant to Industrial Production** Increased productivity and exports in sectors like auto parts, IT and textiles.
- **Role of Private Sector** Enhanced participation of the private sector after abolishing industrial licensing.

Negative Effects

- **Neglect of Agriculture** Decline in agricultural growth leading to rural distress. Reduced public investment in agricultural infrastructure.
- **Uneven Growth in Industrial Sector** Domestic manufacturers face competition from cheaper imports. Inadequate investment in infrastructure hampers industrial growth.
- **Less Employment Opportunities** Despite GDP growth, job creation has not kept pace with economic expansion.
- **Failure of Disinvestment Policies** Disinvestment targets were not met and assets of PSEs were undervalued and sold to private sector.
- **Failure of Fiscal Policies** High tax evasion still persists and reduction in custom duties reduced revenue generation. Tax incentives for foreign investors further diminish tax revenues.
- **Concentration of Growth Process** Growth concentrated only in selected areas in service sectors (telecommunications, IT, finance, etc).

EXAM PATTERN QUESTIONS

Objective Type Questions

Multiple Choice Questions (MCQs)

1. How many days of import cover did India's foreign exchange reserves provide at the peak of the 1991 crisis?

(a) 6 months (b) 3 months
(c) 15 days (d) 1 month

2. Public sector has not performed as much as expected under economic reforms due to

I. lack of competition II. huge losses of PSU
III. managerial inefficiency
IV. political and bureaucratic interference

Codes
(a) I, II and III (b) II, III and IV
(c) I, II, III and IV (d) I, III and IV

3. Which of the following statements accurately reflects the economic crisis of 1991 in India? Competency Based Que

(a) The crisis was primarily triggered by a balance of payments crisis due to rising oil prices and declining foreign exchange reserves
(b) The government's adoption of a closed economy model led to a surplus in the current account, contributing to the crisis
(c) Economic reforms initiated post-crisis included a shift towards protectionism and increased trade barriers
(d) The crisis prompted the Indian government to seek assistance from the neighbouring countries for economic stabilisation

4. Which of the following statements is incorrect regarding the inefficient management of the Indian economy that contributed to the financial crisis?

(a) The government struggled to generate sufficient revenue
(b) The government's revenue consistently exceeded its expenditure
(c) The government borrowed money to meet its consumption needs
(d) The government's expenditure started exceeding its revenue

5. "The 1991 economic reforms were the most significant structural adjustment programme India has ever undergone." – The Economic Times
Which of the following statements is/are correct regarding these reforms? Competency Based Que

I. These reforms focused on deregulation and reducing the role of the state in the economy.
II. The reforms led to the nationalisation of major industries.
III. They involved opening up India's economy to global markets.
IV. They aimed to attract foreign direct investment.

Codes
(a) I and III (b) I, III and IV
(c) II and III (d) I, II, III and IV

6. Which of the following steps were taken during the 1991 economic crisis to stabilise the Indian economy?

I. Devaluation of the Indian Rupee
II. Import restrictions
III. Introduction of LPG reforms
IV. Increase in fiscal deficit Competency Based Que

Codes
(a) I and III (b) II, III and IV
(c) I, II and IV (d) I, II and III

7. Identify, which of the following correctly defines liberalisation. CBSE 2025

(a) Outright sale of part of shares of Public Sector Undertakings (PSUs)
(b) Increased integration with the rest of the world
(c) Removal of restrictions imposed by government on different sectors of the economy
(d) Focus on import substitution

8. Identify, which of the following statement is incorrect about the financial sector reform introduced in 1991? CBSE SQP 2025

(a) Enabled the establishment of private sector banks, Indian as well as foreign
(b) Foreign investment limit in banks was raised to around 74%
(c) Foreign institutional investors were allowed to invest in Indian financial markets
(d) Change in the role of the Reserve Bank of India from facilitator to regulator

9. "India's Financial Sector Reform: SEBI Tightens Regulatory Grip to Curb Fraudulent Activities." – The Financial Express, 5th August, 2018
Which of the following statements correctly reflect the implications of the above headline? Competency Based Que

I. SEBI (Securities and Exchange Board of India) was established as part of the financial reforms under liberalisation.

II. SEBI's primary role is to regulate the stock market and prevent malpractices in capital markets.

III. Financial reforms under liberalisation included the deregulation of interest rates.

IV. SEBI's actions are aimed at protecting investors and ensuring the stability of the financial sector.

Codes

(a) I and IV (b) II and III
(c) I, II and IV (d) All of these

10. The 1991 economic reforms resulted in a reduction of

(a) corporate tax rates
(b) income tax for all individuals
(c) indirect taxes only
(d) tax exemptions

11. The liberalisation of the foreign exchange market is often linked to which of the following economic objectives?

(a) Reducing the fiscal deficit
(b) Increasing import tariffs
(c) Enhancing international trade and investment
(d) Controlling inflation through government regulation

12.

Foreign Exchange Reserves (Percent of GDP)

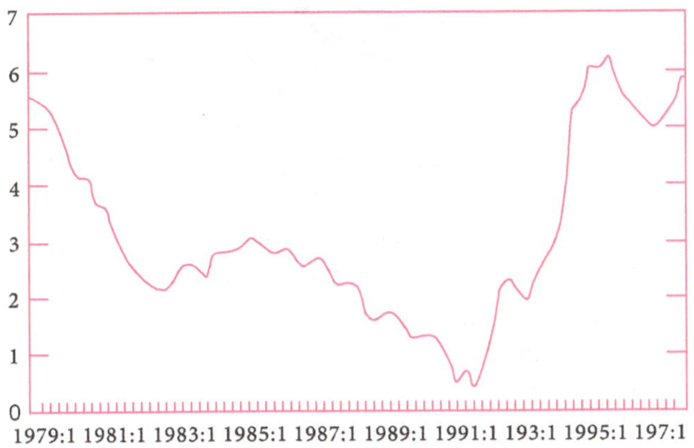

Source *IMF, International Financial Statistics*

The economic reforms of 1991 were initiated as a response to the crisis indicated in the graph. What immediate action was taken by the government to address this situation?

(a) Complete ban on imports
(b) Devaluation of the Indian Rupee
(c) Increase in subsidies
(d) Promotion of import substitution

13. "Demonetisation: Unveiling India's Battle Against Black Money and Corruption."

– The Indian Express, 9th November, 2016

Based on the news headline, which of the following statements is correct? **Competency Based Que**

I. Demonetisation led to the immediate reduction in black money in circulation.

II. The sudden demonetisation of ₹ 500 and ₹ 1,000 notes aimed to curb corruption and counterfeit currency.

III. Demonetisation directly resulted in a significant increase in GDP growth in the subsequent quarter.

IV. The measure was successful in bringing all unaccounted cash into the formal banking system.

Codes

(a) Only II (b) I and IV
(c) Only III (d) II and IV

14. If a registered business in Delhi sells goods to a customer in Haryana as shown in invoice below, which tax will be levied?

Sample GST Invoice

Supplier Details	Invoice Details
Name XYZ Traders	**Invoice Number** INV-001
Address 123 Market Street, Delhi	**Date of Issue** 26th November, 2024
GSTIN 07ABCDE1234F1Z5	**Place of Supply** Delhi
State Code 07 (Delhi)	**Reverse Charge** No

Recipient Details	
Name ABC Retailers	**GSTIN** 06ABCDE5678G1Z2
Address 456 Business Road, Haryana	**State Code** 06 (Haryana)

Description of Goods/ Services	HSN/SAC Code	Quantity	Rate/ Unit (₹)	Amt (₹)
Product A	1001	10	500.00	5,000.00
Product B	2002	5	800.00	4,000.00

(a) CGST and SGST (b) SGST and IGST
(c) Only IGST (d) Only SGST

15. "Historic Tax Reform: GST to Replace a Complex Web of Indirect Taxes." – The Economic Times, 1st July, 2017

Which of the following statements are true regarding the above headline? **Competency Based Que**

I. GST was introduced to bring uniformity in indirect taxation across India.

II. The introduction of GST replaced only the central indirect taxes.

III. GST implementation aimed to boost transparency and reduce tax evasion.

IV. GST has a single tax rate applied uniformly across all goods and services.

Codes

(a) I and III (b) II and IV
(c) I and II (d) All of these

16. **Which of the following is/are advantages of privatisation?**

I. Increased efficiency in operations

II. Reduction in government debt

III. Job security for public sector employees

Codes

(a) Only I (b) Only II

(c) I and II (d) I, II and III

17. **……… refers to the sale of equity of public sector units in the market.**

(a) Liberalisation

(b) Globalisation

(c) Disinvestment

(d) Privatisation

18. **"Privatisation of Air India: A step towards making Indian public sector competitive."**

– The Hindu, October 2022

What was one of the primary objectives of the privatisation policies introduced in 1991? **Competency Based Que**

(a) To increase government control in key sectors

(b) To make public sector units less competitive

(c) To reduce the burden of inefficient public sector enterprises

(d) To completely eliminate the public sector

19. **Opening up the economy to the economies of the world so that Indian economy can compute at international level is called**

(a) liberalisation (b) globalisation

(c) privatisation (d) None of these

20. **As a part of globalisation process, tariff rates were ………… in India.**

(a) raised (b) lowered

(c) not changed (d) abolished

21. **Which of the following statements is against globalisation?**

(a) It will improve allocative efficiency of resources

(b) It will redistribute economic power

(c) It will impose tariff barriers among nations

(d) It will provide updated technology

22. **How can globalisation increase the standard of living of the people in a country?** **CBSE QB; Competency Based Que**

(a) By offering more products to buy

(b) By increasing rural to urban migration

(c) By improving working conditions for factory workers

(d) By making cheaper products available due to increased competition

23.

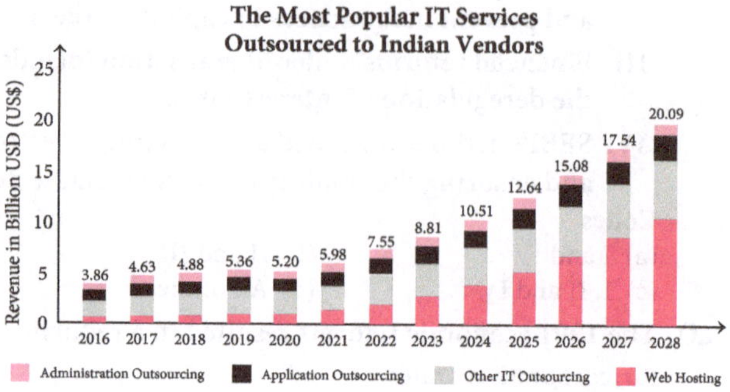

Source *https://mwdn.com/blog/everything-you-wanted-to-know-about-outsourcing-it-services-to-india-in-2023/*

Considering the revenue trends shown, which two categories appear to be the most stable in terms of growth?

(a) Administration Outsourcing and Other IT Outsourcing

(b) Web Hosting and Application Outsourcing

(c) Application Outsourcing and Other IT Outsourcing

(d) Administration Outsourcing and Web Hosting

24.

The image represents a global organisation that has played a crucial role in India's globalisation.

Which of the following best describes the role of this organisation?

(a) IMF provides development loans to countries

(b) WTO enforces rules of trade between nations

(c) IBRD provides financial support for temporary economic crises

(d) World Bank provides financial assistance for development projects

25. **Which of the following falls under the role of the world trade organisation?** **CBSE QB**

(a) Setting the limit for domestic and foreign investments in a country

(b) Mandating the level of tax levied on foreign firms in developing countries

(c) Aiding the development of poor countries by providing infrastructural investment

(d) Providing a platform for member countries to decide future tariff-related strategies

26. .... **was the predecessor organisation to world trade organisation.** CBSE 2020

(a) International Bank for Reconstruction and Development (IBRD)
(b) International Monetary Fund (IMD)
(c) Reserve Bank of India (RBI)
(d) General Agreement on Tariffs and Trade (GATT)

27. The LPG reforms are often credited with which of the following positive outcomes?

(a) Increase in public sector dominance
(b) Surge in foreign direct investment
(c) Nationalisation of key industries
(d) Protectionism in trade policies

28. The LPG reforms of 1991 primarily aimed at

(a) reducing foreign competition
(b) reviving the public sector enterprises
(c) promoting market-driven economy
(d) strengthening import substitution

29. One major criticism of the LPG reforms was

(a) decreased income inequality
(b) rise in unemployment in certain sectors
(c) strengthening of small-scale industries
(d) increase in subsidies for agriculture

30. While the LPG reforms aimed to integrate India into the global economy, which sector faced the most significant adverse effects due to increased global competition?

(a) Agriculture (b) Information technology
(c) Public sector enterprises (d) Banking

31. "India's economic growth story post-1991 reforms hailed globally, but challenges of inequality persist: experts."

Source *The Hindu, 2023*

Which statement inaccurately reflects the impact of LPG reforms? Competency Based Que

(a) LPG reforms enhanced India's global economic standing
(b) LPG reforms fully eradicated income inequality in India
(c) Experts highlight both achievements and unresolved issues from the reforms
(d) Economic growth has accompanied a rise in inequality post-reforms

Direction *Read the case study and answer the questions 32 to 35 on the basis of the same*

"On a morning, a few minutes before 7 AM, Greeshma sat in front of her computer with her headset on and said in accented English 'Hello, Daniella', Second later, she gets the reply, 'Hello, Greeshma'.

The two chatted excitedly before Greeshma said that 'we will work on pronouns today'. Nothing unusual about this that except that Greeshma, 22, was in Kochi and her student Daniella, 13, was at her home in Malibu, California.

Using a simulated whiteboard on their computers, connected by the Internet, and a copy of Daniella's textbook in front of Greeshma, she guides the teenager through the intricacies of nouns, adjectives and verbs. Greeshma, who grew up speaking Malayalam, was teaching Daniella English grammar, comprehension and writing."

32. India is benefitting from liberalisation and integration of world markets. This is due to ....

33. Which sector has enabled geographical integration?

(a) IT (b) Banking
(c) Trade (d) All of these

34. The barriers that restricts trade, are known as ....

35. Globalisation has facilitated

(a) movement of labour (b) movement of technology
(c) movement of capital (d) All of these

Direction *Read the case study and answer the questions 36 to 39 on the basis of the same*

In the early 1990s, India faced a severe economic crisis, including a balance of payments deficit, soaring inflation and stagnant growth. To address this, Finance Minister Manmohan Singh introduced reforms to liberalise the economy, ending the License Raj that stifled private enterprise. Key measures included reducing import tariffs, removing quantitative restrictions and encouraging Foreign Direct Investment (FDI).

Privatisation became a pivotal strategy, focusing on selling government stakes in inefficient Public Sector Enterprises (PSEs) to enhance competitiveness and efficiency. These reforms aimed to integrate India with global markets by lowering trade barriers and participating actively in forums like the World Trade Organisation (WTO).

The reforms resulted in a resurgence of economic growth, with the service sector expanding and foreign investments driving innovation and productivity. However, they also faced criticism for increasing income inequality and overlooking marginalised communities. The socio-economic impacts of these policies continue to spark debates on their inclusivity and sustainability in the long-term.

36. Which of the following was not a primary goal of India's economic reforms initiated in the early 1990s?

(a) Enhancing Foreign Direct Investment (FDI)
(b) Increasing bureaucratic control over industries
(c) Dismantling the License Raj
(d) Promoting private sector participation

37. The increase in GDP growth rates post-reforms can be primarily attributed to

(a) higher taxation on the wealthy
(b) liberalisation and increased foreign investment
(c) nationalisation of key industries
(d) implementation of strict import quotas

38. **The economic reforms initiated in 1991 were a response to a critical .... position and aimed to integrate India into the global economy.**

39. **The growth of the .... sector in the post-reform period has been significant, contributing to a large share of India's GDP and employment opportunities.**

Assertion-Reason

Direction (Q.No. 40 to 49) *Read the following Assertion (A) and Reason (R) and choose the correct alternative from the following*

Alternatives

(a) Both Assertion (A) and Reason (R) are true and Reason (R) is the correct explanation of Assertion (A)
(b) Both Assertion (A) and Reason (R) are true, but Reason (R) is not the correct explanation of Assertion (A)
(c) Assertion (A) is true, but Reason (R) is false
(d) Assertion (A) is false, but Reason (R) is true

40. **Assertion** (A) Structural measures are comprehensive, long-term strategies designed to enhance the fundamental framework and efficiency of an economy.

Reason (R) They are aimed to bring inflation under control.

41. **Assertion** (A) One of the major aims of financial sector reforms was to reduce the role of RBI from regulator to facilitator of financial sector.

Reason (R) Prior to 1991, the financial sector in India was regulated by RBI.

42. **Assertion** (A) Post 1991, India has become the favoured outsourcing destination in the world.

Reason (R) Indian labour have skilled labour force.

CBSE Term I 2021

43. **Assertion** (A) The liberalisation of the Indian economy in 1991 was primarily a response to a balance of payments crisis.

Reason (R) The Indian government aimed to reduce its dependency on foreign aid and enhance economic self-reliance through liberalisation measures.

44. **Assertion** (A) The privatisation of state-owned enterprises has led to a significant decrease in government revenue.

Reason (R) Privatisation typically transfers ownership from the government to private entities, reducing state control over profits.

45. **Assertion** (A) Globalisation has contributed to the environmental degradation in developing countries like India.

Reason (R) Increased industrial activity and foreign investment often lead to higher pollution levels and resource depletion.

46. **Assertion** (A) Globalisation has efficiently managed income inequality within India.

Reason (R) The benefits of globalisation have primarily accrued to skilled workers and urban sectors, while rural and unskilled workers have been left behind.

47. **Assertion** (A) License Permit Raj was a major obstacle for growth of private sector.

Reason (R) Private sector wasted huge amount in obtaining licences, rather than on improving the product, quality and international competitiveness.

CBSE 2024

48. **Assertion** (A) The increase in outsourcing due to globalisation has created job opportunities in India.

Reason (R) Companies from developed nations seek lower labor costs and skilled labour in developing countries, leading to the growth of the service sector in India.

49. **Assertion** (A) The International Monetary Fund (IMF) supports globalisation by providing financial assistance to countries in economic distress.

Reason (R) By investing in infrastructure and human capital, the IMF aims to integrate these countries into the global economy.

Two Statement Based MCQs

Direction (Q.No. 50 to 59) *Read the following statements carefully and choose the correct alternative*

Alternatives

(a) Statement I is correct and Statement II is incorrect
(b) Statement II is correct and Statement I is incorrect
(c) Both the statements are correct
(d) Both the statements are incorrect

50. **Statement I** Inadequate regulatory oversight of financial institutions can significantly heighten the risk of economic crisis, as evidenced by historical financial collapses.

Statement II While stringent regulatory frameworks are essential for stability, they can inadvertently create a false sense of security, potentially leading to riskier behaviours by financial institutions.

51. **Statement I** Economic reforms under liberalisation have made the Indian economy more resilient to global economic shocks.

Statement II Resilience implies that the economy has a better ability to recover, not immunity to all shocks.

52. **Statement I** The liberalisation process in India was primarily driven by the need to reduce fiscal deficits and inflationary pressures.

Statement II Liberalisation has consistently led to increased employment opportunities across all sectors of the Indian economy.

53. **Statement I** The demonetisation of currency was undertaken by Indian government on 8th November, 2016.

Statement II Demonetisation has increased the popularity of e-wallets in India. **CBSE Term I 2021**

54. **Statement I** GST has reduced the rates of existing taxes.

Statement II There is equal share of revenue between Centre and State government under GST.

55. **Statement I** The impact of privatisation on public sector enterprises has always been positive in terms of operational efficiency and profitability.

Statement II Privatisation can sometimes lead to monopolistic practices, harming consumer interests.

56. **Statement I** Globalisation facilitates the flow of capital, goods and services across borders, promoting economic growth.

Statement II Globalisation results in cultural homogenisation, which has no adverse effects on local traditions and identities.

57. **Statement I** Outsourcing is one of the important outcome of globalisation process.

Statement II Owing to globalisation, many Indian companies have expanded their operation abroad. **CBSE 2024**

58. **Statement I** The World Trade Organisation (WTO) plays a crucial role in promoting globalisation by regulating international trade.

Statement II The WTO ensures that all member countries have equal power in decision-making processes.

59. **Statement I** Financial sector is now allowed to take decisions on any matters without consulting the RBI.

Statement II GATT was established in 1923 with 48 member countries. **CBSE 2020 (M)**

Matching

60. **Match the following reforms with their correct outcomes**

	Column I (Reforms)		Column II (Outcomes)
A.	Fiscal reforms	(i)	Simplification of tax structure to improve tax compliance
B.	Financial reforms	(ii)	Introduction of cashless economy measures and UPI system
C.	Demonetisation	(iii)	Improvement of capital markets and banking sector efficiency
D.	GST implementation	(iv)	Reduction in fiscal deficit by controlling unnecessary spending

Codes

	A	B	C	D
(a)	(iv)	(iii)	(ii)	(i)
(b)	(iii)	(i)	(ii)	(iv)
(c)	(i)	(iv)	(ii)	(iii)
(d)	(i)	(iii)	(ii)	(iv)

61. **Match the following** **Competency Based Que**

	Column I		Column II
A.	Steel Authority of India Limited	(i)	Miniratna
B.	Hindustan Aeronautics Limited	(ii)	Maharatna
C.	Bharat Sanchar Nigam Limited	(iii)	Navratna

Codes

	A	B	C
(a)	(i)	(ii)	(iii)
(b)	(ii)	(iii)	(i)
(c)	(iii)	(i)	(ii)
(d)	(ii)	(i)	(iii)

62. **Match the following**

	Column I		Column II
A.	Outsourcing	(i)	Services provided by foreign firms
B.	World Trade Organisation	(ii)	Promotes free trade globally
C.	Foreign Direct Investment	(iii)	Investment in another country
D.	International Monetary Fund	(iv)	Provides financial support globally

Codes

	A	B	C	D
(a)	(i)	(ii)	(iii)	(iv)
(b)	(iv)	(i)	(iii)	(iii)
(c)	(iii)	(ii)	(iv)	(i)
(d)	(ii)	(iv)	(i)	(iii)

63. **Match the following**

	Column I		Column II
A.	Trade liberalisation	(i)	Reducing tariffs and quotas
B.	Financial deregulation	(ii)	Facilitating trade relations
C.	Infrastructure development	(iii)	Allowing free flow of capital
D.	Bilateral and multilateral agreements	(iv)	Building transport and communication networks

Codes

	A	B	C	D		A	B	C	D
(a)	(i)	(ii)	(iii)	(iv)	(b)	(i)	(iii)	(iv)	(ii)
(c)	(iii)	(i)	(iv)	(ii)	(d)	(ii)	(iv)	(i)	(iii)

64. Match the following

Column I		Column II	
A.	Export promotion measures	(i)	Allowed 74% to 100% FDI in some sectors
B.	Liberalised Investment Policy	(ii)	Allowed easier import of goods
C.	Removal of Quantitative Restrictions (QRs)	(iii)	Encouraging SEZs (Special Economic Zones)
D.	Industrial sickness	(iv)	Companies struggling financially due to outdated practices

Codes

	A	B	C	D		A	B	C	D
(a)	(i)	(ii)	(iii)	(iv)	(b)	(i)	(iii)	(ii)	(iv)
(c)	(iii)	(i)	(ii)	(iv)	(d)	(ii)	(i)	(iv)	(iii)

Concept Identification

65. A set of economic policies directed to accelerate the GDP growth.

66. Selling off share capital of PSUs (Public Sector Undertakings) to the private entrepreneurs.

67. System of hiring business services (like services of call centres, transcription, clinical advice, teaching/coaching, etc.) from the outside world.

68. Investment made by foreign banking and non-banking institutions in Indian companies.

69. Physical limit (set by the government) on the quantity of a good that can be imported into the country in a given period of time.

Answers

1. (c) 15 days
2. (c) I, II, III and IV
3. (a) The crisis was primarily triggered by a balance of payments crisis due to rising oil prices and declining foreign exchange reserves
4. (b) The government's revenue consistently exceeded its expenditure
5. (b) I, III and IV
6. (d) I, II and III
7. (c) Removal of restrictions imposed by government on different sectors of the economy
8. (b) Foreign investment limit in banks was raised to around 74%
9. (c) I, II and IV
10. (a) corporate tax rates
11. (c) Enhancing international trade and investment
12. (b) Devaluation of the Indian Rupee
13. (a) Only II
14. (c) Only IGST
15. (a) I and III
16. (c) I and II
17. (c) Disinvestment
18. (c) To reduce the burden of inefficient public sector enterprises
19. (b) globalisation
20. (b) lowered
21. (c) It will impose tariff barriers among nations
22. (d) By making cheaper products available due to increased competition
23. (d) Administration Outsourcing and Web Hosting
24. (b) WTO enforces rules of trade between nations
25. (d) Providing a platform for member countries to decide future tariff-related strategies
26. (d) General Agreement on Tariffs and Trade (GATT)
27. (b) Surge in foreign direct investment
28. (c) promoting market-driven economy
29. (b) rise in unemployment in certain sectors
30. (a) Agriculture
31. (b) LPG reforms fully eradicated income inequality in India
32. opening up of economy
33. (a) IT
34. trade barriers
35. (d) All of these
36. (b) Increasing bureaucratic control over industries
37. (b) liberalisation and increased foreign investment
38. balance of payments
39. services
40. (c) Structural measures are not primarily aimed at controlling inflation, which is often tackled using short-term stabilisation measures like monetary or fiscal policy adjustments.
41. (b) Post 1991, RBI started helping the financial market in its operations.
42. (a) Both Assertion (A) and Reason (R) are true and Reason (R) is the correct explanation of Assertion (A)
43. (a) Both Assertion (A) and Reason (R) are true and Reason (R) is the correct explanation of Assertion (A)

44. (d) While privatisation may reduce direct revenue from state-owned enterprises, it can also lead to increased overall economic growth and tax revenues from the private sector.
Additionally, the government often receives upfront capital from the sale of these enterprises, which can offset any potential decrease in ongoing revenue.
45. (a) Both Assertion (A) and Reason (R) are true and Reason (R) is the correct explanation of Assertion (A)
46. (d) Assertion (A) is false because globalisation has often been criticised for exacerbating income inequality in India, rather than managing it efficiently.
While globalisation has led to economic growth, the benefits have not been evenly distributed, leading to greater disparities between different sectors of society.
47. (a) Both Assertion (A) and Reason (R) are true and Reason (R) is the correct explanation of Assertion (A)
48. (a) Both Assertion (A) and Reason (R) are true and Reason (R) is the correct explanation of Assertion (A)
49. (c) While the IMF does provide financial assistance, it does not typically invest directly in infrastructure or human capital. Instead, its role often involves providing loans that may be contingent on certain economic reforms. Investment in infrastructure and human capital is more commonly associated with organisations like the World Bank.
50. (c) Both the statements are correct
51. (c) Both the statements are correct
52. (a) Employment opportunities have not increased uniformly across all sectors; some sectors have seen job losses due to automation and competition.
53. (c) Both the statements are correct
54. (c) Both the statements are correct
55. (b) The impact of privatisation can vary; while some enterprises have improved, others have struggled.
56. (a) Cultural homogenisation can threaten local traditions and identities.
57. (c) Both the statements are correct
58. (a) The WTO regulates international trade. Decision-making power is often skewed in favour of more economically powerful nations.
59. (a) GATT was established in 1948 with 23 member countries.
60. (a) (iv) (iii) (ii) (i)
61. (b) (ii) (iii) (i)
62. (a) (i) (ii) (iii) (iv)
63. (b) (i) (iii) (iv) (ii)
64. (c) (iii) (i) (ii) (iv)
65. Economic reforms
66. Disinvestment
67. Outsourcing
68. Foreign institutional investment
69. Quota

Subjective Questions

Short Answer Type Questions

1. Explain the circumstances that led to the introduction of the 1991 economic reforms in India.

Or **Why were reforms introduced in India?** NCERT

Ans. There were many reasons due to which economic reforms were a necessity in our country.

These were

(i) **Poor Performance of Industries**
Before the 1990s, the industries were mostly government-owned. The employees did not feel the need to be either competitive or effective because their jobs were secure. The state had the ultimate authority.

(ii) **Adverse Balance of Payments**
One of the biggest factors that played a major role in bringing about the economic reforms was the fact that India's balance of payments were unsustainable.
It was also true that the little foreign exchange with the country was not enough.

(iii) **Rising Fiscal Deficit**
India's fiscal deficit was constantly rising due to the wrong policies and improper implementation of the reforms between 1950 to 1990s.

(iv) **Rising Inflation**
The rate of inflation at the time was immense. Poor and marginalised people of the society did not have enough access to food.
At a massive 13.88%, this inflation rate could not be borne anymore. Liquidity had to be poured into the economy and had to be done very quickly.

2. Explain briefly the meaning of economic reforms. What are the main economic reforms?

Ans. Economic reforms refer to the changes made in the economy with a view to deregulate it and to solve the prevailing economic problems of the country.

In India, economic reforms were introduced in 1991, with the implementation of New Economic Policy.

These reforms can be categorised as

(i) **Stabilisation Reforms**
These reforms were short-term measures which intended to correct disequilibrium in BoP and to check inflation.

(ii) **Structural Reforms**
These are long-term measures which intend to bring efficiency in the working of the economy. These reforms can be categorised as liberalisation, privatisation and globalisation.

3. What is liberalisation? State the main objectives of liberalisation policy.

Ans. It is defined as allowing the private sector companies to operate business transactions in a country with fewer restrictions.

The main objectives of liberalisation policy are

(i) To increase competition among domestic industries.
(ii) To increase foreign capital formation and improve the technology.
(iii) To decrease the debt of the country.
(iv) To encourage cross border trade.
(v) To expand the size of the market.

4. Discuss briefly any two major steps taken by the Government of India on 'financial sector' front under the Economic Reforms of 1991. CBSE 2020

Or **What are your views on the reforms introduced in the financial sector under the New Economic Policy?**

Ans. Financial sector includes financial institutions such as commercial banks, investment banks, stock exchange and foreign exchange market.

The following reforms were initiated in this sector

(i) The banking sector was opened for the private sector. This led to an increase in competition and expansion of services for consumers.
(ii) RBI's role underwent a change from a 'regulator' to a 'facilitator'.

These reforms were much needed and due to these changes, financial sector has witnessed tremendous growth and helped in the development of the economy as a whole.

5. Why did RBI have to change its role from controller to facilitator of financial sector in India? NCERT; CBSE 2024; Competency Based Que

Ans. Before liberalisation, RBI used to manage and control the financial sector that incorporates finance related establishments like commercial banks, investment banks, stock trade activities and foreign exchange market.

With the economic liberalisation and financial sector reforms, RBI expected to move its job from a regulator to facilitator of the budgetary segment.

This infers that financial organisations were allowed to settle on their own choices on numerous issues without speaking with the RBI.

This opened up the entry ways of financial sectors for the private players. The fundamental goal behind the financial changes was to support private area participation, increment in competition and permitting market force to work in the financial segment.

The reform policies led to establishment of private sector banks. Banks have been given freedom to set up new branches and determine the rate of interest to be offered on various deposits.

Banks have been given permission to generate resources from India and abroad through capital market. All this has led to a substantial growth in the financial sector.

6. "The fiscal reforms under the New Economic Policy of 1991 aimed at reducing fiscal imbalances through expenditure control and revenue enhancement" (Ministry of Finance, Government of India).

In light of this, critically assess the role of fiscal reforms in addressing India's fiscal crisis during the early 1990s. Competency Based Que

Ans. The fiscal reforms introduced under the New Economic Policy included several key measures

(i) A reduction in both direct and indirect taxes to stimulate economic activity.
(ii) A deliberate cutback on government expenditure, particularly in areas such as administrative costs and subsidies for food, fertilisers and exports, aimed at reducing the fiscal deficit.
(iii) To encourage compliance and improve efficiency, various tax procedures were simplified to make it easier for taxpayers to meet their obligations.

7. "Globalisation is an essential outcome of liberalisation of an economy." Justify the given statement with a valid explanation. CBSE SQP 2025

Ans. Globalisation, the integration of economies worldwide, is a natural result of liberalisation.

Following points can help to understand

(i) **Access to Global Markets**
Liberalisation opens domestic markets to international trade, encouraging Foreign Direct Investment (FDI).

(ii) **Technological and Knowledge Exchange**
With fewer restrictions, there is increased sharing of technology and expertise among countries.

(iii) **Competitiveness and Growth**
Liberalisation fosters global competition, leading to innovation and higher efficiency in industries.

(iv) **Cultural Exchange**
Enhanced trade and investments promote the exchange of ideas, culture and technology.

Thus, liberalisation sets the stage for globalisation by removing barriers to the movement of goods, services and capital.

8. Examine the impact of the trade and investment policy reforms of 1991 on India's economic trajectory, with particular focus on how these measures facilitated structural transformations and long-term growth. Competency Based Que

Ans. Liberalisation of trade and investment was initiated to increase international competitiveness of industrial production and also the flow of foreign investments and technology into the economy. Prior to these reforms, in order to protect domestic industries, India was following a regime of quantitative restrictions on imports and restrictions of foreign investments.

The trade policy reforms aimed at

(i) dismantling of quantitative restrictions on imports and exports.
(ii) reduction of tariff rates.
(iii) removal of licensing procedures for imports.

Liberalisation led to economic growth by increasing the level of investment in the country.

9. (i) What do you understand by the term 'demonetisation'?

(ii) To what extent has demonetisation transformed the landscape of corruption in India?

Ans. (i) Demonetisation is the act of stripping a currency unit of its status as legal tender. In other words, it means to withdraw (money or the like) from use. The current form of money is pulled from circulation and retired often to be replaced with new notes or coins.
e.g. India demonetised its ₹ 500 and ₹ 1,000 rupee notes on 8th November, 2016. This action affected 86% of all cash in circulation.

(ii) Demonetisation in 2016 aimed to combat corruption by invalidating high denomination notes, promoting transparency and increasing tax compliance.
However, it has not eradicated corruption entirely. While it encouraged a shift towards digital transactions and improved some aspects of financial accountability, corrupt practices have persisted, often adapting to new circumstances.
Therefore, while demonetisation has made some positive contributions towards reducing corruption, it remains a complex issue that requires comprehensive systemic reforms beyond just monetary measures.

10. In November 2016, the Government of India announced the demonetisation of ₹ 500 and ₹ 1,000 currency notes, stating that the move aimed to combat black money, counterfeit currency and corruption.

The sudden announcement led to widespread chaos, affecting various sectors of the economy, individuals and small businesses. Many citizens faced long queues at banks and ATMs, while some sectors experienced immediate disruptions.

Based on the above case study, critically analyse the impact of demonetisation on the Indian economy and answer the following

(i) Give a brief overview of the objectives of demonetisation.

(ii) Discuss any one long-term effect or implication of the demonetisation policy. Competency Based Que

Ans. (i) According to the government, the objectives behind demonetisation policy are

- **To Make India Corruption-free**
Enhance transparency and accountability in the financial system.
- **To Curb Black Money**
Encourage the declaration of unaccounted cash by invalidating high denomination notes.
- **To Control Escalating Price Rise**
Stabilise the economy and reduce inflationary pressures.
- **To Stop the Flow of Funds to Illegal Activities**
Disrupt financing for terrorism and organised crime.

(ii) **Growth of Digital Payments**
Demonetisation accelerated the adoption of digital payment systems in India. The disruption of cash transactions prompted consumers and businesses to explore alternative payment methods, leading to a surge in digital wallets and online banking.

11. **Economic times, July, 2023: "6 years of GST: India's unprecedented indirect tax reform that dared to revolutionise the economic landscape."**

Synopsis: India's introduction of the Goods and Services Tax (GST) marked a significant milestone in the country's taxation history.

The tax base has more than doubled since its implementation in 2017, with revenues experiencing substantial growth.

However, there is still room for more businesses to enroll in GST. There is potential for further growth and harmonisation in the future.

Briefly discuss the concept and components of GST. **Competency Based Que**

Ans. The term GST has been defined in Article 366 (12A) to mean 'any tax on supply of goods or services or both except taxes on supply of the alcoholic liquor for human consumption.'

It is considered as a destination based consumption tax as the final seller in the supply chain passes on the added GST to the consumer.

There are three taxes applicable under this system

(i) **CGST**
It is collected by the central government on an intra-state sale. e.g. Transactions happening within Maharashtra.

(ii) **SGST**
It is collected by the state governments on an intra-state sale. e.g. Transactions happening within Maharashtra.

(iii) **IGST**
It is collected by the central government on an inter-state sale. e.g. Transactions happening between Maharashtra and Tamil Nadu.

12. **Based upon the image given below, explain the role of input tax credit in GST.** **Competency Based Que**

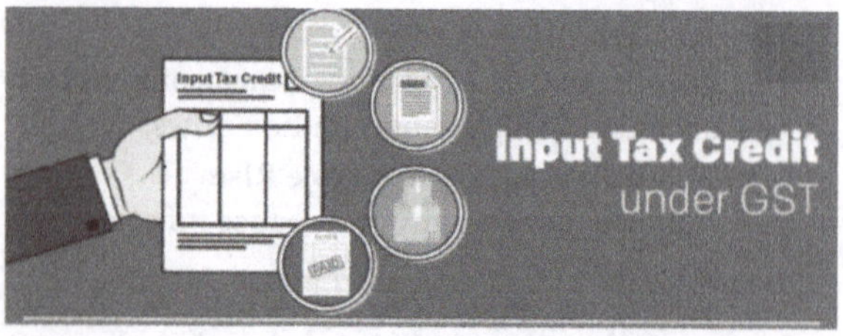

Ans. ITC is a mechanism to avoid cascading of taxes. Cascading of taxes, in simple language, is 'tax on tax'. Under the present system of taxation, credit of taxes being levied by Central Government is not available as set-off for payment of taxes levied by State Governments, and *vice-versa*.

In case of supply of capital goods or plant and machinery, on which ITC is taken, an amount equivalent to ITC availed minus the reduction as prescribed in rules (5% for every quarter or part thereof) shall have to be paid.

13. **The objective of new economic policy was privatisation. Discuss.**

Or **What measures were taken towards privatisation in 1991?**

Ans. The New Economic Policy was introduced with the objective to deregulate the economy and ensure economic development. So, privatisation was crucial for the success of this policy as it ensures high productivity, a competitive environment which promotes innovation and efficiency, diversification of activities and consumer sovereignty.

In order to encourage private sector, following measures have been adopted

(i) The government through its economic policy reduced the number of industries reserved for public sector.

(ii) It has now been planned to reduce the share of public sector investment to 45%. It increases the share of private sector to 55%.

(iii) Financial corporations cannot force the industries for conversion of their loans into equity shares.

(iv) It has now been decided to increase the participation of general public and workers by selling them the shares of public enterprises.

14. **Critically appraise the disinvestment policy initiated by the government during the reforms of 1991.** **CBSE SQP 2025**

Ans. The disinvestment policy of 1991 aimed to reduce the fiscal burden of public sector enterprises (PSEs) and enhance their efficiency by introducing private investment. While it facilitated a market driven approach and reduced inefficiencies, several issues arose.

Benefits

(i) Generated revenue for the government to manage fiscal deficits.

(ii) Improved competitiveness and operational efficiency of some PSEs.

(iii) Encouraged private sector participation in strategic industries.

Challenges

(i) Critics argued that PSEs were undervalued during disinvestment.

(ii) It led to job insecurity among workers.

(iii) There was a lack of transparency in some processes.

Overall, while the policy helped streamline the economy, it faced criticism for its execution and social impact.

15. In your opinion, what are the advantages of privatisation to the economy?

Ans. Advantages of privatisation are

(i) It will introduce efficiency and profitability in Public Sector Undertakings (PSUs).

(ii) It promotes consumer's sovereignty. High degree of consumer's sovereignty implies wider choice and better quality of goods and services.

(iii) It will reduce budgetary deficits which result from expenditure on loss making PSUs.

(iv) It promotes diversification of production. Also, unlike PSUs, private enterprises often generate high profits.

16. Do you think the *Navratna* policy of the government helps in improving the performance of public sector undertakings in India? How?

NCERT; CBSE 2024; Competency Based Que

Ans. Yes, the *Navratna* policy of the government helps in improving the performance of PSUs in India.

The government identifies PSUs and declares them as *Maharatnas, Navratnas* and *Miniratnas* in order to improve their efficiency and enable them to compete globally.

They are given greater managerial and operational autonomy in taking various decisions.

In 2011, about 90 public enterprises were designated with different status. The granting of this special status resulted in better performance of these companies.

17. Identify and explain the concept of economic reforms of 1991 presented in the image given below.

Competency Based Que

Ans. The picture represents 'globalisation'. It refers to the integration of a country's economy with the global economy.

Globalisation was a pivotal aspect of the economic reforms of 1991 and its impact is reflected through the following features

(i) **Free Movement**
It allows for the unrestricted movement of goods, services, capital, labour and resources across nations.

(ii) **Increased Competition**
The primary aim of globalisation is to enhance both domestic and international competition.

(iii) **Market Mechanism**
It involves the extensive application of market mechanisms to facilitate economic activities.

(iv) **Foreign Relationship**
Globalisation fosters dynamic relationships with foreign investors and technology suppliers.

18. "Amazon has been outsourcing to various customer support companies in India to accommodate more local and international buyers and sellers."

In light of the above statement, how has the process of globalisation impacted the Indian economy?

CBSE SQP 2024; Competency Based Que

Ans. The process of globalisation impacted the Indian economy as it

(i) Generates more employment and job opportunities.

(ii) Increases the overall GDP of the country.

(iii) Leads to the formalisation of the employment sector.

(iv) Limits the availability of social security measures for the workers.

19. How do the outcomes of liberalisation and privatisation differ between developed and developing countries in the context of globalisation and what factors influence these differences? **Competency Based Que**

Ans. Liberalisation and privatisation aim to integrate countries into the global economy, but their outcomes can differ significantly between developed and developing countries. This can be understood with the help of following points

(i) **Economic Growth**

Developed Countries Liberalisation attracts Foreign Direct Investment (FDI) and drives economic growth due to established infrastructure and stability.

Developing Countries While it can lead to growth, developing nations often face challenges like political instability and poor infrastructure, resulting in slower economic progress.

(ii) **Employment**

Developed Countries Privatisation may restructure jobs, leading to temporary unemployment but more efficient labor markets over time.

Developing Countries Job losses from privatisation can be significant, with insufficient safety nets for displaced workers, worsening poverty.

(iii) **Access to Services**

Developed Countries Privatisation generally improves service efficiency and quality.

Developing Countries It can limit access to essential services, as profit motives may drive prices up, making them unaffordable for low income populations.

Factors influencing differences

(i) Political stability (ii) Infrastructure

(iii) Regulatory framework

20. India is often called as 'outsourcing destination' of the world. Discuss the prime reasons for this name given to India. CBSE 2020; Competency Based Que

Or

India has certain advantages which makes it a favourite outsourcing destination. What are these advantages? NCERT

Ans. Most multinational corporations and even small companies are outsourcing their services to India because of the following advantages

(i) **Availability of Cheap Labour**
India is a country with a large population and thus, abundant supply of labour. Due to this, labour in India is available at low wage rates.
This helps foreign companies in reducing cost of operation by outsourcing their business processes to India.

(ii) **Skill and Accuracy**
India has a wide pool of talent in the form of educated and trained youth who have the required skill and can work with accuracy in the business processes such as accounting, record keeping, IT consultancy, etc.

(iii) **Continuity and Risk Management**
Periods of high employee turnover add uncertainty to the operations of a company. Outsourcing will provide a level of continuity to the company while reducing the risk that a substandard level of operation would bring to the company.

21. Outsourcing was first recognised as a business strategy in 1989 and became an integral part of business economics throughout the 1990s.

The practice of outsourcing is subject to considerable controversy in many countries. Those opposed argue that it has caused the loss of domestic jobs, particularly in the manufacturing sector.

Supporters say it creates an incentive for businesses and companies to allocate resources where they are most effective and that outsourcing helps to maintain the nature of free-market economies on a global scale.

In this context, why are developed countries opposing outsourcing to India? Competency Based Que

Ans. Developed countries oppose outsourcing of work to India because it results in unemployment in foreign countries and it also reduces the income disparity between the two countries.

Also, outsourcing is opposed by developed countries because it leads to outflow of investments and funds from developed countries to developing countries and as the labour is cheaper in developing countries, so more of the work flows from developed to developing countries which results in unemployment in the developed countries.

22. "NEP stimulated economic growth." Give three arguments in favour and against of this statement.

Ans. Arguments in favour of this statement are

(i) India has become a vibrant economy with the introduction of NEP.
(ii) NEP led to considerable increase in foreign exchange reserves.
(iii) NEP helped to control fiscal deficit.

Arguments against this statement are

(i) It led to urban concentration of growth process.
(ii) This policy encouraged economic colonialism.
(iii) This policy resulted in the spread of consumerism.

23. Agricultural sector appears to be adversely affected by the reform process. Why? NCERT

Or

"Agriculture sector has been adversely affected by the economic reform process." Comment. CBSE 2023

Ans. Due to following reasons, agricultural sector has been adversely affected by the reform process

(i) Public investment in agricultural sector especially in infrastructure which includes irrigation, power, roads, market linkages and research and extension has been reduced in the reform period.
(ii) The removal of fertiliser subsidy has led to increase in the cost of production, which has severely affected the small and marginal farmers.
(iii) Export oriented policies in agriculture have marked a shift from production for the domestic market towards production for the export market focusing on cash crops in lieu of production of foodgrains.

24. Why has the industrial sector performed poorly in the reform period? NCERT

Ans. The industrial sector has performed poorly in the reform period because of the following reasons

(i) Cheaper imports have decreased the demand for domestic industrial goods.

(ii) Globalisation created conditions for the free movement of goods and services from foreign countries that adversely affected the local industries and employment opportunities in developing countries.

(iii) There was inadequate investment in infrastructural facilities such as power supply.

(iv) A developing country like India still does not have the access to developed countries markets because of high non-tariff barriers.

25. What are the major factors responsible for the high growth of the service sector? NCERT

Ans. The major factors responsible for the high growth of the service sector are as follows

(i) **High Income Elasticity of Demand**
It has been noticed that income elasticity of demand for services is more than one. Hence, the demand for services increases at a faster rate than demand for commodities, with the increase in income.

(ii) **Technical and Structural Changes**
The technical and structural changes in the economy, have made it an attractive destination for outsourcing, contributing towards the growth of service sector.

(iii) **Information Technology Revolution**
With the advent of the information technology revolution, it has become possible to deliver services over long distance at a reasonable cost.
Thus, trading in services has increased worldwide, also benefitting India.

(iv) **Economic Reforms in 1991**
Economic reforms initiated in 1991, increased demand for manufacturing industry, thereby benefitting the service sector also.
Liberalisation of financial sector encouraged the growth of financial services. Reforms in certain segments of infrastructure also contributed to the growth of services.

Long Answer Type Questions

26. "The industrial policy framework in India before 1991 was characterised by stringent regulations that restricted private sector participation and emphasised state control over industries."

Given this background,

(i) Discuss about the new economic policy.

(ii) Evaluate the significant transformation of India's industrial policy after the economic reforms of 1991. Competency Based Que

Ans. (i) The New Economic Policy (NEP) refers to the set of economic reforms introduced by the Indian government in 1991 to address a severe economic crisis. The main goals were to liberalise the economy, boost growth and integrate India into the global market.

(ii) The following steps were taken to transform and deregulate the industrial sector

- **Abolition of Industrial Licensing**
Government abolished the licensing requirement of all industries for opening or closing a firm or to decide the amount of goods that could be produced industrial licensing was abolished for almost all product categories except alcohol, cigarettes, hazardous chemicals, industrial explosives, electronics, aerospace and drugs and pharmaceuticals.
- **Contraction of Public Sector**
The number of industries reserved for the public sector was reduced. Presently, only three industries are reserved for public sector. They are railways, atomic energy generation and defence.
- **Dereservation of Production of Goods**
Prior to 1991, production of many goods was reserved for the Small Scale Industries (SSIs). These were dereserved that enabled the participation of any scale of business in these production areas.
- **Price Fixation and Distribution of Products**
A control was established on price fixation and distribution of selected industrial products. In many industries, the market has been allowed to determine the prices.

27. "The liberalisation reforms of 1991 marked a turning point in India's economic history, transforming it from a closed, regulated economy to a more open and competitive market system."

In light of this statement, explain the concept of liberalisation and analyse the key changes introduced by liberalisation. Competency Based Que

Ans. Liberalisation refers to the process of reducing government control and interference in economic activities, allowing for greater freedom in market functioning. In India's case, it involved removing restrictions on production, investment and trade. The primary goals were to enhance competition, increase efficiency and attract foreign investment.

Key changes introduced by liberalisation are

(i) **Industrial Deregulation** (Removal of Licensing)
The government removed the requirement for industries to obtain licenses for most sectors, except a few critical ones (like defense).

(ii) **Encouragement of Private Sector**
This change allowed the private sector to expand, leading to increased entrepreneurship and industrial diversification.

(iii) **Foreign Direct Investment** (FDI) **Reforms**
Foreign investment was welcomed in many sectors, including manufacturing, telecommunications and retail. This brought in foreign capital, new technologies and improved management practices.

(iv) **Trade Policy Reforms** (Reduction in Import)
Import duties were significantly reduced to encourage international trade.
The reduction of trade barriers allowed for greater access to foreign markets and increased the competitiveness of Indian industries globally.

(v) **Financial Sector Reforms** (Autonomy of Banks)
The financial sector was liberalised by granting more autonomy to banks and encouraging the entry of private and foreign banks. Interest rates were deregulated and capital markets were developed to allow more private investment.

In conclusion, liberalisation has had a transformative impact on the Indian economy, driving growth, increasing foreign investment and fostering competitiveness.

28. Distinguish between the following NCERT

(i) **Strategic and minority sale**
(ii) **Bilateral and multilateral trade**
(iii) **Tariff and non-tariff barriers**

Ans. (i) Differences between strategic and minority sale are

Basis	Strategic Sale	Minority Sale
Meaning	Strategic sale involves the sale of minimum 51% stake of a Public Sector Unit (PSU) to the private sector.	Minority sale involves the sale of less than 49% stake of a PSU to the private sector.
Control	The control and management of PSU is transferred to the private sector.	The control and management of PSU remains with the government as it holds the majority stake.

(ii) Differences between bilateral and multilateral trade are

Basis	Bilateral Trade	Multilateral Trade
Meaning	It is a trade agreement between two countries.	It is a trade agreement among more than two countries.
Economic Cooperation	Encourages economic cooperation between two countries.	Encourages globalisation, integrating many countries of the world.

(iii) Differences between tariff and non-tariff barriers are

Basis	Tariff Barriers	Non-tariff Barriers
Meaning	It refers to the taxes imposed on the imports by a country for providing protection to its domestic industries.	It refers to the restrictions other than taxes, imposed on imports by a country for providing protection to its domestic industries.
Purpose	Tariff barriers are allowed by the World Trade Organisation (WTO) to be imposed by its member countries, though at reasonable rates.	Non-tariff barriers like import quotas and voluntary export restraints are now abolished under WTO regime.

29. Discuss the advantages and disadvantages of demonetisation in India.

Ans. Advantages of demonetisation in India are as follows

(i) **Trace Black Money**
Demonetisation has helped the government in tracking black money. The government claimed that large sums of black money were kept hidden by tax evaders and demonetisation has helped it uncover the huge amount of accounted cash.

(ii) **Increase in Tax Revenue**
Due to people disclosing their income by depositing money in their bank accounts, government will get a good amount of tax revenue which can be used to provide good infrastructure, hospitals, roads and many facilities for poor and needy sections of society.

Disadvantages of demonetisation in India are as follows

(i) **Inadequate Supply of New Notes**
The biggest disadvantage of demonetisation has been the chaos and frenzy it created among common people initially. Everyone was rushing to get rid of demonetised notes while inadequate supply of new notes affected the day to day budgets of citizens.

(ii) **Destruction of Old Currency**
Destruction of old currency units and printing of new currency units involve costs, which has to be borne by the government; and if the costs are higher than benefits, there is no use of demonetisation.

30. Explain the advantages and disadvantages of GST in India.

Ans. Following are the advantages of GST in India

(i) **Mitigation of Cascading Effect**
Under the GST administration, the final tax would be paid by the consumer for the goods and services purchased.

However, there would be an unified tax credit structure in place to ensure that there is no slumping of taxes.

(ii) **Elimination of Multiple Layers of Taxation**
One of the advantages of GST is that it integrated different tax levied such as central excise, service tax, luxury tax, special additional duty of customs, etc. into one consolidated tax.

(iii) **Enhanced Productivity of Logistics**
The restriction on inter-state movement of goods has reduced earlier.
Logistic companies had to maintain multiple warehouses across the country to avoid state entry tax on inter-state movements.

Following are the disadvantages of GST

(i) **Negative Impact on Estate Market**
Some economists say that GST in India would negatively impact the real estate market. It would add up 8% cost of new homes.

(ii) **No Reduction in the Number of Tax Layers**
GST reduced tax complexity but did not completely eliminate multiple tax category.

(iii) **Expensive Retail Product**
Some retail products currently have only 4% tax on them. After GST, garments and clothes could become more expensive.

31. What measures have been taken for globalisation of Indian economy?

Ans. The following measures have been taken for globalisation of Indian economy

(i) **Increase in Equity Limit of Foreign Investment**
Equity limit in general, has been raised from 40% to 51%.
Also, in 47 high priority industries and in export trading houses, Foreign Direct Investment (FDI) is allowed upto the extent of 100%.

(ii) **Partial Convertibility**
It means sale and purchase of foreign currency at a price determined by the market forces of demand and supply.
It is called partial convertibility because it is allowed 100% in current account transactions but it is only 51% for capital account transactions.

(iii) **Liberal Foreign Trade Policy**
A long-term liberal trade policy has been implemented which encourages free trade among countries.

(iv) **Reduction in Tariffs**
Custom duties have been reduced drastically. Before 1991, custom duties were as high as 400%, but post 1991, maximum rate of duty is just 10%.

32. "Globalisation has reshaped the economic, social and cultural landscapes of nations, creating both opportunities and challenges for developing countries like India." In the context of this statement, explain the concept of globalisation. Analyse its impact on the Indian economy, highlighting both the positive and negative effects on the economy. Competency Based Que

Or **"Globalisation has been a process for India with only positive results." Defend or refute the given statement with valid explanation.** CBSE 2025

Ans. The statement is refuted. Globalisation refers to the integration of a country's economy with the global economy through trade, Foreign Direct Investment (FDI) and technology exchange. Since the 1990s, India has embraced globalisation, leading to economic growth, increased foreign investments and technological advancements. However, it has also posed challenges such as job insecurity, income disparity, and pressure on domestic industries. Thus, globalisation cannot be seen as a process with only positive results; rather, it has both advantages and disadvantages for the Indian economy.

Positive Effects
Globalisation results in the following benefits for the economy

(i) It helps the economy to adopt new and flexible methods of production.
(ii) It results in raising the productivity of the industrial sector by reducing capital output ratio, increasing exports, raising the efficiency of the workforce, modernising the technology used and increasing capital flow in the country.
(iii) It helps in restructuring the production units of the country towards the production of those goods which the country can produce effectively and efficiently with the use of the domestically available factors of production.
(iv) It helps to increase the flow of foreign capital into the country.
(v) It helps to improve the quality of goods produced in the economy.
(vi) It helps to address the problem of unemployment.

Negative Effects
Globalisation has the following adverse effects on the Indian economy

(i) As a result of globalisation, the local producers stand to lose due to their inability to compete with cheap imports.
(ii) To provide goods and services at competitive prices, producers try to save on costs by lowering the wages, ensuring long working hours and denying the workers various social benefits. This results in mounting unrest among workers.

(iii) Globalisation has also affected the workers of PSUs adversely. They have been affected by budget cuts, privatisation and retrenchment.
(iv) Globalisation has also adversely affected the small businessmen.
(v) Studies have revealed that globalisation has adversely affected nearly half a billion people of South Asia, majority among these are poor people.
(vi) Globalisation has raised the depth of income inequalities.

33. Write a brief note on International Monetary Fund (IMF). Also state its objectives.

Ans. IMF was conceived at the Bretton Woods Conference held in 1944 and set-up in 1946. The main objective of setting-up of such an organisation was to administer a code of good conduct in international liquidity of its member countries and to grant short-term loans to economics, experiencing temporary deficit in Balance of Payments (BoP).

IMF started to function from March, 1947. Its headquarters is located in Washington DC.

There are 189 member countries including India. The highest authority of the IMF is the Board of Governors, which consists of the most part of Ministers of Finance or Central Bank Governors of the member countries.

Each member country appoints one Governor. The board generally meets only once in a year. The main objectives of IMF are as follows

(i) To promote international monetary cooperation.
(ii) To promote exchange stability.
(iii) To assist in the establishment of a multilateral system of payments in respect of current transactions between members and in the elimination of foreign exchange restrictions.
(iv) To give confidence to members by making the general resources of the fund temporarily available to them under adequate safeguards.

34. Write a brief note on International Bank for Reconstruction and Development (IBRD).

Ans. IBRD is popularly known as World Bank. It was set-up in 1944 under Bretton Woods Conference, alongwith IMF, hence these two are known as sister institutions or Bretton Woods' twins.

World Bank is headquartered at Washington DC and has 189 members. The World Bank focuses on making loans to government in order to rebuild railroads, highways and other infrastructure i.e. the areas where private sector enterprises do not take interest.

The main objectives of IBRD are as follows

(i) To help reconstruction of member countries after the Second World War.
(ii) To facilitate the investment of foreign capital for productive purpose.
(iii) To maintain balance growth of international trade and to attain equilibrium in BoP account.
(iv) Motivating governments to act on preventing climate change, controlling communicable diseases, managing international financial crises and promoting free trade.

35. Examine the key achievements of the New Economic Policy in India, in relation to the impacts of Liberalisation, Privatisation and Globalisation (LPG) policies on the economy.

Ans. The New Economic Policy (NEP) of India, initiated in the early 1990s, marked a significant turning point in the country's economic landscape.

With a focus on Liberalisation, Privatisation and Globalisation (LPG), these reforms aimed to transform a largely protected economy into a more vibrant and competitive one.

This transformation can be observed through the following key achievements

(i) The Indian economy has become significantly more dynamic, as evidenced by an upward trend in GDP growth and overall economic activity.
(ii) The LPG policies have effectively stimulated industrial production within the Indian economy.
(iii) Management of the fiscal deficit has improved considerably.
(iv) An increase in the flow of goods and services has contributed to a reduction in the rate of inflation.
(v) The country's foreign exchange reserves have expanded as a result of the LPG policies.
(vi) Following the implementation of LPG policies, there has been a substantial increase in private foreign investment.

In summary, the achievements of the New Economic Policy in India, particularly through the implementation of LPG policies, have significantly reshaped the economic framework of the country.

36. Elaborate how the economic reforms process of India impacted the following CBSE 2024

(i) Agriculture sector (ii) Industrial sector

Ans. The Economic Reforms of 1991 did not benefit the agricultural sector significantly.

The following are the reasons that explain the adverse effects of the economic reforms on India's agriculture sector

(i) **Reduction of Public Investment**
There has been a drastic decrease in the volume of public investment in the agricultural sector.

There has been an acute cutback from the Indian government to provide sufficient irrigation facilities, electricity, information systems, market linkages and roads.

Moreover, investment in agricultural research and development was not as extensive as it was during the green revolution phase.

(ii) **Removal of Subsidies**
Removal of subsidies on fertilisers pushed up the cost of production of agriculture.
This made farming more expensive, thereby, adversely affecting the poor and marginal farmers.

Economic reforms in India have had a significant impact on the industrial sector in several ways

(i) **Liberalisation of Trade and Investment**
Economic reforms in the early 1990s liberalised trade and investment policies, reducing barriers to foreign investment and trade restrictions.
This led to increased competition in the industrial sector, as Indian industries were exposed to international markets and competition from foreign firms.
Domestic industries were forced to become more efficient, innovative and competitive to survive in the global market.

(ii) **Industrial Deregulation**
Reforms also involved deregulation of industries, reducing government control and intervention in industrial activities. This allowed industries more freedom in decision-making, investment and operations.
Industrial deregulation promoted entrepreneurship, innovation and efficiency in the industrial sector by reducing bureaucratic hurdles and promoting market driven practices.

37. Discuss major observations that suggest the negative impacts of Liberalisation, Privatisation and Globalisation (LPG) policies on the Indian economy.

Ans. The following observations illustrate the adverse effects of LPG policies on the Indian economy

(i) **Neglect of the Agricultural Sector**
The agricultural sector has faced significant neglect, leading to a troubling decline in its growth rate. This oversight has resulted in diminished productivity and increased vulnerability for farmers.

(ii) **Fiscal Policy Stress**
The government's fiscal policy has come under considerable strain due to the challenges posed by the LPG framework, resulting in difficulties in managing public finances and meeting developmental needs.

(iii) **Urban Concentration of Growth**
The growth process has concentrated in urban areas, exacerbating regional disparities and neglecting rural development. This urban-centric growth has led to increased migration and strained urban resources.

(iv) **Economic Colonialism**
The expansion of Multinational Corporations (MNCs) has raised concerns about economic colonialism, where domestic markets and industries may become overly reliant on foreign entities, compromising national sovereignty.

(v) **Rise of Consumerism**
The proliferation of MNCs as a result of LPG policies has led to the widespread adoption of consumerism, which can overshadow traditional values and priorities, promoting unsustainable consumption patterns.

(vi) **Lopsided Growth Process**
While LPG has accelerated economic growth, the benefits have not been evenly distributed, resulting in a lopsided growth process that fails to address the needs of all segments of society. This lack of inclusivity has raised concerns about social equity and economic justice.

38. Developed countries have been trying to pursue developing countries to liberalise the trade and allow more flexibility in business policies to provide equal opportunities to multinational firms in their domestic market. International Monetary Fund (IMF) and World Bank helped them in this endeavour.

Liberalisation began to hold its foot on barren lands of developing countries like India by means of reduction in excise duties on electronic goods in a fixed time frame. Indian government did the same and liberalised the trade and investment due to the pressure from World Trade Organisation. Import duties were cut down phase-wise to allow MNC's operate in India on equality basis. As a result, globalisation has brought to India new technologies, new products and also the economic opportunities. Competency Based Que

(i) **Why was Indian economy liberalised in 1991?**
(ii) **Trade liberalisation benefits developed countries more than developing economies. Justify.**

Ans. (i) There were many reasons due to which economic reforms were a necessity in our country.
These were

- **Industrial Sector's Poor Performance**
Before the 1990s, the industries were mostly government owned. The employees did not feel the need to be either competitive or effective because their jobs were secure.

- **Adverse Balance of Payments**
  One of the biggest factors that played a major role in bringing about the economic reforms was the fact that India's Balance of Payments (BoP) were unsustainable.
  It was also true that the little foreign exchange as resources with the country was not enough. There was even an unprecedented rise of 11 percent in the BoP.
- **Rise in Fiscal Deficit**
  India's current account was bleeding. The centre did not have any funds in its hands. The reason for such a deficit was due to factors that were present both externally and internally.
  Suffice to say that the deficit had been a constant since the First Planning Commission's tenure which started in 1950.

(ii) Trade liberalisation promotes free trade, which allows countries to trade goods without regulatory barriers or their associated costs.

This reduced regulation decreases costs for countries that trade with other nations and may, ultimately, result in lower consumer prices because imports are subject to lower fees and competition is likely to increase.

Increased competition from abroad as a result of trade liberalisation creates an incentive for greater efficiency and cheaper production by domestic firms.

This competition might also spur a country to shift resources to industries in which it may have a competitive advantage. For example, trade liberalisation has encouraged the United Kingdom to concentrate on its service sector rather than manufacturing.

39. With the July 1991 budget, there was a clear switch in favour of a move towards an outward-oriented, market based economy. The liberalisation steps initiated in the budget were very comprehensive although the pace remained gradual and there were occasional hiccups.

The 1991 reforms did away with import licensing on all but a handful of intermediate inputs and capital goods. Consumer goods, accounting for approximately 30% of tariff lines, remained under licensing, only a decade later, after a successful challenge by India's trading partners at the World Trade Organisation (WTO), were these goods freed of licensing.

Today, except for a handful of goods that are disallowed on environmental/health/safety grounds, all goods may be imported without a license or other restrictions. With the removal of licensing, the tariff rates became effective restrictions on imports. Therefore, a major task of the reforms has been to lower the tariff rates. Tariff reductions have been mainly confined to non-agricultural, industrial goods.

Therefore, the liberalisation applies strictly to these goods. The reduction in tariffs has been achieved through a gradual compression of the tariff rates. A simultaneous rationalisation of the tariff structure through a reduction in the number of tariff bands helped in this direction. **CBSE 2024 C**

(i) "The trade liberalisation reforms initiated in 1991 budget were very comprehensive."
Justify the given statement explaining any two trade reforms introduced in 1991.

(ii) State any two areas in which tariff reductions were introduced.

Ans. (i) The 1991 economic reforms under liberalisation brought comprehensive changes across industrial, financial, fiscal and foreign exchange sectors, aiming to integrate India into the global economy. The trade liberalisation reforms initiated in 1991 budget were very comprehensive

- **Abolition of Industrial Licensing**
  The government removed industrial licensing for all industries except a few sensitive sectors such as alcohol, hazardous chemicals and drugs, reducing bureaucratic hurdles and encouraging industrial growth.
- **Devaluation of the Indian Rupee**
  To address the balance of payments crisis, the rupee was devalued in 1991, increasing India's export competitiveness and bringing in foreign exchange.

(ii) The two areas in which tariff reductions were introduced are

- **Reduction of Indirect Taxes**
  Indirect tax rates were lowered on goods and services, with the introduction of Goods and Services Tax (GST) in 2017 to unify the tax system.
- **Simplification of Direct Taxes**
  Income and corporate tax rates were lowered to encourage savings and voluntary income disclosures.

SELF ASSESSMENT TEST

Objective Type Questions

1. Which of the following is not a feature of liberalisation in India?
   (a) Reduction in import tariffs
   (b) Expansion of the public sector
   (c) Deregulation of industries
   (d) Encouragement of foreign investment

2. IGST is charged on .... transactions.
   (a) inter-state
   (b) intra-state
   (c) Both (a) and (b)
   (d) None of the above

3. Why privatisation is considered as better policy to improve efficiency of sick PSU's?
   (a) Private sector is more efficient
   (b) Private sector operates for profit
   (c) Private sector provide job security
   (d) Both (a) and (b)

4. The most common route for investment by MNCs in countries around the world is to
   (a) set-up new factories
   (b) buy existing local companies
   (c) form partnership with local companies
   (d) All of the above

5. Which institution oversees the balance of payments and foreign exchange policies in India?
   (a) Reserve Bank of India (RBI)
   (b) Securities and Exchange Board of India (SEBI)
   (c) Ministry of Rural Development
   (d) NITI Aayog

6. What major fiscal policy change in India was linked to IMF's intervention during the 1991 reforms?
   (a) Creation of a unified tax system
   (b) Reduction in fiscal deficit through subsidy cuts
   (c) Abolishment of wealth tax
   (d) Introduction of universal basic income

7. Which of the following statements is/are incorrect?
   I. Outsourcing is an outcome of globalisation.
   II. Reform process has failed to improve the condition of agriculture in India.

   Codes
   (a) Only I (b) Only II
   (c) Both I and II (d) None of these

Answers 1. (b) 2. (a) 3. (d) 4. (d) 5. (a) 6. (b) 7. (b)

Short Answer Type Questions

8. Discuss the support that World Trade Organisation (WTO) provides to its member countries.

9. Define liberalisation. List two measures taken to promote liberalisation in India after 1991.

10. State the measures adopted by the government to promote globalisation.

11. Globalisation is the outcome of liberalisation and privatisation strategies. Explain.

12. "In 1991, the Indian economy encountered severe challenges, requiring immediate attention and decisive actions. The government introduced a series of reforms that marked a significant shift in the country's economic policies."

    Based on the situation described, what were the basic problems that forced India to change its economic policies in 1991?

13. Why should Navratnas not be privatised? Give logical reason.

14. "Privatisation was a significant part of the economic reforms initiated in 1991. Public sector enterprises were either sold to private players or their ownership was diluted to improve efficiency and reduce the financial burden on the government."
    (i) Define privatisation.
    (ii) Explain one method through which privatisation was implemented in India.
    (iii) Discuss one potential benefit and one challenge associated with privatisation.

Long Answer Type Questions

15. Why has the agricultural sector not benefitted from the reform process?

16. How has globalisation affected employment in India? Discuss both positive and negative aspects.

17. Discuss the negative impacts of the LPG policy on the Indian economy.

04

CHAPTER

The development of human resources refers to the increase in the quality of human beings, which can help in the growth and development process of the economy.

▼ YOUR STUDY GOALS

▼ YOUR PRACTICE GOAL

- Objective Type Questions (64 Qs ; MCQs, A-R, Statements, Matching, Concept Identification)
- Subjective Questions (20 SAs, 10 LAs)
- Self Assessment Test (7 MCQs, 7 SAs, 3 LAs)

Human Capital Formation in India

4.1 Concept of Physical Capital and Human Capital

Physical Capital

- All inputs which are required in the production process such as machine, tools and implements, factory buildings, etc. are called *physical capital.*
- Increase in the stock of physical capital leads to economic growth of the country.
- Investment in physical capital is an economic decision.
- e.g. A physical resource like iron can be turned into a physical capital like machine.

Human Capital

- *Human capital* refers to the stock of skill, ability, expertise, education and knowledge available in human beings at a point of time.
- It is needed to effectively use physical capital and also to further produce human capital.
- e.g. A country can convert human resources like students into human capital like doctors, engineers, etc.

Comparison between Physical and Human Capital

The concept of physical capital is the base for conceptualising human capital. There are some similarities between the two forms of capital and some striking dissimilarities as well.

Following points highlight the comparison between these two factors

Basis	Physical Capital	Human Capital
Nature of Formation	Conscious decision by the owner; mainly an economic and technical process.	Partly a social process and partly a conscious decision of the possessor.
Tangibility	Tangible; can be sold easily in the market.	Intangible; cannot be sold in the market.
Separation from Owner	Separable from its owner.	Inseparable from its owner.
Mobility	Completely mobile between countries (except for trade restrictions).	Not perfectly mobile between countries (restricted by nationality, culture, etc).
Creation	Can be imported.	Can be done through conscious policy formulation.
Depreciation	Depreciates over time.	Depreciates but can be avoided with continuous investment (e.g. Education).
Benefits	Creates private benefits only.	Creates both private and social benefits.

How People Become Resource?

People become resource by using their skills, knowledge, productivity and abilities. When human resources are further developed by becoming more educated and healthy, we call it 'human capital formation'.

4.2 Concept of Human Capital Formation

Human capital formation is the process of acquiring and increasing the number of people who have the skills, education and experience which are significant for the economic and political development of a country.

It aims at converting human resources into human capital and to develop man as a creative and productive resource.

Sources of Human Capital Formation

Source	Explanation	Key Points
Investment in Education	Investment in education enhances the productive workforce of a country. It increases their future income as labour skill of an educated person is more than that of an uneducated person.	• Confers higher earning capacity on people. • Gives better social standing and pride. • Enables people to make better choices in life. • Provides knowledge to understand changes taking place in society. • Stimulates innovations. • Facilitates adaptation of new technology.

Source	Explanation	Key Points
Investment in Health	Investment in health ensures a productive labour force and improve the quality of life in the society. It is important because only a healthy worker can contribute towards increasing the capital stock of the country.	• **Preventive Medicine** Prevents the disease through vaccination, anti-disease injections and medications. • **Curative Medicine** Aims at curing a person after he becomes ill, i.e. medical intervention during illness. • **Social Medicine** Aims at spreading awareness about health. • **Other Expenditure** Involves providing clean drinking water, good sanitation facilities, clean and hygienic environment, etc.
On-the-job Training	Firms invest in training to boost labour productivity and insist that workers should work for them for atleast some time in order to recover the cost of training in the form of enhanced productivity.	**Internal Training** (Within office) Worker is trained under the supervision of a skilled worker. **External Training** (Outside office) Trainees are sent outside for formal training.
Migration	People move to places with better job opportunities and salaries. In India, people migrate from rural areas to urban areas. The technically qualified people (like engineers, doctors, etc.) migrate from one country to another in order to get high salaries or to maintain a higher standard of living.	Two kinds of cost are associated with migration • Cost of transportation. • Higher cost of living in the migrated place.
Expenditure on Information	People spend to acquire information relating to labour market, education and health-related information to make informed decisions.	Information helps in better decisions regarding investments in human capital as well as for efficient utilisation of the acquired human capital stock.

Human Capital and Economic Growth

- Economic growth means increase in the real national income of a country. Real national income increases with only increase in the level of output.
- Human capital formation (via education, health, training, migration and job market information) raises individuals' income generating capacity, thus contributing to output growth.
- Human capital formation stimulates **innovations and inventions**, boosting economic growth.
- It helps human resources adapt to **scientific and technological advancements**.
- The relationship between human capital and economic growth is bi-directional.
  It can be depicted as

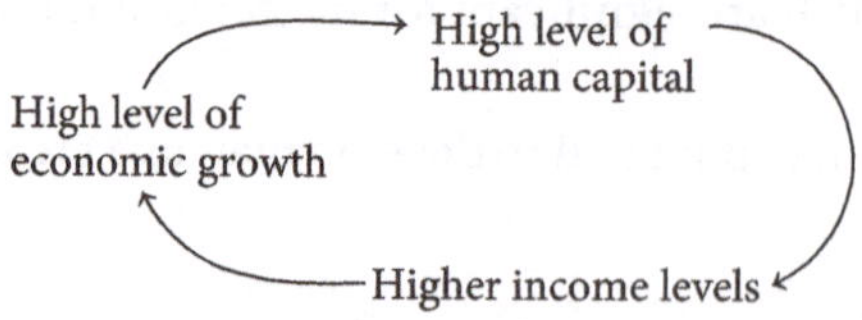

- Developing countries show faster human capital real growth, but per capita real income growth has been slower.
- National Education Policy, 2020 states about world's undergoing rapid changes in knowledge landscape. With scientific and technological advances (e.g. AI, machine learning), many unskilled jobs may be taken over by machines. Also, there will be greater demand for a skilled workforce, particularly in STEM and multidisciplinary areas.
- Climate change and resource challenges will shift the need for new skilled labour towards fields like biology, chemistry, physics, agriculture, climate science and social science.
- India's human capital formation will elevate the economy through a knowledge-based higher growth trajectory.

Human Capital and Human Development

Aspect	Human Capital	Human Development
Focus	Education and health are seen as means to increase labour productivity.	Education and health are integral to overall human well-being.
Primary Goal	Enhancing productivity of labour through education and health investments.	Ensuring people can read, write and lead healthy lives, enabling valued life choices.
View on Investment	Investments in education and health are only justified if they increase economic output and productivity.	Investments in education and health are valued for their role in improving individual well-being, regardless of direct economic returns.
Welfare Perspective	Human capital focuses on economic returns, viewing people primarily as resources that contribute to economic productivity.	Human development views individuals as ends in themselves, emphasising human rights and well-being.
Right to Education and Health	No inherent right to education or health unless it enhances productivity.	Every individual has a right to basic education and healthcare.

4.3 State of Human Capital Formation in India

In India, the most important sources of human capital formation are education and health. The state of human capital formation depends upon the performance of these two sectors. Therefore, government alongwith private institutions, takes substantial steps for the development of these sectors.

Government's role is crucial for the development of these sectors in India because of the following reasons

- Expenditures on education and health make substantial long-term impact and they cannot be easily reversed.
- Individual consumers do not have complete information about the quality of services and their costs.

  In this situation, the providers of education and health services acquire monopoly power and are involved in exploitation. Therefore, government intervenes to ensure that the private providers of these services adhere to the standards set by the government and charge the correct price.
- In India, a large section of the population lives below poverty line. They cannot access the services of private health and education services. Therefore, it is essential that the government provides education and health services free of cost to this section of society.

Regulatory Authorities in Education and Health Sector

- In India, the institutions of **education sector** are facilitated by the ministries of education at the union and state level as well as departments of education and various organisations like National Council of Educational Research and Training (NCERT), University Grants Commission (UGC) and All India Council of Technical Education (AICTE).
- Similarly, the institutions of **health sector** are facilitated by the ministries of health at the union and state level as well as departments of health and various organisations like National Medical Commission and Indian Council for Medical Research (ICMR).

Role of Human Capital Formation

Role	Explanation
Raises Productivity and Production	Skilled and knowledgeable workers use resources more efficiently, increasing production and driving economic growth.
Improves Quality of Life	Human capital formation improves level of education, skill formation, etc. leading to better income, health and overall quality of life, contributing to economic growth.
Raises Life Expectancy	Improved health services and access to nutritious food improves life expectancy by improving longevity of life.
Encourage Innovations	Human capital fosters innovation and capacity to absorb new technologies, promoting further economic growth.
Raises Social Justice and Equality	Improving human capital enhances the productivity of the labour force, leading to better employment opportunities. This increases labour force participation and helps reduce the gap between the rich and poor.

Problems Facing Human Capital Formation

Problem	Details
Rising Population	Rapid population growth, especially in developing countries, reduces per capita access to education, health and other resources.
High Poverty Level	A large portion of the population lives below the poverty line, lacking access to basic education and healthcare, making it difficult to afford higher education and advanced medical treatment.
Brain Drain	Migration of skilled labour in search of better job opportunities and higher salaries slows the human capital formation process in an economy.
Insufficient Manpower Planning	Lack of effective manpower planning leads to a mismatch between the supply and demand of skilled personnel, causing resource wastage.

4.4 Education Sector in India

Education is the most important factor which affects the rate of human capital formation of a country. Through education, individuals are able to earn a living and contribute towards the national income of the country.

Growth in Government Expenditure on Education

Government expenditure on education can be expressed in two key ways

1. **As a Percentage of Total Government Expenditure**
   - Percentage of education expenditure of total government expenditure reflects the priority given to education by the government.
   - During 1952-2014, education expenditure as a percentage of total government spending increased from 7.92% to 15.7%.
2. **As a Percentage of Gross Domestic Product** (GDP)
   - This shows how much of the national income is allocated to education development.
   - During 1952-2014, education expenditure as a percentage of GDP increased from 0.64% to 4.13%.
   - The rise in education expenditure over the years has not been consistent and there has been irregular rise and fall.
   - If we include private expenditure by individuals and philanthropic institutions, the total education expenditure would be significantly higher.

Important Points related to Government Expenditure

- Elementary education takes a major share of total education expenditure.
- The share of higher/tertiary education like colleges, polytechnics, etc. is the least.
- 'Expenditure per student' is higher for tertiary education as compared to elementary education.
- As we expand school education, there is a need for more teachers who are trained in the higher educational institutions, therefore, expenditure on all levels of education should be increased.
- The per capita public expenditure on elementary education differs considerably across states. e.g. In 2014-15, the per capita public expenditure was ₹ 34,651 in Himachal Pradesh and ₹ 4,088 in Bihar.
- The Education Commission (1964-66) had recommended that atleast 6% of GDP should be spent on education.
- However, the current level of expenditure on education is a little over 4% which is highly inadequate.
- The Tapas Majumdar Committee, appointed by the government in 1999, had estimated an expenditure of around ₹ 1.37 lakh crore over 10 years (1998-99 to 2006-07) to bring all Indian children (6-14 years of age) under the purview of school education.

Government's Initiatives to Improve Education in India

The government has taken the following initiatives to improve the level of education in India

1. Right to Education

In 2009, the Government of India has implemented the Right of Children to Free and Compulsory Education Act. This Act makes free education a fundamental right to all children in the age group of 6-14 years.

2. Provision of Education Cess

The government is levying 2% education cess on all union taxes. The revenue from this is spent on providing elementary education in India.

3. Other Measures

The government sanctions a large outlay for the promotion of higher education and new loan schemes for students to pursue higher education.

Educational Achievements in India

The educational achievements in a country are indicated in terms of adult literacy level, primary education completion rate and youth literacy rate. The statistics for these indicators for the last two decades are given in the table below

S.No.	Particulars	1990	2000	2011	2017-18
1.	Adult Literacy Rate (Per cent of people aged 15+)				
	1.1 Male	61.9	68.4	79	82
	1.2 Female	37.9	45.4	59	66
2.	Primary Completion Rate (Per cent of relevant age group)				
	2.1 Male	78	85	92	93
	2.2 Female	61	69	94	96
3.	Youth Literacy Rate (Per cent of people aged 15+ to 24)				
	3.1 Male	76.6	79.7	90	93
	3.2 Female	54.2	64.8	82	90

4.5 Future Prospects in Education

The following areas concerning the Indian education sector needs to be addressed

Area of Concern	Explanation
Education for All : Still a Distant Dream	• While education levels have risen, the number of illiterate individuals still matches India's population as at the time of independence. • The 1950 directive principles aimed for free and compulsory education up to 14 years, but this has still not been achieved. • There is a need for the government to follow this directive to achieve 100% literacy.
Gender Equity : Better than Before	• The literacy gap between males and females is narrowing, indicating progress in gender equity. • Still there is a need to promote women education due to following reasons – Improving economic independence of women. – Enhancing the social status of women. • Positively impact fertility rates and healthcare for women and children. • So, full satisfaction can only be achieved when 100% literacy is realised.
Higher Education : A Few Takers	• The steep Indian education pyramid indicates low participation in higher education. • According to NSSO data (2011-12) – Unemployment rates were 19% for rural male graduates and post-graduates while 16% for urban male graduates and post-graduates. – Nearly 30% of young rural female graduates were unemployed. – In contrast, only 3-6% of primary level educated youth in rural and urban areas were unemployed. – The government should increase funding for higher education and improve the standards of institutions to provide employable skills to students.

Mind Map

HUMAN CAPITAL FORMATION IN INDIA

1 Concept of Physical Capital and Human Capital

Physical Capital It includes all inputs which are required in the production process such as machine, tools and implements, factory buildings, etc.

Human Capital It refers to the stock of skill, ability, expertise, education and knowledge available in human beings at a point of time.

How People become Resource?

People become resource by using their skills, knowledge, productivity and abilities.

2 Human Capital Formation

Human capital formation is the process of acquiring and increasing the number of people who have the skills, education and experience.

Sources

- **Investment in Education** It increases the future income as labour skill of an educated person is more than that of an uneducated person.
- **Investment in Health** It ensures a productive labour force and improve the quality of life in the society.
- **On-the-job Training** Firms invest in training to boost labour productivity and insist that workers should work for them.
- **Migration** People move to places with better job opportunities and salaries.
- **Expenditure on Information** People spend to acquire information relating to labour market, education and health related information.

3 Human Capital and Economic Growth

- Economic growth means increase in the real national income of a country. Real national income increases with only increase in the level of output.
- Human capital formation raises individuals' income generating capacity, thus contributing to output growth.
- Human capital formation stimulates innovations and inventions, boosting economic growth. It helps human resources adapt to scientific and technological advancements.

4 Human Capital and Human Development

- Education and health are seen as means to increase labour productivity in human capital while in human development, they are integral to overall human well-being.
- There is no inherent right to education or health unless human capital enhances productivity.
- Human capital enhances productivity of labour through education and health investments while human development ensures people can read, write and lead healthy lives.

5 State of Human Capital Formation in India

Government's role is crucial for the development of education and health sectors in India because of the following reasons

- Expenditures on education and health make substantial long-term impact and they cannot be easily reversed.
- Individual consumers do not have complete information about the quality of services and their costs. Government intervenes to ensure that the private providers of these services adhere to the standards set by the government and charge the correct price.
- In India, a large section of the population lives below poverty line. Government provides education and health services free of cost to this section of society.

6 Role of Human Capital Formation and Problems

Role

- Raises productivity and production
- Improves quality of life
- Raises life expectancy
- Encourage innovations
- Raises social justice and equality

Problems

- Rising population
- High poverty level
- Brain drain
- Insufficient manpower planning

7 Education Sector in India

Growth in Government Expenditure on Education

1. **As a Percentage of Total Government Expenditure** It reflects the priority given to education by the government. During 1952-2014, education expenditure as a percentage of total government spending increased from 7.92% to 15.7%.
2. **As a Percentage of Gross Domestic Product** (GDP) This shows how much of the national income is allocated to education development. During 1952-2014, education expenditure as a percentage of GDP increased from 0.64% to 4.13%.

Government's Initiatives to Improve Education in India

1. **Right to Education** In 2009, the Government of India has implemented the Right of Children to Free and Compulsory Education Act.
2. **Provision of Education Cess** The government is levying 2% education cess on all union taxes. The revenue from this is spent on providing elementary education in India.
3. **Other Measures** The government sanctions a large outlay for the promotion of higher education and new loan schemes for students to pursue higher education.

Educational Achievements in India

- Adult literacy rate for male and female is 82 and 66 respectively.
- Primary completion rate for male and female is 93 and 96 respectively.
- Youth literacy rate for male and female is 93 and 90 respectively.

8 Future Prospects in Education

- **Education for All : Still a Distant Dream** The 1950 directive principles aimed for free and compulsory education up to 14 years, but this has still not been achieved. There is a need for the government to follow this directive to achieve 100% literacy.
- **Gender Equity : Better than Before** The literacy gap between males and females is narrowing, indicating progress in gender equity. Still there is a need to promote women education due to improving economic independence of women and enhancing the social status of women.
- **Higher Education : A Few Takers** The steep Indian education pyramid indicates low participation in higher education. The government should increase funding for higher education and improve the standards of institutions to provide employable skills to students.

EXAM PATTERN QUESTIONS

Objective Type Questions

Multiple Choice Questions (MCQs)

1. Which of the following would not be considered a part of physical capital?

(a) An automated assembly line in a factory
(b) A company's patents for an innovative manufacturing process
(c) Inventory of raw materials in a production plant
(d) A fleet of delivery trucks used by a logistics company

2. Identify the incorrect statement in context of human capital. **CBSE Term I 2021**

(a) Human capital is intangible in nature
(b) Human capital is perfectly mobile
(c) Human capital is inseparable from its owner
(d) Human capital cannot be sold in market like commodity

3. While physical capital is known to generate .... returns, human capital, shaped by skills, knowledge and experience, tends to offer .... returns. **Competency Based Que**

(a) fixed, variable
(b) constant, diminishing
(c) financial, non-monetary
(d) tangible, intangible

4. Which of the following statements best explains the difference between the concepts shown in image?

(a) 'A' depreciates over time, but 'B' appreciates automatically
(b) 'A' is tangible and can be seen, while 'B' is intangible and manifests in individual capabilities
(c) 'B' is directly related to infrastructure development, whereas 'A' is related to the labour force
(d) 'B' is static once formed, whereas 'A' is dynamic and changes with technological advancements

5. The process of acquiring and increasing the number of persons who have the skills, education and experience which are critical for the economic and political development of a country is called ....

(a) physical capital formation
(b) human capital formation
(c) natural resource development
(d) industrial growth

6. The primary source of human capital formation is ....

(a) physical capital
(b) investment in education
(c) government policies
(d) international trade

7. Which of the following is not a direct component of human capital formation? **Competency Based Que**

(a) Investment in health services
(b) Expenditure on scientific research and development
(c) Migration of skilled workers from India to other countries
(d) Investment in primary and secondary education

8. Identify the incorrect statements regarding human capital formation. **Competency Based Que**

I. Human capital only includes formal education.
II. On-the-job training is a significant source of human capital formation.
III. Health and education are inter-related in human capital formation.
IV. Migration of skilled labour contributes to human capital formation in the home country.

Codes
(a) I and IV
(b) II and III
(c) III and IV
(d) I and II

9. Ms. Ramanpreet has started a new business venture. She intends to spend a huge amount towards 'on-the-job training' of her workers before putting them to work. It exhibits the right step in the direction of human capital formation. Spot which of the following does not directly contributes to the process of human capital formation by Ms Ramanpreet? **CBSE SQP Term I 2021; Competency Based Que**

(a) Adds skills and expertise
(b) Improves efficiency
(c) Ensures gender equity
(d) Increases output productivity

10. **The vaccination campaign for containing Covid-19 is an example of .... medicine.** CBSE Term I 2021

(a) preventive (b) curative
(c) social (d) emotional

11. **"Despite significant investment in education, Country X continues to struggle with slow economic growth and high unemployment rates."**

Which of the following could be the most critical factor behind this paradox? Competency Based Que

(a) The education system in Country X focuses on theoretical knowledge, with little emphasis on practical or job related skills
(b) The high unemployment rates are due to a lack of foreign direct investment in Country X
(c) The population of Country X is growing too rapidly for the education system to keep pace
(d) High investment in education typically results in short-term economic slowdowns before long-term gains are realised

12. **Which five year plan recognised the importance of human capital?**

(a) Tenth (b) Seventh
(c) Sixth (d) Ninth

13. **Which of the following statements is true?**

(a) Major share of education expenditure goes to higher education
(b) No education cess is imposed by the government on all Union taxes
(c) Human development is based on the idea that education and health are integral to human well-being
(d) Education and literacy can be used as synonyms of each other

14. **"India's workforce faces a skills gap: Investment in education and vocational training is critical for economic growth."** – Economic Times, 2024

Based on this headline, which of the following statements are true? Competency Based Que

I. India's workforce requires improved access to education and vocational training to close the skills gap.
II. Economic growth in India depends on the development of a skilled and educated workforce.
III. India's current investment in education and vocational training is sufficient to address the skills gap.
IV. The skills gap is unrelated to economic growth in India.

Codes

(a) Statements I and II are true
(b) Statements II and III are true
(c) Statements III and IV are true
(d) Statements I and IV are true

15. **"Government raises allocation for education by 20% in Union Budget 2024."**

According to data from the Union Budget 2024 and the PIB press release on budget allocations, which of the following is the most accurate interpretation of this allocation? Competency Based Que

(a) It signals a decline in human capital formation
(b) The primary focus is on enhancing physical capital
(c) It highlights the government's emphasis on human capital development
(d) This allocation directly targets industrial growth

16. **"India sees rise in the percentage of population covered by healthcare services: A boost to human capital!"**

Which statement best links healthcare to human capital development? Competency Based Que

(a) Healthcare investment hampers workforce productivity
(b) Enhanced healthcare boosts a nation's physical assets
(c) Healthcare contributes nothing to human capital formation
(d) Better healthcare yields a more productive workforce, enhancing human capital

17. **Identify, which of the following are associated with the problem of human capital formation in India?**

(i) Brain drain
(ii) Low academic standards
(iii) Rising population
(iv) Changes in social outlook CBSE 2023

Codes

(a) (i) and (ii) (b) (ii) and (iii)
(c) (i), (ii) and (iii) (d) (i) and (iv)

18. **The government of India introduced the Right to Education (RTE) Act in the year ...., ensuring free and compulsory education for children between the ages of 6 to 14.**

(a) 2005 (b) 2009
(c) 2010 (d) 2012

19. **"India faces 'educated unemployment', even though the number of educated individuals ready for jobs has increased."**

Which of the following is most likely the reason for this? CBSE SQP Term I 2021; Competency Based Que

(a) The supply of labour is much higher than demand
(b) Investments in health have not taken place proportionally
(c) Although more students are enrolled in schools, there is a high dropout rate
(d) Reverse migration has not been accompanied by alternative employment opportunities

20.

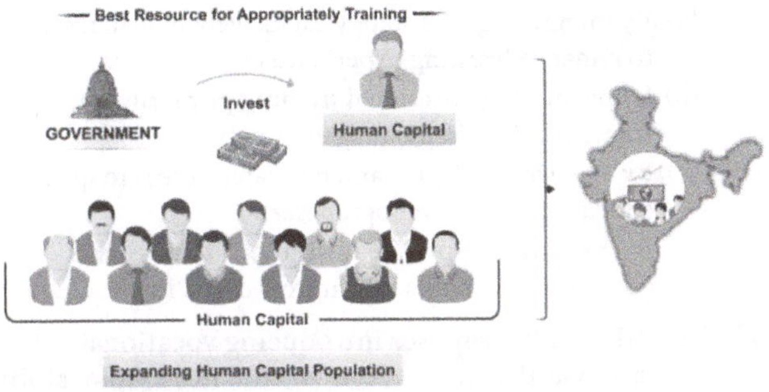

What might be a key indicator of successful government investment in human capital, as implied by the image?

(a) A significant increase in public sector employment
(b) A noticeable improvement in infrastructure projects
(c) A more knowledgeable and skilled workforce driving innovation
(d) An increase in the population size without a focus on skills

21.

Kerala Tops the List

Literacy rates for those aged 7 or more (%)

Top 5 State/UT	Person	Bottom 5 State/UT	Person
Kerala	96.2	UP	73.0
Delhi	88.7	Telangana	72.8
Uttarakhand	87.6	Bihar	70.9
Himachal	86.6	Rajasthan	69.7
Assam	85.9	Andhra	66.4

Source *https://timesofindia.indiatimes.com/education/news/at-96-2-kerala-tops-literacy-rate-chart-andhra-pradesh-worst-performer-at-66-4/articleshow/77990417.cms*

Considering various development indicators, which statement accurately reflects the economic opportunities in Kerala and Andhra Pradesh?

(a) Kerala's educational achievements overshadow its actual job market potential
(b) Kerala's diverse economy contrasts with Andhra Pradesh's agricultural focus
(c) Andhra Pradesh's industrial growth offers more employment than Kerala's diverse sectors
(d) Kerala's economy is primarily agricultural, while Andhra Pradesh is industrialised

22. How does gender equity in education contribute to human capital formation?

(a) It allows for more competition in the job market, leading to fewer job opportunities for men
(b) It ensures that half the population is not excluded from the economic process, leading to increased overall productivity
(c) Gender equity in education only affects social development but has no impact on economic growth
(d) It decreases the total number of individuals pursuing higher education, as more women enter the labour market

Direction *Read the case study and answer the questions 23 to 26 on the basis of the same*

During 1952-2014, education expenditure as percentage of total government expenditure increased from 7.92 to 15.7 and as percentage of GDP increased from 0.64 to 4.13. Throughout this period the increase in education expenditure has not been uniform and there has been irregular rise and fall. To this if we include the private expenditure incurred by individuals and by philanthropic institutions, the total education expenditure should be much higher.

Elementary education takes a major share of total education expenditure and the share of the higher/tertiary education (institutions of higher learning like colleges, polytechnics and universities) is the least.

In 2014-15, the per capita public expenditure on elementary education differs considerably across states from as high as ₹ 34,651 in Himachal Pradesh to as low as ₹ 4,088 in Bihar.

23. How education expenditure as percentage of total government expenditure is related to the percentage of GDP?

(a) Education expenditure as percentage of total government expenditure is directly proportional to percentage of GDP
(b) Education expenditure as percentage of total government expenditure is inversely proportional to percentage of GDP
(c) There is no relation between education expenditure as percentage of total government expenditure and percentage of GDP
(d) There is both direct and inverse relation between education expenditure as percentage of total government expenditure and percentage of GDP

24. During 1952-2014, the increase in education expenditure was …… .

25. The share of higher/tertiary education in total education expenditure is …… .

26. Which of the following is/are the institute(s) of elementary education?

(a) College (b) University
(c) Polytechnic institute (d) School

Direction *Read the case study and answer the questions 27 to 30 on the basis of the same*

India has made significant progress in increasing access to education and healthcare services over the past few decades. The government's initiatives, such as the Right to Education Act and the National Health Mission, have played an essential role in human capital formation.

However, challenges remain, particularly in terms of quality education and healthcare for all.

27. Which government initiative has been a key driver in promoting human capital formation through education?

(a) National Skill Development Mission
(b) Right to Education Act
(c) Swachh Bharat Mission (d) Digital India

28. What is one of the main challenges that India faces in human capital formation, despite significant progress?

(a) Lack of population growth
(b) Poor quality of education and healthcare services
(c) Decline in technological advancements
(d) Decreased government expenditure

29. The National Health Mission is a government initiative aimed at improving healthcare services in India, which is essential for ....

30. One of the primary challenges in India's human capital formation is ensuring the .... of education and healthcare services for all citizens.

Direction *Read the case study and answer the questions 31 to 34 on the basis of the same*

The Government of India, under the National Education Policy 2020, aims to overhaul the education system by focusing on access, equity, quality, affordability and accountability. One of the key highlights is the emphasis on Early Childhood Care and Education (ECCE), ensuring foundational literacy and numeracy by 2025. The policy also aims to increase the Gross Enrolment Ratio (GER) in higher education, including vocational education, from 26.3% in 2018 to 50% by 2035.

Source *Ministry of Education-NEP 2020*

31. Which of the following statements best reflects the intention behind ensuring foundational literacy and numeracy by 2025?

(a) It is a measure to reduce the number of teachers in primary schools
(b) It focuses on enhancing children's ability to read, write, and perform basic arithmetic
(c) It prioritises standardised testing over holistic education approaches
(d) It aims to eliminate early childhood education programmes

32. How does the National Education Policy 2020 intend to address educational inequities?

(a) By integrating technology exclusively in urban schools to enhance learning experiences
(b) By promoting vocational training primarily for economically disadvantaged groups
(c) By ensuring inclusive and equitable access to quality education for all demographics
(d) By encouraging private institutions to take over government schools for improved quality

33. The NEP 2020 proposes introducing vocational education at the .... level to enhance employability and skills among students.

34. By integrating .... into mainstream education, NEP 2020 seeks to equip students with practical skills, contributing directly to economic productivity.

Assertion-Reason

Direction (Q.No. 35 to 44) *Read the following Assertion (A) and Reason (R) and choose the correct alternative from the following*

Alternatives

(a) Both Assertion (A) and Reason (R) are true and Reason (R) is the correct explanation of Assertion (A)
(b) Both Assertion (A) and Reason (R) are true, but Reason (R) is not the correct explanation of Assertion (A)
(c) Assertion (A) is true, but Reason (R) is false
(d) Assertion (A) is false, but Reason (R) is true

35. **Assertion** (A) Physical capital is perfectly mobile between countries except for some artificial trade restrictions.

Reason (R) Physical capital is tangible.

36. **Assertion** (A) An educated person is able to generate more income than an uneducated person.

Reason (R) The labour skill of an educated person is more than that of an uneducated person.

37. **Assertion** (A) Economists emphasise on the need for expanding educational opportunities, as it accelerates development process.

Reason (R) Educated people facilitates adaption of new technology and stimulates innovation. **CBSE Term I 2021**

38. **Assertion** (A) Human capital formation is a flow concept.

Reason (R) Stock is that variable which is measured at a given point of time. **CBSE Term I 2021**

39. **Assertion** (A) Human capital cannot be traded in the market, whereas its services can be traded.

Reason (R) Human capital is intangible in nature. **CBSE 2024 C**

40. **Assertion** (A) Human capital formation in India is solely dependent on government initiatives, which aim to improve literacy and skills across the nation.

Reason (R) Private educational institutions are increasingly becoming vital in providing quality education and addressing gaps in the public education system, particularly in urban areas.

41. **Assertion** (A) The Education Commission (1964-66) had recommended that at least 4% of Gross Domestic Product (GDP) be spent on education.

Reason (R) The Union and State Governments, have been stepping up expenditures in the education sector over the years to fulfil the objective of attaining cent per cent literacy. **CBSE SQP 2025**

42. **Assertion** (A) Insufficient investment in vocational training programmes is a significant barrier to human capital formation in India, leading to a mismatch between educational qualifications and labour market needs.

Reason (R) Consequently, the lack of skilled labour not only limits employment opportunities but also hinders overall economic growth, as industries struggle to find adequately trained workers.

43. **Assertion** (A) The Right to Education Act has significantly improved literacy rates in India, particularly only in urban areas.

Reason (R) The Right to Education Act mandates free and compulsory education for children aged 6 to 14 years, but its implementation has faced challenges in rural areas.

44. **Assertion** (A) Gender equity in education is essential for the holistic development of human capital in India, affecting both social and economic dimensions.

Reason (R) Educating women not only leads to better health outcomes and economic productivity but also fosters social change, reducing gender based disparities in various sectors.

Two Statement Based MCQs

Direction (Q.No. 45 to 54) *Read the following statements carefully and choose the correct alternative*

Alternatives

(a) Statement I is correct and Statement II is incorrect
(b) Statement II is correct and Statement I is incorrect
(c) Both the statements are correct
(d) Both the statements are incorrect

45. **Statement I** Physical capital includes tangible assets like machinery and buildings, while human capital refers to the skills and knowledge possessed by individuals.

Statement II Human capital is considered less important than physical capital for economic growth.

46. **Statement I** Human resources are considered as the source of human capital formation.
Statement II There is a positive relationship between human capital and economic growth.

47. **Statement I** Education is the first component of human development.
Statement II Human development is a narrower concept compared with human capital.

48. **Statement I** Human capital formation plays a crucial role in driving economic growth by enhancing productivity and innovation.

Statement II The primary source of human capital formation in India is through informal vocational training, which is less effective than formal education.

49. **Statement I** Health and nutrition are vital sources of human capital formation, as a healthy population can engage more effectively in educational and economic activities.

Statement II Investment in physical capital, such as infrastructure and technology, is more crucial for human capital formation than investment in health and nutrition.

50. **Statement I** The relationship between human capital and human development is often weak in developing countries, where economic growth can occur without corresponding improvements in education and health outcomes.
Statement II The Human Development Index (HDI) is solely based on economic factors such as GDP per capita and does not take into account education and health indicators.

51. **Statement I** The Gross Enrollment Ratio (GER) in higher education in India has reached international standards, ensuring that most students transition from secondary to tertiary education.

Statement II Despite improvements in GER, the quality of higher education institutions in India varies widely, leading to concerns about the employability of graduates.

52. **Statement I** The government of India has significantly increased its expenditure on education in recent years, reflecting a commitment to enhance human capital formation.
Statement II The educational initiatives in India, such as the Right to Education Act, have had minimal impact on improving literacy rates and educational attainment among children.

53. **Statement I** India has made significant strides in improving literacy rates over the past two decades, with a marked increase in primary school enrollment.

Statement II The 'Education for All' movement in India aims to ensure that every child has access to quality education, regardless of their socio-economic background.

54. Statement I To bolster educational funding, the Government of India implemented the education cess, which allocates additional resources specifically for improving educational infrastructure and services.

Statement II Despite the efforts of the education for all movement, significant barriers still prevent marginalised communities in India from accessing quality education, including socio-economic challenges and cultural factors.

Matching

55. Match the following

Column I	Column II
A. Land	(i) Physical capital
B. People	(ii) Human capital
C. Doctor	(iii) Human resource
D. Factory	(iv) Physical resource

Codes

	A	B	C	D		A	B	C	D
(a)	(i)	(ii)	(iii)	(iv)	(b)	(ii)	(iii)	(iv)	(i)
(c)	(iii)	(iv)	(i)	(ii)	(d)	(iv)	(iii)	(ii)	(i)

56. Match the following

Column I	Column II
A. Adult Male Literacy Rate in 2017-18	(i) 96%
B. Female Primary Completion Rate in 2017-18	(ii) 93%
C. Male Youth Literacy Rate in 2017-18	(iii) 82%

Codes

	A	B	C		A	B	C
(a)	(i)	(ii)	(iii)	(b)	(ii)	(iii)	(i)
(c)	(iii)	(i)	(ii)	(d)	(iii)	(ii)	(i)

57. Match the different forms of health expenditure in Column I with the specific government programmes in Column II **Competency Based Que**

Column I	Column II
A. Preventive medicine	(i) Ayushman Bharat Scheme
B. Curative medicine	(ii) National Immunisation Programme
C. Social medicine	(iii) Jal Jeevan Mission
D. Other expenditure	(iv) Swachh Bharat Mission

Codes

	A	B	C	D		A	B	C	D
(a)	(i)	(ii)	(iii)	(iv)	(b)	(ii)	(i)	(iii)	(iv)
(c)	(iii)	(ii)	(i)	(iv)	(d)	(iv)	(ii)	(i)	(iii)

58. Choose the correct pair **Competency Based Que**

Column I	Column II
A. UGC	(i) Oversees policies relating to education and literacy
B. NCERT	(ii) Coordinates, determines and maintains standards of higher education
C. AICTE	(iii) Regulates technical and management education in India
D. MHRD	(iv) Responsible for education and curriculum development in schools

Codes

(a) A-(i) (b) B-(ii) (c) C-(iii) (d) D-(iv)

59. Arrange the following major educational policy initiatives in India in chronological order

Column I	Column II
A. Right to Education (RTE) Act	(i) 1986
B. National Policy on Education (NPE)	(ii) 2020
C. Sarva Shiksha Abhiyan (SSA)	(iii) 2009
D. New Education Policy (NEP)	(iv) 2001

Codes

	A	B	C	D		A	B	C	D
(a)	(iii)	(i)	(iv)	(ii)	(b)	(i)	(ii)	(iii)	(iv)
(c)	(iii)	(ii)	(iv)	(i)	(d)	(i)	(iii)	(iv)	(ii)

Concept Identification

60. Person who acquires skills through education, training and/or experience, adding to his/her value to the production process.

61. Process of addition made to the stock of skilled and capable people in the country over a period of time.

62. Development of the individuals as valuable personalities by acquiring good education and attaining good health.

63. A method of training where employees learn and acquire new skills while working within their own organisation, under the guidance of experienced colleagues or supervisors.

64. Movement of people across different areas (like from rural to urban areas) of the country in search of job opportunities.

Answers

1. (b) A company's patents for an innovative manufacturing process.
2. (b) Human capital is perfectly mobile
3. (a) fixed, variable
4. (b) 'A' is tangible and can be seen, while 'B' is intangible and manifests in individual capabilities
5. (b) human capital formation
6. (b) investment in education
7. (c) Migration of skilled workers from India to other countries
8. (a) I and IV
9. (c) Ensures gender equity
10. (a) preventive
11. (a) The education system in Country X focuses on theoretical knowledge, with little emphasis on practical or job related skills
12. (b) Seventh
13. (c) Human development is based on the idea that education and health are integral to human well-being
14. (a) Statements I and II are true
15. (c) It highlights the government's emphasis on human capital development
16. (d) Better healthcare yields a more productive workforce, enhancing human capital
17. (c) (i), (ii) and (iii)
18. (b) 2009
19. (a) The supply of labour is much higher than demand
20. (c) A more knowledgeable and skilled workforce driving innovation
21. (b) Kerala's diverse economy contrasts with Andhra Pradesh's agricultural focus
22. (b) It ensures that half the population is not excluded from the economic process, leading to increased overall productivity
23. (a) Education expenditure as percentage of total government expenditure is directly proportional to percentage of GDP
24. changeable
25. minimum
26. (d) School
27. (b) Right to Education Act
28. (b) Poor quality of education and healthcare services
29. human capital formation
30. quality
31. (b) It focuses on enhancing children's ability to read, write and perform basic arithmetic
32. (c) By ensuring inclusive and equitable access to quality education for all demographics
33. secondary
34. vocational education
35. (b) Physical capital can move from one place to another without its owner.
36. (a) Both Assertion (A) and Reason (R) are true and Reason (R) is the correct explanation of Assertion (A)
37. (a) Both Assertion (A) and Reason (R) are true and Reason (R) is the correct explanation of Assertion (A)
38. (b) Both Assertion (A) and Reason (R) are true, but Reason (R) is not the correct explanation of Assertion (A)
39. (a) Both Assertion (A) and Reason (R) are true and Reason (R) is the correct explanation of Assertion (A)
40. (d) While government welfare schemes and policies play a key role, private schools often outperform state schools at primary and secondary levels, making it inaccurate to attribute human capital formation solely to government initiatives.
41. (d) The Education Commission (1964-66) recommended 6% of GDP to be spent on education.
42. (b) Both Assertion (A) and Reason (R) are true, but Reason (R) is not the correct explanation of Assertion (A)
43. (d) The RTE Act has contributed to improvements in literacy rates in India. However, the improvements are more pronounced in urban areas compared to rural regions, where challenges like infrastructure, teacher shortages, etc.

    It is incorrect to say that improvement has been observed only in urban area. Rural areas has also witnessed the growth in education.
44. (a) Both Assertion (A) and Reason (R) are true and Reason (R) is the correct explanation of Assertion (A)
45. (a) Both forms of capital are important for economic development, but human capital is often seen as a primary driver of growth.
46. (c) Both the statements are correct
47. (a) Human capital focuses on the economic value of individuals' skills and knowledge, while human development encompasses a wider range of aspects, including health, education, standard of living and overall well-being.
48. (a) The primary source of human capital formation in India is formal education.
49. (a) Both physical and human capital are interdependent; investment in health and nutrition is essential for effective human capital formation.
50. (a) The HDI is a composite index that includes three key dimensions health, measured by life expectancy at birth; education, measured by mean years of schooling and expected years of schooling and standard of living, measured by Gross National Income (GNI) per capita.

51. (b) GER has reached international standards, which is not entirely true, as many countries have higher enrollment ratios.
52. (a) Initiatives like the Right to Education Act have significantly improved literacy rates and educational attainment.
53. (c) Both the statements are correct
54. (c) Both the statements are correct
55. (d) (iv) (iii) (ii) (i)
56. (c) (iii) (i) (ii)
57. (a) (i) (ii) (iii) (iv)
58. (c) C-(iii)
59. (a) (iii) (i) (iv) (ii)
60. Human capital
61. Human capital formation
62. Human development
63. Internal on-the-job training
64. Migration

Subjective Questions

Short Answer Type Questions

1. Explain the meaning of human capital formation with the help of an example.

Ans. Human capital formation is a process which converts human resources into human capital. It is the process of acquiring and increasing the number of people who have the skills, education and experience which is necessary for the economic development of the country.

e.g. If in the year 2014, the number of doctors and engineers in our country were 4,50,000 and in the year 2015, their number grew to 5,00,000, then it can be said that there is human capital formation to the extent of 50,000 doctors and engineers.

2. "Human resource is the main economic factor." Discuss. Competency Based Que

Ans. Human resource is the most important economic factor than all the other factors of production, *viz.* land, labour, capital and organisation, because it is the only factor which is active.

In the absence of human resource, production in an economy will come to a stand still. Therefore, it is correctly said that human resource is the main economic factor.

3. Interpret the given image to explain the concept of human capital formation. Competency Based Que

Ans. Human capital formation is the process of improving people's skills and knowledge, which leads to overall development in various sectors of the economy.

The image highlights how investing in human capital is essential for societal and economic growth.

(i) **Diverse Human Resources**
The varied colours of the figures represent diversity in human capital, indicating people of different skills, abilities and roles in society.

(ii) **Industrial and Technological Advancements**
The background includes buildings, industries, transportation (bus, plane) and communication systems. These represent sectors that require skilled labour to operate and develop, showcasing how human capital contributes to economic progress.

(iii) **Unity and Collaboration**
The figures are holding hands, symbolising collective effort. This suggests that human capital formation is a collaborative process that involves the combined efforts of individuals, communities and governments.

4. On the basis of the given image, explain the source of human capital formation which may contribute to the economic growth in India. CBSE 2025; Competency Based Que

Or **Explain the role of quality education in human capital formation in a country.** CBSE 2024

Ans. One of the key sources of human capital formation that contributes to economic growth in India, which is highlighted in the image is education.

An educated and skilled workforce enhances productivity, innovation and economic development. The role of education in human capital formation is as follows

(i) An educated society facilitates a better development programme than an illiterate one.
(ii) Education improves productivity and prosperity and also improves the standard of living.
(iii) It does not only contribute towards the growth of the people, but also the development of society as a whole.
(iv) Education increases income and other cultural richness of human capital.

5. How can it be said that health and expenditure on information are crucial for human capital formation, considering that healthier individuals and access to information contribute to higher productivity and innovation? Competency Based Que

Ans. Health and expenditure on information are pivotal for human capital formation as they directly enhance an individual's productivity and efficiency.

Health as a Source of Human Capital Formation

Health is an important source of human capital formation because only a healthy worker can contribute towards increasing the capital stock of the country.

A sick worker, without access to medical facilities is compelled to abstain from work, and there is loss of productivity.

Expenditure on Information as a Source of Human Capital Formation

People spend to acquire information relating to the labour market, education and health institutions, etc. Information relating to job opportunities and educational institutes enables people to increase their earning potential. Therefore, it is also a determinant of human capital formation.

6. "National Education Policy, 2020 of India stresses a lot on in service teachers' training." In the light of the given statement, state and explain any two advantages of such on-the-job trainings in upliftment of education sector of any nation. CBSE 2024; Competency Based Que

Or **"On-the-job training enhances the skills and capabilities of employees, leading to improved performance, adaptability to new technologies, and better alignment with organisational goals." Justify the statement with valid argument.**

Ans. The statement that "on-the-job training enhances the skills and capabilities of employees, leading to improved performance, adaptability to new technologies and better alignment with organisational goals" can be justified through several key arguments

(i) **Skill Enhancement**
On-the-job training helps firms develop employee skills, crucial for human capital formation and increasing productivity.

(ii) **Labour Productivity**
By refining skills, employees can perform tasks more efficiently, contributing significantly to overall organisational output.

(iii) **Team Integration**
This training fosters familiarity among co-workers, enhancing collaboration and communication within teams.

(iv) **Immediate Feedback**
Supervisors can assess employee progress in real time, allowing for quick identification and correction of performance issues.

(v) **Organisational Efficiency**
The skills gained through training improve both individual performance and overall organisational efficiency, driving better alignment with strategic goals.

7. A skilled worker like software professional generates more income than an unskilled worker. Why? Competency Based Que

Ans. A skilled worker generates more income than an unskilled worker mainly because the productivity of an educated and skilled person is higher than an unskilled one. A skilled worker also commands higher earnings and gainful employment.

This is because they cannot be substituted easily, as it takes years to develop a workforce which is skilled in a particular field. On the other hand, an unskilled worker like a rickshaw puller can be easily substituted and such workers easily compromise on lesser earnings.

8. Describe why India is known as a knowledge economy?

Ans. India is known as a knowledge economy due to its focus on leveraging knowledge for economic growth and development. This shift emphasises sectors like IT, education, research and innovation.

Key factors include

(i) **Skilled Workforce**
A large pool of professionals in IT, engineering and medicine drives innovation and productivity.

(ii) **Technological Advancements**
India is a global leader in IT services, with cities like Bengaluru and Hyderabad excelling in tech and outsourcing.

(iii) **Education and Research**
Prestigious institutions like IITs and IIMs produce skilled graduates, while investments in R&D boost sectors like space, biotechnology and pharmaceuticals.

(iv) **Global Outsourcing Hub**
India provides skilled labour and tech solutions worldwide through its strong IT and BPO industries.

9. How can the expenditures related to migration be seen as an investment in human capital, despite the associated costs of relocation and adaptation?

Ans. Expenditure on Migration
People migrate in search of jobs with higher salaries than what they may get in their native places. People from rural areas migrate to urban areas in search of employment. Technically qualified persons, like engineers and doctors, migrate to other countries because of higher earnings in such countries.

Migration in both these cases involves cost of transport, higher cost of living in the migrated places and psychological costs of adapting to a new socio-cultural set-up. The increase in earnings in the new place outweighs these expenditures of migration. Hence, expenditure on migration is a source of human capital formation.

10. Why should migration and social medicine be viewed as investments in human capital? Justify with reasons.
CBSE SQP 2024; Competency Based Que

Ans. Migration occurs when people relocate to new areas in search of better opportunities, despite the high costs involved. The benefits gained from migration often surpass the expenditure, making it an investment in human capital formation.

Social medicine promotes health awareness among the population, resulting in healthier individuals and a more productive workforce. Investing in social medicine directly enhances human capital in the labour market and can therefore be considered an investment in human capital formation.

11. Based on the image given below, explain the role of economic growth, economic development and human capital formation. Competency Based Que

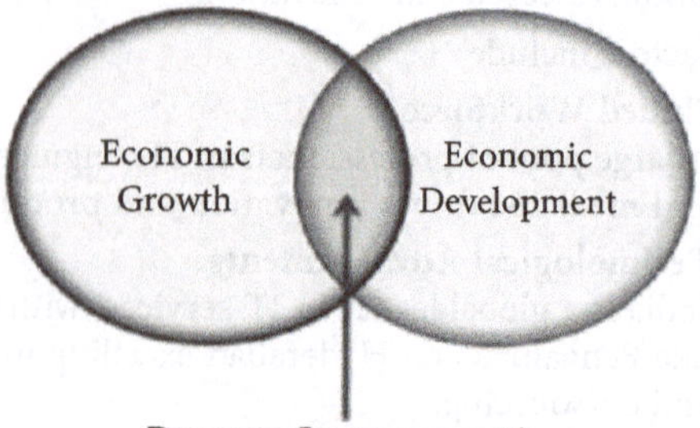

Ans. The process of human capital formation is responsible for economic and human development of the individuals, society and of any country.

Human capital formation increases the economic prosperity of the individual by generating more job opportunities. The economic prosperity brings social equality in a society. Human capital in the economy manages the economic growth of development.

Hence, all researchers consider that human capital is the most important resource of the community, which is more powerful than nature or wealth. In most countries, human capital determines the rate of development, economic, technological and scientific progress.

12. Interpret the image to explain how nurturing human capital contributes to economic growth?
Competency Based Que

Ans. Investment in human capital is believed to be positively related to economic growth. The contribution of human capital formation to economic growth can be explained as follows

(i) **Increase in Labour Productivity**
Investment in human capital through expenditure on education, health, etc. enhances the productivity of labour as they become physically fit and skilled in their jobs. It leads to efficient utilisation of the material inputs and capital. With increase in productivity, output increases at an increasing rate and hence economic growth accelerates.

(ii) **Innovations**
Human capital formation helps in preparing learned scientists and researchers in various subjects who bring out innovative products, technologies and processes and thus add to the economic growth.

(iii) **Capacity to Adopt**
Advanced technology can be adopted only if the skills and knowledge required for using that technology are present in the country.
Investment in education and on-the-job training helps to create these skills and enhances the knowledge base and thus helps in absorption of new technologies which leads to higher production and thus economic growth.

Thus, it is evident that human capital contributes to economic growth in various ways.

13. Examine the role of education in the economic development of a nation. NCERT

Ans. Following points show that education plays a significant role in economic development

(i) Education increases the receptivity of people to modern and scientific ideas. Thus, education increases the efficiency of people.

(ii) It results in greater awareness of available opportunities and mobility of labour.

(iii) It imparts to people knowledge, skills and attitude which would enable them to contribute to the productive programmes.

(iv) It produces skilled and trained personnel needed by the economy. Education prepares individuals as human resources.

14. What are the indicators of educational achievements in a country? NCERT

Ans. The indicators of educational achievements in a country are

(i) Adult literacy level.

(ii) Primary education completion rate.

(iii) Youth literacy rate.

15. "There is a downward trend in inequality world wide with a rise in the average education levels." Comment. NCERT; Competency Based Que

Ans. It is correct that education level reduces global inequality. Education imparts the knowledge and technical skills which enhance the productivity of people.

An educated person possesses higher productivity and efficiency and hence, a relatively higher income earning capacity. The higher income earning capacity and greater acceptability of modern techniques with rise in average education level across the world has raised the living standards and quality of life in the underdeveloped nations.

Distribution of income has become less skewed and income disparity between the rich and the poor is reducing across the world with better earning opportunities available due to rise in education levels.

Governments of different countries have been investing heavily in the education sector as rise in average education levels not only reduce inequality but also other problems like poverty, unemployment and underutilisation of resources.

16. What are the main problems of human capital formation in India? NCERT

Ans. The main problems of human capital formation in India are as follows

(i) **Rising Population**

Rapidly rising population adversely affects the quality of human capital in underdeveloped and developing countries like India. It reduces per head availability of existing facilities like sanitation, employment, drainage, water system, housing, hospitals, education, food supply, nutrition, roads, electricity, etc.

(ii) **Brain Drain**

Migration of highly skilled labour to foreign countries is termed as 'brain drain'. This slows down the process of human capital formation in the domestic economy.

(iii) **Inefficient Manpower Planning**

There is inefficient manpower planning in less developed countries where no efforts have been made either to raise the standard of education at different stages or to maintain the demand and supply of technical labour force. This leads to the wastage of human power and human skill.

(iv) **High Poverty Level**

A large proportion of the population lives below poverty line and do not have access to basic health and educational facilities. A large section of society cannot afford to get higher education or expensive medical treatment for major diseases.

17. Argue in favour of the need for different forms of government intervention in education and health sectors. NCERT

Ans. There is a need for different forms of government intervention in education and health sectors due to the following reasons

(i) Private sector is governed by profit motive and hence does not provide education and health facilities at a reasonable cost which may be affordable to all.

(ii) Standard of education and health needs to be maintained in order to develop human resources effectively and government intervention is needed for this.

(iii) Education and health are essential for social upliftment of backward and weaker sections of the society and government intervention in terms of policy and provision of infrastructure is required in education as well as health sector.

(iv) Regional disparities are prevalent in education and health in India which can be corrected only through government intervention at all levels as private sector would not be forthcoming for establishing schools or hospitals in remote or backward areas.

18. "It would be unclear to say that, the growth of human capital lays the ground for economic growth of a nation."

Do you agree with the given statement? Support your answer with valid illustrations. CBSE SQP 2025

Ans. Yes, an increase in human capital causes economic growth is unclear, owing to the problems pertaining to the estimation of quantifiable relation between the two. Educational yardsticks like years of schooling, teacher-pupil ratio, enrolment rates, etc. may not reflect educational quality accurately. Whereas, human capital measures may show convergence between developing and developed nations. However, there's no empirical evidence to prove income per capita convergence.

Hence, education may improve, but cannot guarantee similar progress in real income across different countries.

19. Discuss the need for promoting women's education in India. CBSE 2023; NCERT

Ans. Women have always been neglected when it comes to education in India. The access to education has always been biased towards male population due to our social system which is patriarchal.

The lack of education has caused exploitation of women and has resulted in a lower social status of women in India.

There is a need to promote women education in India, because of the following reasons

(i) Women education is essential for providing them economic independence and empowering them to save them from exploitation and domestic violence.

(ii) Women education is essential in order to raise the social status of women, so that the quality of life of women can be improved.

(iii) Educating woman helps in promoting family welfare programmes and thus, in population control.

(iv) Educated women are aware of the importance of healthcare and thus, take proper care of their family members contributing in human capital formation.

(v) Educating a woman means educating a family. An educated woman can inculcate moral values in her children and can facilitate their education.

20. "Expenditure on different levels of education in India is in the same proportion". Defend or refute the given statement, giving valid reasons. CBSE 2024 C

Ans. The statement is being refuted. In India, government expenditure on education is not evenly distributed across different levels. Elementary education receives the largest share of public spending, as it is critical for improving literacy rates and providing foundational learning. For instance, in 2014-15, the per capita public expenditure on elementary education varied significantly across states, such as ₹ 34,651 in Himachal Pradesh compared to ₹ 4,088 in Bihar.

In contrast, higher and tertiary education, including colleges and polytechnics, receives a smaller proportion of the total expenditure. However, expenditure per student is higher for tertiary education due to the higher costs involved.

Long Answer Type Questions

21. Explain the various sources of human capital.

Ans. Following are the sources of human capital

(i) **Education**

Investment in education is considered as one of the sources of human capital. Without education, human beings rely solely on physical labour. Investment in education gives human beings additional skills to do the same job.

It converts human beings into human capital, which enhances the labour productivity. This investment in education will ultimately increase the income of human beings in future.

(ii) **Health**

Health is another significant source of human capital. The health of a person affects human capital.

A sick person, without access to medical facilities, is unable to work efficiently leading to productivity loss.

Expenditure on health directly increases the supply of healthy labour force and hence, a source of human capital formation.

The various forms of health expenditure are

- Preventive medicine such as vaccination.
- Curative medicine such as interventions during illness.
- Social medicine such as spread of health literacy.
- Provision of clean drinking water.
- Good sanitation.

(iii) **On-the-job Training**

Firms incur expenditure on providing on-the-job training to their workers. Training imparts technical skills and know-how among the workers while working at the actual work site.

It helps in enhancing the productivity of the workers and facilitates better utilisation of raw materials. It enables workers to absorb values and standards of an organisation.

The workers may be trained by either of the following two methods

- Training within the firm under the supervision of a skilled worker.
- Off-campus training.

(iv) **Migration**

People migrate in search of jobs that fetch them higher salaries than what they may get in their native places. For instance, engineers and doctors migrate to other countries for higher salaries that they may get in such countries.

Migration involves transportation cost, higher cost of living in the migrated place and psychic cost of living in an unknown socio-culture set-up. However, the increased earnings at the new place outweigh the cost of migration. Hence, expenditure on migration is also a source of human capital formation.

(v) **Market Information**

People need to incur expenditure in order to acquire information related to equity markets, labour markets, education, health and other related markets. For instance, expenditure is incurred while collecting information related to education such as form fees, transportation cost, consultancy fee, etc.

22. Education is considered to be an important input for the development of a nation. How? NCERT

Ans. Education is the process of teaching, training, learning, imparting knowledge and developing skills. Education is an important input for the development of a nation in the following ways

(i) **Knowledge and Skills**

A better educated person has greater skills and knowledge which enhances productivity and therefore provides a greater opportunity to work and earn higher income.

(ii) **Rationality**

Education develops thinking process in people and helps them in making rational choices which lead to efficient utilisation of resources resulting in higher productivity.

(iii) **Values and Ethics**

Education inculcates moral values and professional ethics in people, making them law abiding citizens, who contribute towards the well-being of the nation.

(iv) **Adoption of Modern Technology**

Education develops the skills required for understanding and adopting modern technology. This helps in increasing output and growth of the nation.

(v) **Reduction in Income Inequality**

Education enhances the income earning capacity of people from economically backward sections of the country and thus reduces the inequalities in the distribution of income.

(vi) **Standard of Living**

Education raises the living standard of people by enhancing their earning capacity.

(vii) **Participation Rate**

Education makes a greater proportion of population capable of participating in the economic, social and political activities of a nation thus raising the participation of people in the development process.

23. Trace the relationship between human capital and economic growth. NCERT

Or

"Human capital formation gives birth to innovation, invention and technological improvements." Do you agree with the given statement?

Support your answer with valid arguments.

CBSE 2020; Competency Based Que

Ans. Yes, I agree with the given statement. Human capital is believed to be positively related to economic growth though, it is difficult to establish a relation of cause and effect from the growth of human capital to economic growth.

But we can see that human capital formation is related to economic growth in the following manner

(i) **Higher Productivity of Physical Capital**

Human capital increases productivity of physical capital, as skilled workers can handle machines or techniques better than the unskilled workers.

This increased productivity and production leads to economic growth.

(ii) **Innovative Skills**

Human capital facilitates innovation of new methods and techniques of production and this increases the rate of economic growth in the form of increase in GDP.

(iii) **Higher Rate of Participation and Equality**

Human capital formation leads to a higher employment rate. With increase in employment, the productivity rises.

Also, increase in employment opportunities increases the level of income and this helps in reducing inequalities of wealth.

(iv) **Brings Positive Outlook**

The process of human capital formation brings a positive outlook to the society which is different from orthodox and traditional ways of thinking, hence it increases the rate of participation in the workforce leading to an increase in the level of production and GDP.

24. Launched by the Government of India, "NEP 2020 seeks to address the challenges faced by the current education structure and align it with the needs of the 21st century." What are the key objectives and reforms introduced by NEP 2020 to achieve this goal?

Competency Based Que

Ans. NEP 2020 introduces several reforms aimed at modernising and transforming India's education system to meet the challenges of the 21st century. These reforms focus on creating a more holistic, flexible and inclusive education system that nurtures creativity, critical thinking and problem solving skills.

(i) **Holistic Approach**
The policy emphasises a holistic approach to education, integrating various dimensions like critical thinking, creativity and problem solving, ensuring that students are prepared for a rapidly changing world.

(ii) **School Education Changes**
One of the major reforms is the introduction of the National Curriculum Framework for School Education (NCFSE), which replaces the traditional 10+2 system with a more flexible 5 + 3 + 3 + 4 model. This includes

- Foundational Stage (3 years of pre-school + 2 years of Grade 1 and 2)
- Preparatory Stage (Grades 3 to 5)
- Middle Stage (Grades 6 to 8)
- Secondary Stage (Grades 9 to 12)

(iii) **Multilingual Education**
NEP 2020 places a strong emphasis on promoting multilingualism, encouraging students to learn in their mother tongue or regional language up to Grade 5, while also preserving and fostering India's rich cultural heritage.

(iv) **Higher Education Enhancements**
The policy promotes multidisciplinary education in higher education institutions, offering students the freedom to explore subjects across various disciplines. It also supports online education and encourages research and innovation in universities and colleges.

(v) **Vocational Education**
NEP 2020 introduces vocational education from Grade 6 onwards, providing students with practical skills that are critical for employment opportunities and self-reliance.

(vi) **Assessment Reforms**
NEP 2020 shifts the focus from rote learning to competency based assessments, which prioritise the application and understanding of knowledge over memorisation, ensuring that students develop the ability to solve real world problems.

These reforms are designed to make education more relevant, accessible and effective in preparing students for the challenges and opportunities of the 21st century.

25. What are the objectives and functions of NCERT, UGC, AICTE and ICMR?

Ans. Objectives and functions of different organisations are

(i) **National Council of Educational Research and Training** (NCERT)
NCERT is an autonomous organisation set-up in 1961 by the Government of India to assist and advise the Central and State Governments on policies and programmes for qualitative improvement in school education.

(ii) **University Grants Commission** (UGC)
The UGC, set-up in 1953, has the unique distinction of being the only grant giving agency in the country, which has been vested with two responsibilities, i.e. providing funds and coordinating, determining and maintaining standards in institutions of higher education.

(iii) **All India Council for Technical Education** (AICTE)
AICTE was set-up in November, 1945 as a national level apex advisory body to conduct survey on the facilities on technical education and to promote development in the country in a coordinated and integrated manner.

(iv) **Indian Council of Medical Research** (ICMR)
The Indian Research Fund Association (IRFA), re-designated as ICMR in 1949 in New Delhi, is the apex body in India for the formulation, coordination and promotion of biomedical research. It is one of the oldest medical research bodies in the world.

26. "Education commission 1964-66 had recommended that at least 6% of GDP must be spent on education." How far has India been able to achieve the said goal?

CBSE SQP 2020

Or **"Economists believe that India should spend atleast 6% of its GDP on education for achieving desired results." Justify the statement with valid reason.**

CBSE 2020; Competency Based Que

Ans. Yes, the current level of education expenditure is inadequate. It is only 4.13% in comparison to the desired level of 6% of GDP. More than 50 years ago, the education commission has recommended that atleast 6% of GDP should be spent on education, so as to make a noticeable rate of growth in educational achievements.

However, the investment in education expenditure has not been uniform and is marked with regional and gender inequalities.

India has also not been able to achieve the objective of providing free and compulsory education to all children in the age group of 6 to 14 years.

Government's unwillingness to spend 6% of GDP on education has affected this sector adversely, as is enumerated with the help of given statistics

(i) In India, about 30.3 crore people are still illiterate.
(ii) The female literacy rate is 65.46%, which is quite low as compared to male literacy rate of 82.14 per cent.
(iii) There is disparity in education levels of urban and rural areas.

The above said points highlight the need for India to spend atleast 6% of its GDP on education.

27. In your view, is it essential for the government to regulate the fee structure in education and healthcare institutions? If so, why? NCERT

Ans. Education and health are two basic requirements of human beings, so that they may be able to live a life of dignity. It is the responsibility of government to ensure access to education and health facilities even for the poorest of the poor. For this purpose, either the government should itself provide these services through government schools, colleges and hospitals or encourage private sector participation in these sectors.

As India has a vast population which still lacks healthcare and education, it does not seem feasible for government alone to fulfil the requirement in these sectors due to lack of resources. Hence, private sector is allowed to operate in these sectors.

But private sector works with profit as the primary motive and so, if government does not regulate the fee structure in education and healthcare institutions, the fee may become too high to be in affordable limits of common people. This will prevent the purpose of these facilities altogether. Thus, government must intervene and regulate the fee structure of even the private institutes in education and healthcare sectors.

28. "Various initiatives have been taken by the Government of India to improve the education system." Explain these initiatives briefly. Competency Based Que

Ans. The government has taken the following initiatives to improve the level of education in India

(i) **Right to Education**

In 2009, the Government of India has implemented the Right of Children to Free and Compulsory Education Act. This Act makes free education a fundamental right to all children in the age group of 6-14 years.

This landmark legislation aims to eliminate barriers to education, ensuring that every child has access to quality schooling. The RTE Act emphasises not only enrollment but also the retention and completion of education, making it a fundamental right.

(ii) **Provision of Education Cess**

The government is levying 2% education cess on all union taxes. The revenue from this is spent on providing elementary education in India. This initiative ensures that a dedicated fund is available to improve school facilities, teacher training and educational resources, particularly in rural and underserved areas.

By creating a steady financial stream, the government can undertake various educational programmes and infrastructure projects, thus ensuring that the quality of education is not compromised due to lack of funds.

(iii) **Other Measures**

The government sanctions a large outlay for the promotion of higher education and new loan schemes for students to pursue higher education.

A large outlay is sanctioned annually to improve infrastructure in universities and colleges, upgrade facilities and enhance research capabilities.

29. The Indian education system faces several challenges that hinder its progress and development. According to the Annual Status of Education Report (ASER) and studies by organisations such as NITI Aayog and UNESCO, issues such as poor infrastructure, lack of trained teachers, inadequate access to quality education in rural areas and gender inequality are persistent problems.

Additionally, the National Education Policy (NEP) 2020 seeks to address many of these challenges but implementation remains a hurdle.

In the context of this statement,

(i) Critically discuss the major challenges faced by the Indian education system.
(ii) Suggest potential reforms or solutions that could improve the situation. Competency Based Que

Ans. (i) The Indian education system is plagued by several challenges that impact its quality and reach

- **Inadequate Infrastructure**
  Many schools, particularly in rural areas, face issues with basic infrastructure like classrooms, sanitation, electricity and digital connectivity. This creates an environment that is not conducive to learning, especially for girls, who often drop out due to poor hygiene facilities.

- **Shortage of Trained Teachers**
  There is a significant shortage of well-trained teachers, especially in government schools. Many teachers lack proper qualifications and teacher absenteeism is high. In some regions, the student-teacher ratio is also highly skewed, affecting learning outcomes.
- **Access to Quality Education in Rural Areas**
  Students in rural and remote areas suffer from limited access to quality education due to a lack of resources, fewer qualified teachers and fewer opportunities for higher learning.
  Marginalised groups like scheduled castes, scheduled tribes and girls are disproportionately affected.
- **Learning Outcomes**
  Despite increased enrollment, learning outcomes remain poor.
  Studies like ASER report that a large percentage of children in higher grades cannot read or perform basic arithmetic at their expected level, reflecting gaps in the education system's efficacy.

(ii) To improve the Indian education system, targeted reforms are needed to address key challenges. The following solutions aim to ensure better educational outcomes

- **Improving Infrastructure and Digital Access**
  Investments in school infrastructure, especially in rural areas, should be prioritised. This includes providing functional toilets, electricity, internet access and safe classrooms. The government should also work towards closing the digital divide by providing affordable devices and internet for online learning.
- **Enhancing Teacher Training and Recruitment**
  Continuous professional development and training programmes for teachers, coupled with recruitment of well-qualified personnel, would help improve the quality of education. Teacher accountability measures and incentives for good performance can also ensure better teaching practices.

30. World Bank in its report, India and the knowledge economy – Leveraging strengths and opportunities, stated that India should make a transition to the knowledge economy and if it uses its knowledge as much as Ireland does, the per capita income of India will increase from US $ 1,000 in 2002 to US $ 3,000 in 2020. It further states that the Indian economy has all the key ingredients for making this transition such as a critical mass of skilled workers, a well-functioning democracy and a diversified science and technology infrastructure.

Competency Based Que

(i) Name the two independent reports on the Indian economy, which have identified that India would grow faster due to its strength in human capital formation.

(ii) What are the key ingredients of Indian economy for making a transition to the knowledge economy?

Ans. (i) The reports of the Deutsche Bank and World Bank Report on Indian economy. According to these two reports, India would develop faster because of its forte in human capital formation.

According to Deutsche Bank (a German Bank's) report on Global Growth Centres, it has been recognised that India will develop as one of four noteworthy development centers on the planet by 2020.

This report additionally said that between 2005 to 2020, we expect a 40% increase in the average of education in India, to simply over 7 years.

(ii) The following pillars are four critical requisites for a country to be able to fully participate in the knowledge economy

- **Education and Training**
  An educated and skilled population is needed to create, share and use knowledge.
- **Information Infrastructure**
  A dynamic information infrastructure ranging from radio to the internet is required to facilitate the effective communication, dissemination and processing of information.
- **Economic Incentive and Institutional Regime**
  A regulatory and economic environment that enables the free flow of knowledge, supports investment in Information and Communications Technology (ICT) and encourages entrepreneurship is central to the knowledge economy.
- **Innovation Systems**
  A network of research centres, universities, think tanks, private enterprises and community groups is necessary to tap into the growing stock of global knowledge, assimilate and adapt it to local needs and create new knowledge.

SELF ASSESSMENT TEST

Objective Type Questions

1. Expenditure on information and technology is a part of human capital expenditure as a result, India is known as knowledge economy due to development of
   (a) education sector (b) financial sector
   (c) health sector (d) IT sector

2. There is a need to promote education for women in India due to various reasons which include
   (a) it improves economic independence of women
   (b) it improves the social status of women
   (c) it has favourable impact on healthcare of women and children
   (d) All of the above

3. Physical capital .... with time.
   (a) appreciates (b) depreciates
   (c) Either (a) or (b) (d) None of these

4. Which of the following factors is most important for the formation of human capital?
   (a) Economic growth
   (b) Education and skill development
   (c) Increase in physical capital
   (d) Technological progress

5. Which of the following is not a characteristic of human capital?
   (a) Perishable
   (b) Accumulated through education and training
   (c) Can be transferred like physical capital
   (d) Adds value to the production process

6. Which of the following is a government initiative focused on improving healthcare in India?
   (a) Sarva Shiksha Abhiyan (b) Ayushman Bharat
   (c) Skill India Mission (d) Digital India

7. Which of the following statements is/are correct?
   I. Unemployment is a problem of human capital formation.
   II. In India, private expenditure on education is more as compared to government expenditure.

   Codes
   (a) Only I
   (b) Only II
   (c) Both I and II
   (d) None of the above

Answers 1. (d) 2. (d) 3. (b) 4. (b) 5. (c) 6. (b) 7. (c)

Short Answer Type Questions

8. Compare and contrast the concepts of human capital and physical capital.

9. Explain the concept of 'brain drain' and its impact on the process of human capital formation in India. Suggest measures to mitigate its effects.

10. Who regulates the education and health sectors in India?

11. A rural district in India has initiated a development programme focusing on improving the lives of its residents. The government is upgrading local schools, offering free vocational training for youth and organising regular health camps. In addition, community awareness programmes are being conducted to inform people about the importance of sanitation, nutrition and healthcare.

    Based on the case above, explain how the different elements of the programme contribute to the overall development of human capital in the rural area.

12. Why is it essential to improve the standard of higher education?

13. "An educated and healthy workforce is more productive." Explain this statement in the context of human capital formation in India.

14. Is rapidly rising population a constraint in the process of human capital formation? State with reference to the value of human resource.

Long Answer Type Questions

15. The process of human capital formation is closely linked with economic growth. Discuss the impact of human capital formation on the growth and development of the Indian economy, with reference to employment and productivity.

16. Explain briefly the various initiatives taken by the government to improve education in India.

17. "Although the government expenditure on education has increased over the years, yet it is far from satisfactory." Discuss.

05

CHAPTER

Rural development is important for India because even today more than two-third of India's population depends on agriculture which is not generating enough output to provide a decent living for them.

YOUR STUDY GOALS

5.1 Meaning of Rural Development
5.2 Rural Credit
5.3 Rural Banking: A Critical Appraisal
5.4 Agricultural Marketing
5.5 Diversification of Agricultural Activities
5.6 Sustainable Development and Organic Farming

YOUR PRACTICE GOAL

- Objective Type Questions (69 Qs ; MCQs, A-R, Statements, Matching, Concept Identification)
- Subjective Questions (23 SAs, 10 LAs)
- Self Assessment Test (7 MCQs, 7 SAs, 3 LAs)

Rural Development

5.1 Meaning of Rural Development

Rural development is a comprehensive term which essentially focuses on the development of areas that are lagging behind in the overall development of the village economy.

It is a process by which attempts are made to improve the standard of living of rural people.

Key Areas or Challenges in Rural Development

The challenges of rural development can be broadly grouped under two heads

Traditional or Lingering Challenges	Modern or Emerging Challenges
These challenges are being faced for a long time, e.g. Rural credit, agricultural marketing, etc.	These challenges are faced by the rural areas with the changing time, e.g. Organic farming, diversification of farm and non-farm activities, etc.

Areas for Rural Development

- Provision of adequate credit in the rural areas.
- Improving agricultural marketing.
- Problems related to organic farming.
- Honest implementation of land reforms.
- Providing opportunities to diversify farm and non-farm activities in rural areas.
- Development of human resources by providing opportunities for literacy (more specifically female literacy), education and skill development.
- Development of productive resources of each locality.
- Development of human resources by providing health facilities, addressing both sanitation and public health.
- Infrastructure development like electricity, irrigation and transport facilities for agriculture research and information expansion.
- Special measures for alleviation of poverty and bringing about significant improvement in the living conditions of the weaker sections by providing employment.

5.2 Rural Credit

It means providing credit to the farming community. It is the lifeline of the farming activity.
The credit needs of the farming community can be grouped on the basis of purpose and time.

Group	Category	Explanation
Credit Needs Based on Purpose	***Productive Borrowings***	Loans for buying seeds, fertilisers, agricultural equipment and implements.
	Unproductive Borrowings	Loans for social purposes like marriage, festive occasions, illness, death, etc.
Credit Needs Based on Time	***Long-term Credit*** (5 to 20 years)	Loans for acquiring permanent assets such as tractors, land, costly equipment, tubewells, etc.
	Medium-term Credit (12 months to 5 years)	Loans for purchasing machinery, constructing fences, digging wells, etc.
	Short-term Credit (6 to 12 months)	Loans for purchasing seeds, tools, manure, fertilisers, etc. These loans are often provided by cooperatives, moneylenders or banks.

Sources of Rural Credit

Credit in the rural sector is available from two sources

1. Non-institutional Sources

These sources are traditional source of agricultural credit and are not attached to any formal institution. No rules or regulations are applicable to these sources.

The major non-institutional sources of rural credit are moneylenders, friends, relatives, landlords, shopkeepers and commission agents.

Non-institutional sources of rural credit are not encouraged by government because of the following reasons

- They charge high rate of interest.
- They manipulate accounts to keep farmers in **debt-trap**. It is a situation in which farmers borrow more to pay the interest on the previous borrowings and ultimately end up in losing their land.

2. Institutional Sources

These sources of credit operate under the instructions of a formal institution.

The major institutional sources of rural credit are as follows

Source	Explanation
National Bank for Agriculture and Rural Development (NABARD)  NABARD	Set-up in 1982 as an apex body, NABARD coordinates activities of institutions in rural financing. It's main functions are • To grant long-term loans to state government to subscribe the share for cooperative societies' share capital. • To inspect cooperative banks, Regional Rural Banks (RRBs) and primary cooperative societies. • To promote research in agriculture and rural development. • To serve as a refinancing agency for institutions providing finance to rural and agricultural development. • To help tenant farmers and small farmers to consolidate their landholdings.
Commercial Banks	Introduced to agricultural credit under Banking Reforms Act, 1972, these banks provide credit for purchase of inputs, cattle, tractors and more. Post 1969 nationalisation, these banks have increased branches in rural areas.
Regional Rural Banks (RRBs)	Established under the Regional Rural Banks Act of 1976 to cater to the needs of small and marginal farmers, artisans and the weaker sections.
Land Development Banks	Provide long-term loans on the security of land for purchasing tractors, repaying debts, digging tubewells, etc.
Self Help Groups (SHGs)	SHGs provide small-scale loans without formal collateral. They promote savings and offer credit at nominal rates, mainly for consumption purposes. SHGs have empowered women, as nearly 6 crore women became members of 54 lakh women SHGs by May 2019.
Cooperative Credit Societies	These societies are actively engaged in addressing credit needs of the farmers, besides, offering a host of related services. Their main function is to provide timely credit flow to farmers and guidance in agricultural operations.

Micro-credit Programmes

About ₹ 10-15,000 per SHG and additional ₹ 2.5 lakh per SHG as a Community Investment Support Fund (CISF) are provided as part of renovating fund to encourage self-employment for income generation. This credit provision is referred to as micro-credit programmes.

Self Help Group

Role of Cooperatives in Rural Development

- Ensure timely and rapid flow of credit to farmers.
- Spread credit facilities across all regions of the country.
- Provide credit at low rates of interest.
- Eliminate the moneylenders as credit agencies.

5.3 Rural Banking : A Critical Appraisal

There has been rapid expansion of the banking system in rural areas. Rural banking has raised the level of rural farm and non-farm output, income and employment, especially after the green revolution.

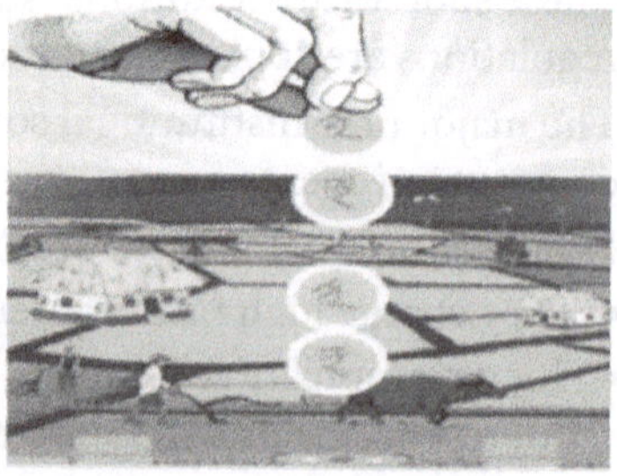

Advantages of Rural Banking

- Farm and non-farm output raised due to credit facilities and advisory services.
- Food security achieved with an abundant buffer stock of grains available now.
- Increased rural employment through availability of credit for self-employment schemes.

Limitations of Rural Banking

- Small and marginal farmers receive only a small portion of institutional credit.
- Rural banking is suffering from high over dues and default rates.
- Inadequate sources of institutional finance to meet the requirements of agricultural credit.
- Regional inequalities in the distribution of institutional credit.
- Apart from commercial banks, there is a lack of development in deposit mobilisation, lending practices and loan recovery in other formal institutions.

To *overcome* the above limitations, banks and farmers need to change their approach

– Banks need to shift from transactional lending to relationship banking.
– Farmers should adopt efficient utilisation of financial resources.

5.4 Agricultural Marketing

It is a process that involves functions of assembling, storage, processing, packaging, transportation, grading and distribution of agricultural commodities throughout the country.

Need of Agricultural Marketing

The need for agricultural marketing arises due to problems faced by farmers, as outlined below

- Farmers face issues of faulty weighing and manipulation of accounts when selling their produce to traders.
- Lack of knowledge about prevailing market prices forces farmers to sell their produce at low prices.
- Farmers often lack proper storage facilities to hold their produce to sell at better price later, leading to about 10% of agricultural produce being wasted.

Therefore, government intervention became necessary to regulate private traders' activities.

Measures taken by Government to Improve Agricultural Marketing

Four measures were initiated to improve the agricultural marketing which are discussed below

1. Regulation of Markets

- First measure is the regulation of markets to create orderly and transparent marketing conditions.
- Regulated markets are established where sale and purchase of produce is monitored by a market committee having government, farmer and trader representatives.
- There is still a need to develop about 27,000 rural periodic markets as regulated market places.

2. Improvement in Physical Infrastructure

- Second measure is to address inadequate infrastructure (roads, railways, warehouses, cold storages, processing units, etc.) to meet growing demand.
- Through this measure, government ensures to enhance physical infrastructure.

3. Cooperative Marketing

- Third measure is to ensure that farmers get a fair price for their produce.
- Government encourages farmers to form producer marketing cooperative societies for better bargaining power.
- Success of milk cooperatives in transforming the social and economic landscape of Gujarat and other parts is testimony to the role of cooperatives.

- Challenges faced by cooperative marketing are
  - Inadequate member (farmers) coverage.
  - Lack of appropriate links between marketing and processing cooperatives.
  - Inefficient financial management.

4. Supportive Policies

Fourth measure taken by government includes supportive policies. These include

Policy	Explanation
Minimum Support Price (MSP)	Guarantees farmers a minimum price by government for their produce, allowing sales above MSP in open markets.
Buffer Stocks Maintenance	Government purchases wheat and rice at MSP to maintain buffer stocks when market prices are low.
Public Distribution System (PDS)	Uses government-purchased stocks to distribute foodgrains and essentials at subsidised prices through fair price shops.

These measures aim to protect farmers' incomes and provide foodgrains at subsidised rate to the poor. However, private trade continues to dominate the agricultural market despite government interventions.

Emerging Alternative Marketing Channels

In India, alternative marketing channels are emerging through which farmers sell their produce directly to consumers, increasing their share in the prices paid by consumers.

Examples of Alternative Channels

- Apni mandi (Established in Punjab, Haryana and Rajasthan)
- Rythu bazars (Focused on vegetables and fruits in Andhra Pradesh)
- Uzhavar sandies (Farmers' markets in Tamil Nadu)
- Hadaspar mandi (Located in Pune)

Contractual Alliances

- National and international fast food chains and hotels are also forming contracts with farmers to supply them farm products of desired quality.
- Farmers receive seeds, inputs and assurances for procurement of produce at pre-decided prices.
- These alternative channels help in
  - Reducing price risks for farmers.
  - Expanding market access for farm products.

5.5 Diversification of Agricultural Activities

It implies the provision of alternate employment opportunities for the labour force engaged in agriculture. Diversification is an emerging challenge in the context of rural development.

It has two aspects

Diversification of Crop Production	Diversification of Productive/Non-farm Activities
• Implies a shift from single cropping to multiple cropping systems. • It may also mean a shift from subsistence to commercial farming. • Important for enhancing overall agricultural productivity. • Reduces risks associated with monsoon failure. • Minimises market risks due to price fluctuations.	• Implies a shift from crop farming to other productive activities such as animal husbandry, fisheries, horticulture, etc. • Focus is on allied activities, non-farm employment and emerging alternatives. • Reduces risk from the agricultural sector. • Provides sustainable livelihood options for rural population. • Enhances ecological balance.

Need for Diversification into Productive/Non-farm Activities

Need for diversification arises due to the following reasons

1. **Seasonal Nature of Agriculture**
   - Agricultural activities are primarily seasonal (e.g. Concentrated in Kharif season).
   - These are limited employment opportunities during the Rabi season, especially in areas with inadequate irrigation facilities.

   Thus, there is a need to focus on allied activities, non-farm employment and other emerging alternatives of livelihood.
2. **Overcrowded Agricultural Sector** As agricultural sector is overcrowded, thus a significant proportion of the growing labour force needs to find alternate employment in non-farm sectors.

Tamil Nadu Women in Agriculture (TANWA)

- It is a project to train the women about the latest agricultural techniques. It involves women in latest agricultural techniques to increase the agricultural productivity and enhance the family income.
- A group of trained women runs a farm in Thiruchirapalli. They make vermicompost and earn a good income.
- Some other groups of women are creating savings through micro-credit system. The accumulated funds are used to promote small-scale household activities, e.g. Production of mushroom, manufacturing of soap, doll making, etc to generate income.

Segments of Productive/Non-farm Activities

Non-farm activities comprise various segments, with some experiencing healthy growth (e.g. Agro processing, food processing, leather and tourism) while others remain at a subsistence level with low productivity. Traditional home-based industries like pottery, craftsmanship handlooms, etc. show potential but lack adequate infrastructure and support.

Some non-farm activities are discussed below

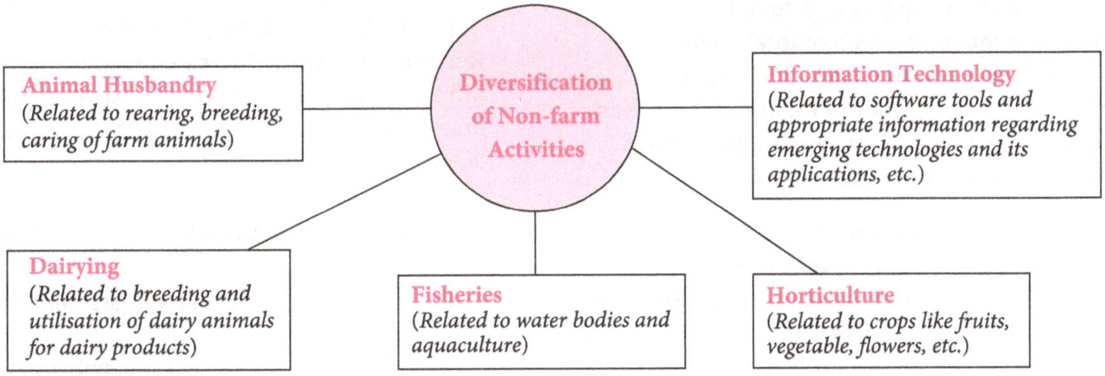

1. Animal Husbandry

- **Farming System** Mixed-crop livestock farming, cattle, goats and poultry are common.
- **Share** Poultry accounts for 61% of livestock production; followed by cattle and buffaloes at 22%.
- **Benefits**
  - Provides income stability, food security transport, fuel and nutrition.
  - Significant employment opportunities for women.
  - Alternative livelihoods for small and marginal farmers.
- **Challenges** Low productivity compared to other countries.
- **Improvements Needed**
  - Better technology and animal breeds to enhance productivity.
  - Enhanced veterinary care and credit access to small and marginal farmers.

2. Dairying

- **Growth** Milk production has increased over ten times (1951-2016) due to ***operation flood***.
- **System of Operation Flood**
  - Farmers can pool their milk produce based on quality.
  - The pooled milk is processed and marketed to urban centers through cooperatives.
  - Farmers are assured of fair prices and stable income from the supply of the milk to urban markets.
- **States Leading in Milk Production** Gujarat, Madhya Pradesh, Uttar Pradesh, Andhra Pradesh, Maharashtra, Punjab, Rajasthan.
- **Diversity** Meat, eggs, wool and other by-products also emerging as important productive sectors for diversification.

3. Fisheries

- **Community Perception** Water bodies regarded as a 'provider' or 'mother'.
- **Production Sources**
  - 65% from inland sources (rivers, lakes, ponds, streams, etc).
  - 35% from marine sources (sea and oceans).
- **Economic Contribution** Today, total fish production accounts for 0.9% of total GDP.
- **Major Producing States** Kerala, Maharashtra, Gujarat, West Bengal, Andhra Pradesh, Tamil Nadu.
- **Workforce** 60% in export marketing and 40% in internal marketing are women.
- **Challenges**
  - Uncontrolled unemployment
  - Low per capita earnings
  - Lack of mobility of labour
  - Indebtedness
  - Illiteracy
  - Inadequate credit facilities
- **Recommendations** Increase credit facilities through cooperatives and SHGs. Also, reorient welfare programmes for long-term gains and sustainability.

4. Horticulture

- **Crop Diversity** Adoption of growing diverse horticulture crops like fruits, vegetables, tubers, flowers, medicinal plants, spices and plantation crops.
- **Economic Impact** Contributes nearly one-third of agricultural output and 6% of GDP of India.
- **Leadership in Production** India is emerged as world leader in producing variety of fruits like mangoes, bananas, coconuts, cashew nuts and is the second largest producer of fruits and vegetables.
- **Benefits**
  - Improved livelihoods, especially for marginalised communities and women.
  - High revenue employment options for women (rural areas) in nursery maintenance, hybrid seed production and food processing.
- **Recommendations** Increase in investment for infrastructure (like electricity, cold storage), marketing linkages, small-scale processing units and technology.

Adoption of Village by Parliamentarians

In October, 2014, The Government of India introduced a new scheme called Saansad Adarsh Gram Yojana (SAGY). Under this scheme

- Members of India's Parliament were required to identify and develop one village from their constituencies.
- To begin with, MPs can develop one village as a model village by 2016 and two more by 2019, covering over 2,500 villages in India.
- As per this scheme, the village can have a population of 3,000-5,000 in the plains and 1,000-3,000 in the hills and should not be MP's own or their spouse's village.
- MPs are expected to facilitate a village development plan, motivate villagers to take up activities and build infrastructure in the areas of health, nutrition and education.

5. Information Technology

- **Revolutionising Sectors** IT has transformed various sectors of the Indian economy, significantly impacting rural areas.
- **Supporting Sustainable Development**
  - IT helps unlock the creative potential and knowledge embedded in the people.

– Enables the government to identify areas at risk of food insecurity and vulnerability through data analysis and appropriate software tools, allowing timely interventions to prevent or reduce likelihood of emergency.

- **Agricultural Management**
  – Assists in predicting weather patterns crucial for farming.
  – Provides expert advice on crop management and pest control.
  – Helps in managing the storage conditions of fertilisers and pesticides.
- **Enhancing Crop Production** Educates farmers about the latest equipment, technologies and resources, leading to improved crop quality and quantity.
- **Employment Generation** IT has the potential to create job opportunities in rural areas, contributing to local economic development.

5.6 Sustainable Development and Organic Farming

Conventional agriculture uses chemical fertilisers and toxic pesticides that penetrate the water resources, harm the livestock, deplete the soil and devastate natural ecosystem.

Thus, there is a need for eco-friendly technology to address these issues and promote sustainable development.

Efforts in evolving eco-friendly technologies are essential and one such technology which is eco-friendly is **organic farming**.

Organic farming is a system of farming that relies upon the use of organic inputs (like green manure, compost, biological pest control, etc.) for cultivation.

This technology restores, maintains and enhances the ecological balance and there is an increasing demand for organically grown food worldwide due to concerns about food safety.

Organic Food

- Gaining popularity globally.
- Command higher price of around 10-100% more than conventional food.
- Many retail chains and super markets are accorded with green status for selling organic products.

Benefits and Limitations of Organic Farming

Benefits	Limitations
• Replaces costly inputs (HYV seeds, chemical fertilisers, etc.) with locally produced cheaper organic inputs thereby improving returns. • Generates income through exports. • Requires more labour, making it suitable for India. • Produces healthier, pesticide-free food with higher nutritional value. • Promotes environmentally sustainable production.	• Requires farmers' awareness and willingness to adopt new technology. • Lacks adequate infrastructure and has marketing challenges. • Lower initial yields compared to modern farming methods. • Thus, small and marginal farmers may struggle with large-scale production. • Organic produce has a shorter shelf life. • Limited options for off-season crop production.

Organically Produced Cotton in Maharashtra

- Cotton, the biggest user of chemical pesticides, is now grown organically. At present, 130 farmers have committed 1,200 hectares of land to grow cotton organically and the cotton produced by them has been found to be of high quality.
- Kisan Mehta, the pioneer of this movement, believe that 78 percent of Indian farmers are marginal farmers who own about less than 0.8 hectares but account for 20 per cent of India's cultivable land. For such farmers, organic agriculture is more profitable in terms of money and soil conservation in the long-run.

Mind Map

RURAL DEVELOPMENT

1 Meaning of Rural Development

Rural development is a process by which attempts are made to improve the standard of living of rural people.

The challenges of rural development can be broadly grouped under traditional or lingering challenges and modern or emerging challenges.

Areas for Rural Development

- Provision of adequate credit in the rural areas.
- Improving agricultural marketing.
- Problems related to organic farming.
- Honest implementation of land reforms.
- Development of human resources.
- Providing opportunities to diversify farm and non-farm activities in rural areas.
- Development of productive resources of each locality.
- Development of human resources by providing health facilities, addressing both sanitation and public health.
- Infrastructure development like electricity, irrigation and transport facilities.
- Special measures for alleviation of poverty.

2 Rural Credit

It means providing credit to the farming community. It is the lifeline of the farming activity. The credit needs of the farming community can be grouped on the basis of purpose and time.

- **Purpose** Productive and unproductive borrowings
- **Time** Long-term, medium-term and short-term credit

Sources

1. **Non-institutional Sources** These sources are traditional source of agricultural credit and are not attached to any formal institution.
2. **Institutional Sources** These sources of credit operate under the instructions of a formal institution. Major sources include National Bank for Agriculture and Rural Development (NABARD), commercial banks, Regional Rural Banks (RRBs), land development banks, Self Help Groups (SHGs) and cooperative credit societies.

3 Rural Banking: A Critical Appraisal

There has been rapid expansion of the banking system in rural areas. Rural banking has raised the level of rural farm and non-farm output, income and employment, especially after the green revolution.

Advantages of Rural Banking

- Farm and non-farm output raised due to credit facilities and advisory services.
- Food security achieved with an abundant buffer stock of grains available now.
- Increased rural employment through availability of credit for self-employment schemes.

Limitations of Rural Banking

- Small and marginal farmers receive only a small portion of institutional credit.
- Rural banking is suffering from high over dues and default rates.
- Inadequate sources of institutional finance to meet the requirements of agricultural credit.
- Regional inequalities in the distribution of institutional credit.
- Apart from commercial banks, there is a lack of development in deposit mobilisation, lending practices and loan recovery in other formal institutions.

4 Agricultural Marketing

It is a process that involves functions of assembling, storage, processing, packaging, transportation, grading and distribution of agricultural commodities throughout the country.

Need

- Farmers face issues of faulty weighing and manipulation of accounts when selling their produce to traders.
- Lack of knowledge about prevailing market prices forces farmers to sell their produce at low prices.
- Farmers often lack proper storage facilities to hold their produce to sell at better price later, leading to about 10% of agricultural produce being wasted.

Measures taken by Government to Improve Agricultural Marketing

- **Regulation of Markets** First measure is the regulation of markets to create orderly and transparent marketing conditions.
- **Improvement in Physical Infrastructure** Second measure is to address inadequate infrastructure to meet growing demand.
- **Cooperative Marketing** Third measure is to ensure that farmers get a fair price for their produce.
- **Supportive Policies** These include minimum support price, buffers stocks maintenance and public distribution system.

5 Diversification of Agricultural Activities

It implies the provision of alternate employment opportunities for the labour force engaged in agriculture. It involves diversification of crop production and diversification of productive/non-farm activities.

Need for Diversification into Productive/Non-farm Activities

- Seasonal nature of agriculture
- Overcrowded agricultural sector

Segments of Productive/Non-farm Activities

- Animal husbandry
- Dairying
- Fisheries
- Horticulture
- Information technology

6 Sustainable Development and Organic Farming

Conventional agriculture uses chemical fertilisers and toxic pesticides that penetrate the water resources, harm the livestock, deplete the soil and devastate natural ecosystem. Thus, there is a need for eco-friendly technology to address these issues and promote sustainable development. Efforts in evolving eco-friendly technologies are essential and one such technology which is eco-friendly is **organic farming.** Organic farming is a system of farming that relies upon the use of organic inputs for cultivation.

EXAM PATTERN QUESTIONS

Objective Type Questions

Multiple Choice Questions (MCQs)

1. **Which of the following is a combination of factors necessary for rural development?**

(a) Agricultural productivity, rural infrastructure, literacy rate
(b) Land reforms, industrial development, human capital formation
(c) Employment generation, education, land concentration
(d) Agricultural diversification, financial inclusion, gender equality

2. **"If India has to make real progress, it has to develop its rural areas."**
Which of the following is incorrect reason for the above mentioned statement?

CBSE Term I 2021; Competency Based Que

(a) Approximately one-third population of rural India still lives in abject poverty
(b) More than 50 per cent of India's population depends on agriculture for their livelihood
(c) Growth rate in the Indian agriculture sector has been quite lower than of other sector
(d) Majority of rural people have access to the basic necessities of life

3. **Which among the following is/are the key challenge(s) in rural development?** **Competency Based Que**

I. Honest implementation of land reforms
II. Development of productive activities
III. Improving agricultural marketing
IV. Enhancing rural financial literacy and access to credit

Codes

(a) I, II and III
(b) II, III and IV
(c) I, III and IV
(d) All of these

4. **Complete the table.**

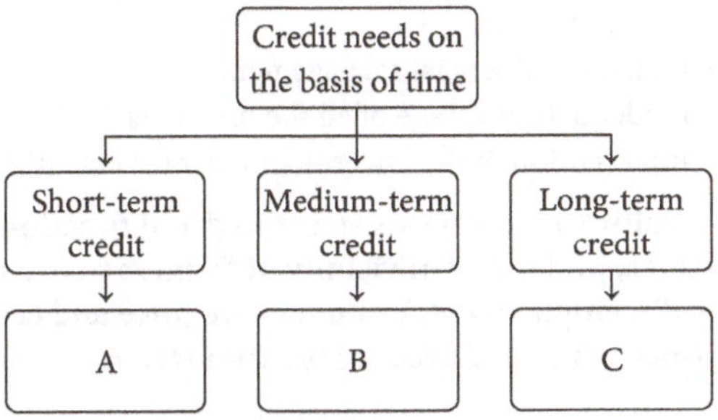

(a) A-3 to 12 months, B-1 to 3 years, C-3 years to 15 years
(b) A-6 to 12 months, B-1 to 5 years, C-5 years to 20 years
(c) A-1 to 12 months, B-1 to 4 years, C-4 years to 10 years
(d) A-3 to 6 months, B-2 to 5 years, C-10 years to 30 years

5. **Which of the following best explains why informal credit sources, such as moneylenders, continue to dominate in rural areas despite the availability of formal banking institutions?** **Competency Based Que**

I. Accessibility
II. Interest rates
III. Trust issues
IV. Government regulations

Codes

(a) I and III
(b) II and IV
(c) I, II and III
(d) All of these

6. **……… is the apex institution which plans and evaluates policies related to rural credit needs.** **CBSE 2023**

(a) Cooperative credit societies
(b) Regional rural banks
(c) Self help groups
(d) NABARD

7. **The institutional structure of rural banking in contemporary India consists of a set of multi-agency institutions, namely, ……… .**

CBSE SQP 2025; Competency Based Que

(i) regional rural banks
(ii) cooperative banks
(iii) land development banks
(iv) commercial banks

Codes

(a) (i) and (iv)
(b) (i), (iii) and (iv)
(c) (i), (ii) and (iii)
(d) (i), (ii), (iii) and (iv)

8. **Distribution of Outstanding Loan of Cultivator Households** (Rural)

S.No.	Credit	1971	2002
(i)	Government	7.1	1.7
(ii)	Cooperative Societies/Banks	22	30.2
(iii)	Commercial Bank	2.4	26.3
(iv)	Traders	8.4	2.6
(v)	Relatives and Friends	13.1	6.2

Sources *NSS 48th Round, Report No. 420 NSS 59th Round, Report No. 501*

Which institutional agency (As given in the above table) has shown the maximum increase in the share of outstanding loan to cultivators? **CBSE Term I 2021; Competency Based Que**

(a) Relatives and friends
(b) Commercial banks
(c) Cooperatives banks
(d) Traders

9. **Headline, Times of India, 2024: "New initiatives in rural credit aim to boost agricultural productivity." Which of the following is a false statement regarding rural credit as per the headline?** **Competency Based Que**

(a) NABARD provides refinancing facilities for rural credit
(b) Kisan Credit Cards (KCC) are issued to ensure easy access to credit
(c) Agricultural credit is exclusively provided by formal sources
(d) Regional Rural Banks (RRBs) play a significant role in providing agricultural loans

10. **The scheme of 'micro finance' is extended through ...... credit provision.** **CBSE 2024**

(a) self help groups
(b) land development banks
(c) regional rural banks
(d) commercial banks

11. **Which of the following statements is not true?**

(a) Self help group was established in 1975
(b) Self help group provides macrofinance to farmers
(c) Self help group charges low rate of interest
(d) Self help group has helped in the empowerment of women

12. **Kavitha, a farmer in rural India, is a recipient of a government scheme named......... .**

This scheme helps her set-up a bank account and provides insurance, overdraft and other social security benefits. **CBSE SQP 2023**

(a) Sansad Adarsh Gram Yojana
(b) Jan Dhan Yojana
(c) Kudumbashree
(d) NABARD

13. **Identify the alternate marketing channel that operates majorly in Punjab, Haryana and Rajasthan.** **CBSE 2024 C**

(a) Apni mandi (b) Hadapsar mandi
(c) Rythu bazars (d) Uzhavar sandies

14. **Which of the following is a challenge faced by rural banking?**

(a) High literacy rates
(b) Urban-centric policies
(c) Excessive competition from urban banks
(d) Improved infrastructure

15. **Identify, which of the following alternative indicates towards incorrect components combination of agricultural marketing system?** **CBSE 2024**

(a) Assembling, storage, processing, packaging
(b) Production, assembling, processing, grading
(c) Assembling, processing, packaging, transportation
(d) Processing, packaging, grading, distribution

16. **Study the following image and identify the measure adopted by the government to improve agricultural marketing.** **CBSE 2025**

(a) Cooperative credit societies
(b) Regulated markets
(c) Transportation facilities
(d) Dissemination of information

17. **The government has introduced a new marketing scheme where farmers can directly sell their produce to consumers, bypassing middlemen. This has led to better profit margins for farmers but has also created concerns regarding the regulation of prices and quality. What is a significant advantage of the new marketing scheme?** **Competency Based Que**

(a) Increased dependency on middlemen
(b) Higher profit margins for farmers
(c) Lower consumer prices due to reduced supply chain costs
(d) Enhanced consumer choice and access to fresh produce

18. **Cooperative marketing societies have faced a downfall in the recent years. Identify which of the following was not a reason behind its downfall.** **CBSE Term I 2021; Competency Based Que**

(a) Lack of coordination between processing and marketing societies
(b) Inefficient financial management
(c) Inadequate coverage of all the members
(d) Intervention of the government is most essential

19. **Agriculture sector needs structured and functional markets, preferably in vicinity of farmers to drive growth, employment, remunerative price and economic prosperity in rural areas of the country.**

Enabling mechanism were also required to be put in place for procurement of agricultural commodities directly from farmers' field and to establish effective linkage between the farm production, the retail chain and food processing industries.

Agriculture being a state subject, a Model APMC Act was formulated and circulated to the States/UTs in the year 2003 for adoption.

What is APMC as highlighted in the above said statement? **Competency Based Que**

(a) Agricultural Produce Market Committee
(b) Agricultural Production and Marketing Circle
(c) Allied Product and Market Committee
(d) None of the above

20. ...... can be classified as one of the alternative sources of diversification from farm output. **CBSE 2024 C**

(a) Green revolution (b) Horticulture
(c) Organic farming (d) Conventional farming

21. A village in India successfully implemented a diversification programme where farmers started growing fruits, vegetables and medicinal plants alongside their traditional crops. This initiative led to a significant increase in household incomes and reduced seasonal unemployment.

Which of the following is a primary benefit observed in this village due to diversification? **Competency Based Que**

(a) Increased reliance on single crops
(b) Higher household incomes
(c) Decreased land productivity
(d) Loss of traditional farming practices

22. What role do cooperatives play in agricultural diversification?

(a) They restrict farmers' choices
(b) They provide financial and technical support
(c) They focus solely on traditional crops
(d) They eliminate market competition

23.

Handicraft Poultry Dairy

Above image indicates which of the following to help generation of sustainable livelihood?

(a) Diversification in production technic
(b) Diversification in the production activities
(c) Agricultural marketing
(d) None of the above

24. White revolution is associated with .... **CBSE 2025**

(a) horticulture (b) fisheries
(c) dairy production (d) animal husbandry

25. Study the following picture

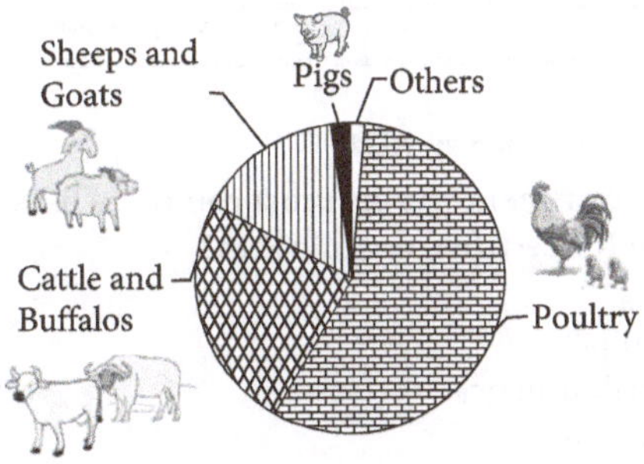

Identify the kind of activities, which may be envisaged under .... as diversification activity. **CBSE 2024**

(a) animal husbandry (b) fisheries
(c) horticulture (d) organic farming

26. During the period 1951-2016, ... led to an increase in the milk production in India by about ten times. **CBSE SQP 2025**

(a) green revolution (b) golden revolution
(c) operation flood (d) industrial revolution

27. Identify the incorrect statement from the following. **CBSE Term I 2021; Competency Based Que**

(a) Horticulture has emerged as a successful sustainable livelihood option for farmers in India
(b) Horticulture is an important sector for potential diversification and value addition in agriculture
(c) India is blessed with supportive climatic and soil conditions for horticulture
(d) Horticulture is the business related to producing, storing and distributing foodgrains

28. IT-enabled 'Smart Agriculture' has been adopted by farmers in a region. While crop yields increased initially, a drought led to significant crop failure.

What IT-based solution could help prevent such losses in the future? **Competency Based Que**

(a) Integrating weather forecasting models with crop management systems
(b) Using blockchain to track and verify farm to market supply chains
(c) Implementing Virtual Reality (VR) to simulate optimal farming practices
(d) Developing mobile applications that teach organic farming techniques

29. .... farming is the system that restores, maintains and enhance the ecological balance. **CBSE 2024**

(a) Conventional (b) Chemical
(c) Organic (d) Multi-layered

30. **Top Ten Countries in terms of Largest Certified Organic Area**

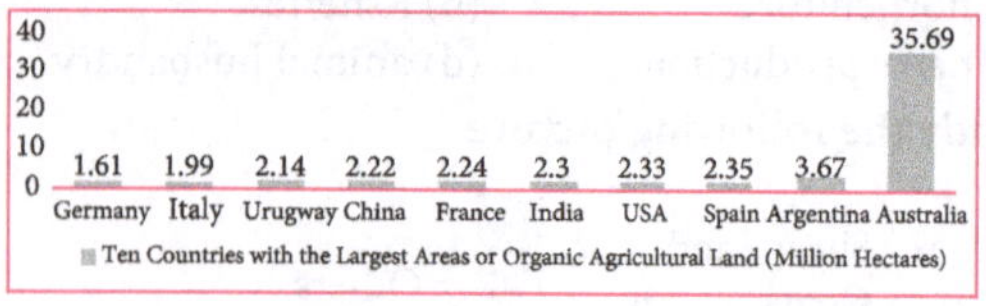

Source *FiBL Survey 2021*

Which continent has the most countries listed in the top ten for certified organic area?

(a) Asia
(b) Europe
(c) North America
(d) Australia

Direction *Read the following case study and answer the questions 31 to 34 on the basis of the same*

ABC village in Bihar was benefitted by Saansad Adarsh Gram Yojana (SAGY). The Government of India introduced this scheme in October, 2014. Under this scheme, Members of India's Parliament need to identify and develop one village from their constituencies.

To begin with, MPs can develop one village as a model village by 2016 and two more by 2019, covering over 2,500 villages in India.

According to the scheme, the village can have a population of 3,000-5,000 in the plains and 1,000-3,000 in the hills and should not be MPs' own or their spouse's village. MP's are expected to facilitate a village development plan, motivate villagers to take up activities and built infrastructure in the areas of health, nutrition and education.

31. **Which of the following statement is correct about the SAGY scheme?**

(a) Under this scheme, a village can be developed as a model village
(b) The village under this scheme should have a maximum population of 5,000 in plains
(c) The village under this scheme should not be MP's own village
(d) All of the above

32. **A village having a population of 3,500 in the hills is .... in SAGY scheme.**

33. **In which year SAGY scheme was introduced by Government of India?**

(a) 2004
(b) 2014
(c) 2008
(d) 2015

34. **Under SAGY scheme villagers are .... to take up activities.**

Direction *Read the following case study and answer the questions 35 to 38 on the basis of the same*

Sunita owns a small farm in Karnataka where she practices organic farming. She switched from conventional farming to organic farming three years ago after realising the harmful effects of chemical pesticides and fertilisers on both the environment and human health.

Since then, she has seen improvements in soil health and crop yield. Sunita uses compost, organic manure and biopesticides made from neem and garlic. However, she faces challenges in marketing her produce because organic products are priced higher and many consumers are not willing to pay the premium. To overcome this, she has started educating consumers about the benefits of organic farming through social media and local farmer markets.

35. **What is one of the key advantages for consumers who buy organic products?**

(a) They are always cheaper than conventional products
(b) Organic products contain fewer preservatives and synthetic chemicals
(c) Organic products are always more attractive in appearance than conventional ones
(d) Organic products are grown with higher amounts of chemical fertilisers

36. **Which of the following is a significant economic challenge for farmers transitioning to organic farming?**

(a) Higher yield in the initial years of organic cultivation
(b) The high cost of organic certification and longer conversion period
(c) Immediate increase in consumer demand for their products
(d) Easier access to government subsidies for organic practices

37. **By switching to organic farming, Sunita has observed improvements in both .... and ....**

38. **To overcome the challenge of marketing her produce, Sunita has begun educating consumers about the .... and .... benefits of organic farming.**

Assertion-Reason

Direction (Q.No. 39 to 48) *Read the following Assertion (A) and Reason (R) and choose the correct alternative from the following*

Alternatives

(a) Both Assertion (A) and Reason (R) are true and Reason (R) is the correct explanation of Assertion (A)
(b) Both Assertion (A) and Reason (R) are true, but Reason (R) is not the correct explanation of Assertion (A)
(c) Assertion (A) is true, but Reason (R) is false
(d) Assertion (A) is false, but Reason (R) is true

39. **Assertion** (A) Rural development in India is a core element for overall development of the nation.

Reason (R) More than two-third of India's population depends on agriculture. **CBSE Term I 2021**

40. **Assertion** (A) During 2014-15, the GVA growth rate of agriculture and its allied sectors was less than 19%.

Reason (R) Decrease in public investment since 1991 was the main reason for this trend.

41. **Assertion** (A) At the time of independence, money lenders exploited small and marginal farmers by lending to them at a high rate.

Reason (R) Such farmers did not have access of institutional sources of credit.

42. **Assertion** (A) Government initiatives like Kisan Credit Card (KCC) scheme aim to meet the credit needs of rural farmers by providing flexible, low-interest loans.

Reason (R) Rural farmers prefer informal sources of credit because of their ease of access and lack of formal procedures.

43. **Assertion** (A) Rural development programmes focus on improving agricultural productivity to raise the income levels of farmers.

Reason (R) Rural areas have abundant non-agricultural employment opportunities, which makes agriculture a secondary source of income for most rural households.

44. **Assertion** (A) Diversification of agriculture is important for sustainable rural development.

Reason (R) Diversification reduces dependency on traditional crops and helps in generating higher incomes through horticulture, dairy and fisheries.

45. **Assertion** (A) Cooperative farming improves productivity and profitability for small and marginal farmers.

Reason (R) In cooperative farming, farmers pool their resources, land and labour, which helps in reducing production costs and increasing efficiency.

46. **Assertion** (A) Microfinance Institutions (MFIs) have become a popular source of agricultural credit for small farmers.

Reason (R) MFIs provide loans without collateral, making credit accessible to those who are traditionally excluded from formal banking systems.

47. **Assertion** (A) Organic farming results in lower yields compared to conventional farming methods.

Reason (R) Organic farming ensures the long-term sustainability of the soil and ecosystem.

48. **Assertion** (A) Organic farming always eliminates the need for pest control.

Reason (R) Organic farming uses natural pest management techniques such as crop rotation and biopesticides.

Two Statement Based MCQs

Direction (Q.No. 49 to 58) *Read the following statements carefully and choose the correct alternative*

Alternatives

(a) Statement I is correct and Statement II is incorrect
(b) Statement II is correct and Statement I is incorrect
(c) Both the statements are correct
(d) Both the statements are incorrect

49. **Statement I** Formal sector in rural areas suffers from growing over dues.

Statement II Post independence, area of operation of informal sector has declined.

50. **Statement I** Institutional sources of rural credit, such as cooperative banks and regional rural banks, provide short-term credit to meet farmers' immediate consumption needs, while non-institutional sources like moneylenders are the major providers of long-term investment credit for rural development.

Statement II The classification of rural credit is based only on the time period for which the credit is provided, categorised into short-term, medium-term and long-term loans, without considering the purpose for which the credit is used.

51. **Statement I** Microfinance Institutions (MFIs) are primarily responsible for providing credit to large-scale industrial sectors in rural areas.

Statement II Microfinance Institutions (MFIs) focus on providing financial services to low income individuals and small-scale enterprises in rural areas to encourage self-employment.

52. **Statement I** Self Help Groups (SHGs) have emerged to fill the gap in formed credit system.

Statement II Formal credit system in India is not only inadequate but also not fully integrated with rural social community development. **CBSE Term I 2021**

53. **Statement I** The cooperative movement in India has been highly effective in empowering small and marginal farmers, ensuring fair prices for their produce and reducing their dependence on middlemen.

Statement II Despite several successful examples, cooperatives in India often face issues like political interference, lack of professional management and unequal distribution of benefits among members.

54. **Statement I** Contract farming in India has empowered small farmers by providing them with direct access to markets, guaranteed prices and protection from market fluctuations.

Statement II Agricultural marketing cooperatives have been successful in eliminating the exploitation of farmers by private traders and middlemen, providing farmers with consistent profits.

55. **Statement I** Non-farm activities have significantly contributed to the economic empowerment of women in rural areas by providing them with independent sources of income.

Statement II The diversification into non-farm activities primarily benefits wealthier households in rural areas, leaving poorer households largely unaffected.

56. **Statement I** The development of fisheries in rural areas can enhance food security and provide alternative livelihoods for communities dependent on agriculture.

Statement II Aquaculture and sustainable fishing practices can enhance rural income and contribute to environmental conservation.

57. **Statement I** The digital divide in rural areas is narrowing, with equal access to IT resources among all demographic groups, including women and marginalised communities.

Statement II The use of mobile technology and apps can facilitate access to agricultural information, financial services and market data for rural farmers.

58. **Statement I** Sustainable development in rural areas solely depends on the use of advanced technology in agriculture, disregarding traditional farming practices.

Statement II Organic farming promotes environmental health and biodiversity, often requiring more labour and time compared to conventional farming methods.

Matching

59. **Match the following types of rural credit with their appropriate examples** **Competency Based Que**

Column I (Type of Credit)		Column II (Example)
A. Short-term credit	(i)	Loans for purchasing agricultural land
B. Medium-term credit	(ii)	Loans for social purpose
C. Long-term credit	(iii)	Loans for farm machinery
D. Unproductive credit	(iv)	Loans for buying seeds

Codes

	A	B	C	D		A	B	C	D
(a)	(iv)	(iii)	(i)	(ii)	(b)	(ii)	(iii)	(iv)	(i)
(c)	(iv)	(ii)	(iii)	(i)	(d)	(i)	(ii)	(iii)	(iv)

60. **Match the following**

Column I		Column II
A. Green revolution	(i)	Fruits production
B. Yellow revolution	(ii)	Milk production
C. White revolution	(iii)	Food grains production
D. Golden revolution	(iv)	Oil seeds production

Codes

	A	B	C	D
(a)	(i)	(ii)	(iii)	(iv)
(b)	(ii)	(iii)	(iv)	(i)
(c)	(iii)	(iv)	(ii)	(i)
(d)	(iii)	(iv)	(i)	(ii)

61. **Match the following**

Column I		Column II
A. Women oriented community based poverty reduction programme implemented in Kerala.	(i)	Tamil Nadu Women in Agriculture (TANWA)
B. It is a project initiated in Tamil Nadu to train women in latest agriculture techniques.	(ii)	Sansad Adarsh Gram Yojana (SAGY)
C. Under this scheme, MPs need to identify and develop one village from their constituencies.	(iii)	*Kudumbashree*

Codes

	A	B	C		A	B	C
(a)	(i)	(ii)	(iii)	(b)	(ii)	(iii)	(i)
(c)	(iii)	(ii)	(i)	(d)	(iii)	(i)	(ii)

62. **Choose the incorrect pair**

Column I		Column II
A. Animal husbandry	(i)	Raising livestock for meat and wool
B. Fisheries	(ii)	Breeding and harvesting fish
C. Horticulture	(iii)	Beekeeping for honey and wax production
D. Dairy farming	(iv)	Milk production and processing

Codes
(a) A-(i) (b) B-(ii)
(c) C-(iii) (d) D-(iv)

63. Match the following key challenges in rural development with their solutions

	Column I		Column II
A.	Lack of irrigation facilities	(i)	Use of modern technologies and seeds
B.	Low agricultural productivity	(ii)	Adult education programmes
C.	Rural unemployment	(iii)	Promoting rural industries
D.	Illiteracy	(iv)	Canal and drip irrigation

Codes

	A	B	C	D
(a)	(i)	(iii)	(ii)	(iv)
(b)	(i)	(ii)	(iii)	(iv)
(c)	(iii)	(iv)	(ii)	(i)
(d)	(iv)	(i)	(iii)	(ii)

Concept Identification

64. A situation in which farmers borrow more to pay the interest on the previous borrowings and ultimately end up in losing their land.

65. A system under which the member farmers are required to pool their produce of milk for collective sale in the market.

66. The collective efforts of farmers or producers who come together to market their products. **CBSE 2020**

67. The process of selling and distributing agricultural products from the farm to consumers. It encompasses various activities, including the buying, selling, grading, storing and transporting of crops and livestock. **CBSE 2020**

68. A situation where lack of agricultural marketing infrastructure often forces the farmers to sell their produce at low prices for fear of spoilage or to pay-off an imminent debt.

69. A process of meeting the needs of the present without compromising the ability of future generations to meet their own needs.

Answers

1. (a) Agricultural productivity, rural infrastructure, literacy rate
2. (d) Many rural areas in India lack access to basic necessities such as proper healthcare, education, sanitation and clean drinking water.
3. (d) All of these
4. (b) A-6 to 12 months, B-1 to 5 years, C-5 years to 20 years
5. (a) I and III
6. (d) NABARD
7. (d) (i), (ii), (iii) and (iv)
8. (b) Commerical banks
9. (c) Agricultural credit is exclusively provided by formal sources
10. (a) self help groups
11. (b) Self help groups are keystone of microfinance, women empowerment and social security in India. It is a village based financial intermediary group with 10-20 local persons for providing small loan amounts.
12. (b) Jan Dhan Yojana
13. (a) Apni mandi
14. (b) Urban-centric policies
15. (b) Production, assembling, processing, grading
16. (b) Regulated markets
17. (b) Higher profit margins for farmers
18. (d) Intervention of the government is most essential
19. (a) Agricultural Produce Market Committee
20. (b) Horticulture
21. (b) Higher household incomes
22. (b) They provide financial and technical support
23. (b) Diversification in the production activities
24. (c) dairy production
25. (a) animal husbandry
26. (c) operation flood
27. (d) Horticulture is the business related to producing, storing and distributing foodgrains
28. (a) Integrating weather forecasting models with crop management systems
29. (c) Organic
30. (b) Europe
31. (d) All of the above
32. not considered
33. (b) 2014
34. inspired
35. (b) Organic products contain fewer preservatives and synthetic chemicals
36. (b) The high cost of organic certification and longer conversion period

37. soil health, crop yield
38. health, environment
39. (a) Both Assertion (A) and Reason (R) are true and Reason (R) is the correct explanation of Assertion (A)
40. (a) Both Assertion (A) and Reason (R) are true and Reason (R) is the correct explanation of Assertion (A)
41. (a) Both Assertion (A) and Reason (R) are true and Reason (R) is the correct explanation of Assertion (A)
42. (b) Both Assertion (A) and Reason (R) are true, but Reason (R) is not the correct explanation of Assertion (A)
43. (c) Most rural households still rely heavily on agriculture as their primary source of income, despite efforts to promote non-agricultural employment.
44. (a) Both Assertion (A) and Reason (R) are true and Reason (R) is the correct explanation of Assertion (A)
45. (a) Both Assertion (A) and Reason (R) are true and Reason (R) is the correct explanation of Assertion (A)
46. (a) Both Assertion (A) and Reason (R) are true and Reason (R) is the correct explanation of Assertion (A)
47. (b) Both Assertion (A) and Reason (R) are true, but Reason (R) is not the correct explanation of Assertion (A)
48. (d) Organic farming does not eliminate the need for pest control entirely. While synthetic pesticides are avoided, organic farmers still face pest challenges and must employ alternative methods like crop rotation or biopesticides to manage pests.
49. (a) Post-independence, the informal sector (money-lenders, unorganised lenders) still holds a significant share in rural areas for providing credit. Its area of operation has not declined significantly; rather, it persists alongside the formal sector.
50. (d) Institutional sources of rural credit, provide both short-term and long-term credit. These banks also fund investment needs for agriculture and rural development. Non-institutional sources primarily provide short-term credit, often for consumption or emergencies.

    The classification of rural credit is not solely based on time period. It is also based on the purpose for which the credit is used, such as production credit for farming inputs and investment credit for equuipment or land development.
51. (b) MFIs of primarily provide credit to low income individuals, not large-scale industrial sectors.
52. (c) Both the statements are correct
53. (c) Both the statements are correct
54. (d) While contract farming offers certain advantages like assured prices, small farmers often face unfavourable contract terms and exploitation from large companies. Agricultural marketing cooperatives, although beneficial in some cases, have not universally eliminated middlemen or ensured consistent profits for farmers due to various structural and governance issues.
55. (a) While non-farm activities empower women economically, they also have the potential to benefit poorer households through diverse income sources.
56. (c) Both the statements are correct
57. (b) While mobile technology is bridging some gaps for rural farmers, the overall digital divide remains a significant challenge, particularly for women and marginalised groups.
58. (b) Sustainable development incorporates both advanced technology and traditional practices, while organic farming indeed promotes environmental health but can be more labour-intensive.
59. (a) (iv) (iii) (i) (ii)
60. (c) (iii) (iv) (ii) (i)
61. (d) (iii) (i) (ii)
62. (c) C-(iii)
63. (d) (iv) (i) (iii) (ii)
64. Debt trap
65. Operation flood
66. Cooperative marketing
67. Agricultural marketing
68. Distress sale
69. Sustainable development

Subjective Questions

Short Answer Type Questions

1. What do you mean by rural development? Bring out the key issues in rural development. NCERT

Ans. Rural development is a comprehensive term which essentially focuses on action for the development of areas that are lagging behind in the overall development of the village economy.

It is a process whereby the standard of living of rural people, especially rural poor people, rises continuously.

Following are the key issues in rural development

(i) Development of the productive resources of each locality.

(ii) Development of human resources by providing opportunities for adult literacy, female literacy, education and skill development.

(iii) Development of human resources by providing health facilities, addressing both sanitation and public health.

(iv) Effective implementation of land reforms.

2. Why rural development has tremendous importance for our country?

Ans. Rural development is of tremendous importance for our country because of the reasons enumerated below

(i) Even today, nearly 70% of the population of India resides in rural areas.

So, if there is growth and prosperity in these areas, it will result in the growth and prosperity of the nation as a whole.

(ii) Rural development will help to create employment opportunities in the rural areas. This will not only raise the standard of living of the rural population, but also check the problem of migration.

(iii) Rural development creates opportunities in rural areas for education and skill development.

This helps to increase efficiency, productivity, mobility, income and standard of living of people.

3. "Understanding the time-bound nature of rural credit is essential for improving access to finance in rural areas."

Discuss the different categories of rural credit based on time period and explain them. Competency Based Que

Ans. Rural credit may be classified as

(i) **Long-term Credit**

These loans are for a period of 5 to 20 years. These loans are required to acquire permanent assets like tractors, land, costly equipment, etc.

(ii) **Medium-term Credit**

These loans are generally for a period of 12 months to 5 years. These loans are required for purchasing machinery, constructing fences and digging wells.

(iii) **Short-term Credit**

These loans are for a period of 6 to 12 months. These loans are required for buying seeds, tools, manure, fertilisers, etc. These loans are given to the needy borrowers by cooperatives, moneylenders and banks.

4. Explain the importance of credit availability in rural development. CBSE 2025, 23

Or **Elaborate the importance of credit in rural development.** CBSE 2024

Ans. The importance of credit in rural development is highlighted in the following points

(i) Credit helps the farmers to commercialise their farming. In other words, commercial farming requires funds that are provided via credit. As the small and marginal farmers produce only for their subsistence, they fail to generate sufficient surplus to reinvest in their lands leading to degradation of the land.

(ii) Secondly, given the long gestation period between sowing and harvesting of the crops, credit is extended to the farmers for meeting their initial requirements of farm inputs like seeds, fertilisers, etc.

(iii) Agriculture continues to depend on uncertain monsoon. Credit is needed to cope with uncertainties of nature or natural calamities.

5. As stated in the economic and political weekly, "In many rural areas, informal lenders are often more accessible than formal financial institutions."

Discuss in brief the characteristics of non-institutional sources of credit. Competency Based Que

Ans. These sources are traditional source of agricultural credit and are not attached to any formal institution. No rules or regulations are applicable to these sources.

The major non-institutional sources of rural credit are moneylenders, friends, relatives, landlords, shopkeepers and commission agents. Non-institutional sources of rural credit are not encouraged by government because of the following reasons

(i) They charge high rate of interest.

(ii) They manipulate accounts to keep farmers in debt-trap.

6. **"According to the National Bank for Agriculture and Rural Development (NABARD), 'our mission is to promote sustainable rural development and support the livelihood of rural populations."**

Discuss the role of NABARD as an institutional source of rural credit, highlighting its key functions to rural development. **Competency Based Que**

Ans. National Bank for Agriculture and Rural Development (NABARD) was set-up in 1982 as an apex body to coordinate the activities of all institutions involved in the rural financing system.

Key functions of NABARD towards rural development are as follows

(i) **Long-term Loans to State Governments** NABARD provides long-term loans to state governments to help them invest in cooperative societies.

(ii) **Inspection of Cooperative Institutions** NABARD inspects cooperative banks, Regional Rural Banks (RRBs) and primary cooperative societies to ensure proper functioning and compliance.

(iii) **Promotion of Agricultural Research** NABARD supports research on agriculture and rural development to encourage innovation and improve practices.

(iv) **Support for Small and Tenant Farmers** NABARD aids small and tenant farmers in consolidating landholdings to boost productivity and stability.

7. **Explain how Kisan Credit Card caters to the credit needs of rural population.**

Ans. Kisan Credit Card (KCC) scheme is an example of a credit facility which was introduced by the government in 1998-99. It facilitates access to credit from commercial banks and Regional Rural Banks (RRBs). Under the scheme, eligible farmers are provided with a Kisan Card and passbook from the relevant bank.

The farmers can make withdrawals and repayments of cash within the credit limit as specified in the Kisan Credit Card (KCC).

8. **"Jan-Dhan-Yojna helps in the rural development." Do you agree with this statement? Explain.** **NCERT; Competency Based Que**

Ans. Jan-Dhan Yojana is a government programme aimed to integrate each and every individual to the formal banking system by opening 'Zero Balance Accounts'. Through this programme, many individuals were actually connected with the formal sector that helped to access easy and affordable credit.

If it is followed at all levels, then it will help in rural development by providing easy and quick credit at affordable rates.

9. **"*Kudumbashree* is a women-oriented community based poverty reduction programme being implemented in Kerala."**

It is an example of which form of institutional credit? Also, explain briefly this form of rural credit. **Competency Based Que**

Ans. It is an example of Self Help Groups (SHGs). Due to the requirement of some kind of collateral or security, vast proportion of poor rural households were automatically out of the institutional credit networks.

Self Help Groups emerged to fill this gap, created by formal credit system. These groups promote thrift in small proportions by a minimum contribution from each member.

From the pooled money, credit is given to needy members on nominal rate of interest, which is repayable in easy instalments. However, borrowings from SHGs are mainly confined to consumption purposes.

10. **Explain the role of micro-credit in meeting credit requirements of the poor.** **CBSE 2023**

Ans. Micro-credit plays an important role in meeting the credit requirements of the poor. Under micro-credit programmes, farmers get adequate credit at cheaper rates. Micro-credit programme promotes thrift in small proportions by a minimum contribution from each member.

From the pooled money, credit is given to the needy members, which is repayable in small instalments at reasonable interest rates. Micro-credit programme removes the need of any kind of collateral. It also helps in women empowerment.

11. **"According to a report by the Reserve Bank of India, rural banking plays a crucial role in enhancing financial inclusion and promoting sustainable development in rural areas."**

Discuss two advantages and two limitations of rural banking in the context of rural development. **Competency Based Que**

Ans. Advantages of rural banking

(i) Advisory services and credit facilities have contributed to higher production levels in both agricultural (farm) and non-agricultural (non-farm) sectors.

(ii) Credit provided for self-employment initiatives has resulted in increased employment opportunities in rural areas, boosting local economies and livelihoods.

Limitations of rural banking

(i) Small and marginal farmers receive only a small fraction of the total institutional credit available, hindering their ability to invest in agricultural activities.

(ii) Rural banking is plagued by significant issues related to overdue loans and high default rates, which affect the overall stability and sustainability of financial institutions.

12. **"Infrastructural development is an essential element to obtain the full potential of the rural sector in India." Justify the given statement with valid arguments.** CBSE 2024; Competency Based Que

Ans. Yes, infrastructure is crucial for realising the rural sector's full potential as it supports production and boosts rural development. It can be understood with the help of following points

(i) **Increases Productivity**
Quality infrastructure improves production and productivity by enabling smooth movement of goods, reducing inefficiencies and ensuring efficient resource utilisation.

(ii) **Generates Linkages in Production**
Infrastructure supports economic growth by creating forward and backward linkages between industries. For instance, better irrigation boosts agriculture, which in turn, benefits industries relying on agricultural raw materials.

(iii) **Expands Market Size**
Efficient transport allows goods to be moved quickly and cost effectively, enabling producers to reach larger domestic and international markets.

13. **Discuss measures initiated by the government to improve agricultural marketing in India.** CBSE 2024

Or **"A sound agricultural marketing system works as the backbone of any agro-system of any nation." Justify the above statement by listing any two steps taken by the Indian government in this direction.** CBSE 2024 C

Ans. The following are the various measures initiated by the Indian government to improve agricultural marketing

(i) **Regulated Markets**
The government came up with the concept of the regulated market where the sale and purchase of the products are monitored by the market committee. The market committee consists of farmers, government agents and traders.

(ii) **Infrastructure Development**
The present infrastructure is not sufficient to meet the growing demands of the farmers. The government of India has provided cold storage and warehouses that help the farmers to sell their products at a time when the price is attractive.

14. **"Over the past few years, India has witnessed a shift from traditional conventional farming to natural/ organic farming."**

Discuss briefly any two reasons behind this shift towards organic produce. CBSE 2024 C

Ans. Two reasons behind the shift towards organic produce are

(i) **Environmental Concerns**
Conventional farming practices use chemical fertilisers and toxic pesticides, which harm water resources, livestock and the natural ecosystem. This has led to a demand for eco-friendly agricultural methods like organic farming, which helps to maintain and restore ecological balance.

(ii) **Rising Demand for Food Safety**
Increasing concerns about food safety and health have driven the demand for organically grown food. Organic produce is perceived to be safer and healthier as it avoids the use of harmful chemical inputs, attracting more consumers globally.

15. **Based upon the image given below, briefly explain the problems of agricultural marketing.** Competency Based Que

Ans. Following are the problems related to agricultural marketing

(i) **Inadequate Transport Facilities**
Transport facilities are highly inadequate in rural India. Only a small number of villages are joined by railways and metalled (pucca) roads to mandies. Produce has to be carried on slow moving transport vehicles like bullock carts.

Such means of transport cannot be used to carry produce too far-off places and the farmer has to dump his produce in nearby markets even if the price obtained in these markets is considerably low.

(ii) **Malpractices in Unregulated Markets**
Even now the number of unregulated markets in the country is substantially large.

Middleman and brokers taking advantage of the ignorance and illiteracy of the farmers, use unfair means to cheat them.

(iii) **Lack of Grading and Standardisation**
Different varieties of agricultural produce are not graded properly. Goods are generally measured in local units that are not standardised.

16. What are the alternative channels available for agricultural marketing? Give some examples. NCERT

Ans. Alternative marketing channels were developed to bring the farmers in direct contact with the consumers.

These channels help in increasing farmers' share in prices paid by the consumers'.

Some examples of these channels are

(i) *Apni Mandi* (Punjab, Haryana and Rajasthan)

(ii) *Hadaspar Mandi* (Pune)

(iii) *Rythu Bazars* (Vegetable and fruit markets in Andhra Pradesh)

(iv) *Uzhavar Sandies* (Farmers markets in Tamil Nadu)

Further, several national and multinational fast food chains are increasingly entering into contracts/alliances with farmers to encourage them to cultivate farm products (vegetables, fruits, etc.) of the desired quality by providing them with seeds and other inputs and also assuring procurement of the products at pre-decided prices.

17. Agricultural diversification includes two aspects; one relates to change in cropping pattern and second relates to a shift of workforce from agriculture to other allied activities and non-agriculture sector.

The need for diversification arises from the fact that there is greater risk in depending exclusively on farming for livelihood.

Diversification towards new areas is necessary not only to reduce the risk from agriculture sector but also to productive sustainable livelihood options to rural area.

In the given context, explain the various aspects of agricultural diversification. Competency Based Que

Ans. Agricultural diversification occurs when more species, plant varieties or animal breeds are added to a given farm or farming community and this may include landscape diversification, i.e. different crops and cropping systems interspersed in space and time.

Aspects of diversification are as follows

(i) The change in the cropping pattern.

(ii) The transformation of the workforce from agricultural work to other associated activities like poultry, livestock, fisheries, etc. and also of the non-agriculture sector.

(iii) For rural people, diversification or focusing on associate activity is important because it gives them an opportunity to earn extra income and overcome poverty.

18. Why is agricultural diversification essential for sustainable livelihoods? NCERT

Ans. Diversification is essential because there is greater risk in depending exclusively on farming for livelihood. It also provides productive and sustainable livelihood options to rural people.

Most of the agricultural employment activities are concentrated in the Kharif season while during the Rabi season, it becomes difficult to find gainful employment in areas lacking in irrigation facilities.

Therefore, expansion into other sectors is essential to provide supplementary gainful employment and in realising higher levels of income for rural people to overcome poverty and other problems.

Hence, there is a need to focus on allied activities, non-farm employment and other emerging alternatives of livelihood for providing sustainable livelihoods in rural areas.

19. Explain the role of non-farm employment in promoting rural diversification. NCERT

Ans. Non-farm sector is an alternative employment opportunity for people in the rural sector.

It has different segments, for example, the traditional household-based industries like pottery barn, handlooms, etc. and dynamic sub-sectors like food processing units, agro-processing units, tourism, etc.

While some of these segments have potential for growth, others may have low productivity. Lack of infrastructure may also be a hindrance for rapid development of the non-farming sector.

On the positive side, the potential for this sector has opened employment opportunities for women as well. The produce from this segment contributes to the growth of GDP.

20. (i) Interpret the given picture based on the Saansad Adarsh Gram Yojana (SAGY) initiated by the Government of India. CBSE SQP 2025; Competency Based Que

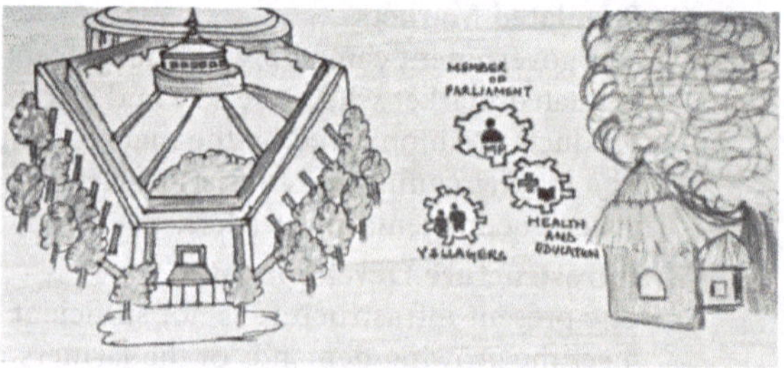

(ii) State any two examples of allied activities.

Ans. (i) The picture represents the implementation of the Saansad Adarsh Gram Yojana (SAGY), where
- Members of Parliament (MPs) adopt and develop a village as a model village.
- The focus areas are health, education and infrastructure.
- The development involves collaboration between MPs, villagers and local government bodies.
- The scheme encourages holistic rural development, motivating villagers to actively participate in improving their own village.

(ii) Two examples of allied activities
- Building infrastructure for health and education, such as primary health centers and schools.
- Promoting sanitation and clean water supply to improve public health.

21. "IT can play a critical role in achieving sustainable development and food security in the 21st century in the country."

Justify the given statement with valid arguments. CBSE 2025; Competency Based Que

Or **"Information technology plays a very significant role in achieving sustainable development and food security." Comment.** NCERT; Competency Based Que

Ans. Information technology plays a very significant role in achieving sustainable development and food security in the following ways

(i) It can act as a tool for releasing the creative potential and knowledge embedded in our people.

(ii) Issues like weather forecasting, crop treatment, fertilisers, pesticides, storage conditions, etc. can be well administered, if expert opinion is made available to the farmers.

(iii) The quality and quantity of crops can be increased manifold, if the farmers are made aware of the latest equipments, technologies and resources.

(iv) It has potential of employment generation in rural areas.

22. What is organic farming and how does it promote sustainable development? NCERT

Or **State the meaning of organic farming. Discuss how does it help in promoting sustainable development.** CBSE 2023

Ans. Organic farming is a sustainable agricultural practice which restores, maintains and enhances the ecological balance. Conventional agriculture uses chemical fertilisers, toxic pesticides, etc. which enter the food supply, penetrate the water resources, harm the livestock, deplete the soil and devastate natural ecosystem. Due to these problems, an eco-friendly technology is required.

Organic farming is an eco-friendly technique of growing crops, which promotes sustainable development. In other words, organic agriculture is a whole system of farming that restores, maintains and enhances the ecological balance and enhances the food safety, thus encouraging the practices towards sustainable development.

23. Enlist some problems faced by farmers during the initial years of organic farming. NCERT

Ans. The problems faced by farmers during the initial years of organic farming are

(i) Organic farming requires inputs like organic manure, bio-fertilisers and organic pesticides.
Though they are cheaper yet farmers find it difficult to get them.

(ii) The yield from organic farming is much less than that of modern agricultural farming.

(iii) The price of organic food is high, so it is difficult to sell them.

(iv) Organic products generally have more blemishes and shorter shelf life.

Long Answer Type Questions

24. Critically evaluate the role of the rural banking system in the process of rural development in India. NCERT

Ans. Rural banking has raised the level of rural farm and non-farm output, income and employment, especially after the green revolution.

The following are the advantages of increase in rural banking facilities

(i) Raising farm and non-farm output by providing services and credit facilities to farmers.

(ii) Generating credit for self-employment schemes in rural areas.

(iii) Achieving food security which is clear from the abundant buffer stocks of grains.

However, the expansion and promotion of rural banking sector has taken a back seat after reforms and it suffers from the following limitations

(i) Small and marginal farmers receive only a very small portion of the institutional credit.

(ii) Rural banking is suffering from the problems of large amount of over dues and default rate.

(iii) The source of institutional finance are inadequate to meet the requirements of agricultural credit.

(iv) There exists regional inequalities in the distribution of institutional credit.

To improve the situation, the banks should build relationship with farmers. Also, the farmers should be made understand the importance of thrift and efficient utilisation of the loaned amount.

25. Explain the steps taken by the government in developing rural markets. NCERT

Ans. Following are the steps taken by the government in developing rural markets

(i) **Regulation of Markets**
The government has established regulated markets where the sale and purchase of the produce is monitored by market committee consisting of representatives of government, farmers and traders. Regulation of markets helps to create orderly and transparent marketing conditions.

(ii) **Improvement in Physical Infrastructure**
Through this measure, the government ensures the improvement in physical infrastructure such as roads, railways, warehouses, cold storages, etc.

(iii) **Cooperative Marketing**
The government encourages farmers to form producer marketing cooperative societies, so that they get better prices of their produce through collective sale.

(iv) **Supportive Policies**
In addition to the above policies, the following supportive policies have also been introduced to develop rural markets

- **Minimum Support Price** (MSP) The government fixes MSP for agricultural output. This policy assures a minimum income to the farmers.
- **Maintenance of Buffer Stock of Wheat and Rice** When market price falls much below the MSP, then government purchases the produce from the farmers at MSP and maintains buffer stock.
- **Distribution of Foodgrains and Sugar** The buffer stocks of foodgrains and sugar are distributed among the poor through the Public Distribution System (PDS) at subsidised prices.

26. "Agricultural cooperative marketing plays a vital role in enhancing the bargaining power of farmers and ensuring fair prices for their produce." Says National Cooperative Development Corporation (NCDC).

Do you agree with the given statement? Explain your answer with suitable arguments. Competency Based Que

Ans. Yes, agricultural cooperative marketing plays a crucial role in empowering farmers by enhancing their bargaining power, ensuring fair prices, providing resources and facilitating access to credit, ultimately contributing to rural development and economic stability.

These are as follows

(i) **Enhancing Bargaining Power**
Agricultural cooperatives allow farmers to combine their produce, increasing their strength in negotiating better prices with buyers.

(ii) **Ensuring Fair Prices**
By marketing through cooperatives, farmers can reach larger markets and secure fair prices, reducing the influence of middlemen.

(iii) **Access to Resources**
Cooperatives provide farmers with important resources like quality seeds, fertilisers and training to improve farming practices.

(iv) **Facilitating Credit Access**
Agricultural cooperatives help farmers access credit from financial institutions, enabling them to invest in their farms and increase productivity.

27. **Stocks in Central Pool on 1st January**

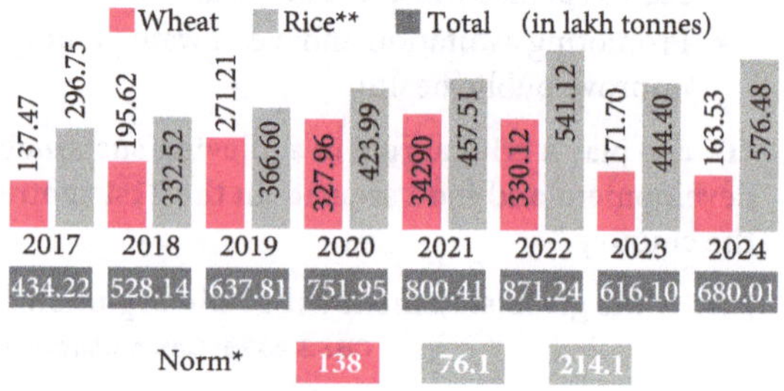

*Minimum operational stock plus strategic reserve for 1st January; "Includes rice equivalent of un-milled paddy

Source *Food Corporation of India*

In reference to above graph, answer the following questions Competency Based Que

(i) **Discuss how buffer stock can influence the agricultural sector.**

(ii) **Discuss the trend of total food stocks in the central pool from 2017 to 2024. What factors could have contributed to the fluctuations over these years?**

Ans. (i) Buffer stock can significantly influence the agricultural sector by providing price stability for farmers.
When the government buys surplus produce, it assures farmers of a guaranteed market and fair prices, encouraging them to invest in better farming techniques and production. This stability can lead to increased agricultural productivity and can prevent distress sales during bumper crop seasons. Furthermore, buffer stock can ensure food security, especially in developing countries, by managing supply and demand effectively.

(ii) From 2017 to 2024, total food stocks in the central pool showed fluctuations, peaking at 800.41 lakh tonnes in 2021, likely due to increased procurement during the Covid-19 pandemic. However, stocks gradually declined to 600.01 lakh tonnes by 2024, primarily due to reduced wheat stocks. Factors contributing to these changes include government procurement policies, climate impacts on wheat production and higher food distribution to meet rising demand.

28. It is stated that "Indian agriculture is no longer a subsistence occupation".

State the value of statement highlighting the diversification of agriculture in India. **Competency Based Que**

Ans. In the pre-independence period and also during the period just after independence, Indian agriculture was characterised by subsistence farming. Under this system, the small landholdings of farmers enabled them to produce just enough to fulfil the needs of their families and to provide seeds for the next sowing season. Farmers did not sell their produce in the market.

However, after independence, the government introduced a number of reforms, such as abolition of *zamindari* system, consolidation of landholdings, etc. which led to substantial increase in agricultural output and led to commercialisation of agriculture.

The farmers started selling their produce in the market for money. This led to improvement in their living conditions. However, this also proved to be insufficient as agricultural infrastructure was not enough to enable agricultural activity all round the year.

This led to the need for encouraging diversification of non-farm activities such as animal husbandry, fishing, etc. These activities helped the farmers to supplement their earning. The value highlighted is the attempt to improve the living standards of the farmers.

29. "The Prime Minister urged to increase the rural income by increasing non-farm activities." Explain how non-farm activities can lead to rise in income of people in rural sector. **CBSE 2020**

Ans. The non-farm sector, particularly in rural areas is being accorded wide recognition in recent years for the following reasons

(i) **Check on Unregulated Migration**
A planned strategy of rural non-farm development may prevent many rural people from migrating to urban industrial and commercial centres.

(ii) **Bridging Rural-Urban Divide**
When the economic base of the rural economy extends beyond agriculture, rural-urban economic gaps are bound to get narrower along with salutary effects in many other aspects associated with the life and aspirations of the people.

(iii) **Employment Generation**
Non-farm rural industries are generally less capital-intensive and more labour absorbing. Thus, they can play a critical role in employment growth in rural areas.

(iv) **Reducing Inequalities**
Rural income distribution is much less unequal in areas where a wide network of non-farm avenues of employment exists.

As the lower strata of rural societies participate much more intensely in non-farm activities, it helps in increasing social mobility.

30. Bring out the importance of animal husbandry, fisheries and horticulture as a source of diversification. **NCERT**

Ans. **Importance of Animal Husbandry**
The following points explain the importance of animal husbandry as a source of diversification

(i) Today, this sector alone provides alternate livelihood options to a significant number of women and over 70 million small and marginal farmers including landless labourers.

(ii) Milk production of the Indian dairy sector has increased by more than five times between 1960-2009 with the successful implementation of 'operation flood'.

(iii) Meat, eggs, wool and other by-products are also emerging as important productive sectors for diversification.

Importance of Fisheries

This sector is important for the reasons enumerated below

(i) Today, total fish production accounts for 0.9 % of the total GDP. Kerala, Gujarat, Maharashtra and Tamil Nadu are the major producers of marine products.

(ii) Fishing has become a source of women empowerment. Even though women are not involved in active fishing, about 60% of the workforce in export marketing and 40% in internal marketing are women.

Importance of Horticulture
This sector is important for the reasons enumerated below

(i) These crops play a vital role in providing food and nutrition, alongwith sustainable employment opportunities.

(ii) During 1991-2003, 'golden revolution' took place. Horticulture became highly productive during this period due to planned investment and the sector emerged as a sustainable livelihood option.

(iii) India has emerged as a world leader in producing a variety of fruits like mangoes, bananas, coconuts, cashew nuts and a number of spices and is the second largest producer of fruits and vegetables.

31. Is it possible to develop information technology as an alternate livelihood option? Give reasons. Competency Based Que

Ans. Yes, Information Technology (IT) can be developed as an alternative livelihood option due to its significant impact on various sectors. Following points will support the statement

(i) **Food Security**
IT helps predict areas of food insecurity and vulnerability, allowing timely planning and intervention.

(ii) **Agricultural Growth**
Farmers get real-time information on weather, soil conditions, market prices and new technologies, improving productivity.

(iii) **Employment Generation**
IT creates job opportunities in rural areas through initiatives like digital services, BPOs and e-commerce.

(iv) **Government Support**
Programmes like Digital India and e-Governance promote IT growth, improving infrastructure and digital literacy.

(v) **Skill Development**
IT training programmes empower rural youth, making them employable in various digital fields.

Thus, IT has proven to be a sustainable livelihood option with the support of government and private initiatives.

32. Identify the benefits and limitations of organic farming. NCERT

Ans. The benefits of organic farming are as follows

(i) Organic farming substitutes costlier agriculture inputs like HYV seeds, chemical fertilisers, pesticides, etc. with locally produced organic inputs that are cheaper and thereby generate good returns on investment.

(ii) It also generates income through exports.

(iii) Due to more labour requirement in organic farming, it is an attractive option for India.

(iv) Organically grown food has more nutritional value than the food grown by chemical farming, thus providing us with healthy food.

The limitations of organic farming are as follows

(i) Inadequate infrastructure and the problem of marketing are major concerns of organic farming which are needed to be addressed to promote organic farming.

(ii) Organic produce have shorter shelf life than sprayed produce.

(iii) Choice in production of off-season crops is quite limited in organic farming.

33. Since ages, farmers in India have taken resource to debt. In the earlier times, the same was from informal sources.

Since Independence with the effort of the government, formal sector activity came into picture. Farmers borrow not only to meet their investment need but also to satisfy their personal needs. Uncertainty of income is caused by factors like crop failure caused by irregular rainfall, reduction in groundwater table other pest attack, etc. These resource push farmers into the clutches of the private money lenders, who charge exorbitant rate of interest which as to their miseries.

Government in India at different times for different reasons, introduced debt relief/waiver scheme.

These schemes were used by the government as a quick means to extricate farmers from their indebtedness, helping to restore their capacity to investment produce.

The cost and benefit of such debt relief scheme is however a widely debated topic among economists.

Some economists argue that such schemes are extremely beneficial to the poor and marginalised farmers while other argue that these schemes add to the fiscal burden to the government.

Some other believes that these schemes may develop the expectation of repeated bailouts among farmers which may spoil the credit culture among farmers.

(i) Explain the importance of credit in rural market.

(ii) What steps can be taken to improve the condition of regional rural banks? Competency Based Que

Ans. (i) The rural economy can grow only if it has adequate flow of finance. It is only capital which can ensure higher productivity in agriculture. Provision of rural credit enables a farmer to buy improved seeds, fertilisers, organic pesticides and equipments. All these inputs help him to increase his agricultural productivity and his income.

So, importance of credit in rural development can be perceived as a means to break the vicious circle of low capital, low productivity and low savings of the rural poor.

(ii) The following steps can be taken to improve the functioning of regional rural banks

- There is a need to increase their authorised capital so that they can expand their business and serve the rural people effectively.
- There is a need to provide them with adequate financial assistance so that they can meet their day-to-day expenses.
- There is a need to attract and retain trained personnel in RRBs by providing them with better working conditions and salaries.

SELF ASSESSMENT TEST

Objective Type Questions

1. Short-term credit is given to the needy borrowers by ....
   (a) cooperatives (b) moneylenders
   (c) banks (d) All of these

2. How Information Technology (IT) plays a crucial role in rural development?
   (a) IT issues weather forecasting, information regarding agricultural inputs and crops treatment
   (b) IT provides latest information of advance agricultural equipments, technology, education and resources
   (c) IT has potential of employment generation in rural areas
   (d) All of the above

3. Which of the following agricultural inputs are used in organic farming?
   I. Bio fertiliser II. Neem pesticide
   III. Chemical insecticide
   IV. Organic manure
   V. High Yield Variety Seeds (HYVS)

   Codes
   (a) I, III, IV (b) I, II, IV
   (c) I, II, III, IV (d) All of these

4. The major goal of Self Help Groups (SHGs) is to
   (a) promote individual savings
   (b) provide large loans to members
   (c) empower rural women and provide micro-credit
   (d) establish large businesses

5. 'Hadaspar Mandi' is an alternative marketing channel operational in
   (a) Punjab (b) Andhra Pradesh
   (c) Pune (d) Tamil Nadu

6. The primary objective of cooperative farming is to
   (a) increase mechanisation
   (b) reduce ownership of land
   (c) pool resources for better productivity
   (d) minimise agricultural loans

7. Which of the following statements is/are incorrect?
   I. Fishing community in India suffers due to industrialisation.
   II. India is highest exporter of flowers in the world.

   Codes
   (a) Only I (b) Only II
   (c) Both I and II (d) None of these

Answers 1. (d) 2. (d) 3. (b) 4. (c) 5. (c) 6. (c) 7. (b)

Short Answer Type Questions

8. Explain the need for agricultural marketing in India.

9. Why are non-institutional sources of credit not encouraged by the government?

10. How is organic farming superior to conventional farming?

11. A Self Help Group (SHG) in a rural village of India was set-up to empower women. The SHG provided small loans to its members, enabling them to start small businesses like tailoring and poultry farming. Over time, the members achieved financial independence and improved their family incomes.

    Based on the case, explain how SHGs contribute to rural development.

12. State any four defects of organic farming.

13. Farmer named Ramesh owns a small piece of land and grows wheat every year. Due to irregular monsoons, his yield has decreased, affecting his income. On advice, he started growing vegetables and rearing goats, which proved to be profitable.

    How does agricultural diversification benefit small farmers like Ramesh?

14. What are the main challenges faced by the rural banking system in India?

Long Answer Type Questions

15. "'The institutional finance plays a vital role in promoting rural development in India." Discuss.

16. Explain the various supportive policies initiated by the government to improve agricultural marketing.

17. A rural village has recently been introduced to high speed internet and a group of farmers is planning to shift from traditional farming to cultivating high value horticultural crops like fruits and vegetables. However, they face challenges like limited technical knowledge and market access.

    Suggest three ways IT services and digital tools can support these farmers in successfully adopting horticulture.

06
CHAPTER

Employment refers to the work performed by individuals in exchange for a wage or salary, contributing to the production of goods and services. It is essential for earning a livelihood and plays a significant role in the economic development of a nation.

YOUR STUDY GOALS

YOUR PRACTICE GOAL

- Objective Type Questions (65 Qs ; MCQs, A-R, Statements, Matching, Concept Identification)
- Subjective Questions (23 SAs, 13 LAs)
- Self Assessment Test (7 MCQs, 7 SAs, 3 LAs)

Employment : Growth, Informalisation and Other Issues

Work is essential for earning a living, providing self-worth and contributing to national income, thus engaging in economic development. People work in various fields, from traditional crafts to modern jobs. Now, technology has also enabled home based production.

We also do work to support those who are dependent on us and helps to address social issues like exploitation, child labour, etc. Recognising the importance of work, Mahatma Gandhi emphasised the value of education and training through work and crafts.

6.1 Some Basic Concepts

Let us understand few basic concepts related to employment

Concept	Explanation
Worker	An individual who is involved in some economic activity to earn a livelihood, including self-employed persons. Worker also includes those who temporarily abstain from work due to illness, injury, bad weather, etc.
Nature of Employment in India	• In India, nature of employment is multifaceted. • Employment can be year round or seasonal; many workers do not receive fair wages. • 471 million strong workforce present in India during 2017-18; 77% being men and rest women. • Women often perform unpaid tasks (like cooking, fetching water, etc.) for which they are not paid wages, thus not categorised as workers.

Concept	Explanation
Labour Supply	It means number of persons willing to work at different wage rates. It depends upon the existing wage rate and is measured in terms of man days.
Labour Force	It means number of persons actually working or willing to work. It does not depend upon the wage rate and is measured in terms of number of days. Labour Force = Persons Working + Persons Available for Work
Workforce	It means number of persons actually working. This measure does not include those persons who are willing to work but are not getting work. Workforce = Labour Force – Number of Persons not Working but are Willing to Work

Participation of People in Employment

The Worker-Population Ratio (WPR) is an indicator used to analyse the employment situation in the country.

Interpretation

- **A *higher WPR*** means greater engagement of people in economic activities (more people are working).
- **A *medium or low WPR*** indicates lower engagement, meaning a higher proportion of the population is not directly involved in economic activities.

Symbolically, $$\text{Worker-Population Ratio} = \frac{\text{Total Number of Workers}}{\text{Total Population}} \times 100$$

The data on rate of participation of people in employment in rural and urban areas, is as follows

Worker-Population Ratio in India, 2017-18

Sex	Worker-Population Ratio		
	Total	**Rural**	**Urban**
Men	52.1	51.7	53.0
Women	16.5	17.5	14.2
Total	**34.7**	**35**	**33.9**

The above table shows the following

- **Worker Participation** 35% of people in India are workers (34% in urban, 35% in rural areas).
- **Employment Opportunities** Rural population have limited resources and fewer job options, restricting their income potential. In contrast, urban people benefit from a variety of employment opportunities suited to their skills and qualifications.
- **Access to Education** Many in rural areas lack access to education or drop out early to join the workforce. Meanwhile, urban areas offer better access to schools, colleges and training institutions, enabling higher educational attainment.
- **Gender Gap** Fewer women participate in economic activities, with only 14% in urban areas and 18% in rural areas.

6.2 Meaning of Employment

Employment means an activity which helps an individual to earn his living.

Employment can be classified as self-employment (self-employed workers) and wage employment (hired workers).

Category	Explanation	Percentage of Workforce
1. **Self-employed Workers**	The workers who own and operate an enterprise to earn their livelihood are known as self-employed workers.	About 52%
2. **Hired Workers**	Those people who are hired by others and are paid wages or salaries as a reward for their services are called hired workers. They can be of two types, i.e. casual wage labourers and regular salaried workers.	—

Category	Explanation	Percentage of Workforce
(i) ***Casual Wage Labourers***	• These are those people, who are not hired by their employers on a regular/permanent basis. • They do not get social security benefits. • e.g. Construction workers.	About 25%
(ii) ***Regular Salaried Workers***	• These include a worker who is engaged by someone or by an enterprise and paid wages on a regular basis. • They get social security benefits. • e.g. Teachers, Chartered Accountants, etc.	About 23%

Distribution of Self-employed and Hired Workers in India

The distribution of self-employed and hired workers across different regions on the basis of region and gender is discussed below

Based on Region (Rural and Urban)

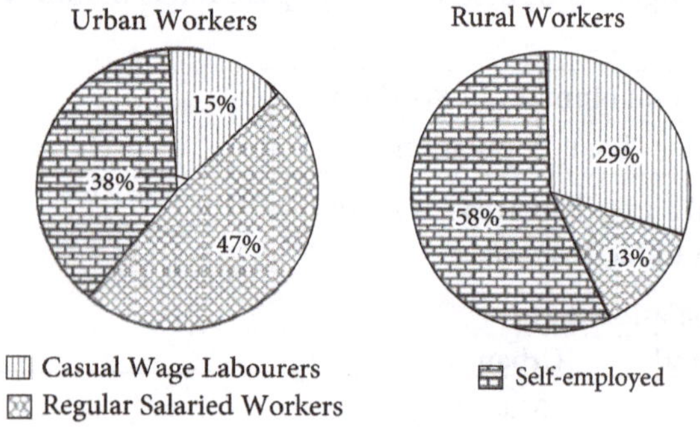

Distribution of Employment by Region

Key Observations

- Self-employment and casual labour are more common in rural areas.
- Urban areas have a higher proportion of regular salaried jobs.
- Rural workers are often self-employed due to dependence on farming.

Based on Gender (Male and Female)

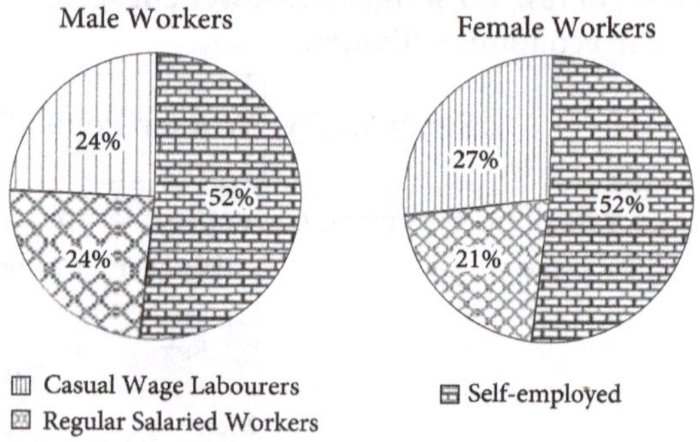

Distribution of Employment by Gender

Key Observations

- Male workers have nearly equal distribution across self-employment, casual labour and salaried jobs.
- Female workers prefer self-employment due to lower mobility in both rural and urban areas.
- Thus, self-employment is a vital source of livelihood for people in India, especially for women.

Employment by Sector

All the productive activities of an economy are divided into primary sector, secondary sector and tertiary sector. The distribution of workforce is as follows

Distribution of Workforce by Industry, 2017-18

Industrial Category	Place of Residence		Sex		Total
	Rural	Urban	Male	Female	
Primary Sector	59.8	6.6	40.7	57.1	44.6
Secondary Sector	20.4	34.3	26.5	17.7	24.4
Tertiary/Service Sector	19.8	59.1	32.8	25.2	31.0
Total	**100**	**100**	**100**	**100**	**100**

Key Observations

- ***Primary Sector Employment***
  - Employs **44.6%** of the total workforce in India.
  - **57.1% of women workers** are concentrated in the primary sector.
  - In rural areas, **59.8%** of the workforce depends on agriculture, forestry and fishing.
- ***Secondary Sector Employment***
  - Employs **24.4%** of the total workforce.
  - Employs **one-third** of the urban workforce.
  - Provides jobs to **20.4%** of rural workers in manufacturing, construction and other industrial activities.
- ***Service Sector Employment***
  - Engages **31%** of the total workforce.
  - Provides jobs to **19.8%** of rural workers.
  - Dominates in urban areas, employing **59.1%** of urban workers.
- ***Rural vs Urban Employment Trends***
  - Agriculture dominates rural employment, while the **service sector** leads in urban areas.
  - A gradual shift is occurring from the primary to secondary and service sectors, especially in urban areas, reflecting economic development trends.

6.3 Growth and Changing Structure of Employment

Overview of Economic Development (1950-2010)

- **Planned Development** For nearly seventy years, India has focused on expanding its economy through increased national output and employment.
- **GDP Growth** From 1950 to 2010, India's Gross Domestic Product (GDP) grew positively and was higher than the employment growth.
- **Employment Growth Rate** During this period, employment increased at a maximum rate of 2% per year, indicating sluggish job creation relative to economic growth.

Trends and Patterns

- **Fluctuations in GDP** Despite overall positive growth, the GDP experienced fluctuations during this period.
- **Decline in Employment Growth** In the late 1990s, employment growth began to decline, returning to levels seen in the early stages of economic planning.
- **Widening Gap** During this period, there has been a growing disparity between GDP growth and employment growth, illustrating a phenomenon known as 'jobless growth'. This indicates that India has managed to produce more goods and services without generating sufficient employment opportunities.

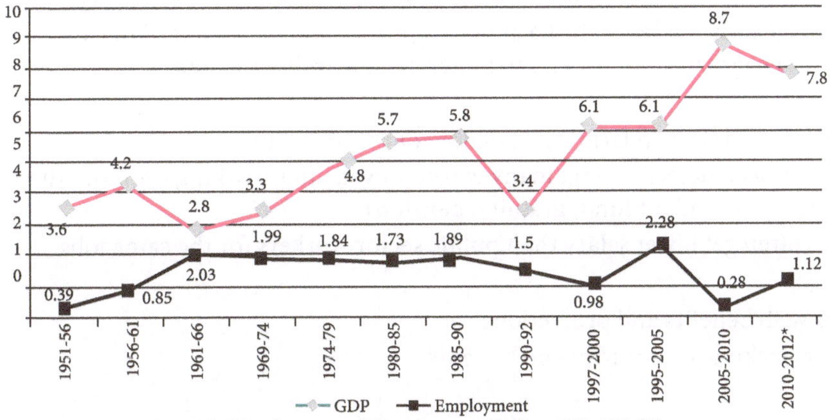

Growth of Employment and Gross Domestic Product, 1951–2012 (%)

Note *This is the period for which comparable and authentic data are available.

Distribution of Workforce in India

The below table will help to understand the effect on different sections of workforce, due to growth pattern of employment and GDP

Trends in Employment Pattern (Sector-wise) **1972-2018** (in %)

Sector	1972-73	2011-2012	2017-2018
Primary	74.3	48.9	44.6
Secondary	10.9	24.3	24.4
Tertiary/Services	14.8	26.8	31.0
Total	**100**	**100**	**100**

Key Observations Shift in Sector Employment (1972-2018)

- 74.3% of the workforce engaged in primary sector in 1972-73 which declined to 44.6% by 2017-18.
- Secondary and tertiary sectors are growing, indicating a substantial shift from farm work to non-farm work.

Casualisation of Workforce

The movement from self-employment and regular salaried employment to casual wage work is known as the process of casualisation of workforce.

The table below shows the status-wise trend in employment pattern

Trends in Employment Pattern (Status-wise) **1972-2018** (in%)

Status	1972-73	2011-2012	2017-2018
Self-employed	61.4	52	52.2
Regular Salaried Employees	15.4	18	22.8
Casual Wage Labourers	23.2	30	25.0
Total	**100**	**100**	**100**

Key Observations

- Over the past few decades (1972-2018), there has been a notable movement towards casual wage work.
- Self-employment remains the largest source of employment despite the trend towards casualisation.

6.4 Informalisation of Indian Workforce

Development Objective Since independence, India aimed to provide decent standard of living through industrialisation, transitioning agricultural workers to better, paying industrial jobs.

Current Reality

- Over 50% of the workforce still relies on farming as major source of livelihood.
- Quality of employment has been deteriorating; many workers even after working for more than 10-20 years, lack basic benefits (like maternity, provident fund, gratuity, pension).
- Private sector employees often get lower salary than public sector workers for the same jobs.

Workforce Structure

- **Formal Sector** Workers with benefits and protections.
- **Informal Sector** Workers lacking job security and benefits.

Key Takeaways

- Despite development efforts, a significant portion of the workforce remains in agriculture.
- Quality of jobs is declining, with many workers deprived of essential benefits.

Formal Sector Vs Informal Sector

Basis	Formal Sector	Informal Sector
Definition	All the public sector establishments and those private sector establishments which employ 10 or more hired workers are called formal sector establishments.	All other establishments i.e. all those private sector establishments which employ less than 10 workers are called informal sector establishments.
Workers	Those who work in such establishments are formal sector workers.	Those who work in such establishments are informal sector workers.
Control	Government exercises control, like labour laws protect employee rights.	No government protection or regulation, thus workers lack rights.
Income and Benefits	Workers enjoy social security benefits and earn more than informal workers.	Workers do not have regular income or social security.
Job Security	Dismissals require compensation and are regulated.	Workers can be dismissed without compensation.
Awareness and Advocacy	Workers are aware of their rights and form trade unions for representation.	Workers have little awareness of rights and no formal representation.
Government Initiatives	Strong emphasis on rights and benefits.	Initiatives underway to modernise and provide social security measures based on ILO recommendations.

Informalisation in Ahmedabad

- Ahmedabad is a prosperous city with its wealth based on the produce of more than 60 textile mills with a labour force of 1,50,000 workers employed in them. These workers had acquired a certain degree of income security, over the time.
- They had secure jobs with a living wage and they were covered by social security schemes protecting their health and old age. They had a strong trade union which represented them not only in disputes but also in activities for the welfare of workers and their families. In the early 1980s, textile mills began to close down all over the country.
- In Ahmedabad, the process of closure was long drawn out and spread over 10 years. Over this period, approximately over 80,000 permanent workers and over 50,000 non-permanent workers lost their jobs and were driven to the informal sector.
- The city experienced an economic recession and public disturbances, especially due to communal riots.
- A whole class of workers was thrown back from the middle class into poverty due to informalisation.

6.5 Meaning of Unemployment

It is a situation in which people who are capable and willing to work are not getting work.

The children below the age of 15 years and adults above the age of 60 years are not part of the working population and hence not considered to be unemployed.

According to **National Statistical Office** (NSO), previously known as National Sample Survey Office (NSSO), unemployment is defined as a situation in which all those who, owing to lack of work, are not working but either seek work through employment exchanges, intermediaries, friends or relatives or by making applications to prospective employers or express their willingness or availability for work under the prevailing condition of work and remunerations.

Employment Data Sources

- Census of India Reports
- NSO's Employment and Unemployment Reports
- Directorate General of Employment and Training Data (Registrations with employment exchanges)

Unemployment reflects the inability of willing workers to find jobs, with significant implications in the Indian economy where many are forced into undesirable work.

Types of Unemployment in India

Following types of unemployment are generally found in India

Type	Definition	Characteristics	Example
Open Unemployment	Occurs when individuals are willing and able to work but cannot find employment.	• Visible and measurable. • Reflects economic conditions.	A qualified engineer searching for job but unable to find any position.
Seasonal Unemployment	Arises during specific seasons when jobs are unavailable, particularly in agriculture.	• Fluctuates with seasons. • Workers may migrate for seasonal jobs temporary in nature.	Farmers unemployed during the off-season after harvest, migrate to cities for work and stay there for sometime, but comeback to village as rainy season begins.
Disguised Unemployment	Exists when additional labour does not contribute to increased output, indicating underutilisation.	• All workers appear to be employed. • No increase in productivity with extra workers.	Five workers on a farm producing the same yield as four; thus fifth worker's contribution is zero.

Causes of Unemployment

Cause	Description
Slow Economic Growth	Slow growth rate fails to generate sufficient employment for the growing labour force.
Rapid Population Growth	The fast rising population creates more job seekers than available job opportunities.
Faulty Employment Planning	Five year plans did not focus adequately on creating jobs, assuming economic growth will take care of unemployment problem.
Excessive Use of Foreign Technology	Heavy reliance on foreign technology has led to technical unemployment due to fewer local jobs.
Lack of Financial Resources	Insufficient funds limit the growth (expansion, diversification) of agriculture and small industries, reducing job creation.
Seasonal Agriculture	Agriculture remains seasonal, leaving workers unemployed for part of the year (3-4 months in a year).
Decay of Cottage and Small Industries	The decline of labour intensive cottage and small industries has resulted in fewer employment opportunities.
Low Savings and Investment	Low rate of capital formation restricts business expansion and the ability to create jobs.
Low Labour Mobility	Social, cultural and familial constraints prevent workers from relocating for job opportunities.

Adverse Effects of Unemployment

Unemployment results in a number of adverse effects which can be classified as economic effects and social effects.

Category	Cause	Explanation
Economic Effects (Measurable in Monetary terms)	***Loss of Output***	Underutilisation of human resources leads to a significant loss in overall output for the economy.
	Loss of Human Resources	Productive capacity of willing individuals is wasted due to unemployment, resulting in a waste of valuable human resources.
	Low Productivity	Increased unemployment leads to greater dependence on agriculture, resulting in lower productivity per worker. This hampers economic growth.
	Low Rate of Capital Formation	Unemployment results in lower income levels, which adversely affects the rate of capital formation.

Category	Cause	Explanation
Social Effects (Visible in form of many social problems)	***Rise in Poverty***	Unemployment correlates with rising poverty levels, as more people lack income and resources.
	Increase in Inequalities	Unemployment exacerbates income and wealth disparities, leading to class conflicts and social injustice.
	Low Standard of Living	Reduced income from unemployment negatively impacts individuals' standard of living.
	Social Unrest	Unemployment can lead to anti-social behaviour and unrest, with individuals resorting to crime (theft, extortion, kidnapping) or even terrorism.
	Results in depression	Unemployed individuals may experience feeling of worthlessness, leading to depression and mental health issues.

Measures/Suggestions to Reduce Unemployment

Following measures can be taken to solve the problem of unemployment in India

- It is essential to increase production in agriculture and industrial sectors.
- The small-scale sector should be encouraged through multiple initiatives such as technical training, supply of raw material, infrastructural facilities, etc.
- Rapid population growth should be reduced so that the additional jobs created do not fall short of new entrants in the labour market.
- The functioning of employment exchanges should be improved.
- Special employment programmes should be implemented which aim to increase the level of employment.
- Government should provide various facilities such as financial assistance, technical training, marketing, etc. to self-employed persons.
- Educational system should be made more vocational and work-oriented.
- Investment should be directed towards areas of production where employment potential is high.

Government and Employment Generation

Since independence, the Union and State Government have played an important role in generating employment or creating opportunities for employment generation.

These efforts can be highlighted through the following points

1. **Direct Employment** The government employs individuals across various departments, operates industries and runs transport services, providing direct job opportunities.
2. **Indirect Employment** When government enterprises increase their production, private enterprises that depend on them for raw materials also raise their output. This in turn, creates more employment opportunities, indirectly generated by government initiatives.

3. **Some of the Key Employment Generation Programmes**
   - **Prime Minister's Rozgar Yojana** Aimed at providing self-employment opportunities.
   - **Sampoorna Gramin Rozgar Yojana** Focused on rural employment generation.
   - **Mahatma Gandhi National Rural Employment Guarantee Act** (MGNREGA) Ensures guaranteed employment for rural households.

   These programmes aim at providing not only employment but also services in areas such as primary health, primary education, rural drinking water, nutrition, assistance for people to buy employment generating assets, development of community assets by generating wage employment, etc.

Mind Map

EMPLOYMENT : GROWTH, INFORMALISATION AND OTHER ISSUES

1 Some Basic Concepts

- **Worker** An individual who is involved in some economic activity to earn a livelihood, including self-employed persons.
- **Nature of Employment in India** Employment can be year round or seasonal.
- **Labour Supply** It means number of persons willing to work at different wage rates.
- **Labour Force** It means number of persons actually working or willing to work.
- **Workforce** It means number of persons actually working.

Workforce = Labour Force – Number of Persons not Working but are Willing to Work

Participation of People in Employment

The Worker-Population Ratio (WPR) is an indicator used to analyse the employment situation in the country.

- A higher WPR means greater engagement of people in economic activities.
- A medium or low WPR indicates lower engagement, meaning a higher proportion of the population is not directly involved in economic activities.

Worker-Population Ratio = (Total Number of Workers/Total Population)×100

2 Employment

Employment means an activity which helps an individual to earn his living. It can be classified as

1. **Self-employed Workers** The workers who own and operate an enterprise to earn their livelihood are known as self-employed workers.
2. **Hired Workers** Those people who are hired by others and are paid wages or salaries as a reward for their services are called hired workers. They can be casual wage labourers and regular salaried workers.

Employment by Sector

- **Primary Sector** Employs 44.6% of the total workforce in India.
- **Secondary Sector** Employs 24.4% of the total workforce.
- **Service Sector** Engages 31% of the total workforce.
- **Rural vs Urban Employment Trends** Agriculture dominates rural employment, while the service sector leads in urban areas.

3 Growth and Changing Structure of Employment

Overview of Economic Development (1950-2010)

- **Planned Development** For nearly seventy years, India has focused on expanding its economy through increased national output and employment.
- **GDP Growth** From 1950 to 2010, India's Gross Domestic Product (GDP) grew positively and was higher than the employment growth.
- **Employment Growth Rate** During this period, employment increased at a maximum rate of 2% per year, indicating sluggish job creation relative to economic growth.

Trends and Patterns

- **Fluctuations in GDP** Despite overall positive growth, the GDP experienced fluctuations during this period.
- **Decline in Employment Growth** In the late 1990s, employment growth began to decline, returning to levels seen in the early stages of economic planning.
- **Widening Gap** During this period, there has been a growing disparity between GDP growth and employment growth, illustrating a phenomenon known as 'jobless growth'.

Casualisation of Workforce

The movement from self-employment and regular salaried employment to casual wage work is known as the process of casualisation of workforce.

4 Informalisation of Indian Workforce

Development Objective Since independence, India aimed to provide decent standard of living through industrialisation, transitioning agricultural workers to better paying industrial jobs.

Current Reality

- Over 50% of the workforce still relies on farming as major source of livelihood.
- Quality of employment has been deteriorating; many workers even after working for more than 10-20 years, lack basic benefits.
- Private sector employees often get lower salary than public sector workers for the same jobs.

Workforce Structure

- **Formal Sector** Workers with benefits and protections.
- **Informal Sector** Workers lacking job security and benefits.

Formal Sector Vs Informal Sector

All the public sector establishments and those private sector establishments which employ 10 or more hired workers are called formal sector establishments while all other establishments which employ less than 10 workers are called informal sector establishments.

5 Unemployment

It is a situation in which people, who are capable and willing to work, are not getting work.

Types of Unemployment in India

- Open unemployment
- Seasonal unemployment
- Disguised unemployment

Causes of Unemployment

- Slow economic growth
- Rapid population growth
- Faulty employment planning
- Excessive use of foreign technology
- Decay of cottage and small industries
- Lack of financial resources
- Seasonal agriculture
- Low savings and investment
- Low labour mobility

6 Measures/Suggestions to Reduce Unemployment

- It is essential to increase production in agriculture and industrial sectors.
- The small-scale sector should be encouraged through multiple initiatives.
- Rapid population growth should be reduced.
- The functioning of employment exchanges should be improved.

Government and Employment Generation

- Direct employment
- Indirect employment

Some of the Key Employment Generation Programmes Prime Minister's Rozgar Yojana, Sampoorna Gramin Rozgar Yojana, Mahatma Gandhi National Rural Employment Guarantee Act (MGNREGA), etc.

EXAM PATTERN QUESTIONS

Objective Type Questions

Multiple Choice Questions (MCQs)

1. The 'workforce' includes
(a) only self-employed workers
(b) only hired workers
(c) all individuals engaged in productive economic activity
(d) only casual workers

2. Which of the following is considered a 'worker' in economic terms? Competency Based Que
(i) A person who is self-employed
(ii) A person who works for others
(iii) A person who contributes to the production of goods and services
Codes
(a) (i) and (ii) (b) (ii) and (iii)
(c) (i) and (iii) (d) (i), (ii) and (iii)

3. Identify, which of the following is the correct formula for calculating 'worker-population ratio'? CBSE 2023
(a) $\frac{\text{Total Labour Force}}{\text{Total Population}} \times 100$
(b) $\frac{\text{Total Workers}}{\text{Total Population}} \times 100$
(c) $\frac{\text{Total Population}}{\text{Total Labour Force}} \times 100$
(d) $\frac{\text{Total Population}}{\text{Total Workers}} \times 100$

4. .... degree of worker-population ratio is better for country.
(a) Lower (b) Higher (c) Moderate (d) Optimal

5. Which of the following statements are true regarding self-employed workers? Competency Based Que
(i) They work for themselves and are not dependent on an employer.
(ii) They usually have less job security compared to hired workers.
(iii) Self-employed workers are always part of the formal sector.
(iv) They can include farmers, artisans and small business owners.
Codes
(a) (i), (ii), (iv) (b) (i), (iii), (iv)
(c) (i), (ii), (iii) (d) (i), (ii), (iii), (iv)

6. The majority of self-employed workers in India are found in
(a) urban areas (b) rural areas
(c) IT sectors (d) manufacturing sectors

7. Two months ago, Shyam was working as part time salesman on commission basis in a company.
Due to his excellent performance, company appointed him as a permanent sales manager on fixed monthly salary. From the point of view of employment, currently he is a Competency Based Que
(a) skilled worker (b) regular salaried worker
(c) unskilled worker (d) casual wage labour

8. In workforce, participation rate for women is .... in rural areas as compared with urban areas.
(a) lower (b) higher
(c) maximum (d) minimum

9. Which of the following is true regarding the sectoral distribution of employment in India? Competency Based Que
(a) Agriculture: Low self-employment, Industry: High self-employment
(b) Agriculture: High self-employment, Industry: Low hired work
(c) Agriculture: High self-employment, Industry: High hired work
(d) Industry: High self-employment, Service: Low hired work

10. Which of the following statements is true based on the pie charts below?

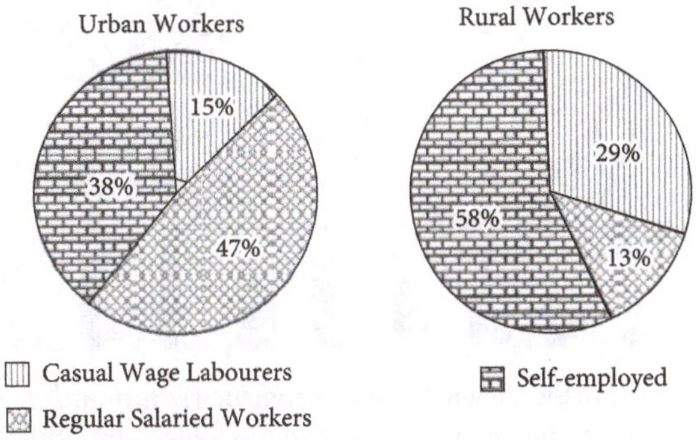

Distribution of Employment by Region

(a) Rural workers have a higher percentage of casual wage labourers than urban workers
(b) Urban workers are mostly employed in self-employed categories
(c) The percentage of self-employed workers is higher in urban areas than rural areas
(d) None of the above

11. Distribution of Workforce by Industry, 2017-18

Industrial Category	Place of Residence		Sex		Total
	Rural	Urban	Male	Female	
Primary Sector	59.8	6.6	40.7	57.1	44.6
Secondary Sector	20.4	34.3	26.5	17.7	24.4
Tertiary/Service Sector	19.8	59.1	32.8	25.2	31.0
Total	**100**	**100**	**100**	**100**	**100**

Based on the data given above, which statement is true regarding the distribution of female workers?
Competency Based Que

(a) Majority of female workers are employed in the tertiary sector
(b) The primary sector employs a higher percentage of females than males
(c) The secondary sector employs the highest percentage of female workers
(d) Urban areas have more female workers in the primary sector than rural areas

12. "Assuming in a hypothetical economy, real gross domestic product recorded a growth rate of 9% during a fiscal year. However, the economy faced a significant challenge in terms of creating an adequate number of employment opportunities." Identify the situation indicated in the given statement and choose the correct option. **CBSE SQP 2025; Competency Based Que**

(a) Casualisation of workforce
(b) Informalisation of workforce
(c) Formalisation of workforce (d) Jobless growth

13.

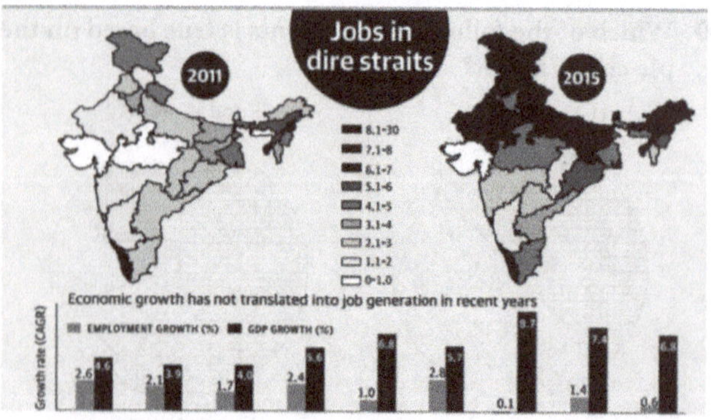

Source *https://www.thehindu.com/news/national/need-for-an-employment-policy-to-solve-jobless-growth/article25041745.ece*

According to the image, which of the following statements is true about economic growth and employment growth?

(a) Employment growth has consistently outpaced GDP growth
(b) Job generation has been higher than economic growth across all years
(c) Both employment and GDP growth have remained constant over time
(d) GDP growth has not translated into proportional job generation

14. Which of the following factors are usually associated with jobless growth?
(i) Technological advancements
(ii) Labour intensive industries
(iii) Automation
(iv) Skill mismatch

Codes
(a) (i), (ii) and (iv)
(b) (i), (iii) and (iv)
(c) (ii) and (iii)
(d) (i) and (iv)

15. "The phenomenon of casualisation in the workforce reflects a trend towards flexible employment contracts." Which of the following implications can be drawn? **Competency Based Que**

(a) Casual employment offers more job security than permanent positions
(b) Workers prefer permanent jobs over casual employment due to stability
(c) Casualisation may lead to increased vulnerability for workers
(d) All workers are transitioning to casual employment models

16. Informalisation of the workforce means

(a) increase in jobs in the formal sector
(b) shift of workers from formal to informal sectors
(c) decline in employment in the agriculture sector
(d) increase in self-employment in the urban areas

17. All the public sector establishments and those private sector establishments which employ .... hired workers or more are called formal sector.

(a) 25 (b) 20 (c) 15 (d) 10

18. Which of the following is a characteristic of the informal sector?

(a) Workers have fixed contracts and social security benefits
(b) Workers are usually paid regular wages
(c) Jobs are often temporary and lack formal contracts
(d) Workers are always hired by large companies

19. **Unemployment is a situation in which people who are ...... and ...... to work but are not getting work.**
(a) incapable and willing
(b) capable and not willing
(c) incapable and not willing
(d) capable and willing

20. **Which of the following is an example of disguised unemployment?**
(a) A teacher losing a job due to school closure
(b) Four people working on a farm where two are required
(c) A person searching for work in the IT sector
(d) An individual waiting for seasonal work

21. **Hidden unemployment can include those working well below their capabilities, those whose positions provide little overall value in terms of productivity or any group that is not currently looking for work but is able to perform work of value and these are not included in official unemployment statistics.**

The above paragraph is indicating Competency Based Que
(a) disguised unemployment
(b) underemployment
(c) structural unemployment
(d) frictional unemployment

22. **The unemployment which is caused by the introduction of new machinery, improvement of production techniques, labour saving devices, etc. is called**
(a) frictional unemployment
(b) casual unemployment
(c) structural unemployment
(d) technological unemployment

23. **Hindustan Times, September 2024**

"The combination of a steady unemployment rate and surging labour force participation indicates that job creation largely kept pace with the influx of new workers into the job market. However, concerns persist about the quality of employment available."

What aspect of the labour market is emphasised as a concern despite the stable unemployment rate? Competency Based Que
(a) Growth in informal employment
(b) Increased participation of women in the workforce
(c) High level of underemployment
(d) Surge in agricultural jobs

24. **One of the major causes of unemployment in India is**
(a) high demand for labour
(b) lack of skill development and training
(c) increase in foreign investment
(d) over-reliance on service sectors

25. **The adverse effects of unemployment include**
(i) Increased poverty levels
(ii) Decline in economic productivity
(iii) Improvement in mental health
(iv) Rise in social unrest
Codes
(a) (i), (ii) and (iii)
(b) (ii), (iii) and (iv)
(c) (i), (ii) and (iv)
(d) (i), (iii) and (iv)

26. **Which measures can be suggested to reduce unemployment?** Competency Based Que
(i) Promoting entrepreneurship
(ii) Increasing the retirement age
(iii) Enhancing skill development programmes
(iv) Offering financial incentives for hiring youth
Codes
(a) (i), (ii) and (iii)
(b) (ii), (iii) and (iv)
(c) (i), (ii) and (iv)
(d) (i), (iii) and (iv)

27. **Which government scheme aims to provide 100 days of guaranteed employment to rural households in India?**
(a) Make in India
(b) Pradhan Mantri Kaushal Vikas Yojana
(c) Mahatma Gandhi National Rural Employment Guarantee Act
(d) Start-up India

Direction *Read the case study and answer the questions 28 to 31 on the basis of the same*

Ritu, a determined rural woman, juggles multiple responsibilities on her family's farm while actively managing household chores.

Her work on the farm allows her to control her schedule, making her an integral part of her family's income generation. Meanwhile, her brother, Ravi, recently transitioned to an urban lifestyle, securing a job as a machine operator in a factory.

While Ravi appreciates the regular pay-check, he often feels constrained by the fixed hours and the monotonous nature of factory work. In contrast, Ritu enjoys the flexibility of working on her own terms, though she faces the uncertainty of seasonal fluctuations in farm income. Their contrasting experiences reflect deeper employment trends in India's rural and urban sectors.

28. **What type of employment does Ritu represent?**
(a) Self-employed in the formal sector
(b) Casual labour in the agricultural sector
(c) Self-employed in the informal sector
(d) Hired worker in the agricultural sector

29. **Ravi, though earning a stable income in the city, feels restricted by the structure of his factory job. His experience illustrates**
(a) the benefits of industrial employment outweigh the drawbacks
(b) a contrast between formal sector security and informal sector flexibility
(c) the rising opportunities for self-employment in urban areas
(d) the freedom that urban employment offers over rural work

30. **Ravi's factory job underscores the urban shift towards .... labour, reflecting the structured environment of industrial employment.**

31. **Ravi's move to an urban area for a factory job exemplifies the migration trend from rural .... work to urban .... work in India.**

Direction *Read the case study and answer the questions 32 to 35 on the basis of the same*

Business Standard, October 2024 "A lasting problem: How can India address its unemployment crisis?"

Unemployment has long been a daunting issue in India, with no government past or present being able to successfully address it. Despite economic growth and numerous promises over the years, millions of young people struggle to find stable employment. But why has unemployment remained such a massive challenge?

India's employment landscape presents a unique set of issues, where agriculture continues to employ nearly 46 per cent of the workforce, especially in rural areas, where many young people lack alternatives. However, these jobs often offer low wages and limited upward mobility.

Many rural youth continue to depend on agriculture, while urban youth, despite better educational qualifications, struggle to find work in industries that can match their skills.

Education is another critical issue. Despite producing 1.5 million engineers annually, up to 80 per cent are deemed unemployable due to skill gaps.

A NASSCOM report warns that India could face a shortage of 1.4 to 1.9 million tech professionals by 2026, further exacerbating the disconnect between education and industry demands.

32. **Which of the following could be a primary reason for the unemployment crisis in India?**
(a) Rapid technological advancements leading to automation
(b) Decrease in the population growth rate
(c) An increase in agricultural output
(d) A rise in global oil prices

33. **How can structural reforms in the education system potentially address India's unemployment crisis?**
(a) By reducing the competition for existing jobs
(b) By increasing the demand for unskilled labour
(c) By improving the alignment between skills taught and market demand
(d) By focusing on theoretical knowledge over practical skills

34. **India's unemployment rate has been exacerbated by rapid ......, which has replaced many traditional jobs.**

35. **One of the suggested solutions for reducing unemployment in India is the improvement of .... to better match the skills of job seekers with market demands.**

Assertion-Reason

Direction (Q.No. 36 to 45) *Read the following Assertion (A) and Reason (R) and choose the correct alternative from the following*

Alternatives
(a) Both Assertion (A) and Reason (R) are true and Reason (R) is the correct explanation of Assertion (A)
(b) Both Assertion (A) and Reason (R) are true, but Reason (R) is not the correct explanation of Assertion (A)
(c) Assertion (A) is true, but Reason (R) is false
(d) Both Assertion (A) and Reason (R) are false

36. **Assertion** (A) The workforce in a country includes all people who are able to work and are working.

Reason (R) The workforce includes only those who are actively engaged in productive activities.

37. **Assertion** (A) The unemployment rate is lower in urban areas than in rural areas in India.

Reason (R) Urban areas provide more diversified employment opportunities, including in the formal sector.

38. **Assertion** (A) Higher percentage of male workers are found in the organised sector employment in India.

Reason (R) In India, females are expected to do household work and unable to devote fixed hours on a regular basis.

39. **Assertion** (A) Services sector in India hasn't generated enough employment over the years.

Reason (R) Even since 1990s, in India the growth rate of GDP has been higher then the growth rate of employment generation.

40. **Assertion** (A) In India, a significant proportion of the female workforce is employed in the informal sector, such as domestic work, street vending and agriculture.

Reason (R) The informal sector provides greater flexibility in working hours and conditions, which is perceived as more suitable for women balancing work with household responsibilities.

41. **Assertion** (A) Contract labourers are often deprived of the privileges and benefits that regular employees in formal sectors enjoy.

Reason (R) The formal sector workforce constitutes a relatively small proportion of India's total labour force.

42. **Assertion** (A) Frictional unemployment is a sign of a dynamic economy.

Reason (R) Frictional unemployment occurs when workers are between jobs or are searching for better job opportunities.

43. **Assertion** (A) Long-term unemployment can result in the erosion of an individual's skills.

Reason (R) When people remain unemployed for long periods, they lose touch with current technologies and industry practices, making it harder for them to find new employment.

44. **Assertion** (A) Unemployment increases the dependency ratio in society.

Reason (R) Unemployed individuals often rely on others for financial support, leading to a higher burden on the working population.

45. **Assertion** (A) The Atmanirbhar Bharat initiative focuses on making India self-reliant and creating more employment opportunities.

Reason (R) The initiative encourages local manufacturing, which in turn increases employment in various industries across the country.

Two Statements Based MCQs

Direction (Q.No. 46 to 55) *Read the following statements carefully and choose the correct alternative*

Alternatives

(a) Statement I is correct and Statement II is incorrect
(b) Statement II is correct and Statement I is incorrect
(c) Both the statements are correct
(d) Both the statements are incorrect

46. **Statement I** A self-employed worker is someone who works for themselves rather than for an employer, such as a farmer, shop owner or a freelancer. They are not covered under the formal employment benefits.

Statement II In India, the proportion of self-employed workers is higher in urban areas compared to rural areas due to better access to resources and infrastructure.

47. **Statement I** Employment is an activity which enables a person to earn means of livelihood for his/her family.

Statement II A worker is the one who contributes to the process of Gross Domestic Product (GDP) by rendering his productive services. **CBSE 2025**

48. **Statement I** Casualisation of the workforce implies that a larger proportion of the workforce is engaged in jobs with secure contracts and stable incomes.

Statement II The growth of the informal sector in India has led to an increase in the casualisation of the workforce, with more people taking up temporary or insecure jobs.

49. **Statement I** Casual workers are hired on a permanent basis and also get social security benefits.

Statement II Workforce comprises, both employed and unemployed person. **CBSE 2024**

50. **Statement I** The informal sector comprises small, unregistered enterprises and workers in this sector usually lack job security and social security benefits.

Statement II The government has made efforts to bring informal workers into the formal sector through initiatives like the Pradhan Mantri Rojgar Yojana (PMRY) and Atal Pension Yojana.

51. **Statement I** Disguised unemployment occurs when more people are employed than required and their marginal productivity becomes zero. This form of unemployment is commonly observed in the agricultural sector in India.

Statement II Open unemployment refers to a situation where a person is not working but is actively seeking work. This type of unemployment is typically found in rural areas where people depend primarily on seasonal work.

52. **Statement I** Seasonal unemployment is mainly found in sectors where production depends on climatic conditions, such as agriculture.

Statement II Seasonal unemployment can be reduced through measures like encouraging multiple cropping and providing alternative employment opportunities during the off-season.

53. **Statement I** Educating the workforce and providing vocational training can be effective measures to reduce structural unemployment.

Statement II The government's role in employment generation includes schemes like Start-Up India, which aim to encourage entrepreneurship and job creation.

54. **Statement I** Rapid economic growth is always sufficient to solve the problem of unemployment in India since it automatically leads to an increase in job creation across all sectors.

Statement II The impact of unemployment is limited to economic aspects and does not significantly affect the social fabric of a society.

55. **Statement I** As per National Sample Survey Organisation (NSSO) unemployment is a situation in which all those who, owing to lack of work, are not working, but seeking work from prospective employers, expressed their willingness to work under the prevailing condition of work and remuneration.

Statement II Disguised unemployment is generally a massive problem in the highly populated country like India. **CBSE 2024**

Matching

56. Match the following

	Column I		Column II
A.	Working population of a country	(i)	Rural-urban divide
B.	Available to work in a country	(ii)	Workforce
C.	Division of workforce based upon region	(iii)	Labour force

Codes

	A	B	C		A	B	C
(a)	(ii)	(iii)	(i)	(b)	(iii)	(ii)	(i)
(c)	(ii)	(i)	(iii)	(d)	(i)	(iii)	(ii)

57. Choose the correct pair form given below

	Column I		Column II
A.	Working during few months in a year	(i)	Disguised unemployment
B.	Working without contribution to output	(ii)	Seasonal unemployment
C.	Growth of employment less than growth of GDP	(iii)	Jobless growth

Codes

(a) A-(i) (b) B-(ii)
(c) C-(iii) (d) All of these

58. Match the following terms with their correct definitions **Competency Based Que**

	Column I		Column II
A.	Labour supply	(i)	Sector of employment where workers do not have job security or formal contracts.
B.	Casualisation of workforce	(ii)	Total number of people who are willing to work at the current wage rate.
C.	Informal sector	(iii)	Workers who run their own businesses or are engaged in their own trade or profession.
D.	Self-employed workers	(iv)	Increasing share of casual workers in the workforce.

Codes

	A	B	C	D		A	B	C	D
(a)	(iii)	(i)	(ii)	(iv)	(b)	(i)	(ii)	(iii)	(iv)
(c)	(ii)	(iv)	(i)	(iii)	(d)	(iv)	(iii)	(i)	(ii)

59. Match the following

	Column I		Column II
A.	Prime Minister's Rozgar Yojana (PMRY)	(i)	Guaranteed 100 days of wage employment
B.	Sampoorna Gramin Rozgar Yojana (SGRY)	(ii)	Promotes rural employment and food security
C.	Mahatma Gandhi National Rural Employment Guarantee Act (MGNREGA)	(iii)	Aims at self-employment for educated youth
D.	Start-Up India	(iv)	Promotes entrepreneurship and innovation

Codes

	A	B	C	D		A	B	C	D
(a)	(iii)	(ii)	(i)	(iv)	(b)	(i)	(iii)	(ii)	(iv)
(c)	(ii)	(iv)	(i)	(iii)	(d)	(iii)	(i)	(iv)	(ii)

Concept Identification

60. The amount of labour that the workers are willing to offer corresponding to different wage rates.

61. A is a worker who is employed on a short-term or temporary basis and is paid for the hours worked or tasks completed.

62. A measure that calculates the proportion of the working age population who are employed or actively engaged in the labour force.

63. A situation when the percentage of casually hired workers in the total workforce tends to rise over time.

64. A situation when people are willing to work at the existing wage rate and are able to work, but are not getting work.

65. A situation wherein the number of workers engaged in a job is much more than actually required to accomplish it. **CBSE 2020**

Answers

1. (c) all individuals engaged in productive economic activity
2. (d) (i), (ii) and (iii)
3. (b) $\frac{\text{Total Workers}}{\text{Total Population}} \times 100$
4. (b) Higher
5. (a) (i), (ii), (iv)
6. (b) rural areas
7. (b) regular salaried worker
8. (b) higher
9. (c) Agriculture: High self-employment, Industry: High hired work
10. (a) Rural workers have a higher percentage of casual wage labourers than urban workers (58% in rural areas vs 15% in urban areas).
11. (b) The primary sector employs a higher percentage of females than males
12. (d) Jobless growth
13. (d) GDP growth has not translated into proportional job generation
14. (b) (i), (iii) and (iv)
15. (c) Casualisation may lead to increased vulnerability for workers
16. (b) shift of workers from formal to informal sectors
17. (d) 10
18. (c) Jobs are often temporary and lack formal contracts
19. (d) capable and willing
20. (b) Four people working on a farm where two are required
21. (a) disguised unemployment
22. (d) technological unemployment
23. (c) High level of underemployment
24. (b) lack of skill development and training
25. (c) (i), (ii) and (iv)
26. (d) (i), (iii) and (iv)
27. (c) Mahatma Gandhi National Rural Employment Guarantee Act
28. (c) Self-employed in the informal sector
29. (b) a contrast between formal sector security and informal sector flexibility
30. hired
31. agricultural, industrial
32. (a) Rapid technological advancements leading to automation
33. (c) By improving the alignment between skills taught and market demand
34. automation
35. vocational training programmes
36. (b) Both Assertion (A) and Reason (R) are true, but Reason (R) is not the correct explanation of Assertion (A)
37. (a) Both Assertion (A) and Reason (R) are true and Reason (R) is the correct explanation of Assertion (A)
38. (a) Both Assertion (A) and Reason (R) are true and Reason (R) is the correct explanation of Assertion (A)
39. (b) Both Assertion (A) and Reason (R) are true, but Reason (R) is not the correct explanation of Assertion (A)
40. (b) Both Assertion (A) and Reason (R) are true, but Reason (R) is not the correct explanation of Assertion (A)
41. (b) Both Assertion (A) and Reason (R) are true, but Reason (R) is not the correct explanation of Assertion (A)
42. (a) Both Assertion (A) and Reason (R) are true and Reason (R) is the correct explanation of Assertion (A)
43. (a) Both Assertion (A) and Reason (R) are true and Reason (R) is the correct explanation of Assertion (A)
44. (a) Both Assertion (A) and Reason (R) are true and Reason (R) is the correct explanation of Assertion (A)
45. (a) Both Assertion (A) and Reason (R) are true and Reason (R) is the correct explanation of Assertion (A)
46. (a) The proportion of self-employed workers is typically higher in rural areas due to agricultural activities and lack of formal employment opportunities, while urban areas have more formal job opportunities.
47. (c) Both the statements are correct
48. (b) 'Casualisation of the workforce' refers to an increase in temporary, informal or part-time employment, which typically leads to less job security and more unstable incomes.
49. (d) Casual workers are typically hired for short-term or temporary work and do not have the same job security as permanent employees. Workforce refers to the number of persons actually working and does not account for those who are willing to work (but not working).
50. (c) Both the statements are correct
51. (a) Open unemployment is typically found in urban areas, not rural areas. Rural areas are more often characterised by seasonal or disguised unemployment.
52. (c) Both the statements are correct
53. (c) Both the statements are correct
54. (d) Rapid economic growth does not always translate into sufficient job creation, especially if the growth is concentrated in capital intensive industries that do not require much labour. In India, economic growth has often been accompanied by jobless growth. Also, unemployment has significant social impacts.
55. (c) Both the statements are correct
56. (a) (ii) (iii) (i)
57. (c) C-(iii)
58. (c) (ii) (iv) (i) (iii)
59. (a) (iii) (ii) (i) (iv)
60. Labour supply
61. Casual wage labourer
62. Worker population ratio
63. Casualisation of workforce
64. Unemployment
65. Disguised unemployment

Subjective Questions

Short Answer Type Questions

1. Ram is an owner of a salon. He is temporarily absent from work due to injury. Can he be considered as worker? Explain. CBSE Term II 2022; Competency Based Que

Ans. Yes, Ram can be considered as worker because he is engaged in work of salon on permanent basis and temporary absentism due to injury does not make him to be considered as unemployed.

Unemployment is a situation in which people who are capable and willing to work are not getting work.

2. Meena is a housewife. Besides taking care of household chores, she works in the cloth shop which is owned and operated by her husband. Can she be considered as a worker? Why? NCERT; Competency Based Que

Ans. Yes, Meena can be considered a worker.
An individual engaged in productive activity to contribute to livelihood or economic value is termed a worker. Meena, despite primarily being a housewife, assists in her husband's cloth shop. The following points explain why Meena qualifies as a worker

(i) **Contribution to Economic Activity**
Meena contributes to the operation of her husband's cloth shop, which is an economic activity. This aligns with the concept of productive work that generates goods or services.

(ii) **Unpaid Work Still Counts**
Even if she is not receiving formal wages for her contribution, her work at the shop adds value to the business, making her an economic participant. In economic terms, unpaid family labour is also considered part of the workforce.

Thus, Meena should be recognised as a worker because her efforts contribute to the family's livelihood and economic productivity.

3. "Neha has been working in a multinational corporation since the past five years on the payroll of the company." Identify and briefly explain the type of employment indicated in the above statement. CBSE 2024; Competency Based Que

Ans. Neha is a regular salaried employee. When a worker is engaged by someone or an enterprise and paid his or her wages on a regular basis, they can be categorised as regular salaried employees.

Such employees are entitled to receive regular compensation from their employer along with other social security benefits.

4. Name the indicator that is generally used for analysing the employment situation in a country. Also discuss its importance. CBSE 2024 C

Ans. Worker-population ratio is an indicator which is used for analysing the employment situation in the country. This ratio is useful in knowing the proportion of population that is actively contributing to the production of goods and services of a country. Higher the worker-population ratio, higher the engagement of people in economic activities and *vice-versa*.

5. "India's demographic dividend can become a demographic disaster if it fails to create jobs for its burgeoning youth population." – The Hindu
In the context of this statement, is employment important for the Indian economy? Competency Based Que

Ans. Yes, employment is crucial for the Indian economy in the context of its demographic dividend for the following reasons

(i) **Utilising Demographic Advantage**
It allows India to harness its large youth population, turning a potential burden into a productive workforce.

(ii) **Economic Growth**
Jobs increase income and consumption, driving economic growth and demand.

(iii) **Poverty Reduction**
Employment directly lifts people out of poverty, ensuring more inclusive development.

(iv) **Social Stability**
Jobs prevent unrest and maintain social harmony by reducing youth frustration.

6. The following table shows the population and worker population ratio for India in 1999-2000. Can you estimate the workforce (rural and urban) for India? NCERT

Region	Estimates of Population (in crore)	Worker-Population Ratio	Estimated Number of Workers (in crore)
Rural	71.88	41.9	$\frac{71.88}{100} \times 41.9 = 30.12$
Urban	28.52	33.7	?
Total	100.40	39.5	?

Ans. Worker-Population Ratio

$$= \frac{\text{Total Number of Workers}}{\text{Total Population}} \times 100$$

$\therefore$ Number of Workers

$$= \frac{\text{Total Population}}{100} \times \text{Worker-Population Ratio}$$

Region	Estimates of Population (in crore)	Worker-Population Ratio	Estimated Number of Workers (in crore)
Rural	71.88	41.9	$\frac{71.88}{100}\times 41.9 = 30.12$
Urban	28.52	33.7	$\frac{28.52}{100}\times 33.7 = 9.61$
Total	100.40	39.5	$\frac{100.40}{100}\times 39.5 = 39.66$

7. Compared to urban women, more rural women are found working. Why? NCERT

Ans. The difference in participation rates is very high between urban and rural women. In urban areas, for every 100 urban females, only about 14 are engaged in some economic activities.

In rural areas, for every 100 rural women, about 18 participate in the employment market. It is common to find that where men are able to earn high incomes, families discourage female members from taking up jobs.

Earnings of urban male workers are generally higher than rural males and so urban families do not want females to work.

Apart from this, many activities of the household in which urban women are engaged, are not recognised as productive work, while women working on farms in the rural areas are considered a part of the workforce if they are being paid wages in cash or in the form of foodgrains.

8. "In a nation like India, self-employment provides an important avenue for employment generation." Defend or refute the given statement with valid arguments. CBSE 2024; Competency Based Que

Ans. The statement is defended. It is justifiable due to several reasons

(i) **Vast Informal Sector**
India has a large informal sector, where many individuals engage in self-employment activities such as street vending, small-scale trading and home based enterprises. This sector provides livelihood opportunities to millions of people who may not have access to formal employment due to factors such as lack of education, skills or employment opportunities.

(ii) **Flexibility**
Self-employment offers flexibility in terms of working hours, location and choice of work. This flexibility is particularly beneficial for individuals who need to balance work with other responsi-bilities such as childcare or caregiving.

(iii) **Addressing Unemployment**
Given the challenges of creating sufficient formal employment opportunities to absorb India's growing workforce, self-employment provides a viable alternative for generating income and reducing unemployment.

9. Why are regular salaried employees more in urban areas than in rural areas? NCERT

Ans. Regular salaried employees are more in urban areas than in rural areas due to following reasons

(i) **Education and Training**
Regular salaried employment requires certain educational qualifications and professional skills. Education and training facilities are not as good in rural areas as in urban areas. Therefore, chances of regular employment are higher for urban people.

(ii) **Infrastructure**
Large companies including MNCs are concentrated in the urban areas due to the presence of economic infrastructure and availability of modern facilities like banks, transport, communication, etc. These companies hire regular salaried employees, which results in concentration their in the urban areas.

(iii) **Agriculture**
Rural population is primarily engaged in agricultural sector and are not willing to take the risk of leaving their farms for regular salaried employment. This is also a reason for regular salaried employment to be less prevalent in rural areas.

10. Elaborate any three reasons owing to which lesser number of women are found in regular salaried employment. CBSE 2024

Or **Why are less women found in regular salaried employment?** NCERT

Ans. Reasons for lesser women participation in regular salaried employment are

(i) **Lack of Education Facilities**
Female education is not given due importance in India and hence a majority of the women in India do not have the educational qualifications and professional skills required for regular salaried employment.

(ii) **Discouragement from Family**
In India, families still do not want female members to step out from the house for work especially if it is for long hours as in regular salaried employment.

(iii) **Wage Discrimination**
Gender-based wage discrimination is prevalent in India which demotivates the women in regular salaried employment and they prefer being at home or going for self-employment opportunities.

11. **Analyse and compare the two images given below** Competency Based Que

Ans. The above two images highlight the women working in rural areas as well as in urban areas. Comparison between these two is as follows

(i) In rural areas, most of the women work in agriculture as compared to females in urban areas where they work more in secondary or tertiary sector.

(ii) Women participation in rural employment is more as compared to women in urban areas.

It is so because earnings of urban workers are generally higher than rural males and so urban families do not want females to work.

(iii) Apart from this, many activities of the household in which urban women are engaged, are not recognised as productive work, whereas women working on farms in the rural areas are considered to be a part of the workforce if they are being paid wages in cash or in the form of foodgrains.

12. **"As an economy grows, the number of employed persons in an economy also increases; however, since 1991 India has come up as an exception to this."**

Do you agree with the given statement? Give valid arguments in support of your answer. CBSE 2024; Competency Based Que

Ans. Yes, after the introduction of economic reforms, in the late 1990s, the Indian economy experienced a rapid rise in the GDP growth rate.

However, employment growth started declining, in spite of rising GDP i.e. India started experiencing the problem of jobless growth. The Indian economy was able to produce more goods and services without a corresponding rise in the number of employed persons.

13. **"Casualisation of the workforce has been on the rise, especially in developing economies, where a significant portion of the labour force is moving into less secure and informal jobs."**

Discuss the concept of 'casualisation of workforce' and its implications on the economy. Competency Based Que

Ans. The 'casualisation of the workforce' refers to a trend where an increasing number of workers are employed in jobs that are temporary, part-time or informal rather than in permanent, secure and well-regulated employment.

This trend is often observed in developing economies but is also seen in developed countries due to changes in labour market policies and globalisation.

Implications for the economy are as follows

(i) **Increased Informality**
As more workers take up informal jobs, it leads to a larger informal sector, which can be harder for governments to regulate and tax, impacting public revenue.

(ii) **Reduced Productivity**
A workforce dominated by casual employment can lead to lower productivity levels as businesses may not invest as much in training and development of temporary workers.

(iii) **Greater Economic Vulnerability**
Economies with a high proportion of casual workers may be more vulnerable to economic shocks, as these workers are the first to lose their jobs during downturns, leading to higher unemployment rates.

14. **Over the last few decades, there has been considerable shift of workforce from self-employment and regular salaried employment to casual wage work. Scholars termed this process of movement as casualisation of workforce.**

Although, self-employment continues to be the major employment provider, but its share is declining and the share of casual workers in employment is increasing.

In this view, give any three reasons of casualisation of workforce. Competency Based Que

Ans. Reasons of casualisation of workforce are as follows (any three)

(i) It is due to lack of opportunities in the organised sector, people start working as casual workers.

(ii) Further the flexibility in terms of working conditions and no special follow-up of labour laws, etc. makes companies to recruit more casual workers.

(iii) The rigid labour regulatory framework of India has proved to be a bottleneck for organisations, from hiring workers and expanding their production.

(iv) Lack of budgetary support also promotes casualisation as in case of education in government schools, various state governments are recruiting casual teachers rather than permanent teachers.

15. Discuss briefly the concept of 'informalisation of workforce' in India. CBSE 2020

Ans. Informalisation of workforce in India implies that there is a continuous decline in the percentage of workforce employed in the formal sector and a corresponding rise in the percentage of workforce employed in informal sector.

With the implementation of the economic reforms in 1991, many workers were dismissed from the formal sector and forced to take up jobs in the informal sector, leading to a considerable rise in the rate of informalisation.

16. Identify the situation depicted in the given image. Suggest the impact of the indicated situation, on the Indian economy. CBSE SQP 2024; Competency Based Que

Ans. The given image depicts the drift of the Indian workforce from the formal sector to the informal sector employment. This situation is popularly known as 'informalisation of the workforce'.

In India, informal sector includes millions of farmers, agricultural labourers, non-farm casual wage labourers, owners of small enterprises and the self-employed people.

The workforce in the informal sector does not get regular income; they do not have any protection or regulation from the government. Workers may be dismissed without any compensation/notice. The government is taking steps to safeguard the interests of the workers in the informal sector.

17. Is it necessary to generate more employment in the formal sector rather than in the informal sector? Why? NCERT; CBSE 2025, 20

Ans. Yes, it is necessary to generate employment in the formal sector rather than in the informal sector because those who work in the informal sector do not get any regular income and do not get protection from the government.

Workers are dismissed without any compensation. Technology used in informal sector is outdated and they also do not maintain any accounts. Workers live in slums or badly built houses. Those who work in the formal sector on the other hand earn more than those in the informal sector and also enjoy social benefits. It is, thus, necessary to generate more employment in the formal sector.

18. Compare and analyse the sector-wise trends in employment, based on following information. CBSE Term II 2022; Competency Based Que

Trends in Employment (Sector-wise)

Sector	1999-2000	2011-12
Primary	60.4	48.9
Secondary	15.8	24.3
Tertiary	23.8	26.8
Total	100	100

Ans. The given table shows the following

(i) **Decline in Primary Sector Employment**
Employment in the primary sector (mainly agriculture) decreased significantly from 60.4% in 1999-2000 to 48.9% in 2011-12, reflecting a shift away from agriculture as a major source of employment.

(ii) **Growth in Secondary Sector Employment**
The secondary sector (industries, manufacturing) saw a substantial increase in employment, rising from 15.8% in 1999-2000 to 24.3% in 2011-12, indicating industrial growth and greater employment opportunities in manufacturing and related sectors.

(iii) **Tertiary Sector Expansion**
Employment in the tertiary (services) sector also grew from 23.8% to 26.8% during the same period, demonstrating the expanding importance of services like IT, finance, education and healthcare in the Indian economy.

19. How is unemployment an economic as well as a social problem?

Ans. Unemployment is both an economic and a social problem. Unemployment is an economic problem because unemployed persons will be consumers only without being a producer.

Non-utilisation of human resources due to unemployment involves double cost of maintenance and loss of output. Unemployment is a social problem in the sense that it causes enormous sufferings to unemployed workers due to their reduced or nil income.

Many social evils like dishonesty, immorality, drinking, gambling, robbery, etc are the outcome of unemployment. It causes social disruption in the society and the government has to incur a heavy unproductive expenditure on law and order.

20. "Unemployment is related to poverty." Comment. Competency Based Que

Ans. Unemployment is related to poverty in following ways

(i) Poor people do not have enough resources for economic purpose. e.g. A poor farmer cannot use the good variety of seeds and equipments.

(ii) Due to poverty, they are not in a position to maintain efficiency and productivity.
Poverty encourages farmers to mortgage their land to moneylenders which in long-run, increases unemployment.

(iii) It is often difficult for poor men to have proper education to improve their mental ability.

Therefore, poor people are not able to get jobs and are unemployed.

21. Define disguised unemployment with a suitable example. CBSE 2024 C

Ans. Disguised unemployment refers to a situation when the person seems to be employed but is not contributing to the output i.e. his marginal productivity is zero.

e.g. Suppose a farmer with four acres of land and two workers can produce 100 quintals of wheat. Even if he employs one more worker, the total output remains unchanged. Hence, the contribution made by the additional worker to the total output is zero and thus can be said to be in a situation of disguised unemployment.

22. Explain the measures to solve unemployment problems.

Ans. Following are the measures to solve the unemployment problem

(i) The government should try to control the population, so that the number of new entrants to the workforce can be reduced.

(ii) The education system of India needs to be reformed to address the problem of unemployment. The emphasis in education should shift from theoretical knowledge to practical skills.

(iii) Agricultural activities should be diversified into fisheries, cattle rearing, horticulture, etc. to generate income and employment opportunities.

(iv) The government should take necessary steps to develop cottage and small industries, both in the rural, as well as, urban areas. These industries are labour intensive and employ more labour, per unit of capital.

23. What role does the government play in generating employment opportunities?

Ans. The government generates employment through direct and indirect efforts. The government makes direct efforts at employing people in various departments for administrative purposes.
It runs various enterprises and when they result in increased output of goods and services, they lead to further increase in employment.

The various private enterprises that are linked to the government enterprises might also benefit from increased output of these enterprises and thus, increase their output and employment also. This way government also indirectly generates employment.

Long Answer Type Questions

24. The Economic Times, August, 2024 "The nature of employment in India has evolved, with rising self-employment, a decrease in regular wage employment and the continued prevalence of casual labour due to the informal economy."

Explain how different forms of employment co-exist in the Indian economy using examples. Discuss how these forms affect the overall labour market and income stability for workers. Competency Based Que

Ans. Employment refers to a situation where individuals engage in work to earn wages or profits. In the context of the Indian economy, employment can be understood through various forms

(i) **Self-employment**
- In self-employment, individuals operate their own business or profession without working for a salary or wage from an employer.
- e.g. A person running a local grocery store or a freelance web designer who works independently.
- **Impact** While self-employment offers flexibility, it can also be risky as income depends on the success of the venture, leading to unstable earnings.

(ii) **Casual Wage Employment**
- Casual workers are hired on a daily or contractual basis and paid wages depending on the hours worked. These jobs are prevalent in the informal sector, which constitutes a significant portion of the Indian labour market.
- e.g. Construction workers or agricultural labourers hired during harvest season.

Such jobs are typically short-term and do not come with job security or benefits like health insurance or pensions.

- **Impact** Casual wage employment creates income insecurity and can leave workers vulnerable to exploitation, but it also serves as a primary source of income for many low skilled labourers.

(iii) **Regular Wage Employment**

- Regular wage employment refers to jobs that provide a steady, periodic income with job security and benefits. These jobs are mostly found in the formal sector, such as government positions or jobs in large private firms.
- e.g. An accountant working for a multinational corporation or a school teacher employed in a public school.
- **Impact** While regular employment provides financial stability, it is becoming less accessible and workers often have to compete for fewer permanent positions.

In conclusion, the co-existence of self-employment, casual wage employment and regular wage employment reflects the complexity of India's labour market. Each form of employment has distinct implications for workers' income stability, security and economic contribution.

25. Refer to the data provided in the table on the worker-population ratio in India, 2017-2018 and answer the following questions. **Competency Based Que**

Worker-Population Ratio in India, 2017-2018

Sex	Worker-Population Ratio		
	Total	Rural	Urban
Men	52.1	51.7	53.0
Women	16.5	17.5	14.2
Total	**34.7**	**35**	**33.9**

(i) **Analyse the nature of employment in India based on the Worker-Population Ratio (WPR) data. Discuss the differences in employment patterns between men and women, and between rural and urban areas.**

(ii) **Using the WPR data, highlight key challenges in the labour market, especially with regard to gender and region based disparities.**

Ans. (i) The Worker-Population Ratio (WPR) data for India in 2017-2018 reveals significant insights into the nature of employment in the country

- **Gender Disparities**
  - The WPR for men is significantly higher at 52.1% compared to just 16.5% for women. This indicates that men are much more likely to be part of the workforce than women.
  - The disparity is consistent across both rural and urban areas. In rural regions, the WPR for men is 51.7% versus 17.5% for women and in urban regions, it stands at 39.0% for men and 14.2% for women.
  - This suggests that women face considerable barriers to employment, including cultural norms, responsibilities at home and lack of access to formal job opportunities.
- **Rural vs Urban Employment Patterns**
  - The total WPR is higher in rural areas (35) compared to urban areas (33.9). This difference is likely due to the availability of informal and agricultural jobs in rural areas, where a larger portion of the population is involved in self-employment or family based agricultural work.
  - Urban areas, with a WPR of 33.9, have more opportunities in formal sectors, but these require skills and education, which may not be accessible to all. The lower WPR in urban areas suggests that the workforce participation does not match the population size, potentially due to a lack of sufficient job creation or higher living costs.

(ii) Key challenges in the labour market are as follows

- **Consistent Gender Gap**
  Women's participation in the workforce is low due to social and economic barriers.
- **Higher WPR in Rural Areas**
  Rural areas show a higher WPR due to more informal and agricultural jobs, while urban areas have a lower WPR. Rural jobs are often low paying and lack security.
- **Urban Job Market Challenges**
  Despite greater opportunities in urban areas, the WPR is lower, indicating issues like skill mismatches, insufficient formal job creation or the cost of living that may make certain jobs unattractive.

26. The following table shows distribution of workforce in India for the year 1972-73. Analyse it and give reasons for the nature of workforce distribution. **NCERT; Competency Based Que**

Place of Residence	Workforce (in millions)		
	Male	Female	Total
Rural	125	69	195
Urban	32	7	39

Ans. From the given table, following points can be noticed about the nature of workforce distribution

(i) Majority of the workforce was residing in the rural areas in India in the year 1972-73. The total workforce was 234 million out of which 195 million workers were from rural areas and 39 million from the urban areas.

Thus, 83% of the total workforce was rural as compared to 17% of the urban workforce.

The reason for this was that a majority of population was living in rural areas during that period.

(ii) The rural workforce comprises of 64% of the male workforce and 36% of female workforce. On the other hand, the urban workforce comprises of about 82% of male workforce and 18% of female workforce. This shows that participation of males in both rural as well as urban areas is higher than that of the females because of lack of opportunities available to women for acquiring education and also the social structure and family norms which did not encourage women to work.

(iii) Another feature of workforce distribution is the difference between urban female workforce and rural female workforce. Females in the rural areas formed 36% of the workforce, whereas, the females in the urban areas formed only 18% of the workforce. This may be attributed to the fact that where men are able to earn high incomes, families discourage female members from taking-up jobs.

Earnings of urban male workers are generally higher than rural males and so the urban families do not want females to work.

Thus, it can be concluded by analysing the above table that majority of the workforce was from the rural areas and there was low female participation rate in the workforce during that period.

27. Study the following chart showing the growth of employment and gross domestic product and analyse the trend of the two variables from 1990-2012.

CBSE SQP 2020; Competency Based Que

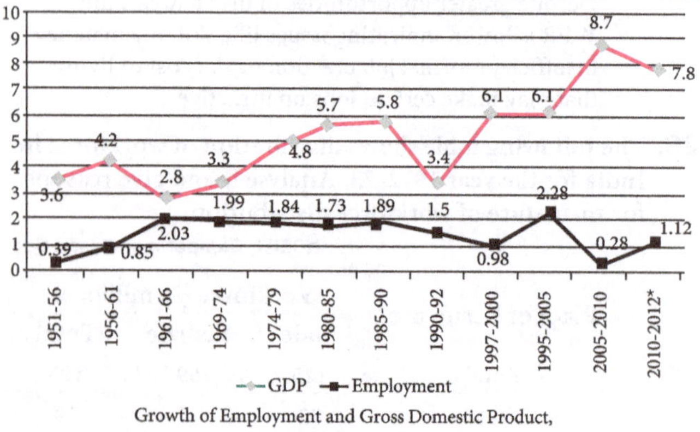

Growth of Employment and Gross Domestic Product, 1951–2012 (%)

Ans. The period between 1990 to 2012 had been significant for India's economic development. Introduction of economic reforms in India has changed everything in India. Variables shown in the given graph show that GDP growth rate has taken an upwards tread over the years whereas the situation of employment growth rate has seen major fluctuations while going down in overall trend.

GDP growth rate has increased from a meagre 3.4% in 1991 to 7.8% in 2012. However the employment growth rate has shown declining trends from 1.5% in 1991 to 1.12% in 2012.

Between the period 1999-2005 the employment generation rate was at peak since independence i.e. 2.28% p.a. with the corresponding GDP growth rate standing at a decent 6.1% p.a. The gap between the two variables is maximum between the period 2005-10 when the employment growth rate hit the lowest in history of independent India i.e. 0.28%. In the same period the GDP growth rate had hit the highest level since independence to the tune of 8.7% p.a. Indian economy has witnessed the peculiar phenomena of 'jobless growth' over all these years.

Learning from the situation government had put in serious efforts on employment front and brought it to a level of 1.12% p.a. between the period 2010-12. In all, the period between 1990-2012 has been highly volatile for the India economy on the two front of GDP and employment growth rate.

28. Economists say that if casualisation increases the earning of the people, then such phenomenon should be welcomed. Suppose a marginal farmer becomes a full-time agricultural labourer.

Do you think he will be happy even if he earns more in his daily wage work?

Or will a permanent and regular worker of the pharmaceutical industry be happy if he becomes a daily wage labourer, even if his overall earnings increase? Discuss. Competency Based Que

Ans. The movement of labour from regular workers to casual wage workers is known as the process of casualisation.

Casualisation is not preferred by the workers, even if it results in increasing their incomes because of the insecurity and social stigma attached to this concept.

A marginal farmer will not be happy to become a full-time agricultural labourer, even if he earns more, because being a farmer is much more prestigious than being an agricultural labourer.

Similarly, working in a pharmaceutical company is considered prestigious than working as a daily wage labourer.

So, a permanent and regular worker of the pharmaceutical company will also not be happy to become a wage labourer.

This leads us to the conclusion that workers consider the work and income collectively and the nature of work gains precedent over income. Therefore, workers resist casualisation even if it results in increase in their income.

29. Differentiate between formal sector and informal sector.

Ans. Differences between formal sector and informal sector are as follows

Basis	Formal Sector	Informal Sector
Meaning	All public and private sector establishments which employ 10 or more hired workers comprise the formal sector.	All establishments which employ less than 10 workers comprise the informal sector.
Government Control	Government exercises control over this sector by passing necessary Acts and formulating rules and regulations.	Government has no control over this sector. Except for the Minimum Wages Act, no other Act is applicable on this sector.
Social Security Benefit	Workers working in this sector are entitled to social security benefits.	Workers working in this sector are not entitled to social security benefits.
Trade Union Formation	The workers working in formal sector have a right to form trade unions.	The workers working in informal sector do not enjoy any such right.
Pay Scale	Formal sector offers better pay scales to its workers.	The pay scales in the informal sector are comparatively low.
Job Security	Workers working in formal sector enjoy job security. They cannot be dismissed without giving them a due notice and/or compensation.	Workers working in informal sector do not enjoy job security. They can be dismissed without a notice and no compensation is offered to them.

30. What do you mean by unemployment? What types of unemployment are found in rural and urban areas of India? Briefly explain.

Ans. Unemployment is a condition where individuals who are willing and able to work do not find employment. In India, various types of unemployment exist in both rural and urban areas, affecting different segments of society.

Below are the major types of unemployment

(i) **Open Unemployment**
This occurs when individuals are actively seeking work but are unable to find any. Despite being capable and willing, they remain fully unemployed. This type of unemployment is common in both rural and urban areas, particularly among daily wage earners.

(ii) **Seasonal Unemployment**
Found mostly in agriculture and seasonal industries like ice-cream and woollen factories, this form of unemployment happens during off-seasons when there is no work available. Workers are employed only during peak seasons and remain unemployed in the slack seasons.

(iii) **Disguised Unemployment**
This type of unemployment occurs when more people are employed than necessary, especially in rural areas. The productivity of these extra workers is either zero or negative, meaning they do not contribute to the overall output. It is common in family run agricultural activities.

(iv) **Industrial Unemployment**
Industrial unemployment affects individuals who lack the necessary skills or education to work in industries, mining, transport, or construction. This has worsened with the migration of rural workers to urban areas in search of jobs, leading to higher unemployment rates in industrial sectors.

(v) **Educated Unemployment**
Due to the rapid expansion of educational institutions, many educated individuals, especially youth, face unemployment. Despite having qualifications, they struggle to find suitable jobs, particularly white-collar positions, due to a mismatch between education and job market needs.

(vi) **Technological Unemployment**
As technology advances, workers who fail to update their skills become obsolete. This form of unemployment arises when workers are replaced by machines or are unable to adapt to new technologies in their field of work.

31. What is seasonal unemployment? Suggest measures for reducing this kind of unemployment in India.

Ans. It refers to a situation where a number of persons are not able to find job in a particular season. It occurs in case of agriculture, ice-cream factories, woollen factories, etc.

Following measures may be suggested to reduce seasonal unemployment

(i) Promotion of multiple cropping, i.e. raising more than one crop on the same piece of land in a year.

(ii) Development of activities allied to agriculture such as animal husbandry, dairy farming, horticulture, etc. to provide extra employment throughout the year.

(iii) Public investment in rural areas in such fields as irrigation, drainage, flood control, land and environment, improvement of rural roads, schools, hospitals, etc.

(iv) Promotion of on-farm investment. Overhaul of machinery, training of farm labour and programmes for eradication of illiteracy during slack seasons.

(v) Mechanisation of peak season activities so that a proportion of the labour force is permanently shifted from agriculture to non-seasonal activities and surplus labour in the slack season is reduced.

(vi) Establishment of a variety of industries which operate at different times of the year so that labour may be kept employed almost throughout the year by shifting from one seasonal industry to another.

32. How is unemployment different from underemployment? How is unemployment measured in India?

Ans. Unemployment is a situation in which people are willing to work and capable to work, but still they are not getting work. Underemployment, on the other hand, is a situation in which an individual is working much below his potential.

As per 27th round of NSO, three types of estimates are available to measure unemployment

(i) **Usual Status Unemployment**

It is measured in number of persons who remained unemployed for a major part of the year.

(ii) **Weekly Status Unemployment**

It is measured in number of persons who did not find any work even for an hour during the week proceeding the survey week.

(iii) **Daily Status Unemployment**

Daily status unemployment is measured in terms of number of man days a person was not getting work on a day during the week proceeding the survey week.

Out of these three, the daily status unemployment concept is most appropriate because it takes into consideration both open and underemployment.

Unemployment Rate by Daily Status

$$= \frac{\text{Daily Status Unemployment}}{\text{Number of Man Days Available}} \times 100$$

33. "According to a recent report by the International Labour Organisation (ILO), the surge in unemployment rates is not only a result of economic downturns but also due to structural changes in industries, automation and shifts in consumer behaviour that require new skill sets."

Discuss the multifaceted causes of unemployment in the current economic landscape contributing to the issue. Competency Based Que

Ans. Unemployment is a complex issue influenced by various factors. The current economic landscape reveals several multifaceted causes of unemployment

(i) **Slow Economic Growth**

In Indian economy, the rate of economic growth is very slow. This slow growth rate fails to provide enough employment opportunities to the rising population. Supply of labour is much more than the available employment opportunities.

(ii) **Rapid Growth of Population**

Continuous increase in population has been a serious problem of India. It is one of the main causes of unemployment. The country has not been able to generate so many employment opportunities for the growing population.

(iii) **Excessive use of Foreign Technology**

There is a lack of scientific and technical research in India due to its high cost.

This has resulted in excessive use of foreign technology which has led to technical unemployment in the country.

(iv) **Lack of Financial Resources**

The expansion and diversification programme of agriculture and small scale industries have suffered because of lack of financial resources.

(v) **Agriculture Still a Seasonal Occupation**

Even after so many years of independence, agriculture in India still does not have access to adequate irrigation facilities, rendering it to be a seasonal occupation.

Due to this, the workforce engaged in farming activities remain unemployed for 3-4 months in a year.

(vi) **Decay of Cottage and Small Industries**

The cottage and small industries are labour intensive and generate a number of employment opportunities.

But the British rule led to their decay and the government of independent India did not initiate adequate measures for their revival. This aggravated the problem of unemployment.

34. "Unemployment not only has economic consequences but also deep-rooted social ramifications. e.g. Long-term unemployment leads to a loss of skills, mental health issues and increases in crime rates. In an economy with persistently high unemployment, this could lead to a decrease in overall productivity, a rise in poverty and greater inequality."

Defend or refute the given statement with valid arguments. Competency Based Que

Ans. The statement is defended. It is supported with following reasons

(i) **Economic Effects**

- **Loss of Output**
  Unemployment is basically underutilisation of the human resources of the country leading to loss of output.
- **Loss of Human Resources**
  Unemployment is a situation in which the productive capacity of able and willing persons is wasted. This leads to a loss of human resources.
- **Low Productivity**
  Unemployment increases the dependence on agriculture and this results in low productivity per labour employed. Low productivity adversely affects the growth rate of the economy.

(ii) **Social Effect**

- **Rise in Poverty**
  Unemployment and poverty are directly correlated. With increase in unemployment, the level of poverty in the country also rises.
- **Increase in Inequalities**
  Unemployment generates inequality in the distribution of income and wealth, thus defying the objective of social justice and resulting in class conflicts between the rich and the poor.
- **Low Standard of Living**
  Unemployment affects the income of an individual adversely and leads to a fall in his standard of living.
- **Social Unrest**
  Long-term unemployment can lead to social unrest, increasing the likelihood of anti-social activities such as theft, extortion and even extremist behaviour.

35. Unemployment is a very serious issue not only in India but in the world. There are hundreds and thousands of people out there who do not have employment.

The problem of unemployment is severe in India because of the growing population and growing demand for jobs. If the country neglects this problem, then it will become the reason for the doom of the nation. Unemployment is a situation in which skilled and talented people wanted to do a job but cannot find the proper job due to several reasons.

There are various type of unemployment in the country including disguised unemployment, open unemployment, technological unemployment and seasonal unemployment, etc.

Worker-population ratio is an indicator which is used for analysing employment situation in the country. In India, the proportion of workforce in the formal sector to total workforce is very high.

Rapid growth of population slows down the economic growth. Further, slow growth of economic sector and fall in the cottage industry are major reasons for unemployment in India.

A large portion of the population is still engaged in the agriculture sector and the sector provides employment in harvest or plantation time only. Further due to heavy dependency of population in the sector leads to underemployment. On the other hand, service sector has contributed the most towards the GDP but not generated enough employment.

Brain drain is another challenge that arises due to high rate of unemployment and poor working condition. This is also a loss of human capital for the economy.

The government has taken the problem seriously and have taken measures to slowly reduce unemployment. Some of the schemes initiated by the government includes IRDP (Integrated Rural Development Programme), DPAP (Drought Prone Area Programme), Jawahar Rozgar Yojana, Employment Assurance Scheme, NRY (Nehru Rozgar Yojana), Training for self-employment, employment exchange, Employment Guarantee Scheme (EGS), development of organised sector, etc. Competency Based Que

(i) In this context, compare unemployment and underemployment.

(ii) Explain how brain drain is a problem of unemployment.

Ans. (i) There is a difference between being unemployed and underemployed. Unemployed means persons don't have a job while underemployment means the job that a person has is inadequate.

Sometimes, the term 'underemployment' is used when talking about people who are working in a lower capacity than one in which they are qualified. However, most often, underemployment is connected to jobs that are lower paid or for a limited number of hours.

The term is also a measure of labour utilisation. When underemployment is high, the workforce is not being utilised to its full potential.

(ii) Brain drain refers to the emigration of highly skilled and educated professionals, such as doctors, engineers and scientists, to other countries in search of better job opportunities, salaries and working conditions. This phenomenon is a serious problem of unemployment because

- **Loss of Skilled Workforce**
  When highly qualified professionals leave, the country loses valuable human capital, leading to a shortage of expertise in key sectors like healthcare, education and technology.

- **Worsening Domestic Unemployment**
  Many skilled individuals leave due to a lack of adequate job opportunities, indicating structural issues in the domestic labour market.
- **Economic Impact**
  The departure of high earning professionals reduces consumer spending and tax revenues, affecting economic growth.
- **Underutilisation of Talent**
  The education and training provided to these professionals become a wasted investment for the country, as they contribute to the growth of foreign economies instead of their own.

Thus, brain drain not only reflects unemployment but also exacerbates it by weakening the country's ability to create and sustain high quality jobs.

36. Employment generation has remained one of the top challenges of Indian policy-makers and over the years, this has only become more complex. India has experienced more or less consistent growth in the structure of the output of the economy, especially after the economic reforms which is measured by gross value added. However, the trend in employment did not reveal a consistent and clear pattern.

These complexities have led to a wide variation in the conclusions drawn by experts and various studies on workforce and employment. Two major sources of data on the workforce and employment have been the

- **decennial population census and**
- **nationwide quinquennial surveys on employment and unemployment by the erstwhile NSSO under the Ministry of Statistics and Programme Implementation (MoSPI), Government of India.**

The nationwide Employment and Unemployment (E&U) surveys have been replaced by the Periodic Labour Force Survey (PLFS) conducted by the National Statistical Office (NSO) of MoSPI, which started in the year 2017-18.

According to NSO, the PLFS data measure the dynamics in labour force participation, workers to population ratio and the employment status along with related, important parameters for both rural and urban areas. Labour force includes persons who were either working (or employed) or those available for work (or unemployed).

Some persons in the labour force are abstained from work for various reasons. Deducting that number from the labour force gives the number of actual workers. These workers are further categorised as persons who are engaged in any economic activity as self-employed or regular wage/salaried and casual labour.

The difference between the labour force and the workforce gives the number of unemployed persons.

The size of the labour force in the country has increased from 485.3 million in the year 2017-18 to 497.4 million in the year 2018-19. The next year, the labour force increased by 8 per cent and reached 537.9 million. This increase was witnessed across male and female populations as well as rural and urban households.

Source *https://www.niti.gov.in/sites/default/files/2022-04/Discussion_Paper _on_Workforce_05042022.pdf (adapted and modified)*

(i) State any two major sources of data on the workforce and employment.

(ii) "The labour force encompasses a broader category than the workforce."
Defend or refute the statement, giving valid reasons in support of your answer.

(iii) "Workers can be categorised into different types depending on their status."
In the light of the given statement, state any one type of employment. **CBSE SQP 2025; Competency Based Que**

Ans. (i) Two major sources of data on the workforce and employment

- **Decennial Population Census**
  - Conducted once every ten years by the Government of India, the census is a comprehensive survey that gathers demographic data, including information on the population size, distribution and other socio-economic characteristics.
  - The census provides basic information about the workforce, including data on the total number of workers, their employment status (such as main or marginal workers) and their economic activity.
- **Nationwide Quinquennial Surveys by NSSO**
  - The National Sample Survey Office (NSSO) conducts detailed surveys on various socio-economic issues, including employment and unemployment, every five years (quinquennial).
  - These surveys provide more granular data about labour market conditions, such as employment by industry, wages, work hours, types of employment (formal vs informal) and the status of unemployment.

(ii) The given statement is defended. Labour force refers to the number of persons who are either employed or unemployed, whereas, workforce refers to all the people who are actively engaged in economic activities.
Hence, labour force is a wider term than the workforce.

(iii) Self-employed are those workers who own and operate an enterprise to earn their livelihood. This includes activities like running a small business, freelancing or practicing a trade independently (e.g. Artisans, consultants or farmers).
Self-employed workers have more control over their work and income but may face greater financial risk and lack job security.

SELF ASSESSMENT TEST

Objective Type Questions

1. Out of the following, who are not considered as worker?

I. Beggar	II. Farmer
III. Teacher	IV. Thief
V. Actor	VI. Gambler
VII. Landless labour	

Codes

(a) I, IV and VI (b) II, III and V
(c) V, IV, II and VII (d) VII, VI, IV and I

2. Developmental strategies in many countries, including India, have aimed at .... the proportion of people depending on agriculture.

(a) increasing (b) equalisation
(c) no changing (d) reducing

3. Women workers constitute .... of the rural workforce.

(a) one-fourth (b) half
(c) one-third (d) three-fourth

4. Which of the following is not a characteristic of informal employment?

(a) Lack of job security
(b) Absence of social security benefits
(c) Fixed working hours
(d) Irregular wages

5. Which of the following is an example of seasonal unemployment?

(a) A software engineer losing their job due to recession
(b) Farmers being unemployed after the harvest season
(c) Workers being replaced due to automation
(d) A fresh graduate searching for their first job

6. The term 'workforce participation rate' refers to

(a) the percentage of the population actively engaged in the workforce
(b) the number of people employed in an organisation
(c) the ratio of unemployed people to the total population
(d) the total number of people working in the informal sector

7. Which of the following statements is/are correct?

I. Women are employed in low paid work due to division of labour between men and women as well as historical and cultural reasons.
II. There has been substantial shift from agriculture to industries and service sector.

Codes

(a) Only I (b) Only II
(c) Both (a) and (b) (d) None of these

Answers 1. (a) 2. (d) 3. (c) 4. (c) 5. (b) 6. (a) 7. (c)

Short Answer Type Questions

8. Explain the difference between organised and unorganised sectors of employment alongwith examples.

9. A rural family of five members owns a small plot of land. All family members, including children, work on this land, but their productivity is low and they earn barely enough to survive.
Identify and explain the type of unemployment in this scenario. Suggest two ways to improve their situation.

10. Why is women's household work not recognised as work?

11. How does the informal sector contribute to the Indian economy despite its challenges?

12. What is meant by 'jobless growth'? Explain its implications for the Indian economy.

13. Can India achieve full employment in the near future? Discuss.

14. How can the problem of educated unemployment be solved?

Long Answer Type Questions

15. Compare and contrast the nature of employment in the primary, secondary and tertiary sectors in India. How does this reflect the stage of economic development?

16. A survey reveals that 60% of urban youth are employed in jobs unrelated to their formal education. Many are underemployed, working fewer hours than they desire or working for lower wages.
(i) Identify the types of employment issues highlighted in this case.
(ii) Suggest three measures the government can take to address them.

17. "Unemployment has far reaching consequences on an economy's performance and societal well-being." Explain the statement with valid reasons.

07

CHAPTER

The environment is the foundation of life on Earth, providing essential resources for survival. Sustainable development offers a path forward, aiming to balance economic growth with ecological preservation.

YOUR STUDY GOALS

YOUR PRACTICE GOAL

- Objective Type Questions (58 Qs ; MCQs, A-R, Statements, Matching, Concept Identification)
- Subjective Questions (21 SAs, 12 LAs)
- Self Assessment Test (7 MCQs, 7 SAs, 3 LAs)

Environment & Sustainable Development

7.1 Meaning of Environment

Environment is defined as the total planetary inheritance and the totality of all resources.

In other words, it is defined as all those conditions and their effects which influence human life. It is the sum total of external forces that affect our existence and quality of life.

Components of Environment

- Biotic components (*Comprising of all living organisms such as trees, humans, forests, etc.*)
- Abiotic components (*Comprising of all non-living components such as air, water, etc.*)

Functions of Environment

Environment performs four vital functions, which are as follows

Function	Explanation
Supply Resources for Production	Environment provides *renewable* (e.g. Trees, fishes) and *non-renewable* (e.g. Fossil fuels) energy resources necessary to carry out for production process. Renewable sources are those which are not depleted with their use while non-renewable sources are those which get exhausted with extraction and use.

Function	Explanation
Assimilates Waste	Environment helps degrade waste generated from production and consumption, preventing its harmful accumulation.
Sustains Life	Essential elements like sun, water, soil and air provided by the environment are crucial for sustaining life.
Enhances Quality of Life	Natural surroundings like forests, rivers, oceans and mountains, etc. provide scenic beauty, peace and enjoyment, thus enhancing human quality of life.

Environmental Crisis

The environment performs its functions without any interruption as long as the demand of these functions is within its **carrying capacity**. This means that

- The rate of extraction of resources is not above the rate of their regeneration.
- Wastes generated are within the assimilating capacity of the environment.

When this is not so, then the environment will not be able to sustain life and this results in *environmental crisis.*

Causes of Environmental Crisis

- Rapid population growth, especially in developing countries.
- High level of consumption and production standards in developed countries resulted in excessive use of resources.

Pre-Industrial Era

Before industrialisation, the demand for environmental resources and waste generation was lower, so pollution remained within the environment's **absorptive capacity**. It is the ability of environment to absorb degradation.

Impact of Industrial Revolution

Population explosion and industrial growth increased the demand for resources and overwhelmed the environment's capacity to regenerate resources leading to environmental crisis.

Reversal of Supply-Demand

Today, the demand for environmental resources has risen sharply, but their supply is limited due to overuse and exploitation, creating a reversal of supply-demand imbalance relationship for environment quality.

Consequences of Environmental Crisis

Consequence	Explanation
Water Scarcity	Development has polluted and dried up rivers and other aquifers, turning water into an economic good.
Resource Depletion	Over-extraction of renewable and non-renewable resources has led to the exhaustion of some of vital resources, increasing the need for expensive technology and research to find new resources.
Health Impact	Declining air and water quality has caused a rise in respiratory and waterborne diseases, leading to increased healthcare costs.
Environmental Issues	Problems like global warming and ozone depletion are adding to the government's financial burden due to the need for mitigation and adaptation measures.
Increased Opportunity Costs	The negative impacts of environmental degradation have led to higher opportunity costs, affecting both economic and social aspects.

Global Environmental Issues

Environment degradation is a global issue. Excessive use of non-renewable resources and high consumption levels have resulted in the problems of global warming and ozone depletion.

Global Warming

The gradual increase in the average temperature of Earth's lower atmosphere is called global warming. Much of the recently observed and projected global warming is human induced.

Causes of Global Warming

Factors that may be contributing to global warming are

- Burning of coal and petroleum products (sources of carbon dioxide, methane, nitrous oxide, ozone).
- Deforestation, which increases the amount of carbon dioxide in the atmosphere.
- Methane gas released in animal waste; and
- Increased cattle production, which contributes to deforestation, methane production and use of fossil fuels.

The atmospheric concentrations of carbon dioxide (CO_2) and methane (CH_4) have increased by 31% and 149% respectively above pre-industrial level since 1750.

Effects of Global Warming

- During the past century, the atmospheric temperature has risen by 1.1° F (0.6° C).
- Disruption of drinking water supplies dependent on snow melts.
- Melting of polar ice has resulted in increase in sea level by several inches and the risk of coastal flooding has increased.
- Extinction of species.
- More frequent tropical storms.
- Increased incidence of tropical diseases.

A United Nations Conference on Climate Change, held in Kyoto, Japan, in 1997, resulted in an international agreement to fight global warming which called for reductions in emissions of greenhouse gases by industrialised nations.

Ozone Depletion

It refers to the phenomenon of reductions in the amount of ozone in the stratosphere.

Causes and Effects of Ozone Depletion

Aspect	Explanation
Causes	High levels of chlorine and bromine compounds in the stratosphere, mainly originated from • Chlorofluorocarbons (CFCs), used in air conditioners, refrigerators and aerosol propellants. • Bromofluorocarbons (Halons), used in fire extinguishers.
Effects	• Increased Ultraviolet (UV) radiation, causing living organism, skin cancer in humans and low production of phytoplankton harming aquatic life. • Damage to terrestrial plants due to increased UV exposure. • Between 1979 to 1990, a 5% reduction in the ozone layer was detected. Since the ozone layer prevents most harmful ultraviolet radiation from passing through the Earth's atmosphere, so it's reduction generated worldwide concern, leading to adoption of the **Montreal Protocol.**

Montreal Protocol

- It is a treaty by the member countries of United Nations to phase out the use of Chlorofluorocarbons (CFCs) which are identified as the main reason of ozone depletion leading to global warming.
- It also bans the use of other ozone depleting chemicals such as carbon tetrachloride, trichoroethane and halons (bromine compounds).
- All the signing countries agreed to freeze the production and consumption of CFC by 2013.
- This has helped in ozone recovery in the stratosphere. India signed this treaty on 17th September, 1992.

7.2 State of India's Environment

India has rich quality and quantity of natural resources. It is clear from the following points

- India has rich quality of soil, hundreds of rivers and tributaries, lush green forests, plenty of mineral deposits beneath the land surface, vast stretch of the Indian Ocean, ranges of mountains, etc.
- Black soil of the Deccan Plateau is particularly suitable for cultivation of cotton. It has lead to concentration of textile industries in this region.
- The Indo-Gangetic Plains spread from Arabian Sea to the Bay of Bengal are one of the most fertile, intensively cultivated and densely populated regions in the world.
- India's forests, though unevenly distributed, provide green cover for majority of its population and natural cover for its wildlife.
- Large deposits of iron-ore, coal and natural gas are found in the country which accounts for nearly 8% of the world's total iron-ore reserves.
- Bauxite, copper, chromate, diamonds, gold, lead, lignite, manganese, zinc, uranium, etc. are also available in different parts of the country.

Challenges to India's Environment

The developmental activities in India have resulted in pressure on its finite natural resources, besides creating impacts on human health and well-being.

The threat to India's environment poses a dichotomy, i.e. threat of poverty induced environmental degradation through cutting down of tress, encroachment into forest land, overgrazing of animals, etc. and, at the same time, threat of pollution from affluence and a rapidly growing industrial sector.

Some of the priority issues are discussed below

Challenges to India's Environment

- Land degradation in India
- Loss of biodiversity
- Air pollution
- Management of fresh water
- Management of solid waste

1. Land Degradation in India

Land degradation means decline in the quality of soil, water or vegetation condition, commonly a result of human activities. Land in India suffers from varying degrees and types of degradation mainly due to excessive use and inappropriate management practices.

Factors responsible for Land Degradation

- Loss of vegetation occurring due to deforestation
- Shifting cultivation and reduction of forest lands
- Non-adoption of adequate soil conservation measures
- Indiscriminate use of agro-chemicals such as fertilisers and pesticides
- Improper planning and management of irrigation systems
- Extraction of groundwater in excess of the regenerative capacity
- Unsustainable fuel, wood and fodder extraction
- Forest fires and overgrazing
- Improper crop rotation
- Poverty of the agriculture-dependent people

2. Loss of Biodiversity

Loss of biodiversity means that some of the species of animals and plants will be lost as a consequence of environmental degradation.

Key Factors of Loss of Biodiversity

- Only 2.5% of world's geographical area is home to 17% of the world's human population and 20% of the world's livestock population.
- Per capita forest land in the country is only 0.06 hectare as against requirement of 0.47 hectare to meet basic needs.
- About 15 million cubic metre forests are cut down each year.

Consequences of Deforestation

- It leads to soil erosion which is being eroded at a rate of 5.3 billion tonnes a year.
- This results in loss of 0.8 million tonnes of nitrogen, 1.8 million tonnes of phosphorus and 26.3 million tonnes of potassium every year.
- According to an estimate provided by Government of India, quantity of nutrients lost due to soil erosion each year ranges from 5.8 to 8.4 million tonnes.
- Loss of various life forms sustained by the forests.

3. Air Pollution

It is the release of pollutants such as gases, particles, biological molecules, etc. into the air that is harmful to human health and the environment.

Pollution from vehicles and industries are the major sources of air pollution.

Vehicle Pollution	Industrial Pollution
• Vehicular emissions are ground level sources and thus, have maximum impact on the general pollution. Number of vehicles has increased from 3 lakh in 1951 to 23 crore in 2016. • In 2016, personal transport vehicles (two wheeler and cars only) constituted about 85% of the total number of registered vehicles thus, contributing significantly to air pollution.	• India is one of the ten most industrialised nations in the world. This status has resulted in unwanted and unanticipated consequences like unplanned urbanisation, pollution and the risk of accidents. • The CPCB (Central Pollution Control Board) has identified seventeen categories of industries as significantly polluting.

4. Management of Fresh Water

Water is an equally important element of life and its pollution is equally serious. Water becomes polluted when chemicals and other waste materials are dumped into it.

Polluted water is the principal cause of diseases like diarrhoea and hepatitis. Thus, the management of fresh water is essential to sustain life.

5. Management of Solid Waste

It is very essential that solid waste should be treated chemically. Efforts should be made for effective management of non-biodegradable waste. Biodegradable waste should also be converted into compost.

Pollution Control Boards

To address major environmental concerns in India i.e. water, air and land pollution, the government set-up the Central Pollution Control Board (CPCB) in 1974.

This was followed by States establishing their own state level boards to address all the environmental concerns.

Key Functions of these Boards

- Investigate, collect and disseminate pollution information, establish standards for emissions and trade effluent.
- Provide technical assistance for pollution control.
- Conduct research relating to problems of water and air pollution and for their prevention, control or abatement.
- Organise awareness programmes through mass media.
- Prepare guidelines for waste treatment.
- Assess air quality through regulation of industries.
- Provide background air quality data for planning
- Monitor water quality in various water bodies (like rivers, wells, lakes, etc).

7.3 Sustainable Development

Sustainable development is the development that will allow all future generations to have a potential average quality of life that is at least as high as which is being enjoyed by the current generation.

This concept was highlighted by the United Nations Conference on Environment and Development (UNCED) as a strategy meeting the needs of present generation without compromising future generations' ability to meet their own needs.

Edward Barbier defines it as enhancing the material living standards of the poor at the grassroots level which is measurable through

- Increased real income
- Improved educational services
- Enhanced healthcare and sanitation
- Better water supply

In specific terms, it aims to

- Decrease absolute poverty by providing secure livelihoods.
- Minimise resource depletion, environmental degradation, cultural disruption and social instability.
- Meet basic needs for employment, food, energy, water and housing.
- Ensure growth in agriculture, manufacturing, power and services to fulfill these needs.

Sustainable Development and Future Generations

The **Brundtland Commission** emphasises the present generation's moral obligation to protect future generations by passing better environment to them. It advocates leaving a stock of 'quality of life' assets no less than what we have inherited.

Present generation can promote development with the help of following practices

- Conservation of natural assets.
- Preservation of the regenerative capacity of ecological systems.
- Avoiding additional costs or risks imposed on future generations.

Chipko/Appiko Movement

- Chipko Movement aimed at protecting forests in the Himalayas. In Karnataka, a similar movement took a different name, 'Appiko', which means 'to hug'.
- In both the movements, villagers helped to save forest resources. When commercial felling by contractors damaged a large number of natural forests, the idea of hugging the trees gave the people hope and confidence that they can protect the forests.
- Due to this incident, the felling discontinued and people saved 12,000 trees. Within months, this movement spread to many adjoining districts.

7.4 Strategies for Sustainable Development

Some strategies for sustainable development are as follows

Strategy	Explanation	Benefits
Use of Non-conventional Energy Sources	Shift from reliance on thermal and hydro power to non-conventional sources like solar, wind and nuclear energy to reduce environmental impacts.	Reduces carbon emissions and pollution, promotes sustainable energy production, less environmental degradation.
LPG and Gobar Gas in Rural Areas	Encourage the use of subsidised Liquefied Petroleum Gas (LPG) and gobar gas plants instead of traditional biomass fuels like wood and dung cakes.	Decreases deforestation and air pollution, provides clean, efficient fuel, produces organic fertiliser from slurry.
CNG in Urban Areas	Adoption of Compressed Natural Gas (CNG) as a fuel in public transport systems, especially in Delhi, has reduced air pollution and improved air quality.	Significantly lowers air pollution, contributes to cleaner urban environments, promotes a shift to cleaner fuels.
Wind Power	Installation of wind turbines in areas with high wind speeds to generate electricity without negative environmental impacts.	Environment friendly energy production, renewable energy source, initial costs offset by long-term benefits.
Solar Power through Photovoltaic Cells	Using photovoltaic cells, solar energy can be converted into electricity. These cells capture sunlight through special materials and transform it into electrical power.	Pollution-free energy production, useful for remote and off-grid areas as well as supports India's efforts in sustainable energy.
Mini-Hydel Plants	Utilise the energy from perennial streams in mountainous regions to power small turbines that generate electricity through mini-hydel plants.	Environment friendly energy production, meets local electricity demand, reduces need for large transmission infrastructure.
Traditional Knowledge and Practices	Promote the return to traditional agricultural, healthcare and other practices that are environmentally sustainable, leveraging local medicinal plants and herbal products.	Preserves biodiversity, supports organic and herbal products, minimises environmental damage from industrial processes.
Bio-composting	Encourage the use of compost made from organic waste instead of chemical fertilisers to enhance agricultural production. Earthworms can speed up the composting process.	Improves soil health, reduces chemical runoff into land and water, helps manage waste, supports organic farming.
Biopest Control	Utilise natural methods for pest control, including plant-based pesticides (e.g. Neem) and encouraging natural predators like birds and snakes, to practice mixed cropping.	Minimises reliance on chemical pesticides, protects soil and water quality, promotes biodiversity and ecosystem balance.

Measures to Achieve Sustainable Development

- Limiting the human population to a level within the carrying capacity of the environment.
- Herman Daly compared the carrying capacity with the 'plimsoll line' of the ship, which is the load limit mark in a ship.
  According to him, if the population exceeds the 'plimsoll line', sustainable development cannot be achieved.
- Technological progress should be input efficient and not input consuming.
- Renewable resources should be extracted on a sustainable basis, i.e. rate of extraction should not exceed rate of regeneration.
- For non-renewable resources, rate of depletion should not exceed the rate of creation of renewable substitutes.
- Inefficiencies arising from pollution should be corrected.

Mind Map

ENVIRONMENT & SUSTAINABLE DEVELOPMENT

1 Environment

Environment is defined as the total planetary inheritance and the totality of all resources. Components include

- **Biotic** Comprise of all living organisms
- **Abiotic** Comprise of all non-living components

Functions

- Supply resources for production
- Assimilates waste
- Sustains life
- Enhances quality of life

2 Environmental Crisis

The environment performs its functions without any interruption as long as the demand of these functions is within its carrying capacity. So, when rate of resource extraction is above rate of regeneration and wastes generated are beyond capacity, then environment will not sustain life, thus resulting in environmental crisis.

Causes

- Rapid population growth, especially in developing countries.
- High level of consumption and production standards in developed countries.

Consequences

- Water scarcity
- Health impact
- Resource depletion
- Environmental issues
- Increased opportunity costs

3 Global Environmental Issues

Environment degradation is a global issue. Excessive use of non-renewable resources and high consumption levels have resulted in the problems of global warming and ozone depletion.

Global Warming The gradual increase in the average temperature of Earth's lower atmosphere is called global warming. Much of the recently observed and projected global warming is human induced.

Effects of Global Warming

- During the past century, the atmospheric temperature has risen by 1.1° F (0.6° C).
- Disruption of drinking water supplies dependent on snow melts.
- Melting of polar ice has resulted in increase in sea level by several inches and the risk of coastal flooding has increased.
- Extinction of species, more frequent tropical storms and increased incidence of tropical diseases.

Ozone Depletion It refers to the phenomenon of reductions in the amount of ozone in the stratosphere.

Causes include high levels of chlorine and bromine compounds in the stratosphere, mainly originated from Chlorofluorocarbons (CFCs) and bromofluorocarbons (Halons).

Effects include increased Ultraviolet (UV) radiation, causing living organism, skin cancer in humans and low production of phytoplankton harming aquatic life and damage to terrestrial plants due to increased UV exposure.

4 State of India's Environment

- India has rich quality of soil, hundreds of rivers and tributaries, lush green forests, plenty of mineral deposits, etc.
- Black soil of the Deccan Plateau has led to concentration of textile industries in this region.
- The Indo-Gangetic Plains are one of the most fertile, intensively cultivated and densely populated regions in the world.
- Large deposits of iron-ore, coal and natural gas are found in the country.
- Bauxite, copper, chromate, diamonds, gold, lead, lignite, manganese, zinc, uranium, etc. are also available in different parts of the country.

5 Challenges to India's Environment

- Land degradation in India
- Loss of biodiversity
- Air pollution
- Management of fresh water
- Management of solid waste

Population Control Boards

To address major environmental concerns in India, i.e. water, air and land pollution, the government set-up the Central Pollution Control Board (CPCB) in 1974. Key functions of these boards are

- Investigate, collect and disseminate pollution information, establish standards for emissions and trade effluent, provide technical assistance for pollution control, etc.
- Conduct research relating to problems of water and air pollution and for their prevention, control or abatement.
- Organise awareness programmes through mass media and prepare guidelines for waste treatment.
- Assess air quality through regulation of industries, provide background air quality data for planning and monitor water quality.

6 Sustainable Development

It is the development that will allow all future generations to have a potential average quality of life that is at least as high as which is being enjoyed by the current generation.

Sustainable Development and Future Generations

The Brundtland Commission emphasises the present generation's moral obligation to protect future generations by passing better environment to them. It advocates leaving a stock of 'quality of life' assets no less than what we have inherited.

Present generation can promote development with the help of following practices

- Conservation of natural assets.
- Preservation of the regenerative capacity of ecological systems.
- Avoiding additional costs or risks imposed on future generations.

7 Strategies for Sustainable Development

- Use of non-conventional energy sources
- LPG and Gobar Gas in rural areas
- CNG in urban areas
- Wind power
- Solar power through photovoltaic cells
- Mini-hydel plants
- Traditional knowledge and practices
- Bio-composting
- Biopest control

Measures to Achieve Sustainable Development

- Limiting the human population
- Technological progress should be input efficient
- Renewable resources should be extracted on a sustainable basis
- Inefficiencies arising from pollution should be corrected

EXAM PATTERN QUESTIONS

Objective Type Questions

Multiple Choice Questions (MCQs)

1. **The environment refers to the total planetary inheritance and the sum total of all .... resources.**

(a) human (b) physical
(c) natural (d) man-made

2. **The environment consists of which of the following?**

(a) Biotic and abiotic components
(b) Only ecosystems and habitats
(c) Only geological and climatic factors
(d) Only energy sources and resources

3. **The environment provides humans with essential life supporting elements like air, water and food. This role of the environment is known as its .... function.**

(a) absorptive (b) regulatory
(c) sustaining (d) ecosystemic

4. **Identify, which of the following is an incorrect function of environment?** CBSE 2023

(a) Supplies resources
(b) Assimilates waste
(c) Land degradation
(d) Provides aesthetic services

5. **The environment performs four vital functions and the environment is able to perform these functions without any interruption as long as the demand on these functions is within its carrying capacity.**

In the given statement 'carrying capacity' implies to

I. **the resource extraction is not above the rate of regeneration.**
II. **wastes generated are beyond the absorptive capacity of the environment.**
III. **the resource extraction is not below the rate of regeneration.**
IV. **the resource and the wastes generated are within the assimilating capacity of the environment.**

Codes Competency Based Que

(a) I, II and IV
(b) Both II and IV
(c) Both I and IV
(d) All of the above

6.

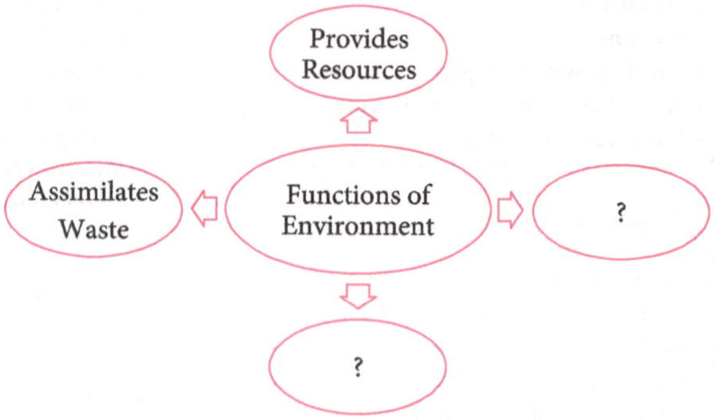

Choose the correct option which indicates the combination of vital functions performed by the environment. CBSE 2024; SQP 2025

(i) **Sustains life**
(ii) **Provides aesthetic services**
(iii) **Generates waste**
(iv) **Provides only renewable resources**

Codes

(a) (i) and (ii)
(b) (ii) and (iii)
(c) (i) and (iv)
(d) (i) and (iii)

7. **Environment and economy are .... and need of each other.**

(a) interdependent (b) independent
(c) dependent (d) complementary

8. **What are the major global environmental issues?**

I. **Global warming**
II. **Ozone depletion**
III. **Development of renewable energy sources**
IV. **Loss of cultural heritage**

Codes

(a) I and II (b) I, II and III
(c) I, II, III and IV (d) II and IV

9. **One of the major consequences of environmental crisis is**

(a) economic growth
(b) sustainable development
(c) loss of biodiversity
(d) improved human health

10.

Refer the given image and analyse the most likely cause of this phenomenon.

(a) Ozone layer recovery
(b) Global warming
(c) Acid rain
(d) Deforestation in tropical regions

11. Which of the following is the primary cause of global warming?

(a) Depletion of the ozone layer
(b) Emission of greenhouse gases
(c) Increase in rainfall
(d) Volcanic eruptions

12. What are the effects of global warming?

I. Rise in sea levels
II. Melting of polar ice caps
III. Increase in agricultural productivity
IV. Extreme weather events Competency Based Que

Codes

(a) I and II (b) I, II and III
(c) I, II, III and IV (d) I, II and IV

13. World Economic Forum According to reports, about 33% of India's GDP comes from sectors that are highly dependent on nature, such as agriculture and forestry.

Source *http://www.weforum.org/agenda/2024/08/india-economy-natural-climate-solution/*

How does this dependency increase India's vulnerability to global warming? Competency Based Que

(a) It reduces the country's carbon emissions significantly
(b) It limits the scope for industrial development in India
(c) It makes the economy highly sensitive to climate change impacts like erratic monsoons
(d) It ensures better adaptability of the agricultural sector to temperature changes

14. Out of the following, what are the correct reasons of high opportunity cost of negative environmental impact?

I. Spending huge amounts on technology and research to explore alternative resource
II. Health costs of degraded environmental quality
III. Global warming
IV. Ozone depletion
V. Industrial revolution Competency Based Que

Codes

(a) I, II, III and IV (b) Both I and II
(c) III, IV and V (d) All of these

15. What is a primary cause of ozone layer depletion?

(a) Greenhouse gases
(b) Chlorofluorocarbons (CFCs)
(c) Carbon monoxide
(d) Sulphur dioxide

16. An article in The New York Times highlights that the depletion of the ozone layer is leading to higher Ultraviolet (UV) radiation levels reaching the Earth's surface.

Which of the following is a consequence of increased UV radiation? Competency Based Que

(a) Reduction in global temperature
(b) Increase in skin cancers and eye cataracts among humans
(c) Enhanced growth of plant species in tropical regions
(d) Decrease in water levels in rivers

17. The Water Diplomat In 2024, the United Nations reported that the Antarctic ozone hole has shown signs of recovery but remains a concern. Which of the following actions would most directly contribute to furthering this recovery?

(a) Reduction in carbon dioxide emissions
(b) Phasing out the use of Hydrofluorocarbons (HFCs)
(c) Promoting electric vehicles
(d) Increasing afforestation efforts

18.

The image shows a drought stricken area, symbolising environmental challenges in rural India. Based on this, which statement best explains the long-term impact of such issues on rural regions?

(a) Urban areas face more severe environmental issues, making rural challenges less significant
(b) Industrial pollution is the primary concern for rural areas
(c) Drought and water scarcity can reduce agricultural output, cause migration and increase poverty
(d) Rural areas are not impacted by environmental challenges, which mainly affect urban regions

19. Interpret the image and identify the major contributor to this environmental issue.

(a) High levels of vehicular emissions
(b) Afforestation drives
(c) Reduced industrial activities
(d) Increase in rainfall

20. India Today: India's air pollution crisis continues to affect over 1 billion people, exposing them to unsafe levels of Particulate Matter (PM2.5).

Source *http://www.indiatoday.in/environment/story/india.faces-mounting-climate-crisis-60-million-at-risk-from-rising-sea-level-2598449-2024-09-12*

Which of the following is a direct consequence of this environmental challenge? **Competency Based Que**

(a) Decline in the population of marine species along India's coastline
(b) Higher instances of respiratory and cardiovascular diseases among urban populations
(c) Increased agricultural yields due to enhanced CO_2 levels
(d) A rise in global agricultural commodity prices

21. .... was set-up in 1974 by the Indian government to address two major environmental concerns *viz.* water and air pollution. **CBSE SQP 2025**

(a) State Pollution Control Board
(b) Central Pollution Control Board
(c) Brundtland Commission
(d) Montreal Protocol

22. What are the major challenges in managing India's freshwater resources?

I. Water scarcity
II. Industrial pollution of water bodies
III. Soil erosion
IV. Excessive reliance on desalination

Codes

(a) I, II and III (b) I and II
(c) I, II and IV (d) I, II, III and IV

23. According to the World Resource Institute, India faces a high level of water stress.

Source *Science Daily*

Which of the following statements is true regarding this situation? **Competency Based Que**

(a) India's water demand will be less than its supply by 2030
(b) Approximately 60% of India's aquifers are expected to be overexploited within the next two decades
(c) Water scarcity is limited to only urban regions in India
(d) Rainwater harvesting is the only method to address this issue

24. Observe the image given below and choose the most appropriate option.

(a) Higher population is a bane for the country
(b) Development is sustainable when there is inter-generational consideration
(c) Growth always stimulates personal development
(d) All of the above

25. Sustainable development focuses on

(a) exclusive economic growth
(b) integrating economic, social and environmental concerns
(c) prioritising industrial development
(d) promoting short-term benefits

26. What are the key strategies for sustainable development?

I. Promotion of renewable energy
II. Sustainable use of resources
III. Increase in industrial production
IV. Conservation of biodiversity

Codes

(a) I, II and III (b) I and II
(c) I, II and IV (d) I, II, III and IV

27. Which of the following is not used as a strategy for sustainable development? **CBSE 2020**

(a) Use of bio-gas (b) Use of solar power
(c) Use of thermal power (d) Use of hydel power

28. The Ministry of Environment, Forest and Climate Change has recently emphasised the importance of adopting a circular economy model in solid waste management.

Which of the following best describes the circular economy approach? **Competency Based Que**

(a) Increasing the production of single-use plastics
(b) Disposing of waste in landfills without segregation
(c) Recycling, reusing and reducing waste generation to create a closed-loop system
(d) Expanding waste-to-energy projects by incinerating waste

Direction *Read the case study and answer the questions 29 to 32 on the basis of the same*

Sustainable development is the synonymous in the minds of many with the colour green and for good reasons.

Twenty years ago, at the First Earth Summit at Rio de Janerio, in Brazil, world leaders set out what today is conventional wisdom SOCIAL AND ECONOMIC HUMAN PROGRESS – cannot be divorced from environmental protection unless both are advanced together, both will flounder together.

Sustainable development is as much about health, education and jobs, as it is about the ecosystems.

It is about ever widening inclusion and movement away from decisions that erode democratic space and do not address social inequality, intolerance and violence.

Sustainable development is about changes that transform impoverished people, communities and countries into informed, educated healthy and productive societies.

It is about wealth creation that generates equality and opportunity. Sustainable development is about consumption and production patterns that respect planetary boundaries; it is also about increasing tolerance and respect for human rights at all levels.

Building on human development legacy that oriented with Economists like Amartya Sen and MahbubUlHaq and was captured by the first Human Development Report in 1990.

United Nations Development Programme (UNDP) has long promoted alternative approaches to measure human progress, along with the Human Development Index (HDI). Today, we are building on this legacy by exploring how to adjust the index to reflect environmental sustainability, so that governments and citizens might better track real progress towards truly sustainable development. This must be our collective objective. **CBSE QB**

29. **Which of the following is not one of the ways to attain the goal of sustainable development?**
(a) Use of cleaner fuels
(b) Use of traditional knowledge and practices
(c) Spreading awareness
(d) Sticking to methods to promote inequalities

30. **State whether the given statement is true or false.**

As per the UNDP Report education and health are the broader issues of human development.

31. **Sustainable development and economic growth are .... (directly/indirectly) related.**

32. **Assertion** (A) Sustainable development is about changes that transform impoverished people, communities and countries into informed, educated, healthy and productive societies.

Reason (R) Sustainable development advocates about wealth creation that generates socio-economic equality and opportunity.

Alternatives
(a) Both Assertion (A) and Reason (R) are true
(b) Both Assertion (A) and Reason (R) are false

Assertion-Reason

Direction (Q.No. 33 to 40) *Read the following Assertion (A) and Reason (R) and choose the correct alternative from the following*

Alternatives
(a) Both Assertion (A) and Reason (R) are true and Reason (R) is the correct explanation of Assertion (A)
(b) Both Assertion (A) and Reason (R) are true, but Reason (R) is not the correct explanation of Assertion (A)
(c) Assertion (A) is true, but Reason (R) is false
(d) Both Assertion (A) and Reason (R) are false

33. **Assertion** (A) Environment helps in the existence of life on earth.

Reason (R) Sun, water, soil and air are a part of environment.

34. **Assertion** (A) Water has become an economic good.

Reason (R) Development has polluted and dried up rivers and other aquifers.

35. **Assertion** (A) The depletion of the ozone layer is linked to the excessive use of Chlorofluorocarbons (CFCs).

Reason (R) CFCs release harmful radiation that directly damages the ozone molecules.

36. **Assertion** (A) Global warming leads to an increase in the average temperature of the earth's atmosphere.

Reason (R) Increased levels of greenhouse gases such as carbon dioxide and methane trap more heat in the earth's atmosphere.

37. **Assertion** (A) Environmental degradation is an inevitable consequence of economic growth.

Reason (R) Higher economic growth leads to increased production, which always results in pollution and resource depletion.

38. **Assertion** (A) Over-exploitation of groundwater resources can lead to land subsidence.

Reason (R) Land subsidence occurs when heavy rainfall causes the soil to absorb too much water.

39. **Assertion** (A) The management of solid waste is a challenge to India's environment.

Reason (R) Proper waste management contributes to soil fertility and increases agricultural productivity.

40. **Assertion** (A) Sustainable development ensures that resources are used judiciously to meet the needs of the present generation without compromising the ability of future generations to meet their own needs.

Reason (R) Sustainable development only focuses on increasing the economic growth of a nation.

Two Statements Based MCQs

Direction (Q.No. 41 to 48) *Read the following statements carefully and choose the correct alternative*

Alternatives

(a) Both the statements are correct
(b) Both the statements are incorrect
(c) Statement I is correct and Statement II is incorrect
(d) Statement I is incorrect and Statement II is correct

41. **Statement I** India supports approximately 17% of the world's human population.

Statement II The high density of population exerts an enormous pressure of India's finite land resources.

42. **Statement I** Biodiversity is crucial for ecosystem stability, providing essential services such as pest control, pollination and climate regulation.

Statement II Developing countries often face more severe consequences from global environmental issues, including loss of biodiversity and increased vulnerability to climate change impacts.

43. **Statement I** Renewable resources can be replenished through human intervention and natural processes.

Statement II Non-renewable resources like coal and petroleum are sustainable as long as technology keeps advancing.

44. **Statement I** The greenhouse effect is a natural process that is essential for maintaining life on earth.

Statement II An enhanced greenhouse effect leads to global warming, which disrupts the earth's climate systems.

45. **Statement I** Global warming is primarily caused by the increase in greenhouse gases such as carbon dioxide (CO_2), methane (CH_4) and nitrous oxide (N_2O) in the atmosphere, which trap heat and raise the earth's temperature.

Statement II The depletion of the ozone layer is a direct result of increased carbon dioxide emissions, which breakdown ozone molecules in the stratosphere.

46. **Statement I** The Montreal Protocol was established to reduce the emission of greenhouse gases and combat global warming.

Statement II The Montreal Protocol aims to phase out the production and consumption of substances that deplete the ozone layer, such as CFCs.

47. **Statement I** Pollution Control Boards monitor industries to ensure compliance with environmental standards.

Statement II The Pollution Control Boards have very small role in promoting public awareness about pollution.

48. **Statement I** Promoting public transportation and reducing reliance on private vehicles are strategies for sustainable urban development.

Statement II Encouraging the use of public transport reduces traffic congestion but has no impact on pollution levels in urban areas.

Matching

49. **Match the following**

Column I		Column II	
A.	Deccan Plateau	(i)	Uses CNG as fuel in public
B.	Indo-Gangetic Plains	(ii)	Suitable for cultivation of cotton
C.	Delhi	(iii)	Densely populated

Codes

	A	B	C		A	B	C
(a)	(i)	(ii)	(iii)	(b)	(ii)	(iii)	(i)
(c)	(iii)	(i)	(ii)	(d)	(iii)	(ii)	(i)

50. **Match the following**

Column I	Column II
A. Per capita forest land	(i) 20% of world's total reserves
B. Iron ore reserves	(ii) 5.8 to 8.4 million tonnes
C. Quantity of nutrients lost	(iii) 0.06 hectare

Codes

	A	B	C		A	B	C
(a)	(i)	(ii)	(iii)	(b)	(ii)	(iii)	(i)
(c)	(iii)	(i)	(ii)	(d)	(iii)	(ii)	(i)

51. **Match the following consequences with the respective environmental crisis**

Column I (Environmental crisis)		Column II (Consequences)	
A.	Deforestation	(i)	Loss of biodiversity
B.	Air pollution	(ii)	Melting glaciers
C.	Soil erosion	(iii)	Desertification of fertile land
D.	Climate change	(iv)	Health issues due to pollution

Codes

	A	B	C	D
(a)	(i)	(ii)	(iii)	(iv)
(b)	(i)	(iii)	(iv)	(ii)
(c)	(i)	(iv)	(iii)	(ii)
(d)	(iii)	(iv)	(i)	(ii)

52. Match the following concepts with their potential challenges in implementation **Competency Based Que**

Column I	Column II
A. Renewable energy	(i) Infrastructure challenges and public awareness
B. Policy frameworks for sustainable development	(ii) Limited reach and engagement in rural areas
C. Waste management system	(iii) Resistance from vested interests and political will
D. Environmental education	(iv) High initial costs and technology adoption issues

Codes

	A	B	C	D		A	B	C	D
(a)	(i)	(ii)	(iii)	(iv)	(b)	(i)	(iii)	(iv)	(ii)
(c)	(iv)	(i)	(iii)	(ii)	(d)	(iv)	(iii)	(i)	(ii)

Concept Identification

53. The total planetary inheritance or the totality of all resources. It includes all the biotic and abiotic factors that influence and depend upon each other. **NCERT Modified**

54. Component of environment include all kinds of living creatures like birds, plants and animals, forests, fisheries which impact human life.

55. The resources which have been provided by the nature in the form of land, air, water, forests, animals, sunshine, etc.

56. The state of balance between the rate at which resources are exploited and the rate at which these are regenerated.

57. Ability of the environment to absorb wastes occurring due to production and consumption activities in the economy.

58. The process of reusing the compost made from organic wastes of different types. **CBSE 2020**

Answers

1. (c) natural
2. (a) Biotic and abiotic components
3. (c) sustaining
4. (c) Land degradation
5. (c) Both I and IV
6. (a) (i) and (ii)
7. (a) interdependent
8. (a) I and II
9. (c) loss of biodiversity
10. (b) Global warming
11. (b) Emission of greenhouse gases
12. (d) I, II and IV
13. (c) It makes the economy highly sensitive to climate change impacts like erratic monsoons
14. (a) I, II, III and IV
15. (b) Chlorofluorocarbons (CFCs)
16. (b) Increase in skin cancers and eye cataracts among humans
17. (b) Phasing out the use of Hydrofluorocarbons (HFCs)
18. (c) Drought and water scarcity can reduce agricultural output, cause migration and increase poverty
19. (a) High levels of vehicular emissions
20. (b) Higher instances of respiratory and cardiovascular diseases among urban populations
21. (b) Central Pollution Control Board
22. (b) I and II
23. (b) Approximately 60% of India's aquifers are expected to be overexploited within the next two decades
24. (b) Development is sustainable when there is inter-generational consideration
25. (b) integrating economic, social and environmental concerns
26. (c) I, II and IV
27. (c) Use of thermal power
28. (c) Recycling, reusing and reducing waste generation to create a closed-loop system
29. (d) Sticking to methods to promote inequalities
30. True
31. directly
32. (a) Both Assertion (A) and Reason (R) are true
33. (a) Both Assertion (A) and Reason (R) are true and Reason (R) is the correct explanation of Assertion (A)
34. (a) Both Assertion (A) and Reason (R) are true and Reason (R) is the correct explanation of Assertion (A)
35. (c) CFCs do not release harmful radiation. Instead, they release chlorine atoms in the stratosphere when exposed to UV radiation and it is these chlorine atoms that cause the breakdown of ozone molecules.

36. (a) Both Assertion (A) and Reason (R) are true and Reason (R) is the correct explanation of Assertion (A)

37. (c) Increased production does not always lead to pollution, sustainable practices and technology can reduce the negative impact on the environment.

38. (c) Land subsidence is typically linked to the removal of groundwater, not an excess of water from rainfall.

39. (b) Both Assertion (A) and Reason (R) are true, but Reason (R) is not the correct explanation of Assertion (A)

40. (c) Sustainable development is not only about economic growth, it also encompasses environmental conservation and social equity.

41. (a) Both the statements are correct

42. (a) Both the statements are correct

43. (c) Non-renewable resources are finite and cannot be considered sustainable, regardless of technological advances.

44. (a) Both the statements are correct

45. (c) Ozone depletion is mainly caused by Chlorofluorocarbons (CFCs) and other ozone depleting substances, not by carbon dioxide emissions. These substances release chlorine and bromine in the stratosphere, which breakdown ozone molecules.

46. (d) The Montreal Protocol is specifically targeted at controlling ozone depleting substances, not directly reducing greenhouse gases.

47. (c) Pollution Control Boards play a significant role in promoting public awareness about pollution through campaigns, educational programmes and dissemination of information.

48. (c) Reducing reliance on private vehicles through public transport can significantly lower air pollution levels by cutting down on emissions.

49. (b) (ii) (iii) (i)

50. (c) (iii) (i) (ii)

51. (c) (i) (iv) (iii) (ii)

52. (d) (iv) (iii) (i) (ii)

53. Environment

54. Biotic or living elements

55. Natural resources

56. Carrying capacity of environment

57. Absorptive capacity of environment

58. Bio-composting

Subjective Questions

Short Answer Type Questions

1. Is environmental crisis a recent phenomenon? If so, why? NCERT; Competency Based Que

Ans. Yes, environmental crisis is a recent phenomenon. In the past, environment was able to perform its functions without any interruption till the resource extraction was not above the rate of regeneration of the resource and the wastes generated were within the assimilating capacity of the environment.

But today, environment fails to perform its vital function of life sustenance resulting in an environmental crisis. The rising population of the developing countries and the affluent consumption and production standards of the developed world have placed a huge stress on the environment. Many resources have become extinct and the wastes generated are beyond the absorptive capacity of the environment. As a result, we are today at the threshold of environmental crisis.

2. Explain carrying capacity of environment with examples.

Ans. Carrying capacity of the environment may be defined as the amount of natural resources which can be drawn from it and the maximum amount of pollutants that can be discharged without damaging it seriously.

e.g. Crude petroleum, the source of petrol and diesel used in motor vehicles is available in limited supply. It cannot be reproduced again.

The present rate of use of these resources, will lead to the depletion of these resources within less than half a century.

Similarly, air pollution has created a problem of ozone depletion. Air pollution has developed a hole exposing human life to the dangerous ultraviolet rays of sun.

Hence, industrial development must be in accordance with the carrying capacity of environment.

3. Explain how the supply-demand reversal of environmental resources account for the current environment crisis. NCERT

Ans. Before the advent of industrial revolution, the rate of resource extraction was less than the rate of regeneration of these resources, i.e. demand was less than supply.

But with expanding population and its growing needs, the demand for resources for both production and consumption went beyond the rate of regeneration of the resources.

This has resulted in a reversal of supply-demand relationship for environmental resources as now there is very high demand for environmental resources and services, but their supply is limited and even these limited resources are being overused and misused.

4. The Times of India, June 2023 "The environment is essential for human survival and development, providing critical natural resources. However, environmental degradation threatens our health, economy and future."

Based on the following statement, explain why the environment is important to us? Competency Based Que

Or **What are the functions of the environment?** NCERT

Ans. The environment is of great importance because it provides essential natural resources that are key to human survival and development/main functions of environment are

(i) **Environment Supplies Resources for Production**
Environment includes those physical resources which are gifted by nature. These resources are used for producing various goods and services.

(ii) **Environment Sustains Life**
Sun, soil, air and water are the essential ingredients of environment for the human life. Absence of these will lead to an end of life on earth.

(iii) **Environment Assimilates Waste**
Production and consumption activity generates wastes. It is generally in the form of garbage which is absorbed by the environment.

(iv) **Environment Enhances Quality of Life**
Environmental surroundings include rivers, oceans, mountains and deserts. Man enjoys these surroundings, adding to the quality of his life.

5. Interpret the image carefully and discuss the different types of pollution shown. Competency Based Que

Ans. Based on the image, the different types of pollution shown are

(i) **Air Pollution**
Represented by the factory chimneys emitting smoke into the air, causing harmful gases and particulate matter to be released into the atmosphere.
This type of pollution affects air quality and human health, contributing to respiratory diseases and environmental issues like global warming.

(ii) **Water Pollution**
Illustrated by industrial waste being dumped into water bodies.
This leads to contamination of rivers, lakes and oceans, harming aquatic life and making water unsafe for consumption and use.

(iii) **Land Pollution**
Depicted by waste and garbage being dumped on the ground.
Improper disposal of solid waste leads to soil contamination, which can affect plant life, wildlife and the quality of agricultural produce.

(iv) **Noise Pollution**
Shown by a person covering their ears due to loud noise from speakers.
Excessive noise from industries, traffic or other sources can cause stress, hearing loss and disrupt ecosystems.

6. How has population explosion and the advent of industrial revolution resulted in environmental crisis?

Ans. With population explosion and with the advent of industrial revolution, to meet the growing needs of the expanding population, the demand for resources for both production and consumption went beyond the rate of regeneration of the resources and the pressure on the absorptive capacity of the environment increased tremendously.

We are now faced with increased demand for environmental resources and services but their supply is limited due to overuse and misuse. Hence, the environmental issues of waste generation and pollution have become critical today.

7. "Today development has become a burden on nature/ environment." Comment. Competency Based Que

Ans. The present thinking with regard to relationship between nature and development is that there should be maximum exploitation of natural resources for development. As a result, people are using nature beyond its carrying capacity and consequently development has become a burden on nature/environment.

Our present technology is creating a number of environmental problems. A number of non-degradable materials are being produced in present day through the production technology.

Following are the some important reasons responsible for the heavy burden on nature

(i) Rise in human population in underdeveloped countries.

(ii) Affluent consumption style in developed countries.

(iii) Misuse of production technology in almost all the countries and poor planning of development.

As a result, there is a reckless use of resources creating negative effects on the society. The negative effects of development on nature are pollution and degradation of resources.

8. "Correction for environmental damages involves opportunity costs." Explain. NCERT; Competency Based Que

Ans. The opportunity cost of correction for environmental damages refers to the huge amount of expenditure incurred on searching for new efficient alternatives.

The heavy intensive and extensive extraction of both renewable and non-renewable resources demands expenditure for exploring new alternative resources in order to avoid an environmental crisis. The discovery of such resources requires heavy investment by the government.

Also, implementation and maintenance of these alternative resources involve very high cost.

e.g. To control air pollution, we need to fit vehicles with catalytic converters which means increased cost of the vehicle. Therefore, the correction for environmental damages involves opportunity cost that is very high.

9. In a recent article published by The Guardian, it was stated, "the planet is warming faster now than at any point in the past 2,000 years, driven largely by human activity."

Do you agree with the statement? Give valid reasons. Competency Based Que

Ans. Yes, I agree with the statement that the planet is warming faster due to human activity. The key reasons are

(i) **Greenhouse Gas Emissions**
Human activities such as burning fossil fuels for energy and transportation release large amounts of Carbon dioxide (CO_2) and methane, which trap heat in the atmosphere, accelerating global warming.

(ii) **Industrialisation**
Since the industrial revolution, human production and consumption patterns have significantly increased greenhouse gas emissions, intensifying the greenhouse effect.

(iii) **Deforestation**
Cutting down forests reduces the earth's natural ability to absorb CO_2, a major greenhouse gas, thereby amplifying the warming process.

(iv) **Agriculture**
Livestock farming produces methane, a potent greenhouse gas and practices like excessive fertiliser use lead to nitrous oxide emissions.

10. Identify the concept shown in the image and discuss its impact on the environment and human health. Competency Based Que

Source *Ozone Cell: Ministry of Environment and Forests, India Students Poster Competition, 2020*

Ans. The concept shown in the image is 'ozone layer depletion'. This refers to the thinning of the ozone layer in the earth's stratosphere, which protects life on earth from harmful Ultraviolet (UV) radiation.

The primary cause is the release of Chlorofluorocarbons (CFCs) and other Ozone Depleting Substances (ODS), which are found in products like refrigerants, aerosols and foam-blowing agents.

Impact on Environment and Health

(i) **Human Health**
Increased UV radiation due to a thinner ozone layer leads to a higher risk of skin cancers, cataracts and weakened immune systems.

(ii) **Environment**
UV rays can reduce crop yields by damaging plants and also affect marine ecosystems by killing plankton, which are crucial for the ocean's food chain.

(iii) **Global Warming**
Ozone depletion can also exacerbate the effects of global warming, as changes in atmospheric chemistry influence climate patterns.

11. Identify the situation depicted in the given figure and explain any one strategy to effectively overcome the problem. CBSE 2024 C; Competency Based Que

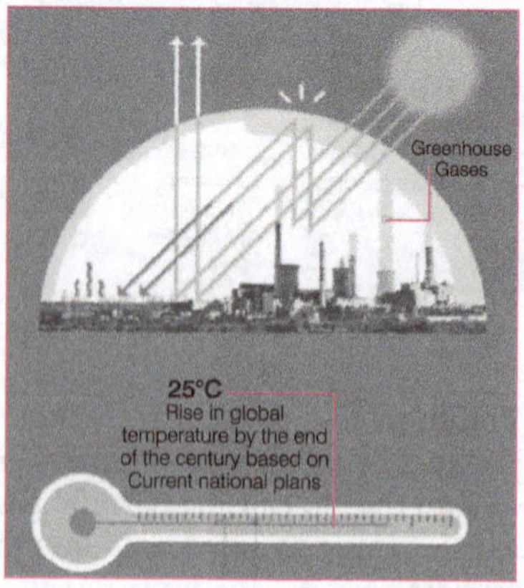

Ans. The situation depicted in the given figure is global warming. One of the strategies to effectively overcome the problem of global warming is the usage of wind energy. Wind power is a popular source of sustainable renewable energy.

In the areas where speed of wind is usually high, windmills can provide electricity without any adverse impact on the environment.

12. "India has abundant natural resources." Substantiate the statement. NCERT; Competency Based Que

Ans. India has abundant natural resources in the terms of rich quality of soil, hundreds of rivers and tributaries, lush green forests, plenty of mineral deposits, vast stretch of Indian ocean, ranges of mountains, etc.

The black soil of the Deccan Plateau is suitable for cultivation of cotton.

The Indo-Gangetic plains are the most fertile regions in the world. India's forests provide green cover for its population and wildlife.

Large deposits of iron-ore, coal and natural gas are found in the country.

13. India's environmental problems pose a dichotomy – they are poverty induced and, at the same time, arise due to affluence in living standards. Is this true? Competency Based Que

Ans. This is true that India's environmental problems pose a dichotomy – they are poverty induced and at the same time arise due to affluence in living standards.

On one hand, population explosion and widespread poverty has led to deforestation in India as the poor people in the rural areas are compelled to cut down trees for earning their livelihood and for use as fuel.

On the other hand, the growing demand for natural resources due to affluence in living standards in the urban areas is also equally responsible for the present environmental degradation.

14. State and discuss any two environmental concerns faced by India in the present times. CBSE 2020

Ans. Two serious environmental concerns faced by India are as follows

(i) **Land Degradation**
Land in India has suffered degradation mainly from unstable use and inappropriate management practices during the development process.

(ii) **Air Pollution**
In India, air pollution is widespread in urban areas where vehicles are the major contributors and in a few other areas which have a high concentration of industries and thermal power plants.

In 2016, personal transport vehicles (two-wheeled vehicles and cars only) constituted about 85% of the total number of registered vehicles. Thus, contributing significantly to total air pollution load.

15. The Government of India is taking several steps to improve the public transport system. The Metro rail network is one such endeavour.

The basic motive behind this strategy is to reduce environmental degradation. What are your views on this strategy? Competency Based Que

Ans. I think that the government's strategy is correct. Improving the public transport system will motivate people to use this mode of transport instead of using their personal vehicles.

This will definitely help to reduce environmental degradation as studies have indicated that emissions of harmful gases from trains per passenger/km are nearly half as that of a car.

Also, one bus emits far fewer fumes than twenty cars. So, air pollution will reduce and the quality of environment will improve.

16. A truck driver had to pay ₹ 1,000 as challan as his truck was emitting black soot.

Why do you think he was penalised? Was it justified? Discuss. Competency Based Que

Ans. To check environmental pollution, the government has imposed fines and penalties on vehicles and industries which cause air pollution.

Since, the truck was emitting black soot, this implies that it was polluting air. Therefore, the truck driver was penalised.

Yes, it was justified because only then the transport operators will adhere to the norms laid down by the government.

17. "Sustainable development is a paradigm shift in development thinking." Comment. Competency Based Que

Ans. Sustainable development implies meeting the basic needs of all and extending to all the opportunity to satisfy their aspirations for a better life, without compromising on the needs of future.

The strategies for sustainable development imply the use of non-conventional sources of energy to minimise the adverse environmental impacts.

Promotion of natural resources, conservation, preserving regenerative capacity of ecological system and avoiding the imposition of environmental rules on future generations would lead to sustainable development.

18. Explain the relevance of intergenerational equity in the definition of sustainable development. NCERT

Ans. Sustainable development makes it obligatory for the development process to be such that the basic needs of not only the present generation, but also of the future generations are taken care of. It becomes the moral duty of this generation to handover the earth to the future generation in good form.

Therefore, if the resources are overused or misused, they will deplete so fast that the production capacity of the future generations would not be sustainable. Sustainable development aims at maximising the welfare of both present and future generations.

It does not mean hindering the existing pace of economic growth, but refers to a judicious or optimum utilisation of resources in such a manner that pace of economic growth sustains with intergenerational equity.

19. Keeping in view your locality, describe any four strategies of sustainable development. NCERT

Ans. Four strategies of sustainable development opted in our locality are

(i) **Use of Eco-friendly Fuel** (CNG, LPG)
The fuels such as petrol and diesel emit huge amount of carbon dioxide that add to the green house impact.

In order to control pollution, the use of CNG and LPG should be promoted. These fuels are cleaner and eco-friendly. Also, pooling of vehicles in the locality should be promoted.

(ii) **Use of Renewable Resources**
India being a tropical country is well endowed with sunlight, water and wind energy.

These natural resources are renewable and pollution free. Thus, attempts should be made to harness solar and wind energy by employing different technologies and to go for rainwater harvesting. It would help in sustainable economic development.

(iii) **Recyclable Products**
The household waste materials like newspapers, old bottles, used batteries, etc. should be accumulated and should be distinguished as biodegradable and non-biodegradable wastes.

The biodegradable wastes are those wastes that can be decomposed and can be used as manure for organic farming.

The non-biodegradable wastes like plastic, etc. should be recycled and re-used. Use of polythene bags should be discouraged.

(iv) **Judicious Use of Electricity**
Electricity is a resource which is used in all households in our locality. It is one such resource which is already in short supply and may not be available to future generations, if we do not start using it judiciously.

Therefore, the easiest strategy for sustainable development is to use power in an efficient manner without wasting it. This can be done by using energy efficient equipments.

20. Under the Delhi Declaration, "the G-20 nations pledged to reach global net zero emissions approximately by mid-century and to triple global renewable energy capacity by 2030."

Discuss briefly the rationale behind the commitment by G-20 nations in the direction of achieving sustainable development.

CBSE SQP 2025; Competency Based Que

Ans. Under the Delhi Declaration, the G-20 member countries pledged to intensify their efforts to address climate change by targeting global net zero emissions by mid-century and significantly expanding renewable energy capacity by 2030.

The rationale behind this commitment lies in the urgent need to mitigate the effects of global warming and promote sustainable development.

By reducing greenhouse gas emissions and transitioning from conventional energy sources (like coal and oil) to renewable alternatives (such as wind and solar power), the G-20 aims to foster a greener economy, protect ecosystems and ensure energy security for future generations. This approach aligns with global goals like the Paris Agreement and UN Sustainable Development targets, which seek to balance economic growth with environmental protection.

21. Analyse the given diagram and explain the relationship between the three interconnected aspects shown. Also, discuss how each of these layers impacts the others and provide examples to illustrate your explanation.

Competency Based Que

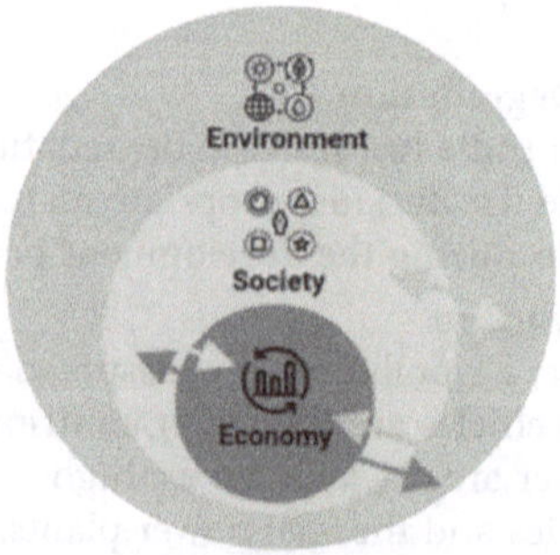

Ans. The diagram illustrates the nested interdependencies between the environment, society and economy. At the core, the economy operates within the society, which in turn exists within the environment. This structure highlights that the economy is dependent on societal structures and both are ultimately constrained by environmental limits.

(i) The environment provides the natural resources and ecosystem services essential for societal survival, such as clean air, water and biodiversity.

(ii) Society regulates how resources are used, balancing needs like health, education and infrastructure, and establishing policies that influence economic activities.

(iii) The economy refers to the system of production, consumption and trade. It thrives by utilising societal resources and is supported by the environment, but its overexploitation can lead to environmental degradation, ultimately affecting societal well-being.

Examples of this dynamic include the impact of industrialisation on pollution (environment), the role of governmental policies in balancing economic growth with environmental sustainability (society) and how overuse of resources, such as fossil fuels, leads to economic and social challenges like climate change and resource depletion (economy).

Long Answer Type Questions

22. Discuss the concept of environment. Also, explain the functions performed by the environment around us.

Ans. Environment is defined as the total planetary inheritance or the totality of all resources. It includes all the biotic (e.g. Birds, animals, plants, forests, etc.) and abiotic (e.g. Water, sun, land, mountains, etc.) factors that influence and depend upon each other.

The environment performs the following four dynamic functions

(i) **Offer Production Resources**
Environment provides us with diverse tangible resources like minerals, water and soil. These are the gifts of nature.
These resources act as an input for converting natural resources into productive and useful things. In other words, environment provides input for production that enhances human life qualitatively.

(ii) **Sustains Life**
Environment provides us with vital ingredients like sun, soil, water and air that are necessary for the survival of life. Absence of these essential elements implies absence of life. It supports biodiversity.

(iii) **Assimilates Waste**
The activities of production and consumption generate waste. This waste in the form of garbage is absorbed by the environment automatically.

(iv) **Enhances Quality of Life**
Environment includes surroundings such as rivers, oceans, mountains and deserts. It provides scenic beauty that man admires in life and adds to the quality of human life.

23. Explain the relationship between environment and the economic development.

Ans. There are two views on how economic development affects environment.

These are

(i) According to first view, economic development degrades our environment by using natural resources for production of goods and services.
Economic development results in pollution in the form of air pollution, water pollution and land pollution.

(ii) According to second view, economic development improves environment quality. The discovery of new materials and sources not only use less of natural resources, but sometimes replace them. Thus, with economic development, degradation of environment decreases.

From the above discussion, we find that relationship between environment and economic development is dynamic and complex. It is difficult to decide whether the economic development leads to degradation of environment or not.

Undoubtedly, economic development leads to excessive extraction of natural resources and generation of pollutants, but it introduces new processes, materials and discoveries. We should be careful and ensure that the economic development should not damage the environment.

24. Explain how the opportunity costs of negative environmental impact are high. NCERT

Ans. Opportunity costs are the costs of the opportunities foregone. By choosing harmful environmental practices, such environmental practices have foregone which produce a positive effect on environment. Such a choice has resulted in increasing the opportunity costs.

The negative environmental impact has high opportunity costs as explained below

(i) Industrial development in the past has polluted and dried up rivers and other aquifers making water an economic good. Also, cleaning up of polluted rivers and replenishing water resources require huge investments.

(ii) The intensive and extensive extraction of both renewable and non-renewable resources has exhausted some of these resources. Huge amount of funds need to be spent on technology and research to explore new resources.

(iii) The health costs of degraded environmental quality are also rising as decline in air and water quality has resulted in increased incidence of respiratory and water-borne diseases.

(iv) Global environmental issues such as global warming and ozone depletion also contribute to increased financial commitments for the government.

Thus, it is clear that the opportunity costs of negative environmental impacts are high.

25. Write a brief note on state of India's environment.

Ans. The rich quality and quantity of natural resources of are stated in following points

(i) India has rich quality of soil, hundreds of rivers and tributaries, lush green forests, plenty of mineral deposits beneath the land surface, vast stretch of the Indian ocean, ranges of mountains, etc.

(ii) Black soil of the Deccan Plateau is particularly suitable for cultivation of cotton. It has led to concentration of textile industries in this region.

(iii) The Indo-Gangetic Plains spread from Arabian Sea to the Bay of Bengal are one of the most fertile, intensively cultivated and densely populated regions in the world.

(iv) India's forests, though unevenly distributed, provide green cover for majority of its population and natural cover for its wildlife.

(v) Large deposits of iron-ore, coal and natural gas are found in the country. India accounts for nearly 8% of the world's total iron-ore reserves.

(vi) Bauxite, copper, chromate, diamonds, gold, lead, lignite, manganese, zinc, uranium, etc. are also available in different parts of the country.

26. In reference to the image, discuss current environmental challenges India is facing.

Ans. India faces numerous environmental challenges, many of which are depicted in the image through contrasting visuals of industrial pollution and sustainable development.

These challenges include

(i) **Land Degradation**

India has experienced significant deforestation due to urbanisation, infrastructure development and agricultural expansion. The image contrasts the loss of green cover with growing industrial areas. Forest loss leads to biodiversity decline, soil erosion and disruptions in the water cycle, which also impacts agriculture and wildlife habitats.

(ii) **Biodiversity Loss**

The loss of forests, pollution and habitat destruction has led to a decline in biodiversity. India, home to rich biodiversity, has seen species' habitats shrink due to human activities.

This not only affects wildlife but also destabilises ecosystems that are crucial for environmental balance and services like pollination, clean water and soil fertility.

(iii) **Air Pollution**

Air pollution is widespread in urban areas of India where vehicles are the major contributors and in few other areas which have a high concentration of industries and thermal power plants. Smoke emissions are of particular concern as they have the maximum impact on the general population.

The carbon emissions into air are causing global warming and respiratory diseases are increasing among the population.

(iv) **Management of Fresh Water**

Water is an equally important element of life and its pollution is equally serious. Water becomes polluted when chemicals and other waste materials are dumped into it.

Polluted water is the principal cause of diseases like diarrhoea and hepatitis. Thus, the management of fresh water is essential to sustain life.

(v) **Management of Solid Waste**

It is essential that solid waste should be treated chemically. Efforts should be made for effective management of non-biodegradable waste. Biodegradable waste should also be converted into compost.

27. How does air pollution contribute to the environmental crisis in India?

Ans. In India, air pollution is widespread in urban areas where vehicles are the major contributors and in a few other areas which have a high concentration of industries and thermal power plants.

Vehicular emissions are of particular concern since these are ground level sources and thus, have the maximum impact on the general population.

The number of motor vehicles has increased from about 3 lakh in 1951 to 23 crore in 2016. In 2016, personal transport vehicles (two-wheeled vehicles and cars only) constituted about 85% of the total number of registered vehicles thus, contributing significantly to total air pollution load.

India is one of the ten most industrialised nations of the world. But this status has brought with it unwanted and unanticipated consequences such as unplanned urbanisation, pollution and the risk of accidents.

The CPCB (Central Pollution Control Board) has identified 17 categories of industries (large and medium scale) as significantly polluting.

28. Give the benefits and limitations of using solar power.

Ans. Following are the benefits associated with solar power

(i) It is relatively easy to install solar panels which help to generate solar power.

(ii) Solar panels, once installed, do not require much maintenance.

(iii) These panels provide sufficient solar power during the long summer days and reduce the problem of power cuts.

Following are the limitations associated with solar power

(i) It is not suitable for areas where sunlight is less or which are generally overcast.

(ii) Solar power is not available at night.

(iii) The initial cost of installing solar panels is high and it requires active consumers participation.

29. Differentiate between economic development and sustainable development.

Ans. The following are the points of difference between economic and sustainable development

Basis	Economic Development	Sustainable Development
Economic Welfare	Economic development refers to the long-term increase in real per capita income and economic welfare.	In sustainable development, besides the increase in real per capita income, the welfare of the present and future generation is taken into consideration.
Use of Natural Resources	It does not account for the exploitation of natural capital.	Sustainable development emphasises on rational utilisation of natural resources.
Use	It is generally used in the context of underdeveloped economies.	It is used for developed, developing as well as underdeveloped economies.
Impact	It lays special focus on the structural, technical and institutional changes in the economy.	It does not lay such focus on the structural, technical and institutional changes in the economy.
Environment Protection	It does not emphasise on environmental protection.	It gives main emphasis on environmental protection.

30. Growing carbon footprint of industries have put power and steel sector in the spotlight as the major contributor to the climate crisis. The challenge of climate change can be tackled only by making our industries and businesses follow practices and processes that reduce their carbon footprint. It can be possible only with green financing.

Green financing aims to increase the level of financial flows (from banking, micro-credit, insurance and investment) from the public, private and not-for-profit sectors to sustainable development priorities.

Global green finance has also started chasing Indian companies. Global development finance institutions and funds are ready to offer long-term support (both equity and debt) at cheap rates to projects like solar energy and hydropower.

Green finance can positively affect environment quality, economic development and financial issues that promote the green economy, such as reducing greenhouse gas emissions, improving energy efficiency or enhancing the organic economy.

On the basis of the given text and common understanding, answer the following questions

CBSE 2025; Competency Based Que

(i) State the meaning and objective of green finance.

(ii) Discuss any two benefits of green financing.

Ans. (i) Green finance refers to financial investments that support environmentally sustainable projects and initiatives. It includes banking, micro-credit, insurance and investment aimed at promoting eco-friendly activities.

Objective of Green Finance The primary objective of green finance is to direct financial resources towards projects that help reduce carbon footprints, improve energy efficiency and support sustainable economic growth. It aims to tackle climate change by encouraging industries and businesses to adopt eco-friendly practices.

(ii) Two key benefits of green financing are as follows
- **Environmental Benefits**
  Green financing helps reduce greenhouse gas emissions, improve energy efficiency and promote renewable energy sources such as solar and hydropower. This leads to better air quality and overall environmental sustainability.
- **Economic Development**
  Green financing encourages investment in sustainable projects, leading to job creation and long-term economic growth. It also provides industries with access to low-cost, long-term financial support, helping them transition to cleaner technologies.

31. **Read the following text carefully and answer questions given below**

Green investment and sustainability are priorities in public policy. India has emerged as a global leader at the front of the climate change. India has pledged to seek solutions for the future.

Government schemes and policies such as Swachh Bharat Mission, Pradhan Mantri Awas Yojana, Smart Cities, Deen Dayal Upadhyay Gram Jyoti Yojana among other, all contribute towards achieving sustainable development goals. The government has contributed to maintain economic growth by introducing and implementing various policies and measures relating to sustainable develop- ment, climate change, energy efficiency and air pollution.

Pradhan Mantri Ujjwala Yojana Scheme, has actively contributed to cleaner air. It has resulted in drastic reduction of respiratory diseases and ultimately death as per recent medical report.

The Jal Jeevan Mission was launched with the objective of achieving water security. We have seen 68 per cent decline in the size of population of various animal species and amphibian over the last 60 years. The issue of greenhouse gases and rising temperature of the earth are a global concern. India is one of those countries that will be affected by the over 2 degree celsius rise in global temperature.

"India has already taken a lot of steps in the area of innovation and development of different production methodologies which are environmentally friendly in the long-run." CBSE Term II 2022; Competency Based Que

Source *The Economic Times : 27th October, 2021*

(i) State and discuss any two steps involved in attaining sustainable development in India.

(ii) From the given text, state any two factors which challenged the carrying capacity of the environment.

Ans. (i) Two steps involved in attaining sustainable development in India are (any two)
- Implementation of Pradhan Mantri Ujjwala Yojana Scheme to clear air. It has resulted in drastic reduction of respiratory diseases.
- Limiting the human population to a level within the carrying capacity of the environment.
- Renewable resources should be extracted on a sustainable basis, i.e. rate of extraction should not exceed rate of regeneration.

(ii) Factors challenging the carrying capacity of the environment are
- Greenhouse gases.
- Raising temperature of earth.

32. **India has aimed to reduce the country's carbon intensity by approximately 45% by 2030. To achieve this 'green finance' plays a vital role. At the initial stages, green finance needs a big push from the government. The Indian government has identified projects worth ₹ 25,000 crore that will be financed by proceeds from sovereign green bonds.**

According to the framework approved by finance ministry, the sovereign green bonds will focus on financing public projects including renewable energy, climate change, clean transportation, sustainable water and waste management and pollution control.

Businesses that take green finance can get benefit in various ways.

It can help them follow different environmental norms and regulations and thus avoid possible fines.

Adopting sustainable developmental practices enhances brand value of businesses. Customers tend to prefer brands that adopt clear sustainable development practices. The energy-efficient and other sustainable development practices promoted by green finance also often help in saving cost, boosting profitability of businesses, etc. CBSE 2024; Competency Based Que

Source *The Economic Times, 22nd April, 2023 (Modified)*

(i) Define sustainable development.

(ii) State the public project areas, where Sovereign Green Bond are focused.

(iii) How can businesses get benefit from green finance?

Ans. (i) Sustainable development can be defined as an approach to the economic development of a country without compromising the quality of the environment for future generations.

(ii) The sovereign green bonds will finance public projects including renewable energy, climate change, clean transportation, sustainable water and waste management and pollution control.

(iii) Businesses that utilise green finance can get benefit in many ways
- It can help them follow different environmental norms and regulations and thus avoid possible fines.
- Adopting sustainable development practices enhances brand value of businesses.
- The energy-efficient and other sustainable development practices promoted by green finance help in saving cost of production, boosting profitability of business.

33. **"We are One Earth, One Future and We Share One Future" is the opening sentence the of the G-20 New Delhi leader's declaration statement.**

In this statement, the leaders pledged to "resolve to fully and effectively implement the 2030 Agenda and the Sustainable Developmental Goals (SDGs)".

The leader's commitments contained in the declaration statement reflect, "the philosophy of living in harmony with our surrounding eco-system."

The declaration recognises the "cascading challenges and crisis that have reversed gains" on the 2030 Agenda of SDG's. The leaders "affirm that no country should have to choose between fighting poverty and fighting for our planet".

The leaders resolved to act
- **accelerate strong, sustainable, balanced and inclusive growth;**
- **accelerate the full and effective implementation of 2030 Agenda;**
- **pursue low carbon and environmentally sustainable development pathways;**
- **pursue reforms for better, comprehensive and more effective finance avenues.**

The leaders commit to "taking collective actions for effective and timely implementation of the G-20, 2023 Action Plan to accelerate progress on the SDG's; including through actions on eliminating hunger and malnutrition, strengthening global health and implementation of One Health approach and delivering quality education." CBSE 2024; Competency Based Que

(i) State and discuss the importance of collective fight in achieving SDGs.

(ii) Discuss briefly the action plan of G-20 leaders in promoting 'One Health' approach.

Ans. (i) The importance of collective action in achieving the Sustainable Development Goals (SDGs) cannot be overstated.

Following points highlight the same
- **Global Challenges Require Global Solutions**
  The SDGs address complex and interconnected global challenges such as poverty, hunger, climate change, inequality and environmental degradation.
  These issues transcend national boundaries and cannot be effectively tackled by any single country or organisation alone.
- **Shared Responsibility**
  The SDGs recognise that achieving sustainable development requires collaboration and partnership among governments, civil society, businesses, academia and international organisations.
  Each stakeholder has a role to play in advancing the SDGs, whether it's setting policies, implementing programmes, mobilising resources or advocating for change.
- **Pooling Resources and Expertise**
  No single entity has all the resources, expertise or capabilities needed to achieve the SDGs on its own.
  Collective action allows for the pooling of resources, expertise and knowledge from diverse stakeholders, enabling more effective and efficient solutions.

(ii) The action plan of G-20 leaders in promoting 'One Health' approach includes
- **Strengthening Global Health Governance**
  G-20 leaders commit to strengthening global health governance structures and mechanisms to facilitate coordination and collaboration among relevant stakeholders, including governments, international organisations, civil society and the private sector.
- **Enhancing Surveillance and Early Warning**
  Systems G-20 leaders pledge to enhance surveillance and early warning systems for detecting and monitoring emerging infectious diseases, zoonotic diseases and anti-microbial resistance.
- **Promoting Multi-sectoral Collaboration**
  G-20 leaders emphasise the importance of multi-sectoral collaboration and coordination across human health, animal health and environmental sectors.

SELF ASSESSMENT TEST

Objective Type Questions

1. .... is the variety of all life forms including animals and plants.
   (a) Biodiversity (b) Universe
   (c) Ecosystem (d) None of these
2. Environment has many resources for us. A resource that can be totally replaced or is always available naturally or that is practically inexhaustible is known as
   (a) conventional resource (b) renewable resource
   (c) non-renewable resource (d) non-conventional resource
3. What are the consequences of environmental crisis?
   (a) Polluted and dried up rivers and other aquifers
   (b) Extinction of vital resources
   (c) Decline in air and water quality
   (d) All of the above
4. In areas where speed of wind is usually high, wind mills can provide electricity without any adverse impact on the environment but it's not yet been explored on a large-scale. What is the correct reason out of the following?
   I. Lack of technological devices
   II. High cost III. Non-availability of land

   Codes
   (a) Only II (b) Both I and II
   (c) Both II and III (d) All of these
5. Which of the following is a key challenge in achieving sustainable development?
   (a) Increasing consumption and minimising waste
   (b) Reducing economic growth to zero
   (c) Balancing economic growth with environmental protection and social equity
   (d) Ignoring the needs of the poor
6. The Kyoto Protocol (1997) is an international agreement that aimed to
   (a) promote biodiversity conservation
   (b) reduce greenhouse gas emissions
   (c) end deforestation globally
   (d) eliminate plastic waste from oceans
7. Which of the following statements is/are incorrect?
   I. Overgrazing by cattle's causes biodiversity loss.
   II. Economic development and sustainable development are same.

   Codes
   (a) Only I (b) Only II
   (c) Both I and II (d) None of these

Answers 1. (a) 2. (b) 3. (d) 4. (b) 5. (c) 6. (b) 7. (b)

Short Answer Type Questions

8. Why is air pollution widespread in urban areas?
9. Explain the concept of sustainable development. How does it differ from conventional development?
10. Give examples of renewable energy sources and their significance for long-term environmental sustainability.
11. Explain the concept of carrying capacity of environment. How does it influence population growth and resource consumption?
12. A developing country is striving to achieve sustainable development while facing challenges such as poverty, environmental degradation and rapid urbanisation. The government has decided to implement strategies that promote economic growth, environmental conservation and social well-being.

    Discuss three key strategies for sustainable development that can be implemented by the government to achieve the set goal.
13. Have people tried to prevent indiscriminate cutting of trees? Discuss the two movements started by them for achieving this objective.
14. The government of a coastal region has implemented a policy to limit industrial activities near marine ecosystems to prevent pollution and preserve biodiversity.
    (i) How does this policy align with the objectives of sustainable development?
    (ii) Discuss the environmental, social and economic aspects of this policy.

Long Answer Type Questions

15. What is the significance of sustainable development? How is it measured?
16. Give the effects of global warming and ozone depletion.
17. India, a rapidly developing nation with a large population, faces numerous environmental challenges. Despite efforts by the government and non-governmental organisations to address these challenges, the country continues to struggle with balancing development and environmental conservation.
    (i) Discuss the major environmental challenges faced by India.
    (ii) How do these challenges affect both the economy and the quality of life of its citizens?

08
CHAPTER

An understanding of the other economies in our neighbourhood is required as all major common economic activities in the region impinge on overall human development in a shared environment.

▼ **YOUR STUDY GOALS**

8.1 Development Strategies of India, China and Pakistan

8.2 Comparative Study of India, China and Pakistan

8.3 An Appraisal of Development Strategies

▼ **YOUR PRACTICE GOAL**

- Objective Type Questions (54 Qs ; MCQs, A-R, Statements, Matching, Concept Identification)
- Subjective Questions (19 SAs, 10 LAs)
- Self Assessment Test (8 MCQs, 7 SAs, 3 LAs)

Comparative Development Experiences of India and its Neighbours

Globalisation has connected nations, leading to regional and global economic groupings like SAARC, EU, ASEAN, G-8, G-20, BRICS, etc. Developing countries study neighbouring economies to assess their own strengths and weaknesses facing competition from both developed and developing nations. This understanding help to promote shared economic growth and human development.

8.1 Development Strategies of India, China and Pakistan

All the three nations have started towards their developmental path at the same time. It can be understood with the help of following points

1. **Political Systems**
   - India is the world's largest democracy, characterised by secularism and liberalism.
   - Pakistan operates under a militarist political power structure.
   - China follows a command economy with centralised control.
2. **Independence and Planning**
   - India and Pakistan became independent in 1947, while People's Republic of China was established in 1949.

- All three countries initiated development planning through five year plans

Aspect	India	Pakistan	China
First Five Year Plan	1951-56	1956 (now called medium-term plan)	1953
Current Plan	Discontinued five year plans after 2017	12th five year plan (2018-23)	14th five year plan (2021-25)

3. **Development Strategies**

   India and Pakistan adopted similar strategies, focusing on expanding the public sector and increasing public expenditure on social development.

4. **Growth and Reforms**
   - Until the 1980s, all the three countries had similar growth rates and per capita incomes.
   - Each country undertook economic reforms at different times
     - China began reforms in 1978.
     - Pakistan started reforms in 1988.
     - India initiated its reforms in 1991.

Development Strategies of India

Key Strategies	Explanation
Sound Trade System	India's 1991 economic reforms introduced globalisation, liberalisation and privatisation, which boosted both global and domestic trade, forming a basis of sound trade system and encouraging economic growth.
Reduction in Poverty	Various poverty alleviation programmes adopted by India helped to improve per capita income, enhance nutrition levels and decrease the percentage of people living in absolute poverty in certain States.
Rural Development	Focused efforts were made to develop underdeveloped rural areas, ensuring overall progress in the rural economy.
Employment Generation	Several economic reforms were launched to generate employment. Many programmes were also initiated with an aim to provide gainful self-employment.

Development Strategies of China

After establishment of People's Republic of China under one party rule, all critical sectors of economy, enterprises and land owned and operated by individuals were brought under government control.

Key Strategies	Explanation
Great Leap Forward (GLF) **Campaign**	Launched in 1958 to industrialise the country on a massive scale. People were encouraged to setup backyard industries and collective farming through communes. However, this campaign faced challenges like severe droughts causing havoc and withdrawal of Russian support in industrialisation process, leading to significant setbacks.
Great Proletarian Cultural Revolution (1966-76)	Initiated by Mao Tse Tung in 1965 to reshape Chinese society. Students and professionals were sent to rural areas to work and learn from the countryside.
1978 Reforms	Reforms were introduced in phases, gradually transitioning China towards a more market-oriented economy. These phases are as follows
(i) ***First Phase***	Focused on agriculture, foreign trade and investment sectors. In agriculture, commune lands were divided into small plots and were allotted to households for use, allowing them to keep income after paying taxes.
(ii) ***Later Phase***	Reforms extended to the industrial sector, allowing private sector firms, township and village enterprises, owned and operated by local collectives, to produce goods. State-Owned Enterprises (SOEs) faced competition during this phase.

Key Strategies	Explanation
(iii) ***Dual Pricing***	Implemented a system where farmers and industrial units bought and sold fixed quantities of input and output at government prices, while surplus could be traded at market prices. Over time, market transactions increased.
(iv) ***Special Economic Zones*** *(SEZs)*	Established to attract foreign investment by offering favourable conditions and incentives for businesses.

Great Leap Forward

Special Economic Zones (SEZs)

Development Strategies of Pakistan

Key Strategies	Explanation
Mixed Economy	Pakistan follows a mixed economy, allowing both public and private sectors to co-exist and contribute to growth.
Import Substitution	Adopted in the late 1950s and 1960s, focusing on industrialisation by protecting domestic industries through tariffs and controlling imports of competing foreign goods.
Green Revolution	Introduced to boost agricultural productivity and achieve self-sufficiency in food production, significantly increasing foodgrain output.
Nationalisation of Capital Goods Industries	In the 1970s, Pakistan nationalised capital goods industries, but later shifted towards denationalisation and encouraging private sector growth in the 1970s and 1980s.
Other Strategies	During the 1970s and 1980s, financial support from Western countries and remittances from the middle-East stimulated economic growth. Government also provided incentives to private sector. Certain reforms were also introduced in 1988.

8.2 Comparative Study of India, China and Pakistan

The comparison of India with Pakistan and China on the basis of demographic indicators, GDP and human development indicators is discussed below

Demographic Indicators

The comparison on the basis of demographic indicators is discussed below

Select Demographic Indicators, 2017-18

Country	**Estimated Population** (in million)	**Annual Growth of Population**	**Density** (per sq km)	**Sex Ratio** (out of 1,000 persons)	**Fertility Rate**	**Urbanisation**
India	1,352	1.03	455	924	2.2	34
China	1,393	0.46	148	949	1.7	59
Pakistan	212	2.05	275	943	3.6	37

Source *World Development Indicators 2019, wwww. worldbank.org*

1. **Population Proportion**
   - Out of every six people in the world, one is Indian and one is Chinese.
   - The population of Pakistan is 212 million, which is about one-tenth of China's (1,393 million) and India's (1,352 million) population.
2. **Population Density**
   - China has the lowest density at 148 per sq km.
   - India's density is 455 per sq km.
   - Pakistan's density is 275 per sq km.
3. **Population Growth Rate**
   - Pakistan has the highest population growth rate at 2.05%.
   - India's population growth rate is 1.03%.
   - China has the lowest population growth rate at 0.46%, influenced by its **one child policy**.
     Implications of China's one child policy are
     – It has resulted in a future projection of more elderly people compared to the young population in China.
     – This led to policy adjustments, allowing couples to have two children.
4. **Sex-ratio**
   - All three countries have a low sex-ratio being biased against females.
   - The sex-ratio is lowest in India (924 females per 1,000 males), followed by Pakistan (943) and then China (949).
5. **Fertility Rate**
   - China has the lowest fertility rate (1.7).
   - Pakistan has the highest fertility rate (3.6).
   - India's fertility rate is moderate at 2.2.
6. **Urbanisation**
   - Urbanisation is highest in China (59% of its population living in urban areas).
   - In India, 34% of the population is urban.
   - In Pakistan, 37% of the population lives in urban areas.

Gross Domestic Product (GDP)

1. **GDP** (measured by Purchasing Power Parity-PPP) **Comparison**
   - China's GDP (PPP) is second largest in the world at US $22.5 trillion.
   - India's GDP (PPP) is US $9.03 trillion, which is approximately 41% of China's GDP.
   - Pakistan's GDP (PPP) is US $0.94 trillion, which is roughly about 11% of India's GDP.

Annual Growth of Gross Domestic Product (%), 1980-2017

Country	1980-90	2015-2017
India	5.7	7.3
China	10.3	6.8
Pakistan	6.3	5.3

Source *Key Indicators for Asia and Pacific 2016, Asian Development Bank, Philippines; World Development Indicators 2018.*

2. **GDP Growth Trends in the 1980s**
   - In the 1980s, China had the highest GDP growth with double-digit rates.
   - Pakistan's GDP growth was moderate, placing it in the middle.
   - India had the lowest growth among the three countries during this time.
3. **GDP Trends from 2015-2017**
   - China and Pakistan experienced a decline in GDP growth during 2015-2017. The decline in Pakistan's growth rate is attributed to the reform processes initiated in 1988 and ongoing political instability.
   - India's GDP growth rate increased during this period, rising from 5.7% to 7.3%.

Sectoral Share of Employment and GVA (GDP)

The sectoral share of employment comparison is discussed below

Agriculture Sector

- In China, due to topographic and climatic conditions, the area suitable for cultivation is only about 10% of its total land area. The total cultivable area in China accounts for 40% of the cultivable area in India.
- There was a shift from 80% workforce in 1980s to 26% of China's workforce being engaged in agriculture and contributing 7% to GVA in China.
- In both India and Pakistan, the contribution of agriculture to GVA was at 16% and 24% respectively.
- In Pakistan, about 41% of people work in agriculture sector whereas in India, it is 43%.

Industrial Sector

- In China, manufacturing sector contributes to GVA at 41% and employ 28% of workforce. In the normal course of development, countries like China first shift their employment and output from agriculture to manufacturing and then to services.
- The proportion of workforce engaged in manufacturing in India and Pakistan were low at 25% and 24% respectively.
- The contribution of industries to GVA is 30% in India and 19% in Pakistan. In India and Pakistan, the shift is taking place directly to the service sector.

Service Sector

- In all the three countries, the service sector is emerging as a major player of development. It contributes highest to GVA, i.e. 54% in case of India, 52% in China and 57% in Pakistan.
- In the 1980s India, China and Pakistan employed 17%, 12% and 27% of its workforce in the service sector, respectively. In 2019, it has reached the level of 32%, 46% and 35%, respectively.

Sectoral Share of Employment and GVA (%), 2018-19

Sector ↓	Contribution to GVA			Distribution of Workforce		
Country →	**India**	**China**	**Pakistan**	**India**	**China**	**Pakistan**
Agriculture	16	7	24	43	26	41
Industry	30	41	19	25	28	24
Service	54	52	57	32	46	35
Total	100	100	100	100	100	100

Source *Human Development Report 2019 : Key Indicators of Asia and Pacific 2019.*

Output Growth in Different Sectors

- Agricultural growth has declined over the past five decades in all the three countries.
- Industrial sector growth rate has also fallen in all three countries.
- Service sector growth between 1980-90 to 2014-18 was increased in India but decreased in China and Pakistan.
- China's growth is driven by both manufacturing and service sector India's growth by service sector while Pakistan experienced a slow down across all sectors.

Trends in Output Growth in Different Sectors, 1980-2018

Period →	1980-90			2014-2018		
Country ↓	**Agriculture**	**Industry**	**Service**	**Agriculture**	**Industry**	**Service**
India	3.1	7.4	6.9	3.1	6.9	7.6
China	5.9	10.8	13.5	3.1	5.3	7.1
Pakistan	4	7.7	6.8	1.7	4.8	5.0

Human Development Indicator

The comparison on the basis of the selected indicators of human development is discussed below

Some Selected Indicators of Human Development, 2017-2019

Item	India	China	Pakistan
Human Development Index (Value)	0.645	0.761	0.557
Rank (based on HDI)	130	87	154
Life Expectancy at Birth (years)	69.7	76.9	67.3
Mean years of Schooling (% aged 15 and above)	6.5	8.1	5.2
Gross National Income Per Capita (PPP US $)	6,681	16,057	5,005
People Below Poverty Line (National)	21.9*	1.7**	24.3*
Infant Mortality Rate (per 1,000 live births)	29.9	7.4	57.2
Maternal Mortality Rate (per 1 lakh births)	133	29	140
Population using at least basic Sanitation (%)	60	75	60
Population using at least basic drinking Water Source (%)	93	96	91
Percentage of Undernourished Children	37.9	8.1	37.6

Note * for the year 2011; for the years 2015.

Source *Human Development Report 2019 and 2020 and World Development Indicators (www.worldbank.org); Key indicators for Asia and the Pacific 2019, Asian Development Bank (ADB).*

- **HDI Rankings** (2017-19) China ranks 87, India 130 and Pakistan 154.
- **Life Expectancy** Highest in China (76.9 years), followed by India (69.7 years) and Pakistan (67.3 years).
- **Mean Years of Schooling** China leads with 8.1%, India has 6.5% and Pakistan 5.2%.
- **Gross National Income per Capita** China's national income is also high ($16,057), followed by India ($6,681), Pakistan ($5,005).
- **Poverty Reduction** China is more effective in reducing poverty compared to India and Pakistan.
- **Infant Mortality Rate** Lowest in China and highest in Pakistan.
- **Maternal Mortality Rate** China (29 women die per 1,00,000 births), whereas in India and Pakistan, 133 and 140 women die respectively.
- **Sanitation and Drinking Water** China outperforms in sanitation while all three provide improved drinking water to most of their population.
- **Undernourished Children** China has the lowest percentage (8.1%), while India (37.9%) and Pakistan (37.6%) have higher rates.

Human Development Index and Liberty Indicators

- Human development indicators are all extremely important indicators, but these are not sufficient.
- Along with these, we also need what may be called 'liberty indicators'. These are a measure of the extent of democratic participation in social and political decision-making.
- Some liberty indicators are measures of the extent of constitutional protection given to rights of citizen or independence of judiciary and the Rule of Law.
- Without including these and giving them overriding importance in the list, the construction of a human development index may be said to be incomplete and its usefulness limited.

8.3 An Appraisal of Development Strategies

Countries often use others' development strategies as models, especially post-reform. Understanding successes and failures of neighbouring nations like China and Pakistan offers valuable insights for shaping economic policies.

Assessment of Structural Reforms in China

The development strategies of China can be understood with the help of its pre-reform period and post-reform period.

Pre-reform Period	Post-reform Period
• Basic health services extended in rural areas. • Equitable foodgrain distribution via the commune system. • Slow growth and lack of modernisation under Maoist rule. • Maoist vision based on decentralisation, self-sufficiency, avoiding foreign tech had failed. • Per capita grain output in 1978 was same as it was in mid-1950, despite land reforms, Great Leap Forward and other initiatives.	• Reforms were first implemented on a small-scale, then expanded. • Improved education, health infrastructure, land reforms, long decentralised planning and existence of small enterprises led to improved social and income indicators. • Agricultural reforms allowed individuals to cultivate land, raising rural prosperity. • Created conditions for phenomenal growth in rural industries and built up strong support base for further reforms.

Assessment of Structural Reforms in Pakistan

The reform process in Pakistan led to worsening of all the economic indicators. As compared to 1980s, growth rate of GDP and its sectoral constituents have not yet improved. Following points highlight the results of structural reforms

- Growth rate of GDP and its sectoral constituents have fallen in 1990s.
- Poverty has risen in Pakistan. In 1960s, there was more than 40% poor in Pakistan which declined to 25% in 1980 and started rising again in the recent decades.
- Agricultural growth and food supply situation were based on good harvest instead of an institutionalised process of technical change. This led to the slow down of growth and re-emergence of poverty.
- Foreign exchange earnings came from remittances from Pakistani workers in the middle-East and the exports of highly volatile agricultural products.
- Dependency on foreign loans increased along with the increased difficulty in paying back the loans.
- However, Pakistan has recovered its economic growth during the last few years. According to Annual Plan 2019-20, there is a growth of 5.5% in the GDP of Pakistan. Agriculture also recorded a growth rate and industrial and service sector grew at 4.9% and 6.2%, respectively.

Conclusion

India's Growth

- It has a democratic system and has seen moderate growth.
- A significant portion of the population still relies on agriculture.
- It has initiated various infrastructure development projects and efforts to improve living standards.

Pakistan's Economic Challenges

- Political instability, reliance on remittances and foreign aid, along with inconsistent agricultural performance have slowed down economic progress.
- In recent years, some macroeconomic indicators have shown positive and moderate growth, indicating economic recovery.

China's Development Approach

- Political freedom remains limited, raising concerns about human rights.
- Over the past four decades, China has successfully combined a market system with strong political control, achieving high growth and poverty reduction.
- China has leveraged the market mechanism to create additional social and economic opportunities while retaining collective ownership of land, ensuring rural social security in rural areas.
- Public investment in social infrastructure before market reforms contributed to improved human development indicators.

Mind Map

COMPARATIVE DEVELOPMENT EXPERIENCES OF INDIA AND ITS NEIGHBOURS

1 Development Strategies of India, China and Pakistan

Developmental Path for All Three Nations

- **Political Systems** India is the world's largest democracy, characterised by secularism and liberalism. Pakistan operates under a militarist political power structure. China follows a command economy with centralised control.
- **Independence and Planning** India and Pakistan became independent in 1947 while People's Republic of China was established in 1949. All three countries initiated development planning through five year plans.
- **Development Strategies** India and Pakistan focused on expanding the public sector.
- **Growth and Reforms** China began reforms in 1978, Pakistan in 1988 and India in 1991.

Development Strategies

India

- Sound trade system
- Rural development
- Reduction in poverty
- Employment generation

China

- Great Leap Forward (GLF) campaign
- 1978 reforms
- Great proletarian cultural revolution

Pakistan

- Mixed economy
- Green revolution
- Import substitution
- Other strategies
- Nationalisation of capital goods industries

2 Comparative Study of India, China and Pakistan

Comparison of India with Pakistan and China can be done on the basis of demographic indicators, GDP and human development indicators.

Demographic Indicators

- **Population Proportion** The population of Pakistan is 212 million, which is about one-tenth of China's (1,393 million) and India's (1,352 million) population.
- **Population Density** (per sq km) China – 148, India – 455, Pakistan – 275.
- **Population Growth Rate** (%) Pakistan – 2.05, India – 1.03, China – 0.46.
- **Sex-ratio** India (924 females per 1,000 males), Pakistan (943), China (949).
- **Fertility Rate** China – 1.7, India – 2.2, Pakistan – 3.6.
- **Urbanisation** (%) China – 59, India – 34, Pakistan – 37.

Sectoral Share of Employment and GVA (GDP)

- **Agriculture Sector** In China, due to topographic and climatic conditions, the area suitable for cultivation is only about 10% of its total land area contributing 7% to GVA. In both India and Pakistan, the contribution of agriculture to GVA was at 16% and 24% respectively.
- **Industrial Sector** In China, manufacturing sector contributes to GVA at 41% and employ 28% of workforce. The contribution of industries to GVA is 30% in India and 19% in Pakistan.
- **Service Sector** In all the three countries, the service sector contributes highest to GVA, i.e. 54% in case of India, 52% in China and 57% in Pakistan.

Human Development Indicator

- **HDI Rankings** (2017-19) China ranks 87, India 130 and Pakistan 154.
- **Life Expectancy Highest in China** (76.9 years), followed by India (69.7 years) and Pakistan (67.3 years).
- **Mean Years of Schooling** China leads with 8.1%, India has 6.5% and Pakistan 5.2%.
- **Gross National Income per Capita** China's national income is also high ($16,057), followed by India ($6,681), Pakistan ($5,005).
- **Poverty Reduction** China is more effective in reducing poverty compared to India and Pakistan.
- **Infant Mortality Rate** Lowest in China and highest in Pakistan.
- **Maternal Mortality Rate** China (29 women die per 1,00,000 births), whereas in India and Pakistan, 133 and 140 women die respectively.
- **Sanitation and Drinking Water** China outperforms in sanitation while all three provide improved drinking water to most of their population.
- **Undernourished Children** China has the lowest percentage (8.1%), while India (37.9%) and Pakistan (37.6%) have higher rates.

3 An Appraisal of Development Strategies

Countries often use others' development strategies as models, especially post-reform. Understanding successes and failures of neighbouring nations like China and Pakistan offers valuable insights for shaping economic policies.

Assessment of Structural Reforms in China

Pre-reform Period

- Basic health services extended in rural areas.
- Equitable foodgrain distribution via the commune system.
- Slow growth and lack of modernisation under Maoist rule.
- Maoist vision based on decentralisation, self-sufficiency, avoiding foreign tech had failed.
- Per capita grain output in 1978 was same as it was in mid-1950, despite land reforms, Great Leap Forward and other initiatives.

Post-reform Period

- Reforms were first implemented on a small scale, then expanded.
- Improved education, health infrastructure, land reforms, long decentralised planning and existence of small enterprises led to improved social and income indicators.
- Agricultural reforms allowed individuals to cultivate land, raising rural prosperity.
- Created conditions for phenomenal growth in rural industries and built up strong support base for further reforms.

Assessment of Structural Reforms in Pakistan

- Growth rate of GDP and its sectoral constituents have fallen in 1990s.
- Poverty has risen in Pakistan. In 1960s, there was more than 40% poor in Pakistan which declined to 25% in 1980 and started rising again in the recent decades.
- Agricultural growth and food supply situation were based on good harvest instead of an institutionalised process of technical change.
- Foreign exchange earnings came from remittances from Pakistani workers in the middle-East and the exports of highly volatile agricultural products.
- Dependency on foreign loans increased along with the increased difficulty in paying back the loans.
- Agriculture also recorded a growth rate and industrial and service sector grew at 4.9% and 6.2%, respectively.

EXAM PATTERN QUESTIONS

Objective Type Questions

Multiple Choice Questions (MCQs)

1. Economic reforms were introduced in the year .... in India and in the year .... in Pakistan. **CBSE 2024**

(a) 1978, 1988 (b) 1988, 1978
(c) 1978, 1991 (d) 1991, 1988

2. Mao initiated the 'great leap forward' movement in the year .... **CBSE 2025**

(a) 1951 (b) 1955
(c) 1958 (d) 1962

3. Which of the following country/countries followed the five year planning structure of economic development? **CBSE 2025**

(i) India (ii) China
(iii) Pakistan (iv) USA

Codes

(a) (i), (ii) and (iii) (b) (ii) and (iii)
(c) (i) and (iv) (d) Only (iv)

4. In 1965, Mao introduced the .... under which students and professionals were sent to work and learn from the countryside. **CBSE 2024 C**

(a) great leap forward campaign
(b) commune system
(c) great proletarian cultural revolution
(d) medium-term development plan

5. Which of the following points is/are true regarding China's development strategies? **Competency Based Que**

I. China's state-led economic planning was central to early industrialisation.
II. The privatisation of agriculture boosted China's early growth in rural areas.
III. China's economic reforms in 1978 shifted focus towards market mechanisms.
IV. China's reforms led to high levels of income inequality in rural areas.

Codes

(a) I and III (b) I, III and IV
(c) II and IV (d) I, II and III

6. Under the economic reforms introduced in China in 1978, ... were set-up to attract foreign investors. **CBSE 2024 C**

(a) remittance zones (b) land zones
(c) special commune zones (d) special economic zones

7. In China, under ...., peasants were provided with pooled land to create larger fields that could yield greater output and they shared farm implements. **CBSE 2025**

(a) joint farming system (b) commune system
(c) great proletarian cultural revolution
(d) green revolution

8. .... is geographically the largest nation among India, China and Pakistan and its density is .... among the three nations. **CBSE 2024 C**

(a) China, highest (b) Pakistan, lowest
(c) India, lowest (d) China, lowest

9. China's demographic problem of 4-2-1, resulted in a higher proportion of elderly individuals compared to the younger population. This was primarily due to the implementation of .... **CBSE SQP 2025**

Or .... measure introduced in China led to the decline in its population as well as sex-ratio. **CBSE 2024 C**

(a) great leap forward campaign
(b) great proletarian cultural revolution
(c) one child norm
(d) Special Economic Zones

10. Identify the correct combination of GDP growth performance (average annual growth rate) in the last few decades among India, China and Pakistan.

I. China's GDP growth outpaced India and Pakistan in 1980-90.
II. India has maintained a higher growth rate than Pakistan post-2000s.
III. Pakistan's growth rate surpassed India in the 1980s.
IV. Pakistan and China had similar growth rates in the 2015-17. **Competency Based Que**

Codes

(a) I and II (b) I and II
(c) II and III (d) I, II and III

11. Which of the following statements about sectoral employment and Gross Value Added (GVA) are true?

I. The agricultural sector employs the highest percentage of the workforce in all three countries.
II. The services sector contributes more than 50% to the GDP of India.
III. China's industrial sector contributes more to GVA than its agricultural sector.

IV. Pakistan's services sector is the major contributor to employment. **Competency Based Que**

Codes
(a) I, II and III (b) II and III
(c) I and IV (d) II, III and IV

12. **Which of the following sectors has shown the highest growth rate in India between period of 2014-2017?**
(a) Agriculture (b) Industry
(c) Services (d) Construction

13. **Choose the correct arrangement in terms of better Human Development Index (HDI) rank among India, China and Pakistan during years 2017-2019.** **Competency Based Que**
(a) India ranks higher than China, which ranks higher than Pakistan
(b) Pakistan ranks lower than China, but higher than India
(c) China ranks higher than India, which ranks higher than Pakistan
(d) China ranks lower than Pakistan, but higher than India

14. **Some Selected Indicators of Human Development, 2017-2019**

Item	India	China	Pakistan
Human Development Index (Value)	0.645	0.761	0.557
Rank (based on HDI)	130	87	154
Life Expectancy at Birth (years)	69.7	76.9	67.3

Based on the data in the table showing life expectancy at birth for China and India, what could the gap in life expectancy suggest about the differences between the two countries? **Competency Based Que**
(a) China likely has a more developed healthcare system and better overall living conditions compared to India
(b) The life expectancy difference is solely due to geographical factors and cannot be significantly influenced by policy changes
(c) India's economic performance is stronger than China's, despite having a lower life expectancy
(d) Life expectancy is unrelated to a country's development policies

15. **........... indicator may be defined as the measure of the extent of demographic participation in social and political decision-making in a country.** **CBSE 2025, 24**
(a) Economic (b) Health
(c) Demographic (d) Liberty

16. **Identify the incorrect statement from the following.** **CBSE 2023**
(a) China's economic growth rate is better than that of Pakistan
(b) Pakistan is behind India in HDI ranking
(c) One child policy norm was adopted in Pakistan
(d) In 1991, India adopted new economic reforms

17. **India and Pakistan were such a young country post-independence and succeeding governments were so fragile that they felt the need to promote their own agricultural programmes to maintain their political popularity. The story of the Green Revolution in India and Pakistan is the story of rice and wheat, hunger and governmental response to suffering.**

In comparison with India, Pakistan enjoyed greater success of green revolution due to which of the following reasons? **Competency Based Que**
(a) Geographical advantages
(b) Political advantages
(c) External advantages (d) All of the above

18. **As per the image given below, in which year growth rate of Indian economy and Chinese economy was similar?**

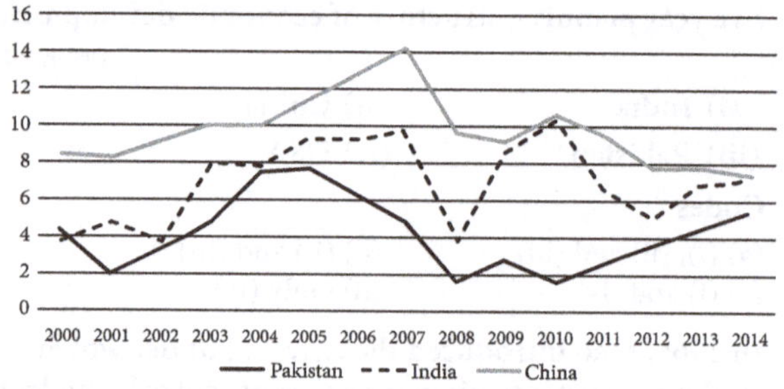

Source *https://www.researchgate.net/figure/CIP-GDP-growth-comparison_fig1_290449904)*
(a) 2000
(b) 2010
(c) 2014
(d) Both (b) and (c)

19. **......... and .... are the reasons for the slowdown of the Pakistan economy since independence.**
(i) Political instability
(ii) Over dependence on remittances from abroad
(iii) Stable performance of agriculture sector
(iv) Growth of service sector **CBSE SQP 2023**

Codes
(a) (i) and (ii) (c) (iii) and (iv)
(b) (ii) and (iii) (d) (i) and (iv)

20. **One of the key differences between the development strategies of China and Pakistan is** **Competency Based Que**
(a) China's rapid industrialisation vs Pakistan's slow industrial growth
(b) China's emphasis on agriculture vs Pakistan's focus on services
(c) Pakistan's focus on foreign trade vs China's isolation
(d) None of the above

Direction *Read the case study and answer the questions 21 to 24 on the basis of the same*

The economic trajectories of India, China and Pakistan over the past few decades reveal distinct approaches to development, shaped by various historical and political factors. India has embraced a mixed economy model, where both public and private sectors coalesce to drive growth. This model has enabled India to leverage state resources while fostering private entrepreneurship.

In stark contrast, China's path shifted dramatically in 1978, when it introduced significant reforms that transitioned its economy towards a 'socialist market economy'.

This strategy combined state intervention with opportunities for private enterprise, leading to unprecedented industrial growth. Meanwhile, Pakistan has navigated a more tumultuous economic landscape characterised by nationalisation in the 1970s, which aimed to control key industries and banks.

Over time, Pakistan's economic policies have oscillated between nationalisation and liberalisation, impacting its growth trajectories in agriculture, industry and services. Each country has thus experienced unique challenges and achievements, reflected in their respective human development outcomes.

21. **What was a crucial element of China's economic strategy after 1978 that contributed to its rapid growth?**
(a) Emphasis on privatising all state-owned enterprises
(b) Integration of market principles into a primarily state controlled economy
(c) Sole reliance on agricultural output for economic stability
(d) A shift towards a completely free market capitalist system

22. **Which statement best reflects the nature of Pakistan's economic policy during the 1970s?**
(a) It prioritised liberal trade policies to enhance economic growth
(b) It strictly followed a socialist market model similar to China's
(c) It adopted a balanced approach between privatisation and state-control
(d) It focused on nationalising major industries to assert government control

23. **India's development strategy has traditionally been characterised by a mixed economy model, where both the .... and .... sectors have played a key role.**

24. **China's reforms after 1978 resulted in rapid growth in the ...... sector, contributing significantly to its GDP.**

Assertion-Reason

Direction (Q.No. 25 to 34) *Read the following Assertion (A) and Reason (R) and choose the correct alternative from the following*

Alternatives
(a) Both Assertion (A) and Reason (R) are true and Reason (R) is the correct explanation of Assertion (A)
(b) Both Assertion (A) and Reason (R) are true, but Reason (R) is not the correct explanation of Assertion (A)
(c) Assertion (A) is true, but Reason (R) is false
(d) Assertion (A) is false, but Reason (R) is true

25. **Assertion** (A) The developmental experiences of India and Pakistan have a lot of similarities.
Reason (R) Both India and Pakistan laid emphasis on creating a large private sector. **CBSE 2024**

26. **Assertion** (A) China's economic reforms led to rapid industrialisation, transforming it into a global manufacturing hub.
Reason (R) China's reforms emphasised rapid industrialisation without allowing foreign investment in the country.

27. **Assertion** (A) China's Special Economic Zones (SEZs) played a crucial role in attracting Foreign Direct Investment (FDI).
Reason (R) SEZs in China were established with the aim of isolating foreign investors from the rest of the Chinese economy to maintain state control.

28. **Assertion** (A) Import substitution strategy promotes self-reliance in the economy by encouraging domestic industries to produce goods previously imported.
Reason (R) Import substitution strategy focuses on producing goods domestically that were previously imported to reduce dependency on foreign markets.

29. **Assertion** (A) Pakistan's growth rate during the 1960s was higher than that of India.
Reason (R) Pakistan followed an outward looking growth strategy that emphasised trade liberalisation during this period.

30. **Assertion** (A) The green revolution led to the rise in the production of foodgrains.
Reason (R) It led to mechanisation and increase in public investment in infrastructure.

31. **Assertion** (A) In 1970s, there was low population growth in China.
Reason (R) China introduced the one-child norm in late 1970s.

32. **Assertion** (A) India has a higher life expectancy compared to Pakistan.

Reason (R) Life expectancy is directly related to the quality of healthcare services in a country.

33. **Assertion** (A) India has a higher share of employment in agriculture compared to China.

Reason (R) India has been slower in shifting its workforce from agriculture to the industrial and service sectors.

34. **Assertion** (A) China's human development indicators, such as life expectancy and literacy rates, are significantly better than those of India and Pakistan.

Reason (R) China has consistently allocated a larger share of its GDP to social sectors like education and healthcare compared to India and Pakistan.

Two Statements Based MCQs

Direction (Q.No. 35 to 44) *Read the following statements carefully and choose the correct alternative*

Alternatives

(a) Statement I is correct and Statement II is incorrect
(b) Statement II is correct and Statement I is incorrect
(c) Both the statements are correct
(d) Both the statements are incorrect

35. **Statement I** Great Proletarian Cultural Revolution was introduced in China in 1950's.

Statement II China's growth is mainly contributed by the manufacturing sector. **CBSE 2023**

36. **Statement I** China has used the market mechanism to create additional social and economic opportunities for its citizens.

Statement II In China, social infrastructure created by the government brought positive results in human development indicators. **CBSE 2024**

37. **Statement I** China, has used market system mechanism without loosing political commitment to create additional social and economic opportunities.

Statement II India, Pakistan and China have similar physical endowments but totally different political systems. **CBSE 2024**

38. **Statement I** The liberalisation of trade in India post-1991 resulted in a higher share of exports in GDP compared to China's share of exports in its GDP during the 1990s.

Statement II China's exports surpassed those of India due to its strategic positioning in the global supply chain and emphasis on manufacturing.

39. **Statement I** During the late 1970s and 1980s, Pakistan transitioned from a state led economic approach to a more liberalised policy framework.

Statement II The adoption of a highly controlled and regulated economic system post-independence hindered Pakistan's early economic growth.

40. **Statement I** In the early years of planning, India's strategy focused on import substitution and self-reliance to reduce dependency on foreign goods.

Statement II China's Great Leap Forward (GLF) was a successful strategy that significantly improved agricultural productivity in the 1950s.

41. **Statement I** The dependency ratio in China is lower than that in India and Pakistan due to the one child policy and slower population growth.

Statement II A lower dependency ratio always indicates a better standard of living for the country.

42. **Statement I** In Pakistan, the share of the industrial sector in GDP is higher than that of the service sector.

Statement II The majority of Pakistan's labour force is employed in the industrial sector due to the country's focus on manufacturing.

43. **Statement I** In India, the service sector contributes the highest share to the Gross Value Added (GVA), but a large proportion of the population is still engaged in agriculture.

Statement II China has a higher proportion of its workforce in the industrial sector compared to India and Pakistan.

44. **Statement I** India has a higher Human Development Index (HDI) ranking than Pakistan due to better education and health indicators.

Statement II China's HDI rank is higher than both India and Pakistan due to its greater emphasis on social infrastructure.

Matching

45. Choose the correct pair from given below

Column I		Column II
A.	Great proletarian culture	(i)	India
B.	Special economic zone	(ii)	Pakistan
C.	Public sector with leading role	(iii)	China

Codes

(a) A-(i) (b) B-(ii)
(c) C-(iii) (d) All the pairs are incorrect

46. **Match the following**

Column I	Column II
A. Lowest rate of agricultural output growth 2014-18	(i) China
B. Lowest GDP between 2015-17	(ii) India
C. Highest workforce in service sector in 2018-19	(iii) Pakistan

Codes

	A	B	C
(a)	(ii)	(iii)	(i)
(b)	(iii)	(ii)	(i)
(c)	(ii)	(i)	(iii)
(d)	(i)	(iii)	(ii)

47. **From the events given in Column I and facts given in Column II about China, choose the correct pair** **CBSE 2024**

Column I	Column II
A. Structural transformation	(i) Limited urbanisation
B. Great leap forward campaign	(ii) Reduced globlal demand for chinese products
C. Less stress of usage on natural resources	(iii) Low density of population
D. Slowdown in GDP, since 2014	(iv) Aimed at massive industrasation

Codes

(a) A-(i) (b) B-(ii)
(c) C-(iii) (d) D-(iv)

48. **Match the development path of India, China and Pakistan Column I and Column II**

Column I	Column II
A. India's economic policy (1947-1990)	(i) Led to rapid urbanisation and economic growth
B. China's economic reforms	(ii) Economic reforms in 1978
C. Pakistan's industrialisation	(iii) Mixed economy with public sector dominance
D. China's development strategy	(iv) Adopted import substitution industrialisation initially

Codes

	A	B	C	D
(a)	(iii)	(ii)	(iv)	(i)
(b)	(i)	(ii)	(iii)	(iv)
(c)	(ii)	(iii)	(iv)	(i)
(d)	(iii)	(i)	(iv)	(ii)

49. **Match the events with correct timeline in Column I and Column II**

Column I	Column II
A. Special Economic Zones set-up in China	(i) 1991
B. Economic reforms in India	(ii) 1953
C. Nationalisation of capital goods industries in Pakistan	(iii) 1979
D. First Five Year plan in China	(iv) 1970

Codes

	A	B	C	D
(a)	(iii)	(ii)	(iv)	(i)
(b)	(iii)	(ii)	(i)	(iv)
(c)	(ii)	(iii)	(iv)	(i)
(d)	(iii)	(i)	(iv)	(ii)

Concept Identification

50. China's campaign to rapidly industrialise and collectivise agriculture, resulting in catastrophic famine and the deaths of millions.

51. Number of infants dying before reaching one year of age per 1,000 live births in a year.

52. A composite index prepared by United Nations Development Programmes (UNDP) which includes quantitative aspects of per capita GDP and the quality aspects of performance in health and education.

53. A geographical region that has economic laws different from a country's typical economic laws to attract foreign investment, offering benefits like tax breaks, etc.

54. An economic theory that compares the relative value of different currencies by determining the cost of the same goods and services in each country.

Answers

1. (d) 1991, 1988
2. (c) 1958
3. (a) (i), (ii) and (iii)
4. (c) great proletarian cultural revolution
5. (b) I, III and IV
6. (d) special economic zones
7. (b) commune system
8. (d) China, lowest
9. (c) one child norm
10. (d) I, II and III
11. (b) II and III
12. (c) Services
13. (c) China ranks higher than India, which ranks higher than Pakistan
14. (a) China likely has a more developed healthcare system and better overall living conditions compared to India
15. (d) Liberty
16. (c) One child policy norm was adopted in China.
17. (a) Geographical advantages
18. (d) Both (b) and (c)
19. (a) (i) and (ii)
20. (a) China's rapid industrialisation vs Pakistan's slow industrial growth
21. (b) Integration of market principles into a primarily state-controlled economy
22. (d) It focused on nationalising major industries to assert government control
23. public, private
24. industrial
25. (c) Both India and Pakistan laid emphasis on creating a large public sector.
26. (c) Foreign investment was a key part of China's reform process, especially in special economic zones.
27. (c) SEZs were not aimed at isolating foreign investors; rather, they were meant to integrate foreign investment with the domestic economy to promote export led growth.
28. (a) Both Assertion (A) and Reason (R) are true and Reason (R) is the correct explanation of Assertion (A)
29. (c) Pakistan's strategy was more inward looking, focusing on import substitution rather than trade liberalisation.
30. (b) Both Assertion (A) and Reason (R) are true, but Reason (R) is not the correct explanation of Assertion (A)
31. (a) Both Assertion (A) and Reason (R) are true and Reason (R) is the correct explanation of Assertion (A)
32. (a) Both Assertion (A) and Reason (R) are true and Reason (R) is the correct explanation of Assertion (A)
33. (a) Both Assertion (A) and Reason (R) are true and Reason (R) is the correct explanation of Assertion (A)
34. (a) Both Assertion (A) and Reason (R) are true and Reason (R) is the correct explanation of Assertion (A)
35. (d) Great Proletarian Cultural Revolution was introduced in China in 1965. China's growth is mainly contributed by the service sector followed by manufacturing sector.
36. (c) Both the statements are correct
37. (c) Both the statements are correct
38. (b) Although India's trade liberalisation led to an increase in the share of exports in GDP, it did not surpass China's export share. China's export to GDP ratio was much higher due to its aggressive export led growth strategy.
39. (c) Both the statements are correct
40. (a) China's Great Leap Forward (GLF), initiated in 1958, aimed to rapidly transform the country into an industrial power. However, the GLF led to severe agricultural disruption and a massive famine, making it a failure rather than a success.
41. (a) A lower dependency ratio does not necessarily guarantee a better standard of living, as it depends on factors like economic opportunities, quality of education and healthcare.
42. (d) In Pakistan, the service sector contributes a larger share to GDP compared to the industrial sector, similar to India. Additionally, a significant portion of Pakistan's labour force is employed in agriculture, not industry. The industrial sector's contribution to employment is smaller compared to agriculture.
43. (c) Both the statements are correct
44. (c) Both the statements are correct
45. (d) All the pairs are incorrect
46. (a) (ii) (iii) (i)
47. (c) C-(iii)
48. (a) (iii) (ii) (iv) (i)
49. (d) (iii) (i) (iv) (ii)
50. Commune system
51. Infant mortality rate
52. Human development index
53. Special Economic Zones (SEZs)
54. Purchasing Power Parity (PPP)

Subjective Questions

Short Answer Type Questions

1. Explain any three similarities in the development strategies of India, Pakistan and China.

Ans. India, China and Pakistan have many similarities in their development strategies which are as follows

(i) All the three countries had started planning their development strategies in similar ways. India announced its five year plan in 1951-56, while Pakistan announced its first five year plan in 1956, which is now called medium-term plan. China announced its first five year plan in 1953.

(ii) India and Pakistan adopted similar strategies such as creating a large public sector and raising public expenditure on social development.

(iii) Till the 1980s, all the three countries had similar growth rates and per capita incomes.

2. "India's growth trajectory has shifted towards a services led economy, with rapid expansion in IT and digital sectors, while Pakistan remains largely agrarian with a struggling industrial base. Meanwhile, China's growth, after decades of industrialisation, is increasingly transitioning towards high tech industries and domestic consumption."

Source *The Times of India*

Referring to the given statement, discuss your observations on the structure of growth in India, Pakistan and China. Competency Based Que

Ans. Following observations highlight the structure of growth in India, Pakistan and China

(i) **Mixed Economy *vs* Statism**
India and Pakistan have adopted a mixed economy model of growth, where both the public and private sectors play a role. In contrast, China follows a model of Statism, with the government playing a dominant role in controlling the economy and guiding its development.

(ii) **Sectoral Focus**
India and Pakistan have relied more on the tertiary sector (services), especially in areas like IT and digital services for India and agriculture and services for Pakistan. On the other hand, China's economy has relied heavily on the secondary sector (manufacturing and industry) for its GDP growth.

(iii) **Contribution to GDP**
In China, the secondary sector (manufacturing and industrial sectors) contributes significantly more to GDP than in India and Pakistan, where the tertiary sector is the main contributor.
This reflects China's historical emphasis on industrialisation, while India and Pakistan have seen their service sectors expand more rapidly.

3. In a recent article published by The Economic Times, it was stated, "India's development strategy must focus on inclusive growth, improving infrastructure and boosting human capital to sustain long-term economic progress."

Justify the statement with valid arguments. Competency Based Que

Ans. India's development strategy aims to achieve balanced and sustainable growth by addressing key challenges in various sectors of the economy. Some of the prominent strategies of India are discussed below

(i) **Sound Trade System**
India initiated economic reforms in 1991 and introduced globalisation, liberalisation and privatisation as measures to encourage global and domestic trade. These reforms formed a basis of a sound trade system and encouraged economic growth.

(ii) **Reduction in Poverty**
India has adopted several poverty alleviation programmes to reduce poverty in India. This helped in increasing per capita income and rise in nutrition level of poor. This led to a subsequent fall in percentage of absolute poor in some states.

(iii) **Rural Development**
Under this strategy, India adopted various measures for the development of areas that were lagging behind in the rural economy. By concentrating on key areas, overall rural development was ensured.

(iv) **Employment Generation**
Several economic reforms were initiated to generate employment in the country.
Many employment generation programmes were also initiated with an aim to provide gainful self-employment.

4. The 1960s, Chinese Communist Party leader Mao Zedong came to feel that the current party leadership in China, as in the Soviet Union, was moving too far in a revisionist direction, with an emphasis on expertise rather than on ideological purity. Mao's own position in government had weakened after the failure of his 'Great Leap Forward' (1958-60) and the economic crisis that followed.

In this context, briefly explain the objectives of great leap forward. Competency Based Que

Ans. Great leap forward, in Chinese history, was the campaign undertaken by the Chinese communists between 1958 and early 1960 to organise its vast population, especially in large-scale rural communes, to meet China's industrial and agricultural problems.

The Chinese hoped to develop labour intensive methods of industrialisation, which would emphasise manpower over machines and capital expenditure.

Thereby, it was hoped, the country could bypass the slow and more typical process of industrialisation through gradual accumulation of capital and purchase of heavy machinery.

The great leap forward approach was epitomised by the development of small backyard steel furnaces in every village and urban neighbourhood, which were intended to accelerate the industrialisation process.

5. "The reform process implemented in the late 1970s, commonly known as China's open door policy, encompassed a wide range of reforms across sectors like agriculture, investment, industry, etc. These reforms played a pivotal role in driving the rapid growth of the Chinese economy over subsequent decades."

In the light of the given text, discuss any two reforms responsible for the rapid economic growth of China. **CBSE SQP 2025; Competency Based Que**

Ans. The fast paced economic growth in China can be traced back to the following reforms introduced in 1978

(i) In the initial phase, reforms were initiated in agriculture, foreign trade and investment sectors. For instance, in agriculture commune lands were divided into small plots, which were allocated to individual households.
They were allowed to keep all income from the land after paying stipulated taxes.

(ii) In the subsequent phase, reforms were initiated in the industrial sector. Private sector firms, in general and township and village enterprises, in particular, were allowed to produce goods. At this stage, state owned enterprises were made to face competition.

6. "China permitted 100% equity investment by foreign investors in most sectors, making it an attractive hub for infrastructure investments."

In light of statement, discuss how China's economy is exposed to the global market. **Competency Based Que**

Ans. Following points highlight the global exposure of the economy of China

(i) **Foreign Investment**
China allowed 100% equity investment for foreign investors across most sectors, promoting significant foreign capital inflows.

(ii) **Labour Flexibility**
Foreign investors were given the freedom to manage labour, including 'hire and fire' policies, making China's labour market more competitive.

(iii) **Shift from Protectionism**
China shifted from an inward looking, protectionist policy to one that encourages growth through competition, integrating itself more deeply into the global economy.

7. "Special Economic Zone (SEZ) increases foreign investment." Explain.

Ans. A Special Economic Zone (SEZ) is a geographical region that has economic laws different from a country's typical economic laws. Usually, the goal is to increase foreign investment.

Special economic zones attract investors since they offer high quality infrastructure facilities and support services. Besides allowing duty free import of capital goods and raw materials, attractive fiscal incentives and simpler customs, banking and other procedures are offered in such zones.

8. Evaluate any two factors that led to the rapid growth in economic development in China. **CBSE 2025**

Or **Evaluate the various factors that led to the rapid growth in economic development in China.** **NCERT**

Ans. China's rapid economic development can be attributed to several key factors. The major factors that contributed significantly are

(i) **Economic Reforms and Open Door Policy** (1978)
The Chinese government introduced market oriented reforms under the leadership of Deng Xiaoping. These reforms included privatisation of agriculture, promotion of private enterprises and encouragement of foreign investments. The Open Door Policy allowed China to integrate into the global economy, boosting trade and industrial growth.

(ii) **Investment in Infrastructure and Human Capital**
The Chinese government heavily invested in modern infrastructure, such as roads, railways and power supply, which facilitated industrial growth. Additionally, focus on education and skill development created a highly productive workforce, leading to increased efficiency and innovation in various sectors.

(iii) **Land Reforms and Agricultural Productivity**
The Chinese government implemented land reforms, withdrawing the communal farming system.

These factors played a crucial role in making China one of the fastest growing economies in the world.

9. Describe the path of developmental initiatives taken by Pakistan for its economic development. NCERT

Ans. For economic development, Pakistan followed the mixed economy model in which public and private sectors co-exist. The different policies adopted by Pakistan are stated below

(i) A variety of regulated policy frameworks were introduced in the late 1950s and 1960s.
(ii) Protection of domestic consumer goods industries through tariff barriers.
(iii) The introduction of green revolution and mechanisation in agriculture sector.
(iv) Public investment in infrastructure in selected areas.
(v) Nationalisation of capital goods industries was introduced in 1970s.
(vi) In 1980s, the policy of denationalisation and encouragement to private sector was adopted.
(vii) In 1988, economic reforms were initiated in the economy.

10. From the given data, compare and analyse annual growth of population and urbanisation of China and Pakistan, with valid reasons.
CBSE 2024; Competency Based Que

Demographic Indicators, 2017-18

Country	Estimated Population (in million)	Annual Growth of Population	Population Density (per sq km)	Sex Ratio	Fertility Rate	Urbanisation
India	1352	1.03	455	924	2.2	34
China	1393	0.46	148	949	1.7	59
Pakistan	212	2.05	275	943	3.6	37

Ans. Following points highlight the comparison between two countries

(i) **Annual Growth Rate of Population**
Although China is the largest populated country but a strong positive point for China is that, its annual growth rate of population is just 0.46% per annum while that of Pakistan is 2.05% per annum.

(ii) **Urbanisation**
China is comparatively more urbanised than Pakistan. The rate of urbanisation in China is 59% while that in Pakistan is 37%.
The degree of urbanisation depicts the standard and quality of living of people of a particular country.
Also, this confirms the shift in the economic structure of an economy.
Higher degree of urbanisation reveals higher industrialisation and development of tertiary sector in the economy.

11. What similar developmental strategies have India and Pakistan followed for their respective developmental paths? NCERT

Or **Briefly explain any two similar developmental strategies opted by India and Pakistan for their respective developmental path.** CBSE Term II 2022

Ans. India and Pakistan have followed following similar strategies in their respective development plans

(i) India and Pakistan both started their development process on the basis of economic planning after getting independence in 1947.
(ii) Both of them have adopted the mixed economic system involving the co-existence of both the public and the private sector.
(iii) Both the countries relied more on the public sector for initiating the process of growth and development.
(iv) Both of them introduced economic reforms around the same time to strengthen their economies. Pakistan initiated reforms in 1988 and India followed in 1991.
(v) They both have announced five year plans for growth and development.

12. "Scholars find son preference as a common phenomenon in India, Pakistan and China." Justify the given statement in the light of skewed sex-ratio.
CBSE 2024; Competency Based Que

Ans. Both rural and urban populations have economic and traditional incentives to prefer sons over daughters. Sons are preferred as they provide the primary financial support to the parents.
A woman changes her surname to her husband's surname after marriage. For some families, ones daughter-in-law's name instead of a daughter's name would be added in the book of family tree.
Therefore, if a family had no son, the fortune and name of the family would have no legal heirs. The choice of small families also affects the people's views on the sex of their child.

13. Compare and analyse the given data of India and China, with valid reasons.
CBSE 2020; Competency Based Que

Country	Annual Growth Rate of Population (2015)	Gender Ratio (Per thousand males)
India	1.2%	929
China	0.5%	941

Source *World Development Indicators, 2015.*

Ans. **Annual Growth Rate of Population** (2015)
The annual growth rate of population in India is high at 1.2%. China has a low growth rate at 0.5%.

The low growth rate can be attributed to the adoption of one child policy by China. Also, the high growth rate in India implies that the population of India will exceed China's population by 2050.

Gender Ratio

Gender ratio in both the countries is low, but in India it is even lower than China. A low gender ratio indicates that both the countries are male dominated.

14. What is the important implication of the 'one child norm' in China? NCERT

Ans. The important implications of the 'one child norm' are

(i) Low population growth.

(ii) Decline in the sex-ratio.

(iii) After a few decades, there will be more elderly people in proportion to young people.

(iv) In the long-run, China will have to provide more social security measures with fewer workers.

15. Compare and analyse the following information related to Annual Growth of Gross Domestic Product (GDP) of India and China. CBSE 2023; Competency Based Que

Annual Growth of Gross Domestic Product

Country	1980-90	2015-2017
India	5.7	7.3
China	10.3	6.8

Source *Asian Development Bank, Philippines; World Development Indicators, 2018.*

Ans. The given data shows that China has gained economic strength over the years.

When many developed countries were finding it difficult to maintain a growth rate of even 5%, China was able to maintain near double-digit growth during the decade of 1980s.

The growth rate of China has reduced to an average of 6.8%, over the period 2015-17. In the recent past, India has posted a decent rise in the growth rate.

While India had maintained a reasonable growth rate of 5.7% in the decade of 1980's, it has shown great calibre and character in the period 2015-17 by registering an average growth rate of 7.3%.

Nevertheless, Indian elephant has to travel a long distance before it could present itself as a real threat to the growth story of the Chinese dragon.

16. On the basis of the data given below, outline and discuss the shift in employment and output for India and China. CBSE 2024 C; Competency Based Que

Sectoral Share of Employment and GVA (%), 2018-19

Sector ↓	Contribution to GVA			Distribution of Workforce		
Country →	India	China	Pakistan	India	China	Pakistan
Agriculture	16	7	24	43	26	41
Industry	30	41	19	25	28	24
Service	54	52	57	32	46	35
Total	100	100	100	100	100	100

Source *Human Development Report 2019 : Key Indicators of Asia and Pacific 2019*

Ans. The given data pertains to the sectoral share of employment and Gross Value Added (GVA).

(i) Due to topographic and climatic conditions, the cultivable area in China is relatively smaller than that of India.

Hence, the contribution of the agricultural sector to the GVA in China is 7% employing 26% of its workforce, whereas in India it is 16% employing 43% of its workforce.

(ii) Owing to rapid industrialisation in China, the contribution of the industrial sector to GVA stands at 41% with 28% of the workforce as against corresponding figures of 30% and 25% in India.

(iii) Both the nations have similar contribution of the service sector to GVA standing at 52% and 54% with corresponding 46% and 32% to the workforce, respectively in China and India.

17. Define the liberty indicator. Give some examples of liberty indicators. NCERT, CBSE 2024

Or **Define 'liberty indicator' with the help of an example and state its importance.** CBSE Term II 2022

Ans. 'Liberty indicators' are those indicators which represent the degree of civil and political freedom to individuals in a country. They should also be considered alongwith indicators of income, health and education in the human development index.

One such indicator has actually been added as a measure is 'the extent of democratic participation in social and political decision-making' but it has not been given any significance.

Some other 'liberty indicators' are measures of 'the extent of constitutional protection given to rights of citizens' or 'the extent of constitutional protection of the Independence of the Judiciary and the Rule of Law' which have not been introduced in HDI till now.

Without including such indicators and giving them adequate weightage, the construction of a human development index remains incomplete and its usefulness remains limited.

18. "To measure the extent of development in an economy, liberty indicators should be considered along with other socio-economic parameters."
Do you agree with the given statement? Give valid reasons in support of your answer.
CBSE SQP 2025; Competency Based Que

Ans. Yes, measurement of the development level in an economy is a comprehensive approach where liberty indicators should be considered along with other socio-economic parameters.

Liberty indicators measure the extent of democratic participation in social and political decision-making. These indicators are significant as they reflect the degree of civil liberties, political rights and economic freedom within a society. With the incorporation of liberty indicators, policy-makers can gain a more holistic understanding of an economy's development status.

19. Give reasons for the slow growth and re-emergence of poverty in Pakistan. **NCERT**

Ans. The reasons for the slow down of growth and re-emergence of poverty are as given below

(i) The agricultural growth was not the result of technology improvement. Rather, it was based on good climatic conditions. When the conditions were good, the economic growth showed positive trends and *vice-versa.*

(ii) In Pakistan, a considerable part of foreign exchange came from remittances from Pakistani workers in the Middle-East.

(iii) In Pakistan, there is more dependence on foreign borrowings and increasing difficulty in paying back the loans.

(iv) Inadequate infrastructure for manufacturing sectors.

Long Answer Type Questions

20. Write a brief note on the following international organisations

(i) SAARC	**(ii) ASEAN**
(iii) European Union	**(iv) G-8**
(v) G-20	**(vi) BRICS**

Ans. (i) **SAARC**

South Asian Association for Regional Cooperation (SAARC) was established on 8th December, 1985 to encourage cooperation among member countries in the fields of agriculture, health, population control, anti-terrorism measures, rural development, science and technology and narcotics control.

Afghanistan, Bangladesh, Bhutan, India, Maldives, Nepal, Sri Lanka and Pakistan are its members. It was formed on the proposal of Zia-Ur-Rehman, the then President of Bangladesh. Its headquarter is in Kathmandu.

(ii) **ASEAN**

Association of South East Asian Nation (ASEAN) was created on 8th August, 1967 by Indonesia, Malaysia, the Philippines, Singapore and Thailand with objectives to accelerate economic growth, social progress, regional stability and to resolve their differences peacefully.

Subsequently, Brunei, Cambodia, Laos, Myanmar and Vietnam also joined this association. It is headquartered at Jakarta.

(iii) **European Union**

It is a political and economic union of 27 member states that is primarily located in Europe. It was formed to develop an internal single market regulated by a same set of laws to ensure free movement of people, goods and services between the member nations. A common currency 'Euro' circulates in all the member nations. Austria, France, Germany, Italy, Spain and Sweden are important member nations. Brussels is the defacto capital of the European Union.

(iv) **G-8**

It is an inter-governmental political forum of the industrialised economies of the world, which are democratic in character. Initially, formed in 1975, with six member countries, *viz.* France, Germany, Italy, Japan, the United Kingdom and the United States, this association came to be known as G-8 with the inclusion of Canada in 1976 and of Russia in 1997.

However, in 2014 Russia has been expelled from the membership of G-8, temporalily. This forum represents about 65% of the world economy.

(v) **G-20**

It is an international forum comprising of the governments and Central Bank governors of 20 major economies. It was founded in 1999 with an objective to study, review and promote high level discussions of measures to promote international financial stability.

The members include 19 individual countries, *viz.* Argentina, Australia, Brazil, Canada, China, France, Germany, India, Indonesia, Italy, Japan, South Korea, Mexico, Russia, Saudi Arabia, South Africa, Turkey, the United Kingdom, The United States, alongwith the European Union.

(vi) **BRICS**

It is the acronym representing association of five major emerging national economies, *viz.* Brazil, Russia, India, China and South Africa. All the member countries are leading developing or newly industrialised countries and are characterised by their fast growing economies and those who significantly influence their regional affairs.

It was formed in 2011 and works on the principles of non-interference, equality and mutual benefit.

21. Briefly discuss the various development strategies pursued by China.

Ans. After the establishment of People's Republic of China under one party rule, all the critical sectors of the economy, enterprises and land owned and operated by individuals were brought under government control. Certain development strategies of China are discussed below

(i) **Great Leap Forward** (GLF) **Campaign**
This campaign was initiated in 1958. It aimed at industrialising the country on a massive scale. People were encouraged to set-up industries in their backyards.
In rural areas, communes were started. Under the commune system, people collectively cultivated lands.
In 1958, there were 26,000 communes which covered almost all the farm population. However, this campaign met with many problems, some important among them are

- A severe drought caused havoc in China, killing about 30 million people.
- Due to a political conflict, Russia withdrew its professionals from China which were sent to help in the industrialisation process.

(ii) **Great Proletarian Cultural Revolution** (1966-76)
In 1965, Mao Tse Tung started a cultural revolution on a large-scale. In this revolution, students and professionals were sent to work and learn from the countryside.

(iii) **1978 Reforms**
Since 1978, China began to introduce many reforms in different phases. These are as follows

- **First Phase**
In this phase, the reforms were initiated in agriculture, foreign trade and investment sectors. In agriculture, commune lands were divided into small plots which were allocated (for use, not ownership) to individual households. They were allowed to keep all income from the land after paying taxes.
- **Later Phase**
In this phase, reforms were initiated in industrial sector. Private sector firms, township and village enterprises which were owned and operated by local collectives were allowed to produce goods.
- **Dual Pricing**
The reform process also involved dual pricing i.e. prices were fixed in two ways. The farmers and industrial units were required to buy and sell fixed quantities of inputs and outputs on the basis of prices fixed by the government and the rest were purchased and sold at market prices.
- **Special Economic Zones** (SEZs)
In order to attract foreign investors, special economic zones were set-up.

22. Critically appraise the development strategies of Pakistan.

Ans. The development strategies of Pakistan are discussed below

(i) **Mixed Economy**
Pakistan follows a mixed economy system where both public and private sectors co-exist.

(ii) **Import Substitution**
Pakistan adopted a regulatory policy framework in the late 1950s and 1960s for import substitution based industrialisation. The policy combined tariff protection for manufacturing of consumer goods together with direct import controls on competing foreign goods.

(iii) **Green Revolution**
It was introduced to increase the productivity and self-sufficiency in food. This increased the output of foodgrains. This had changed the agrarian structure dramatically.

(iv) **Nationalisation of Capital Goods Industries**
In 1970s, nationalisation of capital goods industries took place. Pakistan then shifted its policy orientation in 1970s and 1980s when the importance was given to denationalisation and the encouragement of private sector.

(v) **Other Strategies**
During 1970s and 1980s, Pakistan received financial support from Western countries and remittances from emigrants to the middle-East.
This helped the country in stimulating economic growth. Government also offered incentives to the private sector. This had created a climate for new investments. In 1988, certain reforms were also initiated in the country.

23. Mention the salient demographic indicators of China, Pakistan and India. NCERT

Ans. The salient demographic indicators of China, Pakistan and India are discussed below

(i) The population of Pakistan is very small and accounts for roughly about one-tenth of China or India.
China is the largest nation and geographically occupies the largest area among the three nations, therefore its density is the lowest.

(ii) Population growth is highest in Pakistan, followed by India and China.

(iii) Sex-ratio is biased against females in all three countries. In recent times, all three countries are trying to adopt various measures to improve the situation.

Due to one child norm, after few decades there will be more elderly people in proportion to young people.

(iv) The fertility rate is low in China and very high in Pakistan as compared to India.

(v) Urbanisation is high in China with India and Pakistan having only 34% and 37% of its people living in urban areas respectively.

24. Comment on the growth rate trends witnessed in China and India in the last two decades. NCERT

Ans. China has the second largest GDP (PPP) of $ 22.5 trillion whereas India's GDP (PPP) is $ 9.03 trillion. When many developed countries were finding it difficult to maintain a growth rate of even 5%, China was able to maintain near double-digit growth for more than two decades.

Its growth rate in 1980-90 was 10.3% and for 2015-2017, it was 6.8%. In the 1980-90, China was having double-digit growth and India was stuck at 5.7% decadal growth rate. This rate showed improvement in 2015-2017 at 7.3%.

As far as sectorwise contribution to growth is concerned, in 2018-19, contribution of agriculture to GDP in China was 7% while in India it was 16%.

On the other hand, manufacturing contributes to GDP in China at 41%, whereas in India manufacturing sector contributes at around 30%.

In the last two decades, the growth of agriculture sector has declined in both the countries. In the industrial sector, China has maintained a double-digit growth rate, whereas for India industrial growth rate has declined.

25. Compare and contrast the development of India, China and Pakistan with respect to some salient human development indicators. Competency Based Que

Ans. India, China and Pakistan show varying levels of progress in human development indicators. China leads in most metrics, including life expectancy, education and income, while India and Pakistan lag behind in comparison.

This analysis highlights the differences in development among the three countries which are as follows

(i) China is moving ahead of both India and Pakistan in terms of indicators of human development.

(ii) Based on HDI of 2017-19, China ranked 87 while India and Pakistan stand at 130 and 154 respectively.

(iii) China has the highest life expectancy of 76.9 years followed by India (69.7 years) and Pakistan (67.3 years).

(iv) Mean years of schooling is highest in China with 8.1%. It is 6.5% and 5.2% for India and Pakistan respectively.

(v) Gross national income per capita is also high in China (US $ 16,057) followed by India (US $ 6,681) and Pakistan (US $ 5,005).

(vi) China is ahead of India and Pakistan in reducing proportion of people below the poverty line and also their performance in sanitation.

(vii) Infant mortality rate is low in China and highest in Pakistan.

(viii) For one lakh births, in China only 29 women die whereas, in India and Pakistan, 133 and 140 women die respectively.

(ix) All the three countries report providing improved drinking water sources for most of its population.

(x) China has the lowest percentage of undernourished children i.e. 8.1% while India and Pakistan have 37.9% and 37.6% of undernourished children.

26. Write a note on assessment of structural reforms in China.

Ans. The development strategies of China can be understood with the help of its pre-reform period and post-reform period, which are as follows

Pre-reform Period

(i) There was massive extension of basic health services in rural areas.

(ii) Through the commune system, there was more equitable distribution of foodgrains.

(iii) There was slow pace of growth and lack of modernisation in the Chinese economy under the Maoist rule.

(iv) Maoist vision of economic development based on decentralisation, self-sufficiency and avoiding foreign technology had failed.

(v) Despite extensive land reforms, collectivisation, the great leap forward and other initiatives, the per capita grain output in 1978 was the same as it was in the mid-1950s.

Post-reform Period

(i) Each reform measure was first implemented at a smaller level and then extended on a massive scale.

(ii) Establishment of infrastructure in the areas of education and health, land reforms, long existence of decentralised planning and existence of small enterprises had helped positively in improving the social and income indicators in the post reform period.

(iii) Agricultural reforms, by handing over plots of land to individuals for cultivation, brought prosperity to a vast number of poor people.

It created conditions for the subsequent phenomenal growth in rural industries and built-up a strong support base for more reforms.

27. Mention about the assessment of structural reforms in Pakistan briefly.

Ans. The reform process in Pakistan led to worsening of all the economic indicators. As compared to 1980s, the growth rate of GDP and its sectoral constituents have not yet improved.

Following points highlight the results of structural reforms in Pakistan

(i) Growth rate of GDP and its sectoral constituents have fallen in 1990s.

(ii) Poverty has risen in Pakistan. In 1960s, there was more than 40% poor in Pakistan which declined to 25% in 1980 and started rising again in the recent decades.

(iii) Agricultural growth and food supply situation in Pakistan were based on good harvest instead of an institutionalised process of technical change.

When there was a good harvest, the economy was in good condition, when it was not, the economic indicators showed stagnation or negative trends. This led to the slowdown of growth and re-emergence of poverty.

(iv) Foreign exchange is an essential component for any country. In Pakistan, foreign exchange earnings came from remittances from Pakistani workers in the Middle-East and the exports of highly volatile agricultural products.

(v) The dependency of Pakistan on foreign loans is increasing and the difficulty in paying back the loans is also increasing.

(vi) However, Pakistan has recovered its economic growth during the last few years. According to Annual Plan 2019-20, there is a growth of 5.5% in the GDP of Pakistan. Agriculture also recorded a growth rate and industrial and service sector grew at 4.9% and 6.2%, respectively.

28. Sino-Pak Friendship Corridor

The China-Pakistan Economic Corridor (CPEC) has deepened the decades-long strategic relationship between the two nations. But it has also sparked criticism for burdening Pakistan with mountains of debt and allowing China to use its debt-trap diplomacy to gain access to strategic assets of Pakistan.

The foundations of CPEC, part of China's Belt and Road Initiative, were laid in May, 2013. At the time, Pakistan was reeling under weak economic growth. China committed to play an integral role in supporting Pakistan's economy.

Pakistan and China have a strategic relationship that goes back decades. Pakistan turned to China at a time when it needed a rapid increase in external financing to meet critical investments in hard infrastructure, particularly power plants and highways. CPEC's early harvest projects met this need, leading to a dramatic increase in Pakistan's power generation capacity, bringing an end to supply side constraints that had made rolling blackouts a regular occurrence across the country.

Pakistan leaned into CPEC, leveraging Chinese financing and technical assistance in an attempt to end power shortages that had paralysed its country's economy. Years later, China's influence in Pakistan has increased at an unimaginable pace.

China as Pakistan's Largest Bilateral Creditor China's ability to exert influence on Pakistan's economy has grown substantially in recent years, mainly due to the fact that Beijing is now Islamabad's largest creditor. According to documents released by Pakistan's finance ministry, Pakistan's total public and publicly guaranteed external debt stood at $ 44.35 billion in June, 2013, just 9.3 percent of which was owed to China.

By April, 2021, this external debt had ballooned to $ 90.12 billion, with Pakistan owing 27.4 percent — $ 24.7 billion — of its total external debt to China, according to the International Monetary Fund (IMF).

Additionally, China provided financial and technical expertise to help Pakistan build its road infrastructure, expanding North-South connectivity to improve the efficiency of moving goods from Karachi all the way to Gilgit-Baltistan (PoK).

These investments were critical in better integrating the country's ports, especially Karachi, with urban centers in Punjab and Khyber-Pakhtunkhwa provinces.

Despite power asymmetries between China and Pakistan, the latter still has tremendous agency in determining its own policies, even if such policies come at the expense of the long-term socio-economic welfare of Pakistani citizens.

Source *https://www.usip.org/publications/2021/ 05/ pakistans-growing-problem-its-china-economic-corridor-modified*

(i) Outline and discuss any two economic advantages of China Pakistan Economic Corridor (CPEC) accruing to the economy of Pakistan.

(ii) Analyse the implication of bilateral 'debt-trap' situation of Pakistan *vis-a-vis* the Chinese economy.

CBSE SQP Term II 2022; Competency Based Que

Ans. (i) Economic advantages of China Pakistan Economic Corridor (CPEC) to the economy of Pakistan are

- China provided financial and technical expertise to help Pakistan build its road infrastructure, supporting employment and income in the economy.
- CPEC has led to a massive increase in power generation capacity of Pakistan. It has brought an end to supply-side constraints in the nation, which had made blackouts a regular phenomenon across the country.

(ii) China has become famous for its 'debt-trap diplomacy' in recent times. Under this, China provides financial and technical expertise/assistance to help various nations to bring them under its direct or indirect influence. The first and the foremost implication of the diplomacy is that Beijing has now become Islamabad's largest creditor.

According to documents released by Pakistan's finance ministry, its total public external debt stood at $ 44.35 billion in June 2013, just 9.3 percent of which was owed to China. By April 2021, this external debt had ballooned to $ 90.12 billion, with Pakistan owing 27.4 percent — $ 24.7 billion — of its total external debt to China, according to the IMF. This clearly indicates diplomacy.

29. **In 1950, Pakistan's per person GDP was US $ 1,268, which was almost 50 percent greater than India that year. However, in the backdrop of sustained political uncertainty and upheaval, Pakistan stagnated throughout the 1950s while a politically stable India grew.**

As a result, by 1960, India had almost caught up with Pakistan in per capita GDP terms with the per capita income gap having shrunk to 15 per cent.

Unfortunately, from 1964, India went into two decades of economic stagnation while Pakistan, under the military rule of Ayub Khan, opened up to foreign capital which funded a period of rapid industrialisation and economic growth, albeit at the cost of worsening inequality. By 1984, Pakistan's per capita income was more than double that of India's. Pakistan's slow down began in the 1980s during the military regime of Zia-u-Haq. Zia enabled and institutionalised Islamic nationalism in Pakistan.

In recent times, specifically in 2022, Pakistan floods in summer cause over $ 30 billion dollars in economic losses in Pakistan. At the end of March, 2022, the State Bank of Pakistan's reserves stood at $ 11.425 bn, but they gradually tanked to an almost four-year low of $ 6.715 bn on 2nd December.

Pakistan's forex reserves were equal to just five weeks of merchandise imports. In January 2023, for the first time, the CEO of Pakistan's largest bank, Habib comments publicly on the prevailing economic situation.

He said it could be a 'Big Blow' to the economy if the stakeholders didn't make the right decisions swiftly. Even smallest institutions need timely execution.

(i) What led to downfall of Pakistan economy after 1950?

(ii) What were the reasons for the growth of Pakistan's economy during 1980s?

Competency Based Que

Ans. (i) Since independence, the economy of Pakistan has always been in vicissitudes (many changes) situations.

Even though during initial years of the partition, the country faced lot of hardships, but during Gen. Ayyub Khan's era, the country has managed 5.82% average growth rate from 1958-1969. Soon after the partition, Pakistan had started to lay its foundations. Meanwhile, the country did not get the proper distribution of resources as the assets were divided in the ratio of 17 to India and 5 to Pakistan of which bulk of the irrigated land was in Pakistan and major canal system, the military division was 65 to 35 percent in the favour of India.

During that time, Pakistan was a dominant underdeveloped agrarian with a little share of services, manufacturing and infrastructure, backed with millions of refuges.

Some people criticise that Ayub Khan's non-liberal policies of bureaucratic capitalism model has increased income inequality and this rapid development with the exploitation of East Pakistan and labour class ended with a political disability.

(ii) Pakistan's economy recovered significantly during the 1980s via a policy of deregulation as well as an increased inflow of foreign aid and remittances from expatriate workers.

Under Muhammad Zia-ul-Haq, "many of the controls on industry were liberalised or abolished, the balance of payments deficit was kept under control and Pakistan became self-sufficient in all basic foodstuffs with the exception of edible oils."

As a result, Pakistan's rate of GDP growth rose to an average of 6.5 percent per annum in the 1980s.

A tremendous boost to economic activity was provided by rising worker remittances, which reached a peak of US $ 3 billion in 1982-83, equivalent to 10 percent of the gross national product of Pakistan. Zia also successfully negotiated with the United States for larger external assistance.

In addition to supplying direct aid to Pakistan, the US and its allies funnelled about US $ 5-7 billion to the Afghan Mujahideen through Pakistan, further uplifting the local economy.

SELF ASSESSMENT TEST

Objective Type Questions

1. Due to introduction of 'one-child policy', China's fertility rate decline from .... to .... births.
   (a) 3 to 1 (b) 2 to 1
   (c) 3 to 1.7 (d) None of these

2. China has a very less proportion of cultivable land due to which of the following reason(s)?
   (a) Topographic condition (b) Climatic condition
   (c) Economic condition (d) Both (a) and (b)

3. Apart from instructions of international agencies, which other reasons forced Pakistan to implement economic reforms?
   (a) Political instability
   (b) Over-dependency on foreign aid
   (c) Volatile performance of agriculture
   (d) All of the above

4. Public sector was given leading role in .... during initial phase of industrialisation.
   (a) India (b) Pakistan
   (c) China (d) Both (a) and (b)

5. As of 2017-18, which of the following countries has the highest population?
   (a) India
   (b) China
   (c) Pakistan
   (d) All have the same population

6. What is a significant reason for the lower poverty levels in China compared to India and Pakistan?
   (a) Greater reliance on agriculture
   (b) Faster industrialisation
   (c) Higher population growth rate
   (d) Higher foreign aid

7. Which of the following statements is/are correct?
   I. India has shown improvement in access to sanitation over the year.
   II. The density of population is highest in China compared with three countries.

   Codes
   (a) Only I
   (b) Only II
   (c) Both I and II
   (d) None of the above

8. **Statement I** Pakistan's economic development has been affected by political instability.
   Statement II Pakistan has a higher literacy rate than India.

   Alternatives
   (a) Statement I is correct and Statement II is incorrect
   (b) Statement II is correct and Statement I is incorrect
   (c) Both the statements are correct
   (d) Both the statements are incorrect

Answers 1. (c) 2. (d) 3. (d) 4. (d) 5. (b) 6. (b) 7. (a) 8. (a)

Short Answer Type Questions

9. State any three points that are common in the development strategy of China, Pakistan and India.
10. Among the three sectors of economy, which sector became the driving force for achieving a higher growth rate in India and China? Justify your answer.
11. How has the one-child policy contributed to China's economic development? Mention one positive and one negative impact.
12. Comment on the areas where India and Pakistan have failed in context to development.
13. "Despite a higher growth rate in recent decades, India still lags behind China in terms of HDI and life expectancy." Discuss two key factors contributing to this disparity.
14. Compare the trends in sectoral contribution to GDP in India, China and Pakistan.
15. Discuss the impact of demographic trends on the economic development of India and Pakistan.

Long Answer Type Questions

16. What are the economic strengths and weaknesses of India and China?
17. Give a brief account of the development initiatives taken by Pakistan for its economic development.
18. Critically analyse the structural reform in China by comparing its economic structure, policy framework and development indicators before and after the reforms.

PROJECT WORK

Meaning of Project

The word project comes from the Latin word 'Projectum' which means 'before an action'. At school level, a project is a research assignment given to a student which generally requires a larger amount of effort and more independent work than that is involved in a normal assignment.

It requires students to undertake their own fact finding endeavours, either from library, or from the internet or by means of primary data collection.

Utilities of Making a Project

Following points state the uses/utility of project work

(*i*) To provide information about the development and growth of institutions, business products and government activities.

(*ii*) To provide information to the consumers about the prices of commodities, quality and uses, etc of a product as per their interest.

(*iii*) It is helpful in estimating the preferences of consumers for petrol car or diesel car, telephone or mobile phone, etc.

(*iv*) Project report is helpful for the shareholders, who may be interested in knowing the earning of an enterprise and possibility of getting dividend.

(*v*) To help in the policy formulation about the economic and social development of any country.

Thus, we can say that project work may help marketers, shareholders, economists, consumers and government in effective and efficient decision-making.

Steps Towards Making a Project

The following steps are adviced to be taken while developing a project

1. *Identifying a Problem or an Area of Study*

At the outset, you should be clear about what you want to study. On the basis of your objective, you will proceed with the collection and processing of the data.

2. *Choice of Target Group*

The choice or identification of the target group is important for framing a project. This will also help in identifying those persons on whom you focus your attention.

3. *Collection of Data*

Data regarding project report should be collected using primary or secondary data or both the methods. Primary data can be collected by personal interviews or by mailing questionnaire. Secondary data are usually used when there is shortage of time, money and manpower resources and information is easily available.

4. *Organisation and Presentation of Data*

After collecting the data, project report can be presented using statistical tables, graphs or diagrams.

5. *Analysis and Interpretation*

Statistical measures like measures of central tendency, measures of disperson and correlation may be used as per the requirements of your analysis.

6. *Preparing a Project Report*

A project report is prepared for communicating the findings of the project.

Project Report

A project is presented with the help of a project report. The project report contains a detailed statement of the findings of the analyser. It should be prepared with great care and consideration. *A project report should*

- be handwritten
- be concise and clear
- have diagrammatic presentation
- have a length of 25 to 30 pages
- have topics with suitable headings
- end up with conclusion

Elements of Project Report

A good project report should contain the following elements

Title Page

This should include the project title, name of the company on which you are conducting your research and name of the student. You can also list the name of your school, class and subject teacher.

Acknowledgement

It is usual to thank those individuals, who have provided particularly useful assistance, technical or otherwise, during your project.

Content Page

This should list the main sections and sub-sections of your report. Choose self-explanatory titles with their respective pages and use double spacing for clarity.

Introduction

This is one of the most important component of the project report. It should begin with a clear statement of what the project is about, so that the nature and scope of the project can be understood by a reader. It should summarise everything which you set out to achieve and provide a clear summary of the project's background, relevance and main contributions. The introduction should set the context for the project and should provide the reader with a summary of the key things to look out for in, the remainder of the report.

Background

The background section of the report should set the project into action, it specifies the problem of the company, what remedial actions were taken by the company and what are its effects.

Body of Report

The central part of the report usually consists of three or four sections detailing the technical work undertaken during the project. The structure of these sections is highly project dependent. They can reflect the chronological development of the project. It includes the detailed description regarding the matter of the project.

Evaluation

This might involve quantitative and qualitative evaluation such as expressibility, functionality, ease-of-use, etc of a product. At some point, you should also evaluate the strengths and weaknesses of what you have done. It includes certain questionnaires, sampling test which help in evaluating the result on the basis of truths and facts.

Conclusion

The conclusion should list the things, which have been learnt as a result of the work you have done. It shows the ultimate response of the project undertaken by a student. It should be expressive and impressive so that a reader would clearly evaluate the result and rate you on the basis of your presentation.

Bibliography

In this section, you should mention the details of all the secondary sources, *i.e.*, magazines, newspapers, reports, internet links, etc. used for developing the project.

Assessment of Project

As per CBSE guidelines, the project will be assessed on the following parameters

S.No.	Heading	Marks Allotted
1.	Relevance of the topic	3
2.	Knowledge Content/Research Work	6
3.	Presentation Technique	3
4.	Viva	8
	Total	**20 Marks**

Sample Project

EVOLUTION OF MONEY

Name : ....

Class : ....

Roll No. : ....

School : ....

Submitted by .... Submitted to ....

Acknowledgement

I would like to extend my sincere and heartfelt obligation towards all those who have helped me in making this project. Without their active guidance, help, cooperation and encouragement, I would not have been able to present the project on time.

I am extremely thankful and pay my gratitude to my teacher Mr/Ms .... for his/her valuable guidance and support for completion of this project.

I extend my gratitude to my Principal Mr/Ms .... for the moral support extended during the tenure of the project.

I also acknowledge with a deep sense of reverence, my gratitude towards my parents, other faculty members of the school and friends for their valuable suggestions given to me in completing this project.

Date...........

....

Name of Student

Certificate

This is to Certify that the project work

.... is the bonafide work of

.... (Name of the student) who carried out the work under

my supervision.

____

(Name and Signature of
Teacher/Supervisor)

Contents

Objectives of the Project

I choose the topic 'Evolution of Money', as this topic is not very much explored and also reflects how human and nature have developed. I was intrigued by this topic and wanted to learn more about it. This project provided me with that opportunity.

More specifically, I have undertaken this project with following objectives

- To understand the basic meaning of money.
- To know about different money forms.
- To know about how scarcity of materials and convenience of humans shaped the forms of money.
- To understand the different kinds of different money form.
- To analyse the advantages and disadvantages of different forms of money.

Introduction to Money

To overcome the drawbacks of barter system and to smoothen the process of exchange, an intermediary was necessary, which was acceptable to both parties i.e., buyer and seller, such an intermediary is known as money.

Growther defines money as, "It is anything that is generally acceptable as a means of exchange and which at the same time acts as a measure and store of value."

Characteristics of Money

- Money is generally accepted as a medium of exchange.
- Stability of value in money is a major feature of money.
- A good form of money should have easy transportability.
- Money should be durable for a long period of time.

Evolution of Money

Money is the most useful and necessary invention. Money as we see it in its present form, has evolved after a long process of evolution.

It is derived from the latin word 'Moneta'. The source of evolution of money is lost. Money is developed according to the needs and requirements. Each time money is evolued, it removed the drawbacks of previous form of money.

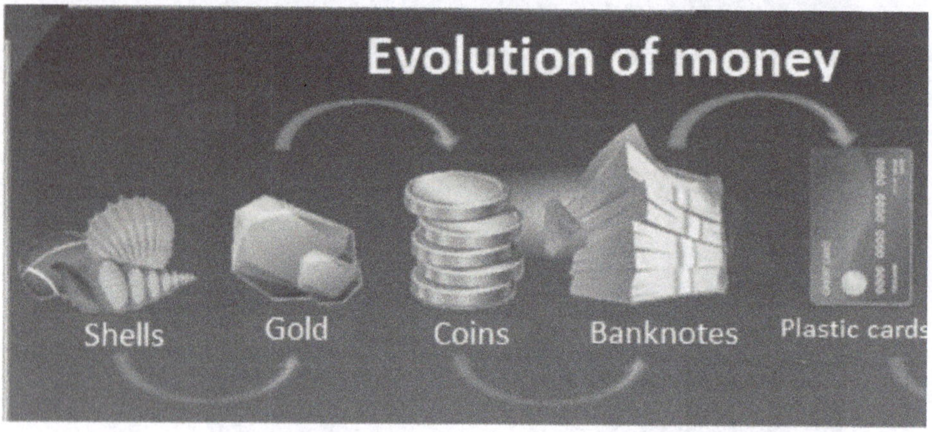

Stages of Evolution of Money

Stages of evolution of money can be understood with the help of the chart given below:

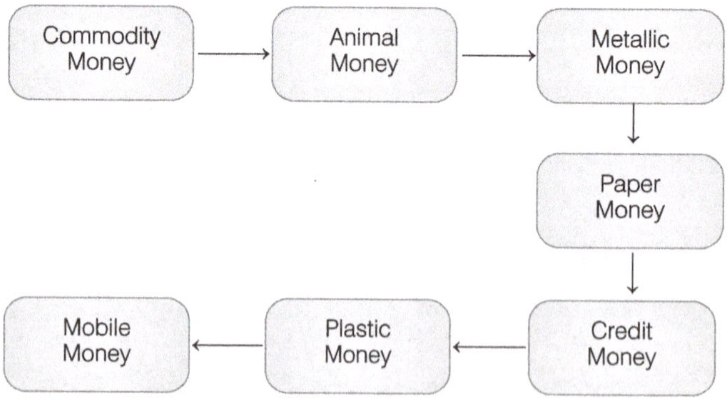

Commodity Money

Commodity money is money whose value comes from a commodity of which it is made. It consists of objects that have value in themselves as well as value in their use as money.

Numerous commodities in various times and places have been effectively utilised as this form of tried and true currency. This type of money used is called commodity money.

Besides gold and silver, peoples, nations and empires have employed salt, chocolate beans, copper, decorative belts, shells, cigarettes and even large stones.

Animal Money

In the early days of civilisation in the primitive farming, communities' money took the form of animals. Animals such as goats, bulls, rabbits were used as a medium of money. This form of money is called animal money. This is not a very known form of money. It was used only for a very less period of times. At time of monarchy, it was used by kings pertaining to transactions with other kingdoms. Nomadic hunters also used this form of money.

Metallic Money

Metallic money is 'money made of some metal'. With the drawbacks of commodity money and with economic advancement of the people, metals came to be used as money.

This money existed during the town economy stage or during the pre-machine age. In the beginning iron, copper, tin, bronze, nickel, lead, gold, silver, etc. were used. The final choice however was in favour of gold and silver due to their scarcity. Initially, pieces of gold and silver of different sizes and shapes were used. Metallic money was used earlier in the form of unstandardised bullion. Later, metallic coins were developed.

Advantages of Metallic Money

Metallic money has some advantages which are as follows

- It was durable.
- It had ornamental and decorative value.
- It could be stored.
- It had steady demand and supply.
- Subdivision of metallic money was possible.
- It was readily acceptable as a medium of exchange.

Disadvantages of Metallic Money

Metallic money also has some disadvantages which are as follows

- It was necessary to carry metallic money in bulk in case of large transactions.
- It needed to be split up at every stage of exchange.
- It was difficult to assess the actual value of metals.
- The pieces of metal were not uniform in weight, size, shape, value, etc and therefore had to be weighed at every stage of exchange.

Paper Money

Paper money is a medium of exchange for goods or services within an economy. It is printed on paper, rather than in coin form. Only paper money has value printed on it. When the demand or fashion faded for goods from which earlier metallic money was made (beaver pelts, shells, peppercorns, tulip bulbs) or more people found that they really needed more of one commodity and less of other, these systems became cumbersome. Paper money solves this problem because it is exchangeable for any good or service that people want.

Types of Paper Money

Following are the types of paper money

- **Representative Paper Money** It is that money which is fully backed by equivalent metallic reserves.
- **Convertible Paper Money** It is that money which is convertible into coins on demand.
- **Inconvertible Paper Money** When government of a country does not bear any responsibility of its conversion into gold or silver, then it is termed as inconvertible paper money. It is accepted because it is declared as legal tender by currency issuing authority. It is currently in circulation in India.

Advantages of Paper Money

Paper money has some advantages which are as follows

- It is economical, since it substitutes a less expensive material than metal for money and conserves metal.
- It is easily and quickly increased as the printing press is more expeditious than the mine.
- It has fiscal advantages like in emergencies, before taxes can be laid or bonds sold, paper money may be run-off in anticipation of taxes or receipts from sales of bonds.
- It is more convenient than metallic money as it is light in weight and the weight does not increase with the amount. Also, it is easy to conceal and carry.
- It provides a certain elasticity to the currency if used in appropriate manner.

Disadvantages of Paper Money

Paper money also has some disadvantages which are as follows

- The greatest has been pointed out - the high probability of overissue, with consequent disturbance of contracts and foreign exchanges.
- The government may also suffer as it is a heavy purchaser and pays like other individuals. In case of higher prices due to inflation, the government expenditures are increased, and as a result the public debt is expanded.
- The area of circulation of paper money is very limited as gold can be accepted internationally but paper is accepted only in the country issuing it. Thus, it cannot be used in international settlements.
- Paper money has less stability of value also, for the reason that it has only one use, namely, its monetary use. The metals, on the other hand have an equal or greater use in the arts, for which the demand is relatively constant, as much as social usages change slowly and the demand for silver or gold utensils shifts but little.

Credit Money

It refers to the deposits with banks which can be withdrawn at any time the depositor likes or has the facility to transfer it to someone else through a bank cheque. Although, cheque in itself is not money, it is therefore known as near money as it performs the same function as money.

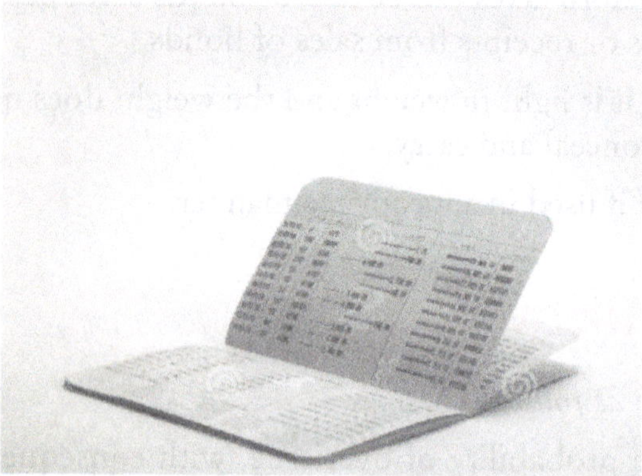

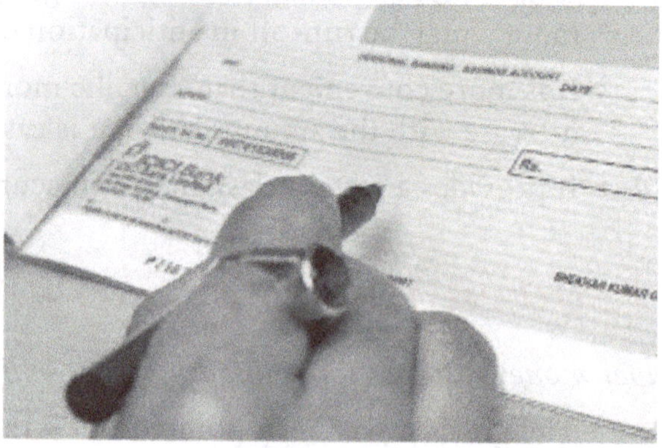

Plastic Money

Plastic money refers to the money we hold in the form of hard plastic cards. The various cards can be cash cards, credit cards, debit cards, pre-paid cash cards and store cards. Through these cards, we can make purchases. Plastic money was introduced in 1950s and is known as polymer money. These cards are made from plastic and from this source itself, the name 'plastic money' is originated.

Types of Plastic Money

Following are the types of plastic money

- **Credit Card** This card allows cashless payment with a set spending limit. Payment is made after the purchase. It imparts flexibility in payments.
- **Charge Card** This card allows cashless payment without a set spending limit. It does not allow credit facility. Most well known charge cards are American Express, Diners Club, etc.
- **Debit Card** This card is directly linked to the cardholder's bank account. At the time of payment, amount, is debited immediately from bank account. It does not allow credit facility. Maestro and VISA are the few examples of known debit cards.
- **Customer Card/Store Card** (PLCC) This card facilitate payment and credit function. PLCC can be used only at specific places. Well known customer cards are Media markt, myOne, etc.
- **Prepaid Card/Gift Card** Use of this card is required to get it topped up with credit before use. This card also does not provide credit or instalment facility. American Express, VISA are known prepaid cards.

Advantages of Plastic Money

Plastic money consists of number of advantages. *Few of them are as follows*

- Plastic money is very convenient to carry and put very less load while carrying.
- Plastic money has facilitated e-commerce by making online payments possible with just few clicks of mouse.
- Plastic money is less risky as compared to cash. It is generally protected with a password, so unauthorised access is denied.
- Credit cards also provide option of buying on credit and paying later. This is very effective function in case of emergencies.

Disadvantages of Plastic Money

Despite of many advantages, plastic money has some disadvantages too, which are as follows

- Plastic money is usually not acceptable at small outlets.
- Use of cards can also be risky in some cases, especially in case of online transactions.
- It cannot be used for all daily needs such as paying vegetable vendor, milkman, etc.

Mobile Money

Mobile money is a new form of money which generally refers to the payment services operated under financial regulation and performed via mobile phones. Instead of paying with cash, cheque or credit cards, a customer can use a mobile wallet to pay for a wide range of goods and services.

A mobile wallet is a payment service that enables users to make payment to merchants for utility bills, book tickets, transfer money and other such transactions.

A customer can also use this means to transfer money to another person. It is the latest electronic banking innovation and revolution changing the lives of millions across the globe.

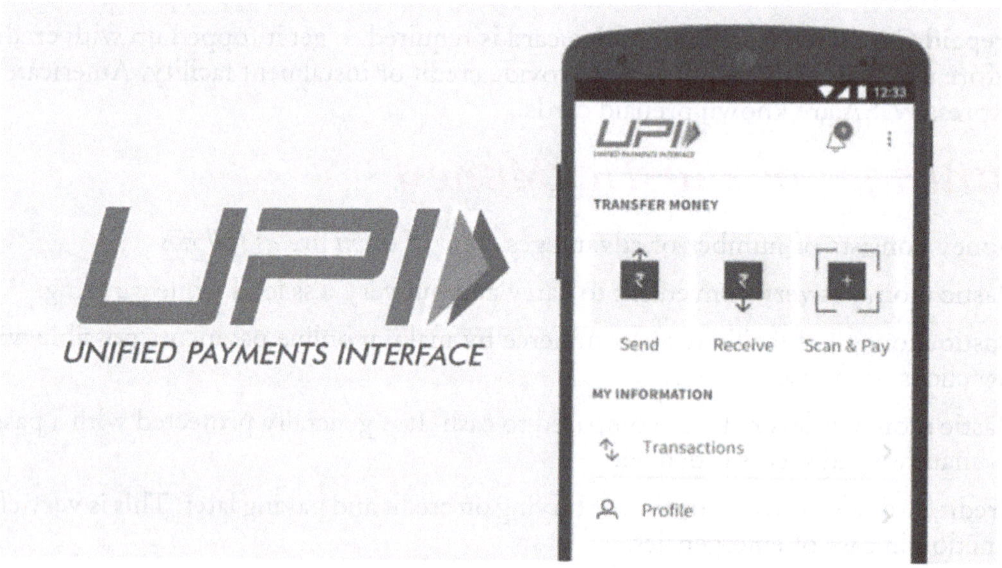

Conclusion

This project leads us to the conclusion that money has gradually evolved. It has taken a lot of time for money to come into form in which it exists today. From using heavy metals to light paper as a currency, humans have played a major role in its evolution. Human need, wants and requirements have largely contributed in its changed forms. In all of these forms, one thing remain constant i.e. general acceptance.

We also come to the conclusion that mobile money is just the beginning of what technology can do for emerging markets, which is being adopted world wide in different ways.

Viva Voce Questions

1. ***Why have you chosen this project?***

Ans. I have chosen this project because I wanted to know more about how money evolved.

2. ***What do understand by 'money' in economics?***

Ans. Anything which is generally acceptable as a means of exchange and which at the same time acts as a measure and store of value.

3. ***What is the particular feature in each form of money?***

Ans. Money is generally accepted as a means of exchange.

4. ***From where, the word 'Money' has come?***

Ans. Money is derived from Latin word 'Moneta'.

5. ***What is the major cause behind the evolution of money?***

Ans. Drawbacks in the previous forms of money caused better form of money to evolve.

6. ***After barter system, what was first time used as money?***

Ans. Different commodities such as sea shells, cigarettes, stones, etc were used as money.

7. ***Name the animals that were used as money.***

Ans. Goats, bulls, rabbits were used as money in ancient times.

8. ***In which age, metallic money came into existence?***

Ans. Metallic money existed during town economy state or pre–machine age.

9. ***What kind of metals were used as metallic money?***

Ans. Copper, tin, bronze, gold, silver, etc were used as metallic money.

10. ***What was the major drawback of metallic money that lead to its downfall?***

Ans. Bulky nature of metal and inconvenience in carrying it led to its downfall.

11. ***Name the three types of paper money.***

Ans. Representative paper money, convertible paper money and inconvertible paper money are types of paper money.

12. ***Which type of paper money is currently in circulation in India?***

Ans. Inconvertible paper money is currently in circulation in India.

13. ***What is the advantage of paper money over metallic money?***

Ans. Paper money is lighter in weight, easier to conceal and carry than metallic money.

14. ***Give the meaning of representative paper money.***

Ans. It is that money which is fully backed by equivalent metallic reserves.

15. ***How paper money proved to be disadvantageous in terms of international trade?***

Ans. Paper money cannot be used in international settlements, it can only be accepted in country issuing it, thus proving to be disadvantageous.

16. ***Explain the merit of paper money as 'economical'.***

Ans. Paper money is made up of a less expensive material. So, it is described as 'economical'.

17. ***What do you understand by credit money?***

Ans. It refers to the deposits with banks which can be withdrawn on demand through a cheque or otherwise.

18. ***Give an example of near money.***

Ans. Cheque is an example of near money as it performs the same function as money.

19. ***What are the different kinds of cards that are used as plastic money?***

Ans. Cash cards, credit cards, debit cards, pre-paid cash cards and store cards are usually used as plastic money.

20. ***What is the other name for plastic money?***

Ans. Plastic money is also known as polymer money.

21. ***Name two most well known charge cards.***

Ans. American Express and Diners club are well known charge cards.

22. ***Maestro and VISA are famous for which plastic money?***

Ans. Maestro and VISA are famous debit cards.

23. ***What is the major disadvantage of plastic money?***

Ans. Plastic money is not acceptable at small outlets.

24. ***Which facility is available now with coming of plastic money?***

Ans. Plastic money has facilitated 'E-commerce'.

25. ***What do you understand by mobile money?***

Ans. Mobile money is a form of money through which customers can pay for various goods and services using their mobile phones without paying through cash, cheque or credit cards.

SUGGESTED PROJECTS

Students can also choose the projects from the given suggestions

1. Project (Option one) : What going Around us

These projects provide an opportunity to the learner to explore various economic issues from his/her day to day life and also issues which are of broader perspective. The following projects can be undertaken.

1. Micro and small scale industries
2. Food supply channel in India
3. Contemporary employment situation in India
4. Disinvestment policy of the government
5. Goods and Service Tax Act and its Impact on GDP
6. Health expenditure (of any state)
7. Human Development Index

[The above list is not exhaustive]

2. Project (Option Two) : Analyse any concept from the syllabus

These projects provide opportunity to the learners to develop economic reasoning vis-a-vis to the given concept from the syllabus.

The following projects can be undertaken

1. Methods of calculating national income
2. Credit creation and money multiplies
3. Central Bank and its functions
4. Government budget and its components
5. Budget deficit
6. Exchange rate systems
7. Foreign exchange market
8. Balance of payments

[The above list is not exhaustive]

SAMPLE QUESTION PAPER 1

A Highly Simulated Sample Question Paper for CBSE Class XII Examination

ECONOMICS

Time : 3 Hours **Max. Marks : 80**

General Instructions

1. This question paper contains 34 questions. All questions are compulsory.
2. This question paper contains two sections : Section A – Macroeconomics, Section B – Indian Economic Development
3. This paper contains 20 Multiple Choice Questions of 1 mark each.
4. This paper contains 4 Short Answer Type I Questions of 3 marks each to be answered in 60 to 80 words.
5. This paper contains 6 Short Answer Type II Questions of 4 marks each to be answered in 80 to 100 words.
6. This paper contains 4 Long Answer Type Questions of 6 marks each to be answered in 100 to 150 words.

Section-A

(Introductory Macroeconomics)

1. Complete the table given below (1)

Rounds	Initial Deposits	Legal Reserve (20%)	Excess Reserve
I	10,000	...	...
II	...	1,600	...

(a) 2,500, 8,500, 8,500, 6,900
(b) 2,000, 8,000, 8,000, 6,400
(c) 3,000, 7,000, 7,000, 4,000
(d) 4,000, 6,000, 6,000, 4,000

2. "The Reserve Bank of India (RBI) Act enjoins the RBI to set out deviations of actual inflation outcomes from projections, if any and the underlying reasons thereof. The April 2023 MPR had projected inflation at 5.1 per cent for Q_1 : 2023-24 and 5.4 per cent for Q_2. In Q_2 (July-August), the actual outcome at 7.1 per cent exceeded the projection by 170 bps due to a steep rise in vegetables prices, particularly those of tomatoes. In fact, vegetable prices and even overall food prices registered the highest month over month increase in the current CPI series (2012 = 100) in July, resulting in the projection error."

Source *https://www.rbi.org.in/Scripts/Publications View.aspx?id=22050#CP12*

Based on given statement, actual inflation trends in Q_2: 2023-24 ....projections, signals policy-makers to .... (1)

(a) surpass, purchase securities from OMO
(b) fall behind, increase the government spending
(c) surpass, increase the bank rate
(d) fall behind, decrease the CRR

3. Which of the following best represents the sequence of evolution of money? (1)

(a) Coins, barter goods, paper currency, digital payments
(b) Barter goods, coins, paper currency, digital payments
(c) Digital payments, barter goods, coins, paper currency
(d) Paper currency, coins, barter goods, digital payments

4. **Statement I** The value of investment multiplier always varies between 0 and 1.

Statement II The minimum value of investment multiplier is one when MPC equals zero and maximum value equals one when MPC equals one. (1)

Alternatives

(a) Statement I is correct and Statement II is incorrect
(b) Statement II is correct and Statement I is incorrect
(c) Both the statements are correct
(d) Both the statements are incorrect

5. Which of the following is not a measure to correct deficient demand? (1)

(a) Increasing government spending
(b) Lowering taxes
(c) Expanding public investment
(d) Raising interest rates

6. Which of the following statements is correct? (1)

(i) The consumption function is linear when MPC is constant.

(ii) Autonomous consumption can be zero in certain cases.

(iii) A higher MPC leads to a steeper consumption function.

(iv) The consumption function is downward sloping when income increases.

Codes

(a) (i) and (iv) (b) (i), (ii) and (iii)

(c) (i) and (iii) (d) (i), (iii) and (iv)

7. ...... is also known as the 'controller of credit' in India. (1)

(a) State Bank of India (b) HDFC Bank

(c) Central Bank of India (d) Reserve Bank of India

8. Developing countries like India prepares a deficit budget as the developmental needs are more of these countries. Suppose for a hypothetical country, the total receipts of the government are given as ₹ 3,000 crore and total expenditure are given as ₹ 4,500 crore. What will be the amount of fiscal deficit? (1)

(a) ₹ 4,500 crore (b) ₹ 3,000 crore

(c) ₹ 1,500 crore (d) Can't be determined

9. Capital transfers of balance of payments account are ...... in nature. (1)

(a) recurring (b) non-recurring

(c) regular (d) Both (a) and (c)

10. **Assertion** (A) Public goods are non-rival and non-excludable in nature.

Reason (R) Public good is provided by the government for the general public without any discrimination. (1)

Alternatives

(a) Both Assertion (A) and Reason (R) are true and Reason (R) is the correct explanation of Assertion (A)

(b) Both Assertion (A) and Reason (R) are true, but Reason (R) is not the correct explanation of Assertion (A)

(c) Assertion (A) is true, but Reason (R) is false

(d) Assertion (A) is false, but Reason (R) is true

11. Given the following data, find net value added at factor cost by Buta Singh (a farmer) producing wheat. (3)

Particulars	₹ (in crores)
Sale of Wheat by the Farmer in the Local Market	6,800
Purchase of Tractor	5,000
Procurement of Wheat by the Government from the Farmer	200
Consumption of Wheat by the Farming Family during the Year	50
Expenditure on the Maintenance of Existing Capital Stock	100
Subsidy	20

Or

"GDP is considered as measure of mass welfare of a country." Do you agree? Give reason in support of your answer.

12. Reserves scaled up by $14.721 billion during a week in October last year which was also the month when it hit a two-year low of 524.52 billion while in October 2021, the reserves touched an all time high of $645 billion. Other things remaining constant, explain the impact of the same on the national income. (3)

13. Answer the following questions based upon the information given below

Autonomous investment = ₹ 100 crore

Autonomous consumption = ₹ 50 crore

50 percent of the additional income is spent on consumption

(i) Determine the equilibrium level of income.

(ii) Calculate the saving and consumption expenditure at equilibrium level of national income. (4)

14. "There are various components of money supply as used by the RBI." Do you agree with the given statement? Give reason in support of your answer. (4)

15. This extract has been taken from The Economic Times dated 30th December, 2020.

Any political party which forms government at the centre has certain social, political and economic responsibilities.

When it comes to budgeting, identifying areas of weakness helps the government to allocate resources in a useful and sustainable manner. This is one of the most fundamental objectives behind framing a government budget. It's important for the government to ensure that funds reach where they are required the most.

(i) On the basis of the given extract and your understanding, explain the importance of preparing a government budget. (3)

(ii) State the components of government budget. (1)

Or "An increase in tax rates on higher income group reflects an economic value of equality of social welfare." Do you agree with the given statement? Give reason. (4)

16. In 2021-22, India's per capita income saw a modest increase compared to previous years, reflecting growth challenges due to global disruptions and local economic factors. The per capita income stood at ₹ 1,45,000, marking a 4.5% rise from the previous year.

However, despite the overall increase, income disparities remain significant, with wealth concentrated in certain segments of the population. The services sector contributed the largest share to national income, followed by the industrial sector, while agriculture, although vital for employment, lagged behind in terms of contribution to the overall income.

Gross Domestic Capital Formation (GDCF) remained a key metric in evaluating economic growth, with investments in fixed assets showing growth. However, variations in inventories often impact the net growth of GDCF. Policy-makers emphasise balanced growth across sectors to ensure equitable income distribution and sustainable economic development.

(i) "Unpaid domestic work performed by individuals is included in the national income." Defend or refute the statement with a valid reason. (3)

(ii) "Gross Domestic Capital Formation (GDCF) can indicate the growth potential of an economy." Defend or refute the statement with a valid reason. (3)

17. (i) Look at the figure given below and identify the gap EB assuming OM as full employment output. Based upon your identification, explain any two remedies to deal with the situation. (3)

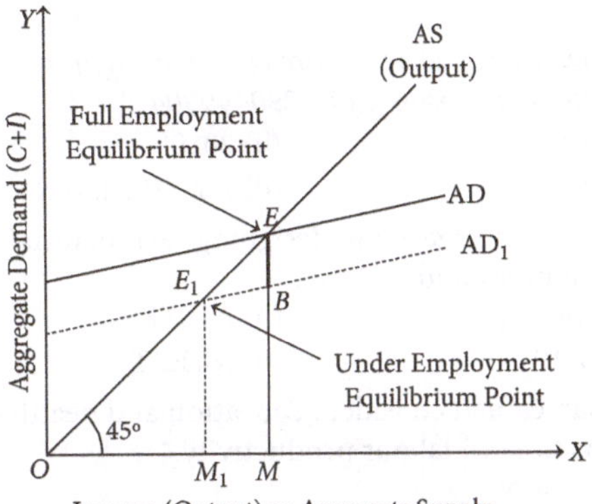

(ii) Covid-19 has significantly impacted the income level of the households and thus have reduced the level of consumption and investment expenditures thereby lowering AD. Examine the economic implication of increase in government investment expenditure when the economy is in such a situation. (3)

Or (i) Given consumption function $C = 100 + 0.75Y$ (where C = Consumption expenditure and Y = National income) and investment expenditure ₹ 2050. Calculate

(a) Equilibrium level of national income.

(b) Consumption expenditure at equilibrium level of national income.

(ii) In poor countries like India, people spend a high percentage of their income so that APC and MPC are high. Yet, value of multiplier is low. Why?

Section-B
(Indian Economic Development)

18. Which of the following was not the main reason for food shortage in India after partition? (1)

(a) Low productivity of Indian agriculture

(b) Food surplus areas of West Pakistan and Sindh region went to Pakistan

(c) Excessive use of chemical based fertilisers

(d) All of the above

19. ...... has emerged as an escape route for the agricultural workers. (1)

(a) Taking up jobs in the service sector

(b) Rural non-farm sector

(c) Becomes a moneylender with provision of loans at higher rate of interest

(d) All of the above

20. Which of the given statements are correct with regard to commercialisation of agriculture? (1)

(i) Production for self-consumption

(ii) Production of cash crops instead of food crops

(iii) Production of crops for sale in the market

(iv) Commercialisation of agriculture have improved the economic status of majority of farmers

Codes

(a) (i) and (iv) (b) (ii) and (iii)

(c) (ii) and (iv) (d) (iii) and (iv)

21. As per the image given below, in which year growth rate of Indian economy and Chinese economy was similar? (1)

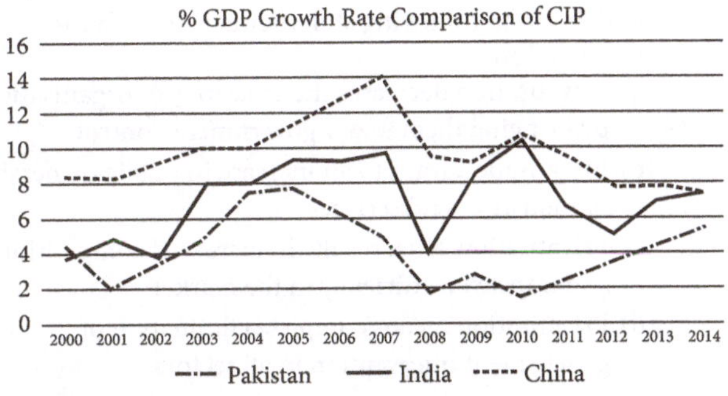

Source *https://www.researchgate.net/ figure/CIP-GDP-growth-comparison_fig1_ 290449904*
(a) 2000 (b) 2010
(c) 2014 (d) Both (b) and (c)

22. .... is engaged in designing text material up to the senior secondary level. (1)
(a) UGC (b) AICTE
(c) ICMR (d) NCERT

23. Human capital considers education and health as a means to ...... labour productivity. (1)
(a) increase
(b) decrease
(c) constant
(d) Either increase or decrease

24. Amit runs a small-scale textile unit in a rural part of India. His unit employs 30 local villagers and produces handmade fabrics that are exported to urban markets. The business not only supports Amit and his family but also provides a source of income for the workers, enhancing their standard of living.

Which of the following correctly describes the role of small-scale industries in Amit's case? (1)
(a) Generating employment opportunities and reducing rural unemployment
(b) Fostering large-scale industrial production and international competition
(c) Increasing dependence on imported raw materials
(d) Limiting economic development to urban areas

25. **Assertion** (A) Contribution by Indian agriculture in employment is highest till date.

Reason (R) The contribution of agriculture to GDP is not the highest in Indian economy. (1)

Alternatives
(a) Both Assertion (A) and Reason (R) are true and Reason (R) is the correct explanation of Assertion (A)
(b) Both Assertion (A) and Reason (R) are true, but Reason (R) is not the correct explanation of Assertion (A)
(c) Assertion (A) is true, but Reason (R) is false
(d) Assertion (A) is false, but Reason (R) is true

26. Which of the following statements is true about privatisation? (1)
(a) Privatisation decreases the efficiency of organisations by bringing them under government control
(b) Privatisation leads to an increase in public ownership of industries and services
(c) Privatisation often results in increased competition and improved efficiency in the market
(d) Privatisation means complete elimination of government intervention in all sectors

27. **Statement I** Agricultural diversification takes place in two forms, one in production method and second in production type.

Statement II Diversification in production type is also seasonal in nature. (1)

Alternatives
(a) Statement I is correct and Statement II is incorrect
(b) Statement II is correct and Statement I is incorrect
(c) Both the statements are correct
(d) Both the statements are incorrect

28. Based upon the image given below, briefly explain the concept of agricultural marketing in India. (3)

29. "There are various means by which countries are trying to strengthen their own domestic economies." Defend or refute the statement with valid explanation. (3)

Or

"Chinese structural reform process have always been appreciated for its success with no failures." Defend or refute the statement with valid explanation.

30. (i) "The environment performs its functions without any interruption as long as the demand of these functions is within its carrying capacity." In the light of the given statement, give the meaning of carrying capacity and explain how population explosion has resulted in depletion of natural resources. (3)
(ii) State any one alternative channel available for agricultural marketing with example. (1)

31. Answer the following questions
(i) Give any two objectives for the introduction of GST in Indian context.
(ii) Why were the benefits of green revolution restricted to few states and few crops in initial stage of planning? (4)

Or

State with reason whether the following statements are true or false
(i) There has been a decline in growth rate of agricultural sector during the reform period.
(ii) There were several hurdles faced by the land reform and land ceiling legislation during the pre-reform period.

32. Over the last four decades, there has been considerable shift of workforce from self-employed and regular salaried employment to casual wage work. Scholars termed this process of movement from self-employment and regular salaried employment to casual work as casualisation of workforce. In this context, explain the phenomenon of casualisation of workforce in India. (4)

33. (i) Given lines have been taken from an IMF article on "Five things to know about the informal economy" published on 28th July, 2021.
"The informal economy is a global and pervasive phenomenon. Some 60% of the world's population participates in the informal sector. Although, mostly prevalent in emerging and developing economies, it is also an important part of advance economies". Having understood the extent of informal economy, can you suggest some reasons for increased formalisation and working in the formal sector. (3)

(ii) You are residing in a village. If you are asked to advise the village panchayat, what kinds of activities would you suggest for the improvement of your village which would also generate employment? (3)

Or (i) "Information technology can play a critical role in achieving sustainable development and food security in the twenty-first century." Is the statement correct? Give reasons in support of your answers.

(ii) Explain any two problems related to human capital formation in India.

34. Read the following text carefully and answer the given questions on the basis of the same and common understanding

In the first five-year plan of India, more emphasis was given on agriculture. During the plan, there was a favourable monsoon.

As a result, the progress of agriculture during the first plan was very much satisfactory.

However, in the second five year plan more emphasis was given on industries rather than on agriculture. Besides due to the failure of monsoon, agricultural production suffered a set-back. There was scarcity of foodgrains and it had to be imported from abroad.

In order to solve the food problem, a programme was launched from the third five-year plan. This programme was known as the Intensive Agriculture District Programme (IADP). In 1960-61, seven districts in India were covered under this programme.

Only those districts were selected which had assured irrigation facilities. The main thrust of this programme was to apply improved seeds, chemical fertiliser, pesticides, etc. in irrigated areas and to raise productivity of land. Encouraged by the success of this programme, it was extended to cover more areas.

From the middle of the 1970s, this programme has been used on a wide scale and under its impact agricultural production, particularly of foodgrains, has increased rapidly.

There were three basic pillars of the new programme i.e. use of High Yielding Varieties (HYV) of seeds, extension of minor irrigation projects and use of chemical fertilisers and insecticides.

This new programmes was known as the new agricultural strategy or HYV technology.

As a result of the adoption of this new technology, agricultural production and productivity has increased so rapidly that it has been described as a revolution, specially with the production of wheat and rice.

Since the advent of the green revolution, the country has avoided famine even during adverse weather conditions. India has become self-sufficient in foodgrains.

(i) Why Intensive Agricultural District Programme (IADP) launched and what were the importance of this programme? (3)

(ii) "The new strategy of green revolution was accepted as a central point to solve the food crisis prevailing in the country." Comment. (3)

Answers

1. (b) 2,000, 8,000, 8,000, 6,400
2. (c) surpass, increase the bank rate
3. (b) Barter goods, coins, paper currency, digital payments
4. (d) Both the statements are incorrect
5. (d) Raising interest rates
6. (c) (i) and (iii)
7. (d) Reserve Bank of India
8. (d) Can't be determined
9. (b) non-recurring
10. (a) Both Assertion (A) and Reason (R) are true and Reason (R) is the correct explanation of Assertion (A)
11. ₹ 6,970 crore
13. (i) ₹ 300 crore
    (ii) ₹ 100 crore
18. (c) Excessive use of chemical based fertilisers
19. (b) Rural non-farm sector
20. (b) (ii) and (iii)
21. (d) Both (b) and (c)
22. (d) NCERT
23. (a) increase
24. (a) Generating employment opportunities and reducing rural unemployment
25. (b) Both Assertion (A) and Reason (R) are true, but Reason (R) is not the correct explanation of Assertion (A)
26. (c) Privatisation often results in increased competition and improved efficiency in the market
27. (a) Statement I is correct and Statement II is incorrect

SAMPLE QUESTION PAPER 2

A Highly Simulated Sample Question Paper for CBSE Class XII Examination

ECONOMICS

Time : 3 Hours **Max. Marks : 80**

General Instructions

1. This question paper contains 34 questions. All questions are compulsory.
2. This question paper contains two sections : Section A – Macroeconomics, Section B – Indian Economic Development
3. This paper contains 20 Multiple Choice Questions of 1 mark each.
4. This paper contains 4 Short Answer Type I Questions of 3 marks each to be answered in 60 to 80 words.
5. This paper contains 6 Short Answer Type II Questions of 4 marks each to be answered in 80 to 100 words.
6. This paper contains 4 Long Answer Type Questions of 6 marks each to be answered in 100 to 150 words.

Section-A

(Introductory Macroeconomics)

1. Balance of trade refers to balance of export and import of .... (1)

(a) invisible items (b) visible items

(c) Both (a) and (b) (d) Neither (a) nor (b)

2. "The announcements made in the Union Budget FY24, such as a single window IT system for registrations and delegating powers under the SEZ Act to IFSCA to avoid dual regulations, will enhance the ease of doing business. The IFSC is expected to emerge as a preferred gateway for global capital flows into and out of the country."

In reference to above statement, the measures such as simplifying registration processes and delegating powers under the SEZ Act to IFSCA, are expected to boost global capital flows. How would such capital flows be classified in government accounts? (1)

(a) Capital expenditure

(b) Revenue expenditure

(c) Capital receipt

(d) Revenue receipt

3. A government budget is prepared for a fiscal year running from .... (1)

(a) 1st April to 31st March

(b) 1st July to 30th June

(c) 1st April to 31st December

(d) 1st January to 31st December

4. Chalks and dusters purchased by school is an example of .... (1)

(a) intermediate goods

(b) final goods

(c) consumption goods

(d) capital goods

5. Complete the table given below (1)

Export of Goods	Import of Goods	Surplus/Deficit
100 cr	......	–200 cr
......	400 cr	200 cr

(a) 300 cr, 600 cr

(b) 600 cr, 300 cr

(c) 600 cr, 400 cr

(d) 400 cr, 600 cr

6. **Statement I** Balance of payments records transactions only by the residents of the country

Statement II Balance of trade is the component of the capital account of BoP. (1)

Alternatives

(a) Statement I is correct and Statement II is incorrect

(b) Statement II is correct and Statement I is incorrect

(c) Both the statements are correct

(d) Both the statements are incorrect

7. The 'court fee receipt' will be categorised uner .... components of the budget. (1)
(a) revenue receipt and tax receipts
(b) revenue receipt and non-tax receipts
(c) capital receipt and interest payment
(d) capital receipt and scholarship

8. **Assertion** (A) The incidence and impact of both direct and indirect taxes are unavoidable.

Reason (R) Direct taxes are generally progressive in nature in countries with high income inequalities. (1)

Alternatives
(a) Both Assertion (A) and Reason (R) are true and Reason (R) is the correct explanation of Assertion (A)
(b) Both Assertion (A) and Reason (R) are true, but Reason (R) is not the correct explanation of Assertion (A)
(c) Assertion (A) is false, but Reason (R) is true
(d) Assertion (A) is true, but Reason (R) is false

9. Which of the following is the correct objective of the government budget? (1)
(i) The government budget aims to promote economic growth by increasing investment and production.
(ii) One of the key objectives of the government budget is to reduce income and wealth inequality.
(iii) The budget helps in the reallocation of resources to priority sectors for social welfare.
(iv) The government budget has no role in addressing economic issues.

Codes
(a) (i), (ii) and (iii)
(b) (i) and (iv)
(c) (iii) and (iv)
(d) Only (ii)

10. A government budget shows primary deficit of ₹ 4,680 crore. The government expenditure on interest payment is ₹ 620 crore. How much is the fiscal deficit? (1)
(a) ₹ 4,680 (b) ₹ 4,060 (c) ₹ 5,300 (d) ₹ 7,548

11. In February, the government projected that Indian economy would grow 7% in 2022-23. But this is likely to be revised in the months and years ahead, and the final figure won't be known for at least three years. That final figure can be significantly different. Such revisions in GDP have important policy implications as the GDP data goes into the budget making process, affecting the way the government plans its finances and allocates money to schemes.

The nominal GDP is considered as a better measure compared with real GDP. Defend of refute the statement with suitable justification. (3)

12. State whether the following statements are true or false. Give reasons for your answer. (3)
(i) Difference between value of exports and imports of goods and services is called balance of trade.
(ii) External assistance is not recorded in balance of payments account.

Or If BoP of a country is – ₹ 100 crore and total payments are ₹ 500 crore, find out the total receipts.

13. In an economy, $C = 300 + 0.5Y$ and $I =$ ₹ 600 (where $C =$ Consumption, $Y =$ Income or investment). Compute the following
(i) The equilibrium level of income
(ii) Consumption at equilibrium level (4)

14. Giving reasons, state whether the following statements are true or false (4)
(i) There is an inverse relationship between the value of marginal propensity to save and investment multiplier.
(ii) When the value of average propensity to save is negative, the value of marginal propensity to save will also be negative.

Or

What is the sum of expenditure on consumption and investment in an economy called? State its components.

15. India's core inflation remains elevated at 6.2%, raising concerns about cost push pressures and demand side imbalances in the economy. There is an urgent need for policy interventions to stabilise prices.

–Financial Express, April, 2024

(i) Identify and explain any three monetary measures that the Reserve Bank of India can implement to correct the situation. (3)
(ii) State any two causes of the situation indicated in the above news report. (1)

16. (i) "While using the expenditure method to calculate national income, it is essential to account for various precautions to avoid inaccuracies." Defend or refute the statement, with the help of valid reasons. (3)
(ii) Explain how shall the payment of electricity bill by a school be treated while estimating national income? (3)

Or

(i) Calculate 'net domestic product at factor cost' from the given data

S.No.	Particulars	₹ (in crores)
(i)	Net Factor Income to Abroad	30
(ii)	Sales	2,000
(iii)	Subsides	20

S.No.	Particulars	₹ (in crores)
(iv)	Consumption of Fixed Capital	50
(v)	Net Current Transfer to Abroad	(−)10
(vi)	Closing Stock	100
(vii)	Opening Stock	200
(viii)	Intermediate Costs	1,000
(ix)	Indirect Tax	150

(ii) What treatment is assigned to the 'payment of interest on borrowings' by general government?

17. XYZ Bank is a prominent financial institution in a growing city, catering to both individuals and businesses. For years, the bank has been playing a vital role in the economic landscape by providing essential financial services.

It operates under strict regulations and ensures that customers' funds are safe while contributing to the economy's growth.

The bank has built a strong relationship with local residents, offering them a safe place to store their money and also providing opportunities to earn interest on their deposits. Additionally, XYZ Bank supports economic development by offering various types of loans. e.g. It provides personal loans to individuals who wish to purchase homes or vehicles and business loans to companies looking to expand or invest in new projects. These loans are crucial in stimulating economic activity, as they enable individuals to meet their needs and businesses to grow.

Over time, XYZ Bank has become a central player in supporting the region's economic growth, providing financial products that help individuals achieve their goals while enabling businesses to thrive and contribute to the overall economy.

(i) How does XYZ Bank contribute to economic growth through its lending activities? (3)

(ii) Discuss the forms of deposits commercial bank offers to its customers. (3)

Section-B
(Indian Economic Development)

18. Three-tier system of rural cooperative credit societies is .... (1)

(a) central cooperative banks
(b) state cooperative banks
(c) primary agricultural credit societies
(d) All of the above

19. **Statement I** China announced its first economic reforms in the year 1953.

Statement II India initiated its new economic policy in the year 1988. (1)

Alternatives

(a) Statement I is correct and Statement II is incorrect
(b) Statement II is correct and Statement I is incorrect
(c) Both the statements are correct
(d) Both the statements are incorrect

20. "Since independence, India has witnessed a considerable fall in the infant mortality rate in India." Identify which of the following is not to be one of the reasons for the fall in the infant mortality rate? (1)

(i) Improvement in health facilities over the years.
(ii) Improvement in educational standards over the years.
(iii) Fall in standard of living of the population of the nation over the years.
(iv) Technological expansion over the years.

Codes

(a) (iii) and (iv) (b) (i) and (ii)
(c) Only (iii) (d) (ii) and (iv)

21. **Assertion** (A) Privatisation process leads to a change in management with a change in ownership.

Reason (R) Change in management is not a necessary condition for the process of privatisation. (1)

Alternatives

(a) Both Assertion (A) and Reason (R) are true and Reason (R) is not the correct explanation of Assertion (A)
(b) Both Assertion (A) and Reason (R) are true, but Reason (R) is the correct explanation of Assertion (A)
(c) Assertion (A) is false, but Reason (R) is true
(d) Assertion (A) is true, but Reason (R) is false

22. The 'operation flood' programme was successfully implemented in the year .... (1)

(a) 1892 (b) 1970
(c) 1982 (d) 1995

23. A farmer in a semi-arid region grows wheat in the winter and maize during the rainy season. This strategy helps to manage the variability in rainfall. Which of the following best describes this approach? (1)

(a) Monoculture farming
(b) Crop diversification
(c) Pesticide reliance
(d) Soil degradation

24. Which of the following statements correctly reflects a comparative analysis of the economies of India, China and Pakistan? **(1)**

(a) China experienced significant GDP growth starting in the early 1980s

(b) India's GDP growth rebounded after the implementation of the New Economic Policy 1991

(c) The economic reforms in Pakistan were largely similar to those in India

(d) All three countries made the private sector the central focus of their economies

25. The long-term planning process similar to India is known as .... **(1)**

(a) national development strategy

(b) perspective planning

(c) strategic development plans

(d) long-term economic vision

26. About ...... per cent of female workforce is employed in the primary sector in India. **(1)**

(a) 47 (b) 57 (c) 67 (d) 77

27. Identify the policy measure with respect to China. **(1)**

(a) SEZ (b) GLF

(c) Dual price (d) Commune system

28. Observe the given figure carefully and answer the question that follows

What was the offer before green revolution and why Indian farmers were not ready for the same offer after green revolution? **(3)**

29. "Composition of foreign trade of any country tells us about the nature of commodities that are exported and imported." What can you state about the composition of foreign trade at the time of independence? **(3)**

Or What was the two-fold motive behind the systematic deindustrialisation affected by the British in pre-independent India?

30. (i) "Under the colonial regime, the real motive behind the development of infrastructure was to meet various colonial interests."

Accept/Refute the above statement. Give reason in support of your answer. **(3)**

(ii) State any one drawback of providing agricultural subsidy. **(1)**

31. Elucidate the functions of Central Pollution Control Board (CPCB) to address the environmental concerns in India. **(4)**

Or

"Indiscriminate felling of trees led to environmental problems." Do you agree? Give reason to justify your answer.

32. On the basis of the following data, answer the following questions **(4)**

Country	Urbanisation	Infant Mortality Rate (Per 1,000 live births)
India	33	38
Pakistan	39	66

(i) Comment on the infant mortality rate among India and Pakistan.

(ii) "Pakistan is more urbanised than India." Do you agree?

33. (i) "We have a moral obligation to hand over the planet earth in good order to the future generation."

Do you agree with the above statement? Suggest any measures to achieve the above obligation. **(3)**

(ii) Organic farming is a way to a sustainable development. Do you agree? Justify. **(3)**

Or (i) "The reform process initiated in the early 1990s resulted in a decline in the number of workers employed in the formal sector." Critically analyse.

(ii) Women workforce is biased towards self-employment. Explain why?

34. India's land is undergoing degradation or desertification. In 2011-2013, it stood at 29.3 per cent of the total land, representing an increase of 0.57 per cent (which is 1.87 million hectares in area) compared with 2003-2005, according to a report-cum-atlas by ISRO's Space Applications Centre.

Soil erosion due to water and wind, and degradation of vegetation cover were the main processes that has led to land degradation.

Almost 90 per cent of the states experienced a rise-notably Delhi and the North-Eastern states in land degradation in 2011-2013 compared with 2003-2005 while four states showed slight decreases in land degradation.

Reclaiming degraded lands will require a strict land use policy and better watershed management initiatives, say experts.

Land degradation can exacerbate climate change and threaten agricultural productivity, water quality, biodiversity, sustainable development and the living conditions of humans and wildlife, among other effects.

Globally, a third of our land is degraded, affecting 3 billion people and it is expected to worsen with rising demand for food.

(i) What is land degradation? State the factors responsible for land degradation. (3)

(ii) State and discuss three principal causes of environmental degradation. (3)

Answers

1. (b) visible items

2. (c) Capital receipt

3. (a) 1st April to 31st March

4. (a) intermediate goods

5. (a) 300 cr, 600 cr

6. (d) Both the statements are incorrect

7. (a) revenue receipt and tax receipts

8. (c) Assertion (A) is false, but Reason (R) is true

9. (a) (i), (ii) and (iii)

10. (c) ₹ 5,300

12. *Or* ₹ 400 crore

13. (i) 1,800 (ii) 1,200

16. *Or* (i) ₹ 2,070 crore

18. (d) All of the above

19. (a) Statement I is correct and Statement II is incorrect

20. (b) (i) and (ii)

21. (a) Both Assertion (A) and Reason (R) are true and Reason (R) is not the correct explanation of Assertion (A)

22. (b) 1970

23. (b) Crop diversification

24. (b) India's GDP growth rebounded after the implementation of the New Economic Policy 1991

25. (b) perspective planning

26. (b) 57

27. (b) GLF

SAMPLE QUESTION PAPER 3

A Highly Simulated Sample Question Paper for CBSE Class XII Examination

ECONOMICS

Time : 3 Hours **Max. Marks : 80**

General Instructions

1. This question paper contains 34 questions. All questions are compulsory.
2. This question paper contains two sections : Section A – Macroeconomics, Section B – Indian Economic Development
3. This paper contains 20 Multiple Choice Questions of 1 mark each.
4. This paper contains 4 Short Answer Type I Questions of 3 marks each to be answered in 60 to 80 words.
5. This paper contains 6 Short Answer Type II Questions of 4 marks each to be answered in 80 to 100 words.
6. This paper contains 4 Long Answer Type Questions of 6 marks each to be answered in 100 to 150 words.

Section-A
(Introductory Macroeconomics)

1. **Statement I** Consumption and saving curves are complementary curves.

Statement II APC can be even less than one and APS can be more than one. (1)

Alternatives

(a) Statement I is correct and Statement II is incorrect
(b) Statement II is correct and Statement I is incorrect
(c) Both the statements are correct
(d) Both the statements are incorrect

2. "A company located in India receives a loan from a company located abroad." How is this transaction be recorded in India's balance of payments account? (1)

(a) Credit side of current account
(b) Debit side of current account
(c) Credit side of capital account
(d) Debit side of capital account

3. Money supply in the economy is a .... concept. (1)

(a) stock (b) flow
(c) constant (d) None of these

4. Devaluation refers to .... in price of domestic currency in terms of all foreign currencies under fixed exchange rate regime. (1)

(a) increase (b) decrease
(c) No change (d) Either (a) or (b)

5. Which of the following aggregates are correct? (1)

(i) $GDP_{FC} = GDP_{MP}$ – Net Indirect Taxes
(ii) $NDP_{FC} = GDP_{MP}$ +Net Indirect Taxes – Depreciation
(iii) $NNP_{FC} = GNP_{MP}$ – Net Indirect Taxes – Depreciation
(iv) $GNP_{MP} = GDP_{MP}$ – Net Factor Income from Abroad

Codes

(a) (ii) and (iii) (b) (i) and (iv)
(c) (i), (iii) and (iv) (d) (iii) and (iv)

6. The saving at different levels of income is given in the following schedule

Income (₹ Cr)	0	200	400	600	800	1,000
Saving (₹ Cr)	–120	–60	0	60	120	180

Saving function will be (1)

(a) $S = -60 + 0.7Y$ (b) $S = -120 + 0.3Y$
(c) $S = -100 + 0.5Y$ (d) $S = -120 + 0.7Y$

7. Imagine you deposit ₹ 1,000 in a commercial bank. The bank keeps 10% of this as reserve and lends out the remaining amount. This process continues with other depositors as well.

What is the amount of loans created in the economy after 3rd round of lending? (1)

(a) ₹ 900 (b) ₹ 729 (c) ₹ 810 (d) ₹ 2,439

8. **Assertion** (A) A deficit in the balance of trade indicates an excess of imports over exports of services.

Reason (R) A trade surplus helps to increase foreign exchange reserves. (1)

Alternatives

(a) Both Assertion (A) and Reason (R) are true and Reason (R) is the correct explanation of Assertion (A)

(b) Both Assertion (A) and Reason (R) are true, but Reason (R) is not the correct explanation of Assertion (A)

(c) Assertion (A) is true, but Reason (R) is false

(d) Assertion (A) is false, but Reason (R) is true

9. If the Marginal Propensity to Consume (MPC) is high, the value of the investment multiplier .... and the impact of an initial increase in investment on income .... (1)

(a) rises, rises (b) falls, rises

(c) rises, falls (d) falls, falls

10. In 2023-24, India's economic growth was shaped by resilient domestic demand and cautious global economic conditions. The services sector, contributing 55% to the economy, remained a key driver, while capital expenditure by the central government tripled compared to 2019-20, focusing on infrastructure. However, global uncertainties, including falling demand from trading partners and volatility in commodity prices, posed risks to external trade. India's fiscal deficit reduced from 6.4% of GDP in 2022-23 to 5.6% in 2023-24, reflecting higher tax revenues and controlled expenditures.

The industrial sector grew by 9.5%, but agriculture slowed to 1.4%, partly due to poor monsoons.

Source *Economic Survey 2023-24*

In the context of aggregate demand, which component played a significant role in driving India's economic growth in 2023-24? (1)

(a) Government expenditure

(b) Net exports

(c) Private consumption expenditure

(d) Investment expenditure by the private sector

11. The net domestic product at market price of an economy is ₹ 4,500 crore. The capital stock is worth ₹ 4,000 crore and it depreciates at the rate of 10% per annum.

Indirect taxes amount to ₹ 150 crores, subsidies amount to ₹ 20 crores, factor income from rest of the world is ₹ 400 crores and to rest of the world is ₹ 600 crores. Find out the gross national product at factor cost. (3)

12. "Many large Multinational Corporations (MNCs) have recently shifted their investments from China and have started their production in India, thereby boosting the Make in India plans of the government."

Presuming others factors being constant, discuss the effects of the given statement on foreign exchange rates with reference to the Indian economy. Use diagram. (3)

Or

Indian investors lend abroad. Answer the following questions

(i) In which sub-account and on which side of the balance of payments account, such lending is recorded? Give reasons.

(ii) Explain the impact of this lending on market exchange rate. Use diagram.

13. The equilibrium level of income in an economy is ₹ 5,000 crore. The autonomous consumption expenditure is equal to ₹ 250 crore and investment expenditure ₹ 1,000 crore.

Calculate consumption expenditure at equilibrium level of national income, Marginal Propensity to Save (MPS), saving function and investment multiplier. (4)

14. (i) "To boost falling demand in the economy, the Reserve Bank of India recently reduced reverse repo rate." Elaborate the rationale (objectives) behind the steps taken by the central bank. (3)

(ii) State the difference between repo rate and reverse repo rate. (1)

Or

Define credit multiplier. What role does it play in determining the credit creation power of the banking system? Use a numerical illustration to explain. (4)

15. (i) Distinguish between bank money and high power money. (2)

(ii) Explain 'difficulty in storing wealth' problem faced in the barter system of exchange. (2)

16. (i) From the following data, calculate national income by income method and expenditure method (3)

Particulars	₹ (in crores)
Private Final Consumption Expenditure	2,000
Net Capital Formation	400
Change in Stock	50
Compensation of Employees	1,900
Rent	200
Interest	150

Particulars	₹ (in crores)
Operating Surplus	720
Net Indirect Taxes	400
Employers' Contribution to the Social Security Schemes	100
Net Exports	20
Net Factor Income from Abroad	(–) 20
Government Final Consumption Expenditure	600
Consumption of Fixed Capital	100

(ii) Suppose a ban is imposed on consumption of tobacco. Examine its likely effects on GDP and welfare. (3)

17. The Government of India's budget is an important tool for managing the country's economy. It outlines the government's revenue and expenditure for the upcoming year. In the 2024-25 budget, the government has emphasised boosting economic growth, with a particular focus on infrastructure development, education and healthcare.

One of the key proposals is the increased allocation for infrastructure projects, including roads, railways and airports, which is expected to boost employment and improve connectivity across the country.

The budget also includes provisions for subsidies in various sectors, including agriculture and food security. Moreover, the government has introduced new tax reforms aimed at enhancing tax compliance and increasing revenue generation. These reforms are expected to create a more transparent taxation system and provide a boost to the economy. The 2024-25 budget also projects a reduction in fiscal deficit to 4.5% of GDP, as the government continues its efforts to maintain fiscal discipline while promoting growth.

(i) Why is the increased allocation for infrastructure projects considered a capital expenditure? (3)

(ii) How does the government's proposal to reduce the fiscal deficit contribute to economy? (3)

Or (i) "Taxation is an effective tool to reduce the inequalities of income." Justify the given statement with valid reasons.

(ii) Explain the distinction between fiscal deficit and primary deficit.

Section-B
(Indian Economic Development)

18. Prior to India's independence, stagnation in agriculture sector was mainly caused by .... (1)

(a) investment in technology
(b) investment in agriculture facilities
(c) advanced infrastructural facilities
(d) land settlement system

19. The Great Leap Forward(GLF) programme was initiated by China to develop their .... sector. (1)

(a) agriculture (b) industry
(c) trade (d) None of these

20. Observe the image given below and identity the planning objective. (1)

(a) Growth (b) Self-reliance
(c) Modernisation (d) Equality

21. **Statement I** NABARD was set-up in 1982 as an apex body to coordinate the activities of all institutions involved in the rural financial system.

Statement II Credit plays a crucial role in rural development and informal credit is on the rise post-independence. (1)

Alternatives

(a) Statement I is correct and Statement II is incorrect
(b) Statement II is correct and Statement I is incorrect
(c) Both the statements are correct
(d) Both the statements are incorrect

22. .... was initiated by the chairman of Chinese Communist Party, Mao Zedong in 1965. (1)

(a) Great Leap Forward
(b) Commune System
(c) Proletarian Cultural Revolution
(d) Economic Reforms in China

23. A child enrolled in a school that provides both basic education and healthcare services experiences improvements in academic performance, as well as better health due to improved nutrition and access to preventive care. This scenario best illustrates the concept that (1)

(a) education and health are mutually reinforcing and interconnected.
(b) health services are unrelated to academic performance.
(c) education alone is sufficient for improving a child's well-being.
(d) only physical education programmes contribute to overall health improvements.

24. Read the statements given below and choose the correct one(s) in the context of comparative development (1)

(i) Density of population of India is more than that of China and Pakistan.
(ii) In all the three countries (India, China and Pakistan), service sector contributes highest share of GVA (GDP).
(iii) Pakistan has outperformed India in the rate of urbanisation.

Codes

(a) (i) and (ii)
(b) (i) and (iii)
(c) (ii) and (iii)
(d) (i), (ii) and (iii)

25. Which of the following statements is incorrect regarding the environmental crisis? (1)

(a) Human activities, such as deforestation and fossil fuel consumption, are central to the acceleration of climate change and extreme weather patterns
(b) The depletion of essential natural resources, including water and arable soil, has minimal long-term implications for ecological stability and human survival
(c) The erosion of biodiversity exacerbates ecosystem instability, undermining vital services like food production and climate regulation
(d) Pollution from industrial, agricultural and urban sources significantly contributes to environmental degradation and public health crises globally

26. **Assertion** (A) More proportion of female workforce is employed in the primary sector as compared to proportion of male workforce.

Reason (R) Male workforce get opportunities in both secondary and service sectors. (1)

Alternatives

(a) Both Assertion (A) and Reason (R) are true and Reason (R) is the correct explanation of Assertion (A)
(b) Both Assertion (A) and Reason (R) are true, but Reason (R) is not the correct explanation of Assertion (A)
(c) Assertion (A) is true, but Reason (R) is false
(d) Assertion (A) is false, but Reason (R) is true

27. Tatas paid ₹ 2,700 crore in cash and assumed ₹ 15,300 crore in debt from the airline. The transaction also involves the sale of Air India Express and its ground handling subsidiary, AISATS. The above situation indicates .... (1)

(a) disinvestment
(b) privatisation
(c) liberalisation
(d) None of the above

28. Interpret the given picture on account of current environmental challenges. (3)

Source *http://www.theenvironmentalblog. org/current-environmental-issues*

29. "Compared to the 1970s, there has hardly been any change in the distribution of workforce across various industries." Comment. (3)

Or

"Use of chemical fertilisers to compensate food shortage, gives food dividends at one time in the form of increased production but becomes a disaster later in the form of adverse effects on health."

How can we overcome this problem?

30. Compare and analyse the following information related to contribution to GDP (GVA) and distribution of workforce in different sectors in India, China and Pakistan. (4)

Sectoral Share of GVA (GDP) and Employment (%) 2018-19

Sector	Contribution to GVA (GDP)			Distribution of Workforce		
	India	**China**	**Pakistan**	**India**	**China**	**Pakistan**
Agriculture	16	7	24	43	26	41
Industry	30	41	19	25	28	24
Services	54	52	57	32	46	35
Total	100	100	100	100	100	100

31. (i) Distinguish between tariff and non-tariff barriers.
(ii) Why has the industrial sector performed poorly in reform period? (4)

Or

"In light of the escalating climate crisis and rampant resource depletion, it is imperative that the global community collectively adopts a multidimensional approach to sustainable development, which not only prioritises economic growth but also integrates social equity and environmental stewardship, thereby ensuring that the legacy we leave for future generations is one of resilience and sustainability."

— Adapted from an article in The Guardian discussing the urgent need for comprehensive sustainable development strategies.

(i) Discuss any three strategies to implement sustainable development. (3)
(ii) Discuss any one measure to achieve sustainable development. (1)

32. State whether the following statements are true or false with valid arguments. (4)
(i) Human capital benefits only the owner and the not the society.
(ii) In India, higher education takes a major share of total education expenditure.

33. (i) "There are no benefits of diversification of agriculture activities."
Do you agree? Explain your view with reason. (3)
(ii) Distinguish between green revolution and golden revolution. (3)

Or

(i) "Economic development depends on the effective utilisation of human capital in a country."
Do you agree with the given statement? Support your answer with valid arguments.
(ii) Victor is able to get work only for 2 hours in a day. Rest of the day, he is looking for work. Is he unemployed? Why?

34. Read the following text carefully and answer the given questions on the basis of the same and common understanding

The green revolution was a period that began in the 1960s during which agriculture in India was converted into a modern industrial system by the adoption of technology, such as the use of High Yielding Variety (HYV) seeds, mechanised farm tools, irrigation facilities, pesticides and fertilisers.

Mainly led by agricultural scientist MS Swaminathan in India, this period was part of the larger green revolution endeavor initiated by Norman E Borlaug, which leveraged agricultural research and technology to increase agricultural productivity in the developing world.

Under premiership of leader Lal Bahadur Shastri, the green revolution within India commenced in 1968, leading to an increase in foodgrain production, especially in Punjab, Haryana and Uttar Pradesh.

Major milestones in this undertaking were the development of high yielding varieties of wheat and rust resistant strains of wheat.

The long-term effects of green revolution have been analysed by environmentalists like Vandana Shiva and others who say that it caused greater environmental, financial and sociological problems like droughts, rural indebtedness and farmer suicides.

Reports have shown soil deterioration from the use of chemicals which has led to the collapse of agricultural systems in many regions of the country and negatively affected the farmers, food and water supply.

Source *www.wikipedia.org.*

(i) Why was green revolution implemented and how did it benefits the farmers? (3)
(ii) Justify the following statement with valid explanation
"Green revolution enabled the government to procure sufficient foodgrains to build its stocks that could be used during time of shortage." (3)

Answers

1. (a) Statement I is correct and Statement II is incorrect
2. (c) Credit side of capital account
3. (a) stock
4. (a) increase
5. (b) (i) and (iv)
6. (b) $S = -120 + 0.3Y$
7. (b) ₹ 729
8. (d) Assertion (A) is false, but Reason (R) is true
9. (a) rises, rises
10. (a) Government expenditure
11. ₹ 4,570 crore
16. (i) ₹ 2,600 crore
18. (d) land settlement system
19. (b) industry
20. (d) Equality
21. (a) Statement I is correct and Statement II is incorrect
22. (c) Proletarian Cultural Revolution
23. (a) education and health are mutually reinforcing and interconnected.
24. (d) (i), (ii) and (iii)
25. (b) The depletion of essential natural resources, including water and arable soil, has minimal long-term implications for ecological stability and human survival
26. (b) Both Assertion (A) and Reason (R) are true, but Reason (R) is not the correct explanation of Assertion (A)
27. (b) privatisation

CBSE
Examination Paper 2025

ECONOMICS

Time : 3 Hours **Max. Marks : 80**

General Instructions

1. This question paper contains 34 questions. All questions are compulsory.
2. This question paper contains two sections : Section A – Macroeconomics, Section B – Indian Economic Development
3. This paper contains 20 Multiple Choice Questions of 1 mark each.
4. This paper contains 4 Short Answer Type I Questions of 3 marks each to be answered in 60 to 80 words.
5. This paper contains 6 Short Answer Type II Questions of 4 marks each to be answered in 80 to 100 words.
6. This paper contains 4 Long Answer Type Questions of 6 marks each to be answered in 100 to 150 words.

Section A
(Introductory Macroeconomics)

1. If the value of investment multiplier (K) is 5, the relevant saving function would be .... (1)

(a) $S = -60 + 0.25\,Y$ (b) $S = -60 + 0.75\,Y$
(c) $S = -60 + 0.20\,Y$ (d) $S = -60 + 0.60\,Y$

2. Identify, which of the following items will not be included in estimating national income of India. (1)

(a) Salary to Indian residents working at the Russian Embassy in India
(b) Income generated from smuggling
(c) Payments to farm workers in the form of foodgrains
(d) Interest paid by a firm to a bank

3. If an upward sloping straight line consumption function makes an intercept at the Y-axis at a positive coordinate, it implies that Marginal Propensity to Consume (MPC) .... and Average Propensity to Consume (APC) .... as the income increases. (1)

(a) remains constant, rises
(b) rises, rises
(c) remains constant, falls
(d) falls, falls

4. **Assertion** (A) Other things remaining constant, devaluation of domestic currency may lead to rise in national income of the nation.

Reason (R) Devaluation of domestic currency refers to reduction in the value of domestic currency by the government with respect to foreign currency under the fixed exchange rate system. (1)

Alternatives

(a) Both Assertion (A) and Reason (R) are true and Reason (R) is the correct explanation of Assertion (A)
(b) Both Assertion (A) and Reason (R) are true, but Reason (R) is not the correct explanation of Assertion (A)
(c) Assertion (A) is true, but Reason (R) is false
(d) Assertion (A) is false, but Reason (R) is true

5. Central bank can decrease the money supply in the economy by .... (1)

(a) lowering the cash reserve
(b) increasing the bank rate
(c) lowering the bank rate
(d) purchase of G-Secs (Government Securities)

6. If the total credit created by the banks is ₹ 500 and reserve ratio is 20%, the value of primary deposits would be .... (1)

(a) ₹ 200 (b) ₹ 300
(c) ₹ 100 (d) ₹ 500

7. Using the given information, complete the following table **(1)**

Income (Y) (in ₹ crore)	Savings (in ₹ crore)	Consumption (in ₹ crore)	Average Propensity to Consume (APC)
0	...(i)...	30	—
100	0	...(ii)...	1
200	30	170	0.85
300	60	240	0.8

(a) −30, 120 (b) 30, 120 (c) 0, 70 (d) −30, 100

8. Identify, which of the following is not a source of demand for foreign exchange. **(1)**
(a) Imports of goods and services
(b) Gifts by Indians to their families living abroad
(c) Indian tourists visiting foreign countries
(d) Loans from rest of the world

9. Suppose in an economy, planned spendings are greater than planned outputs.
Identify the correct option with respect to effects on the economy. **(1)**
(i) Decrease in planned inventories in the economy.
(ii) Rise in national income.
(iii) Decrease in real output level in the economy.
(iv) Decrease in employment level in the economy.

Codes
(a) Only (i) (b) (i) and (ii)
(c) (iii) and (iv) (d) (ii), (iii) and (iv)

10. **Statement I** The price of a given currency in terms of another is known as bank rate.
Statement II Demand curve for foreign exchange is a downward sloping curve. **(1)**
Alternatives
(a) Statement I is correct and Statement II is incorrect
(b) Statement I is incorrect and Statement II is correct
(c) Both the statements are correct
(d) Both the statements are incorrect

11. Distinguish between autonomous transactions and accommodating transactions in the balance of payments of the economy. **(3)**

12. Calculate domestic income (NDP_{FC}) from the data given below **(3)**

S.No.	Particulars	₹ (in lakh)
(i)	Gross National Product at Market Price	2,500
(ii)	Consumption of Fixed Capital	200
(iii)	Goods and Services Tax	20
(iv)	Subsidies	50
(v)	Net factor Income from Abroad	50
(vi)	Changes in Stocks	30
(vii)	Unexpected Loss of a Fixed Asset	500

Or Define Net Factor Income from Abroad (NFIA) and discuss its components.

13. (i) Estimate the value of Aggregate Demand (AD) in an imaginary economy. **(3)**
(a) Autonomous investment (I_0) = ₹ 100 crore
(b) Marginal Propensity to Save (MPS) = 0.2
(c) Level of income (Y)= ₹ 4,000 crore
(d) Autonomous consumption expenditure ($\overline{C}$) = ₹ 50 crore
(ii) State the meaning of propensity to consume. **(1)**

14. "An economy is operating at under employment level of income." What does this situation indicate? Discuss any one fiscal measure to tackle this situation. **(4)**

Or Elaborate using a hypothetical numerical example, how a given initial increase in investment affects the level of final income of the economy.

15. "In the 1990s, on the advice of Reserve Bank of India (RBI), the Government of India took a decision of hypothecation of gold reserves to different nations."
In the light of above statement, discuss briefly the role of central bank as banker, agent and advisor to the government. **(4)**

16. Government provides certain goods and services which cannot be provided by the market mechanism. Examples of such goods are national defence, roads, government administration, etc. which are referred to as public goods.
There are two major differences between public and private goods. One, the benefits of public goods are available to all and are not only restricted to one particular consumer. e.g. If a person wears a shirt, it will not be available to others. It is said that this person's consumption stands in rival relationship to the consumption of others.
However, if we consider a public park or measures to reduce air pollution, the benefits will be available to all. One person's consumption of a good does not reduce the amount available for consumption for others and so several people can enjoy the benefits, that is, the consumption of many people is not 'rivalrous'.
Two, in case of private goods, anyone who does not pay for the goods can be excluded from enjoying its benefits.

If you do not buy a ticket, you will not be allowed to watch a movie at a local cinema hall.

However, in case of public goods, there is no feasible way of excluding anyone from enjoying the benefits of the good. That is why public goods are called non-excludable.

Even if some users do not pay, it is difficult and sometimes impossible to collect fees for the public good. These non-paying users are known as 'free-riders'. Consumers will not voluntarily pay for what they can get for free and for which there is no exclusive title to the property being enjoyed.

The link between the producer and consumer which occurs through the payment process is broken and the government must step in to provide for such goods.

On the basis of the given text and common understanding, answer the following questions

(i) Describe how the government's role in providing public goods impacts community welfare. (3)

(ii) Define free-riders. Explain the challenges posed by the free-riders in the context of public goods. (3)

17. (i) Suppose, there are only three firms in a hypothetical economy, *viz.* A, B and C. During a given period of time, the following transactions were under, taken by them.

(a) Firm A sold goods worth ₹ 2,000 to Firm B and ₹ 1,200 to Firm C.

(b) Firm B sold goods worth ₹ 1,100 to Firm A and ₹ 3,500 to Firm C.

(c) Firm C sold to households for final consumption, goods worth ₹ 5,700.

Estimate the value of Net Domestic Product at Market Price (NDP_{MP}) assuming depreciation to be ₹ 120. (3)

(ii) Explain the likely impact of construction of 2,000 new schools providing high quality education in a, nation on gross domestic product and welfare in an economy. (3)

Or (i) Distinguish between Real Gross Domestic Product (GDP) and Nominal Gross Domestic Product (GDP).

(ii) As per a news dated 11th April, 2023 : "Electric vehicle sales crossed one million mark in FY 2023." Analyse its impact on Gross Domestic Product (GDP) and economic welfare.

Section-B
(Indian Economic Development)

18. Assertion (A) The year 1921 is called as the year of great divide.

Reason (R) After the year 1921, India experienced a sharp rise in its population growth rate. (1)

Alternatives

(a) Both Assertion (A) and Reason (R) are true and Reason (R) is the correct explanation of Assertion (A)

(b) Both Assertion (A) and Reason (R) are true, but Reason (R) is not the correct explanation of Assertion (A)

(c) Assertion (A) is true, but Reason (R) is false

(d) Assertion (A) is false, but Reason (R) is true

19. Mao initiated the 'great leap forward' movement in the year .... (1)

(a) 1951 (b) 1955

(c) 1958 (d) 1962

20. "The Indian government adopted a policy of fixing maximum land holding limit (ownership) for an individual." (1)

It is commonly known as ....

(a) green revolution (b) land ceiling

(c) marketable surplus (d) golden revolution

21. Study the following image and identify the measure adopted by the government to improve agricultural marketing (1)

(a) Cooperative credit societies

(b) Regulated markets

(c) Transportation facilities

(d) Dissemination of information

22. Identify, which of the following correctly defines liberalisation. (1)

(a) Outright sale of part of shares of Public Sector Undertakings (PSUs)
(b) Increased integration with the rest of the world
(c) Removal of restrictions imposed by government on different sectors of the economy
(d) Focus on import substitution

23. In China, under ...., peasants were provided with pooled land to create larger fields that could yield greater output and they shared farm implements. (1)

(a) joint farming system
(b) commune system
(c) great proletarian cultural revolution
(d) green revolution

24. White revolution is associated with .... (1)

(a) horticulture
(b) fisheries
(c) dairy production
(d) animal husbandry

25. .... indicator may be defined as the measure of the extent of demographic participation in social and political decision-making. (1)

(a) Economic (b) Liberty
(c) Health (d) Demographic

26. **Statement I** Employment is an activity which enables a person to earn means of livelihood for his/her family.

Statement II A worker is the one who contributes to the process of Gross Domestic Product (GDP) by rendering his productive services. (1)

Alternatives

(a) Statement I is correct and Statement II is incorrect
(b) Statement I is incorrect and Statement II is correct
(c) Both the statements are correct
(d) Both the statements are incorrect

27. Which of the following country/countries followed the five year planning structure of economic development? (1)

(i) India (ii) China
(iii) Pakistan (iv) USA

Codes

(a) (i), (ii) and (iii)
(b) (ii) and (iii)
(c) (i) and (iv)
(d) Only (iv)

28. "During the British rule, contribution of industrial sector to the Gross Domestic Product (GDP) remained very low." Justify the given statement with valid arguments in support of your answer. (3)

Or "The real motive behind infrastructural development under the British rule was not to provide basic amenities to the people of India but to subserve various colonial interests."

Do you agree with the given statement? Give valid reasons in support of your answer.

29. On the basis of the given image, explain the source of human capital formation which may contribute to the economic growth in India. (3)

30. Evaluate any two factors that led to the rapid growth in economic development in China. (4)

31. "IT can play a critical role in achieving sustainable development and food security in the 21st century in the country."

Justify the given statement with valid arguments. (4)

Or

Explain the importance of credit availability in rural development.

32. "It is necessary to generate more employment in the formal sector rather than in the informal sector."

Justify the given statement with valid arguments. (4)

33. (i) "Globalisation has been a process for India with only positive results."

Defend or refute the given statement with valid explanation. (3)

(ii) "The goal of equity was served by 'abolition of intermediaries' in agriculture in the post independence period."

Do you agree with the given statement? Support your answer with valid explanation. (3)

Or

(i) "Farm subsidies put a huge burden on the government finances, but are necessary for poor and marginal farmers."

Justify the given statement with valid explanation.

(ii) Discuss briefly the role of small-scale industries in generating of employment and equity in India under the planning period.

34. Growing carbon footprint of industries have put power and steel sector in the spotlight as the major contributor to the climate crisis.

The challenge of climate change can be tackled only by making our industries and businesses follow practices and processes that reduce their carbon footprint. It can be possible only with green financing.

Green financing aims to increase the level of financial flows (from banking, micro-credit, insurance and investment) from the public, private and not-for-profit sectors to sustainable development priorities.

Global green finance has also started chasing Indian companies. Global development finance institutions and funds are ready to offer long-term support (both equity and debt) at cheap rates to projects like solar energy and hydropower.

Green finance can positively affect environment quality, economic development and financial issues that promote the green economy, such as reducing greenhouse gas emissions, improving energy efficiency or enhancing the organic economy.

(i) State the meaning and objective of green finance. (3)

(ii) Discuss any two benefits of green financing. (3)

Answers

1. (c)

$$K = \frac{1}{1-MPC}$$

$$5 = \frac{1}{1-MPC}$$

$$1-MPC = \frac{1}{5}$$

$$1-MPC = 0.2$$

$$MPC = 0.8$$

$$MPS = 1-0.8 = 0.2$$

2. (b) Income generated from smuggling

3. (a) remains constant, rises

4. (b) Both Assertion (A) and Reason (R) are true, but Reason (R) is not the correct explanation of Assertion (A)

5. (b) increasing the bank rate

6. (c) Credit Multiplier $= \frac{1}{\text{Reserve Ratio}}$

Total Credit = ₹ 500

Reserve Ratio = 20% *or* 0.20

So, Multiplier $= \frac{1}{0.20} = 5$

Now, Total Credit = Primary Deposits × Money Multiplier

500 = Primary Deposits × 5

∴ Primary Deposits = ₹ 100

7. (d) Savings = Income – Consumption

8. (d) Loans from rest of the world

9. (b) (i) and (ii)

10. (b) The price of a given currency in terms of another is called the exchange rate.

11. Differences between autonomous and accommodating transactions of balance of payments are as follows (any three)

Basis	Autonomous Transactions	Accommodating Transactions
Meaning	These transactions are those which are made with a view to earn profit.	These transactions are taken up by government to keep BoP balanced.
Recorded	These are recorded in both i.e. current and capital account of BoP.	These are recorded only in capital account of BoP.
Alternate Name	These are also known as above the line transactions.	These are also known as below the line transactions.
Undertaken By	These are undertaken by both government and private sector.	These are undertaken only by government sector.
Example	Export of intellectual property.	Receiving foreign aid, foreign exchange reserves accumulation.

12. Net National Product at Market Price (NNP_{MP})

= Gross Domestic Product at Market Price (GDP_{MP}) − Depreciation = 2,500 − 200 = ₹ 2,300 lakh

Net National Product at Market Price (NNP_{MP})

= Net Domestic Product at Market Price (NDP_{MP}) + Net Factor Income from Abroad (NFIA)

⇒ Net Domestic Product at Market Price (NDP_{MP})

= 2,300 − 50 = ₹ 2,250 lakh

Now, Net Domestic Product at Factor Cost (NDP_{FC})

= Net Domestic Product at Market Price (NDP_{MP}) − Goods and Services Tax + Subsidies

= 2,250 − 20 + 50 = ₹ 2,280 lakh

Or Net factor income from abroad is the difference between the factor income earned from abroad by normal residents of a country (i.e. India) and the factor income earned by non-residents (foreigners) in the domestic territory of that country (i.e. India).

Following are its three main components
(i) Net compensation of employees.
(ii) Net income from property and entrepreneurship (rent, interest, profit).
(iii) Net retained earnings of resident companies abroad.

13. (i) Given, autonomous investment = ₹ 100 crore
Marginal Propensity to Save (MPS) = 0.2
Level of Income (Y) = ₹ 4,000 crore
Autonomous Consumption Expenditure ($\overline{C}$) = ₹ 50 crore
Marginal Propensity to Consume (MPC) = 1 − MPS = 1 − 0.2 = 0.8

We know that,

or $AD = C + I$

$AD = \overline{C} + MPC\,(Y) + I_0$

$= 50 + 0.8\,(4{,}000) + 100$

$= 50 + 3{,}200 + 100 =$ ₹ 3,350 crore

(ii) Marginal propensity to consume is the ratio of change in consumption expenditure (ΔC) to change in income (ΔY).

So, $$MPC = \frac{\Delta C}{\Delta Y}$$

14. This situation indicates that the economy is facing 'deficient demand'.
Deficient demand occurs when aggregate demand is less than aggregate supply. It is shown in the diagram.
In the diagram, full employment level of demand is indicated by AD_1.
If demand level happens to be AD_2, the gap between AD_1 and AD_2 is equal to *ab*. Deficient Demand is indicated by *abc*.

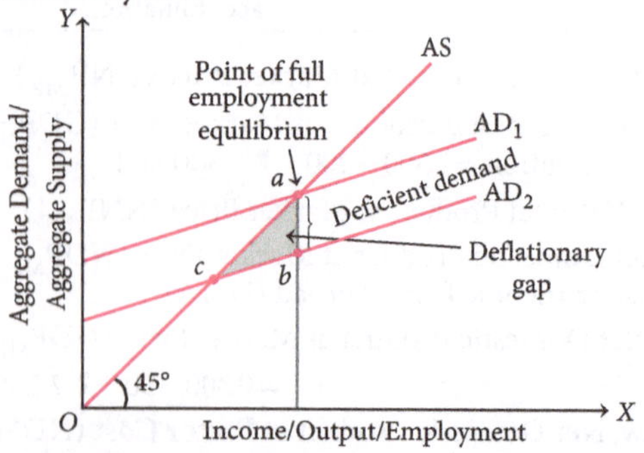

One effective fiscal measure to address this issue is 'increasing government expenditure'.

Or The effect of an initial increase in investment on the final income of an economy can be explained using the investment multiplier concept. The multiplier (K) is given by

$$K = 1/1 - MPC$$

Where MPC (Marginal Propensity to Consume) represents the fraction of additional income that households spend on consumption.

Numerical Example

Suppose an economy experiences an initial increase in investment of ₹ 100 crores and the MPC = 0.8.
The multiplier (K) is calculated as

$$K = 1/1 - 0.8 = 1/0.2 = 5$$

The total increase in income is given by
Total Income = $K \times$ Initial Investment
Thus, an initial investment of ₹ 100 crore leads to a final income increase of ₹ 500 crore in the economy due to the multiplier effect. This happens because the additional investment generates income, which increases consumption, further boosting demand and production.

15. The Central Bank plays a crucial role as the banker, agent and advisor to the government. It helps in managing the financial transactions of the Central and State Governments, implements monetary policies and provides expert guidance on economic matters.

(i) **As a Banker**
The Central Bank maintains the government's accounts, provides short-term loans and advances and manages public debt by issuing and redeeming government securities.

(ii) **As an Agent**
It carries out financial transactions on behalf of the government, such as buying and selling government securities in the open market. It also manages the issuance of new currency and foreign exchange reserves.

(iii) **As an Advisor**
It advises the government on monetary policy, inflation control, credit regulation and overall economic stability. The Central Bank provides recommendations to frame policies that ensure growth and financial stability in the economy.

16. (i) The government plays a crucial role in providing public goods, which significantly enhances community welfare in the following ways

(a) **Ensuring Availability for All**
Public goods like roads, national defence, and pollution control benefit everyone equally. Since they are non-rivalrous, one person's use does not reduce availability for others.

(b) **Addressing Market Failure**
Due to the free-rider problem, private firms may not supply these goods, as people can benefit without paying.

The government ensures their provision, preventing market failure and maintaining essential services.

(c) **Enhancing Quality of Life**

Public goods improve safety, infrastructure and environmental conditions, fostering economic growth and overall well-being. This leads to a more stable and prosperous society.

By providing public goods, the government ensures fairness, accessibility and long-term community welfare.

(ii) Free-riders are individuals who benefit from a public good without contributing to its cost. Since public goods are non-excludable, people may choose not to pay, knowing they cannot be denied access.

This creates several challenges

(a) **Underfunding of Public Goods**

If many people avoid paying, the government may struggle to raise enough resources to maintain or improve public goods.

(b) **Overuse and Degradation**

Since individuals do not bear direct costs, public goods like parks or roads may be overused, leading to congestion or depletion.

(c) **Burden on the Government**

The government must use tax revenue or public funds to finance these goods, which can strain financial resources.

To address the free-rider problem, the government uses taxation and regulations to ensure that public goods are funded and accessible to all.

17. (i) Value Added by Firm A = Sales (to B and C) − Purchases + Change in Stock

$= (2{,}000 + 1{,}200) - 1{,}100$

$= ₹\ 2{,}100$

Value Added by Firm B = Sales (to A and C) − Purchases

$= (3{,}500 + 1{,}100) - 2{,}000 = ₹\ 2{,}600$

Value Added by Firm C = Sales (to Market) − Purchases (from A and B)

$= 5{,}700 - (1{,}200 + 3{,}500) = ₹\ 1{,}000$

Now, GDP_{MP} = Value Added by Firm A + B + C

$= 2{,}100 + 2{,}600 + 1{,}000 = ₹\ 5{,}700$

So, $NDP_{MP} = GDP_{MP}$ − Depreciation

$= 5{,}700 - 120 = ₹\ 5{,}580$

(ii) The construction of 2,000 new schools providing high quality education will have a positive impact on both Gross Domestic Product (GDP) and welfare in the economy

(a) **Increase in GDP**

The construction process will create jobs, boosting income and demand. In the long-run, a better educated workforce enhances productivity, innovation and economic growth, leading to a higher GDP.

(b) **Improved Human Capital**

High quality education develops skilled workers, increasing employability and wages. This leads to higher earnings and better economic opportunities.

(c) **Enhanced Welfare**

Education improves living standards by reducing poverty and inequality. An educated population makes better health and social choices, leading to overall well-being and sustainable economic development.

Or (i) Differences between real gross domestic product and nominal gross domestic product are

Basis	Nominal GDP	Real GDP
Definition	GDP at current prices, representing the market value of final goods and services produced within a country during an accounting year, using current year prices.	GDP at constant prices, representing the market value of final goods and services produced within a country during an accounting year, using base year prices.
Price Changes	Affected by inflation or deflation.	Adjusted for inflation, reflecting actual production changes
Usefulness	Useful for current economic analysis and comparisons within the same year.	Useful for long-term comparisons and assessing real economic growth.

(ii) The rise in Electric Vehicle (EV) sales crossing one million in FY 2023 has a significant impact on Gross Domestic Product (GDP) and economic welfare

(a) **Increase in GDP**

Higher EV sales boost production, creating demand for raw materials, labour and services. This leads to increased industrial output, job creation and overall economic growth.

(b) **Technological Advancement and Investment**
Growth in the EV sector encourages innovation, research and investment in infrastructure like charging stations, further strengthening the economy.

(c) **Improved Economic Welfare**
EV adoption reduces air pollution, leading to better public health and a cleaner environment. Lower fuel dependency also enhances energy security, contributing to long-term sustainable development.

18. (a) Both Assertion (A) and Reason (R) are true and Reason (R) is the correct explanation of Assertion (A)

19. (c) 1958

20. (b) land ceiling

21. (b) Regulated markets

22. (c) Removal of restrictions imposed by government on different sectors of the economy

23. (b) commune system

24. (c) dairy production

25. (b) Liberty

26. (c) Both the statements are correct

27. (a) (i), (ii) and (iii)

28. During British rule, the contribution of the industrial sector to India's Gross Domestic Product (GDP) remained very low due to the following reasons

(i) **Deindustrialisation**
The British followed a policy of systematically destroying India's traditional handicraft industries by imposing heavy duties on Indian exports while allowing free imports of British manufactured goods. This led to a decline in indigenous industries.

(ii) **Lack of Modern Industries**
The British did not promote large-scale industrialisation in India. The limited industries that developed were mainly focused on raw material extraction for British industries, rather than manufacturing finished goods in India.

(iii) **Lack of Capital Goods Industries**
The British did not establish capital goods industries such as iron and steel, which are essential for industrial development. As a result, India remained dependent on Britain for machinery and equipment, hindering industrial growth.

Due to these reasons, India's industrial sector remained underdeveloped, contributing minimally to GDP during British rule.

Or Yes, the real motive behind infrastructural development under British rule was to serve colonial interests rather than to benefit the Indian people.

The following reasons support this statement:

(i) **Facilitating British Trade**
Railways, roads and ports were primarily developed to transport raw materials from different parts of India to ports for export to Britain and to distribute British manufactured goods within India. They were not meant to promote Indian industries.

(ii) **Strengthening British Control**
The British built railways and telegraph systems to improve communication and administration, enabling them to quickly suppress revolts and maintain effective control over India.

(iii) **Neglect of Social Infrastructure**
While transport infrastructure was developed, basic amenities like health, education and sanitation were largely ignored, proving that the British were not concerned with improving the standard of living of Indians.

Thus, infrastructural development under British rule was designed to serve their economic and political interests rather than to benefit the Indian population.

29. One of the key sources of human capital formation that contributes to economic growth in India, which is highlighted in the image, is education. An educated and skilled workforce enhances productivity, innovation and economic development.

The role of education in human capital formation is as follows

(i) An educated society facilitates a better development programme than an illiterate one.

(ii) Education improves productivity and prosperity and also improves the standard of living.

(iii) It does not only contribute towards the growth of the people, but also the development of society as a whole.

(iv) Education increases income and other cultural richness of human capital.

30. China's rapid economic development can be attributed to several key factors. The major factors that contributed significantly are

(i) **Economic Reforms and Open Door Policy** (1978)
The Chinese government introduced market oriented reforms under the leadership of Deng Xiaoping. These reforms included privatisation of agriculture, promotion of private enterprises and encouragement of foreign investments. The Open Door Policy allowed China to integrate into the global economy, boosting trade and industrial growth.

(ii) **Investment in Infrastructure and Human Capital**

The Chinese government heavily invested in modern infrastructure, such as roads, railways and power supply, which facilitated industrial growth. Additionally, focus on education and skill development created a highly productive workforce, leading to increased efficiency and innovation in various sectors.

These factors played a crucial role in making China one of the fastest growing economies in the world.

31. Information technology plays a very significant role in achieving sustainable development and food security in the following ways

(i) It can act as a tool for releasing the creative potential and knowledge embedded in our people.

(ii) Issues like weather forecasting, crop treatment, fertilisers, pesticides, storage conditions, etc. can be well administered, if expert opinion is made available to the farmers.

(iii) The quality and quantity of crops can be increased manifold, if the farmers are made aware of the latest equipments, technologies and resources.

(iv) It has potential of employment generation in rural areas.

Or The importance of credit in rural development is highlighted in the following points

(i) Credit helps the farmers to commercialise their farming. In other words, commercial farming requires funds that are provided via credit. As the small and marginal farmers produce only for their subsistence, they fail to generate sufficient surplus to reinvest in their lands leading to degradation of the land.

(ii) Secondly, given the long gestation period between sowing and harvesting of the crops, credit is extended to the farmers for meeting their initial requirements of farm inputs like seeds, fertilisers, etc.

(iii) Agriculture continues to depend on uncertain monsoon. Credit is needed to cope with uncertainties of nature or natural calamities.

32. Yes, it is necessary to generate employment in the formal sector rather than in the informal sector because those who work in the informal sector do not get any regular income and do not get protection from the government.

Workers are dismissed without any compensation. Technology used in informal sector is outdated and they also do not maintain any accounts. Workers live in slums or badly built houses.

Those who work in the formal sector on the other hand earn more than those in the informal sector and also enjoy social benefits. It is. thus, necessary to generate more employment in the formal sector.

33. (i) The statement is refuted, as it has also led to several challenges, which are as follows

(a) **Rising Inequality**

Globalisation has widened the gap between the rich and the poor, benefiting urban areas more than rural regions.

(b) **Threat to Small Industries**

Small-scale industries and local businesses struggle to compete with multinational corporations, leading to job losses.

(c) **Economic Vulnerability**

Increased dependence on global markets makes India susceptible to international financial crises and economic fluctuations.

Thus, globalisation has not been entirely positive for India, as it has also created economic and social challenges.

(ii) No, I do not agree with the given statement.

The government's abolition of intermediaries, particularly the zamindari system, was heralded as a transformative reform aimed at empowering farmers by transferring land ownership directly to the tiller of land.

The policy of 'land to the tiller' was based on the idea that the cultivators will take more interest as they will have more incentive to invest in increasing output if they are the owners of the land.

On the positive side, the abolition intended to enhance agricultural productivity by motivating farmers to invest in their land, as they would directly benefit from any increased output.

However, the goal of equity was not fully served by abolition of intermediaries due to following reasons

(a) In some areas, the former zamindars continued to own large areas of land by making use of some loopholes in the legislation.

(b) Even when the tillers got ownership of land, the poorest of the agricultural labourers did not benefit from land reforms.

In conclusion, while the abolition of intermediaries was framed as a progressive step toward achieving equitable land distribution, a critical analysis reveals that its implementation fell short of its ambitious goals.

Or

(i) Farm subsidies impose a significant financial burden on the government. However, they are crucial for small and marginal farmers in India due to the following reasons

(a) **Financial Support**

Most Indian farmers have limited resources. Subsidies help them afford essential inputs like seeds and fertilisers, preventing financial distress.

(b) **Risk Mitigation**

Agriculture is unpredictable due to monsoons and market fluctuations. Subsidies act as a safety net, ensuring stable livelihoods.

(c) **Food Security**

Subsidies maintain agricultural production, preventing food shortages and price hikes.

(d) **Preventing Rural Distress**

Without subsidies, farmers may quit agriculture, leading to migration and urban unemployment.

Thus, despite the financial burden, subsidies are crucial for sustaining small farmers and ensuring food security.

(ii) The roles of small-scale industries in India can be described as follows

(a) **Generation of Employment**

Small-scale industries serve as a significant employment generator in India. Employment is a crucial determinant of a nation's growth. Hence, the promotion and development of small-scale industries can lead to increased job opportunities, further promoting national growth.

(b) **Lower Capital Requirement**

Unlike large-scale industries, small-scale industries require less capital. In countries like India, where capital is limited, small-scale industries can help to maintain a balance.

(c) **Resource Utilisation and Entrepreneurial**

Skill development small-scale industries provide opportunities for entrepreneurial skill development, especially among the rural populace who do not have access to large-scale industries. These sectors also utilise resources available in rural areas, promoting rural development.

34. (i) Green finance refers to financial investments that support environmentally sustainable projects and initiatives. It includes banking, micro-credit, insurance and investment aimed at promoting eco-friendly activities.

Objective of Green Finance

The primary objective of green finance is to direct financial resources towards projects that help reduce carbon footprints, improve energy efficiency and support sustainable economic growth. It aims to tackle climate change by encouraging industries and businesses to adopt eco-friendly practices.

(ii) Two key benefits of green financing are as follows

(a) **Environmental Benefits**

Green financing helps reduce greenhouse gas emissions, improve energy efficiency and promote renewable energy sources such as solar and hydropower. This leads to better air quality and overall environmental sustainability.

(b) **Economic Development**

Green financing encourages investment in sustainable projects, leading to job creation and long-term economic growth. It also provides industries with access to low cost, long-term financial support, helping them transition to cleaner technologies.